The
Dramatic Festivals
of Athens

The
Dramatic Festivals
of Athens

BY

SIR ARTHUR PICKARD-CAMBRIDGE

OXFORD
AT THE CLARENDON PRESS
1953

Oxford University Press, Amen House, London E.C.4

GLASGOW NEW YORK TORONTO MELBOURNE WELLINGTON
BOMBAY CALCUTTA MADRAS KARACHI CAPE TOWN IBADAN

Geoffrey Cumberlege, Publisher to the University

PRINTED IN GREAT BRITAIN

PREFACE

My first words must be an expression of deep regret at the loss to scholarship through the deaths of two most active and fruitful students of the Greek Theatre and Drama, to whom I am personally very deeply indebted. The one, Ernst Fiechter, died at St. Gallen on 19 April 1948, his invaluable work on the theatres of Greece still unfinished. We had recently entered upon what promised to be a most interesting and profitable correspondence, and I hoped great things of his future studies; but the correspondence suddenly ceased and some weeks later came the news of his death. His last published writing in his lifetime was a discriminating but most kindly review of my own *Theatre of Dionysus*, which in his posthumously published volume on the theatre in the Piraeus he treats with even greater kindness. The other, Heinrich Bulle, had escaped, carrying the manuscripts of an unfinished book, when his house in Würzburg was bombed; but the manuscripts were mostly destroyed in a later raid from the air, and he died from a heart-attack brought on by the shock. The last few years have also taken from us A. Körte, H. Schleif, and L. Deubner, all of whom are greatly missed by those who are pursuing the same studies.

The present work concludes, so far as I have been able to do it, the task which I set myself many years ago, and to the fulfilment of which the *Theatre of Dionysus* (1946) was the first instalment. I hope that the two books will be treated as, in a sense, one. I have tried so far as I could to avoid overlapping, and have referred back freely to the earlier work. On the other hand, readers of the present volume may find some small amount of repetition between the several chapters. I had to choose between this and the insertion of a number of cross-references which would have been inconvenient to readers, especially to any who might be interested in the subject of a particular chapter and might not want to turn backwards and forwards.

I have sometimes travelled away from the subject of the Athenian Dramatic Festivals, but the reader is not bound to follow; the Table of Contents will furnish him with sufficient warnings. My excuse for the last chapter is the want of any brief and satisfactory treatment known to me in English writings of a very interesting subject.

It has been my object throughout to keep as closely as possible to evidence, and to state this evidence fully enough to enable the reader to judge for himself of the value of the conclusions drawn from it. Scholarship has suffered much in the last half-century from a lack of scruple in this respect, leading, as it often has, to attractive but erroneous theories and to the suggestion of connexions and 'derivations' which cannot be substantiated. I fear that the constant reference to evidence is inconsistent with elegant essay-writing, but it seems to me to be a service that needs to be rendered, and I have tried, in a modest way, to render it—how imperfectly, I do not need to be told.

But though this attempt is based upon direct personal study of evidence, I am deeply grateful to other workers in the same field for the help which I have derived from their writings, and have tried to acknowledge it in my notes. I must express my special thanks for generous assistance in the choice and collection of illustrations to Sir John Beazley and Professor T. B. L. Webster, and to Dr. Margarete Bieber for her ready consent to my use of materials contained in her own works. I have also received welcome help from Mr. Bernard Ashmole and other members of the staff of the Department of Greek and Roman Antiquities at the British Museum. My obligations to authors and publishers for permission to reproduce illustrations and to the authorities of Museums for leave to figure objects under their care are very numerous and are acknowledged in their place. If I have accidentally failed to obtain any consent for which I should have asked, I hope that the oversight may be pardoned.

A. W. P.-C.

CONTENTS

II. THE GREAT OR CITY DIONYSIA

Contents

III. THE ACTORS

IV. COSTUME

Contents . xiii

§ 11. κοθορνός—meaning and use at different periods.   *pages* 233-4
Dress in comedy §§ 12-14.   234-8
  § 12. Brief survey.   234-5
  § 13. The φλύακες vases.   235-6
  § 14. Survival of mimes.   237-8

V. THE CHORUS

A. THE CHARACTER, FUNCTIONS, AND MOVEMENTS OF THE CHORUS   239-51
  § 1. Importance of the chorus in the play.   239-41
  § 2. Number of the chorus.   241-2
  § 3. Occasional second chorus.   242-3
  § 4. Costumes of the chorus.   243-5
  § 5. Movements of the tragic chorus.   245-9
  § 6. Movements of the comic chorus.   249-50
  § 7. Delivery by whole chorus, semichoruses, or single choreutai.   250-1

B. DANCING IN DRAMA   251-62
  § 1. Greek views on dancing.   251-3
  § 2. Use of hands in dancing.   253-4
  § 3. The σχήματα of the dance.   254-5
  § 4. History of dramatic dancing.   255-6
  § 5. Dancing during Stasima.   256-7
  § 6. ἐμμέλεια.   258-9
  § 7. σίκιννις.   259-60
  § 8. ὑπόρχημα.   260-2

C. MUSIC IN DRAMA   262-7

VI. THE AUDIENCE

§ 1. Number in the audience.   268
§ 2. Women and children in the audience.   268-70
§ 3. Payments for admission.   270-3
§ 4. Theatre-tickets.   273-5
§ 5. Prohedria and reserved seats.   275-8
§ 6. Behaviour of audience.   278-81
§ 7. Judgement and taste of audience.   281-5

VII. THE ARTISTS OF DIONYSUS

§ 1. Early professionalism.   286-7
§ 2. The Artists under Alexander and his successors; reasons for organization.   287-9

Contents

LIST OF ILLUSTRATIONS

5278   b

I

THE LESSER FESTIVALS

A. THE ANTHESTERIA

THE oldest of the Festivals of Dionysus at Athens was the Anthesteria, extending over the 11th, 12th, and 13th of the month Anthesterion (about the end of February), these days being known respectively as Πιθοίγια, Χόες, and Χύτροι. (Each day began for religious purposes on the previous evening.) Although this festival has little direct connexion with the history of the drama, it is necessary to study it briefly, because some elements in it have been wrongly connected with dramatic festivals—in particular, its association with the precinct of Dionysus ἐν Λίμναις, and the procession which escorted Dionysus in a car resembling a ship—and the study may help to place the dramatic festivals in the general setting of the worship of Dionysus at Athens.

1. The following are the principal texts bearing on the Anthesteria:

(1) Thucyd. ii. 15. τὸ δὲ πρὸ τοῦ (i.e. before the ξυνοικισμός brought about by Theseus) ἡ ἀκρόπολις ἡ νῦν οὖσα πόλις ἦν, καὶ τὸ ὑπ᾽ αὐτὴν πρὸς νότον μάλιστα τετραμμένον. τεκμήριον δέ· τὰ γὰρ ἱερὰ ἐν αὐτῇ τῇ ἀκροπόλει καὶ ἄλλων θεῶν ἐστι καὶ τὰ ἔξω πρὸς τοῦτο τὸ μέρος τῆς πόλεως μᾶλλον ἵδρυται, τό τε τοῦ Διὸς τοῦ Ὀλυμπίου καὶ τὸ Πύθιον καὶ τὸ τῆς Γῆς καὶ τὸ ⟨τοῦ⟩ ἐν Λίμναις Διονύσου, ᾧ τὰ ἀρχαιότερα Διονύσια [τῇ δωδεκατῇ] ποιεῖται ἐν μηνὶ Ἀνθεστηριῶνι, ὥσπερ καὶ οἱ ἀπ᾽ Ἀθηναίων Ἴωνες ἔτι καὶ νῦν νομίζουσιν. ἵδρυται δὲ καὶ ἄλλα ἱερὰ ταύτῃ ἀρχαῖα. καὶ τῇ κρήνῃ τῇ νῦν μὲν τῶν τυράννων οὕτως σκευασάντων Ἐννεακρούνῳ καλουμένῃ, τὸ δὲ πάλαι φανερῶν τῶν πηγῶν οὐσῶν Καλλιρρόῃ ὠνομασμένῃ, ἐκείνη [ἐκεῖνοί, Bekker] τε ἐγγὺς οὔσῃ τὰ πλείστου ἄξια ἐχρῶντο, καὶ νῦν ἔτι ἀπὸ τοῦ ἀρχαίου πρό τε γαμικῶν καὶ ἐς ἄλλα τῶν ἱερῶν νομίζεται τῷ ὕδατι χρῆσθαι. καλεῖται δὲ διὰ τὴν παλαιὰν ταύτῃ κατοίκησιν καὶ ἡ ἀκρόπολις μέχρι τοῦδε ἔτι ὑπ᾽ Ἀθηναίων πόλις.

In l. 4 after ἀκροπόλει Classen inserts καὶ τὰ τῆς Ἀθηνᾶς, which must in any case be understood.

(2) Eur. *Iph. Taur.* 947 ff.

πρῶτα μέν μ᾽ οὐδεὶς βροτῶν
ἑκὼν ἐδέξαθ᾽, ὡς θεοῖς στυγούμενον·

B

οἳ δ' ἔσχον αἰδῶ, ξένια μονοτράπεζά μοι
950 παρέσχον, οἴκων ὄντες ἐν ταὐτῷ στέγει,
σιγῇ δ' ἐτεκτήναντ' ἀπροσφθεγκτόν μ', ὅπως
δαιτὸς γενοίμην πώματός τ' αὐτοῖς δίχα,
ἐς δ' ἄγγος ἴδιον ἴσον ἅπασι βακχίου
μέτρημα πληρώσαντες εἶχον ἡδονήν . . .
958 κλύω δ' Ἀθηναίοισι τἀμὰ δυστυχῆ
τελετὴν γενέσθαι, κἄτι τὸν νόμον μένειν
χοῆρες ἄγγος Παλλάδος τιμᾶν λέων.

(3) Aristoph. *Ach.* 960–1.

ἐκέλευσε Λάμαχός σε ταυτησὶ δραχμῆς
ἐς τοὺς Χοᾶς αὐτῷ μεταδοῦναι τῶν κιχλῶν.

Schol. εἰς τοὺς Χοᾶς· εἰς τὴν ἑορτὴν τῶν Χοῶν. ἐτελεῖτο δὲ
Πυανεψιῶνος ὀγδοῇ, οἱ δὲ Ἀνθεστηριῶνος δεκάτῃ. φησὶ δὲ Ἀπολλόδωρος Ἀνθεστήρια καλεῖσθαι κοινῶς τὴν ὅλην ἑορτὴν Διονύσῳ ἀγο-
μένην, κατὰ μέρος δὲ Πιθοιγίαν, Χοᾶς, Χύτραν. καὶ αὖθις, ὅτι Ὀρέστης
μετὰ τὸν φόνον εἰς Ἀθήνας ἀφικόμενος, ἦν δὲ ἑορτὴ Διονύσου Ληναίου,
ὡς μὴ γένοιτό σφισιν ὁμόσπονδος ἀπεκτονὼς τὴν μητέρα, ἐμηχανήσατο
τοιόνδε τι Πανδίων, χοᾶ οἴνου τῶν δαιτυμόνων ἑκάστῳ παραστήσας,
ἐξ αὐτοῦ πίνειν ἐκέλευσε μηδὲν ὑπομιγνύντας ἀλλήλοις, ὡς μήτε ἀπὸ
τοῦ αὐτοῦ κρατῆρος πίοι Ὀρέστης μήτε ἐκεῖνος ἄχθοιτο καθ' αὑτὸν
πίνων μόνος. καὶ ἀπ' ἐκείνου Ἀθηναίοις ἑορτὴ ἐνομίσθη οἱ Χόες.

(4) Ibid. 1000–2.

ΚΗΡΥΞ. ἀκούετε λέῳ· κατὰ τὰ πάτρια τοὺς Χοᾶς
πίνειν ὑπὸ τῆς σάλπιγγος· ὃς δ' ἂν ἐκπίῃ
πρώτιστος, ἀσκὸν Κτησιφῶντος λήψεται.

Schol. V. ἐν ταῖς Χοαῖς ἀγὼν ἦν περὶ τοῦ ἐκπιεῖν τινὰ πρῶτον χοᾶ,
καὶ ὁ πιὼν ἐστέφετο φυλλίνῳ στεφάνῳ καὶ ἀσκὸν οἴνου ἐλάμβανεν.
πρὸς σάλπιγγος δ' ἔπινον.

Schol. R. ἐτίθετο δὲ ἀσκὸς πεφυσημένος ἐν τῇ τῶν Χοῶν ἑορτῇ,
ἐφ' οὗ τοὺς πίνοντας πρὸς ἀγῶνα ἑστάναι, τὸν πρῶτον πίνοντα δὲ ὡς
νικήσαντα λαμβάνειν ἀσκόν, ἔπινον δὲ μέτρον τι οἷον χοᾶ.

(5) Ibid. 1076–7.

ὑπὸ τοὺς Χοᾶς γὰρ καὶ Χύτρους αὐτοῖσί τις
ἤγγειλε λῃστὰς ἐμβαλεῖν Βοιωτίους.

Schol. Θεόπομπος τοὺς διασωθέντας ἐκ τοῦ κατακλυσμοῦ ἑψῆσαί
φησι χύτραν πανσπερμίας· ὅθεν οὕτω κληθῆναι τὴν ἑορτήν, καὶ θύειν
τοῖς Χουσὶν Ἑρμῇ χθονίῳ, τῆς δὲ χύτρας οὐδένα γεῦσαι. τοῦτο δὲ
ποιῆσαι τοὺς περισωθέντας, ἱλασκομένους τὸν Ἑρμῆν καὶ περὶ τῶν
ἀποθανόντων. ἤγετο δὲ ἡ ἑορτὴ Ἀνθεστηριῶνος τρίτῃ ἐπὶ δέκα, ὡς

Φιλόχορος. Ἄλλως· ἐν μιᾷ ἡμέρᾳ ἄγονται οἵ τε Χύτροι καὶ οἱ Χόες ἐν
Ἀθήναις, ἐν ᾧ πᾶν σπέρμα εἰς χύτραν ἑψήσαντες θύουσι μόνῳ τῷ
Διονύσῳ καὶ Ἑρμῇ. οὕτω Δίδυμος.

(Cf. Phot. s.v. Ὑδροφόρια· ἑορτὴ πένθιμος Ἀθήνησιν ἐπὶ τοῖς ἐν
τῷ κατακλυσμῷ ἀπολομένοις, ὡς Ἀπολλώνιος.)

(6) Aristoph. *Ach.* 1224–5.

> ὡς τοὺς κριτάς με φέρετε· ποῦ 'στιν ὁ βασιλεύς;
> ἀπόδοτέ μοι τὸν ἀσκόν.

Schol. δηλοῖ ὡς ἄρα τὴν ἐπιμέλειαν ὁ βασιλεὺς εἶχε τῆς ἁμίλλης τοῦ
χοός, καὶ τὸ ἆθλον ἐδίδου τῷ νικήσαντι, τὸν ἀσκόν.

(7) Aristoph. *Knights* 95.

> ἀλλ' ἐξένεγκέ μοι ταχέως οἴνου χοᾶ.

Schol. practically repeats the story of Orestes and Pandion as
in Schol. Aristoph. *Ach.* 961.

(8) Aristoph. *Frogs* 211–19.

> λιμναῖα κρηνῶν τέκνα,
> ξύναυλον ὕμνων βοὰν
> φθεγξώμεθ', εὔγηρυν ἐμὰν ἀοιδάν,
>   κοὰξ κοάξ,
> ἢν ἀμφὶ Νυσήιον
> Διὸς Διόννυσον ἐν
> Λίμναισιν ἰαχήσαμεν,
> ἡνίχ' ὁ κραιπαλόκωμος
> τοῖς ἱεροῖσι Χύτροισι
> χωρεῖ κατ' ἐμὸν τέμενος λαῶν ὄχλος.

Schol. on l. 216. ἀπὸ τῶν ἑαυτῶν λιμνῶν μεταφέρουσιν ἐπὶ τὸν ἐν
Λίμναις Διόνυσον λεγόμενον. Λίμναι δὲ χωρίον τῆς Ἀττικῆς, ἐν ᾧ
Διονύσου ἱερόν. Λίμνη· τόπος ἱερὸς Διονύσου, ἐν ᾧ καὶ οἶκος καὶ νεὼς
τοῦ θεοῦ. Καλλίμαχος ἐν Ἑκάλῃ 'Λιμναίῳ δὲ χοροστάδας ἦγον ἑορτάς'.
Schol. on l. 218. Χύτροι· ἑορτὴ παρ' Ἀθηναίοις. ἄγεται δὲ παρὰ
ταύτην τὴν αἰτίαν, ἣν καὶ Θεόπομπος ἐκτίθεται γράφων οὕτως,
' διασωθέντας οὖν τοὺς ἀνθρώπους, ἧπερ ἐθάρρησαν ἡμέρᾳ, τῷ ταύτης
ὀνόματι προσαγορεῦσαι καὶ τὴν ἑορτὴν ἄπασαν. ἔπειτα θύειν αὐτοῖς
ἔθος ἔχουσι, τῶν μὲν Ὀλυμπίων θεῶν οὐδενὶ τὸ παράπαν, Ἑρμῇ δὲ
χθονίῳ, καὶ τῆς χύτρας, ἣν ἕψουσι πάντες οἱ κατὰ τὴν πόλιν, οὐδεὶς
γεύεται τῶν ἱερέων, τοῦτο δὲ ποιοῦσι τῇ ἡμέρᾳ, καὶ τοὺς τότε παρα-
γενομένους ὑπὲρ τῶν ἀποθανόντων ἱλάσασθαι τὸν Ἑρμῆν'. ἤγοντο δὲ
ἀγῶνες αὐτόθι οἱ Χύτρινοι καλούμενοι, καθά φησι Φιλόχορος ἐν τῇ
ἕκτῃ τῶν Ἀτθίδων.

4 *The Lesser Festivals*

(9) Isaeus, *Or.* viii. 35. Κίρων γὰρ ἐκέκτητο οὐσίαν, ὦ ἄνδρες, ἀγρὸν μὲν Φλυῆσι . . . οἰκίας δ᾽ ἐν ἄστει δύο, τὴν μὲν μισθοφοροῦσαν, παρὰ τὸ ἐν Λίμναις Διονύσιον, χιλίας εὑρίσκουσαν, τὴν δ᾽ ἑτέραν, ἐν ᾗ αὐτὸς ᾤκει.

(10) Skylax (?) *Peripl.* 112 (*Geogr. Gr.* i. 94). τὰ γὰρ πλάσματά (sc. κέραμος Ἀττικὸς καὶ χόες) ἐστιν ὤνια ἐν τοῖς Χουσὶ τῇ ἑορτῇ.

(11) Pseudo-Dem. *in Neaeram*, §§ 73–78. καὶ αὕτη ἡ γυνὴ ὑμῖν ἔθυε τὰ ἄρρητα ἱερὰ ὑπὲρ τῆς πόλεως, καὶ εἶδεν ἃ οὐ προσῆκεν αὐτὴν ὁρᾶν ξένην οὖσαν, καὶ τοιαύτη οὖσα εἰσῆλθεν οἷ οὐδεὶς ἄλλος Ἀθηναίων τοσούτων ὄντων εἰσέρχεται ἀλλ᾽ ἢ ἡ τοῦ βασιλέως γυνή, ἐξώρκωσέν τε τὰς γεραρὰς τὰς ὑπηρετούσας τοῖς ἱεροῖς, ἐξεδόθη τε τῷ Διονύσῳ γυνή, ἔπραξεν δὲ ὑπὲρ τῆς πόλεως τὰ πάτρια τὰ πρὸς τοὺς θεούς, πολλὰ καὶ ἅγια καὶ ἀπόρρητα. . . . (§ 74) . . . τὸ γὰρ ἀρχαῖον, ὦ ἄνδρες Ἀθηναῖοι, δυναστεία ἐν τῇ πόλει ἦν καὶ ἡ βασιλεία τῶν ἀεὶ ὑπερεχόντων διὰ τὸ αὐτόχθονας εἶναι, τὰς δὲ θυσίας ἁπάσας ὁ βασιλεὺς ἔθυε, καὶ τὰς σεμνοτάτας καὶ ἀρρήτους ἡ γυνὴ αὐτοῦ ἐποίει, εἰκότως, βασίλιννα οὖσα. (§ 75) ἐπειδὴ δὲ Θησεὺς συνῴκισεν αὐτοὺς καὶ δημοκρατίαν ἐποίησεν καὶ ἡ πόλις πολυάνθρωπος ἐγένετο, τὸν μὲν βασιλέα οὐδὲν ἧττον ὁ δῆμος ᾑρεῖτο . . . τὴν δὲ γυναῖκα αὐτοῦ νόμον ἔθεντο ἀστὴν εἶναι καὶ μὴ ἐπιμεμειγμένην ἑτέρῳ ἀνδρὶ ἀλλὰ παρθένον γαμεῖν, ἵνα κατὰ τὰ πάτρια θύηται τὰ ἄρρητα ἱερὰ ὑπὲρ τῆς πόλεως . . . (§ 76) καὶ τοῦτον τὸν νόμον γράψαντες ἐν στήλῃ λιθίνῃ ἔστησαν ἐν τῷ ἱερῷ τοῦ Διονύσου παρὰ τὸν βωμὸν ἐν Λίμναις (καὶ αὕτη ἡ στήλη ἔτι καὶ νῦν ἕστηκεν, ἀμυδροῖς γράμμασιν Ἀττικοῖς δηλοῦσα τὰ γεγραμμένα), μαρτυρίαν ποιούμενος ὁ δῆμος . . . ὅτι τήν γε θεῷ γυναῖκα δοθησομένην καὶ ποιήσουσαν τὰ ἱερὰ τοιαύτην ἀξιοῦμεν εἶναι. καὶ διὰ ταῦτα ἐν τῷ ἀρχαιοτάτῳ ἱερῷ τοῦ Διονύσου καὶ ἁγιωτάτῳ ἐν Λίμναις ἔστησαν, ἵνα μὴ πολλοὶ εἰδῶσιν τὰ γεγραμμένα· ἅπαξ γὰρ τοῦ ἐνιαυτοῦ ἕκαστου ἀνοίγεται, τῇ δωδεκάτῃ τοῦ Ἀνθεστηριῶνος μηνός. . . . (§ 78) βούλομαι δ᾽ ὑμῖν καὶ τὸν ἱεροκήρυκα καλέσαι, ὃς ὑπηρετεῖ τῇ τοῦ βασιλέως γυναικί, ὅταν ἐξορκοῖ τὰς γεραρὰς ⟨τὰς⟩ ἐν κανοῖς πρὸς τῷ βωμῷ, πρὶν ἅπτεσθαι τῶν ἱερῶν, ἵνα καὶ τοῦ ὅρκου καὶ τῶν λεγομένων ἀκούσητε. . . .

ΟΡΚΟΣ ΓΕΡΑΡΩΝ

ἁγιστεύω καὶ εἰμὶ καθαρὰ καὶ ἁγνὴ ἀπὸ ⟨τε⟩ τῶν ἄλλων τῶν οὐ καθαρευόντων καὶ ἀπ᾽ ἀνδρὸς συνουσίας, καὶ τὰ θεοίνια καὶ τὰ ἰοβάκχεια γεραρῶ (Dobree for MSS. γεραίρω) τῷ Διονύσῳ κατὰ τὰ πάτρια καὶ ἐν τοῖς καθήκουσι χρόνοις.

Cf. Bekk. *Anecd.* i. 231. 32. γεραιραί· ἱερεῖαι κοινῶς, ἰδίως δὲ παρὰ τοῖς Ἀθηναίοις αἱ τῷ Διονύσῳ τῷ ἐν Λίμναις τὰ ἱερὰ ἐπιτελοῦσαι, ἀριθμῷ δεκατέσσαρες.

Etym. Magn. 227. 35. γεραιραί· παρὰ Ἀθηναίοις γυναῖκές τινες

ἱεραί, ἃς ὁ βασιλεὺς καθίστησιν ἰσαρίθμους τοῖς βωμοῖς τοῦ Διονύσου,
διὰ τὸ γεραίρειν τὸν θεόν. οὕτω Διονύσιος ὁ Ἁλικαρνασεύς.

(12) Aristotle, *Ἀθ. Πολ.* iii. ᾤκησαν δὲ οὐχ ἅμα πάντες οἱ ἐννέα ἄρχοντες,
ἀλλ᾽ ὁ μὲν βασιλεὺς εἶχε τὸ νῦν καλούμενον Βουκολίον, πλησίον τοῦ
Πρυτανείου (σημεῖον δέ· ἔτι καὶ νῦν γὰρ τῆς τοῦ βασιλέως γυναικὸς
ἡ σύμμιξις ἐνταῦθα γίνεται τῷ Διονύσῳ καὶ ὁ γάμος), ὁ δὲ ἄρχων τὸ
Πρυτανεῖον, ὁ δὲ πολέμαρχος τὸ Ἐπιλυκεῖον.

(13) Callimachus, *Aitia*, fr. 1.

> ἠὼς οὐδὲ πιθοιγὶς ἐλάνθανεν οὐδ᾽ ὅτε δούλοις
> ἦμαρ Ὀρέστειοι λευκὸν ἄγουσι Χόες·
> Ἰκαρίου καὶ παιδὸς ἄγων ἐπέτειον ἀγιστόν,
> Ἀτθίσιν οἰκίστη, σὸν φάος, Ἠριγόνη
> ἐς δαίτην ἐκάλεσσεν ὁμήλικας.

(14) Dion. Hal. *Antiq.* VII. lxxii. 11. ἐφεῖται γὰρ τοῖς κατάγουσι τὰς νίκας
ἰαμβίζειν τε καὶ κατασκώπτειν τοὺς ἐπιφανεστάτους ἄνδρας αὐτοῖς
στρατηλάταις, ὡς Ἀθήνησι τοῖς πομπευταῖς τοῖς ἐπὶ τῶν ἀμαξῶν
πρότερον ἅμα σκώμμασι παροχουμένοις, νῦν δὲ ποιήματα ᾄδουσιν
αὐτοσχέδια.

Cf. Harpokr. s.v. πομπείας καὶ πομπεύειν· ἀντὶ τοῦ λοιδορίας καὶ
λοιδορεῖν. Δημοσθένης δὲ ἐν τῷ ὑπὲρ Κτησιφῶντος. μεταφέρει δὲ ἀπὸ
τῶν ἐν ταῖς Διονυσιακαῖς πομπαῖς ἐπὶ τῶν ἀμαξῶν λοιδορουμένων
ἀλλήλοις.

(15) Plutarch, *Quaest. Conv.* i. 613 b. εἰ μὲν οὖν ὥσπερ οἱ τὸν Ὀρέστην
ἑστιῶντες, ἐν θεσμοθετείῳ σιωπῇ τρώγειν καὶ πίνειν ἐμέλλομεν, ἦν τι
τοῦτο τῆς ἀμαθίας οὐκ ἀτυχὲς παραμύθιον.

(16) Ibid. ii. 643 a. καίτοι τίν᾽ ἔχει διαφορὰν ἢ κύλικα καταθέντα τῶν
κεκλημένων ἑκάστῳ καὶ χοῦν, ἐμπλησάμενον οἴνου, καὶ τράπεζαν
ἰδίαν ὥσπερ οἱ Δημοφωντίδαι τῷ Ὀρέστῃ λέγονται, πίνειν κελεῦσαι
μὴ προσέχοντα τοῖς ἄλλοις;

(17) Ibid. iii. 655 e. τοῦ νέου οἴνου Ἀθήνησι μὲν ἑνδεκάτῃ μηνὸς κατ-
άρχονται, Πιθοίγια τὴν ἡμέραν καλοῦντες· καὶ πάλαι γ᾽ ὡς ἔοικεν
εὔχοντο, τοῦ οἴνου πρὶν ἢ πιεῖν ἀποσπένδοντες, ἀβλαβῆ καὶ σωτήριον
αὐτοῖς τοῦ φαρμάκου τὴν χρῆσιν γενέσθαι.

(18) Athen. iv. 130 d. σὺ δὲ μόνον ἐν Ἀθήναις μένων εὐδαιμονίζεις τὰς
Θεοφράστου θέσεις ἀκούων, θύμα καὶ εὔζωμα καὶ τοὺς καλοὺς ἐσθίων
στρεπτούς, Λήναια καὶ Χύτρους θεωρῶν. (Part of quotation from
Hippolochos, a disciple of Theophrastus.)

(19) Ibid. x. 437 b–e. Τίμαιος δέ φησιν ὡς Διονύσιος ὁ τύραννος τῇ τῶν
Χοῶν ἑορτῇ τῷ πρώτῳ ἐκπιόντι χοᾶ ἆθλον ἔθηκε στέφανον χρυσοῦν·

καὶ ὅτι πρῶτος ἐξέπιε Ξενοκράτης ὁ φιλόσοφος καὶ λαβὼν τὸν χρυσοῦν
στέφανον καὶ ἀναλύων τῷ Ἑρμῇ τῷ ἱδρυμένῳ ἐπὶ τῆς αὐλῆς ἐπέθηκεν,
ᾧπερ εἰώθει καὶ τοὺς ἀνθινοὺς ἑκάστοτε ἐπιτιθέναι στεφάνους ἑσπέρας
ἀπαλλασσόμενος ὡς αὑτόν· καὶ ἐπὶ τούτῳ ἐθαυμάσθη. τὴν δὲ τῶν
Χοῶν ἑορτὴν τὴν Ἀθήνησιν ἐπιτελουμένην Φανόδημός φησι Δημο-
φῶντα τὸν βασιλέα βουλόμενον ὑποδέξασθαι παραγενόμενον τὸν Ὀρέστην Ἀθήναζε, πρὸς δὲ τὰ ἱερὰ οὐ θέλων αὐτὸν προσιέναι οὐδ’ ὁμόσπον-
δον γενέσθαι μήπω δικασθέντα ἐκέλευσε συγκλεισθῆναί τε τὰ ἱερὰ καὶ
χοᾶ οἴνου ἑκάστῳ παρατεθῆναι, τῷ πρώτῳ ἐκπιόντι εἰπὼν ἆθλον
δοθήσεσθαι πλακοῦντα. παρήγγειλέ τε καὶ τοῦ πότου παυσαμένους
τοὺς μὲν στεφάνους οἷς ἐστεφάνωντο πρὸς τὰ ἱερὰ μὴ τιθέναι διὰ τὸ
ὁμορόφους γενέσθαι τῷ Ὀρέστῃ, περὶ δὲ τὸν χοᾶ τὸν ἑαυτοῦ ἕκαστον
περιθεῖναι καὶ τῇ ἱερείᾳ ἀποφέρειν τοὺς στεφάνους πρὸς τὸ ἐν Λίμναις
τέμενος, ἔπειτα θύειν ἐν τῷ ἱερῷ τὰ ἐπίλοιπα. καὶ ἔκτοτε τὴν ἑορτὴν
κληθῆναι Χοᾶς. τῇ δὲ ἑορτῇ τῶν Χοῶν ἔθος ἐστὶν Ἀθήνησι πέμπεσθαι
δῶρά τε καὶ τοὺς μισθοὺς τοῖς σοφισταῖς, οἵπερ καὶ αὐτοὶ συνεκάλουν
ἐπὶ ξένια τοὺς γνωρίμους, ὥς φησιν Εὐβουλίδης ὁ διαλεκτικὸς ἐν
δράματι Κωμασταῖς οὕτως

> σοφιστιᾷς, κάκιστε, καὶ Χοῶν δέῃ
> τῶν μισθοδώρων, οὐκ ἀδείπνων ἐν τροφῇ.

Ἀντίγονος δ’ ὁ Καρύστιος ἐν τῷ περὶ τοῦ Διονυσίου βίου τοῦ Ἡρα-
κλεώτου τοῦ ἐπικληθέντος Μετατιθεμένου φησὶ τὸν Διονύσιον τοῖς
οἰκέταις συνεορτάζοντα ἐν τῇ τῶν Χοῶν ἑορτῇ κτλ. (An unedifying
anecdote follows.)

(20) Athen. xi. 465 a. Φανόδημος δὲ πρὸς τῷ ἱερῷ φησι τοῦ ἐν Λίμναις
Διονύσου τὸ γλεῦκος φερόντας τοὺς Ἀθηναίους ἐκ τῶν πίθων τῷ θεῷ
κιρνάναι, εἶτ’ αὐτοὺς προσφέρεσθαι· ὅθεν καὶ Λιμναῖον κληθῆναι τὸν
Διόνυσον ὅτι μιχθὲν τὸ γλεῦκος τῷ ὕδατι τότε πρῶτον ἐπόθη κεκρα-
μένον. διόπερ ὀνομασθῆναι τὰς [πηγὰς] Νύμφας καὶ τιθήνας τοῦ
Διονύσου, ὅτι τὸν οἶνον αὐξάνει τὸ ὕδωρ κιρνάμενον. ἡσθέντες οὖν τῇ
κράσει ἐν ᾠδαῖς ἔμελπον τὸν Διόνυσον, χορεύοντες καὶ ἀνακαλοῦντες
Εὔαν τε καὶ Διθύραμβον καὶ Βακχευτὰν καὶ Βρόμιον.

(21) Ibid. 495 a–c. Κράτης δὲ ἐν δευτέρῳ Ἀττικῆς διαλέκτου γράφει
οὕτως· οἱ χόες πελίκαι, καθάπερ εἴπομεν, ὠνομάζοντο· ὁ δὲ τύπος ἢ
τοῦ ἀγγείου πρότερον μὲν τοῖς Παναθηναϊκοῖς ἐοικώς, ἡνίκα ἐκαλεῖτο
πελίκη, ὕστερον δὲ ἔσχεν οἰνοχόης σχῆμα, οἷοί εἰσιν οἱ ἐν τῇ ἑορτῇ
παρατιθέμενοι, ὁποίους δή ποτε ὄλπας ἐκάλουν, χρώμενοι πρὸς τὴν
τοῦ οἴνου ἔκχυσιν, καθάπερ Ἴων ὁ Χῖος ἐν Εὐρυτίδαις φησὶν

> ἐκ ξαθέων πιθακνῶν ἀφύσσοντες ὄλπαις
> οἶνον ὑπερφίαλον κελαρύζετε.

νυνὶ δὲ τὸ μὲν τοιοῦτον ἀγγεῖον καθιερώμενόν τινα τρόπον ἐν τῇ ἑορτῇ παρατίθεται μόνον, τὸ δ' εἰς τὴν χρείαν πῖπτον μετεσχημάτισται, ἀρυταίνῃ μάλιστα ἐοικός, ὃ δὴ καλοῦμεν χοᾶ. (Crates' date is *c.* 210 B.C.)

(22) Diog. Laert. iv. 8 (on Xenokrates). καὶ χρυσῷ στεφάνῳ τιμηθέντα ἐπάθλῳ πολυποσίας τοῖς Χουσὶ παρὰ Διονυσίῳ ἐξιόντα θεῖναι πρὸς τὸν ἱδρύμενον Ἑρμῆν, ἔνθαπερ τιθέναι καὶ τοὺς ἀνθινοὺς εἰώθει. (See No. 19 above.)

(23) Philostratus, *Heroic.* xii. 2. (Αἴας παῖδα) τήν τε ἄλλην ἔτρεφε τροφήν, ἣν Ἀθηναῖοι ἐπαινοῦσι, καὶ ὅτε Ἀθήνησιν οἱ παῖδες ἐν μηνὶ Ἀνθεστηριῶνι στεφανοῦνται τῶν ἀνθέων τρίτῳ ἀπὸ γενέας ἔτει, κρατῆράς τε τοὺς ἐκεῖθεν ἐστήσατο καὶ ἔθυσεν ὅσα Ἀθηναίοις ἐν νόμῳ.

(24) Schol. on Hesiod, *Op.* 336. καὶ ἐν τοῖς πατρίοις ἐστὶν ἑορτὴ Πιθοίγια, καθ' ἣν οὔτε οἰκέτην οὔτε μισθωτὸν εἴργειν τῆς ἀπολαύσεως τοῦ οἴνου θεμιτὸν ἦν, ἀλλὰ θύσαντας πᾶσι μεταδιδόναι τοῦ δώρου τοῦ Διονύσου.

(25) Zenobius (in Codex Athous, 14th cent.). θύραζε Κᾶρες, οὐκ ἔτ' Ἀνθεστήρια· φασὶν ὅτι οἱ Κᾶρές ποτε μέρος τῆς Ἀττικῆς κατέσχον· καὶ εἴ ποτε τὴν ἑορτὴν τῶν Ἀνθεστηρίων ἦγον οἱ Ἀθηναῖοι, σπονδῶν αὐτοῖς μετεδίδοσαν καὶ ἐδέχοντο τῷ ἄστει καὶ τοῖς οἰκίαις, μετὰ δὲ τὴν ἑορτὴν τινῶν ὑπολελειμμένων ἐν ταῖς Ἀθήναις, οἱ ἀπαντῶντες πρὸς τοὺς Κᾶρας παίζοντες ἔλεγον· θύραζε Κᾶρες, οὐκ ἔτ' Ἀνθεστήρια.

To this, two collections of proverbs, in a Bodleian and a Vatican MS., both of the fifteenth century, add: τινὲς δὲ οὕτως φασὶ θύραζε Κῆρες, οὐκ ἔνι Ἀνθεστήρια.

(26) Photius. τὰ ἐκ τῶν ἁμαξῶν. . . . Ἀθήνησι γὰρ ἐν τῇ τῶν Χοῶν ἑορτῇ οἱ κωμάζοντες ἐπὶ τῶν ἁμαξῶν τοὺς ἀπαντῶντας ἔσκωπτόν τε καὶ ἐλοιδόρουν. τὸ δ' αὐτὸ καὶ τοῖς Ληναίοις ὕστερον ἐποίουν. (So also Suidas.)

(27) Photius. μιαρὰ ἡμέρα· ἐν τοῖς Χουσὶν Ἀνθεστηριῶνος μηνός, ἐν ᾧ δοκοῦσιν αἱ ψυχαὶ τῶν τελευτησάντων ἀνιέναι, ῥάμνον (MSS. ῥάμνῳ) ἕωθεν ἐμασῶντο καὶ πίττῃ τὰς θύρας ἔχριον.

(28) Id. ῥάμνος· φυτὸν ὃ ἐν τοῖς Χουσὶν ὡς ἀλεξιφάρμακον ἐμασῶντο ἕωθεν. καὶ πίττῃ ἐχρίοντο τὰ δώματα· ἀμίαντος γὰρ αὕτη. διὸ καὶ ἐν ταῖς γενέσεσι τῶν παιδῶν χρίουσι τὰς οἰκίας εἰς ἀπέλασιν τῶν δαιμόνων.

(29) Id. θύραζε Κᾶρες, οὐκέτ' Ἀνθεστήρια· ἣν οἱ μὲν διὰ πλῆθος οἰκετῶν Καρικῶν εἰρῆσθαί φασιν, ὡς ἐν τοῖς Ἀνθεστηρίοις εὐωχουμένων αὐτῶν καὶ οὐκ ἐργαζομένων. τῆς οὖν ἑορτῆς τελεσθείσης λέγειν ἐπὶ τὰ ἔργα ἐκπέμποντας αὐτούς· θύραζε Κᾶρες, οὐκέτ' Ἀνθεστήρια. τινὲς δὲ οὕτως

τὴν παροιμίαν φασί· θύραζε Κῆρες, οὐκ ἔνι Ἀνθεστήρια, ὡς κατὰ τὴν
πόλιν τοῖς Ἀνθεστηρίοις τῶν ψυχῶν περιερχομένων. (Suidas repeats
this.)

(30) Suidas, s.v. Χόες. Contains nothing which is not in (3) above,
though in longer or shorter form.

(31) *I.G.* ii². 1672 (l. 204) (in the accounts of the ἐπιστάται Ἐλευσινόθεν
for 329/8 B.C.). εἰς Χόας δημοσίοις ἱερεῖον ΔΔΗΗ.

(32) Inscr. from Miletus (*Rev. Ét. Gr.* 1919, p. 262), l. 21. τοῖς δὲ
Καταγωγίοις κατάγειν τὸν Διόνυσον τοὺς ἱερεῖς καὶ τὰς ἱερείας τοῦ
Διονύσου τοῦ Βακχίου μετὰ τοῦ ἱερέως καὶ τῆς ἱερείας πρὸ τῆς ἡμέρας
μέχρι τῶν . . . τῆς πόλεως. (Date 276–275 B.C.)

(33) *Inschr. von Priene* 174. 19. ἐχέτω δὲ καὶ στολὴν (ὁ ἱερεὺς) ἣν ἂμ
βούληται καὶ στέφανον χρυσοῦν μῆνα Ληναιῶνα καὶ Ἀνθεστηριῶνα·
καὶ τοῖς Καταγωγίοις καθηγήσεται τῶν συγκαταγόντων τὸν Διόνυσον.
(2nd cent. B.C.)

(34) Philostratus, *Vit. Soph.* I. xxv. πέμπεται γάρ τις μηνὶ Ἀνθεστηριῶνι
μετάρσια τριήρης ἐς ἀγοράν, ἣν ὁ Διονύσου ἱερεὺς οἷον κυβερνήτης
εὐθύνει πείσματα ἐκ θαλάττης λύουσαν. (This was at Smyrna in
the reign of Hadrian.)

(35) *I.G.* ii². 1368, ll. 111 ff. (The Iobacchoi of Athens, 2nd cent. A.D.).
ἱερεὺς δὲ ἐπιτελείτω τὰς ἐθίμους λιτουργίας Στιβάδος καὶ ἀμφιετηρίδος εὐπρεπῶς καὶ τιθέτω τὴν τῶν Καταγωγίων σπονδὴν Στιβάδι
μίαν καὶ θεολογίαν, ἣν ἤρξατο ἐκ φιλοτειμίας ποιεῖν ὁ ἱερασάμενος
Νεικόμαχος.

(36) Philostratus, *Vit. Apoll.* III. xiv. θεῶν δὲ ἀγάλμασιν ἐντυχεῖν φασιν, εἰ
μὲν Ἰνδοῖς ἢ Αἰγυπτίοις, θαῦμα οὐδέν, τὰ δέ γε ἀρχαιότατα τῶν παρ'
Ἕλλησι, τό τε τῆς Ἀθηνᾶς τῆς Πολιάδος καὶ τὸ τοῦ Ἀπόλλωνος τοῦ
Δηλίου καὶ τὸ τοῦ Διονύσου τοῦ Λιμναίου καὶ τὸ τοῦ Ἀμυκλαίου, καὶ
ὁπόσα ὧδε ἀρχαῖα, ταῦτα ἱδρύεσθαί τε τοὺς Ἰνδοὺς καὶ νομίζειν
Ἑλληνικοῖς ἤθεσι, φασὶ δ' οἰκεῖν τὰ μέσα τῆς Ἰνδικῆς.

(37) Ibid. IV. xxi. ἐπιπλῆξαι δὲ λέγεται περὶ Διονυσίων Ἀθηναίοις, ἃ
ποιεῖταί σφισιν ἐν ὥρᾳ τοῦ Ἀνθεστηριῶνος· ὁ μὲν γὰρ μονῳδίας
ἀκροασόμενος καὶ μελοποιίας παραβάσεών τε καὶ ῥυθμῶν, ὁπόσοι
κωμῳδίας τε καὶ τραγῳδίας εἰσίν, ἐς τὸ θέατρον ξυμφοιτᾶν ᾤετο,
ἐπεὶ δὲ ἤκουσεν ὅτι αὐλοῦ ὑποσημήναντος λογισμοὺς ὀρχοῦνται καὶ
μεταξὺ τῆς Ὀρφέως ἐποποιίας τε καὶ θεολογίας τὰ μὲν ὡς Ὧραι, τὰ
δὲ ὡς Νύμφαι, τὰ δὲ ὡς Βάκχαι πράττουσιν, ἐς ἐπίπληξιν τούτου
κατέστη.

2. The passage quoted above (No. 23) from the *Heroicus* of
Philostratus suggests that the name of the Anthesteria is derived
from the wearing of a crown of flowers by boys and girls who
were just passing out of infancy. This is confirmed by a vase-
painting (Fig. 1)[1] of the late fifth century showing a garlanded
little boy carrying a vessel of the characteristic shape of the
χοῦς, and by an inscription[2] on a relief commemorating a boy
who had died just before he could be crowned at the festival
and describing him as ἡλικίης Χοικῶν, ὁ δὲ δαίμων ἔφθασε τοὺς
Χοῦς. Hesychius[3] records that at Rhodes maidens just ripe for
marriage were called ἀνθεστηριάδες. Pausanias[4] mentions a
Διόνυσος Ἄνθιος as worshipped at Phlya, and an Ἀνθιστήρ in an
inscription[5] of the second century B.C. at Thera is conjectured
to be a Bacchic hero or the god himself.[6]

3. On the first day of the festival, called Πιθοίγια, people
gathered near[7] the Sanctuary of Dionysus ἐν Λίμναις, opened the
πίθοι—the jars containing the wine of last autumn's grapes—and
drank it after pouring libations of it to Dionysus. Their slaves
shared in the drinking and the merry-making of the feast.[8]

4. The second day, the Χόες, was celebrated by drinking
throughout the city, vessels of a peculiar shape being appropriated to the ceremony,[9] and a drinking-match, announced by
sound of trumpet, was solemnly conducted by the archon
basileus at the θεσμοθετεῖον.[10] The ritual was based upon that
which, according to tradition, had been observed when Orestes
was entertained at Athens before he had been purified of murder;
to avoid contamination each drinker had a separate vessel, and
all drank in silence.[11] In the contest in the θεσμοθετεῖον the prize

[1] Klein, *Vasen mit Lieblingsinschriften*, p. 136, No. 1; Deubner, *Attische Feste*, Taf. 13, No. 4.
The boy depicted is also pushing a toy wagon, which Deubner aptly compares with the
ἁμαξίς presented (in Aristophanes, *Clouds* 864) by Strepsiades to Pheidippides at the Diasia.
For the part played by children in the festival see below, p. 10.

[2] *I.G.* iii[1]. 1342 (= Kaibel, *Epigr. Gr.* 157).

[3] s.v. ἀνθεστηριάδες.

[4] I. xxxi. 4.

[5] *I.G.* xii. 3. 329.

[6] Other Choes are depicted here by the kindness of Sir John Beazley, Mrs. S. P. Karouzou,
and Dr. H. A. Thompson (see *Am. J. Arch.* l (1946), and *Hesperia*, xviii (1949)).

[7] πρὸς τῷ ἱερῷ (Phanodemus *ap.* Athen. xiii. 465 a), not *in* the ἱερόν, which was only open
on the next day. (So also Deubner, op. cit., pp. 127–9.)

[8] Miss J. E. Harrison's attempt to connect the Πιθοίγια with the cult of the dead (*Prolegomena*, pp. 43 ff.) is answered by Farnell (*Cults*, v, pp. 221 ff.), and Deubner (op. cit., p. 95).

[9] Athen. xi. 495 a–c. (Passage 21 on pp. 6–7 above.)

[10] Plut. *Quaest. Conviv.* i, p. 613 b. (Passage 15 above.)

[11] Passages 3, 16, 19 above.

was a skin full of wine.[1] In unofficial drinking-matches on the same day there were cakes and garlands as prizes, and the revellers generally, at the end of the day, took the garlands which they wore, wound them round their χόες, brought them to the priestess in charge of the sanctuary ἐν Λίμναις, and poured libations of the rest of the wine.[2] A vase (a χοῦς) of the early fourth century in the Louvre (Fig. 2c) is thought to represent the priestess receiving a youth who comes to dedicate his garland.

Miss G. M. A. Richter has published[3] two vases in the New York Metropolitan Museum of Art (Figs. 3 and 4) of about 420 B.C., each of the characteristic form of the χοῦς, depicting (as she suggests) a reveller at the Anthesteria—the one while he is dancing, with two youthful companions (one of whom holds his clothes), the other at the moment when, having well drunk, he is trying to re-enter his own house—if indeed it is not the house of a hetaira. He ought of course to have taken his χοῦς by this time to the priestess, but it is probable that the revels which succeeded the drinking-match at the Choes went on for some time after the day called Χύτροι had technically begun.[4] Miss Richter also notes that the museum contains a number of miniature jugs of the same type which, she conjectures, may have been used by children taking part in the festival, and Mrs. S. P. Karouzou[5] publishes some Athenian examples of 'children's choes' (Figs. 1b, 2a) of the same class as those depicted in Figs. 1a, 2b, showing children playing. A stele on one of the vases perhaps indicates that one of the children thought of had died.

A delightful picture (Fig. 5)[6] on a chous in the Vlasto Collec-

---

[1] That the festival included ἀσκωλιασμός, leaping upon a full wineskin, is stated by Schol. on Aristoph. *Ach.* 1000, but this is probably due to a confusion with other festivals, arising out of the fact that the full wineskin was awarded as a prize.   [2] Athen. xi. 437 c.

[3] *Bull. New York Metrop. Mus. of Art*, xxxix (1939), pp. 231–2.

[4] In the scene in Aristoph. *Ach.* 1071–142, Lamachus is called out for military duties owing to warning of a raid ὑπὸ τοὺς Χοᾶς καὶ Χύτρους, while Dikaiopolis prepares for a drinking-match (with his χοῦς, l. 1133), evidently like that of the Anthesteria. See Immerwahr, *Trans. Am. Phil. Ass.* lxxvii (1946), pp. 247 ff.

[5] *Am. J. Arch.* l (1946), pp. 123–39. She makes a very interesting attempt to show that on another such vase (her Fig. 10) the children are performing a parody of the Orestes story which is connected with the festival, but her argument, though very ingenious, is not (to me) quite convincing, nor is her suggestion that the ἀγῶνες χυτρινοί were originally the contests of children at the festival. (This is not consistent with the very slight literary evidence; see below, p. 15.) This is not the place to discuss further the part played by children in the festival, but reference may be made to Deubner, op. cit., pp. 238 ff. It has been suggested that the very small choes may have been seasonal presents for children—like Easter eggs.

[6] Published by kind permission of Mrs. Jean Serpieri, the present owner of the Vlasto Collection.

a   *b*

c

FIG. I. ATTIC CHOES

a   *b*

c

FIG. 2. ATTIC CHOES

FIG. 3. REVELLER AT CHOES

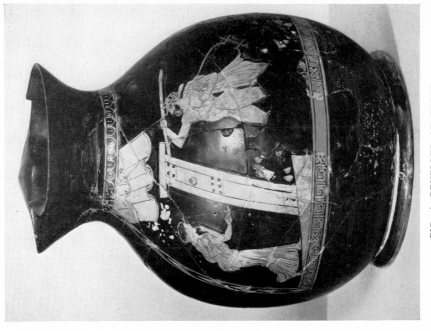

FIG. 4. REVELLER AT CHOES

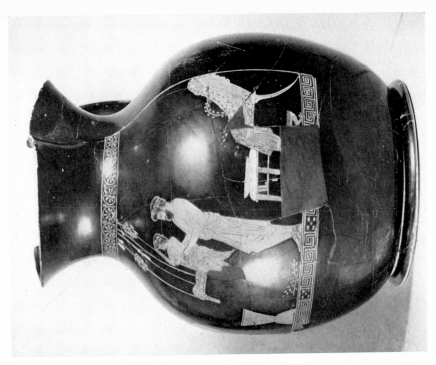

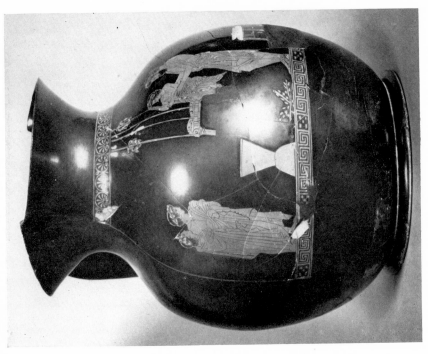

FIG. 5. INFANT ON SWING

tion by the Eretria painter shows a little boy garlanded and lightly held on a swing by his father, while two older garlanded children look on. Sir John Beazley, to whom I am indebted for photographs of this, interprets the scene as a ceremony of purification, probably by fumes from the vessel in the centre.

The sanctuary ἐν Λίμναις was open on this day only in the year, and the revellers continued to frequent it until the evening, when, strictly speaking, the day called Χύτροι had already begun.[1] In the sanctuary—doubtless in an inner chamber[2]—there took place the secret ceremonies, conducted by the fourteen γεραιραί, preparatory to the sacred marriage of the βασίλιννα, the wife of the archon βασιλεύς, to Dionysus.[3] The marriage itself was celebrated (by what symbolism we do not know) in the Βουκόλιον,[4] which stood near the Πρυτανεῖον; the site of this is still a matter of controversy. It was doubtless a piece of fertility-magic, and symbolized the union of the god of fruitfulness with the community represented by the wife of its religious head.

5. Whether or not there is a connexion between these ceremonies and the procession, represented on a number of vase-paintings, in which Dionysus was escorted riding in a car shaped like a ship on wheels, has been keenly disputed.[5] What is represented is plainly the arrival of Dionysus in Athens from overseas—whether from Thrace or Lydia or Euboea—and Deubner makes out a strong case for the connexion with the Anthesteria, based on a comparison of a number of vases with the evidence of ancient notices (quoted above) and of ceremonies of the

[1] Aristoph. *Frogs* 218. (Passage 8 above.)

[2] Schol. on Aristoph. *Frogs* 216 mentions that the temple contained the οἶκος and νεὼς τοῦ θεοῦ.

[3] Pseudo-Dem. *in Neaer.* §§ 73–78. (Passage 11 above.) For the nature of these ceremonies see Farnell, *Cults*, v, pp. 217 ff., and Deubner, op. cit., pp. 100 ff. It has been conjectured that the archon βασιλεύς himself may have impersonated the god. This ἱερὸς γάμος is possibly the subject of a vase-painting in the British Museum (Deubner, op. cit., Taf. 10, Figs. 1 and 2 and p. 101; cf. Farnell, *Cults*, v, p. 260).

[4] Aristotle, *Ἀθ. Πολ.* iii. The expression used by Aristotle, τὸ νῦν καλούμενον Βουκόλιον, may imply that he knew an earlier name for the building. The American excavators have made a strong case for placing the Prytaneion (mentioned in Paus. i. xviii, § 3) on the NW. slope of the Acropolis, below the precinct of Aglauros. See *Hesperia*, iv (1935), pp. 470–1; xviii (1949), p. 129. For earlier controversy see Judeich, *Topogr. Athen.*, pp. 296–8.

[5] Cf. my *Dith. Trag. Com.*, pp. 114 ff., Figs. 4–7 (and Figs. 6–8 here). I am now more inclined to support the connexion with the Anthesteria, but it must always remain possible that the painters are representing a popular subject, without direct dependence on any festival or ritual. Deubner (op. cit., pp. 104, 149) argues from the fact that the Iobaccheion at Athens (passage 35 above) was built over part of the remains of the precinct ἐν Λίμναις that the Καταγώγια celebrated by the Iobacchoi may have been a survival of the return of Dionysus in a ship-car at the Anthesteria centuries before.

type called Καταγώγια (the 'bringing home' of Dionysus) in a number of Ionian states, in some of which a connexion with the local Anthesteria is affirmed; these states include Smyrna, Ephesus, Miletus, Priene, and others.[1]

If the Anthesteria really included a procession of this kind, it may have escorted the god to the Βουκόλιον, though this is no

Fig. 6. Dionysiac procession

more than a conjecture. The car of Dionysus may have been followed by the wagons from which the revellers shouted their jests,[2] while the crowd retaliated in like manner—a form of merriment which is attested both for the Anthesteria and for the Lenaia, as well as for the procession to Eleusis before the mysteries. (It was perhaps a common feature of popular processions at Athens, and may have been apotropaic in its original intention, though such an explanation is scarcely necessary.)

6. The third day of the festival, called Χύτροι, began on the evening of the day called Χόες. There is consequently some confusion here and there in the attribution of particular ceremonies to one day or the other. Thus Aristophanes (*Frogs* 217–19, passage 8 above) speaks of the revels as occurring on the Χύτροι—and this was probably correct, though they began with the

[1] On the arrival by sea, besides references given in passages 32 ff. above and in *Dith. Trag. Com.*, pp. 114 ff., cf. O. Kern, *Rel. der Gr.* i, p. 232; Wilam.-Moell. *Glaube der Hell.* ii, p. 4; Deubner, op. cit., p. 111, etc.; Lesky, *Mitt. Ver. Klass. Phil. in Wien*, 1925, pp. 11–24, and *Wiener Stud.* xlvii (1929), pp. 3 ff. For Ephesus vide Maas, *Orpheus*, pp. 55 ff. and 61. On Καταγώγια generally see Nilsson in *Jahrb. Arch.* xxxi (1916), pp. 309 ff.

[2] Photius, s.v. τὰ ἐκ τῶν ἁμαξῶν; Harpokr. s.v. πομπείας and πομπεύειν (quoted above, p. 5). Suidas, s.v. τὰ ἐξ ἁμαξῆς, records a peculiar (and perhaps more serious) form of vituperation from a wagon at Alexandria (see Farnell, *Cults*, v, p. 212).

drinking-match on the Χόες—and Photius refers to the Χόες as the day on which the ghosts wandered; such confusions are not unnatural, and there may in practice have been some over-lapping; but it seems probable that, speaking generally, the cheerful ceremonies connected with the Χόες came to an end about sunset, and that the Χύτροι which then began was a day of a quite different character, devoted to the cult of the dead, and that Dionysus had little part in it.[1] The day was named after the pots of a kind of porridge, composed of various kinds of grain, offered to Hermes Χθόνιος,[2] with intercessions for the dead—particularly, we are told, for those who perished in Deukalion's flood.[3] It was a day of gloom, a μιαρά or ἀποφρὰς ἡμέρα, on which ghosts were abroad, and cathartic measures (such as the chewing of buckthorn and the smearing of houses with pitch) were taken as a precaution against them. At the end of the day the cry was uttered, θύραζε Κᾶρες or θύραζε Κῆρες, οὐκέτ' Ἀνθεστήρια.

This cry has been the subject of much controversy. If it was originally θύραζε Κᾶρες—an order to the country slaves, who had come in to the city to share in the feast, to go back to work—it may easily have become a colloquial phrase for recalling idle slaves to their task; and the literary evidence suggests that Κᾶρες was the original form of the phrase. Zenobius (second century A.D.), who got his material from Didymus' work πρὸς τοὺς περὶ προοιμίων συντεταχότας (Didymus' own source being possibly the collection of proverbs in forty books made by Demon in the third century B.C.) seems to have included this form only, though two collections of proverbs in manuscripts slightly later than the principal manuscript of Zenobius (evidently copying Photius, as their reproduction of the misreading ἔνι for ἔτ' shows) add the other version, θύραζε Κῆρες, and explain it by the expulsion of

---

[1] It is very doubtful whether the Ἀγῶνες Χυτρινοί (see below) were an essential or original part of the festival.

[2] That the offering was made to Dionysus as well as to Hermes is stated on the authority of Didymus in the schol. on Aristoph. *Ach.* 1076 (passage 5 above), but it can hardly be doubted that the words Διονύσῳ καί are a mistaken insertion: in fact μόνῳ could not make sense with τῷ Διονύσῳ καὶ Ἑρμῇ (it would have to be μόνοις). On the text of the scholia bearing on the Χύτροι see F. T. Tausend, *Studien zu Attischen Festen* (Würzburg, 1920). For the possible connexion of certain vases with this ceremony see Karouzou, *Am. J. Arch.* l (1946), pp. 122–3.

[3] See passages quoted above, Nos. 5, 8, 28. It is possible that the Ὑδροφορία, the pouring of libations of water to these same victims of the flood, was also a ceremony of the Χύτροι: see Deubner, op. cit., p. 113.

the ghosts who wandered about the city during the festival. The evidence, however, that the word κῆρες was ever applied to the souls of the dead, apart from this passage, is extremely slight. Hesychius has κῆρες· ψυχαί· συμφοραί· μοῖραι θανατηφόροι, and Suidas κήρ· ψυχή, καὶ θανατηφόρος μοῖρα. καὶ κῆρες, θανατηφόροι μοῖραι . . . κὴρ δὲ καὶ ἡ ψυχή, διότι διὰ πυρός ἐστι· τὸ γὰρ ἔμφυτον θερμόν, τοῦτο ψυχή. 'εἰμὶ δὲ κὴρ τυμβοῦχος, ὁ δὲ κτείνας με Κόροιβος'[1] (but no stress can be laid on this, as the κὴρ τυμβοῦχος is the figure on the tombstone, not the deceased). Further, there is no other evidence of the expulsion of ghosts in Athens, though it was performed in other parts of Greece, as in many other European countries, and there is something to be said for the suggestion that θύραζε Κῆρες may have arisen under the influence of Roman religion, when such expulsion regularly took place at the Lemuria. A further difficulty arises from the fact that the proverb forms an iambic trimeter. There is no ground for Crusius's statement that this was a traditional metre of liturgical formula, and the line as it stands—with Κᾶρες—may come from some comedy, even if something of the sort was said at the Anthesteria. No final solution seems possible.[2]

How a day of evil omen came to be attached to the cheerful Dionysiac festival we do not know. That it was probably separate at first is shown by the fact that there is no hint of anything like it in any of the parallel festivals in Ionian states of which brief records survive. The Anthesteria as a whole was plainly a cheerful feast, and there is reason to think that it dates from before the migration from Greece to Asia Minor of the Ionian tribes who all celebrated it at the same time.[3] If so, and if it was originally an Ionian festival, there is nothing surprising in the absence from it of dramatic elements, or performances which might grow into drama, since the roots of drama were for the most part in Dorian soil.[4]

[1] *Anth. Pal.* vii. 154 (author and date unknown).

[2] See especially O. Crusius, *Analecta critica ad paroemiographos Graecos* (1883); Nilsson in *Eranos*, xv (1915), pp. 181 ff.; Malten in Pauly–W. *Real-Encycl.*, Suppl. iv, s.v. 'Ker'; and Ganszyniec in *Eranos*, xlv (1947), pp. 100–13. The suggestions that Κῆρες may be applied to ghosts metaphorically ('ye evil things'), or that κᾶρες may be Doric for κῆρες, are very unconvincing; as is also Deubner's treatment of the line as a combination of ritual phrases in other metres, accidentally forming an iambic trimeter.

[3] The objection that this implies a worship of Dionysus in Greece earlier than is often recognized is met by Deubner, op. cit., pp. 122–3.

[4] I do not here discuss the possible connexion of the ceremony called αἰώρα with the Χύτροι, on account of the space which would be required. See Deubner, *Att. Feste*, pp. 118 ff.,

7. The only direct point of contact between the Anthesteria and the Greek Drama in classical times is that furnished by the so-called Ἀγῶνες Χυτρινοί which were restored after an unspecified period of abeyance by a law of Lycurgus in the third quarter of the fourth century B.C. The principal authority for this is found in Plutarch (?), *Vit. X Orat.* 841 f. εἰσήνεγκεν δὲ καὶ νόμους, τὸν μὲν περὶ τῶν κωμῳδῶν, ἀγῶνα τοῖς χύτροις ἐπιτελεῖν ἐφάμιλλον ἐν τῷ θεάτρῳ καὶ τὸν νικήσαντα εἰς ἄστυ καταλέγεσθαι, πρότερον οὐκ ἐξόν, ἀναλαμβάνων τὸν ἀγῶνα ἐκλελοιπότα. This can hardly refer to anything but a contest of comic actors, the victor in which acquired the right to act at the ensuing Dionysia ἐν ἄστει.[1] For tragedy the choice of the three protagonists was the duty of the archon, but the successful protagonist of the previous year had a right to be selected; subordinate actors were chosen by the poets themselves.[2] Presumably the contest at the Χύτροι was limited to protagonists, though there is no definite statement to this effect. The notice of Plutarch is confirmed by the scholiast[3] on Aristophanes' *Frogs*, l. 218, with his quotation from Philochorus (c. 280 B.C.). The nature of the contests is unrecorded. It does not seem likely that these ἀγῶνες were an essential part of the Anthesteria, the nature of which has been described above. They cannot have been an original part, because the Anthesteria was a much older festival than the Dionysia ἐν ἄστει.[4] But the festival fell at a time which would be convenient for the choice of actors for the Dionysia a few weeks later, and a time of public holiday-making would also be suitable, and so the contests may naturally have been 'thrown in' on the third day of the festival.

8. There is a reference in Philostratus' life of Apollonius[5] to dances in costume at the Anthesteria which shocked Apollonius, who had apparently expected to hear singing and recitation of selections from tragedy and comedy. These performances

and Karouzou, *Am. J. Arch.* l (1946), p. 122 and refs. there given, and Immerwahr, *Trans. Am. Phil. Ass.* lxxvii (1946), pp. 254 ff. But see above (pp. 10, 11 and Fig. 5).

[1] Other interpretations are shown to be impossible by O'Connor, *Chapters in the History of Actors and Acting in Ancient Greece* (1908), pp. 54–55. The conjecture that the privilege won by the victorious actor was that of producing the Old Comedy acted at each Dionysia from 339 B.C. onwards (i.e. from the time of Lycurgus) would be attractive, but the words ἀναλαμβάνων τὸν ἀγῶνα ἐκλελοιπότα seem to exclude it.

[2] Suidas, s.v. νεμήσεις ὑποκριτῶν, and below, p. 94.   [3] Passage 8 on p. 3.

[4] The 'theatre' in which the Dionysia ἐν ἄστει were celebrated cannot have been there before the sixth century B.C. See *Theatre of Dionysus in Athens*, ch. i.

[5] IV. xxi. (Passage 37 on p. 8.)

occurred in the intervals of recitations of Orphic poems. If any or all of these things formed part of the Anthesteria of the first century A.D., the festival must have changed much. These performances may have replaced the ἀγῶνες Χυτρινοί on the Χύτροι. It is possible that the original character of the festival had long been forgotten, and it was probably not long after this that the sanctuary ἐν Λίμναις was partly destroyed and replaced by the Iobaccheion of which some remains are still to be seen.

9. There can be no serious doubt that the Anthesteria were identical with the ἀρχαιότερα Διονύσια mentioned by Thucydides. His words admit of no other interpretation. But some scholars[1] have found a difficulty in his use of the comparative, which, they think, means that Thucydides knew only *two* Dionysiac festivals, an earlier and a later, and that as the later must have been the Great Dionysia, the earlier must have been the Lenaia which must accordingly have been, wholly or in part, identical with the Anthesteria and must have taken place ἐν Λίμναις.

In reply it may be shown (1) that the inference from the use of the comparative is unwarranted, (2) that the identification of the Anthesteria and the Lenaia is contrary to the evidence.

(1) Even if the use of the comparative implied a comparison between two terms only, these two terms might be (*a*) the Anthesteria, (*b*) the rest of the Dionysiac festivals treated as a group of more recent institutions. But in fact there are other passages in classical Greek literature in which the comparative of words denoting age, etc., is used of the oldest, not of two, but of several. Nilsson[2] collects the following instances:

Lys. x. 5. ὁ γὰρ πρεσβύτερος ἀδελφὸς Πανταλέων ἅπαντα παρέλαβε καὶ ἐπιτροπεύσας ἡμᾶς τῶν πατρῴων ἀπεστέρησεν.

Id. xiii. 67. ἦσαν τοίνυν οὗτοι, ὦ ἄνδρες δικασταί, τέτταρες ἀδελφοί· τούτων εἷς μὲν ὁ πρεσβύτερος κτλ.

Xen. *Cyr.* v. i. 6. ὡς δ' ἡμῶν ὁ γεραίτερος εἶπε.[3] (The context shows that a number of persons were concerned.)

Theocr. xv. 139. οὔθ' Ἕκτωρ, Ἑκάβας ὁ γεραίτερος εἴκατι παιδῶν.

---

[1] Gilbert, Dörpfeld, Capps, and others. I have discussed the matter in Appendix C to Haigh's *Attic Theatre* (ed. iii), but on certain points prefer the present statement of the case.

[2] *Studia de Dionysiis Atticis*, p. 54. Homeric instances can be found in Kühner–Gerth, *Gr. Gramm.*, § 349, p. 3.

[3] The reading γεραίτερος is far better supported than γεραίτατος. Grammarians and editors tend to 'emend' such comparatives into the supposed orthodox superlative, as, for example, in Aelian, *Var. H.* ii. 41, etc.

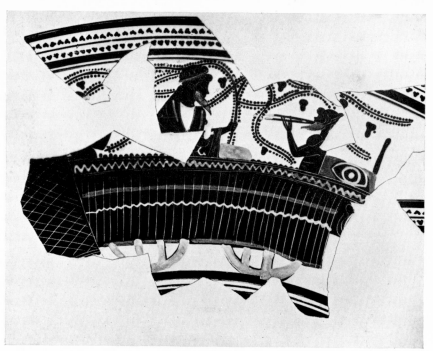

a

b

FIG. 7. DIONYSIAC PROCESSION

FIG. 8. DIONYSUS AT SEA

It may, however, be suggested that for some considerable period there *were* only two Dionysiac festivals, the Anthesteria and the Lenaia, and that therefore on the strictest view of the comparative, the former would be τὰ ἀρχαιότερα, and might continue to be so spoken of even after the institution of the Great Dionysia, if no one was pedantic enough to change the appellation to the superlative.[1]

(2) The Lenaia were celebrated in the month Gamelion (elsewhere called Lenaion), the Anthesteria in Anthesterion:[2] and in inscriptions the two festivals are plainly treated as distinct; e.g. in the accounts of money laid out on each festival in 329–328 B.C.,[3] and in an inscription of 193–192 B.C.[4] which separates the Lenaia from the Χύτροι. Photius, Suidas, etc., in explaining the σκώμματα ἐκ τῶν ἀμαξῶν, after referring to the custom at the Χόες, add τὸ δ' αὐτὸ καὶ τοῖς Ληναίοις ὕστερον ἐποίουν. Nothing could be clearer.[5]

That the character of the two festivals was quite different will be seen from the account of the Lenaia to be given in the next section of this chapter, where the connected problem of the place of the Lenaian performance will also have to be discussed.

10. The remaining question in regard to the Anthesteria concerns the site of the precinct ἐν Λίμναις, and for this the only first-hand evidence is that of Thucydides.[6] He is explaining that the earliest city (before Theseus) was quite small, consisting only of what in his own day was called the Acropolis, together with the area beneath it in a direction more or less south. This latter expression must refer to the area on the southern and southwestern slope of the Acropolis, then included within the same city-wall as the Acropolis itself—the area known as Pelargikon. This he confirms by noting that the temples of other gods

[1] But it is impossible to follow Capps's distinction (*Class. Philol.* IV. i) of ἀρχαιότερα ('ancient', 'primitive') from παλαιότερα (prior in time) and the conclusions which he draws from it. Aeschines, *in Ctes.* § 50, uses both words in exactly the same sense.

[2] Nilsson, op. cit., pp. 1–37, completely disproves Gilbert's attempt to prove that the names of the months were changed and the festivals transferred from one month to another.

[3] *C.I.A.* ii². 1672.

[4] Ibid. 2130; cf. Nilsson, op. cit., pp. 42–44. He quotes other equally conclusive passages (p. 143).

[5] The schol. on Aristoph. *Ach.* 961 certainly refers to the Χόες as a festival of Διόνυσος Ληναῖος, but other accounts do not; the scholiasts are far from impeccable, and (as has often been suggested) ΛΗΝΑΙΟΥ is an easy corruption of ΛΙΜΝΑΙΟΥ.

[6] II. xv, see above, p. 1.

(besides Athena) all fell within this small city, being on the Acropolis, and that the oldest sanctuaries outside this original city were also close to it—πρὸς τοῦτο τὸ μέρος[1] τῆς πόλεως μᾶλλον ἵδρυται—they 'were built with reference to—or close to—this part of Athens' (τῆς πόλεως being the Athens *of Thucydides' own day*)—namely, the sanctuaries of Olympian Zeus, the Pythion, the sanctuary of Ge and that of Dionysus ἐν Λίμναις, and other old sanctuaries; that the fountain originally called Kallirrhoe, but now (since Peisistratus' day) called Enneakrounos, was in the same neighbourhood; and that hence the Acropolis (which with the additional area on the south was the original city) was still commonly called πόλις. One of these sanctuaries may certainly be identified with the Pythion close to the Klepsydra below the north-west corner of the Acropolis (well known from Euripides, *Ion* 283 ff. and Strabo ix. 2), quite near which, as Strabo's description shows, was an Olympion.[2] The location of the Sanctuary of Ge is less certain; it is often thought to have been that of Γῆ Κουροτρόφος[3] at the south-west corner of the Acropolis, but there are other possibilities.[4] As for the other old sanctuaries, Pausanias[5] mentions the Temple of Demeter and Kore (possibly included in the Eleusinion, along with the image of Triptolemus, which Pausanias mentions in the same breath) and that of Eukleia, which was a memorial of the victory of Marathon. Near these—and near enough to be the main water-supply of the original city—was the fountain Kallirrhoe or Enneakrounos, which most scholars have been content to identify (after Dörpfeld) with the fountain at the foot of the Pnyx, of which the remains are well known; but the American excavators place it at the south-west corner of the Agora which they are in process of uncovering, in the hollow to the north of

---

[1] πρὸς τοῦτο τὸ μέρος: not 'to the south of the original city' but 'close to this part of Athens'. It would be absurd to think of Thucydides as referring in the words which follow to the sanctuaries a long way to the south—nearly a kilometre from Agora—the Olympion well-known from the columns still standing, with a Pythion near it and a spring called Kallirrhoe (no doubt called after the old one when the settlement by the Ilissus was made and the old Kallirrhoe had lost the name and was called Enneakrounos). See J. E. Harrison, *Primitive Athens*, pp. 153–4.

[2] ἐτήρουν δ' ἐπὶ τρεῖς μῆνας, καθ' ἕκαστον μῆνα ἐπὶ τρεῖς ἡμέρας καὶ νύκτας ἀπὸ τῆς ἐσχάρας τοῦ Ἀστραπαίου Διός· ἔστι δ' αὕτη ἐν τῷ τείχει μεταξὺ τοῦ Πυθίου καὶ τοῦ Ὀλυμπίου. See especially A. Keramopoullos, Ἀρχ. Δελτ. xii (1929), pp. 86–98 for the identification of the Olympion.   [3] Paus. I. xxii. 3.

[4] See Broneer in *Hesperia*, xi (1942), p. 260, and below, p. 20.

[5] I. xiv. I.

the Areopagus.[1] In either case, Thucydides' remarks would be substantially true.

Where, then, was the Dionysion ἐν Λίμναις?[2] Three theories have been propounded:

(1) *That it was on the Ilissus*, near the spring Kallirrhoe and the Olympieion of Peisistratus and Hadrian. This is really ruled out by the distance from the entrance of the Acropolis (about 980 yards) and from the greater part of the original city. It derives its plausibility only from the fact that there was a duplication of names between the sanctuaries in this region and those at and near the north-west portion of the Acropolis. It is also extremely doubtful (according to the geologists) whether the region by the Ilissus was ever a region of marshy ground,[3] such as the title ἐν Λίμναις and the chorus of the *Frogs* require. (The latter implies *real* marshy ground.)

(2) *That it was close to (or just south of) the site of the Theatre of Dionysus*. Those who (like Carroll) hold this view base it mainly on a combination of the statement of Thucydides that it was in the ἐν Λίμναις that the ἀρχαιότερα Διονύσια were celebrated and an expression in the speech against Neaera—ἐν τῷ ἀρχαιοτάτῳ ἱερῷ Διονύσου καὶ ἁγιωτάτῳ ἐν Λίμναις—with Pausanias' state-ment[4] that the ἀρχαιότατον ἱερόν of Dionysus was πρὸς τῷ θεάτρῳ. But whereas down to the fourth century the original precinct ἐν Λίμναις, wherever it was, remained in being, it had certainly disappeared by the time of Pausanias, who in describ-ing Athens as he found it would naturally give the title of ἀρχαιότατον ἱερόν to the oldest temple which he found existing, viz. the older Temple of Dionysus in the theatre precinct. His expression gives no guidance as to the place of the ἐν Λίμναις.

Carroll's further argument that Thucydides is naming the ancient sanctuaries in the order of their localities (an unproved assumption) and that the ἐν Λίμναις must therefore be farther

---

[1] See Shear in *Hesperia*, iv (1935), p. 360; Broneer, ibid. xi (1942), p. 260; Vanderpool, ibid. xviii (1949), p. 133. Anti (*Teatri Greci Arcaici*, ch. vii, esp. p. 190) argues against the American view of Enneakrounos, but Thompson (*Am. J. Phil.* lxix (1948), pp. 451 ff.) replies sufficiently.

[2] For discussion of this subject see esp. Dörpfeld's account of his excavations in *Att. Mitt.* xx (1895), pp. 161 ff. (closely followed by J. E. Harrison, *Primitive Athens*); H. von Prott in *Ath. Mitt.* xxiii (1898), pp. 205 ff.; M. Carroll in *Class. Rev.* xix (1905), pp. 325–8 and Excursus III of his edition of Pausanias' *Attica*, and Dörpfeld, *Ath. Mitt.* xlvi (1921), pp. 81 ff.

[3] See H. von Prott, ibid. xxiii (1898), pp. 213–14, and refs. there given.

[4] I. xx. 3. The next sentence shows that he is thinking of temples in the theatre precinct only.

away from the Olympion and Pythion than the Sanctuary of
Γῆ Κουροτρόφος, at the south-west corner of the Acropolis, is
rendered very unsafe by the fact that it is only a conjecture that
this particular Sanctuary of *Γῆ* was the one referred to by the
historian, and that it is at least probable that there was one
nearer the Olympion and Pythion, north-west of the Acropolis.[1]

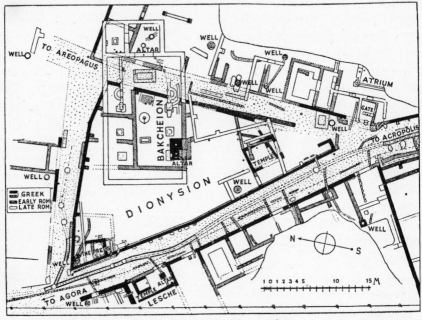

FIG. 9. Plan of Dionysian precinct

He is also extremely doubtful whether the requisite swampy
ground can be found at any period known to us in the neighbourhood of the theatre.

(3) *That it was in the precinct excavated by Dörpfeld* in 1894 to the
west of the Acropolis in the hollow enclosed by the western
slopes of the Acropolis, and the Areopagus and the Pnyx. This
was, as the authorities require, outside the earliest, or Thesean,
city-wall, but included in the later city, as a passage of Isaeus
proves the *ἐν Λίμναις* to have been.[2] There is no doubt that this
was in early times a swampy region, though it ceased to be so
in the course of time, probably because it was drained or filled

---

[1] See Broneer, *Hesperia*, xi (1942), p. 260. The further excavation and study of the ground
north-west of the Acropolis may throw light on the question.
[2] viii. 35.

up or both. There is an interesting confirmation of this in a passage of Strabo,[1] often misunderstood, in which he seems to be quoting the region of the Athenian Dionysion ἐν Λίμναις as a parallel to a district just outside Amyklai, which was also called Λίμναι because it had once been marshy, but was no longer so. The masonry of Dörpfeld's precinct also shows that the floor-level had been raised at some time, doubtless to accommodate it to a raising of the level outside.

The authorities for the Dionysion ἐν Λίμναις state that the precinct contained a νεώς and an οἶκος,[2] and that there was a βωμός, with an inscribed στηλή close to it.[3] Dörpfeld's precinct satisfies both these conditions. There is a small temple at the south end, and at the north-west corner a building partly occupied by a winepress. Not too much stress must be laid on the winepress (ληνός), which Dörpfeld claims as a proof that the precinct was Dionysiac (and was in fact the Λήναιον).[4] There are other winepresses in the neighbourhood, and the fact that no other known sanctuary of Dionysus contains one could be interpreted in more than one way.[5] But about the νεώς and the οἶκος there is no doubt; and one of the most conspicuous objects in the precinct is the foundation of an altar-table mounted on four low pillars,[6] with grooves in the foundation which can scarcely be intended for anything but the reception of στηλαί. The polygonal masonry of the lower strata of the walls,[7] and the geometrical

---

[1] VIII. v. ὑποπέπτωκε δὲ τῷ Ταϋγέτῳ ἡ Σπάρτη ἐν μεσογαίᾳ καὶ Ἀμύκλαι, οὗ τὸ Ἀπόλλωνος ἱερόν, καὶ ἡ Φᾶρις. ἔστι μὲν οὖν ἐν κοιλοτέρῳ χωρίῳ τὸ τῆς πόλεως ἔδαφος, καίπερ ἀπολάμβανον ὄρη μεταξύ· ἀλλ᾽ οὐδέν γε μέρος αὐτοῦ λιμνάζει, τὸ δὲ παλαιὸν ἐλίμαζε τὸ προαστεῖον καὶ ἐκάλουν αὐτὸ Λίμνας, καὶ τὸ τοῦ Διονύσου ἱερὸν ἐν Λίμναις ἐφ᾽ ὑγροῦ βεβηκὸς ἐτύγχανε, νῦν δ᾽ ἐπὶ ξηροῦ τὴν ἵδρυσιν ἔχει. The words τὸ Δ. ἱερὸν ἐν Λίμναις must surely refer to the well-known Δ. ἐν Λίμναις, i.e. the one at Athens. Cf. H. F. Tozer, *Selns. from Strabo* (1893), p. 212, and F. Bölte, *Ath. Mitt.* xxxiv (1909), pp. 391-2. (The latter suggests that Strabo's authority was Apollodorus of Athens); cf. also Dörpfeld, ibid. xlvi (1921), p. 83.

[2] Schol. on Aristoph. *Frogs* 216 (above, p. 3); cf. Harpokr. and Suid. s.v. ἐν Λίμναις Διόνυσος.   [3] Pseud.-Dem. *in Neaer.* § 76 (above, p. 4).

[4] This word is not really connected with ληνός, see below, p. 27.

[5] Dörpfeld ingeniously gets round the inappropriateness of a ληνός in a precinct only open on one day in February (not a season when a winepress would be used) by suggesting that the officials must have had access to the precinct at other times, though the public were excluded (*Ath. Mitt.* xlvi (1921), p. 86).

[6] The slab of a similar altar-table, found in an Attic village in 1880 and inscribed to Dionysus Αὐλωνεύς, is described ibid. v (1880), p. 116, but as it appears to be of early imperial date, it is hardly worth mention here. But Dörpfeld notes (ibid., p. 168) that such altars are also found on vases, especially in connexion with Dionysus.

[7] Dörpfeld's full description in *Ath. Mitt.* xx (1895) should be consulted, or Miss J. E. Harrison's summary in her *Primitive Athens*, from which Fig. 9 is borrowed by permission of the Cambridge University Press.

vases found, point to the altar and the temple being of the seventh or early sixth century B.C. (The winepress found is of the fourth century, but there are traces of an earlier one and of other structures below it.) The Dionysiac character of the precinct is rendered the more probable by the fact that when it was destroyed or remodelled, a Dionysiac sanctuary—that of the Iobacchoi—was built over it in the second century A.D.,[1] and the facts that there appears to have been only one small entrance to the precinct in its earlier days[2] and that there is an almost complete absence of dedications and inscriptions dating from pre-imperial times are entirely in accordance with the statement that it was then open only once a year. It would appear, then, extremely likely that the precinct was in fact the Dionysion ἐν Λίμναις, though there is no ground for going farther, with Dörpfeld, and identifying it also with the Lenaion. This will be discussed later.

B. THE LENAIA

1. The Lenaia took place in the month which was called Gamelion in Athens, and Lenaion in Ionian states generally. It corresponded roughly to January. The following are the principal texts which bear directly or indirectly on the festival:

(1) Hesiod, *Op.* 504.

> μῆνα δὲ Ληναιῶνα, κάκ᾽ ἤματα βουδόρα πάντα,
> τοῦτον ἀλεύασθαι.

Schol. (*a*) μῆνα δὲ Ληναιῶνα· Πλούταρχος οὐδένα φησὶ μῆνα Ληναιῶνα καλεῖσθαι παρὰ Βοιωτοῖς· ὑποπτεύει δὲ ἢ τὸν Βουκάτιον αὐτὸν λέγειν . . . ἢ τὸν Ἑρμαῖον, ὅς ἐστι μετὰ τὸν Βουκάτιον καὶ εἰς ταὐτὸν ἐρχόμενος τῷ Γαμηλιῶνι, καθ᾽ ὃν καὶ τὰ Λήναια παρ᾽ Ἀθηναίοις. Ἴωνες δὲ τοῦτον οὐδ᾽ ἄλλως, ἀλλὰ Ληναιῶνα καλοῦσι.

(*b*) . . . Ληναιὼν δὲ εἴρηται διὰ τὸ τοὺς οἴνους ἐν αὐτῷ εἰσκομίζεσθαι· οὗτος δὲ ὁ μὴν ἀρχὴ χειμῶνός ἐστιν· οἱ δὲ Ληναιῶνα φάσκουσιν αὐτὸν καλεῖσθαι διὰ τὰ Λήναια, ἅ ἐστιν ἔρια καὶ προβατοδόραν καὶ αἰγιοδόραν καλοῦμεν. ἢ ἐπειδὴ Διονύσῳ ἐποίουν ἑορτὴν τῷ μηνὶ τοῦτο, ἣν Ἀμβροσίαν ἐκάλουν.

[This note appears here in various forms and also in Hesych. and *Etym. Magn.* s.v. Ληναιών.]

---

[1] It is here that the great inscription of this thiasos (*I.G.* ii[2]. 1368) was found.
[2] Dörpfeld, *Ath. Mitt.* xx (1895), p. 166.

(2) Schol. on Aristoph. *Ach.* 378. τὰ δὲ Λήναια ἐν τῷ μετωπώρῳ ἤγετο, ἐν οἷς οὐ παρῆσαν οἱ ξένοι, ὅτε τὸ δρᾶμα τοῦτο οἱ Ἀχαρνεῖς ἐδιδάσκετο.

[This is only worth quoting as showing how small may be the value of scholia.]

(3) Bekk. *Anecd.* i, p. 235. Διονύσια· ἑορτὴ Ἀθήνησι Διονύσου. ἤγετο δὲ τὰ κατ᾽ ἀγροὺς μηνὸς Ποσειδεῶνος, τὰ δὲ Λήναια Γαμηλιῶνος, τὰ δὲ ἐν ἄστει Ἐλαφηβολιῶνος.

(Hesych. s.v. Διονύσια repeats this, but instead of Γαμηλιῶνος writes μηνὸς Ληναιῶνος. Schol. on Plato, *Rep.* 475 d writes μηνὸς Μαιμακτηριῶνος.)

(4) Aristoph. *Ach.* 202.

> ἄξω τὰ κατ᾽ ἀγροὺς εἰσίων Διονύσια.

Schol. ἄξω τὰ κατ᾽ ἀγρούς· τὰ Λήναια λεγόμενα. ἔνθεν τὰ Λήναια καὶ ὁ ἐπιλήναιος ἀγὼν τελεῖται τῷ Διονύσῳ. Λήναιον γάρ ἐστιν ἐν ἀγροῖς ἱερὸν τοῦ Διονύσου, διὰ τὸ †πλεκτοὺς ἐνταῦθα γεγονέναι, ἢ διὰ τὸ πρῶτον ἐν τούτῳ τῷ τόπῳ ληνὸν τεθῆναι.

Cf. Steph. Byz. Λήναιος· ἀγὼν Διονύσου ἐν ἀγροῖς ἀπὸ τῆς ληνοῦ. Ἀπολλόδωρος ἐν τρίτῳ Χρονικῶν καὶ ληναϊκός καὶ ληναιεύς. ἔστι δὲ καὶ δῆμος.

(5) Aristoph. *Ach.* 504–6.

> αὐτοὶ γάρ ἐσμεν οὑπὶ Ληναίῳ τ᾽ ἀγών,
> κοὔπω ξένοι πάρεισιν· οὔτε γὰρ φόροι
> ἥκουσιν, οὔτ᾽ ἐκ τῶν πόλεων οἱ ξύμμαχοι.

Schol. (a) χειμῶνος γὰρ λοιπὸν ὄντος εἰς τὰ Λήναια καθῆκε τὸ δρᾶμα, εἰς δὲ τὰ Διονύσια ἐτέτακτο Ἀθήναζε κομίζειν τὰς πόλεις τοὺς φόρους, ὡς Εὔπολίς φησιν ἐν Πόλεσιν.

(b) ὁ τῶν Διονυσίων ἀγὼν ἐτελεῖτο δὶς τοῦ ἔτους, τὸ μὲν πρῶτον ἔαρος ἐν ἄστει, ὅτε καὶ οἱ φόροι Ἀθήνησιν ἐφέροντο, τὸ δὲ δεύτερον ἐν ἀγροῖς, ὁ ἐπὶ Ληναίῳ λεγόμενος, ὅτε ξένοι οὐ παρῆσαν Ἀθήνησι· χείμων γὰρ λοιπὸν ἦν.

(6) Schol. on Aristoph. *Ach.* 961 (relating the story of Orestes' visit, says) ἦν δὲ ἑορτὴ Διονυσίου Ληναίου. [See above, p. 2.]

(7) Aristoph. *Ach.* 1155.

> ὅς γ᾽ ἐμὲ τὸν τλήμονα Λήναια χορηγῶν ἀπέλυσεν ἄδειπνον.

(8) Id. *Knights* 546–8.

> παραπέμψατ᾽ ἐφ᾽ ἕνδεκα κώπαις
> θόρυβον χρηστὸν ληναΐτην,
> ἵν᾽ ὁ ποιητὴς ἀπίῃ χαίρων.

Schol. ληναΐτην· ἑορτὴ παρὰ τοῖς Ἀθηναίοις τὰ Λήναια, ἐν ᾗ μεχρὶ νῦν ἀγωνίζονται ποιηταὶ συγγράφοντές τινα ᾄσματα τοῦ γελασθῆναι χάριν· ὅπερ ὁ Δημοσθένης εἶπεν ἐξ ἁμάξης· ἐπὶ ἁμαξῶν γὰρ οἱ ᾄδοντες καθήμενοι λέγουσί τε καὶ ᾄδουσι τὰ ποιήματα.

Suidas s.v. ἐξ ἁμαξῆς repeats this schol. and adds: λέγεται καὶ ληναΐτης ὁ χορὸς ὁ τῶν Ληναίων. (*Vide* also (10) below.)

(9) Aristoph. *Frogs* 479.

καλεῖ θεόν.

Schol. . . . τὸ δὲ κάλει θεόν τινες οὕτως ἀποδεδώκασιν. ἐν τοῖς Ληναϊκοῖς ἀγῶσι τοῦ Διονύσου ὁ δᾳδοῦχος κατέχων λαμπάδα λέγει 'καλεῖτε θεόν' καὶ οἱ ὑπακούοντες βοῶσι 'Σεμελήι᾽ "Ιακχε πλουτοδότα'.

(10) Photius. τὰ ἐκ τῶν ἁμαξῶν . . . Ἀθήνησι γὰρ ἐν τῇ τῶν Χοῶν ἑορτῇ οἱ κωμάζοντες ἐπὶ τῶν ἁμαξῶν τοὺς ἀπαντῶντας ἔσκωπτόν τε καὶ ἐλοιδόρουν· τὸ δ' αὐτὸ καὶ τοῖς Ληναίοις ὕστερον ἐποίουν. (So also Suidas.)

(11) *Law of Euegoros* (*ap.* Dem. *Meid.* § 10).[1] Εὐήγορος εἶπεν· ὅταν ἡ πομπὴ ᾖ τῷ Διονύσῳ ἐν Πειραιεῖ καὶ οἱ κωμῳδοὶ καὶ οἱ τραγῳδοὶ καὶ ἡ ἐπὶ Ληναίῳ πομπὴ καὶ οἱ τραγῳδοὶ καὶ οἱ κωμῳδοί, καὶ τοῖς ἐν ἄστει Διονυσίοις ἡ πομπὴ καὶ οἱ παῖδες καὶ ὁ κῶμος καὶ οἱ κωμῳδοὶ καὶ οἱ τραγῳδοί, καὶ Θαργηλίων τῇ πομπῇ καὶ τῷ ἀγῶνι μὴ ἐξεῖναι μήτε ἐνεχυράσαι μήτε λαμβάνειν ἕτερον ἑτέρου μηδὲ τῶν ὑπερημέρων ἐν ταύταις ταῖς ἡμέραις.

(12) *I.G.* ii². 1496. (*a*) ll. 68 ff. [334–333 B.C.] [ἐκ τοῦ δερ]ματικοῦ. [ἐπὶ Κτησ]ικλέους ἄρχοντος ἐγ Διονυσίων τῶν ἐμ Πειραιεῖ παρὰ βοωνῶν ΗΗΗΔΡ καὶ τὸ περιγενόμενον ἀπὸ τῆς βοωνίας ΗΗΓΔΔΔ, ἐγ Διονυσίων τῶν [ἐπὶ] Ληναίῳ παρὰ μυστηρίων ἐπιμελητῶν. . . .

(*b*) ll. 105–6 [333–332 B.C.] ἐγ Διονυσίω]ν τῶν ἐπὶ Ληναίῳ π[αρὰ στρατηγῶν] ΗΡΙΙΙ.

[This inscription contains the accounts of the ταμίαι τῆς θεοῦ.]

(13) Ibid. 1672. 182 ff. [329–328 B.C.]. λόγος ἐπιστατῶν Ἐλευσινόθεν καὶ ταμιῶν τοῖν θεοῖν ἐπὶ τῆς Πανδιονίδος ἕκτης πρυτανείας . . . ἐπαρχὴ Δήμητρι καὶ Κόρῃ καὶ Πλούτωνι Π, ἐπιστάταις ἐπιλήναια εἰς Διονύσια θῦσαι ΔΔ . . . εἰς Χόας δημοσίοις ἱερεῖον ΔΔΡΡ.

(14) Aristot. Ἀθ. Πολ. lvii. ὁ δὲ βασιλεὺς πρῶτον μὲν μυστηρίων ἐπιμελεῖται [μετὰ τῶν ἐπιμελητῶν ὧν] ὁ δῆμος χειροτονεῖ, δύο μὲν ἐξ Ἀθηναίων ἀπάντων, ἕνα δ' [ἐξ Εὐμολπιδῶν, ἕνα] δ' ἐκ Κηρύκων. ἔπειτα Διονυσίων τῶν ἐπιληναίων· ταῦτα δέ ἐστι [πομπὴ καὶ ἀγών·

---

[1] The date of Euegoros is unknown. Stahl, *De Euegori lege disputatio* (1893), which I have been unable to obtain, places it in the fourth century B.C.

τ]ὴν μὲν οὖν πομπὴν κοινῇ πέμπουσιν ὅ τε βασιλεὺς καὶ οἱ ἐπιμεληταί,
τὸν δὲ ἀγῶνα διατίθησιν ὁ βασιλεύς· τίθησι δὲ καὶ τοὺς τῶν λαμπάδων
ἀγῶνας ἅπαντας· ὡς δ᾿ ἔπος εἰπεῖν καὶ τὰς πατρίους θυσίας διοικεῖ
οὗτος πάσας.

(15) Pollux viii. 90. ὁ δὲ βασιλεὺς μυστηρίων προέστηκε μετὰ τῶν ἐπιμελητῶν καὶ Ληναίων καὶ ἀγώνων τῶν ἐπὶ λαμπάδι, καὶ τὰ περὶ τὰς
πατρίους θυσίας διοικεῖ.

(16) *I.G.* ii². 2130 (*c.* A.D. 192–3). βασιλεὺς ... ἐπετέλεσεν τὸν ἀγῶνα τῶν
Ληναίων καὶ ἑστίασε τοὺς συνεφήβους καὶ τοὺς περὶ τὸ Διογένειον
πάντας.

(17) Alkiphron, *Epist.* iv. xviii, § 10 (Schepers). ἐγὼ δὲ τὰς θηρικλείους
καὶ τὰ καρχήσια καὶ τὰς χρυσίδας καὶ πάντα τὰ ἐν ταῖς αὐλαῖς ἐπί-
φθονα, παρὰ τούτοις ἀγαθὰ καλούμενα, τῶν κατ᾿ ἔτος Χοῶν καὶ τῶν
ἐν τοῖς θεάτροις Ληναίων καί τῆς χθίζης ὁμολογίας καὶ τῶν τοῦ
Λυκείου γυμνασίων καὶ τῆς ἱερᾶς Ἀκαδημείας οὐκ ἀλλάττομαι.

(18) Hippolochus (*c.* 310 B.C.) *ap.* Athen. iv. 130 d. σὺ δὲ μόνον ἐν
Ἀθήναις μένων εὐδαιμονίζεις τὰς Θεοφράστου θέσεις ἀκούων, θύμα
καὶ εὔζωμα καὶ τοὺς καλοὺς ἐσθίων στρεπτούς, Λήναια καὶ Χύτρους
θεωρῶν.

(19) Clem. Alex. *Protrept.* i. 2 (p. 4 Stählin). ἀλλὰ γὰρ τὰ μὲν δράματα
καὶ τοὺς ληναΐζοντας ποιητάς, τέλεον ἤδη παροινοῦντας, κιττῷ που
ἀναδήσαντες, ἀφραίνοντας ἐκτόπως τελετῇ βακχικῇ, σὺν καὶ τῷ ἄλλῳ
δαιμόνων χορῷ, Ἑλικῶνι καὶ Κιθαιρῶνι κατακλείσωμεν γεγηρακό-
σιν κτλ.

    Schol. ληναΐζοντας· ἀγροικικὴ ᾠδὴ ἐπὶ τῷ ληνῷ ᾀδομένη, ἣ καὶ
αὐτὴ περιεῖχεν τὸν Διονύσου σπαραγμόν, πάνυ δὲ εὐφυῶς καὶ χάριτος
ἐμπλέως τὸ κιττῷ ἀναδήσαντες τέθεικεν, ὁμοῦ μὲν τὸ ὅτι Διονύσῳ τὰ
Λήναια ἀνάκειται ἐνδειξάμενος, ὁμοῦ δὲ καὶ ὡς παροινίᾳ ταῦτα καὶ
παροινοῦσιν ἀνθρώποις καὶ μεθύουσιν συγκεκρότηται.

(20) Heraclitus *ap.* Clem. Alex. *Protrept.* ii. 34 (p. 26 Stählin). ὡυτὸς δὲ
Ἅιδης καὶ Διόνυσος, ὅτεῳ μαίνονται καὶ ληναΐζουσιν.

    Schol. ληναΐζουσιν· βακχεύουσιν· λῆναι γὰρ αἱ βάκχαι. Cf. (21)
and (31) below.

(21) Hesych. λῆναι· βάκχαι Ἀρκάδες (i.e. they were so called in Arcadia).

(22) Id. ἐπὶ Ληναίῳ ἀγών· ἔστιν ἐν τῷ ἄστει Λήναιον περίβολον ἔχον
μέγαν καὶ ἐν αὐτῷ Ληναίου Διονύσου ἱερόν, ἐν ᾧ ἐπετελοῦντο οἱ ἀγῶνες
Ἀθηναίων πρὶν τὸ θέατρον οἰκοδομηθῆναι.

(23) Id. Λίμναι· ἐν Ἀθήναις τόπος ἀνειμένος Διονύσῳ, ὅπου τὰ †Λαια
(? Λήναια) ἤγετο.

(24) Demosth. *de Cor.* § 129. ἢ ὡς ἡ μήτηρ τοῖς μεθημερινοῖς γάμοις ἐν τῷ κλεισίῳ τῷ πρὸς τῷ καλαμίτῃ ἥρῳ χρωμένη τὸν καλὸν ἀνδρίαντα καὶ τριταγωνιστὴν ἄκρον ἐξέθρεψέ σε;

Schol. (*a*) τὸ δὲ ἱερὸν αὐτοῦ (sc. τοῦ καλαμίτου ἥρωος) ἐστι πρὸς τῷ Ληναίῳ (*B.C.H.* i, 1877, p. 142).

(*b*) κλισίον· τὸ οἴκημα . . . ἐν τῇ ἀγορᾷ.

(25) Photius. Λήναιον· περίβολος μέγας Ἀθήνησιν ἐν ᾧ τοὺς ἀγῶνας ἦγον πρὸ τοῦ τὸ θέατρον οἰκοδομηθῆναι ὀνομάζοντες ἐπὶ Ληναίῳ. ἔστιν δὲ ἐν αὐτῷ καὶ ἱερὸν Διονύσου Ληναίου.

(26) Id. ἴκρια. τὰ ἐν τῇ ἀγορᾷ ἀφ' ὧν ἐθεῶντο τοὺς Διονυσιακοὺς ἀγῶνας πρὶν ἢ κατασκευασθῆναι τὸ ἐν Διονύσου θέατρον.

(Cf. Pollux viii. 175. ἰκριοποιοὶ δ' εἰσιν οἱ πηγνύντες τὰ περὶ τὴν ἀγορὰν ἴκρια.)

(27) Photius. ὀρχήστρα· πρῶτον ἐκλήθη ἐν τῇ ἀγορᾷ· εἶτα καὶ τοῦ θεάτρου τὸ κάτω ἡμικύκλιον, οὗ καὶ οἱ χοροὶ ᾖδον καὶ ὠρχοῦντο.

(28) Schol. on Aristoph. *Plut.* 954. οὐκ ἐξῆν δὲ ξένον χορεύειν ἐν τῷ ἀστικῷ χορῷ· ἐν δὲ τῷ Ληναίῳ ἐξῆν· ἐπεὶ καὶ μέτοικοι ἐχορήγουν.

(29) Plato, *Protag.* p. 327 d. ἀλλ' εἶεν ἄγριοί τινες, οἷοί περ οὓς πέρυσι Φερεκράτης ὁ ποιητὴς ἐδίδαξεν ἐπὶ Ληναίῳ.

(30) Anon. *de Com.* a¹, ll. 6 ff. (Kaibel, *Fr. Com.*, p. 7). τὴν αὐτὴν (sc. τὴν κωμῳδίαν) δὲ καὶ τρυγῳδίαν φασὶ διὰ τὸ τοῖς εὐδοκιμοῦσιν ἐπὶ Ληναίῳ γλεῦκος δίδοσθαι, ὅπερ ἐκάλουν τρύγα, ἢ ὅτι μήπω προσωπείων ηὑρημένων τρυγὶ διαχρίοντες τὰ πρόσωπα ὑπεκρίνοντο.

(31) Inscr. from Kyme 791 Schw. ὑπὺ τεῖ κλίνει τούτει λῆνος ὕπυ.

(Wilam. *Glaube der Hell.* ii, p. 63, says that λῆνος here can only mean an initiated βάκχος; cf. (20) above.)

2. For a long time it was assumed that the festival called Lenaia, the place of its celebration, the Lenaion, and the god worshipped, Dionysus Lenaios, were so named from a connexion with the winepress, ληνός, though the mere existence of a ληνός in the sanctuary ἐν Λίμναις (up to then identified with the Lenaion), and of others in the neighbourhood, was obviously inconclusive, even allowing for the fact that other known shrines of Dionysus are not known to have included winepresses; winepresses are common objects in a vine-growing country, and the special reference to the winepress and its god in January or February was not obviously appropriate. Consequently an

alternative derivation[1] of these words, not from ληνός, but from
λῆναι, known to be an appellation of bacchanals or maenads,
has found more general favour. It was pointed out that the
normal form of the adjective derived from ληνός would be
λήνειος (cf. Καδμεῖος, οἰκεῖος, βάκχειος, ἵππειος, etc.), whereas
adjectives of the -αιος form are usually connected with feminine
substantives of the first declension (βίαιος, ἀγοραῖος, δίκαιος,
etc.). The argument is not absolutely conclusive, because a very
few feminines in -ος have corresponding adjectives in -αῖος, e.g.
νῆσος (νησαῖος), ὁδός (ὁδαῖος), χέρσος (χερσαῖος), and ληνός might
conceivably be one of these; but these adjectives (except
χερσαῖος) are very rare, and some other feminines in -ος have
adjectives in -ειος, e.g. κόπρος (κόπρειος), λήκυθος (ληκύθειος,
Callimachus), κέλευθος (κελεύθειος, Pausanias and Hesychius),
μίλτος (μιλτεῖος, *Anth. Pal.* vi. 63), etc. So that the derivation
from λῆναι has at least the balance of probability; and if so, we
have to do with the festival, sanctuary, and god of the maenads or
women worshippers of Dionysus. The use of the word ληναΐζουσιν
by Heraclitus as the equivalent of βακχεύουσι strongly supports
this view, and Clement of Alexandria uses ληναΐζοντας of inspired
or frenzied poets, though the scholiast on his words gives the
derivation from ληνός, probably quoting it from elsewhere, as
ληναΐζοντας cannot be paraphrased as ἀγροικικὴ ᾠδή. In an
inscription of the third century B.C. from Halikarnassos (*Inscr.
in Brit. Mus.*, No. 902) Dionysus is θεᾶν ληναγέτας Βακχᾶν.

Another line of investigation has been thought to suggest the
nature of their worship.

3. In 1912 Frickenhaus[2] described and illustrated a large
number of vases (to which others could be added),[3] ranging
over the whole of the fifth century B.C., which, while differing
in details, are almost all[4] clearly inspired by the cult of Dionysus
in the form of a bearded mask set upon a wooden pillar; the
pillar is clothed with varying degrees of decoration; the god
is crowned with ivy to which (or to some other part of his
decoration) are attached thin cables of the type known as
πλακοῦντες, and the adornment sometimes includes grapes. The
worship is performed by women in various stages of ecstasy,

---

[1] First suggested by Ribbeck, *Anfänge u. Entwicklung des Dionysoskultes in Attica*, p. 13.
[2] In a Winckelmanns-Programm, *Lenäen Vasen*.
[3] e.g. Deubner, 'Eine neue Lenäen Vase', in *Jahrb. Arch.* xlix (1934), pp. 1–5.
[4] In a few of these the idol is not depicted, though the ritual seems to be of the same type.

with thyrsi, torches, flutes, and tympana, and, on one of the
earlier (*c.* 490–480 B.C.) of all the vases, the work of the artist
Makron and the potter Hieron (Fig. 10), one carries a kid. On
a series of Attic stamnoi of the fifth century, in front of the idol,

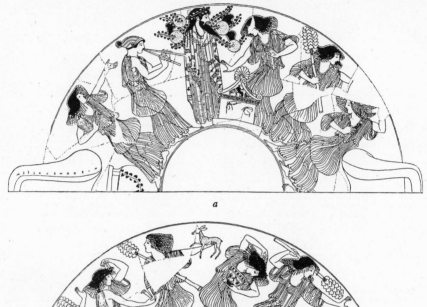

a

b

FIG. 10. Kylix of Makron from Vulci

there is commonly a table, usually bearing two large stamnoi,
out of which one or two of the women are dipping wine with
a ladle to fill the skyphoi which some of them carry, and probably also the kantharos represented on some of the vases, for
the god (see Figs. 11 and 12).[1] Such may be taken to be the
essential elements in the worship. The painters, however, are
not closely tied to the details of any ritual actually performed,
since some of the pictures include naked satyrs (e.g. Fig. 13),[1]

[1] Stamnoi from Falerii (in Villa Papa Giulio, *c.* 480–450 B.C.) and Gela (at Oxford,
c. 460–450 B.C.). Cf. also fig. 15 from Vulci in B.M., about 440 B.C.

a

b

FIG. II. ATTIC STAMNOI

FIG. 12. Stamnos from Gela

Fig. 14. Stamnos in Goluchow

FIG. 13. ATTIC STAMNOS IN LOUVRE

and on one of the most informative, a stamnos from Nuceria
of about 420–410 B.C. (Fig. 16), the women bear names which
could be associated with imaginary Maenads, but not with living
women worshippers—Dione, Maenas, Thaleia, Choreia. On
another,[1] though the ritual was plainly one for women, there
is a man with a crooked stick. Further, one of the stamnoi
(Fig. 14),[2] of about 430 B.C., while lacking the idol, shows a
woman carrying a garlanded infant who is stretching out his
arms to another woman (a figure of great dignity and beauty).
Some have been tempted to compare this infant with the Dionysus Liknites aroused[3] by the Thyiades at Delphi, but that was
a spring ceremony, the Lenaia a winter one, and the character
of the scene does not in any way support the comparison. However this may be, Frickenhaus has no doubt that this cult of
the pillar-god, which in some respects recalls that with which
the god, under the names Καδμεῖος or Περικιόνιος, was worshipped in Thebes, was the ritual of the Lenaia, and was a
nocturnal (and therefore torchlit) worship of the god by women
behaving as Maenads at this festival, and that it came with the
god from Thebes.[4] He further identifies the god with the
Athenian Διόνυσος ᾿Ορθός, to whom legend attributed the invention of mixing wine with water;[5] but in fact this mixing is
only suggested (and even then perhaps not quite certainly) on
one of the vases in Frickenhaus's collection.[6] The point need not
be further discussed here, since we are primarily concerned with
the ascription of the ritual to the Lenaia, in which Frickenhaus
is supported by Deubner.[7]

That the vases are not to be connected with the Anthesteria,
as Nilsson supposed,[8] these scholars prove beyond doubt. The
shape of the vessels depicted is quite different from that of those
which were used at the Anthesteria, and there are really no

[1] Frickenhaus, op. cit., Taf. v, Nr. 27.
[2] In Goluchow, in the Czartoryski Collection, see Beazley, *Vases in Poland*, pp. 51 ff.,
who believes the infant to be a satyr.
[3] According to Plutarch, *Is. et Osir.* xxxv.
[4] Wilamowitz, *Glaube der Hell.* ii, p. 80, notes that the Περικιόνιος of Thebes was not masked,
but was a simple pillar covered with ivy; cf. Eur. *Antiope*, fr. 23, εἶδον δὲ θαλάμοις . . . βουκόλων
κομῶντα κισσῷ στῦλον Εὐίου θεοῦ; the schol. on Eur. *Phoen.* 651 refers the ivy-clad god to
περικιόνιος. Wilam. suggests that the στῦλος may have come from Thebes, the mask from
Naxos (cf. Athen. iii. 78 c for Naxian masks, and the discussion by Wrede, 'Der Masken-Gott'
in *Ath. Mitt.* liii (1928), pp. 80–89).
[5] Philochorus *ap.* Athen. ii. 38 c.   [6] No. 24.
[7] Op. cit., pp. 127–32.   [8] *Jahrb. Arch.* xxxi (1916), pp. 328 ff.

reliable points of contact. It is unnecessary to resume that discussion here. For the connexion with the Lenaia the case rests on the argument that the Lenaia was a festival of λῆναι or Maenads, that it is such a festival that is represented on the vases, that we know of no other public festival of the kind,[1] and that the festival must have been a well-known one to be reproduced on so many vases. (Deubner successfully answers Robert's objection to the appearance of grapes in a January festival.) These facts do not constitute proof, but they do afford a strong probability in favour of the view that the Lenaia did include such a temperately ecstatic worship of Dionysus in the form of a masked and draped pillar as the vases depict.[2] There must remain a certain doubt whether the vases do not cover two distinct forms of ritual—the one, represented on the kylix of Makron and the stamnos from Nuceria, being worship of a much more markedly ecstatic kind, the other a much more sober performance (itself very variable in details); and if so, it would be natural to associate the former with the λῆναι of the Lenaia—unless the two sets of vases represent earlier and later stages in the ceremonies of the same festival. A striking vase by the Eretria painter,[3] of which Sir John Beazley has kindly lent me a photograph (Fig. 17), may well show a yet earlier stage—the preparation of the mask of Dionysus, though the costume of the women is somewhat more decorative than on Frickenhaus's vases. That the worship was nocturnal is rendered likely, though not absolutely certain,[4] by the torches shown on the vases and the mention of the δᾳδοῦχος in one of the records of the festival.[5] Frickenhaus also notices[6] that an Attic festival-calendar gives, for the month Gamelion, the instruction κιττώσεις Διόνυσον, which recalls the ivy-crowned pillar-god of the vases.[7]

4. There have been several conjectures as to the meaning of

[1] The βακχεῖον referred to at the beginning of Aristophanes' *Lysistrata* was evidently (from the context) that of a private society. See schol. ad loc. καὶ γὰρ πολλὰς ἑορτὰς αἱ γυναῖκες ἔξω τῶν δημοτελῶν ἦγον ἰδίᾳ συνερχόμεναι.

[2] For further discussion see Robert, *Gött. gel. Anz.* 1913, pp. 366 ff., and Petersen, *Rh. Mus.* 1913, pp. 239 ff., in addition to references already given.

[3] Published by kind permission of Mrs. Jean Serpieri, the owner of the Vlasto Collection. See also Beazley, *Att. Redfig. Vas.*, p. 725, No. 11.

[4] See Aristoph. *Thesmoph.* 280, and the scene in Eur. *Bacch.* 145 ff.

[5] See p. 24, passage 9.

[6] Op. cit., p. 29.

[7] *I.G.* ii². 1367; but the inscription is of the first century A.D., and cannot carry much weight in regard to a time five or six centuries earlier.

FIG. 15. ATTIC STAMNOS IN BRITISH MUSEUM

FIG. 16a. ATTIC STAMNOS FROM NUCERIA

FIG. 16*b*. ATTIC STAMNOS FROM NUCERIA

FIG. 17. OINOCHOE OF ERETRIA PAINTER

a celebration conducted by Maenads at a festival in January.
Farnell suggests that it was intended to rouse or strengthen the
sleeping god, like other winter festivals known to anthropo-
logists. There seems little direct support for this in the meagre
evidence, and the ivy-clad pillar-god is hardly in keeping with
this idea. Others lay more stress on the fact that the archon
basileus was associated in the conduct of the festival with
officials of the Eleusinian mysteries—the ἐπιμεληταί and the
δᾳδοῦχος—and that according to a scholiast on Aristophanes'
Frogs the δᾳδοῦχος, torch in hand, bade the worshippers call
upon the god (καλεῖτε θεόν), and that they responded with the
cry Σεμελήι᾽ ῎Ιακχε πλουτοδότα. This would not, however, justify
the belief, which some hold, that it was the birth of Dionysus
as son of Semele that was commemorated, because the Iakchos
of the mysteries was a young man, and πλουτοδότα is perhaps
less appropriate to an infant.[1] Even if on one of Frickenhaus's
'Lenaean vases' there is a woman holding out the infant to
another, it is not certain that the infant was (as Frickenhaus
thinks) Dionysus or Iakchos, and not her own human infant
which she had brought with her to the meeting or, as Sir John
Beazley believes, a satyr. Nor would it be right to infer that
Semele herself had any part in the celebration. It is therefore
impossible to say with confidence what there was in common
between the Lenaia and the Eleusinia.[2] These dances in the
winter season were probably like the trieteric 'orgies' of
Thyiades on Mount Parnassus and elsewhere, though they were
annual, and (if the vases are any guide) less wild.

Another connexion with mystic rites of a different kind, the
omophagy or devouring of the slain Dionysus, as in the Cretan
mysteries of Zagreus, appears to be indicated by the scholiast on
Clement of Alexandria, who interprets Clement's use of the word
ληναΐζοντας by speaking of ἀγροικικὴ ᾠδὴ ἐπὶ τῷ ληνῷ ᾀδομένη,
ἣ καὶ αὐτὴ περιεῖχεν τὸν Διονύσου σπαραγμόν. But the meaning
of the note is obscure; περιεῖχεν probably only implies the

[1] It would take us too far to discuss this last point in relation to the birth of Ploutos as child of Demeter.

[2] Some may infer from the juxtaposition of names in *I.G.* ii². 1672, ll. 182 ff. (see above, p. 24), that Demeter, Kore, and Pluto may have been associated with the Lenaia; but the epistatai who contributed to the Lenaia also (l. 204) contributed to the Χόες, so that the proof of a *particular* connexion with the Lenaia is not strong. The calendar of festivals at Mykonos (Dittenb. *Syll.*³ 1024) shows that the three deities received sacrifices there in the month Lenaion, but this was at a late date (*c.* 200 B.C.).

mention of this σπαραγμός in the chant, and the rest of the note seems to indicate that, whatever was done, it was done by ivy-crowned *men* in a state of intoxication and has nothing to do with the women's performance It seems doubtful whether we know enough to reconcile these isolated records, or to go beyond the comparative certainty that the Lenaia included mystical elements which were in some way the concern of the officials of Eleusis, and very probably a nocturnal worship of Dionysus by women, such as the vases depict. There is certainly no sufficient ground for Dr. A. B. Cook's theory[1] that there was an elaborate passion-play, that the Lenaia went on to represent the re-birth of the god (as the dithyramb, he imagines, at the Dionysia, ten months before, represented his begetting), and that the passion-play at the Lenaia was the origin of tragedy.[2]

If the celebration came to Athens from the north—from Macedonia or Thrace—whence the worship of Dionysus by wild women came into Greece, it may well have come by way of Thebes.[3] It must have established itself at Athens before the Ionian migrations from Attica into the various Ionian towns in which (together with the name of the month Lenaion) it is recorded to have been observed.

5. The passages quoted above show that the festival included a πομπή—a procession conducted by the archon basileus and the epimeletai, and the σκώμματα ἐκ τῶν ἁμαξῶν, which were a feature of the Choes, were afterwards introduced into the Lenaia. The scholiast on Aristophanes' *Knights* 546 seems to include among these σκώμματα songs of a ludicrous kind composed by poets. The wagons doubtless formed part of the πομπή.

---

[1] *Zeus*, i, pp. 685 ff. I have replied to this at length in *Dith. Trag. Com.*, pp. 208–18.

[2] The treatment of words connected with the Lenaia by G. W. Elderkin (*Archaeological Papers*, v, 1943) seems to rest almost entirely on false etymologies and unfounded conjectures. But as he identifies the Ἴακχος of the Lenaian chant with the dismembered Zagreus, it may be noted that there is no hint of a σπαραγμός of Iakchos before Lucian, Περὶ ὀρχήσεως, 39, and that the name, so far from connoting cries of pain, is always associated with cries of joy and hope. (It is comparatively rarely that the verb ἰαχεῖν, with which he associates the name, expresses a cry of grief or fear; it is most commonly a battle-cry or shout of applause.) His interpretation of ληνός as the 'mangling-place' of grapes, with λῆναι as the 'manglers' or 'tearers of the god', identifies two very different processes. Grapes are not 'torn asunder', and ληνός seems to mean primarily a vessel of a particular shape, whether a winepress or any other (see L. and S.). There is not the least reason to suppose that παλαιοῦ πένθεος in Pindar, fr. 113, relates to sufferings of Iakchos (of which nothing else is known).

[3] The invocation of Iakchos as son of Semele confirms this. Farnell, op. cit., p. 213, suggests that it may have been learned by the Ionians in the Boeotian period of their history, before they came to Attica. There is much that is uncertain here.

There is no evidence of any phallic elements in the procession or the festival. Inscriptions show that there was a sacrifice, but give no details. There is also no evidence of a κῶμος,[1] and if in fact the Lenaia had much in common with the Eleusinia, it can well be understood that revels and phallic ritual would be absent, though the σκώμματα with their apotropaic intention were present in both celebrations.

6. The inscriptions which are usually cited with reference to the Lenaia in places outside Athens are all of relatively late dates and throw little or no light on the Athenian festival; most merely mention the month Lenaion in dating a decree or prescribing a sacrifice or whatever it may be.[2] Two inscriptions suggest a possible connexion of the festival in these places with mystic rites—one from Mykonos[3] (dated by Dittenberger about 200 B.C.) prescribes for the 10th of Lenaion sacrifices to Demeter, Kore, and Zeus Bouleus, and for the 12th δυωδεκατεῖ Διονύσῳ Ληνεῖ ἐτήσιον· ὑπὲρ καρπῶν Διὶ Χθονίῳ Γῇ Χθονίῃ δερτὰ μέλανα ἐτήσια: the other from Magnesia on the Maeander[4] of the second century A.D., which seems to refer to a private religious society, and gives instructions to the officials ὥστε τῷ Ληνεῶνι τὰ εἰθισμένα αὐτοῖς προσφέρεσθαι ὑπὸ τῶν μυστῶν. But it would be rash to draw any inferences from these facts to the cults of Athens many centuries earlier. An inscription from Astypalaia[5] gives a variant for the name of the month τοὶ πρυτάν[ιες] [τοὶ πρυτανεύον]τες Ληναιοβάκχιον στεφανωσάντων αὐτὸν τοῖς Διονυ[σίοις ἐν τῷ ἀγῶνι] τῶν τραγῳδῶν, and may possibly allude to a contest of tragedies at a Lenaian festival. A very fragmentary record[6] seems to commemorate victories of actors and poets at the Lenaia in Rhodes, probably in the first century B.C. An

---

[1] Deubner, op. cit., p. 133, argues for a κῶμος in which men wore women's costumes and women men's; but this depends upon his connexion (which seems unproved) of a group of vases published by Buschor with this festival (Buschor, *Jahrb. Arch.* xxxviii–xxxix (1923–4), pp. 128 ff.).

[2] *C.I.G.* 3664 (Kyzikos) mentions the months Lenaion and Anthesterion (the names are nearly all Roman); *C.I.G.* 3641b (l. 17) mentions dues payable to Asklepios at Lampsakos in the month Lenaion; *C.I.G.* 3137 (l. 34) dates a decree (of the time of Seleucus) μηνὸς Ληναιῶνος. Inscriptions from Samos (*B.C.H.* 1881, p. 480, probably of the second century B.C.) and Delos (ibid., p. 26 = *I.G.* xi. 203 A, ll. 31 ff.: 269 B.C.) also mention the month, as does one of the Greek inscriptions in the British Museum (vol. iii, No. 477, col. E, ll. 70 and 72), of the second century B.C. (about).

[3] Dittenberger[3], No. 1024, see above, p. 33, n. 2.

[4] Kern, *Inscr. of Magn. on M.*, No. 117.

[5] *C.I.G.* 2483. It is a decree in honour of Arkesilas.

[6] *I.G.* xii. 125.

inscription of the second century B.C. from Priene, quoted above,[1] refers to the costume of the priest of Dionysus in the months of Lenaion and Anthesterion.

7. The Lenaian festival at Athens was held mainly in the Lenaion, ἐπὶ Ληναίῳ. As to where this was, two different traditions appear in the scholia and lexicographers. According to one, the Lenaion was ἐν ἀγροῖς, outside the city-walls. So says the scholiast on Aristophanes, *Acharnians* 202 and 504, and also Stephanus of Byzantium, who claims the authority of Apollodorus, though whether Apollodorus is his authority for the words ἐν ἀγροῖς or only for the words ἀπὸ τῆς ληνοῦ which follow them cannot be determined. Dramatic contests at the Lenaia were always in historical times distinguished from the Great Dionysia ἐν ἄστει. But the expression ἐν ἄστει seems to have been primarily used of the Great Dionysia in contrast to the ἐν ἀγροῖς of the Rural Dionysia, and this may have been its original use, as it is not at all certain that organized dramatic contests were not held at the Rural Dionysia earlier than at the Lenaia. (This will be referred to later.) The statement that the Lenaia were held ἐν ἀγροῖς may be, as Deubner suggests,[2] due to a mistaken conflation of the facts that the *Acharnians* was acted at the Lenaia and that in this play (at l. 202) Dikaiopolis proposes to enact τὰ κατ’ ἀγροὺς Διονύσια (of course in pretence).[3] The rest of the evidence points to the place of the celebration being in the market-place, which was, of course, in the city, and was to the north-west of the Acropolis. Hesychius (repeated almost verbally by Photius) describes the Lenaion as a place ἐν ἄστει, having a large circumference, and having in it the ἱερόν—temple or precinct—of the Lenaian Dionysus, in which 'the contests of the Athenians' (evidently dramatic contests) were held, before the theatre was built. Photius also speaks of the ἰκρία—the wooden stands—from which the spectators watched 'the Dionysiac contests' before the theatre was built, as ἐν ἀγορᾷ—in the market-place—and the existence of a place in the Agora called ὀρχήστρα[4] confirms this. Further, Demosthenes[5] associates the misbe-

---

[1] p. 8.

[2] Op. cit., p. 124. I think this is a better account than that given in my *Dith. Trag. Com.*, p. 238.

[3] As a Christmas dinner might be acted in a play produced at midsummer. (This would not prove that Christmas was a midsummer festival.)

[4] Plato, *Apol.* 26 e; Phot. s.v. ὀρχήστρα.   [5] *de Cor.* § 129.

haviour of Aeschines' mother with the κλείσιον adjoining the sanctuary of the ἥρως καλαμίτης, and the scholiasts on the passage say (1) that this κλείσιον was in the Agora, and (2) that the ἱερόν of the ἥρως καλαμίτης adjoined the Lenaion. It seems therefore safe to place the Lenaion in the Agora, though its exact site still remains to be determined by the American excavators. In this large precinct there must have taken place the earliest dramatic performances, whatever they were like, and the nocturnal celebrations of the λῆναι: the πομπή must have gone through the streets outside also.

There is no evidence for connecting the Lenaia with the Sanctuary of Dionysus ἐν Λίμναις except (1) the corrupt passage of Hesychius, s.v. Λίμναι· ἐν Ἀθήναις τόπος ἀνειμένος Διονύσῳ, ὅπου τὰ λαια ἤγετο, where most scholars accept the emendation of λαια to λήναια.[1] Such evidence is too shaky to set against that which has just been stated. (2) A scholiast on Aristophanes, *Acharnians* 961,[2] who in describing the visit of Orestes to Athens which led to the institution of the peculiar ritual of the Choes says ἦν δὲ ἑορτὴ Διονύσου Ληναίου. But none of the other versions of the story make any allusion to Dionysus Ληναῖος, the scholiasts on Aristophanes are by no means free from mistakes, and Nilsson[3] may be right in thinking that Ληναίου is a textual error for Λιμναίου,[4] the title of the god as connected with the Anthesteria.

8. When Aristotle[5] speaks of the ἀγών at the Lenaia as being managed by the archon basileus—apparently without the assistance of the Eleusinian officials who helped him in the conduct of the πομπή—he presumably refers to the dramatic contests of the fourth century; Aristophanes also,[6] in 425 B.C., had described the dramatic contest as ὁ ἐπὶ Ληναίῳ ἀγών, and as a domestic festival at which there were no strangers or allies present. (The seas were still too stormy, and it was not till some three months

---

[1] Even if there was a ληνός in the precinct ἐν Λίμναις, it would not prove anything, if (as is practically certain) the word Λήναιον has nothing to do with ληνός. The attempt of C. Anti, *Teatri Greci arcaici*, chs. vi, vii, to prove that the Lenaic theatre is to be placed in the trapezoidal area adjoining the temple ἐν Λίμναις, and that most of Aristophanes' plays were acted here and not in the Theatre of Dionysus will not bear investigation.

[2] Quoted above, p. 2.

[3] *Studia de Dionysiis Atticis*, p. 57.

[4] This appellation of Dionysus is attested by Callimachus, Phanodemus, and Philostratus (see above, pp. 3, 8).

[5] Ἀθ. Πολ. lvii.

[6] *Ach.* 504.

later that they were easily navigable.[1]) The evidence of inscriptions makes it practically certain that the organization of contests at the Lenaia in tragedy and comedy (parallel to those at
the City Dionysia) goes back no farther than the middle of the
fifth century B.C.—about 442 B.C. in tragedy, about 432 in
comedy—and for what happened before that evidence is lacking.
It is possible that the performances were more on the scale of
those of the Dionysia ἐν ἀγροῖς of the Rural demes, none of which
seem to have celebrated the Lenaia,[2] and that it was comparatively late that they became more ambitious and were transferred
from the market-place to the Theatre of Dionysus. (The date of
this transference is nowhere recorded, but possibly it may have
followed the Periclean improvements in the theatre, about 445
B.C.[3]) It would be then that the inscriptional record (following
the new official status of the festival) might naturally begin.[4]
How the contests were organized (under the archon basileus)
before this remains unknown. It may have been from the first
that comic performances were more important at this festival
than tragic (the reverse being the case at the City Dionysia).[5]
In the fifth century only two tragic poets competed, each with
two tragedies but no satyric play. The great tragic poets seldom
appeared at the Lenaia; Sophocles did so a few times;[6] a victory
of Agathon in 416 is recorded—his first.[7] In the fourth century
Dionysius won at this festival his only success with a tragedy,[8]
and victories were won by Astydamas and Achaeus.[9] On the
other hand, the great comic poets seem to have competed in-
differently at either festival, though even in comedy a special
prestige attached itself to a City victory, if we may judge by

---

[1] Theophr. *Char.* iii τὴν θάλατταν ἐκ Διονυσίων πλόιμον εἶναι. See below, p. 56.

[2] See Farnell, *Cults*, v, p. 213. The dates of the Rural Dionysia may, as he suggests, have
been adjusted so as to enable citizens and country-dwellers to attend both festivals. The
Rural Dionysia seem to have been normally in December (see below).

[3] Dörpfeld, *Ath. Mitt.* xx (1895), p. 183, thinks that the transference may have taken place
a century later, when Lycurgus built or altered the theatre. But it seems improbable that the
theatre should not have been used for the comedies of the great comic poets at the Lenaia as
well as at the Dionysia, though the contest might well continue to retain the name of ἐπὶ
Ληναίῳ ἀγών. Pollux iv. 121 speaks of καὶ Διονυσιακὸν θέατρον καὶ Ληναϊκόν as if they were
distinct, but there is no indication of the date of which he is thinking.

[4] See below, p. 72 and Appendix.

[5] They may have developed out of dramatic elements—disguises, impersonations, etc.—in
the πομπή and the σκώμματα ἐκ τῶν ἁμαξῶν.

[6] See Haigh, *Tragic Drama of the Greeks*[3], p. 128, n. 4.

[7] Plato, *Symp.* 173 a; Athen. v. 217 a.

[8] Diod. Sic. xv. 74.   [9] See below, p. 116.

Aristophanes' disappointment[1] at failing to win one with the
Clouds, after his two Lenaian victories. As at the City Dionysia,
five comic poets competed, each with one play, except during
a short period in the Peloponnesian war when the number was
reduced to three. That the Lenaian festival was less highly
regarded than the City Dionysia is probably the reason why at
the former, but not at the latter, aliens might sing in the choruses
and resident aliens could be choregoi.[2]

There were contests of tragic actors and comic actors—the
best in each category being awarded a prize—almost, if not
quite, from the time at which the inscriptional record began;[3]
but there is no evidence that old plays were ever acted as they
were at the City Dionysia, and in the period best known to us
there was no performance of dithyrambs, and no such performance is mentioned in the Law of Euegoros;[4] but early in the
third century an inscription[5] does record a dithyrambic victory
at the Lenaia.

It is not certain when the contests came to an end. The monument set up by Xenokles[6] as agonothetes in 306 B.C. proves their
continuance after the abolition of choregia. The list of victorious
tragic poets at the Lenaia[7] goes down only to about 320 B.C.,
but as the victorious tragic actors' list goes down to the end
of the third century (and may have gone farther) the contest of
poets doubtless also continued. The extant didaskalic record[8] of
comedy at the Lenaia terminated soon after 288 B.C., but the
list of victorious comic poets[7] continues beyond 150 B.C.

9. An inscription[9] of a date later than the beginning of the
third century B.C. found at Rhamnus is of interest as showing
apparently that at that time there was a cult of Dionysus
Ληναῖος there. Καλλισθένης Κλεοβούλου Προσπάλτιος χειροτονηθεὶς
ἐπὶ τὴν παραλίαν στεφανωθεὶς ὑπὸ τῆς βουλῆς καὶ τοῦ δήμου
Διονυσίῳ Ληναίῳ ἀνέθηκεν. But the interpretation is not perfectly
clear; it at least assumes that Kallisthenes of the Prospaltian
deme had some reason for commemorating at Rhamnus a

---

[1] *Clouds*, 520 ff.   [2] Schol. Aristoph. *Plut.* 394; Plutarch, *Phok.* 30.
[3] See below, pp. 72–73.   [4] See above, p. 24.
[5] *C.I.A.* ii². 3779 Νικοκλῆς ... Ληναία διθυράμβῳ; but Nikokles (of Tarentum) was a citharode
(ὃς ἐπὶ μέγιστον δόξης κιθαρῳδῶν ἁπάντων ἦλθεν, Paus. I. xxxvii. 2), not a flute-player, and
this does not look like an ordinary dithyrambic contest. There was no such contest at the
Lenaia in the time of Demosthenes (*in Meid.* § 10).
[6] *C.I.A.* ii². 3073. See p. 121.   [7] *I.G.* ii². 2325.
[8] Ibid. 2319. See below, p. 110.   Πρακτικά, 1891, p. 16.

distinction conferred by the Council and People of Athens, and we do not know the history of the stone.

C. THE RURAL DIONYSIA

1. The festivities called τὰ κατ᾽ ἀγροὺς Διονύσια were celebrated, at least normally,[1] in the month Poseideon, which corresponds roughly to December. The central feature was a κῶμος escorting a phallus held aloft, and this was no doubt in origin designed to promote or encourage the fertility of the autumn-sown seed or of the earth in general, at the time when it seemed to be slumbering. When the special association with Dionysus began is not known; the rite was probably far more primitive than the worship of Dionysus in Attica, and had nothing directly to do with wine; the vintage was long past, and the new wine was not yet fit to be broached; this was left for the Πιθοίγια some two or three months later; but there need be no doubt that in the merry-making which accompanied the festival plenty of wine was drunk, and in historical times these rural festivals were regarded as being held in honour of Dionysus. Nor is it known at what date dramatic performances first came to be associated with some or all of them.

The festivals were organized by each deme for itself in historical times (with one possible exception), and at least in the early fourth century they were not held everywhere on the same date in Poseideon, since Plato[2] speaks of people going from one of the festivals to another to gratify their desire for entertainment, and at this time, when troupes of actors travelled from one to another with their repertoire of plays, time must have been allowed for their movements.

In Plutarch's day[3] slaves had their share in the enjoyment and made the most of it, as they doubtless did in Attica centuries before.

2. In addition to the phallic procession, of which more is to

---

[1] Farnell, *Cults*, v, p. 206, suggests that in Ikaria the festival may have taken place in the spring, but this seems very doubtful. That the usual date was in Poseideon is stated definitely by Theophrastus, *Char.* iii, and by the scholiasts to Aeschines, *in Tim.* § 43, and Plato, *Rep.* 475 d, and this is confirmed by inscriptions (*I.G.* ii². 1183 and 1496). See below, pp. 42, 47.

[2] *Rep.* 475 d ὥσπερ δὲ ἀπομεμισθωκότες τὰ ὦτα ἐπακοῦσαι πάντων χορῶν περιθέουσι τοῖς Διονυσίοις οὔτε τῶν κατὰ πόλεις οὔτε τῶν κατὰ κώμας ἀπολειπόμενοι.

[3] Plut. *non posse suav. vivi sec. Epicurum* 1098 b καὶ γὰρ οἱ θεράποντες ὅταν Κρόνια δειπνῶσιν ἢ Διονύσια κατ᾽ ἀγρὸν ἄγωσι περιιόντες, οὐκ ἂν αὐτῶν τὸν ὀλολυγμὸν ὑπομείναις καὶ τὸν θόρυβον, ὑπὸ χαρμονῆς καὶ ἀπειροκαλίας τοιαῦτα ποιούντων καὶ φθεγγομένων.

be said immediately, it is commonly stated that one of the amusements of these festivals was ἀσκωλιασμός—the attempt to jump or stand on an oiled and full wineskin. The game is described fully by Pollux,[1] without reference to any particular festival, and the scholiast on Aristophanes' *Ploutos* 1129 speaks of Ἀσκώλια as ἑορτή, ἐν ᾗ ἐνήλλοντο τοῖς ἀσκοῖς εἰς τιμὴν τοῦ Διονύσου, though it may be doubted whether there was a separate festival for this simple amusement; it probably entered into many festivals. The argument generally used to connect it particularly with the Rural Dionysia is derived from a passage of Virgil's second Georgic (380 ff.) which mentions it in the same breath as rural dramatic contests in Attica:

> non aliam ob culpam Baccho caper omnibus aris
> caeditur et veteres ineunt proscaenia ludi,
> praemiaque in gentes pagos et compita circum
> Thesidae posuere, atque inter pocula laeti
> mollibus in pratis unctos saluere per utres.

The argument is perhaps not quite conclusive, but lends some additional likelihood to what was in any case probable.

3. The only definite information about the procession at the Rural Dionysia is that which is derived from the scene in Aristophanes' *Acharnians*,[2] in which Dikaiopolis carries through an imitation (on a much reduced scale) of the procession. It is headed by his daughter as κανηφόρος, carrying as an offering a cake or flat loaf on which she pours porridge with a ladle; behind her is the slave Xanthias as φαλλοφόρος (with another slave), carrying the phallos upright on a pole, and lastly Dikaiopolis himself representing the body of revellers and singing a chant to Phales, the personified symbol of fertility and greeted as the companion of Bacchus. Whether some of the Attic demes may have offered more costly or varied sacrifices we do not know. Plutarch's words[3] may or may not include a reference to Attica as well as to his native Boeotia—ἡ πάτριος τῶν Διονυσίων ἑορτὴ τὸ παλαιὸν ἐπέμπετο δημοτικῶς καὶ ἱλαρῶς, ἀμφορεὺς οἴνου καὶ κληματίς, εἶτα τράγον τις εἷλκεν, ἄλλος ἰσχάδων ἄρριχον ἠκολούθει κομίζων, ἐπὶ πᾶσι δ' ὁ φαλλός. There were many types of phallic procession in the Hellenic world, but none

---

[1] ix. 121. [2] ll. 241–79.
[3] *De cupid. divit.* 527 d. It is doubtful whether δημοτικῶς conveys any reference to celebration by demes.

of those described by Athenaeus[1] are brought by him into
any connexion with the Rural Dionysia.[2] In this festival the
customs may well have varied from deme to deme. Nor is it
possible to say whether it was at the Rural Dionysia (as Deubner
appears to assume) that κῶμοι of different demes competed, still
less to derive comedy from these κῶμοι in particular. There are
references[3] to contests between separate groups of revellers, each
under its κώμαρχος, such as may have figured in any festivities
in which κῶμοι were included, but without any special mention
of the Rural Dionysia. Pollux[4] mentions a dance called τετράκωμος which he tentatively connects with 'the Athenian
τετράκωμοι'—four demes which must have competed with each
other, but again we are not told on what occasions.

4. It cannot be regarded as certain that all references to
'Dionysia' or to dramatic competitions in the demes refer necessarily to the Rural Dionysia in Poseideon, which, it might be
supposed, being in midwinter, might not be an appropriate
time for dramatic performances in the open air, though suitable
enough for a primitive κῶμος, and in some of the demes—at
Ikaria, the Peiraeus, Salamis, and Eleusis, for instance—the
festival appears to have been of a more important character
than in others. But in the Peiraeus at least it does seem in fact
to have been held, late in the fourth century, in Poseideon,[5] and
also at Myrrhinus. The management of the festival was probably
in most demes the duty of the demarch, who was appointed by
the State for the festival in the Peiraeus, as was the archon who

---

[1] xiv. 621 d–622 d. The passage and the question of the relation of comedy to the phallic
κῶμος are discussed in my *Dith. Trag. Com.*, pp. 228 ff.

[2] Heraclitus, fr. 127 (Byw.) may have in view some celebrations like those of the Rural
Dionysia: εἰ μὴ γὰρ Διονύσῳ πομπὴν ἐποιεῦντο καὶ ὕμνεον ᾆσμα αἰδοίοισι, ἀναιδέστατα εἴργαστ'
ἄν· ὡυτὸς δὲ Ἀίδης καὶ Διόνυσος ὅτεῳ μαίνονται καὶ ληναΐζουσι.

[3] See Deubner, op. cit., p. 136, n. 2. He quotes *I.G.* ii². 1303 (330–329 B.C.): Ξυπεταίονες
ἐνίκων, Ἀριστοφῶν ἦρχε, κώμαρχοι (three names follow), and ibid. 3104 ἐπὶ Θεοφράστου
ἄρχοντος Ἀντιφάνης . . . κωμαρχῶν ἐνίκα (at Acharnai, in the middle or late fourth century
B.C.); cf. Palaios in *Polemon*, iii (1929), pp. 44 ff., and Roussel in *C.R. Acad. Inscr.* 1929, pp. 195–
9, who conjectures that these inscriptions may refer to some Dionysiac festival organized by
several demes in common.

[4] iv. 105 ὁ δὲ τετράκωμος, τὸ τῆς ὀρχήσεως εἶδος, οὐκ οἶδ' εἴ τι προσῆκον ἦν τοῖς Ἀθήνησι
τετρακώμοις, οἳ ἦσαν Πειραιεῖς Φαληρεῖς Ξυπεταίονες Θυμοιτάδαι.

[5] In *I.G.* ii². 1496, in the accounts of the ταμίαι of Athena and the ἐπιμεληταί established
by Lycurgus, the entries with regard to the Dionysia in the Peiraeus must fall in this month,
as the arrangement is chronological and these entries immediately precede the entry for the
Lenaia which fell in Gamelion. (The mention of the Great Dionysia—in Elaphebolion—
follows shortly afterwards.) The date of the inscription is 334–333 B.C. For Myrrhinus (ibid.
1183) see also below, p. 47.

was entrusted at Salamis with the same duty;[1] with the latter were associated special ἐπιμεληταί. The demarch is mentioned in connexion with the Dionysia at Eleusis in the middle of the fourth century in an inscription (*I.G.* ii². 1186) which is worth quoting in illustration of the importance attached to the Dionysia there:

Καλλίμαχος Καλλικράτους εἶπεν· ἐπειδὴ Δαμασίας Διονυσίου Θηβαῖος οἰκήσας Ἐλευσῖνι κόσμιός τε ὢν διατετέλεκε καὶ φιλανθρώπως ἔχει πρὸς πάντας τοὺς ἐν τῷ δήμῳ οἰκοῦντας καὶ αὐτὸς καὶ οἱ μαθηταὶ αὐτοῦ, καὶ Διονύσια ποιούντων Ἐλευσινίων καὶ ἐφιλοτιμήθη πρὸς τοὺς θεοὺς καὶ τὸν δῆμον τῶν Ἀθηναίων καὶ Ἐλευσινίων, ὅπως ὡς κάλλιστα γένηται τὰ Διονύσια, καὶ παρασκευάσας τοῖς αὐτοῦ τέλεσι χορους δύο, τὸν μὲν παιδῶν τὸν δὲ ἀνδρῶν, ἐπέδωκεν τῇ Δήμητρι καὶ τῇ Κόρῃ[2] καὶ τῷ Διονύσῳ· δεδόχθαι Ἐλευσινίοις ἐπαινέσαι Δαμασίαν Διονυσίου Θηβαῖον σωφροσύνης ἕνεκα καὶ εὐσεβείας τῆς πρὸς τὼ θέω καὶ στεφανῶσαι αὐτὸν χρυσῷ στεφάνῳ ἀπὸ Χ δραχμῶν. ἀνειπάτω δὲ αὐτὸν ὁ μετὰ Γνάθιν δήμαρχος Διονυσίων τῶν Ἐλευσῖνι τοῖς τραγῳδοῖς. . . . ἔστω δὲ αὐτῷ προεδρία καὶ ἀτέλεια ὧν εἰσιν κύριοι Ἐλευσίνιοι . . . καὶ ἐπιμέλεσθαι αὐτοῦ ὁ δήμαρχος ὁ ἀεὶ δημαρχῶν ὅτου ἂν δέηται· ἐλέσθαι δὲ αὐτίκα μάλα ὅστις ἐπιμελήσεται ὅπως ἂν ἀναγραφῇ τόδε τὸ ψήφισμα καὶ σταθῇ ἐν τῷ Διονυσίῳ κτλ.

(One would like to know more of this Damasias of Thebes, whose κοσμιότης and σωφροσύνη so much impressed the Eleusinians, in addition to his piety and munificence.)[3] In *I.G.* ii². 3090 is an Eleusinian record of an occasion on which two synchoregoi won the victory at Eleusis in both tragedy and comedy, the poets being Sophocles and Aristophanes. This must mean that the festival at Eleusis was of special importance,

---

[1] Aristot *Ἀθ. Πολ.* liv κληροῦσι δὲ καὶ εἰς Σαλαμῖνα ἄρχοντα καὶ εἰς Πειραιέα δήμαρχον, οἳ τὰ Διονύσια ποιοῦσι ἑκατέρωθι καὶ χορηγοὺς καθίστασιν· ἐν Σαλαμῖνι δὲ καὶ τὸ ὄνομα τοῦ ἄρχοντος ἀναγράφεται (sc. as well as that of the χορηγοί). The 'archon' at Salamis is also mentioned in *I.G.* ii². 1008 (ll. 82 ff.), where the crown awarded to the κοσμητής of the Ephebi is to be proclaimed Διονυσίων τῶν ἐν Σαλαμῖνι τραγῳδῶν ἐν τῷ ἀγῶνι, τῆς δὲ ποιήσεως τοῦ στεφάνου καὶ ἀναγορεύσεως ἐπιμεληθῆναι τὸν ἄρχοντα καὶ τὸν στρατηγὸν καὶ τοὺς ἐπιμελητάς. (So also ibid. 1011, late in the second century b.c.)

[2] The association of Demeter and Kore in their own sacred place with Dionysus seems natural enough. That the association was somewhat close is suggested by the schol. on Aristoph. *Frogs* 343—καὶ μὲν δὴ Διονύσου ἐν Ἐλευσῖνι ἱερόν ἐστι καὶ ἐν Διονυσίοις ἐτελεῖτο τὰ μυστήρια, but no details are recorded or there may be some confusion in the scholion. The mysteries of Eleusis were celebrated in the autumn. Diodorus iii. xiv. 7 records a legend that Dionysus and Demeter entered Attica together, and that the first seat of their cult was Eleusis.

[3] In *I.G.* ii². 1187 (middle of the fourth century) a crown awarded to Derkylos is similarly to be proclaimed Ἐλευσῖνι ἐν τῷ θεάτρῳ τραγῳδῶν τῷ ἀγῶνι, and in ibid. 1193 a crown for Smikythion, and in ibid. 1189 (334–333 b.c.) a resolution in honour of the Ephebi and their σωφρονιστής is to be similarly announced.

unless the plays produced were repeated performances of plays already performed in the city. (The inscription runs Γνᾶθις Τιμοκήδους Ἀναξανδρίδης Τιμαγόρου | χορηγόντες κωμωιδοῖς ἐνίκων | Ἀριστοφάνης ἐδίδασκεν | ἑτέρα νίκη τραγωιδοῖς | Σοφοκλῆς ἐδίδασκεν. See below, p. 54.)

5. At Aixone it was the custom in the fourth century B.C. to order the proclamation of crowns for deserving citizens in the theatre and to erect (under the supervision of the demarch) a monument recording the honour. The most interesting of these decrees[1] is as follows:

Φιλοκτήμων Χρέμητος εἶπε· ἐπειδὴ οἱ χορηγοὶ οἱ ἐπὶ Χρέμητος ἄρχοντος Δημοκράτης Εὐφιλήτου καὶ Ἡγησίας Λυσιστράτου καλῶς καὶ φιλοτίμως ἐχορήγησαν Αἰξωνεῦσιν, ἐπαινέσαι αὐτοὺς καὶ στεφανῶσαι χρυσῷ στεφάνῳ ἀπὸ ⌐ΙΙΙ . . . δραχμῶν ἑκάτερον φιλοτιμίας ἕνεκα καὶ ἐπιμελείας τῆς εἰς τοὺς δημότας· δοῦναι δὲ αὐτοῖς καὶ εἰς θυσίαν τὸν δήμαρχον Δωρόθεον καὶ τοὺς ταμίας Δ δραχμὰς ἀπὸ τῆς προσόδου τῶν δημοτῶν· ἀναγράψαι δὲ τόδε τὸ ψήφισμα τὸν δήμαρχον Δωρόθεον εἰς στήλην λιθίνην καὶ στῆσαι εἰς τὸ θέατρον, ὅπως ἂν εἰδῶσιν οἱ μέλλοντες χορηγεῖν Αἰξωνεῦσι ὅτι τιμήσει αὐτοὺς ὁ δῆμος ὁ Αἰξωνέων τοὺς εἰς ἑαυτοὺς φιλοτιμουμένους.

An inscription found at Glyphada in Attica in 1941 and probably to be dated 313/12 B.C. (the archonship of Theophrastus in that year being slightly more probable than the archonship of Theophrastus in 340–339) contains a decree in honour of two choregoi at Aixone, Auteas and Philoxenides, and forms part of a striking monument (Fig. 18)[2] which is adorned with five masks of the Middle or New Comedy type. The inscription runs:

Γλαυκίδης Σωσίππου εἶπεν· ἐπειδὴ οἱ χορηγοὶ Αὐτέας Αὐτοκλέους καὶ Φιλοξενίδης Φιλίππου καλῶς καὶ φιλοτίμως ἐχορήγησαν, δεδόχθαι τοῖς δημόταις στεφανῶσαι αὐτοὺς χρυσῷ στεφάνῳ ἑκάτερον ἀπὸ ἑκατὸν δραχμῶν ἐν τῷ θεάτρῳ τοῖς κωμῳδοῖς τοῖς μετὰ Θεόφραστον ἄρχοντα, ὅπως ἂν φιλοτιμῶνται καὶ οἱ ἄλλοι χορηγοὶ οἱ μέλλοντες χορηγεῖν, δοῦναι δὲ αὐτοῖς

---

[1] *I.G.* ii². 1198 (326–325 B.C.), cf. Nos. 1197, 1200, and 1202 (all late fourth century).

[2] The date is the same as that of *I.G.* ii². 1202, as is shown by the occurrence in both of the names of the same archon, proposer, and demarch. In favour of the date 313–312 B.C., rather than 340 B.C., is the reference (in No. 1202) to Aristokrates, son of Aristophanes, the proposer of a decree (No. 1201) in 317–316 B.C. in honour of Demetrius of Phalerum. On the other hand, Auteas was already known from ibid. 2492, of about 345 B.C., and a Philippos Αἰξωνεύς from ibid. 2752, and from Plut. *Vit. X Orat.* 843 a, where his daughter is said to have married the son of Lycurgus the orator. The masks which adorn the monument on which the inscription is carved are not sufficiently distinctive of either Middle or New Comedy to afford a certain clue. I am indebted for a photograph of this monument to Mr. J. M. Cook. The inscription is published and discussed in *Ath. Mitt.* lxvi (1941), pp. 218 f., but I have not so far been able to procure the next number of this periodical, in which the masks were to be discussed. Cf. also Webster in *J.H.S.* lxxi. 222, n. 7.

FIG. 18. MONUMENT AT AIXONE

καὶ εἰς θυσίαν δέκα δραχμὰς τὸν δήμαρχον Ἡγησιλέων καὶ τοὺς ταμίας,
ἀναγράψαι δὲ καὶ τὸ ψήφισμα τόδε τοὺς ταμίας ἐν στήλῃ λιθίνῃ καὶ στῆσαι
ἐν τῷ θεάτρῳ, ὅπως ἂν Αἰξωνεῖς ἀεὶ ὡς κάλλιστα ⟨τὰ⟩ Διονύσια ποιῶσιν.

These and other decrees indicate considerable enthusiasm for
the drama in this little place in the fourth century.[1]

6. At Ikaria, also in the fourth century, a decree[2] was passed
honouring the demarch and the choregoi for their performance
of their duties: Κάλλιππος εἶπεν· ἐψηφίσθαι Ἰκαριεῦσιν ἐπαινέσαι
Νίκωνα τὸν δήμαρχον καὶ στεφανῶσαι κιττοῦ στεφάνῳ, καὶ ἀνειπεῖν
τὸν κήρυκα ὅτι στεφανοῦσιν Ἰκαριεῖς Νίκωνα καὶ ὁ δῆμος ὁ Ἰκαρι-
έων τὸν δήμαρχον, ὅτι καλῶς καὶ δικαίως τῷ Διονύσῳ τὴν ἑορτὴν
ἐποίησεν καὶ τὸν ἀγῶνα· ἐπαινέσαι δὲ καὶ τοὺς χορηγοὺς Ἐπικράτην
καὶ Πραξίαν καὶ στεφανῶσαι κιττοῦ στεφάνῳ καὶ ἀνειπεῖν καθάπερ
τὸν δήμαρχον. (Ikaria was a small village, and its crowns are
of ivy, not of gold, but ivy was sacred to Dionysus.) There were
traditions which associated Ikaria with the advent of Dionysus
into Attica, with the beginnings both of tragedy and comedy,[3]
and also with an autumn festival, but we have no indication
of the date of the Rural Dionysia. An inscription[4] containing
the accounts of the treasury of Dionysus at Ikaria in the fifth
century, unfortunately in a very fragmentary condition, shows
both by its references to χορηγοί and otherwise that there were
regularly organized dramatic festivals at that time, for which
payments were provided out of the treasury and arrangements
were made for ἀντίδοσις; and in the fourth century various
choregoi set up monuments to commemorate their victories;
from two of these it appears that three choregoi might collabo-
rate. These inscriptions[5] include:

(1) Ἄρχιππος Ἀρχεδέ[κτου] νικήσας ἀνέθηκε τῷ Διονύσῳ· Νικόστρατος
ἐδίδασκε. It is disputed whether this Nikostratos was the third son
of Aristophanes or a dithyrambic poet of the same name.

(2) Ἔργασος Φανομάχου | Φανόμαχος Ἐργάσου | Διόγνητος Ἐργάσου |
τραγῳδοῖς χορηγήσαντες | νικῶντες ἀνέθεσαν. The victors are a
father and two sons.

(3) Ἁγνίας Ξάνθιππος Ξανθίδης νικήσαντες ἀνέθεσαν. Here it is assumed
that χορηγοῦντες or some equivalent is to be understood.

---

[1] No. 1200 is part of a decree in honour of two choregoi, Leontios and Glaukon, in 317–316
B.C. in practically the same terms as No. 1198. See also the appendix to this chapter.
[2] *I.G.* ii². 1178.   [3] See *Dith. Trag. Com.*, pp. 102 ff.
[4] *I.G.* ii². 186–7. Whether the ἀντίδοσις—the exchange of goods between rival claimants
to exemption from χορηγία—was on the same lines as at Athens, the inscription in its fragmentary state does not show.   [5] Ibid. 3094, 3095, 3098.

A father and two sons appear again as synchoregoi at Aegilia :[1]
Τιμοσθένης Μειξωνίδου, Μειξωνίδης Τιμοσθένους, Κλεόστρατος
Τιμοσθένους χορηγοῦντες νικήσαντες ἀνέθεσαν τῷ Διονύσῳ τἄγαλμα
καὶ τὸμ [βωμόν]. Family pride in dramatic victories appears
again in an epigram found in an inscription[2] from Anagyrus
(Vari) probably of the second half of the fourth century:

> ἡδυγέλωτι χορῷ Διονύσια σύμ ποτε ἐν[ίκων]
> μνημόσυνον δὲ θεῷ νίκης τόδε δῶρον [ἔθηκα],
> δήμῳ μὲν κόσμον, ζῆλον πατρὶ κισσοφο[ροῦντι],
> τοῦδε δ' ἔτι πρότερος στεφανηφόρον [εἷλον ἀγῶνα].

(These victories, however, were probably won at the Dionysia
at Athens, not at Anagyrus, like those mentioned in the inscription from Aixone discussed in the Appendix.)

7. The records already quoted will have given an idea of the
performances at the organized festivals in the demes. Tragedy
is mentioned frequently. Whether the more important tragic
poets produced new plays at the Rural Dionysia is unknown,
though Euripides is said to have competed at the Peiraeus; but
doubtless many lesser poets did so, and there may have been
many repetitions of old masterpieces and other plays which had
already been performed in the city.[3] There is a record[4] of dithyramb at Acharnai, where the same choregos served for both
comedy and dithyramb, and an early-fourth-century inscription[5]
probably refers also to dithyramb:

---

[1] *I.G.* ii². 3096. The names appear from *I.G.* i². 769 to be those of demesmen from Aegilia.
There are no other records of three synchoregoi. The number of choregoi at Ikaria was
sometimes two or sometimes one, as the inscriptions quoted show. The inscription from
Eleusis, *I.G.* ii². 3090, earlier than 406–405 B.C., records two synchoregoi there, who served
for both tragedy and comedy and won in each. (See above, p. 43.) Some inscriptions from
Aixone (Nos. 1198 and 1200) and Acharnai (No. 3092), all of the fourth century, record
two synchoregoi. At Eleusis (No. 310) and Paeania (No. 3097), both of the fourth century,
single choregoi are commemorated, and also (probably rather later) at Rhamnus. (See
below, p. 47, n. 4.)

[2] *I.G.* ii². 3101.

[3] Demosthenes taunts Aeschines with his acting of a part in the *Hecuba* (*de Cor.* § 267), and
this must have been in one of the demes. It was for a tour round the demes that (according
to Demosthenes, *de Cor.* § 262) he joined a troupe of bad actors.

[4] *I.G.* ii². 3106: . . . Δημ]οστράτου νικήσας ἀνέθηκ[ε κυκλίῳ] χορῷ καὶ κωμῳδοῖς. Χάρης
Θηβαῖος ηὔλει. Σπευσεάδης (?) Ἀθηναῖος [ἐδίδασκε].

[5] Ibid. 3092. No satisfactory explanation has been given of the last line. It has been suggested that the reference is to a victory gained subsequently and added to the record; but
the whole inscription appears to have been engraved at the same time. Others imagine that
Polychares may have assisted Ariphron, but if so the record is unique. Ariphron was a well-
known lyric poet, and Dikaiogenes, though primarily a tragic poet, is stated by Harpokration
and Suidas (s.v.) to have composed dithyrambs also.

Μνησίστρατος Μίσγωνος   Μνησίμαχος Μνησίστρατο
Διοπείθης Διοδώρου ἐχόρηγον   Θεότιμος Διοτίμο ἐχόρηγον
Δικαιογένης ἐδίδασκεν   Ἀρίφρων ἐδίδασκεν
           Πολυχάρης Κώμωνος ἐδίδασκεν.

An inscription recording the provision of men's and boys' choruses at Eleusis by Damasias of Thebes has already been quoted at length,[1] as also has an inscription from Ikaria which probably refers to a lyric victory.[2] Inscriptions speak of comedy at Eleusis[3] and at Rhamnus.[4]

8. As for the non-dramatic parts of the festivals, a procession (πομπή) and sacrifice are mentioned at Eleusis in 165–164 B.C.,[5] in addition to the ἀγών in the theatre, and in the Peiraeus in 329–328 B.C. and later (see below). At Myrrhinus a special assembly was held after the Dionysia to deal with matters arising out of the festival; the date was the 19th of Poseideon.[6] A decree[7] of the deme of Peiraeus in honour of Kallidamas in the first half of the third century shows that those who were given the honour of front seats in the theatre were ceremonially escorted to their places by the demarch: εἶναι δὲ αὐτῷ προεδρίαν ἐν τῷ θεάτρῳ, ὅταν ποιῶσι Πειραιεῖς τὰ Διονύσια, οὗ καὶ αὐτοῖς Πειραιεῦσι κατανεῖμαι, καὶ εἰσαγέτω αὐτὸν ὁ δήμαρχος εἰς τὸ θέατρον καθάπερ τοὺς ἱερεῖς καὶ τοὺς ἄλλους οἷς δίδοται ἡ προεδρία παρὰ Πειραιέων. The award of προεδρία is recorded in the inscriptions of a number of demes (Aixone, Myrrhinus, Eleusis), but nowhere else with this special mark of honour attached to it.[8]

9. The celebration of the Dionysia ἐν ἀγροῖς at Phlya is mentioned in Isaeus' eighth oration, § 15, where it is said of Kiron that εἰς Διονύσια εἰς ἀγρὸν ἦγεν ἀεὶ ἡμᾶς (in § 35 it is stated that

---

[1] Above, p. 43.   [2] p. 45.

[3] *I.G.* ii². 3100 (middle of fourth century) Ἀθηνόδωρος Γο.... χορηγῶν κωμῳδ[...

[4] Ibid. 3108 (probably fourth century) Ῥαμνούσιος ... κωμῳδοῖς (unless this refers to a victory in the city), and 3109 (early third century) Μεγακλῆς Μεγακλέους Ῥαμνούσιος ἀνέθηκεν Θέμιδι στεφανωθεὶς ὑπὸ τῶν δημοτῶν δικαιοσύνης ἕνεκα ἐπὶ ἱερείας Καλλιστοῦς καὶ νικήσας παισὶ καὶ ἀνδράσι γυμνασιαρχῶν καὶ Φειδοστράτης Νεμέσει ἱερείας ... καὶ κωμῳδοῖς χορηγῶν. Χαιρέστρατος Χαιρεδήμου Ῥαμνούσιος ἐποίησε.

[5] Ibid. 949 ἐπειδὴ Πάμφιλος Ἄ[ρχοντος] κατασταθεὶς δήμαρχος εἰς τὸν ἐπὶ Πέλοπος ἄρχοντος ἐνίαυτ[ον τοῖς Διονυσί]οις ἔθυσεν τῷ Διονύσῳ καὶ τὴν πομπὴν ἔπεμπεν καὶ ...... τον, ἔθηκεν δὲ καὶ τὸν ἀγῶνα ἐν τῷ θεάτρῳ κτλ.

[6] Ibid. 1183 τῇ δὲ ἐνάτῃ ἐπὶ δέκα τοῦ Ποσειδεῶν[ος] μην[ὸς χρηματίζε]ιν πε[ρὶ Διο]νυσίων. Wilhelm, *Urkunden*, p. 238, suggests ἀγορὰν ποιεῖν for χρηματίζειν.

[7] *I.G.* ii². 1214.

[8] Wilhelm, op. cit., pp. 235 ff., proposes restorations of certain inscriptions which would make them refer to the regulation of προεδρία at the Peiraeus and the payment of entrance-money.

Κίρων ἐκέκτητο οὐσίαν ἀγρὸν μὲν Φλυῆσι), καὶ μετ' ἐκείνου τε ἐθεωροῦμεν καθημένοι παρ' αὐτόν κτλ. The festival at Kollytos (close to Athens) was the scene of Aeschines' performance of the part of Oinomaos, which (according to Demosthenes) he murdered,[1] and of an insult directed against Timarchos by the actor Parmenon in the course of a comedy which he was acting.[2] An inscription from Paeania records (in the middle of the fourth century) a victory as choregos in a tragedy of [Δημ]οσθένης Δ[ημαινέτ]ου Παιανιεύς, possibly a relation of the orator.

10. The festival in the Peiraeus appears to have been more important than any of the other Rural Dionysia. It has already been noted that the official in charge of it was appointed by the State,[3] and in the Law of Euegoros, quoted by Demosthenes in his prosecution of Meidias,[4] it is mentioned along with the Lenaia and the City Dionysia as a period during which the exaction of debts and taking of security were forbidden. Euripides is said to have produced plays for competition there which attracted Socrates to see them,[5] and the expenses on sacrifices offered there were a matter of public concern.[6] It was a compliment to ambassadors from other states to give them special places at this festival :[7] κατανεῖμαι δὲ αὐτοῖς (sc. ambassadors from Kolophon) καὶ θ[έαν τὸν ἀρχιτέκτο]να εἰς τὰ Διονύσια τὰ Πειραϊκά. The officials of the Eleusinian mysteries seem also to have had an interest in the festival and in 329–328 B.C. contributed to the cost of a sacrifice :[8] εἰς Διονύσια τὰ ἐν Πειραιεῖ ἐπιστάταις εἰς θυσίαν ΔΔ. A decree of about the same date[9] orders the ἀγορανόμοι to see that the streets are in proper condition for the procession : ἐπιμεληθῆναι τοὺς ἀγορανόμους τῶν ὁδῶν τῶν πλατειῶν, ᾗ ἡ πομπὴ

---

[1] Dem. de Cor. § 180. Demochares, Demosthenes' nephew, εἰ ἄρα πιστευτέον αὐτῷ λέγοντι περὶ Αἰσχίνου, said that Aeschines was tritagonist for the tragic poet Ischander, and fell down when, in the part of Oinomaos, he was pursuing Pelops, and had to be picked up by the chorus-trainer Sannior (*Vit. Aesch.* ii). The poet of the *Oinomaos*, according to this passage, must have been Ischander (who is called τραγῳδιοποιός), not Sophocles as is frequently stated (e.g. by Pearson, Soph. *Fr.* ii, p. 125; Goodwin, commentary on *de Cor.* ad loc.; Haigh, *Att. Th.*[3], p. 29).

[2] Aeschin. in Timarchum, § 157.　　　　　　　　　　　[3] Aristotle, Ἀθ. Πολ. liv.

[4] Dem. in Meid. § 10; see above, p. 24, for the text of the law.

[5] Aelian, *Var. Hist.* ii. 13 καὶ Πειραιοῖ δὲ ἀγωνιζομένου τοῦ Εὐριπίδου καὶ ἐκεῖ κατῄει (sc. ὁ Σωκράτης). It is not stated whether these were new plays or old ones repeated.

[6] *I.G.* ii². 1496, l. 70 [ἐγ Διο]νυσίων τῶν [ἐμ Πει]ρα[ιεῖ παρὰ] βοωνῶν ΗΗΗΔΙ, καὶ τὸ περιγενόμενον ἀπὸ τῆς βοωνίας ΗΗΓΔΔΔ . . . (Accounts of the ταμίαι of Athena, 334–333 B.C.)

[7] Ibid. 456, ll. 32 ff.

[8] Ibid. 1672 (Accounts of the Epistatai of the Eleusinia).

[9] Ibid. 380 (320–319 B.C.).

πορεύεται τῷ Διὶ τῷ Σωτῆρι καὶ τῷ Διονύσῳ, ὅπως ἂν ὁμαλισθῶσιν καὶ κατασταθῶσιν ὡς βέλτιστα. Then, except for the decree conferring προεδρία on Kallidamas in the third century, there is a long gap in our knowledge of the festival: but from 118–117 B.C. onwards it is frequently mentioned in a series of decrees[1] relating to the duties performed by the epheboi, who appear to have regularly sacrificed a bull which they took in procession[2] to the festival and in 106–105 B.C. to have dedicated a φιάλη to the god costing 100 drachmae. (They performed similar duties at the City Dionysia and the Eleusinia.) An inscription of 116–115 B.C.[3] shows that the epheboi escorted the statue of Dionysus to the theatre in the Peiraeus as they did in Athens.

11. Deubner[4] has made a study of a sculptured frieze embodied in a wall of the little church of Hagios Eleutherios in Athens, in which the chief festivals or characteristic qualities or operations of the seasons are represented by symbolical figures or groups of figures, arranged in chronological order from Pyanopsion to Boedromion. In the place corresponding to Poseideon appears a group of judges sitting at a table bearing five crowns, and on the ground two fighting-cocks and a palm-branch. Deubner takes the whole to symbolize the contests of the Rural Dionysia. (Other symbols which follow are interpreted as referring to the Lenaia in Gamelion.) The date of the frieze may fall in the second or first century B.C. or, as some archaeologists think, not before the Imperial period. In any case, if correctly interpreted, the frieze is a record of the continued interest in the Rural Dionysia down to a comparatively late date.

12. The Rural Dionysia were doubtless among the 'great occasions' of the year in the country demes, celebrated with different degrees of elaboration in the several localities according to their traditions and their means, and though some of them,

---

[1] Ibid. 1008 (118–117 B.C.), 1011 (106–105 B.C.), 1028 (100–99 B.C.), 1029 (94–93 B.C.), 1039 (c. 83–73 B.C.).

[2] e.g. in No. 1028 παρήγαγον δὲ καὶ τοῖς Ἐλευσινίοις βοῦς τροφίας δύο καὶ ἔθυσαν καὶ τοῖς Πειραίοις τῷ Διονύσῳ ταῦρον καὶ ἔθυσαν, τοῖς τε Διονυσίοις ἕτερον βοῦν ὡς ὅτι κάλλιστον παρήγαγον τῇ πομπῇ ὃν καὶ ἔθυσαν ἐν τῷ ἱερῷ καὶ ἐπὶ τούτοις ἅπασιν ἐκαλλιέρησαν; and in No. 1011 ὁμοίως δὲ καὶ τῷ ἐν Πειραιεῖ Διονύσῳ θύσαντες ἀνέθηκαν φιάλην ἀπὸ δραχμῶν ἑκατόν.

[3] *Hesperia*, xvi (1947), p. 171: εἰσήγαγον δὲ τήν τε Παλλάδα καὶ τὸν Διόνυσον ἔν τε Πειραιεῖ καὶ ἐν ἄστει καὶ ἐβουθύτησαν ἐν ἑκατέρᾳ τῶν πόλεων κτλ.

[4] *Att. Feste*, pp. 138, 248 ff. and Plates 34 ff. Deubner's study is based on earlier accounts by Robert, Svoronos, and others.

such as those of the Peiraeus, which was virtually a city function, and of Eleusis, Salamis, and Ikaria, were more important
than others, the local patriotism of other demes is attested by
a number of inscriptions, of which those of Aixone are the most
striking. It may be that the general knowledge of the subjects
of tragedy, which Aristophanes seems to assume, was fostered by
these festivals. His allusions are mostly to plays performed
recently in Athens itself, but a wider knowledge of the main
themes of the tragic poets is attested by Antiphanes[1] in the
fourth century, who complains of the necessity under which, by
comparison, the comic poets laboured of having to invent their
own stories and persons. The actors' companies which toured
the demes in the fourth century may have been undistinguished
as actors, but the evidence of Demosthenes and others that they
performed the tragedies of the great masters is clear,[2] and seems
(like that of Antiphanes) to contradict the statement of Aristotle
in the *Poetics*[3] (at about the same date) that even the well-known
stories were well known to few, though they pleased everyone.

However this may be, it is interesting to notice that a great
part of the evidence from inscriptions about the Rural Dionysia
comes from the fourth century B.C. This may, of course, be an
accident, but it may point (as Antiphanes does) to the special
popularity of the drama at this period—the period in which the
great work associated with the name of Lycurgus was being
carried out in the theatre at Athens and theatres were springing
up in many parts of Greece, while famous actors, like Neoptolemus, were becoming important personages and taking part
in diplomatic exchanges between states.[4]

13. Few of the theatres which may have once existed in the
Attic demes have left any traces. The oldest extant remains in
all probability are those of Thorikos,[5] where they must be earlier
than the date of any dramatic performances, and seem to go
back at least to the middle of the sixth century B.C. There are

[1] Fr. 191 (Kock). See also below, p. 284.

[2] e.g. *de Cor.* § 262—which, unless Demosthenes greatly exaggerates, shows that bad
actors might be pelted by the audience without mercy. See also above, p. 46.

[3] ch. ix ὥστ' οὐ πάντως ἂν εἴη ζητητέον τῶν παραδεδομένων μύθων, περὶ οὓς αἱ τραγῳδίαι
εἰσίν, ἀντέχεσθαι. καὶ γὰρ γελοῖον τοῦτο ζητεῖν, ἐπεὶ καὶ τὰ γνώριμα ὀλίγοις γνώριμά ἐστιν, ἀλλ'
ὅμως εὐφραίνει πάντας.   [4] See below, p. 286.

[5] See Dörpf. u. Reisch, pp. 109–11; Bulle, *Unters. zu den Gr. Theatern*, pp. 9 ff., 210,
Taf. 1, 2; Arias, *Il Teatro greco fuori di Atene*, pp. 24 ff.; Flickinger, *Gk. Theater*, p. 227 and
figs. 70, 71; Caputo in *Dioniso*, iii (1933), pp. 301 ff.; iv, p. 90; Anti, *Teatri greci arcaici*,
pp. 45–48 (with criticisms in *Class. Rev.* lxii (1948), p. 125); Dilke, *B.S.A.* xlv, pp. 25 ff.

FIG. 19. VIEW OF THEATRE AT THORIKOS

remains of several lines of steps which may have served for
spectators of choral dances or of any kind of festal performance
or for attenders at a public assembly. The form of this auditorium (see Plan) is unlike that of any other theatre, and its size
was increased at some time[1] later than the original building by

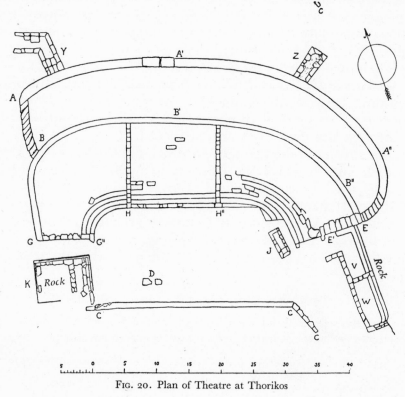

FIG. 20. Plan of Theatre at Thorikos

an addition (A) higher up on the rising ground. The area in front
of the steps was terraced up to a level and no doubt in time
served for dramatic presentations, and it was bounded on the
side farthest from the steps by a wall (D) of which some slight remains are visible. There are also the remains of a small temple (K),
an altar (J), and what is sometimes regarded as a βουλευτήριον or
council-chamber.

The principal remains at Rhamnus[2] are three stone seats or

[1] Perhaps when Thorikos was fortified by the Athenians in 410–409 B.C. (Xen. *Hellen.*
I. ii. 1).
[2] See Bulle, op. cit., pp. 1–4, Taf. 1; Arias, op. cit., pp. 22–24; Anti, op. cit., pp. 146–8;
ke, *B.S.A.* xlv, pp. 25 ff.

thrones—probably there were originally seven—dedicated to Dionysus by the priest of the Hero Archegetes;[1] they stand on a base of local marble and, together with what was a row of stelai in a line with them on a similar base, formed a front row behind which the crowd could stand on the rising ground, and the performances could be given on the levelled ground in front. The remains are considered to belong to the fourth century, and though the place doubtless served for the public meetings of the little village and Bulle thinks he can locate the council-chamber, it is definitely called a theatre in inscriptions.[2]

At Ikaria[3] there seems to have been a similar row of thrones, standing between the main body of spectators and the performers. Two pairs of thrones of crude workmanship are still to be seen and there are traces of an altar.

The theatre in the Peiraeus[4] in which the Dionysia were celebrated, and to which the inscriptions quoted in this chapter belong, was on the peninsula of Munychia, and has disappeared entirely. It figures occasionally in the history of the classical period.[5] The later theatre at Zea, built probably in the second century B.C., though of some interest in the history of the development of the Greek theatre, does not come within the scope of this chapter.[6]

APPENDIX ON *I.G.* II². 3091 (AIXONE)

IT is extremely doubtful whether this much-discussed inscription[7] has any reference to the Rural Dionysia at all. It was discovered near Aixone

[1] *I.G.* ii². 2849 ἀνέθηκεν Διονύσῳ ἱερεὺς ἥρω ἀρχηγέτου . . . καὶ στεφανωθεὶς ὑπὸ τῆς βουλῆς καὶ τῶν δημοτῶν καὶ τῶν στρατιωτῶν.

[2] P.A.E. 1891, 16 ἀναγράψαι δὲ τόδε τὸ ψήφισμα ἐν στήλῃ λιθίνῃ καὶ στῆσαι ἐν τῷ θεάτρῳ (4th cent.).

[3] See Bulle, op. cit., pp. 4 ff., Taf. 1; Arias, op. cit., pp. 19–21; Anti, op. cit., pp. 144–6; Dilke, loc. cit., pp. 30 ff.   [4] pp. 48–49.

[5] Thucyd. viii. 93 οἱ δὲ ἐν αὐτῷ ὁπλῖται τόν τε Ἀλεξικλέα ὃν ξυνέλαβον ἀφέντες καὶ τὸ τείχισμα καθελόντες εἰς τὸ πρὸς τῇ Μουνυχίᾳ θέατρον ἐλθόντες; Lysias xiii. 32 ἐπειδὴ ἡ ἐκκλησία Μουνυχίασιν ἐν τῷ θεάτρῳ ἐγένετο; Xen. *Hellen.* II. iv. 32 ἀπέκτειναν (sc. the soldiers of Epaminondas) τριάκοντα τῶν ψιλῶν, τοὺς δ᾽ ἄλλους κατεδίωξαν πρὸς τὸ Πειραιοῖ θέατρον.

[6] See Dörpfeld u. Reisch, pp. 97–100; Bulle, op. cit., pp. 203–4; Arias, op. cit., pp. 15–18; and my *Theatre of Dionysus at Athens*, pp. 139, 144, 181–3, 217–18. An inscription, *I.G.* ii². 2334, headed οἵδε ἐπέδωκαν εἰς τὴν κατασκευὴν τοῦ θεάτρου and containing a long list of donors is said to belong to the second half of the second century B.C.

[7] Published by Palaios in *Polemon*, i, pp. 161 ff. For discussion see *New Chapters in Gk. Lit.*, Third Series, pp. 69 ff.; Wilamowitz, *Hermes*, lxv (1930), pp. 243–5; M. Guarducci, *Riv. di Fil.* viii (1930), pp. 202 ff.; ix (1931), pp. 283 ff.; xiv (1936), pp. 283 ff.; M. Fromhold-Treu, *Hermes*, lxix (1936), pp. 324 ff.; Körte, *Gnomon*, xi (1935), pp. 632 ff.; Vitucci, *Dioniso*, vii (1939), pp. 216 ff. What is said in the text is what now seems most probable in the light of the discussion, and differs in some points from my conclusions in *New Chapters*, loc. cit.

FIG. 21. THEATRE AT RHAMNUS

FIG. 22. THEATRE AT IKARIA

at Palaiochori, apparently on the site of Halai Aixonides, rather than
that of Aixone itself,[1] inscribed on a cylindrical block of white marble
which was probably the base of a statue. It runs:

> Ἐ[πιχάρης χορηγῶν ἐνίκα κ]ωμῳδοῖς
> Ἐχφαντίδης ἐδίδασκε Πείρας
> Θρασύβολος χορηγῶν ἐνίκα κωμῳδοῖς
> Κρατῖνος ἐδίδασκε Βουκόλους
> Θρασύβολος χορη[γ]ῶν ἐνίκα τραγῳδοῖς
> Τιμόθεος ἐδίδασκε Ἀλκμέωνα Ἀλφεσίβο[ιαν
> Ἐπιχάρης χορηγῶν ἐνίκα τραγῳδοῖ[ς
> Σοφοκλῆς ἐδίδασκε Τηλέφειαν.

It is now generally agreed that the date of the inscription, as determined
by the form of the letters and the orthography, is early in the fourth
century, probably about 380 B.C.[2] At this date the monument commemorated the choregic victories of Epichares and Thrasybulus; the
victories must have been won at different festivals, as there would not
have been *two* victors either in tragedy or in comedy at the same festival.
Whether the victories are in chronological order it is impossible to say.
Inscriptions make it clear that Ekphantides' earliest victory at the City
Dionysia fell between 457 and 454 B.C., and that he either took no part or
won no victory in the Lenaian contests, which were first state-organized
about 442 B.C., so that he probably died before this. (Geissler dates his
Σάτυροι between 445 and 440 B.C., but on somewhat inconclusive grounds.)
The date of Cratinus' Βουκόλοι is quite uncertain.[3] Hesychius' gloss,
which is often quoted as showing that the play was refused a chorus by
the archon, does not necessarily mean this, and in its corrupt condition
affords no safe basis of argument.[4] Timotheos, otherwise unknown as
a tragic poet, may or may not have been identical with the famous lyric
poet. The Τηλέφεια of Sophocles, probably a trilogy dealing with the
story of Telephus,[5] is not recorded elsewhere.

It seems clear (despite the arguments of M. Guarducci) that the
formula ἐδίδασκε is only used in inscriptions of plays produced by the
authors in person; and though it is quite possible that greater as well as
lesser poets may occasionally have produced plays in the demes in person[6]

[1.] See Fromhold-Treu, loc. cit.

[2] M. Guarducci argues for an earlier date but quite unconvincingly.

[3] See *New Chapters*, Third Series, p. 74.

[4] e.g. the argument that having been refused at Athens, he may have presented it at
Aixone. Even if he were refused by the archon for the Dionysia, he may have obtained a
chorus next year—or from the βασιλεύς for the Lenaia.

[5] The plays were probably the Ἀλεάδαι, Μυσοί, and Ἀχαιῶν Σύλλογος. See *New Chapters*,
Third Series, pp. 76 ff.; Fromhold-Treu, loc. cit.; and below, p. 82.

[6] Euripides certainly did so. See above, p. 46. Whether the very large numbers of plays
attributed e.g. to Antiphanes and Menander are to be accounted for by their following this
practice remains uncertain.

—either for the first time or in repetition of performances in the city—it seems more likely that the record is that of *choregic* victories gained in Athens in the last half of the fifth century by Epichares and Thrasybulus, demesmen of Aixone, and commemorated either by themselves in their old age or by their family or deme early in the fourth century, perhaps after their deaths. The victory with the two plays of Timotheos must have been won at the Lenaia, when each poet presented only two tragedies. The Τηλέφεια, if it was a trilogy or tetralogy, must have been performed at the City Dionysia.

The alternative supposition—that so many famous poets of the fifth century should all have chosen Aixone as the place for the production of their plays by themselves—seems less likely; and, if so, the inscription throws no light on the Rural Dionysia at Aixone, but only on the enthusiasm of its citizens for the drama in the fourth century—a thing which is attested by other inscriptions.

It has often been supposed that another record of the local commemoration in a deme of a choregic victory by its citizens at a festival in Athens is found in an inscription at Eleusis, which is generally interpreted as meaning that the two synchoregoi[1] named were victorious with the *Frogs* of Aristophanes in 406–405 B.C. and the *Oedipus Coloneus* of Sophocles in 402–401 B.C., and thereafter erected this monument at Eleusis. But Wilhelm is certain that the lettering is earlier than 405 B.C., and that the inscription is better interpreted as above, as referring to a festival at Eleusis. It is in any case very improbable that the same pair of synchoregoi, both from Eleusis, would have been victorious *at Athens* in two years so close to each other. The inscription runs:[2] [Γ]νᾶθις Τιμοκήδους Ἀναξανδρίδης Τιμαγόρου | χορηγοῦντες κωμῳδοῖς ἐνίκων | Ἀριστοφάνης ἐδίδασκεν | ἑτέρα νίκη τραγῳδοῖς | Σοφοκλῆς ἐδίδασκεν.

An inscription from Salamis,[3] of the early part of the fourth century, is probably of the same kind: Διόδωρος Ἐξηκεστίδου νικήσας χορῷ παίδων. Παιδέας ἐδίδασκε. Τηλεφάνης ηὔλει Μεγαρεύς. Φιλόμηλος ἦρχε.

---

[1] See Körte in *Gnomon*, xi (1935), pp. 634–5. Synchoregia was introduced in Athens in 406–405 B.C., and Capps (*Hesperia*, xii, p. 5) proves fairly certainly that it lasted there for that one year only (see below, p. 88). It must have been abolished at latest by 399–398 B.C. for the City Dionysia (ibid.).

[2] *I.G.* ii². 3090; see above, p. 44.

[3] *I.G.* ii². 3093. ἦρχε means that he was the local official appointed to conduct the festival. See Aristotle, Ἀθ. Πολ. liv, and above, pp. 40, 42. For Telephanes see *Dith. Trag. Com.*, pp. 73, 75, and *Anth. Pal.* vii. 159.

II

THE CITY DIONYSIA

1. THE last of the Athenian festivals of Dionysus to be instituted was known as the 'City Dionysia'[1] by contrast with the Rural festivals, and as the 'Great Dionysia'[2] on account of the importance which soon attached to it. It might also be called τὰ Διονύσια[3] without further qualification. It was instituted in honour of Dionysus Eleuthereus, whose image had been brought to Athens from Eleutherai, on the borders of Attica and Boeotia, and stood in the older temple of Dionysus within the theatre precinct. The date and the circumstances of the transfer of the image to Athens are not certain, but it was said to have been brought by an otherwise unknown Pegasos, who was probably a missionary of the cult of the god. In Athens, as in some other places in Greece,[4] the god was not well received, and the men of Athens were smitten with a disease from which (it was said) they only freed themselves (on the advice of an oracle) by manufacturing φαλλοί in honour of the god.[5]

A passage of Pausanias[6] seems to date the mission of Pegasos in the time of the legendary Amphiktyon, King of Athens, and in another passage[7] he records that the people of Eleutherai voluntarily transferred themselves from the Boeotian to the

---

[1] Διονύσια τὰ ἀστικά, Thucyd. v. 20; Διονύσια τὰ ἐν ἄστει, Law of Euegoros (Demosth. *Meid.* § 10) and many inscriptions, e.g. *I.G.* ii². 840, 851, 900, etc. Hence also such phrases as ἐν ἄστει διδάσκειν, διδασκαλία ἀστική, εἰς ἄστυ καθιέναι, νίκη ἀστική, etc.

[2] Διονύσια τὰ μεγάλα, Aristot. Ἀθ. Πολ. lvi, and (for example) *I.G.* ii². 654, 682.

[3] Διονύσια, Aristot. Ἀθ. Πολ. lvi, and (for example) *I.G.* ii². 1006, 1028, 1183, etc.

[4] Including Eleutherai itself, where the daughters of the eponymous Eleuther were driven mad by the god when he was insulted by them (Suidas, s.v. Μελαναιγίς). Eleuther himself then organized the worship of Dionysus. (Hygin. *Fab.* 225 'Eleuther primus simulacrum Liberi patris constituit, et quemadmodum coli deberet ostendit.')

[5] Schol. on Aristoph. *Ach.* 243 Πήγασος ἐκ τῶν Ἐλευθερῶν (αἱ δὲ Ἐλευθεραὶ πόλις ἐστὶ Βοιωτίας) λαβὼν τοῦ Διονύσου τὸ ἄγαλμα ἧκεν εἰς τὴν Ἀττικήν· οἱ δὲ Ἀθηναῖοι οὐκ ἐδέξαντο μετὰ τιμῆς τὸν θεόν. ἀλλ' οὐκ ἀμισθί γε αὐτοῖς ταῦτα βουλευσαμένοις ἀπέβη. (The story of their punishment follows.)

[6] I. ii. 5 μετὰ δὲ τὸ τοῦ Διονύσου (i.e. Dionysus Μελπόμενος) τέμενός ἐστιν οἴκημα ἀγάλματα ἔχον ἐκ πηλοῦ, βασιλεὺς Ἀθηναίων Ἀμφικτύων ἄλλους τε θεοὺς ἑστιῶν καὶ Διόνυσον. ἐνταῦθα καὶ Πήγασός ἐστιν Ἐλευθερεύς, ὃς Ἀθηναίοις τὸν θεὸν εἰσήγαγε.

[7] I. xxxviii. 8 πρότερον μὲν γὰρ Ἐλευθερεῦσιν ὅροι πρὸς τὴν Ἀττικὴν ἦσαν· προσχωρησάντων δὲ Ἀθηναίοις τούτων, οὕτως ἤδη Βοιωτίας ὁ Κιθαιρών ἐστιν ὄρος. προσεχώρησαν δὲ Ἐλευθερεῖς οὐ πολέμῳ βιασθέντες, ἀλλὰ πολιτείας τε ἐπιθυμήσαντες παρὰ Ἀθηναίων καὶ κατ' ἔχθος τὸ Θηβαίων. ἐν τούτῳ τῷ πεδίῳ ναός ἐστι Διονύσου, καὶ τὸ ξόανον ἐντεῦθεν Ἀθηναίοις ἐκομίσθη τὸ ἀρχαῖον· τὸ δὲ Ἐλευθεραῖς ⟨τὸ⟩ ἐφ' ἡμῶν ἐς μίμησιν ἐκείνου πεποίηται.

Athenian alliance; but there is no reason for connecting the advent of the god with this political change (of which the date is unknown). The action of Pegasos was probably an incident in the gradual spread of Dionysiac cults throughout Greece, which was unconnected with political motives.[1] What seems certain is that it was in the sixth century that the festival became important, probably through the policy of Peisistratus. That it was a relatively late institution is indicated by the fact that it was not controlled by the archon basileus, the successor of the kings as the supreme religious official of Athens,[2] but by the archon eponymos. He had charge of the procession and of the dramatic and dithyrambic contests, with the assistance of his two πάρεδροι, and (for the procession) of ten ἐπιμεληταί. The latter were originally appointed by vote of the Assembly and paid their own expenses, but in Aristotle's time[3] were chosen by lot, one from each tribe, and received 100 minae from the State for the necessary equipment. The archon and ἐπιμεληταί continued to perform their functions even when the duties of the choregoi had been handed over to an agonothetes.[4]

2. The importance of the festival was derived not only from the performances of dramatic and lyric poetry but from the fact that it was open to the whole Hellenic world and was an effective advertisement of the wealth and power and public spirit of Athens, no less than of the artistic and literary leadership of her sons. By the end of March the winter was over, the seas were navigable,[5] and strangers came to Athens from all parts for business or pleasure.[6] After the founding of the Delian

---

[1] The attempt of Vollgraff (*Ath. Mitt.* xxxii (1907), pp. 567 ff.) to prove that the statue of Eleuthereus was not brought to Athens before 420 B.C., and was then placed in the *new* Temple of Dionysus, rests on unprovable assumptions and is sufficiently answered by Farnell, *Cults*, v, pp. 227–9.

[2] He first appears as taking part in the festival in an inscription in the middle of the second century A.D. (*I.G.* ii². 2046) in which he is mentioned as offering τῷ Διονύσῳ τὴν ἐν τῇ πομπῇ θυσίαν.

[3] Aristot. Ἀθ. Πολ. lvi. The πάρεδροι are mentioned both by Aristotle and in a laudatory inscription in honour of the archon and πάρεδροι of the year 284/3 B.C. (*Hesperia*, vii, p. 100). The ἐπιμεληταί also are joined in such a vote of thanks in *I.G.* ii². 668 (282–281 B.C.). In the time of Theophrastus one of the contentions of those who favoured oligarchy was that the archon ought to manage the festival-procession without being hampered by ἐπιμεληταί representing the demos (*Char.* 26).　　　　　　　　[4] *I.G.* ii². 896. See below, pp. 68, 93.

[5] One of the typical remarks of the ἀδολέσχης in Theophrastus, *Char.* 3, is τὴν θάλατταν ἐκ Διονυσίων πλόιμον εἶναι. But in the time of Demetrius (Plut. *Demetr.*, p. 894 b) the procession was prevented by a snow-storm. The theatre of Dionysus was sheltered from the north wind by the Acropolis, but it can still be cold in Athens in March and April.

[6] Aeschines, *in Ctes.* § 43, speaks of proclamations at the Dionysia as taking place ἐναντίον

League the allies of Athens brought their tribute at this season, and the surplus revenues were displayed in the theatre.[1] At the same period, before the performance of the tragedies began, the orphaned children of those who had fallen in battle for Athens, such as had reached a suitable age, were caused to parade in the theatre in full armour and receive the blessing of the People. (This practice appears no longer to have been followed in the time of Aeschines and Demosthenes.)[2] The festival was also made the occasion for the proclamation of honours conferred upon citizens or strangers for conspicuous services to Athens;[3] and it was a natural time for the visits of ambassadors from other states for business requiring publicity.[4] The festival was a time of holiday; prisoners were released on bail to attend the festival and sometimes took the chance of escaping.[5] The Law of Euegoros, quoted by Demosthenes,[6] forbade legal proceedings and distraint or taking of security for debt during this and some other festivals; but the date of the law is unknown, and it is possible that in the fifth century the holding of an Assembly was not excluded.[7]

πάντων τῶν Ἑλλήνων, and Demosthenes, in Meid. § 74, complains that Meidias insulted him ἐναντίον πολλῶν ξένων καὶ πολιτῶν. For the presence of strangers at the City Dionysia, in contrast with the Lenaia, see Aristoph. Ach. 505–6, and above, pp. 23, 37.

[1] Eupolis, Πόλεις, fr. 240 K. (with schol. on Aristoph. Ach. 378, 504); cf. Isocr. de Pace, § 82 ἐψηφίσαντο τὸ περιγιγνόμενον τῶν πόρων ἀργύριον διελόντες κατὰ τάλαντον εἰς τὴν ὀρχήστραν τοῖς Διονυσίοις εἰσφέρειν, ἐπειδὰν πλῆρες ᾖ τὸ θέατρον· καὶ τοῦτ' ἐποίουν καὶ παρεισῆγον τοὺς παῖδας τῶν ἐν πολέμῳ τετελευτηκότων, ἀμφοτέροις ἐπιδεικνύοντες, τοῖς μὲν συμμάχοις τὰς τιμὰς τῆς οὐσίας αὐτῶν ὑπὸ μισθωτῶν εἰσφερομένας, τοῖς δ' ἄλλοις Ἕλλησι τὸ πλῆθος τῶν ὀρφάνων καὶ τὰς συμφορὰς τὰς διὰ τὴν πλεονεξίαν ταύτην γιγνομένας.

[2] Aeschines, in Ctes. § 154 τίς γὰρ οὐκ ἂν ἀλγήσειεν ἄνθρωπος Ἕλλην καὶ παιδευθεὶς ἐλευθερίως, ἀναμνησθεὶς ἐν τῷ θεάτρῳ ἐκεῖνό γε, εἰ μηδὲν ἕτερον, ὅτι ταύτῃ ποτὲ τῇ ἡμέρᾳ μελλόντων ὥσπερ νυνὶ τῶν τραγῳδῶν γίγνεσθαι, ὅτε εὐνομεῖτο μᾶλλον ἡ πόλις καὶ βελτίοσι προστάταις ἐχρῆτο, προελθὼν ὁ κῆρυξ καὶ παραστησάμενος τοὺς ὀρφάνους ὧν οἱ πατέρες ἦσαν ἐν τῷ πολέμῳ τετελευτη-κότες, νεανίσκους πανοπλίᾳ κεκοσμημένους, ἐκήρυττε τὸ κάλλιστον κήρυγμα καὶ προτρεπτικώτατον πρὸς ἀρετήν, ὅτι τούσδε τοὺς νεανίσκους, ὧν οἱ πατέρες ἐτελεύτησαν ἐν τῷ πολέμῳ ἄνδρες ἀγαθοὶ γενόμενοι, μέχρι μὲν ἥβης ὁ δῆμος ἔτρεφε, νυνὶ δὲ καθοπλίσας τῇδε τῇ πανοπλίᾳ, ἀφίησιν ἀγαθῇ τύχῃ τρέπεσθαι ἐπὶ τὰ ἑαυτῶν καὶ καλεῖ εἰς προεδρίαν. τότε μὲν ταῦτ' ἐκήρυττεν, ἀλλ' οὐ νῦν.

[3] This provision occurs in many inscriptions. See below, p. 82, n. 9. The proclamation was made before the tragedies began. Aeschines, in Ctes. § 41, speaks as if the practice of making proclamations at the festival had sometimes been abused; cf. Demosth. de Cor. § 120.

[4] In Thucyd. v. 23 the oath of alliance between Athens and Sparta is to be renewed annually by the ambassadors of Sparta at the Dionysia.

[5] As, according to Demosth. in Androt. § 68, Androtion's father did. The schol. ad loc. says ἔθος ἦν παρὰ τοῖς Ἀθηναίοις ἐν τοῖς Διονυσίοις καὶ τοῖς Παναθηναίοις τοὺς δεσμώτας ἀφίεσθαι τοῦ δεσμοῦ ἐν ἐκείναις ταῖς ἡμέραις παρασχόντας ἐγγυητάς.   [6] See above, pp. 24, 48.

[7] In Thucyd. iv. 118 the Athenians are said to have ratified the truce with Sparta in 423 B.C. in the Assembly on the 14th of Elaphebolion, but it is disputed whether this date fell within the festival period at that time; see below, p. 64. In Thucyd. v. 23 it is not stated at what point in the Dionysia, or before what persons or body the treaty with Sparta was to be renewed, but the renewal may well have required an Assembly.

3. As a rite preliminary to the festival, though perhaps not considered part of the festival itself,[1] there was a re-enactment of the original advent of Dionysus from Eleutherai. The statue of Dionysus Eleuthereus was taken to a temple in the neighbourhood of the Academy, on the road to Eleutherai, and placed by the ἐσχάρα there. There sacrifice was offered,[2] and hymns were sung,[3] and the statue was escorted back to the theatre in a torchlight procession in which the leading part was taken by the epheboi, the young men of military age. The dates of the ephebic inscriptions[4] which are the authority for these statements are late in the second or early in the first century B.C.; but the re-enactment of the god's advent does not look like an afterthought and probably goes back to the earliest days of the festival when, after his first cold welcome, it was desired to make amends by doing him special honour. Whether the statue thus brought to the theatre was left there till the end of the festival is not recorded. It may well have been returned to the temple in preparation for the sacrifices to which the πομπή (probably on the next day) led up,[5] and have been brought back daily to the theatre for the performances at which it was certainly present.[6] The temple in the Academy is de-

[1] In I.G. ii². 1006 (123–122 B.C.) the εἰσαγωγή of the god is evidently distinguished from the Dionysia in the strict sense and from the πομπή, which was part of the festival proper. εἰσήγαγον δὲ καὶ τὸν Διόνυσον ἀπὸ τῆς ἐσχάρας εἰς τὸ θέατρον μετὰ φωτός· καὶ ἔπεμψαν τοῖς Διονυσίοις ταῦρον ἄξιον τοῦ θεοῦ, ὃν καὶ ἔθυσαν ἐν τῷ ἱερῷ τῇ πομπῇ, ἐφ' ᾧ καὶ ἐστεφανώθησαν ὑπὸ τοῦ δήμου.

[2] Among others by the epheboi: ibid. 1011 εἰσήγαγον δὲ καὶ τὸν Διόνυσον ἀπὸ τῆς ἐσχάρας θύσαντες τῷ θεῷ, καὶ ἀνέθηκαν φιάλην κατασκευάσαντες τῷ θεῷ ἀπὸ δραχμῶν ἑκατόν. Cf. also the inscription printed in *Hesperia*, xvi (1947), p. 171 (dated 116–115 B.C.; it is part of the same inscription as I.G. ii². 1009).

[3] Alkiphron iv. xviii. 16 (Schepers), where the fictitious Menander says ἐμοὶ γένοιτο τὸν Ἀττικὸν ἀεὶ στέφεσθαι κισσὸν καὶ τὸν ἐπ' ἐσχάρας ὑμνῆσαι κατ' ἔτος Διόνυσον. Herodes Atticus (early second century A.D.) is said by Philostratus (*Vit. Soph.*, p. 549) to have given a feast of drink on a large scale to citizens and strangers at the Kerameikos, on the way to the Academy: ὁπότε δὲ ἥκοι Διονύσια καὶ κατίοι εἰς Ἀκαδήμιαν τὸ τοῦ Διονύσου ἕδος ἐν Κεραμεικῷ ποτίζων ἀστοὺς ὁμοίως καὶ ξένους κατακειμένους ἐπὶ στιβάδων κισσοῦ. But this was doubtless a late perversion of a festival which had lost its meaning.

[4] Other inscriptions are I.G. ii². 1028 (quoted above, p. 49) (100–99 B.C.), and 1008 (119–118 B.C.) καὶ εἰσήγαγον τὸν θεὸν ἀπὸ τῆς [ἐσχάρας εἰς τὸ θέατρον μετὰ φωτὸς κ]α[ὶ ἔπεμψαν ταῦρον τοῖς Διονυσίοις τῇ πομ]πῇ καὶ θύσαντες ἐπὶ τού[τοις ἅπασιν ἐκαλλιέρησαν]: cf. also 1030 (94–93 B.C.) παρήγαγον δὲ καὶ τῇ πομπῇ τῶν Διον[υσίων ἕτερον βοῦν . . . καὶ ἔθυσαν] τοῖς θεοῖς ἐν τοῖς ἱεροῖς ὑπέρ τε τοῦ δήμου καὶ παίδων καὶ γυναικῶν, and 1039 (83–73 B.C.) ἔθυσαν δὲ τά τε Προηρόσια καὶ μυστήρια καὶ Πειραιὰ καὶ Διονύσια παραστήσαντες ὡς κάλλιστα θύματα.

[5] The bull was sacrificed ἐν τῷ ἱερῷ, in the sacred precinct, but not, of course, in the theatre. This was doubtless the climax of the procession.

[6] See Aristoph. *Knights* 536, *Frogs* 809, etc.; Philostr. *Vit. Apoll.* iv. xxii; Dio Chrys. xxxi. 121 (p. 631 R.), etc.

scribed by Pausanias as a small one.¹ It may have existed for
this particular purpose alone. It is difficult to draw any conclusion from the fact that the altar was an ἐσχάρα (a low altar,
hollowed out at the top) and not a βωμός or a θυμέλη. The uses
of the several terms were not kept rigidly separate.²

There has been much discussion, some of it of a speculative
and rambling character, of the εἰσαγωγὴ ἀπὸ τῆς ἐσχάρας.³ The
account given above attempts to keep closely to the evidence,
and the same principle will be observed in regard to the πομπή,
the procession with which the Dionysia in the strict sense began,
and the κῶμος, which, whatever its nature, is clearly separated
from the πομπή in the Law of Euegoros.

4. The πομπή was essentially a religious procession leading
up to the sacrifices in the sacred precinct of Dionysus.⁴ The
sacrifice of a bull, which was led in the procession, by the
epheboi (in the second and first centuries B.C. but probably also
earlier) has already been mentioned, and no doubt many other
victims were offered.⁵ Many bloodless offerings were also made,
and these were carried in the procession in a variety of vessels
borne by men and women, both citizens and resident aliens.
There were κανηφόροι (bearers of golden baskets of offerings),
who were maidens of noble birth.⁶ They may have led the
procession, as in the 'Rural Dionysia' in the *Acharnians*. The
ὀβελιαφόροι (carrying the loaves known as ὀβελίαι) and the
σκαφηφόροι and ὑδριαφόροι and ἀσκοφόροι who are mentioned
as taking part in Dionysiac functions⁷ probably acted in this

¹ Paus. I. xxix. 2 καὶ ναὸς οὐ μέγας ἐστίν, ἐς ὃν τοῦ Διονύσου τοῦ Ἐλευθερέως τὸ ἄγαλμα ἀνὰ
πᾶν ἔτος κομίζουσιν ἐν τεταγμέναις ἡμέραις.
² See Gow, *J.H.S.* xxxii (1912), pp. 213 ff.; Nilsson, *Jahrb. Arch.* xxxi (1916), pp. 37–38;
Picard, *Comptes R. Acad. Inscr. et Belles Lettres*, 1936, pp. 111 ff. (summarizing conclusions
of F. Robert).
³ e.g. Nilsson, *Jahrb. Arch.* xxxi (1916), pp. 309 ff.; Stengel, ibid., pp. 340 ff.; Bethe,
Hermes, lxi (1926), pp. 459 ff.; Pfuhl, *de Athen. pompis sacris*, pp. 74 ff.; etc. (Frickenhaus's
article in *Jahrb. Arch.* xxvii (1912), pp. 80 ff., belongs to the eccentricities of scholarship.)
By far the best summary is that of Deubner, *Att. Feste*, p. 139.
⁴ ἐν τῷ ἱερῷ or ἐν τοῖς ἱεροῖς in the ephebic inscriptions quoted above.
⁵ This is suggested by the high value placed on the skins of the sacrificed victims in *I.G.*
ii². 1496.
⁶ Schol. on Aristoph. *Ach.* 241 κατὰ τὴν τῶν Διονυσίων ἑορτὴν παρὰ τοῖς Ἀθηναίοις αἱ
εὐγενεῖς παρθένοι ἐκανηφόρουν. ἦν δὲ ἐκ χρυσοῦ πεποιημένα τὰ κανᾶ, ἐφ' ὧν τὰς ἀπαρχὰς ἁπάντων
ἐτίθεσαν. In *I.G.* ii². 896 (185 B.C.) a certain Zopyrus is praised for sending his daughter
οἴσουσαν τὸ ἱερὸν κανοῦν τῷ θεῷ κατὰ τὰ πάτρια.
⁷ Poll. xi. 75 ὀβελίαι δ' ἄρτοι οὓς εἰς Διονύσου ἔφερον οἱ καλούμενοι ὀβελιαφόροι; cf. Athen.
iii. 111 b ἐκαλοῦντο δὲ καὶ ὀβελιαφόροι οἱ ἐν ταῖς πομπαῖς παραφέροντες αὐτοὺς (sc. τοὺς
ὀβελίας) ἐπὶ τῶν ὤμων (Antiphanes in the fourth century wrote a comedy called Ὀβελιαφόροι);
Suid. s.v. ἀσκοφορεῖν· ἐν ταῖς Διονυσιακοῖς πομπαῖς, τὰ μὲν ὑπὸ τῶν ἀστῶν ἐπράττετο, τὰ δὲ

greatest of Dionysiac processions. Colour was lent to the procession by the scarlet gowns of the μέτοικοι and the gorgeous robes of the choregoi of the lyric and dramatic performances which were to follow. Alcibiades on one occasion walked in a purple robe,[1] and part of Demosthenes' grievance against Meidias was that Meidias had broken into a goldsmith's shop and partly destroyed the golden crown and gold-embroidered cloak in which Demosthenes had intended to parade as choregos.[2] When Plutarch[3] spoke of the lavish display of the Dionysiac processions in his own time as compared with the original simplicity of the rustic festivals, he must have overlooked the magnificence of the Athenian processions of the fifth and fourth centuries B.C. (some 500 to 600 years earlier); but it is not in fact clear of what places or periods he is speaking. At least one of the primitive elements of Dionysiac worship which Plutarch mentions was conspicuous in the Dionysiac procession, the carrying of φαλλοί in honour of the god.

The direct evidence for this practice is indeed slight and depends upon the conjectural completion of inscriptions, but is probably sufficient. About the year 446–445 B.C. it was ordained that the new colony of Brea should annually send a phallos to the City Dionysia;[4] this is not likely to have been an isolated

---

τοῖς μετοίκοις ποιεῖν ὑπὸ τῶν νομοθετησάντων προσετέτακτο. οἱ μὲν οὖν μέτοικοι χιτῶνας ἐνεδύοντο χρῶμα ἔχοντας φοινικοῦν καὶ σκάφας ἔφερον· ὅθεν σκαφηφόροι προσηγορεύοντο. οἱ δὲ ἀστοὶ ἐσθῆτα εἶχον ἣν ἐβούλοντο καὶ ἀσκοὺς ἐπ' ὤμων ἔφερον· ὅθεν ἀσκοφόροι ἐκαλοῦντο; Suid. s.v. σκαφηφόροι (without express reference to the Dionysia)· . . . Δημήτριος γοῦν ἐν γ′ Νομοθεσίας φησίν, ὅτι προσέταττεν ὁ νόμος τοῖς μετοίκοις ἐν ταῖς πομπαῖς αὐτοὺς μὲν σκάφας φέρειν, τὰς δὲ θυγατέρας αὐτῶν ὑδρεῖα καὶ σκιάδεια; Zenob. v. 95 συντομώτερος σκάφης· παροιμία ἐπὶ τῶν σκάφας φερόντων μετοίκων . . . ἐπειδὴ οἱ μέτοικοι σκάφας ἔφερον ἐν ταῖς πομπαῖς; Poll. iii. 55 μέτοικος ὁ τὸ μετοίκιον συντελῶν· τὸ δ' ἦν δυοκαίδεκα τῷ δημοσίῳ δραχμαὶ καὶ τῷ γραμματεῖ τριώβολον. σκαφηφόρος· οὕτω δὲ τοὺς μετοίκους ὠνόμαζον, καὶ τὰς γυναῖκας αὐτῶν ὑδριαφόρους, ἀπὸ τοῦ ἔργου ἑκατέρους.

[1] Athen. xii. 534 c ὅτε δὲ χορηγοίη πομπεύων ἐν πορφυρίδι, εἰσιὼν εἰς τὸ θέατρον ἐθαυμάζετο οὐ μόνον ὑπὸ τῶν ἀνδρῶν ἀλλὰ καὶ ὑπὸ τῶν γυναικῶν.

[2] Dem. *in Meid.* § 22 (evidence of the goldsmith Pammenes) ἐκδόντος δέ μοι Δημοσθένους, ᾧ μαρτυρῶ, στέφανον χρυσοῦν ὥστε κατασκευάσαι καὶ ἱμάτιον διάχρυσον ποιῆσαι, ὅπως πομπεύσαι ἐν αὐτοῖς τὴν τῶν Διονυσίων πομπήν κτλ.

[3] *de Cupid. divit.* 527 d ἡ πάτριος τῶν Διονυσίων ἑορτὴ τὸ παλαιὸν ἐπέμπετο δημοτικῶς καὶ ἱλαρῶς, ἀμφορεὺς οἴνου καὶ κληματίς, εἶτα τράγον τις εἷλκεν, ἄλλος ἰσχάδων ἄρριχον ἠκολούθει κομίζων, ἐπὶ πᾶσι δ' ὁ φαλλός· ἀλλὰ νῦν ταῦτα παρεώραται καὶ ἠφάνισται, χρυσωμάτων περιφερομένων καὶ ἱματίων πολυτελῶν καὶ ζευγῶν ἐλαυνομένων καὶ προσωπείων, οὕτω τἀναγκαῖα τοῦ πλούτου καὶ τὰ χρήσιμα τοῖς ἀχρήστοις κατακέχωσται καὶ τοῖς περίττοις. See above, p. 41.

[4] *I.G.* i². 46 βοῦν δὲ καὶ [. . . . . . a]γειν ἐς Παναθήναια τὰ μεγάλ[α καὶ ἐς Διονύσι]α φαλλόν. A decree of 278–277 B.C., *I.G.* ii². 673, providing for the safe conduct of a procession (the nature of which is not indicated) includes the words τῆς φαλλαγ[ωγίας]. Phalloi were also carried at the Dionysia at Delos; see Nilsson, *Gr. Feste*, pp. 280–2, and Vallois, *B.C.H.* xlvi (1922), pp. 94–112, who gives a full account.

emblem, and the carrying of phalloi would be reminiscent of the placation of the god after his original arrival in Athens.[1]

The route taken by the procession is unknown. At some time during the festival there were dances of choruses at various altars, and especially at that of the Twelve Gods in the Agora, and these are connected by scholars either with the εἰσαγωγὴ ἀπὸ τῆς ἐσχάρας or with the πομπή. There is no evidence to show which is correct, but Xenophon mentions the dances in a passage which is primarily about πομπαί.[2]

It may be assumed that the procession was enlivened by satirical songs such as were sung on all such occasions at Athens, and that these were not entirely prompted by the desire to avert the evil eye.[3] It is also related that Demetrius of Phalerum was greeted with a laudatory poem when as archon he conducted the procession.[4] Naturally the procession might also be the occasion of such encounters and love-affairs as Menander often took as the starting-point of his plots.[5]

5. Of the κῶμος nothing distinctive is known. No doubt it was a much less formal proceeding than the πομπή, and it is at least probable that the πομπή took place in the morning—most likely on the 9th of Elaphebolion,[6] before the dithyrambs were performed—and the κῶμος, if it was a revel-procession, in the evening, perhaps on the same day.[7]

---

[1] See above, p. 55.

[2] Xen. *Hipparch*. iii. 2 τὰς μὲν οὖν πομπὰς οἴομαι ἂν καὶ τοῖς θεοῖς κεχαρισμενωτάτας καὶ τοῖς θεαταῖς εἶναι εἰ ὅσων ἱερὰ καὶ ἀγάλματα ἐν τῇ ἀγορᾷ ἐστι, ταῦτα ἀρξάμενοι ἀπὸ τῶν Ἑρμῶν κύκλῳ περὶ τὴν ἀγορὰν καὶ τὰ ἱερὰ περιελαύνοιεν τιμῶντες τοὺς θεούς, καὶ ἐν τοῖς Διονυσίοις δὲ οἱ χοροὶ προσεπιχαρίζονται ἄλλοις τε θεοῖς καὶ τοῖς δώδεκα χορεύοντες. The site of the Altar of the Twelve Gods was on the north side of the Agora (*J.H.S.* 1934, p. 185); the altar itself was found in 1887 and is in the National Museum, and the base of the dedication to the Twelve Gods by Leagros, who died in 464 B.C., was discovered in 1934 (*Hesperia*, iv, pp. 355 ff.). See also ibid. xvi (1947), p. 198, for discovery of additional fragments.

[3] See Harpokr. s.v. πομπείας κτλ. (quoted above, p. 5).

[4] Athen. xii. 542 e ἐν δὲ τῇ πομπῇ τῶν Διονυσίων, ἣν ἔπεμψεν ἄρχων γενόμενος, ᾖδεν ὁ χορὸς εἰς αὐτὸν ποιήματα Σείρωνος τοῦ Σολέως, ἐν οἷς ἡλιόμορφος προσηγορεύετο, 'ἐξόχως δ' εὐγενέτας ἡλιόμορφος ζαθέοις ἄρχων σε τιμαῖσι γεραίρει'.

[5] Menander, fr. 558 K. Διονυσίων μὲν ἦν | πομπή . . . | ὁ δέ μ' ἠκολούθησεν μεχρὶ τοῦ πρὸς τὴν θύραν· | ἔπειτα φοιτῶν καὶ κολακεύων ἐμέ τε καὶ | τὴν μήτερ' ἔγνω μ' . . . .

[6] See Wilamowitz, *Herakl*. ii. 49, though Robert conjectures that it was in the evening (*G.G.A.* 1899, p. 543).

[7] This is suggested by the order of events as enumerated in the Law of Euegoros. But recent views on the word κῶμος in the law make it the equivalent of χοροὶ ἀνδρῶν, which were at first the only performances in the festival and are named in the law under their original name, though in the same place (after οἱ παῖδες) as in the inscriptional record, *I.G.* ii². 2318. This is doubtful (see pp. 24, 63, 104); but if it is correct, then there was no κῶμος in the sense of 'revel-procession' distinct from the πομπή.

6. The order of the events composing the festival cannot be determined with certainty in all respects. It is clear from the evidence that has been given that the εἰσαγωγή of the god from the temple in the Academy was a preliminary ceremony, and was distinct from the πομπή, which was an essential part of the festival itself. For the rest, the evidence is as follows:

(1) Aeschines, *in Ctes*. §§ 66–68. Δημοσθένης . . . γράφει ψήφισμα . . . (67) . . . ἐκκλησίαν ποιεῖν τοὺς πρυτάνεις τῇ ὀγδόῃ ἱσταμένου τοῦ ἐλαφηβολιῶνος μηνός, ὅτ᾿ ἦν τῷ Ἀσκληπιῷ ἡ θυσία καὶ ὁ προαγών, ἐν τῇ ἱερᾷ ἡμέρᾳ, ὃ πρότερον οὐδεὶς μέμνηται γενόμενον . . . . (68) . . . ἐνταῦθ᾿ ἕτερον ψήφισμα νικᾷ Δημοσθένης, ἐν ᾧ γράφει μὴ μόνον ὑπὲρ τῆς εἰρήνης ἀλλὰ καὶ συμμαχίας ὑμᾶς βουλεύσασθαι, μὴ περιμείναντας τοὺς πρέσβεις τοὺς ὑμετέρους, ἀλλ᾿ εὐθὺς μετὰ τὰ Διονύσια τὰ ἐν ἄστει, τῇ ὀγδόῃ καὶ ἐνάτῃ ἐπὶ δέκα.

Schol. ad loc. ἐγίγνοντο πρὸ τῶν μεγάλων Διονυσίων ἡμέραις ὀλίγαις ἔμπροσθεν ἐν τῷ ᾠδείῳ καλουμένῳ τῶν τραγῳδῶν ἀγὼν καὶ ἐπίδειξις ὧν μέλλουσι δραμάτων ἀγωνίζεσθαι ἐν τῷ θεάτρῳ· δι᾿ ὃ ἐτύμως προάγων καλεῖται. εἰσίασι δὲ δίχα προσώπων οἱ ὑποκριταὶ γυμνοί.

(The nature of the Proagon will be discussed later.)

From these passages it appears that in 346 B.C. on the 8th of Elaphebolion there were held the feast of Asklepios (introduced into Athens in 420 B.C.)[1] and the Proagon,[2] and that Demosthenes (at least according to Aeschines) wrongfully had an assembly called on a ἱερὰ ἡμέρα. The passage might equally be held to show that the day was *not* so sacred as absolutely to prohibit an assembly in case of emergency; and in fact a ἱερὰ ἡμέρα was not necessarily ἀποφράς 'closed to civil business',[3] and there are a number of recorded instances of assemblies held on various days during the Dionysian period of Elaphebolion.

(2) Demosthenes, *in Meid*. §§ 8–10, shows that (in 348 B.C.) the law ordered that on the day following the Pandia a special assembly should be held in the theatre, to discuss the conduct of the Dionysiac festival by the archon and any alleged offences in the course of the festival—these to be the subject of προβολαί. The Law of Euegoros (quoted in § 10) speaks of the elements

---

[1] Körte, *Ath. Mitt.* xviii (1893), p. 246, and xxi (1896), p. 315. In *I.G.* ii². 1496 the items referring to the Asklepieia precede those referring to the Dionysia.

[2] It is not known where the Proagon was held before Pericles built the Odeum (*c.* 444 B.C.).

[3] This is pointed out by Ferguson (*Hesperia*, xvii, p. 134). His view that the 9th of Elaphebolion was a day of inaction in the ritual of the Dionysia, and that the festival proper may have begun on the 10th, is not so convincingly proved; but if he is right some of the calendar-dates suggested in the text would have to be moved on by one day.

of the City Dionysia as ἡ πομπὴ καὶ οἱ παῖδες καὶ ὁ κῶμος καὶ οἱ κωμῳδοὶ καὶ οἱ τραγῳδοί. (The date of this law is unknown; it may not have been enacted before the fourth century: see p. 24.)

(3) Thucydides iv. 118. On the 14th of Elaphebolion in 423 B.C. the Athenians in full assembly ratified the treaty with Sparta. Allen argues that this proves that the festival must therefore have been over before the 14th. But we do not know what the law as regards assemblies during the festival may have been in 423 B.C. Even if the Law of Euegoros was already in force, it only forbids proceedings for debt, and against it are to be set the possibility (see above on Aeschin. *in Ctes.* § 67) that an assembly might be held if necessary and the fact that, according to Thucyd. v. 23, the annual renewal of the treaty with Sparta was fixed for the Dionysia, so that presumably not all public business was excluded.

(4) Aristophanes, *Birds* 786 ff., on any straightforward interpretation shows that in 414 B.C. comedies were acted in the afternoons of the same days as were devoted to tragedies; and as this year fell within the period when only three comedies were performed (not five),[1] we can infer that three days were taken up each with three tragedies, a satyric play, and a comedy. The passage runs:

αὐτίχ' ὑμῶν τῶν θεατῶν εἴ τίς ἐσθ' ὑπόπτερος,
εἶτα πεινῶν τοῖς χοροῖσι τῶν τραγῳδῶν ἤχθετο,
ἐκπτόμενος ἂν οὗτος ἠρίστησεν ἐλθὼν οἰκάδε,
κᾆτ' ἂν ἐμπλησθεὶς ἐφ' ἡμᾶς αὖθις αὖ κατέπτετο.

(There is really no excuse for the emendation τρυγῳδῶν, nor for taking ἐφ' ἡμᾶς to refer to anything but 'comedy', as distinct from the τραγῳδοί.)

The conclusions to which the evidence seems to point are:[2]

   i. That during the whole Classical period there was a preparatory day (in the fourth century the 8th of Elaphebolion)

[1] See below, pp. 64, 83. Five comedies competed in 429 B.C. when Kallias won fourth place (*I.G.* xiv. 1097) and again in the fourth century; but three only in 425 and during the greater part of the Peloponnesian War.

[2] The best general summary of the conflicts of opinion on the subject will be found in J. T. Allen's paper, *On the Program of the City Dionysia during the Peloponnesian War* (University of California Press, 1938), with whose conclusions I am in agreement, except on one or two points. I do not repeat the very full references which he gives to the literature of the subject, as I am mainly concerned here to consider what emerges from the actual (very meagre) evidence.

on which the Proagon was held (though if the schol. on Aeschines is right, this might be 'a few days' before the main festival). The Asklepieia were also celebrated on this day, and in the latter part of the day there was the εἰσαγωγή of Dionysus ἀπὸ τῆς ἐσχάρας.

ii. That the first day of the festival proper began with the πομπή, which may have occupied several hours early in the day. Then followed the dithyrambic choruses, five of boys, five of men, and in the evening the κῶμος. (This would not make too full a day, if we may assume that each chorus would not occupy more than half an hour or so—after which no one would probably be too tired for the fun of the κῶμος, if it was in fact a special 'event'.)

iii. That during the Peloponnesian War the succeeding three days (probably the 10th, 11th, and 12th) would each be given to three tragedies, a satyric play, and a comedy.

iv. That before and after the Peloponnesian War, when there were five comedies, four days would be required (the 10th to the 13th), and probably the five comedies occupied one day, the tragedies three; there is no evidence to show which came first.[1]

v. That when the acting of old plays singly, or of one satyric play for the whole festival, was introduced, or the number of plays was varied (as happened at some periods),[2] the calendar was naturally modified.

vi. That the Pandia followed on the day after the conclusion of the Dionysia, i.e. probably on the 14th (possibly on the 13th during the Peloponnesian War).

vii. That on the day after the Pandia the special assembly in the theatre was held.

The shortening of the programme during the Peloponnesian War may have been intended to save both time (one day less

---

[1] In the Law of Euegoros tragedies are mentioned before comedies for the Lenaia, comedies before tragedies for the City Dionysia, as in the great inscription *I.G.* ii². 2318. But in both places the order may either be that of performance or that of relative importance at the particular festival—or both. There are obviously also ways of arranging the 'events', so as to assign one comedy to each of five days (cf. my *Dith. Trag. Com.*, p. 218), e.g. by giving one day to boys' choruses and a comedy, and another to men's choruses and a comedy; but these would be very short days compared with those which contained three tragedies, a satyric play, and a comedy, and I do not now favour this view. For the eccentric views of Dr. A. B. Cook (*Zeus*, i, pp. 645 ff.) cf. my review in *Class. Rev.* xxix (1915), p. 84.

[2] These changes will be noted later: see pp. 71–73.

being required) and expense, at a time when military operations and the building of ships would necessarily be the first
considerations.[1]

To complete this sketch of the order of proceedings at the
Dionysia it should be added (1) that the day's ceremonies began
at daybreak;[2] (2) that at some point, probably very early in the
proceedings, the theatre was purified by the offering of a
sucking-pig[3] by persons called περιστίαρχοι or περιεστίαρχοι;
(3) that libations were poured, apparently by the strategoi;[4]
(4) that the proclamation of crowns bestowed on citizens, the
display of tribute from subject states, and the parade and ex-
hortation of the children of citizens who had fallen in battle
took place before the performance of tragedies,[5] though of these
ceremonies only the proclamation of crowns was still observed
in the latter part of the fourth century; (5) that each 'event' in
the competition was announced by sound of trumpet.[6]

7. It may be convenient to consider at this point the little
that is known about the Proagon which preceded and the
Ecclesia which followed the festival. The passage already quoted
from Aeschines[7] shows that in 346 B.C. the Proagon took place
on the 8th of Elaphebolion, though the scholiast on the same
passage seems to suggest that it might be a day or two earlier.[8]
The scholiast describes the ceremony as ἀγὼν καὶ ἐπίδειξις ὧν
μέλλουσι δραμάτων ἀγωνίζεσθαι ἐν τῷ θεάτρῳ and as being held
in the Odeum. (His ' ἀγών ' is probably a mistake, arising from
his interpreting προάγων as 'a preliminary contest', rather than as
'a ceremony preliminary to the contest'.) The scholiast on Aristophanes' *Wasps* 1104, speaks of the Odeum as τόπος θεατροειδής,
ἐν ᾧ εἰώθασι τὰ ποιήματα ἀπαγγέλλειν πρὸ τῆς εἰς τὸ θέατρον
ἀπαγγελίας; and it is generally agreed that it is to this ceremony

---

[1] So J. T. Allen, op. cit., pp. 40–41. Ferguson (*Hesperia*, xvii, pp. 131 ff.) discusses the
alterations in the order of the festival made by Demetrius Poliorketes in certain years, and
the combination for a short time of the Dionysia and the Demetrieia; but these were violations
of the normal arrangement, which was doubtless re-established later.

[2] ἅμα τῇ ἡμέρᾳ (Aeschin. *in Ctes.* § 76); ἕωθεν (Demosth. *in Meid.* § 74).

[3] Suid. s.v. καθάρσιον; Pollux viii. 104.

[4] Plut. *Kimon* 8 (see below, p. 96).

[5] Aeschin. *in Ctes.* §§ 153–4; Isocr. *de Pace*, § 82. See above, p. 57.

[6] Pollux iv. 88, where the custom is said to have been instituted by the failure of the actor
Hermon to appear at the right moment. The incident mentioned in Aristoph. *Ach.* 11–13
probably refers to the Proagon, when the several competitors were summoned by the herald.

[7] *in Ctes.* § 67.

[8] Or, if Ferguson is right, that the Dionysiac festival proper did not begin till the 10th
(see above, p. 62). But the scholiast is a very unsafe authority.

that Plato refers when he speaks of Agathon's brave appearance at it—*Sympos.* 194 a ἐπιλήσμων μεντἂν εἴην, ὦ Ἀγάθων . . . εἰ ἰδὼν τὴν σὴν ἀνδρείαν καὶ μεγαλοφροσύνην ἀναβαίνοντος ἐπὶ τὸν ὀκρίβαντα μετὰ τῶν ὑποκριτῶν καὶ βλέψαντος ἐναντία τοσούτῳ θεάτρῳ, μέλλοντος ἐπιδείξεσθαι σαυτοῦ λόγους καὶ οὐδ᾽ ὁπωστιοῦν ἐκπλαγέντος κτλ. It seems that each poet mounted a temporary platform with his actors and announced the subjects of the plays which he was about to produce.[1] A touching incident occurred at the Proagon after the news of the death of Euripides had been received, when Sophocles appeared in mourning and brought in his chorus and actors without the customary garlands, and the audience burst into tears.[2] Actors who appeared in the Proagon did not wear masks or costumes.[3]

References in inscriptions[4] are generally taken to imply that the Proagon before the Dionysia was not the only one, and that there was a Proagon also before the Lenaia. Whether there was a Proagon at all before the building of the Odeum by Pericles (about 444 B.C.) and, if so, where it was held, remains unknown. There is no evidence to support Müller's view[5] that the Proagon was held in the Odeum in the Agora, near the Enneakrounos; he argues that in the round Periclean Odeum half the spectators would only see the actors' backs; but the Periclean Odeum was not round,[6] and ὀκρίβας probably indicates a temporary platform.[7]

8. The law regarding the Ecclesia after the festival has already been mentioned. What purports to be its text is given by Demosthenes in the speech against Meidias (§ 8) : τοὺς πρυτάνεις ποιεῖν ἐκκλησίαν ἐν Διονύσου τῇ ὑστεραίᾳ τῶν Πανδίων. ἐν δὲ ταύτῃ χρηματίζειν πρῶτον μὲν περὶ ἱερῶν, ἔπειτα τὰς προβολὰς παραδιδότωσαν τὰς γεγενημένας ἕνεκα τῆς πομπῆς ἢ τῶν ἀγώνων τῶν

---

[1] As Haigh noted (*Att. Theat.*, p. 68), λόγος is used of the subjects or plots in Aristoph. *Wasps* 54 and *Peace* 50, and in Hesych. s.v. λόγος· ἡ τοῦ δράματος ὑπόθεσις. It is also so used in the *Poetics* of Aristotle. The schol. on *Wasps* 1104 is probably not strictly correct in using the phrase τὰ ποιήματα ἀπαγγέλλειν, if the verb is used in the same sense as ἀπαγγελία in πρὸ τῆς εἰς τὸ θέατρον ἀπαγγελίας.

[2] *Vit. Eurip.* λέγουσι δὲ καὶ Σοφοκλέα, ἀκούσαντα ὅτι ἐτελεύτησε, αὐτὸν μὲν ἱματίῳ φαιῷ ἤτοι πορφυρῷ προελθεῖν, τὸν δὲ χορὸν καὶ τοὺς ὑποκριτὰς ἀστεφανώτους εἰσαγαγεῖν ἐν τῷ προάγωνι καὶ δακρῦσαι τὸν δῆμον.

[3] Schol. Aeschin., *in Ctes.* § 67.

[4] e.g. *I.G.* ii². 780, l. 15 ἐπετέλεσε δὲ καὶ τοὺς προάγωνας τοὺς ἐν τοῖς ἱεροῖς κατὰ τὰ πάτρια (of an agonothetes in 246–245 B.C.). But the interpretation cannot be regarded as certain.

[5] *Gr. Bühnenalt.*, p. 365.

[6] Cf. *Theatre of D.*, pp. 1, 2 (and refs. there), and Dilke in *B.S.A.* xliii (1948), pp. 185–6.

[7] Cf. *Theatre of D.*, pp. 72–73.

ἐν τοῖς Διονυσίοις, ὅσαι ἂν μὴ ἐκτετισμέναι ὦσιν.[1] On this Demosthenes comments (§ 9): ὁ μὲν νόμος οὗτός ἐστιν, ὦ ἄνδρες Ἀθηναῖοι, καθ' ὃν αἱ προβολαὶ γίγνονται, λέγων, ὥσπερ ἠκούσατε, ποιεῖν τὴν ἐκκλησίαν ἐν Διονύσου μετὰ τὰ Πάνδια, ἐν δὲ ταύτῃ ἐπειδὰν χρηματίσωσιν οἱ πρόεδροι περὶ ὧν διῴκηκεν ὁ ἄρχων, χρηματίζειν καὶ περὶ ὧν ἄν τις ἠδικηκὼς ᾖ περὶ τὴν ἑορτὴν ἢ παρανενομηκώς—καλῶς, ὦ ἄνδρες Ἀθηναῖοι, καὶ συμφερόντως ἔχων ὁ νόμος, ὡς τὸ πρᾶγμα αὐτὸ μαρτυρεῖ. The Law of Euegoros, which he next quotes, forbidding proceedings against debtors during certain festivals, concludes: ἐὰν δέ τις τούτων τι παραβαίνῃ, ὑπόδικος ἔστω τῷ παθόντι, καὶ προβολαὶ αὐτοῦ ἔστωσαν ἐν τῇ ἐκκλησίᾳ τῇ ἐν Διονύσου ὡς ἀδικοῦντος, καθὰ περὶ τῶν ἄλλων ἀδικούντων γέγραπται.

The first duty of the Assembly was to scrutinize the conduct of the officials responsible for the festival. An inscription published by the American excavators of the Agora[2] shows that in 284–283 B.C. this duty was still taken seriously:

ἔδοξεν τῷ δήμῳ· Ἀγύρριος Καλλιμέδοντος Κολλυτεὺς εἶπεν· ἐπειδὴ Εὔθιος ἄρχων γενόμενος τάς τε θυσίας ἔθυσεν τοῖς θεοῖς κατὰ τὰ πάτρια καὶ τῆς πομπῆς τῷ Διονύσῳ ἐπεμελήθη φιλοτίμως καὶ τἆλλα πάντα ἔπραξεν τὰ περὶ τὴν ἀρχὴν δικαίως πειθόμενος τοῖς τε νόμοις καὶ τοῖς ψηφίσμασιν τῆς βουλῆς καὶ τοῦ δήμου καὶ διὰ ταῦτα αὐτὸν καὶ πρότερον ὁ δῆμος ἐπήνεσεν καὶ ἐστεφάνωσεν ἐν τῇ ἐκκλησίᾳ τῇ ἐν Διονύσου, ὅπως ἂν οὖν πᾶσιν φανερὸν ᾖ ὅτι ὁ δῆμος καὶ νῦν καὶ εἰς τὸν λοιπὸν χρόνον τιμήσει τοὺς δικαίως ἄρχοντας τὰς ἀρχὰς καὶ κατὰ τοὺς νόμους· ἀγαθῇ τύχῃ δεδόχθαι τῷ δήμῳ ἐπαινέσαι Εὔθιον κτλ.

After the scrutiny of the archon came the προβολαί—the complaints laid by individuals before the Assembly of misconduct on the part of unofficial persons or of injuries received during the festival. The προβολή was not strictly a judicial proceeding but the delation of offenders to the Assembly, and if the Assembly accepted a motion that the accused had transgressed the law or the sanctity of the festivals, the complainant's hands were greatly strengthened in any judicial proceedings which he might subsequently take. Such was the προβολή which Demosthenes threatened to bring against Meidias in 349, when publicly assaulted

---

[1] It is very doubtful whether the text of the law is genuine. The prytanes did indeed convoke the Assembly, but the business was conducted by the πρόεδροι (or their ἐπιστάτης for the day), and παραδιδότωσαν is post-classical for παραδόντων. The last words of the law can only mean 'unless the complainant has been paid his damages'; but ἐκτίνειν προβολήν is an odd expression.　　　　　　　　　　　　　　　[2] *Hesperia*, vii, p. 100.

by him and otherwise injured, while he was in office as choregos.[1]
(In fact the case was settled by a compromise, and the speech
was not delivered.) Among other instances of προβολή, Demosthenes mentions one in which the charge was that the accused
had used violence to prevent a man from taking his seat in the
theatre,[2] and another[3] in which a certain Ktesikles, after a
προβολή, was condemned to death for carrying a whip in the
festal procession and striking one of his personal enemies with
it while intoxicated.

There are inscriptions which illustrate the nature of the resolu-
tions (other than motions of censure) passed by the Assembly
held in the theatre after the festival. In 342 B.C. there was a
decree[4] in honour of the Boulé for its care of the εὐκοσμία of the
theatre—one of the very few indications that the Council was
specially concerned with the festival, and indicating probably
its responsibility for the maintenance of order. (In another
inscription[5] not many years later there is a reference to οἱ
λαχόντες ἐπιμεληταὶ τῆς εὐκοσμίας τῆς περὶ τὸ θέατρον.) In 245
B.C. there was a decree[6] commending and rewarding the agonothetes who had supervised the festival; and in 185 B.C. a resolution[7] commending Zopyrus for sending his daughter Timothea
to officiate as kanephoros at the festival, οἴσουσαν τὸ ἱερὸν κανοῦν
τῷ θεῷ κατὰ τὰ πάτρια, and also honouring the ἐπιμεληταὶ τῆς
πομπῆς for their conduct of the procession in conjunction with
the archon.[8] Evidently their functions had not been superseded
(as those of the choregoi had) by the institution of the agonothetes.

9. Apart from scattered notices, our information as regards
the performances of lyric choruses and of plays at Athens de-

---

[1] *in Meid.* § 1 προὐβαλόμην ἀδικεῖν τοῦτον περὶ τὴν ἑορτήν, οὐ μόνον πληγὰς ὑπ’ αὐτοῦ λαβὼν
τοῖς Διονυσίοις, ἀλλὰ καὶ ἄλλα πολλὰ καὶ βίαια παθὼν παρὰ πᾶσαν τὴν χορηγίαν.

[2] Ibid. § 178; this case, though the Assembly passed a vote of censure on the man, was
not brought into court.   [3] Ibid. § 180.

[4] *I.G.* ii². 223 Κηφισοφῶν Καλλιβίου Παιανιεὺς εἶπεν· ἐπειδὴ ἡ βουλὴ ἡ ἐπὶ Πυθοδότου
ἄρχοντος καλῶς καὶ δικαίως ἐπεμελήθη τῆς εὐκοσμίας τοῦ θεάτρου, ἐπαινέσαι αὐτὴν καὶ στεφανῶσαι
χρυσῷ στεφάνῳ κτλ. Cf. *Theatre of D.*, p. 136.

[5] *I.G.* ii². 354.   [6] Ibid. 780.

[7] Ibid. 896. See above, p. 59.

[8] Ξένων Ἀσκληπιάδου Φλυάσιος εἶπεν· ἐπειδὴ οἱ χειροτονηθέντες ἐπιμεληταὶ τῆς πομπῆς ἐπὶ
Ζωπύρου ἄρχοντος τάς τε θυσίας ἔθυσαν τοῖς θεοῖς οἷς πάτριον ἦν, ἔπεμψαν δὲ καὶ τὴν πομπὴν
μετὰ τοῦ ἄρχοντος ὡς ἠδύναντο φιλοτιμότατα, ἐπεμελήθησαν δὲ καὶ τῶν ἄλλων ὧν καθῆκεν
αὐτοῖς· ἀγαθῇ τύχῃ δεδόχθαι τῷ δήμῳ ἐπαινέσαι τοὺς ἐπιμελητὰς τῆς πομπῆς καὶ στεφανῶσαι
ἕκαστον αὐτῶν κτλ. This inscription was ordered to be erected ἐν τῷ τεμένει τοῦ Διονύσου,
τὸ δὲ γενόμενον ἀνάλωμα εἰς ταῦτα μερίσαι τὸν ταμίαν τῶν στρατιωτικῶν.

pends upon two fragmentary but reliable sources—the series of inscriptions contained in the latest edition of the *Corpus* (together with one or two since discovered), and the statements of Alexandrian scholars contained in the 'Arguments' prefixed to many plays in our editions. Both these sources can be taken as reporting accurately the official records kept by the archons at Athens. A few statements are also found in the Parian Marble, an important chronological inscription of about 260 B.C., which, though not without its problems, is generally trustworthy.

It may be assumed that an official record was kept from the date when the festival was organized (or reorganized) under state-management in the form in which it was celebrated throughout the fifth century; but it is doubtful whether any of the inscriptions which we possess is an exact transcript of this record, though it is the information contained in it that they all report or rearrange. In the latter half of the fourth century B.C. Aristotle busied himself, probably between 334 B.C. and his death, with the records of lyric and dramatic performances, and for the history up to about 334 or a little later all subsequent recorders doubtless depended on him, bringing his chronicle up to date for subsequent periods. The Alexandrian scholars of the third century—among them Eratosthenes and Lycophron—devoted great attention to the history of the Athenian drama, and Callimachus' Πίναξ κατὰ χρόνους τῶν ἀπ' ἀρχῆς γενομένων διδασκάλων must have been a standard work.

Besides official records and the compilations of professional scholars, there were also many monuments erected by victorious choregoi and others, of which some few fragments have come down to us.

The main inscriptional records will be found in the Appendix to this chapter, with some necessary notes on each type of inscription, but a brief general account may be given here.

10. The work of Aristotle on the subject was contained in three books, enumerated in the catalogue of his writings given by Diogenes Laertius,[1] Νῖκαι Διονυσιακαί α', Περὶ τραγῳδιῶν α', Διδασκαλίαι α'. The title of the first is given by Hesychius as Νικῶν Διονυσιακῶν ἀστικῶν καὶ Ληναϊκῶν α', showing that the one

---

[1] Diog. L. v. 26. Aristotle also prepared a list of Pythian victors, in conjunction with Kallisthenes, for the Temple of Apollo at Delphi; this was engraved at the public expense in 331 B.C. (see Homolle, *B.C.H.* xxii. 261, 631; Bourguet, ibid. xxiv. 504; and Dittenberger, *Syll.*³ 915).

book covered both festivals, but otherwise there is no information about the book and no quotation from its remains. Nothing is known of the book Περὶ τραγῳδιῶν. But the Διδασκαλίαι no doubt took its title from the official language of the festival. The poet was said διδάσκειν τραγῳδίαν or κωμῳδίαν, his function as teacher of his chorus and actors was termed διδασκαλία, and at least from Alexandrian times onwards his work collectively might be called διδασκαλία, and the official records were an enumeration of the several διδασκαλίαι of each festival; the same ground was doubtless covered by Aristotle. That Aristotle's Διδασκαλίαι included the records of dithyrambs as well as of tragedy and comedy is proved by late allusions to the work.[1] One or two references suggest that its contents were not exactly identical with those of any of the extant inscriptions: e.g. he is said to have noted that there were two poets named Κινησίας, and it is thought by some that, unlike the inscriptions, he referred to certain tetralogies by their collective names—Πανδιονίς or Οἰδιπόδεια—though the inference is by no means certain.[2] It is interesting that he entered a *Rhesus* as a genuine play of Euripides,[3] though it is not proved that this was the extant play.

11. Of the inscriptions the most discussed, *I.G.* ii². 2318, generally referred to by scholars as *Fasti*, unfortunately lacks two or possibly three of its opening columns, and it is uncertain with what year it began, though it claims to go back to the beginning of the κῶμοι in honour of Dionysus,[4] whatever this expression means. It certainly would not have gone back as far as 534 B.C., in or about which year Thespis won a prize for tragedy[5]—under what kind of organization is not recorded. It may have gone back as far as 509 or 508 B.C., when Hypodikos is said to have produced the first dithyrambic chorus of men[6]— the first, perhaps, under a democratic régime, as Lasos seems to have preceded him under the tyrants—but perhaps the most

---

[1] Harpokr. s.v. διδάσκαλος· ὅτι γὰρ Παντακλῆς ποιητής, δεδήλωκεν Ἀριστοτέλης ἐν ταῖς διδασκαλίαις (Pantakles was a dithyrambic poet of the latter half of the fifth century B.C.); and schol. on Aristoph. *Birds* 1379 ὁ δὲ Ἀριστοτέλης ἐν ταῖς διδασκαλίαις δύο (sc. Κινησίας) φησὶ γεγονέναι.

[2] Ibid. 282 εἴη ἂν οὖν τὸν ἔποπα ἐσκευοποιηκὼς τῇ Πανδιονίδι τετραλογίᾳ, ἣν καὶ Ἀριστοτέλης ἐν ταῖς διδασκαλίαις ἀναγράφει; and schol. on Plato, *Apol.* 18 b, καὶ ὁ Μέλητος Οἰδιπόδειαν ἔθηκεν, ὡς Ἀριστοτέλης διδασκαλίαις. See below, p. 81.

[3] Arg. Eur. *Rhesus*. All extant refs. to Aristotle's Διδασκαλίαι are collected by V. Rose, *Aristot. Fragm.*, Nos. 618–30.

[4] See Appendix, pp. 104 ff.   [5] *Marm. Par.*, Epoch 43.

[6] Ibid., Epoch 46; see my *Dith. Trag. Com.*, p. 25.

probable view places the beginning of the record in or about
501 B.C. (It is possible that it was about this time that satyric
plays were brought into the contests, but there is no certainty
about this.) The first extant entry in the inscription refers to the
year 472 B.C. (An earlier column must have recorded the beginning of the contest of comic poets with the victory of Chionides in 486 B.C.) For each year the inscription recorded (in the
same order) (1) archon's name, (2) tribe victorious with boys'
chorus, and choregos, (3) tribe victorious with men's chorus, and
choregos, (4) victorious choregos and poet in comedy, (5) victorious choregos and poet in tragedy. In 447 B.C. the name of
the tragic actor who won the prize is added, and it must have
been inserted in two previous years, since another inscription
places the success of the first victor, Herakleides, in 449. The
entries for 386 and 339 B.C. respectively record the first occasions
of the performance of an old tragedy and an old comedy, but
the inscription never notices the name of a dithyrambic poet
or a victorious comic actor or a satyric play performed singly.
The extant portions end in the year 328 B.C.; the inscription
may have been continued until some twenty years later, when
the appointment of an agonothetes put an end to the choregic
system, or may have ended earlier.

12. We have next a number of fragments (*I.G.* ii². 2319–23)
which are generally grouped under the title of Διδασκαλίαι. They
were practically all found on the southern slope of the Acropolis,
and formed part of a building (possibly, as Reisch conjectures,
erected by an agonothetes in 278) which included both this
record and the lists of victors to be referred to in the next para-
graph. This didaskalic record began in the fifth century and
appears to have been originally compiled soon after 288 B.C.;
after which it was supplemented (No. 2323) by records of
comedies at the Dionysia extending over the rest of the third
and most of the second centuries. The main inscription (Nos.
2319–22) was arranged in the order (1) tragedies at the
Dionysia, (2) comedies at the Dionysia, (3) comedies at the
Lenaia, (4) tragedies at the Lenaia; and in each category were
entered (*a*) archon's name, (*b*) the names of the poets in order
of success, and the name of each play with which each poet
competed and of the protagonist who acted in it. (In the record
of tragedies the satyric play with which, after a certain date,

the performances opened and its poet, and the old tragedy performed and its protagonist, preceded the enumeration of the competing poets and plays; and in the record of comedies the old comedy produced was similarly entered.) Each year's record in each category closed with the name of the victorious actor. The remains of these didaskaliai are very incomplete, but it happens that they attest a number of interesting facts showing, for example, that (1) the competition of tragedies at the Lenaia began only about 432 B.C.: two tragedies only, and no satyric play, were offered by each poet; (2) in 340 B.C. the tragic poets at the Dionysia also offered only two tragedies each, instead of the usual three—it is not known why; (3) in many years of the second century B.C. the competition of comedies at the Dionysia was omitted, and it may have become triennial instead of annual. On the architraves of the building on which the didaskaliai were engraved there were inscribed lists of victorious tragic poets, tragic actors, comic poets, and comic actors at the Dionysia and the Lenaia—eight lists in all—the names being placed in order of the poet's or actor's first victory at the festival, and the number of his victories at that festival added. Before the name of Aeschylus (whose first victory was won in 484 B.C.) about ten lines are missing in the list of tragic poets at the Dionysia; the list of comic poets at the same festival doubtless began with Chionides in 486, though the first few lines of the list are missing. Other lists show that the contest of tragic actors at the Dionysia began in 449, when Herakleides was victorious; and that at the Lenaia contests of comedy, and probably contests of comic actors also, began in or about 442, and contests of tragic actors about 432.

13. Another kind of record, probably compiled by Alexandrian scholars, survives in some fragments of an inscription found in Rome (*I.G.* xiv. 1097, 1098). This record, taking poet by poet in order and perhaps going back to the first performances of comedy at each of the two festivals, contained lists of the comedies of each poet in order of the places (first, second, etc.) awarded to each play, Dionysian placings being entered before Lenaian. The extant fragments refer to Telekleides, Lysippos, and Anaxandrides.

14. Another fragment of an inscription discovered by the American investigators of the Agora is part of a record of the

actors placed first, second, or third in each of the contests in old comedy, old satyr-plays, and old tragedy, and is interesting as proving that instead of the presentation of a single old play of each kind there was a contest between the old plays of each kind, or at least between their actors, and that at this date (254 B.C.) satyric plays were treated in the same way as tragedies and comedies—an illustration of the special interest which seems to have been taken in satyric drama in the third century.

The inscriptions on some private monuments are quoted in the Appendix to this chapter and in various notes.

15. It may be convenient to give here briefly, at the cost of some repetition, the main chronological conclusions to be drawn from the inscriptions, reserving discussion for the Appendix:

City Dionysia

Contest of tragic poets: began with Thespis *c.* 534 B.C., but under what organization is uncertain; continued into imperial times.

Contest of comic poets: probably began 486 B.C. (Suidas, s.v. Chionides); continued at least to about 120 B.C.

Contest of tragic actors: began 449 B.C.; latest extant names *c.* 280 B.C., but may have continued much later.

Contest of comic actors: began between 329 and 312 B.C.; continued at least to 120 B.C.

Performance of old tragedies: first performance in 386 B.C.; part of the regular programme in 341–339 B.C. and quite possibly from 386 B.C. onwards.

Performance of old comedies: first performance in 339 B.C.; part of the regular programme either at once or at least by 311 B.C.

Single satyric play at beginning: first extant record in 341 B.C.

In 254 B.C. there were contests of old comedies, old satyric plays, and old tragedies, with a prize for the successful actor in each kind.

Lenaia

Contest of tragic poets: began *c.* 432 B.C.; continued to end of second century B.C.

Contest of comic poets: began *c.* 442 B.C.; continued to a date later than 150 B.C.

Contest of tragic actors: began *c.* 432 B.C.; extant record goes to end of third century B.C.

Contest of comic actors: began *c.* 442 B.C.; probably continued till after 150 B.C.

16. The inscriptions considered give practically no information about the performances of dithyrambs after 328 B.C., and Wilamowitz[1] supposed that the contests for the prize in dithyramb at the Dionysia ceased when choregoi were superseded by an agonothetes in the last decades of the fourth century. But we do not in fact know how the appointment of the agonothetes may have affected the tribal organization of the dithyrambic choruses. The fact upon which Wilamowitz relies, viz. that the didaskalic inscription,[2] erected probably soon after 280 B.C., does not mention either choregoi or dithyrambs, proves nothing, as it does not mention them for the earlier period either, when they were certainly regular, and his assumption that the compiler, knowing that there was no contemporary interest in such things, omitted them for the earlier period also is entirely unwarranted. He also thinks[3] that tribal contests ceased because amateurs, such as the tribal choruses must have been, were not equal to the highly elaborate music of the day; that the flute-player, the virtuoso, brought his own troupe of singers with him; and that the Athenian Διονύσου τεχνῖται, who were professional, did not work on tribal lines. But highly elaborate music was in vogue, and the predominance of the flute-player was already marked, more than a century earlier, when the tribal contests were certainly regular. Moreover, performances of dithyrambs were continually held in many parts of Greece[4] in the third and second centuries B.C, and even down to the third century A.D.,[5] and it is most unlikely that they should have been degraded from their position in Athens itself, whatever changes of form or organization they may have suffered. In fact an inscription not many years before A.D. 100[6] suggests that the Oineid tribe had just won a victory with a dithyramb at the Dionysia, and that its expenses had been generously defrayed by Philopappus. A list of twenty-five choreutai is given, a chorus of only half the classical κύκλιος χορός, and not all of them members of the tribe; it was probably professional, but the tribal contest, even

---

[1] *Gött. gel. Anz.* 1906, p. 614.   [2] *I.G.* ii². 2319; see below, pp. 110 ff.
[3] I partly repeat here what I said in *Dith. Trag. Com.*, pp. 239–40.
[4] See ibid., pp. 75 ff.   [5] Cf. *Theatre of D.*, p. 245.
[6] *I.G.* ii. 3112 ἡ Οἰνηὶς φυλὴ διὰ τῶν εὖ ἀγωνισαμένων χορῷ Διονυσιακῷ τὸν ἄρχοντα καὶ ἀγωνοθέτην Γάιον Ἰούλιον Ἀντίοχον Ἐπιφανῆ Φιλόπαππον Βησαιέα τῆς εἰς ἑαυτὴν εὐεργεσίας ἕνεκα. ἐδίδασκε Μοιραγένης, ἐχορήγει Βούλων, οἱ Μοιραγένους Φυλάσιοι. ἐπεστάτει Μένανδρος Φυλάσιος, ηὔλει Φίλητος Μενίσκου Κολωνῆθεν, ἐχόρευον [about 25 names], ἐμελοποίει Μουσικό[ς]. The functions of the χορηγός and ἐπιστάτης can only be conjectured.

with hired professionals, evidently continued. But an inscription of the second century A.D.[1] does show that the tribal contest had then been abandoned, that all the choregoi joined in one show and one monument, and that the word ἐνίκα had lost its proper meaning. Other inscriptions[2] name a number of tribes jointly as victorious, and a letter[3] of Hadrian to a congress of τεχνῖται Διονύσου seems to refer to the performance of many dithyrambs at the City Dionysia.

17. The first step in the preparation for the contest of dithyrambs was the selection of a choregos from each of the ten tribes, of which five provided the choruses of men, five those of boys.[4] How the tribe selected its choregos is not clear, but the choice was made a month after the last festival,[5] and it appears that the ἐπιμεληταὶ τῆς φυλῆς, of whose functions little is known, had some responsibility in the matter, as had also the archon in virtue of his general supremacy in all that concerned the festival, and when the arrangements broke down in 349 B.C. in the Pandionid tribe, the archon and the ἐπιμελήταί scolded each other, until the situation was saved by Demosthenes, who volunteered to serve as choregos for the tribe.[6] The choregos for a

---

[1] Ibid. 3114 (Kaibel, *Epigr.* 927) ὁ δῆμος ἐνίκα· Λούκιος Φλάυιος Φλάμμας Κυδαθηναιεὺς ἦρχε. | πάντες χοραγοὶ πᾶς τε φυλέτας χορὸς | ἄγαλμα δήμῳ Κέκροπος ἐστάσαντό με | ἑκούσιοι μεθέντες ἐξ ἀγωνίας, | ὡς μὴ φέροι τις αἶσχος ἀποκισσούμενος. | ἐγὼ δ' ἑκάστῳ τόσσον εὐκλείας νέμω | καθ' ὅσσον αὐτῷ ξυνὸς ὢν ὀφείλομαι.

[2] *I.G.* ii². 3117, 3118.

[3] Ibid. 1105.

[4] Schol. on Aesch. *in Tim.* § 11 ἐξ ἔθους Ἀθηναῖοι (κατέστησαν) κατὰ φυλὴν πεντήκοντα παίδων χορὸν ἢ ἀνδρῶν, ὥστε γενέσθαι δέκα χορούς, ἐπειδὴ καὶ δέκα φυλαί. λέγονται δὲ οἱ διθύραμβοι χοροὶ κύκλιοι καὶ χορὸς κύκλιος. (On the meaning of κύκλιος see *Dith. Trag. Com.*, pp. 48–49.) Cf. Isaeus, *Or.* v, § 36 οὗτος γὰρ τῇ μὲν φυλῇ εἰς Διονύσια χορηγήσας τέταρτος ἐγένετο (i.e. was placed fourth in the contest); Plut. *Vit. X Orat.* 835 b ἐχορήγησε κυκλίῳ χορῷ τῇ αὐτοῦ φυλῇ ἀγωνιζομένη διθυράμβῳ.

[5] Argt. II to Dem. *in Meid.* (after some very confused matter) παυομένης δὲ τῆς ἑορτῆς ἐν τῷ πρώτῳ μηνὶ προὐβάλλοντο οἱ χορηγοὶ τῆς μελλούσης ἑορτῆς. The records of a choregos serving for two tribes together probably refer to dithyrambs at the Thargelia (as certainly in Antiphon, *de Chor.* § 11); e.g. Dem. *in Lept.* § 28 τίνα ῥαστώνην τοῖς πολλοῖς ὁ σός, ὦ Λεπτίνη, ποιεῖ νόμος, εἰ μιᾶς ἢ δυοῖν φυλαῖν ἕνα χορηγὸν καθίστησιν, ὃς ἀνθ' ἑνὸς ἄλλου τοῦθ' ἅπαξ πονήσας ἀπαλλάξεται; on which the schol. says that ἐξηγήσαντό τινες ὡς ἐν τοῖς Θαργηλίοις δυοῖν φυλαῖν εἷς μόνος καθίστατο χορηγός· τοῖς δὲ μεγάλοις Διονυσίοις πλείονος αὐτῷ γενομένης τῆς δαπάνης, εἷς χορηγὸς ἑκάστης φυλῆς καθίστατο. Cf. *I.G.* ii². 3063–72 (all of the fourth century B.C.).

[6] Dem. *in Meid.* § 13 ἐπειδὴ γάρ, οὐ καθεστηκότος χορηγοῦ τῇ Πανδιονίδι φυλῇ, τρίτον ἔτος τουτί, παρούσης δὲ τῆς ἐκκλησίας, ἐν ᾗ τὸν ἄρχοντ' ἐπικληροῦν ὁ νόμος τοῖς χοροῖς τοὺς αὐλητὰς κελεύει, καὶ κατηγοροῦντος τοῦ μὲν ἄρχοντος τῶν ἐπιμελητῶν τῆς φυλῆς, τῶν δ' ἐπιμελητῶν τοῦ ἄρχοντος, προελθὼν ὑπεσχόμην ἐγὼ χορηγήσειν ἐθελοντὴς καὶ κληρουμένων πρῶτος αἱρεῖσθαι τὸν αὐλητὴν ἔλαχον. Before the middle of the fifth century the flute-player is said to have been engaged and paid by the poet, his part not having yet attained its later importance; cf. Plut. *de Mus.* 30 ἀλλὰ γὰρ καὶ αὐλητικὴ ἀφ' ἁπλουστέρας εἰς ποικιλωτέραν μεταβέβηκε μουσικήν·

chorus of boys had to be over forty years of age, but Lysias'
21st Oration shows that there must have been exceptions.[1] How
the choregos obtained his poet is nowhere clearly stated; there
was obviously some competition for the best poets, and choregoi may have drawn lots for the order of choice between the
available poets, as in the fourth century they certainly did,
at an assembly at which the archon presided, for the order of
choice between the flute-players.[2] It was obviously a disadvan-
tage to be drawn last, when only one poet or flute-player was
left. It is very remarkable that the inscriptional records make
no mention of the poet, though among the poets who competed
at Athens were Pindar, Simonides, and Bacchylides, and it is
also noteworthy that a large proportion of the dithyrambic poets
at the Athenian Dionysia, whose names are known to us in the
fifth and fourth centuries, were not of Athenian birth. Nor in
fact were most of the famous flute-players; but the advantage
of a good flute-player was rated very highly.

Having got his poet and his flute-player, the choregos had to
select his chorus from among the members of his tribe.[3] That the
selection rested with himself is nowhere expressly stated with
reference to the Dionysia, but it may be inferred from the fact
that it was certainly so at the Thargelia;[4] and an inscription[5]
referring to the choregos for tragedy at Ikaria may be tentatively
reconstructed so as to imply that the choregos chose his singers
there. He could obviously employ skilled assistance in the selection, though the actual evidence for this is uncertain.[6] He had

τὸ γὰρ παλαιόν, ἕως εἰς Μελανιππίδην τὸν τῶν διθυράμβων ποιητήν, συμβέβηκεν παρὰ τῶν
ποιητῶν λαμβάνειν τοὺς αὐλητὰς τοὺς μισθούς, πρωταγωνιστούσης δηλονότι τῆς ποιήσεως, τῶν
δ' αὐλητῶν ὑπηρετούντων τοῖς διδασκάλοις· ὕστερον δὲ καὶ τοῦτο διεφθάρη.

[1] Aristot. *Ἀθ. Πολ.* lvi; Aeschin. *in Timarch.* § 11; Lysias, *Or.* xxi, §§ 1–5.

[2] Aristoph. *Birds* 1403–4 ταυτὶ πεποίηκας ἐμὲ τὸν κυκλιοδιδάσκαλον | ὃς ταῖσι φυλαῖς
περιμάχητός εἰμ' ἀεί; cf. Antiphon, *Or.* vi, § 11 (choice of dithyrambic poets by lot for the
Thargelia).

[3] The restriction to members of the tribe appears to have held good only for dithyramb,
not for tragedy and comedy.

[4] Antiphon, loc. cit., speaks of the pains which he took in collecting his dithyrambic
chorus of boys for the Thargelia: τὸν χορὸν συνέλεξα ὡς ἠδυνάμην ἄριστα, οὔτε ζημιώσας οὐδένα
οὔτε ἐνέχυρα βίᾳ φέρων οὔτε ἀπεχθανόμενος οὐδένι. This suggests that pressure might sometimes be brought to bear.

[5] *I.G.* i². 186–7. The words τραγῳδοὺς κατέλεγεν ('enrolled') are certain.

[6] Haigh, *Att. Th.*³, p. 60, says that an agent so employed was called χορολέκτης; but the
word, when it actually occurs, seems to mean the leader of the chorus, who gave them the
ἐνδόσιμον or starting-note (Hecataeus *ap.* Aelian, *N.A.* xi. 1, cf. xv. 5), and the word may
well mean the conductor or assembler of the chorus, without implying that he had selected
them. Pollux, iv. 106, mentions but does not define the word.

also to provide them with a room for training and rehearsals,[1] and above all he had to secure a good chorus-trainer (χορο-διδάσκαλος). No small part of Demosthenes' grievance against Meidias lay in Meidias' attempt to corrupt his chorus-trainer.[2]

Xenophon[3] testifies to the importance of a skilled choice of singers and trainer, when he mentions the victorious career of Antisthenes as choregos, despite his lack of all personal knowledge of music and of training. The members of the dithyrambic chorus had to be citizens by birth, and might be challenged, as those of Demosthenes' chorus were by Meidias,[4] though Demosthenes disputed the legality of the proceeding. Apparently members of a men's chorus were exempt from military service.[2] The chorus, whether of men or boys, received not only musical training but also physical, in a care for their diet which might result in excess.[5] Success naturally depended largely upon the leader of the chorus (the koryphaios),[6] but much depended also on the readiness of the choregos to spend his money lavishly. A stingy choregos (like Dikaiogenes who is pilloried by Isaeus)[7] might disgrace himself and his tribe, while magnificence in the costumes of himself and his chorus evidently helped towards victory. Demosthenes boasts[8] of the gold-embroidered robe and golden crown which he had had made for himself, and the golden crowns intended for his chorus—all damaged by Meidias, who broke into the goldsmith's house. Other passages in the

---

[1] διδασκαλεῖον (Antiphon, loc. cit.) ; also called χορηγεῖον (Poll. ix. 1, 2) : cf. Xen. *Hiero* ix. 43; *de Rep. Ath.* i. 13 ; Bekker, *Anecd. Gr.* 72. 17.

[2] *in Meid.* § 15.

[3] *Memor.* III. iv, §§ 3, 4 καὶ ὁ Σωκράτης ἔφη· 'Ἀλλὰ καὶ φιλόνικος Ἀντισθένης ἐστίν, ὃ στρατηγῷ προσεῖναι ἐπιτηδεῖόν ἐστιν. οὐχ ὁρᾷς ὅτι καὶ ὁσάκις κεχορήγηκε πᾶσι τοῖς χοροῖς νενίκηκε;' 'Μὰ Δί',' ἔφη ὁ Νικομαχίδης, 'ἀλλ' οὐδὲν ὅμοιόν ἐστι χοροῦ τε καὶ στρατεύματος προεστάναι.' 'Καὶ μήν,' ἔφη ὁ Σωκράτης, 'οὐδὲ ᾠδῆς γε ὁ Ἀντισθένης οὐδὲ χορῶν διδασκαλίας ἔμπειρος ὢν ὅμως ἐγένετο ἱκανὸς εὑρεῖν τοὺς κρατίστους ταῦτα.'

[4] *in Meid.* § 56; cf. Andokid. *in Alcib.* § 20 κελεύοντος δὲ τοῦ νόμου τῶν χορευτῶν ἐξάγειν ὃν ἄν τις βούληται ξένον ἀγωνιζόμενον. The speaker narrates an assault by Alcibiades on one of the choreutai of Taureas, ὃς ἀντιχόρηγος ἦν Ἀλκιβιάδῃ παισί.

[5] Plut. *de Glor. Ath.* 349 a ; cf. Suid. s.v. φαρυγγίνδην· ὡς ἀριστίνδην· σκώπτοντες γὰρ τὴν γαστριμαργίαν τῶν χορευτῶν Ἀττικοὶ οὕτω λέγουσι. (Neither passage seems to refer to dithyrambic choruses as distinct from tragic and comic.)

[6] Dem. *in Meid.* § 60 ἴστε δὲ δήπου τοῦθ', ὅτι τὸν ἡγέμον' ἂν ἀφέλῃ τις οἴχεται ὁ λοιπὸς χορός.

[7] Isaeus, *Or.* v, § 36; cf. Plut. *Dem.* xxix ἐδόκει γὰρ ἀνταγωνίζεσθαι τῷ Ἀρχίᾳ τραγῳδίαν ὑποκρινόμενος, εὐημερῶν δὲ καὶ κατέχων τὸ θέατρον ἐνδείᾳ παρασκευῆς καὶ χορηγίας κρατεῖσθαι.

[8] Dem., *in Meid.* §§ 16, 22, etc.; cf. Antiphanes, fr. 204 (K.), of a choregos who ruined himself by his expenditure on his chorus, and χορηγὸς αἱρεθεὶς | ἱμάτια χρυσᾶ παρασχὼν τῷ χορῷ ῥάκος φορεῖ; see p. 78 n. 1.

orators[1] estimate the cost of a men's chorus at 50 minae and of a
boys' chorus at 15, as against 30 minae for a tragic chorus (which
was much smaller than a dithyrambic) and 16 for a comic.[2]

The dithyrambic chorus, who did not wear masks, danced in
circular formation in the orchestra, doubtless with the altar as
their centre.

18. The successful choregos received, as the representative of
his tribe,[3] a tripod which he erected at his own expense upon
a monument, with an appropriate inscription. Such tripods
were carried by the well-known monuments of Lysikrates (334
B.C.)[4] and Thrasyllus (319 B.C.),[5] and the course of a 'Street of
the Tripods' is described by Pausanias,[6] leading in all probability
to the Propylaeum which gave entrance to the theatre.[7] Long
before this a tripod dedicated by the Antiochid tribe in 476 B.C.
bore an epigram[8] of Simonides, who had composed the victorious dithyramb when he was eighty years old, and other
epigrams of the same period suggest that the victorious poet
may have been escorted home in procession, crowned with
flowers and gay ribbons;[9] but the evidence that the prize for
dithyramb was a bull never refers directly to Athens.[10] In the
time of Demosthenes the victorious choregos was crowned in the
theatre.[11] It should be added that it does not appear to have

---

[1] Lysias, *Or.* xxi, §§ 1, 2. The fifty included the cost of the tripod; cf. Dem. *in Meid.* § 156,
and Plut. *de Glor. Ath.* 349 b (speaking of choregoi) καὶ τούτων τοῖς μὲν ἡττηθεῖσι περιῆν
προσυβρίσθαι καὶ γεγονέναι καταγελάστους· τοῖς δὲ νικήσασιν ὁ τρίπους ὑπῆρχεν, οὐκ ἀνάθημα
τῆς νίκης, ὡς Δημήτριός φησιν, ἀλλ' ἐπίσπεισμα τῶν ἐκκεχυμένων βίων καὶ τῶν ἐκλελοιπότων
ἐπιτάφιον οἴκων. [2] For choregia in general see also below, pp. 87 ff.
[3] Lysias, *Or.* xxi, § 5; Dem. *in Meid.* § 5; cf. schol. on Aeschin. *in Tim.* § 10.
[4] The inscription (*I.G.* ii². 3042) runs: Λυσικράτης Λυσιθείδου Κικυννεὺς ἐχορήγει. Ἀκα-
μαντὶς παίδων ἐνίκα. Θεών ηὔλει. Λυσιάδης Ἀθηναῖος ἐδίδασκε. Εὐαίνετος ἦρχε. For the monument see E. A. Gardner, *Ancient Athens*, pp. 399–405 and fig. 23.
[5] *I.G.* ii². 3056 Θράσυλλος Θρασύλλου Δεκελεὺς ἀνέθηκε χορηγῶν νικήσας ἀνδράσιν Ἱππο-
θωντίδι φυλῇ. Εὔιος Χαλκιδεὺς ηὔλει. Νέαιχμος ἦρχεν. Καρκίδαμος Σώτιος ἐδίδασκεν; cf. *Theatre
of D.*, pp. 138, 169. For a dedication in the same year by Nikias (*I.G.* ii². 3055) see below,
p. 79.
[6] Paus. I. xx, § 1 ἔστι δὲ ὁδὸς ἀπὸ τοῦ πρυτανείου καλουμένη Τρίποδες, ἀφ' οὗ δὲ καλοῦσι τὸ
χωρίον. ναοὶ θεῶν εἰς τοῦτο (i.e. for such a purpose) μεγάλοι, καί σφισι ἐφεστήκασι τρίποδες,
χαλκοῖ μέν, μνήμης δὲ ἄξια περιέχοντες εἰργασμένα; cf. Judeich, *Topogr. Ath.*, pp. 305–6. (The
monument of Thrasyllus stands, not in this street, but in the κατατομή above the theatre.)
[7] See *Theatre of D.*, p. 2, and refs. there.
[8] *Epigr.* 147.
[9] Especially ibid. 148 (not in fact by Simonides himself). See *Dith. Trag. Com.*, pp.
26, 52.
[10] Simon. *Epigr.* 145, 172; Pind. *Olymp.* xiii. 18; schol. on Plat. *Rep.* 399. See *Dith. Trag.
Com.*, pp. 6, 7, 52.
[11] This is implied in Dem. *in Meid.* § 63 ἀλλὰ τοῖς νόμοις καὶ τῇ τῶν ἄλλων βουλήσει συγχωρῶν
ἠνείχετο καὶ νικῶντα καὶ στεφανούμενον τὸν ἐχθρὸν ὁρᾶν. (The reference is to two rival choregoi.)

FIG. 23. MONUMENT OF LYSIKRATES

FIG. 24. THE SACRIFICE OF IPHIGENEIA

see p. 170)

been necessary in the Classical period that each tripod should be mounted on a separate monument; Nikias (the statesman) is said by Plutarch[1] to have erected the monument described as ὁ τοῖς χορηγικοῖς τρίποσιν ὑποκείμενος ἐν Διονύσου νεώς, and whether these tripods were all won by himself on different occasions or not, they must have been grouped on the roof of the temple.

19. It seems that there were two great periods in the history of dithyramb at Athens. The first was in the early part of the fifth century—the time of Simonides, Pindar, and Bacchylides. Some remains of the poems written by the two latter for Athens have survived. At this time the poetry was of the highest literary merit and the music subordinated to it; but already, if the fragment of Pratinas is rightly interpreted,[2] the flute was striving to gain the mastery, and with Melanippides, probably about the middle of the century, succeeded in achieving this despite strong criticism from persons of conservative taste. This predominance of the flute and of highly elaborate music, to the detriment of the words, was characteristic of the second period of famous dithyrambic writers[3]—Melanippides, Phrynis, Kinesias, Timotheus, Philoxenus, and others, down to the middle of the fourth century, after which no names of distinguished poets are recorded, though famous flute-players are often mentioned. It appears that a flute-player might perform for competition an old dithyramb, as the *Elpenor* and the Αἴας ἐμμανής of Timotheus of Miletus were performed after his death by Pantaleon of Sikyon and Timotheus of Thebes respectively.[4] The details of the reorganization consequent upon the substitution of an agonothetes for choregia towards the end of the fourth century are unknown, but it has already been indicated[5] that the tribes retained their interest in dithyramb as late as the first or second century A.D.

20. Throughout the fifth century B.C. and probably, apart

---

[1] Plut. *Nik.* iii, § 3. The identification of this monument has given rise to much controversy. See *Theatre of D.*, p. 29 and refs. there.

[2] *Dith. Trag. Com.*, pp. 28 ff., and see especially Athen. xvi. 617 b.

[3] *Dith. Trag. Com.*, pp. 52, 72 ff. (for importance of the flute-player at different periods).

[4] *I.G.* ii². 3055 Νικίας Νικοδήμου Ξυπεταιῶν ἀνέθηκε νικήσας χορηγῶν Κεκροπίδι παίδων· Πανταλέων Σικυώνιος ηὔλει· ᾆσμα Ἐλπήνωρ Τιμοθέου· Νέαιχμος ἦρχεν (i.e. 319 B.C.); and Lucian, *Harmonides*, § 1 ὥσπερ ὅτε καὶ σύ, ὦ Τιμόθεε, τὸ πρῶτον ἐλθὼν οἴκοθεν ἐκ Βοιωτίας ὑπηύλησας τῇ Πανδιονίδι καὶ ἐνίκησας ἐν τῷ Αἴαντι τῷ ἐμμανεῖ, τοῦ ὁμωνύμου σοι ποιήσαντος τὸ μέλος, οὐδεὶς ἦν ὃς ἠγνόει τοὔνομα, Τιμόθεον ἐκ Θηβῶν.

[5] pp. 74, 75 above. The history of dithyramb is much more fully treated in *Dith. Trag. Com.*, pp. 1–82. (I have not seen C. del Grande, *Ditirambographi* (1946).)

from a few exceptional years, through the earlier part of the fourth century also, each tragic poet who entered the contest for the prize in tragedy presented four plays, of which the fourth was normally a satyric play, until at some date before 341 B.C. a single satyric play came to be presented at the beginning of the programme and each tragic poet offered at most three plays only. The didaskalic inscription records three plays apiece in 341, but only two in 340; the reason for this exception is unknown. By this time the acting of an old tragedy, presented by an actor before the competition of new tragedies, was already regular, and various experiments may have been tried with a view to controlling the total length of the day's performances.

The rule by which during the fifth century and for some time afterwards each poet offered four plays was probably due to the same need; and it was necessary in the interests of fair competition, as well as for the sake of the time-table, that each poet should know what was expected of him and that the programme should be constructed on a well-understood plan. The two alleged exceptions in the fifth century were probably not such. (1) In 467 B.C.—the year when Aeschylus was victorious with the *Laius, Oedipus, Seven against Thebes*, and *Sphinx*—thesecond place was taken by Aristias, who (according to the Hypothesis of the *Seven against Thebes*) competed Περσεῖ, Ταντάλῳ, Παλαισταῖς σατύροις τοῖς Πρατίνου (τοῦ) πατρός; but Professor Garrod[1] is convincing when he suggests that there has been an omission here (through haplography) of Ἀνταίῳ after Ταντάλῳ. (Aristias is known otherwise to have written an *Antaios*.)[2] (2) The scholiast on Aristophanes' *Frogs* 67[3] says that the son of Euripides presented three of his father's plays after his father's death, but the fact that the scholiast does not mention the satyric play does not necessarily mean that the official records did not, or that none was offered.

How long before Aeschylus the rule of four plays may have been in force there is no evidence to show. There is no certain explanation of Suidas' statement that Pratinas exhibited 50 plays of which 32 were satyric;[4] Suidas' numbers are never very reliable and we do not know whence he derived them; they may

---

[1] *Class. Rev.* xxxiv (1920), p. 130.   [2] Aristias, fr. 1 (N.).

[3] οὕτω καὶ αἱ διδασκαλίαι φέρουσι τελευτήσαντος Εὐριπίδου τὸν υἱὸν αὐτοῦ δεδιδαχέναι ὁμωνύμως ἐν ἄστει Ἰφιγένειαν τὴν ἐν Αὐλίδι, Ἀλκμέωνα, Βάκχας.

[4] See *Dith. Trag. Com.*, p. 93.

often depend on the number of titles known to the Alexandrian scholars or preserved in the Alexandrian library. But there is no reason to doubt that Aeschylus regularly followed the rule.

21. It is usual also to speak of Aeschylus not simply as presenting four plays but as a writer of tetralogies or (if the satyric play is disregarded) of trilogies. The name τετραλογία probably originated in reference to oratory and denoted a group of four λόγοι (speeches) concerned with the same case, like those of Antiphon, and it is not known to have been applied to tragedy before the time of the Alexandrian scholars Aristarchus and Apollonius, who also were the first to use τριλογία in this application.[1] The words are very rarely found, but they seem to have been used only of groups of plays connected in subject, such as the *Oresteia*, the *Lycurgeia* of Aeschylus[2] and of Polyphrasmon,[3] the *Pandionis* of Philokles, and the *Oedipodeia* of Meletos. The *Supplices*, *Seven against Thebes*, and *Prometheus Vinctus* are also each part of such tetralogies, and Wecklein and others have collected some of the titles of lost plays of Aeschylus into similar groups with more or less probability, such as the Μυρμίδονες, Νηρηίδες, and Φρύγες ἢ Ἕκτορος Λύτρα (with choruses of attendants on Achilles, Thetis, and Priam); the Ὅπλων Κρίσις, Θρήισσαι, and Σαλαμίνιοι (presenting the story of Ajax); the Ἀργεῖοι, Ἐλευσίνιοι, and Ἐπίγονοι (the story of the Argive attack on Thebes); the Κάβειροι, Ὑψιπύλη, and Ἀργώ (the Argonautic expedition). The Μέμνων and Ψυχοστασία may have belonged to one trilogy, the Τήλεφος and Μυσοί to another, and so on. But Aeschylus also at times presented four independent plays. It is, for instance, impossible to regard the Φινεύς, Πέρσαι, Γλαῦκος Ποτνιεύς, and the satyric Προμηθεύς as a tetralogy,[4] and the satyric play was probably often independent of the trilogy to which it was attached.

---

[1] Schol. on Aristoph. *Frogs* 1124 τετραλογίαν φέρουσι τὴν Ὀρέστειαν αἱ διδασκαλίαι Ἀγαμέμνονα Χοηφόρους Εὐμενίδας Πρωτέα σατυρικόν. Ἀρίσταρχος καὶ Ἀπολλώνιος τριλογίαν λέγουσι χωρὶς τῶν σατυρικῶν. This does not of course imply that the word τετραλογία was found in the διδασκαλίαι, any more than does the schol. on *Birds* 281 οὗτος ὁ Φιλοκλῆς ἔποπα ἐσκεύασεν ἐν τῇ Πανδιονίδι τετραλογίᾳ . . . εἴη ἂν οὖν τὸν ἔποπα ἐσκευοποιηκὼς τῇ Πανδιονίδι τετραλογίᾳ ἣν καὶ Ἀριστοτέλης ἐν ταῖς Διδασκαλίαις ἀναγράφει, or schol. on Plato, *Apol.* 18b καὶ ὁ Μέλητος Οἰδιπόδειαν ἔθηκεν, ὡς Ἀριστοτέλης Διδασκαλίαις. Whether Aristotle (and the διδασκαλίαι) used the collective titles *Oresteia*, *Pandionis*, *Oidipodeia*, etc., remains uncertain (see above, p. 70).

[2] Schol. on Aristoph. *Thesm.* 135 τὴν τετραλογίαν λέγει Λυκούργειαν Ἠδωνοὺς Βασσαρίδας Νεανίσκους Λυκοῦργον τὸν σατυρικόν.

[3] Arg. to Aesch. *Septem* (partly quoted above, p. 80) . . . γ´ Πολυφράσμων Λυκουργείᾳ.

[4] Despite the attempt of Donaldson, *Gk. Theatre*, pp. 118–19, to find connexions.

Whether Sophocles ever composed a connected tetralogy or trilogy is uncertain. Some think that the Τηλέφεια ascribed to him in an inscription from Aixone may have been a trilogy including the Ἀλεάδαι, Μυσοί, and Ἀχαιῶν Σύλλογος,[1] but it is evident that what was characteristic of him was the development of the independent single play, and this must be the meaning of the confused remark of Suidas on him: καὶ αὐτὸς ἦρξεν τοῦ δρᾶμα πρὸς δρᾶμα ἀγωνίζεσθαι ἀλλὰ μὴ τετραλογίαν.[2] He certainly presented, as a rule, four independent plays. So, as a rule, did Euripides, but there seems to have been sometimes a connexion of subject between his three tragedies, e.g. in 415 B.C. between the *Alexandros*, *Palamedes*, and *Troades*,[3] and in 410 B.C. between the *Chrysippos*, *Oinomaos*, and *Phoinissai*.[4] Aelian[5] tells the story of Plato the philosopher that he composed a 'tetralogy', which he was on the point of getting acted at the Dionysia, when Socrates persuaded him to burn it. It is not worth while to discuss whether Suidas' confused notice[6] of Nikomachus of Alexandreia Troas ascribes a trilogy to him.

22. It has already been noted that the number of the plays sometimes varies in the fourth century, and the recorded numbers of plays by Theodektes,[7] Aphareus, and others is not exactly divisible by three or four; but the value of these records is uncertain, and some poets, such as Chairemon, composed plays for reading, not for performance.[8] The competitions went on, and proclamations of honours were made and crowns bestowed καινοῖς τραγῳδοῖς or τραγῳδῶν ἐν τῷ ἀγῶνι at the Dionysia down to the Imperial period,[9] but the history of the regulations

---

[1] See above, p. 54, and *New Chapters in Gk. Lit.* iii, pp. 76 ff.

[2] τετραλογίαν is Meursius's emendation for στρατολογεῖσθαι or στρατολογίαν. Suidas (or his authority) cannot have meant that Sophocles exhibited only one play at each festival, or that on each day of the festival each poet produced one play only. (See Haigh, *Att. Th.*, p. 17 n.)

[3] Cf. B. Snell, 'Euripides' *Alexandros*' (*Hermes*, Einzelschr. 1937).

[4] See Robert, *Oedipus*, pp. 396 ff.

[5] *Var. Hist.* ii. 30; cf. Diog. L. iii. 5. According to ibid. 56 Plato was said by Thrasyllus κατὰ τὴν τετραλογίαν ἐκδοῦναι τοὺς διαλόγους ... τὰ δὲ τέτταρα δράματα ἐκαλεῖτο τετραλογία. (The intervening words are probably interpolated and in any case are nonsense.)

[6] See P. Wiesmann, *Das Problem der tragischen Tetralogie*, p. 32.

[7] Theodektes is said to have written 50 tragedies and competed 13 times, Aphareus to have composed 35 tragedies (besides others of disputed genuineness) and competed 8 times (Suid. s.v. Θεοδέκτης; Plut. *Vit. X Orat.* 839 d). [8] Aristot. *Rhet.* III. xi.

[9] See *I.G.* ii². 555 (c. 305 B.C.), 646 (295–294 B.C.), 682 (c. 274 B.C.), 851 (before 224–223 B.C.), 956 (161–160 B.C.), 957 (158–157 B.C.), 958 (154 B.C.); and many of the series of ephebic inscriptions, ibid. 1006 (122–121 B.C.) to 1043 (38–37 B.C.), e.g. Nos. 1006, 1009, 1011, 1028, 1029, 1030, 1039, 1042, 1043.

for the production of plays is no longer traceable. By the time of Dio Chrysostom[1] (about A.D. 100) most, though apparently not all, of the plays performed were old, but in Lucian's day (late in the second century) the composition of new plays had ceased.[2]

23. Comedy was later than tragedy in obtaining recognition by the State, though plays had been given earlier by performers at their own charges[3]—whether at one of the regular Dionysiac festivals or not we are not told. The first victory in a State-recognized contest was won by Chionides in 486 B.C.,[4] and it must have been at the Dionysia, because Lenaian contests in comedy were only introduced in or about 442 B.C. The first victory mentioned in the extant portion of the inscription *I.G.* ii². 2318 is that of Magnes in 472.

Each poet offered one play only at each festival (whether Dionysia or Lenaia), at least during the fifth and probably the fourth century. The statement that Aristophanes offered two plays at the Lenaia in 422 B.C.—the *Proagon* and the *Wasps*—depends upon a passage[5] in the Argument to the *Wasps* which is certainly corrupt and has never been emended in any way which commands agreement, but the possibility of such an exceptional occurrence cannot be absolutely ruled out. In 288 B.C. the didaskalic inscription (*I.G.* ii². 2319) records the obtaining

---

[1] *Or.* 19 ἥ τε φωνὴ (of the actors) μείζων . . . ἥ τε λέξις οὐκ αὐτοσχέδιος . . . ἀλλὰ ποιητῶν ἐπιμελῶς καὶ κατὰ σχολὴν πεπονηκότων. καὶ τά γε πολλὰ αὐτῶν ἀρχαῖά ἐστι, καὶ πολὺ σοφωτέρων ἀνδρῶν ἢ τῶν νῦν. (Cf. *Or.* 57.)

[2] Lucian, *Encomium Demosth.* 27 καὶ τῷ Διονύσῳ τὸ μὲν ποίησιν καινὴν ποιεῖν ἐκλέλειπται, τὰ δὲ προτέροις συντεθέντα τοῖς νῦν εἰς μέσον κομίζουσι χάριν οὐκ ἐλάττω φέρει; and *de Salt.* 27 (the actor) μονῆς τῆς φωνῆς ὑπεύθυνον παρέχων ἑαυτόν· τὰ γὰρ ἄλλα τοῖς ποιηταῖς ἐμέλησε πρὸ πολλοῦ ποτε γιγνομένοις.

[3] Aristot. *Poet.* v καὶ γὰρ χορὸν κωμῳδῶν ὀψέ ποτε ὁ ἄρχων ἔδωκεν, ἀλλ' ἐθελονταὶ ἦσαν.

[4] Suidas s.v. Χιωνίδης· Ἀθηναῖος, κωμικὸς τῆς ἀρχαίας κωμῳδίας, ὃν καὶ λέγουσι πρωτ-αγωνιστὴν γενέσθαι τῆς ἀρχαίας κωμῳδίας, διδάσκειν δὲ ἔτεσιν ὀκτὼ πρὸ τῶν Περσικῶν (i.e., if the reckoning is inclusive, 486 B.C.: *vide* Capps, *Introd. of Comedy into the City Dionysia*, p. 9, and *Hesperia*, xii (1943), p. 10; and *Dith. Trag. Com.*, pp. 286–7). If contests in tragedy began in 502 B.C. (or earlier) Aristotle's ὀψέ ποτε would be sufficiently justified. (See above, p. 71.) Chionides and Magnes are coupled together by Aristotle, *Poet.* iii, in a context which implies that they were the first recognized Athenian comic poets. For πρωταγωνιστήν see Rees, *The Rule of Three Actors in the Classical Drama*, pp. 31 ff., and below, pp. 93–97, 133.

[5] ἐδιδάχθη ἐπὶ ἄρχοντος Ἀμεινίου διὰ Φιλωνίδου ἐν τῇ πόλει ὀλυμπιάδι. β' ἦν. εἰς Λήναια. καὶ ἐνίκα πρῶτος Φιλωνίδης Προάγωνι. Λεύκων Πρέσβεσι τρίτος. Kanngiesser's emendation ἐν τῇ πθ' ὀλυμπιάδι ἔτει β' is highly probable; but if he is right in continuing καὶ ἐνίκα πρῶτος· Φιλωνίδης Προάγωνι δεύτερος (i.e. δεύ· omitted by haplography before Λεύκων), the case for the production of two plays by Aristophanes (through Philonides) goes. But there are many other emendations, which are conveniently summarized in Starkie's edition of the *Wasps*, pp. 391–2.

of the second and third places, also at the Lenaia, by Diodorus, though some scholars prefer to suppose that there were two comic poets of that name.

The number of comic poets who competed at each festival was always five,[1] except during part of the Peloponnesian War, when it was reduced to three,[2] probably owing to financial depression in Athens and possibly also to save a day.[3] The first performance of an old comedy, produced by an actor outside the competition, is recorded to have been given at the Dionysia in 339 B.C.,[4] and in 311[5] an old comedy appears as a regular part of the programme and so it continued through most of the second century B.C. (There is no record of old plays performed at the Lenaia.) The extant inscriptional record comes to an end about 143 B.C., but new comedies (and old) doubtless continued to be produced at Athens, as they were elsewhere, until the first century of the Christian era.[6] The contest of comedies, however, evidently lost some of its original popularity and importance about the beginning of the second century B.C., and, from the fact that in four places in the didaskalic inscription[7] for that century it was omitted (οὐκ ἐγένετο) for two years running, Reisch[8] conjectures that it had become triennial instead of annual. This goes somewhat beyond the extant evidence, but is not impossible.

24. The choice of the poets to be allowed to compete at both Dionysia and Lenaia rested with the archon ἐπώνυμος.[9] To him the poets 'applied for a chorus' (χορὸν αἰτεῖν); on what principles or evidence he made his choice and assigned the chorus (χορὸν διδόναι) we are never told; but Cratinus[10] (who had himself been

---

[1] This is proved for 434 B.C. by *I.G.* xiv. 1097, for 388 B.C. by the Argt. to Aristophanes' *Ploutos*, for 311 B.C. by *I.G.* ii². 2323 a, and for various dates in the third and second centuries by ibid. 2323. Cf. also Aristot. Ἀθ. Πολ. lvi.

[2] See Argts. to Aristoph. *Clouds*, *Peace*, and *Birds* (covering the period 423–405 B.C.).

[3] See above, pp. 64, 83.

[4] *I.G.* ii². 2318 ἐπὶ Θεοφράστου παλαιὸν δρᾶμα πρῶτον παρεδίδαξαν οἱ κωμῳδοί.

[5] Ibid. 2323 a (the play was the Θησαυρός of Anaxandrides).

[6] A brief sketch of theatrical performances outside Athens from the third century onwards is given in *Theatre of D.*, pp. 240–6. See also below, Ch. VII.

[7] *I.G.* ii². 2323, cols. iii–vi.

[8] *Zeitschr. öst. Gym.*, p. 299.

[9] The phrase χορὸν ἔδωκεν is found in Aristot. *Poet.* v (see above, p. 83). Suidas' gloss s.v. χορὸν δίδωμι is unintelligible. χορὸν αἰτεῖν occurs in Aristoph. *Knights* 513.

[10] Cratinus, Βουκόλοι, fr. 15 (K.) ὃς οὐκ ἔδωκ' αἰτοῦντι Σοφοκλέει χορὸν | τῷ Κλεομάχου δ', ὃν οὐκ ἂν ἠξίουν ἐγώ | ἐμοὶ διδάσκειν οὐδ' ἂν εἰς Ἀδώνια. (Κλεομάχου is Dobree's emendation for Κλεομάχῳ; cf. Cratinus, Ὧραι, fr. 256 ἴτω δὲ καὶ τραγῳδίας | ὁ Κλεομάχου διδάσκαλος, | παρατιλτριῶν ἔχων χορὸν | Λυδιστὶ τιλλόντων μέλη | πονηρά. Athenaeus, xiv. 638 d, shows that both fragments refer to Gnesippus.)

refused a comic chorus)¹ attacks an archon for preferring the dissolute poet Gnesippus to Sophocles. A passage of Plato's *Laws* (vii. 817 d) suggests that each poet read specimens of his work to the archon (νῦν οὖν, ὦ παῖδες . . . ἐπιδείξαντες τοῖς ἄρχουσι πρῶτον τὰς ὑμετέρας παρὰ τὰς ἡμετέρας ᾠδάς, ἂν μὲν τὰ αὐτά γε ἢ καὶ βελτίω τὰ παρ᾽ ὑμῶν φαίνηται λεγόμενα, δώσομεν ὑμῖν χορόν, εἰ δὲ μή, ὦ φίλοι, οὐκ ἄν ποτε δυναίμεθα). There appears to have been no limit of age for tragic or comic poets.² Sophocles first produced a play when he was twenty-eight, Euripides when he was twenty-six, and Aristophanes first produced a comedy in his own name (the *Knights*) when he was only about twenty and had already had three other plays produced in the name of Kallistratos. Much later, Menander put on a comedy while still an ἔφηβος,³ and perhaps was the first to do so.

25. It was usual for a poet to produce his own plays, and there are very few exceptions among tragic poets. Aristophanes hints that Iophon was helped in his plays by his father Sophocles, but that is not quite the same thing.⁴ In the fourth century, however, Aphareus won two Dionysiac victories with plays produced in the name of Dionysius and two Lenaian victories in other names.⁵ But in comedy the practice was not infrequent. Aristophanes' *Banqueters*, *Babylonians*, *Acharnians*, and *Lysistrata* were produced by Kallistratos, his *Wasps* and *Frogs* by Philonides, his *Birds* by one or other of these two friends, and his last two plays, the Κώκαλος and Αἰολοσίκων, by his son Araros, whom he desired to commend to the spectators.⁶ The *Autolycus* of Eupolis was produced by Demostratus,⁷ and in the fourth century Philippus, son of Aristophanes, brought out plays for Eubulus.⁸ There is no

¹ Hesych. πυρπερέγχει· Κρατῖνος ἀπὸ διθυράμβου ἐν Βουκόλοις ἀρξάμενος, ἐπειδὴ χορὸν οὐκ ἔλαβε παρὰ τοῦ ἄρχοντος †ἐστιν οὗ ἠτήρει†. Emendations are uncertain.

² The statement of schol. on Aristoph. *Nub.* 510 (that a man under forty was allowed μήτε δρᾶμα ἀναγινώσκειν ἐν θεάτρῳ μήτε δημηγορεῖν) is a confused reminiscence of the rule that the choregos to a chorus of boys must be over forty. Anyhow the poet did not 'read his play'.

³ Anon. *de Com.* (Kaibel, *Fragm.*, p. 9) ἐδίδαξε δὲ πρῶτος ἔφηβος ὢν ἐπὶ Φιλοκλέους ἄρχοντος (321 B.C.). The emendation πρῶτον seems hardly necessary, though commonly accepted. *I.G.* ii². 2323 a records that a poet (probably Ameinias) ἔφηβος ὢν ἐνεμήθη in 311 B.C.

⁴ Aristoph. *Frogs* 73–79; with schol. which at most records a suspicion.

⁵ Plut. *Vit. X Orat.* 939 d ἀρξάμενος δ᾽ ἀπὸ Λυσιστράτου διδάσκειν ἄχρι Σωσιγένους ἐν ἔτεσιν εἰκοσιοκτὼ διδασκαλίας ἀστικὰς καθῆκεν ἓξ καὶ δὶς ἐνίκησε διὰ Διονυσίου καθείς, καὶ δι᾽ ἑτέρων ἑτέρας δύο Ληναϊκάς.

⁶ Arg. iv to Aristoph. *Plout.* καὶ τὸν υἱὸν αὐτοῦ συστῆσαι Ἀραρότα δι᾽ αὐτῆς τοῖς θεαταῖς βουλόμενος, τὰ ὑπόλοιπα δύο δι᾽ ἐκείνου καθῆκε, Κώκαλον καὶ Αἰολοσίκωνα.

⁷ Athen. v. 216 d.

⁸ *Vit. Aristoph.* (*Proleg.* xiii, ed. Dindorf).

reason to suppose that there was any concealment in these cases, except possibly in that of Araros, and even the sale of plays to others by Plato (the comic poet) to relieve his poverty was admitted by himself in his *Peisandros*.[1] The *Wasps*, though produced by Philonides, contains words (1016 ff.) which are obviously spoken by Aristophanes on his own behalf.

A poet's reason for employing someone else to produce his plays may have been (as with Aristophanes) the natural diffidence of a young man,[2] or the realization that composition and production may well require different qualifications. Kallistratos may have had special experience, and a good poet may often have been glad to escape the labour of teaching his performers and rehearsing his play, with all the attendant business.

Where, as in the case of plays brought out for Aristophanes by Kallistratos and Philonides, there was no concealment, it is natural that the prize should go to the real composer of the play and that he should be recorded as the victor, and (after long and keen controversy on the subject) it now seems clear that it is the real poet, not his deputy, whose name appears in extant inscriptions. For the fourth century this is certain; Aphareus, whose only two victories were won in the name of Dionysius, is himself credited with these in the list of poets victorious at the Dionysia,[3] and the inscription recording the places taken by Anaxandrides' plays[4] mentions one produced for him by Anaxippus.[5] For the fifth century, the name of Aristophanes is restored with practical certainty in the list of victors at the Dionysia between those of Hermippus and Eupolis,[6] it being now proved that the first victory of Aristomenes, the other candidate for the place, fell much later.

[1] Fr. 99 (K.); see Suid. s.v. Ἀρκάδας μιμούμενοι, and other refs. given by Kock. (The Arcadians were proverbially said to have won military victories for others but never for themselves.)

[2] See Aristoph. *Knights* 512–14; *Clouds* 528–31.

[3] *I.G.* ii². 2325.   [4] *I.G.* xiv. 1098.

[5] Or possibly Dioxippus.

[6] *I.G.* ii². 2325. Hermippus' first Dionysiac victory was won in 435 (ibid. 2318) and that of Eupolis in 424, and Aristophanes' first victory (on which his place in the list depends) was doubtless with the *Babylonians* produced by Kallistratos in 426. There is no need to follow the controversy in detail, as these instances seem to be sufficient and there is nothing to set against them; but see especially Capps, *Am. J. Phil.* xxviii (1907), pp. 89 ff., and *Hesperia*, xii, p. 3; Dittmer, *Fragments of Athenian Comic Didascaliae found in Rome*, pp. 44–46, 51–53; Geissler, *Chronologie der altatt. Komödie*, pp. 2 ff.; Oellacher in *Wiener Stud.* 1916, pp. 101 ff.; Wilhelm, *Urkunden*, pp. 107, etc.; Jachmann, *de Aristotelis didascaliis*.

It still, of course, remains possible that the official record of the archon may have entered the name of the producer, and that the producer may have formally received the prize (though it may be doubted whether he would have been allowed to retain it); and in that case the compilers of the records for our inscriptions, at a later date, may have corrected the archon's entries by substituting the names of the actual poets; but there is no evidence that it was so. After the death of Aeschylus the Athenian people gave permission for the production of his plays in competition with those of living poets,[1] and this may have been the point of his claim in Aristophanes' *Frogs* (866 ff.) that his poetry had not died with him like that of Euripides; but it is not known how in this case the record was worded. If in some lists, Athenian or Alexandrian, such victories were entered in his own name, and in others in that of the producer, this might account for the fact that while he is said to have won thirteen victories (all Dionysian, since tragic contests at the Lenaia had not begun in his lifetime) Suidas says that some credited him with twenty-eight.

26. The appointment of the choregoi, upon whom the success of the poets' work in the competition might largely depend,[2] was one of the first duties of the archon eponymos on entering upon office.[3] At some date in the fourth century (before the composition of Aristotle's *Constitution of Athens* in 325 B.C. or thereabouts) the appointment of choregoi for comedy was transferred to the tribes. The expense of the choregia, as will be explained shortly, might be very heavy, and the duty was a λητουργία laid upon the richest citizens in turn. Any citizen so called upon might demand that another whom he considered better able to discharge the duty should do so, or else exchange property with himself; or he might claim to be excused, e.g. on the ground that he was already discharging another λητουργία or for some other

---

[1] Philostr. *Vit. Apoll.* VI. xi ὅθεν πατέρα μὲν αὐτὸν τῆς τραγῳδίας ἡγοῦντο, ἐκάλουν δὲ καὶ τεθνεῶτα εἰς Διονύσια, τὰ γὰρ Αἰσχύλου ψηφισαμένων ἀνεδιδάσκετο καὶ ἐνίκα ἐκ καινῆς; cf. *Vit. Aesch.* Ἀθηναῖοι δὲ τοσοῦτον ἠγάπησαν Αἰσχύλον ὡς ψηφίσασθαι μετὰ θάνατον αὐτοῦ τὸν βουλόμενον διδάσκειν τὰ Αἰσχύλου χορὸν λαμβάνειν. So in Aristoph. *Ach.* 9–12 (over thirty years after Aeschylus' death) a spectator (probably at the Proagon) is expecting the name of Aeschylus to be called, and is annoyed at being put off with Theognis.

[2] See above, pp. 75 ff., where this is emphasized in relation to dithyramb. (Choregoi for dithyramb were appointed by the tribes.)

[3] Aristot. Ἀθ. Πολ. lvi ἔπειτα χορηγοὺς καθίστησι τρεῖς ἐξ ἁπάντων Ἀθηναίων τοὺς πλουσιωτάτους· πρότερον δὲ καὶ κωμῳδοῖς καθίστη πέντε, νῦν δὲ τούτοις αἱ φυλαὶ φέρουσι. The archon then τὰς ἀντιδόσεις ποιεῖ καὶ τὰς σκήψεις εἰσ⟨άγει?⟩.

sufficient reason. Such questions were settled by the archon. But it was not always easy to find a sufficient number of choregoi,[1] and at one moment of financial stress, in the year 406–405 B.C., the duties of each choregos, both in tragedy and comedy, were divided between two synchoregoi[2]—an arrangement of which we have already noticed instances in the records of Rural Dionysia. This expedient was probably confined to the one year —at least there is no hint of anything further—and to the Dionysia, and Capps has made it clear that the inscription *I.G.* ii². 2318 can best be reconstructed, as regards the relevant columns, on this supposition.[3] Lysias' client in his 21st Oration was choregos, not synchoregos, for comedy in 402 B.C., and the inscription just quoted attests the existence of choregia, not synchoregia, from 398 to 329 B.C.[4]

27. It might happen that a public-spirited citizen volunteered to bear the expense of a tragic or comic chorus (as Demosthenes undertook that of a dithyramb).[5] The client of Lysias, who has just been mentioned, undertook eight choruses in nine years,

[1] See above (in reference to dithyramb), p. 75.

[2] Schol. on Aristoph. *Frogs* 406 ἔοικε δὲ παρεμφαίνειν ὅτι λιτῶς ἤδη ἐχορηγεῖτο τοῖς ποιηταῖς. ἐπὶ γοῦν τοῦ Καλλίου τούτου φησὶν Ἀριστοτέλης ὅτι σύνδυο ἔδοξε χορηγεῖν τὰ Διονύσια τοῖς τραγῳδοῖς καὶ κωμῳδοῖς· ὥστε ἴσως ἦν τις καὶ περὶ τὸν Ληναϊκὸν ἀγῶνα συστολή. (It should be noticed that this is only a conjecture by the scholiast, and that there is no other evidence to support it.) χρόνῳ δ' ὕστερον οὐ πολλῷ τινι καὶ καθάπαξ περιεῖλε Κινησίας τὰς χορηγίας· ἐξ οὗ καὶ Στράττις ἐν τῷ εἰς αὐτὸν δράματι ἔφη 'σκηνὴ μὲν τοῦ χοροκτόνου Κινησίου'. What Kinesias is supposed to have done does not appear, but the epithet 'murderer of choruses' probably refers to the badness of his poetry, not to any action connected with choregia, and that he took any such action may easily be a false inference by the scholiast or his authority. Certainly Kinesias did not 'abolish' choregia for good, as Aristotle's Ἀθ. Πολ. lvi proves, but he may have initiated some hostile action—cf. schol. on *Frogs* 153 ὁ Κινησίας ἐπραγματεύσατο κατὰ τῶν κωμικῶν ὡς εἶεν ἀχορήγητοι.

[3] *Hesperia*, xii, pp. 5–8. It has commonly been stated that synchoregia must have continued until 401 B.C. at least, on the strength of an inscription from Eleusis (*I.G.* ii². 3090; see above, p. 54) which runs: [Γ]ναθις Τιμοκήδους Ἀναξανδρίδης Τιμαγόρου | χορηγοῦντες κωμῳδοῖς ἐνίκων | Ἀριστοφάνης ἐδίδασκε | ἑτέρα νίκη τραγῳδοῖς | Σοφοκλῆς ἐδίδασκεν. Jachmann, Körte, Kirchner, and others have assumed that the inscription refers to the City Dionysia and to the younger Sophocles, who produced his father's *Oedipus Coloneus* in 401 B.C. (Argt. *Oed. Col.*). But the inscription seems obviously to be one of a number of records of Rural Dionysia, at which synchoregia seems not to have been uncommon (e.g. *I.G.* ii². 1198, 1200, 3092, 3095, 3096—of which the last two record *three* synchoregoi at Rural Dionysia; see above, p. 45 ff.). Further, Wilhelm is certain that this inscription is shown by the script to be earlier than 406–405 B.C. Accordingly there is no obstacle to Capps's view (op. cit., p. 8) that synchoregia was only in force for the one year 406–405 B.C.

[4] So do *I.G.* ii². 3042 (334 B.C.), 3055, and 3056 (319 B.C.). The explanation of the dropping of the chorus in Aristophanes' later days by the unwillingness of choregoi to come forward, as given by Platonius and in the *Life* of Aristophanes, is probably not more than guess-work. (Kaibel, *Com. Gr. Fr.*, p. 5, and Dübner, *Proleg. de Com.*, pp. xiii, xxviii.) Cf. *Theatre of D.*, pp. 160–7, and Maidment's discussion in *Class. Quart.* 1935. See also below, p. 75.

[5] See above, p. 75.

and his speech¹ gives some valuable information as to the expense involved—30 minae for choregia in tragedy in 410, 50 minae for a dithyrambic chorus of men (and the erection of the tripod) in 409, more than 15 minae for a boys' chorus in 404, 16 minae for a comedy in 402, besides expenditure at other festivals. Another client of Lysias,² named Aristophanes, gives the cost of two tragic choregiai about 392 B.C. as 50 minae. At a later date Demosthenes³ says that it was common knowledge that a men's chorus was much more expensive than a tragic; this may have been mainly because of the larger number of singers,⁴ and also, perhaps, because of the temptation to extravagant ostentation which dithyramb seems to have offered.⁵ But a good deal evidently depended upon the ambition or generosity of the choregos himself, who might be either liberal or mean in the matter of costumes, or in supplying many or few mute characters to form a retinue for the chief persons in the play, and so on. Nikias is said by Plutarch to have won popularity by his lavish expenditure as choregos, and never to have failed to win the prize. It was possible to hire second-hand costumes,⁶ but there were apparently limits to extravagance set by good taste. Aristotle treats an over-showy treatment of a comic chorus as characteristic of the βάναυσος.⁷ Plutarch⁸ tells a story of an actor who refused to appear unless the choregos gave him the retinue befitting the part of a queen; Melanthios the choregos shouted to him that a single maidservant was retinue enough for the wife of Phokion, and that he should not give himself airs.

The chief expense which fell upon the choregos was that of the training of the chorus, including the provision of costumes and the payment of salaries to the singers in the chorus and to their trainer, and probably (for tragedy and comedy, though not for dithyramb)⁹ to the flute-player also; and he doubtless

---

¹ Lysias, *Or.* xxi, §§ 1–5.   ² Id. xix, §§ 29, 42.
³ *in Meid.* § 156.
⁴ Though each tragic chorus (and choregos) had to serve for a whole tetralogy (see Argt. to Aesch. *Agam.*).   ⁵ See above, p. 77.
⁶ Pollux vii. 78 τοὺς δὲ τὰς ἐσθῆτας ἀπομισθοῦντας τοῖς χορηγοῖς οἱ μὲν νέοι ἱματιομίσθας ἐκάλουν, οἱ δὲ παλαιοὶ ἱματιομισθωτάς.
⁷ *Eth. Nic.* IV. ii ἐν γὰρ τοῖς μικροῖς τῶν δαπανημάτων πολλὰ ἀναλίσκει καὶ λαμπρύνεται παρὰ μέλος, οἶον ἐρανιστὰς γαμικῶς ἑστιῶν, καὶ κωμῳδοῖς χορηγῶν ἐν τῇ παρόδῳ πορφύραν εἰσφέρων, οἶον οἱ Μεγαρεῖς. (It is not quite clear to what practice Aristotle refers.)
⁸ Plut. *Phok.*, ch. xix.
⁹ In dithyramb also the flute-player was paid by the poet until about the middle of the fifth century (id., *de Mus.* xxx, and see above, p. 76). Athen. xiv. 617 b records that both

had the deciding voice in the provision of any special scenery which might be required.[1] It is probable that the choregos was also responsible for such additional choruses as that of the huntsmen in the prologue of the *Hippolytus*, the προπομποί in the *Eumenides*, and the shepherds in Euripides' *Alexandros*, and in comedy the chorus of frogs in Aristophanes' play, and Agathon's chorus in the *Thesmophoriazousai*, though—as Haigh suggests—the two latter, and the huntsmen's chorus in the *Hippolytus*, may have been sung behind the scenes by members of the regular chorus, while mute figures appeared before the spectators.[2] But in fact we hear less of any meanness on the part of choregoi than of pride in the generous carrying out of an important public service, and the sanctity attached to the holder of the office. The archon appears to have been entitled to put some kind of pressure upon an inefficient choregos,[3] but no instance of this seems to be recorded, unless one is to be inferred from a fragment of Eupolis,[4] εἶδες χορηγὸν πώποτε ῥυπαρώτερον τοῦδε; The thorough training of a dramatic chorus was evidently regarded as a matter of some public importance, apart from its artistic attraction. Athenaeus,[5] speaking of the latter half of the fifth century B.C., says:

ἦν γὰρ τὸ τῆς ὀρχήσεως γένος τῆς ἐν τοῖς χοροῖς εὔσχημον τότε καὶ μεγαλοπρεπὲς καὶ ὡσανεὶ τὰς ἐν τοῖς ὅπλοις ἀπομιμούμενον. ὅθεν καὶ Σωκράτης ἐν τοῖς ποιήμασιν τοὺς κάλλιστα χορεύοντας ἀρίστους φησὶν εἶναι τὰ πολέμια, λέγων οὕτως

οἳ δὲ χοροῖς κάλλιστα θεοὺς τιμῶσιν, ἄριστοι
ἐν πολέμῳ.

σχεδὸν γὰρ ὥσπερ ἐξοπλισία τις ἦν ἡ χορεία καὶ ἐπίδειξις οὐ μόνον τῆς λοιπῆς εὐταξίας ἀλλὰ καὶ τῆς τῶν σωμάτων ἐπιμελείας.

singers and flute-players were μισθοφόροι in the time of Pratinas (αὐλητῶν καὶ χορευτῶν μισθοφόρων κατεχόντων τὰς ὀρχήστρας), though it is not stated who paid them.

[1] Demosthenes' feigned dream (Plut. *Dem.* 29, quoted above, p. 77) illustrates the possibility of the failure of an actor through want of χορηγία.

[2] It is sometimes stated by modern writers that any additional provision made by a choregos over and above what was normally expected of him was termed παραχορήγημα. The meaning of this word is discussed below (p. 138); in its few occurrences it seems to mean simply a special or additional provision (χορηγεῖν in its secondary sense of 'supply') without any necessary reference to a χορηγός in the technical sense.

[3] Xen. *Hiero* ix. 4 καὶ γὰρ ὅταν χοροὺς ἡμῖν βουλώμεθα ἀγωνίζεσθαι, ἆθλα μὲν ὁ ἄρχων προτίθησιν, ἀθροίζειν δὲ αὐτοὺς προστέτακται χορηγοῖς καὶ ἄλλοις διδάσκειν, καὶ ἀνάγκην προστιθέναι τοῖς ἐνδεῶς τι ποιοῦσιν.

[4] Fr. 306 (K.). But for an instance in the case of dithyramb see Isaeus, *Or.* v. 36 (and above, p. 77).   [5] xiv. 628 e–f.

The scholiast on Aristophanes' *Clouds* (l. 339) says that the description of a huge feast in that passage τείνει πρός τε τοὺς παρὰ τοῖς χορηγοῖς ἐστιωμένους καὶ πρὸς τοὺς ἐν πρυτανείῳ ἀεὶ δειπνοῦντας, and this may refer to the good living of a chorus in training.[1] There is, however, a reference in Aristophanes' *Acharnians*[2] to the failure of Antimachus to feast his chorus at the end of the Lenaia. There was probably a customary banquet given by the choregos to his chorus after the Dionysia, though the only banquet recorded on such an occasion is that given by Agathon as a successful poet, and that was probably quite unofficial.

It does not appear that the choregos had any expense in connexion with the actors proper, nor is there any indication that he was responsible for their costumes, as he was for those of the chorus. The honorarium paid to each poet, whether successful or not, as well as the prize given to the victorious poet, were also the affair of the State. (The amounts of these are unknown, but the allusions[3] to the cutting down of the payments to comic poets seem to imply that such payments were made, and could be altered, by the Assembly. What prizes were given for the victors besides the ivy crown is unknown.)

28. By the middle of the fourth century, if not before, there was probably a class of professional singers from whom the choregos chose; Aristotle notes that tragic and comic choruses might consist of the same persons.[4] But, once selected, they had to be trained. The trainer (χοροδιδάσκαλος) had to be a citizen, though there were exceptions such as that of Sannio, who had been disfranchised but evidently continued his career as a trainer of choruses for tragedy.[5] The earliest generation of dramatic poets taught their own choruses, inventing the dances as they required; and both Phrynichus and Aeschylus were famous for their skill in this.[6] Aeschylus also employed the

---

[1] For the luxury of a dithyrambic chorus, see above, p. 77.

[2] 1153–5 ὅς γ' ἐμὲ τὸν τλήμονα Λήναια χορηγῶν ἀπέλυσεν ἄδειπνον.

[3] Aristoph. *Frogs* 367 ἢ τοὺς μισθοὺς τῶν ποιητῶν ῥήτωρ ὢν εἶτ' ἀποτρώγει. (The schol. says that the reference is to the reduction of the poets' payments by Archinus and Agyrrhius.) Cf. Hesych. s.v. μισθός· τὸ ἔπαθλον τῶν κωμικῶν . . . ἔμμισθοι δὲ πέντε ἦσαν. In the dithyrambic contests instituted by Lycurgus in honour of Poseidon in the Peiraeus, the prizes for the choruses placed first, second, and third were to be 10, 8, and 6 minae respectively.

[4] Aristot. *Pol.* iii. iii. 1276 b. It may be assumed that the selection of the chorus rested with the choregos; see above, p. 76.   [5] Demosth. *in Meid.* § 58.

[6] Athen. i. 22 a φασὶ δὲ καὶ ὅτι οἱ ἀρχαῖοι ποιηταί, Θέσπις, Πρατίνας, Κρατῖνος, Φρύνιχος, ὀρχησταὶ ἐκαλοῦντο διὰ τὸ μὴ μόνον τὰ ἑαυτῶν δράματα ἀναφέρειν εἰς ὄρχησιν τοῦ χοροῦ, ἀλλὰ καὶ

services of Telestes, whom Athenaeus describes both as χοροδιδάσκαλος[1] and as ὁ Αἰσχύλου ὀρχηστής,[2] and as having special skill
in regard to the movements of his hands and in realistic imitation. Plutarch[3] tells how Euripides rebuked a man who showed
his amusement when the poet was singing over to his chorus
one of his odes written in the mixolydian mode.

A trainer employed by a poet (who was himself the διδάσκαλος
in the strict sense) might be termed ὑποδιδάσκαλος.[4] But the
training of choruses no doubt became a professional business in
time, and the professional trainers usurped the title of διδάσκαλος
with no sign of subordination, except perhaps at Athens where
they may still have been called ὑποδιδάσκαλοι, even when producing an old play, out of respect for the original composer.

The disciplining of the dramatic choruses, as distinct from
their training, is stated by Suidas[5] to have been the task of
specially elected officials. Some may be tempted to connect this
with a statement of Athenaeus[6] that the chorus were given
drinks both before and after their performance.

29. During the régime of Demetrius of Phalerum at Athens
(317–307 B.C.), the choregia was abolished, and the Dionysian
festival placed under the management of an agonothetes elected
annually and provided with funds for the performance of his
duties. The exact date of the change is unknown. The old belief
that it occurred immediately after the death of Antipater in
319 B.C. rests on a misinterpretation of a passage in Plutarch's
life of Phokion,[7] where the title is used in a general sense and

ἔξω τῶν ἰδίων ποιημάτων διδάσκειν τοὺς βουλομένους ὀρχεῖσθαι; Athen. i. 21 d, e καὶ Αἰσχύλος
δὲ . . . πολλὰ σχήματα ὀρχηστικὰ αὐτὸς ἐξευρίσκων ἀνεδίδου τοῖς χορευταῖς. Χαμαιλέων γοῦν
πρῶτον αὐτόν φησι σχηματίσαι τοὺς χοροὺς ὀρχηστοδιδασκάλοις οὐ χρησάμενον, ἀλλὰ καὶ αὐτὸν
τοῖς χοροῖς τὰ σχήματα ποιοῦντα τῶν ὀρχήσεων. Cf. Plut. *Symp. Quaest.* VIII. ix, § 3 καίτοι καὶ
Φρύνιχος ὁ τῶν τραγῳδιῶν ποιητὴς περὶ αὐτοῦ φησιν ὅτι 'σχήματα δ' ὄρχησις τόσα μοι πόρεν,
ὅσσ' ἐνὶ πόντῳ | κύματα ποιεῖται χείματι νὺξ ὀλοή'.

[1] Athen. i. 21 f.
[2] Ibid. 22 a Τελέστης ὁ Αἰσχύλου ὀρχηστὴς οὕτως ἦν τεχνίτης ὥστε ἐν τῷ ὀρχεῖσθαι τοὺς
Ἑπτὰ ἐπὶ Θήβας φανερὰ ποιῆσαι τὰ πράγματα δι' ὀρχήσεως. (See below, p. 256.)
[3] *De Recta Ratione Audiendi*, p. 46 b.
[4] Phot. s.v. ὑποδιδάσκαλος· ὁ τῷ χορῷ καταλέγων· διδάσκαλος γὰρ ὁ ποιητής, ὡς Ἀριστοφάνης.
Cf. Plato, *Ion* 536 a, and below, p. 312.
[5] Suid. s.v. ἐπιμεληταί· ἐπιμεληταὶ ἐχειροτονοῦντο τῶν χορῶν ὡς μὴ ἀτακτεῖν τοὺς χοροὺς
ἐν τοῖς θεάτροις.
[6] xi. 464 f καὶ τοῖς χοροῖς εἰσιοῦσιν ἐνέχεον (sc. οἱ Ἀθηναῖοι) πίνειν, καὶ διηγωνισμένοις, ὅτε
ἐξεπορεύοντο ἐνέχεον πάλιν.
[7] ch. 31 ὁ δὲ (sc. Φωκίων) τούτων μὲν οὐκ ἐφρόντιζεν, ἐντυγχάνων δὲ Νικάνορι καὶ διαλεγό-
μενος εἴς τε τἆλλα τοῖς Ἀθηναίοις πρᾷον αὐτὸν καὶ κεχαρισμένον παρεῖχε, καὶ φιλοτιμίας τινὰς
ἔπεισε καὶ δαπάνας ὑποστῆναι γενόμενον ἀγωνοθέτην. Nicanor undertook the expense of various
festivals, but this does not mean that he was elected official ἀγωνοθέτης of the Dionysia.

without special reference to the Dionysia. Inscriptions of 319 B.C. show that choregia was still in existence in that year,[1] and on the other hand the monument of Xenokles in 306 B.C.[2] was erected by him as agonothetes and begins with the words ὁ δῆμος ἐχορήγει. It refers to the Lenaia, but it is unlikely that the new system was not applied at the same time to the City Dionysia. Demetrius may have instituted it in 309 B.C., when as archon he would have been responsible for this and other festivals.

The reason for the change may have been simply the burdensomeness of the choregia, falling upon a smaller number of men than formerly and those poorer than rich men had been in earlier days;[3] a similar change was applied by Demetrius to the Panathenaia,[4] the Thargelia, and probably to other festivals, both literary and gymnastic,[5] the supervision of the performances being for most purposes transferred to an agonothetes—whether to one for all festivals at this date or to several is not known.[6] But that the archon and the ἐπιμεληταί retained some of their functions at the Dionysia even after the institution of the agonothetes is shown by inscriptions already quoted[7] in another connexion. When Hadrian was in Athens in A.D. 126 he performed the office of agonothetes with distinction.[8]

30. As regards the choice of actors in tragedy and comedy, four periods seem to be distinguishable:

(1) Originally the poet acted in his own play,[9] and this is

---

[1] See above, p. 88.　　　　　　　　　　[2] *I.G.* ii². 3073; see Appendix, p. 121.

[3] That an agonothetes and an ἐπιμελητής might incur a considerable amount of personal expenditure, even when ὁ δῆμος ἐχορήγει, is shown by *I.G.* ii. 314 καὶ εἰς ταῦτα πάντα ἐκ τῶν ἰδίων ἀναλώσας πολλὰ χρήματα, though it cannot be decided how much of this was voluntary, as some of it certainly was. The passage does not refer to the Dionysia by name.

[4] The statement of Ferguson, *Hellenistic Athens*, p. 57, that Demetrius transferred the contests of Homeric rhapsodists from the Panathenaia to the Dionysia goes beyond the evidence of Athen. xiv. 620 b τοὺς δὲ νῦν Ὁμηριστὰς ὀνομαζομένους πρῶτος εἰς τὰ θέατρα παρήγαγε Δημήτριος ὁ Φαληρεύς. At a later date the Διονύσου τεχνῖται included professional reciters of epic, but not necessarily at the Dionysia.

[5] For the general political background of these changes see Ferguson, op. cit., ch. ii, and Tarn, in *Cambr. Anc. Hist.* vi, pp. 495 ff. The changes were not reversed when Demetrius Poliorketes came into power in 307 B.C. Demetrius of Phalerum as a Peripatetic may have shared Aristotle's objection to χορηγίαι and certain other liturgies (Aristot. *Pol.* viii (v). 1309ª13 ff. and 1320ᵇ4), as tending to dissipate the funds in the hands of the rich with no corresponding benefit to the State.

[6] See Ferguson in *Klio*, viii (1908), pp. 345 ff.

[7] p. 56 above. Dedications by agonothetai are found in *I.G.* ii². 3073 and later.

[8] Ibid. 1105, and Dio Cass. lxix. 16 τά τε Διονύσια τὴν μεγίστην παρ' αὐτοῖς ἀρχὴν ἄρξας ἐν τῇ ἐσθῆτι τῇ ἐπιχωρίῳ λαμπρῶς ἐπετέλεσε.

[9] Aristot. *Rhet.* iii. i ὑπεκρίνοντο γὰρ αὐτοὶ τὰς τραγῳδίας οἱ ποιηταὶ τὸ πρῶτον; Plut. *Solon* xxix ὁ Σόλων . . . ἐθεάσατο Θέσπιν αὐτὸν ὑποκρινόμενον, ὥσπερ ἔθος ἦν τοῖς παλαιοῖς.

particularly recorded of Thespis. That Aeschylus also acted in person, whether only before or also after he introduced a second actor (as he had already done in the earliest extant plays), is at least probable.[1] Cratinus may have acted in his own comedies.[2]

(2) The poet employed professional actors, selected by himself. So Aeschylus employed Kleandros and afterwards Mynniskos as second and third actors.[3] Sophocles regularly employed Tlepolemos,[4] and was said to have had the special capacities of his actors in view in composing his plays.[5] The *Life* of Euripides states that Kephisophon acted for Euripides, but only on the authority of Thomas Magister, which carries little weight.[6] In comedy Krates was said to have acted in the plays of Cratinus[7] before he composed plays on his own account, and Pherekrates in those of Krates.[8]

(3) Three protagonists for tragedy were chosen by the State— it is not known how, but presumably by the archon—and allocated by lot to the poets. It is natural to connect this change with the introduction of prizes for actors, in tragedy at the Dionysia certainly in 449 B.C. and at the Lenaia possibly about 432 B.C., though there is no direct evidence about this. In tragedy at least, the actor who won the prize was entitled to be one of the three competitors in the following year.[9] There is less certainty about the method of selection of comic actors. In the third quarter of the fourth century Lycurgus is said[10] to have revived the contest of comic actors at the Χυτροί, the victor in which had the right to act at the ensuing Dionysia, but this only provided for one of the five protagonists, and when or how long this method had

---

[1] He must have done so, if the statement in the *Life* of Sophocles, that Sophocles was the first to abandon the practice, is correct (πρῶτον μὲν καταλύσας τὴν ὑπόκρισιν τοῦ ποιητοῦ διὰ τὴν ἰδίαν μικροφωνίαν). The parts which Sophocles took as a harp-player in the *Thamyris* and a ball-player in the *Nausicaa* were doubtless mute parts.

[2] This may perhaps be inferred from Athenaeus 22a.

[3] *Vit. Aesch.* ἐχρήσατο δ' ὑποκριτῇ πρῶτον μὲν Κλεάνδρῳ, ἔπειτα καὶ τὸν δεύτερον αὐτῷ προσῆψε Μυννίσκον τὸν Χαλκιδέα· τὸν δὲ τρίτον ὑποκριτὴν αὐτὸς ἐξεῦρεν, ὡς δὲ Δικαίαρχος ὁ Μεσσήνιος, Σοφοκλῆς. See below, p. 132.

[4] Schol. Aristoph. *Clouds* 1267.

[5] Ister, quoted in *Vit. Soph.*

[6] Other references to Kephisophon say nothing of his having been an actor.

[7] Schol. Aristoph. *Knights* 537; Anon. *de Com.* (Kaibel), p. 7.

[8] Ibid., p. 8.

[9] Hesych., Suid., and Phot. s.v. νεμήσεις ὑποκριτῶν· οἱ ποιηταὶ ἐλάμβανον τρεῖς ὑποκριτὰς κλήρῳ νεμηθέντας ὑποκρινομένους τὰ δράματα, ὧν ὁ νικήσας εἰς τοὐπιὸν ἄκριτος παρελαμβάνετο. The phrase ὑποκρίνεσθαι τὸ δρᾶμα is used only of protagonists; there is no direct evidence about the selection of the second and third actors for each poet.

[10] Plut. *Vit. X Orat.* 841 f. See above, p. 15.

previously been in vogue is unknown; nor is it possible to say how comic actors were chosen for the Lenaia—where the comic actors' prize was probably instituted about 442 B.C.—or for the Dionysia generally either from the beginning or from the institution of the prize for comic actors between 329 and 312 B.C. But there is no reason to doubt that each poet received his actor by lot. Under the system in vogue for tragedy, the actor allocated to each poet probably acted in all four of his plays. The didaskalic inscription[1] shows that at the Lenaia in 418 B.C. both the tragedies presented by each of the two rival poets were acted by Lysikrates and Kallippides respectively, and the same system was probably applied to the Dionysia. But, as the poets themselves became less famous than the great three had been and actors developed greater professional skill, it was obviously felt that it was not fair to give one poet the advantage of the best actor in all his plays, and the system was changed.

(4) Three tragic actors were chosen as before, but each acted in a single tragedy of each poet, so that in 341, when Astydamas, Euaretos, and Aphareus each competed with three tragedies at the Dionysia, each had the services of the three actors, Thettalos, Neoptolemos, and Athenodoros, in one play.[2] It was shortly after this that Aristotle stated that the actors were now more important than the poets.[3]

It may be presumed that the five comic actors selected were still assigned to the poets by lot, but at a late period we occasionally find the same actor serving two poets. So in 288 B.C. Aristomachos acted for both Simylos and Diodoros, and in 155 Damon played not only for both Chairion and Biottos but also in the old play which preceded the competition, while Kallikrates acted for both Philokles and Timoxenos.

It is not definitely known how the second and third actors for each group of tragedies were chosen or paid. (Presumably the protagonists were paid by the State.) Demosthenes[4] taunts Aeschines with hiring himself out as 'tritagonist' to the actors Simylos and Socrates, but this was for the Rural Dionysia and probably for the acting of old plays only. It seems likely that for rural festivals the whole body of performers (who might

---

[1] *I.G.* ii². 2319.

[2] Ibid. 2320. In the following year Astydamas, Timokles, and Euaretos each offered two plays only; the two actors were Thettalos and Neoptolemos.

[3] *Rhet.* III. i μεῖζον δύνανται νῦν τῶν ποιητῶν οἱ ὑποκριταί.   [4] *de Cor.* § 262.

be a troupe habitually acting together) was assembled by the protagonist.

31. But the importance of the protagonist in the Athenian festivals seems almost excessive, when we remember not only the possibility of a play being spoiled by the bad acting of secondary characters, but the heavy demands made upon these secondary characters in a Greek play.[1] It is the protagonist alone who is said to 'act the play', both in inscriptions[2] and in literature,[3] and only the protagonist could win the prize for acting. It is, however, noteworthy that the prize did not necessarily go to the actor of the successful plays. The didaskalic inscription already quoted[4] illustrates this: the successful tragedies were acted by Lysikrates, but the prize for acting went to Kallippides, and about 183 B.C. Onesimus won the actor's prize with the Ναυαγός of Paramonos, which only took second place in the contest of comedies.

32. The public performance of lyric choruses and of drama at Athens took the form of a contest, and elaborate precautions were taken to secure fairness in the selection of the judges and in their performance of their duties. The exact methods adopted have been the subject of much controversy, but an account can be given which reconciles the few passages of ancient writers which bear on the subject. Plutarch,[5] describing how in 468 B.C. the archon by a bold stroke set aside the regular procedure, shows incidentally in part what this procedure must have been:

ἔθεντο δὲ εἰς μνήμην αὐτοῦ (Kimon) καὶ τὴν τραγῳδίαν κρίσιν ὀνομαστὴν γενομένην. πρώτην γὰρ διδασκαλίαν τοῦ Σοφοκλέους ἔτι νέου καθέντος, Ἀψεφίων ὁ ἄρχων, φιλονεικίας οὔσης καὶ παρατάξεως τῶν θεατῶν, κριτὰς μὲν οὐκ ἐκλήρωσε τοῦ ἀγῶνος, ὡς δὲ Κίμων μετὰ τῶν συστρατήγων προελθὼν εἰς τὸ θέατρον ἐποιήσατο τὰς νενομισμένας σπονδάς, οὐκ ἀφῆκεν αὐτοὺς ἀπελθεῖν, ἀλλ' ὁρκώσας ἠνάγκασε καθίσαι καὶ κρῖναι δέκα ὄντας, ἀπὸ φυλῆς μίας ἕκαστον (or, as Helbig, ἀπὸ φυλῆς ἕνα ἑκάστης). ὁ μὲν οὖν ἀγὼν καὶ διὰ τὸ τῶν κριτῶν ἀξίωμα τὴν φιλοτιμίαν (? φιλονικίαν or τῇ φιλοτιμίᾳ) ὑπερέβαλε, νικήσαντος δὲ τοῦ Σοφοκλέους κτλ.

The point in the theatrical proceedings at which the archon must have called in the generals to help must have been just before the performances of tragedy, when the audience (who had probably seen the Proagon and formed their prejudice in

---

[1] See pp. 133 f., 139 f.   [2] See pp. 108 ff.   [3] e.g. Dem. *de Fals. Leg.* § 246.
[4] *I.G.* ii². 2319.   [5] *Kimon*, ch. 8.

favour of particular competitors) was vehemently proclaiming its preferences, and would evidently put pressure on the judges if they were drawn by lot in the regular manner from the ten now representing each of the ten tribes (see below). Instead of drawing one name from each urn, the archon called on the ten strategoi, each of whom also represented one tribe, so that at least the tribal character of the selection was preserved—a bold experiment, but one whose felicitousness, together with the popularity of the returning generals, might well capture the good-will of the excited crowd.[1] (The only difficulty is as to the nature of the 'accustomed libations' offered by the generals, and the point in the proceedings at which they were offered, and there is no information available for solving this.)

33. Further details of the method of selection, especially in its earlier stages, are found in passages of the orators:

Isocr. xvii, §§ 33–34. Πυθόδωρον γὰρ τὸν σκηνίτην καλούμενον, ὃς ὑπὲρ Πασίωνος ἅπαντα καὶ λέγει καὶ πράττει, τίς οὐκ οἶδεν ὑμῶν πέρυσιν ἀνοίξαντα τὰς ὑδρίας καὶ τοὺς κριτὰς ἐξελόντα τοὺς ὑπὸ τῆς βουλῆς ἐμβληθέντας; καίτοι ὅστις μικρῶν ἕνεκεν καὶ περὶ τοῦ σώματος κινδυνεύων ταύτας ὑπανοίγειν ἐτόλμησεν, αἳ σεσημασμέναι μὲν ἦσαν ὑπὸ τῶν πρυτάνεων, κατεσφραγισμέναι δ᾽ ὑπὸ τῶν χορηγῶν, ἐφυλάττοντο, ἔκειντο δ᾽ ἐν ἀκροπόλει, τί δεῖ θαυμάζειν, εἰ κτλ.

Lysias iv. 3. ἐβουλόμην δ᾽ ἂν μὴ ἀπολαχεῖν αὐτὸν κριτὴν Διονυσίοις, ἵν᾽ ὑμῖν φανερὸς ἐγένετο ἐμοὶ διηλλαγμένος, κρίνας τὴν ἐμὴν φυλὴν νικᾶν· νῦν δ᾽ ἔγραψε μὲν ταῦτα εἰς τὸ γραμματεῖον, ἀπέλαχε δέ. καὶ ὅτι ἀληθῆ ταῦτα λέγω, Φιλῖνος καὶ Διοκλῆς ἴσασιν, ἀλλ᾽ οὐκ ἔστιν αὐτοῖς μαρτυρῆσαι μὴ διομοσαμένοις περὶ τῆς αἰτίας ἧς ἐγὼ φεύγω, ἐπεὶ σαφῶς ἐγνῶτ᾽ ἂν ὅτι ἡμεῖς ἦμεν αὐτὸν οἱ κριτὴν ἐμβαλόντες καὶ ἡμῶν εἵνεκα ἐκαθίζετο.

Demosth. *in Meid.* § 17. καὶ οὐδ᾽ ἐνταῦθα ἔστη τῆς ὕβρεως, ἀλλὰ τοσοῦτον αὐτῷ περιῆν, ὥστε τὸν ἐστεφανωμένον ἄρχοντα διέφθειρε, τοὺς χορηγοὺς συνῆγεν ἐπ᾽ ἐμέ, βοῶν, ἀπειλῶν, ὀμνύουσι παρεστηκὼς τοῖς κριταῖς . . . . § 18. . . . καίτοι . . . προδιαφθείρας τοὺς κριτὰς τῷ ἀγῶνι τῶν ἀνδρῶν . . . ἐμοὶ μὲν ὕβρισεν τὸ σῶμα, τῇ φυλῇ δὲ κρατούσῃ τὸν ἀγῶνα αἰτιώτατος τοῦ μὴ νικῆσαι ἐγένετο.

34. From these passages it appears that:

(1) Before the festival (or before the particular contest) the Council drew up a list of names selected from each of the ten

---

[1] Though the victory awarded to Sophocles on this occasion was his first, he was already well known and popular in Athens, and there seems to be no sufficient reason to discredit the story.

tribes. What qualifications were required we are not told, but it is clear that the choregoi were present and had a voice in the selection, and that a choregos could (like Lysias' client) get someone pledged to support him put on the list, and that violence (like that of Meidias) might be brought to bear to influence the selection. That there was any demand for critical capacity seems unlikely. Aristophanes (*Ekkl.* 1154 ff.) divides the judges into the two classes of σοφοί and ἡδέως γελῶντες, and claims the support of both.

(2) The names were then placed in ten urns, each containing the names selected from one tribe. These urns were sealed both by the prytanes who presided at the Council and by the choregoi, and deposited in the Acropolis in the custody of the public treasurers. It was a capital offence to tamper with them, though on the occasion described by Lysias it appears to have been done.

(3) At the beginning of the contest for which the judges were required, the ten urns were placed in the theatre, and the archon drew one name from each. The ten persons selected swore to give an impartial verdict.[1] (Here Meidias again attempted to influence them.) At the end of the contest each wrote his order of merit on a tablet; the tablets were placed in an urn, from which the archon drew five at random,[2] and on these five tablets the issue of the contest was decided.

35. It is obvious that the ten judges who heard the contest officially might be influenced by the clamour of partisans in the theatre, and Plato refers to this in the *Laws* :[3]

οὔτε γὰρ παρὰ θεάτρου δεῖ τόν γε ἀληθῆ κριτὴν κρίνειν μανθάνοντα καὶ ἐκπληττόμενον ὑπὸ θορύβου πολλῶν καὶ τῆς αὐτοῦ ἀπαιδευσίας, οὔτ' αὖ γιγνώσκοντα δι' ἀνανδρίαν καὶ δειλίαν ἐκ ταὐτοῦ στόματος οὗπερ τοὺς θεοὺς ἐπεκαλέσατο ἐκ τούτου ψευδόμενον ἀποφαίνεσθαι ῥαθύμως τὴν κρίσιν· οὐ γὰρ μαθητὴς ἀλλὰ διδάσκαλος, ὥς γε τὸ δίκαιον, θεατῶν μᾶλλον ὁ κριτὴς καθίζει καὶ ἐναντιωσόμενος τοῖς τὴν ἡδονὴν μὴ προσηκόντως μηδὲ ὀρθῶς ἀποδιδοῦσι θεαταῖς.[4]

---

[1] This oath is referred to in Pherecrates, fr. 96 (K.) and Aristoph. *Ekkl.* 1160, where the judges are bidden μὴ ἐπιορκεῖν.

[2] The tablet of the friend of Lysias' client was not drawn (ἀπέλαχε), and so his promise could not be fulfilled.

[3] ii. 659 a: cf. iii. 700 c–701 b, where some of the same points are made, and particularly the protest against the ἄμουσοι βοαὶ πλήθους and the κρότοι ἐπαίνους ἀποδιδόντες which prevailed in his own day. (See below, p. 279.)

[4] Cf. Lucian, *Harmon.* 2 καὶ γὰρ οὖν ἐν τοῖς ἀγῶσιν οἱ μὲν πολλοὶ ἴσασι κροτῆσαί ποτε καὶ συρίσαι, κρίνουσι δὲ ἑπτὰ ἢ πέντε ἢ ὅσοι δή. The reference in ἑπτά is no longer explicable.

A story, true or false, is told by Aelian[1] that at the first performance of the *Clouds* the audience noisily demanded that the
judges should place Aristophanes' name first on their lists; but
the poet was unsuccessful. The influence of the audience or of
powerful persons may have been all the greater because it was
known how each judge voted. Thus Alcibiades won the victory
with a boys' chorus because (according to Andokides[2]) τῶν
κριτῶν οἱ μὲν φοβούμενοι οἱ δὲ χαριζόμενοι νικᾶν ἔκριναν αὐτόν,
and Menander, frequently defeated by Philemon by unfair
means, asked Philemon if he were not ashamed of defeating him
so often.[3] Aristophanes himself shows some consciousness of the
influence of the spectators, e.g. in the *Birds* (ll. 444–5):

> ὄμνυμ᾽ ἐπὶ τούτοις πᾶσι νικᾶν τοῖς κριταῖς
> καὶ τοῖς θεαταῖς πᾶσι,

and there was even sufficient possibility of the use of bribery (as
there was with a popular jury) for Aristophanes to disown it.[4]

36. That the final verdict was that of five judges is confirmed
by lexicographers and grammarians.[5] The name of the victorious poet was proclaimed by the herald,[6] and he was crowned
in the theatre by the archon with a crown of ivy.[7]

There is nothing to show whether the same ten judges acted
in all three contests at each festival, or how the prize for the
best actor, when it was introduced, was awarded. How far the
judges may have been influenced by the fear of penalties it is
impossible to say: Aeschines[8] refers to the trial of judges of
cyclic choruses (καὶ τοὺς μὲν κριτὰς τοὺς ἐκ τῶν Διονυσίων ἐὰν μὴ
δικαίως τοὺς κυκλίους χοροὺς κρίνωσι ζημιοῦτε), but says nothing
of judges of tragedy or comedy. (The reference may be to the

---

[1] *Var. Hist.* ii. 13.   [2] *in Alcib.* § 20.

[3] Aul. Gell. *N.A.* xvii. 4 (see below, pp. 280, 283).   [4] *Ach.* 557–9.

[5] Zenob. iii. 64 ἐν πέντε κριτῶν γούνασι κεῖται· παροιμιῶδες οἷον ἐν ἄλλων ἐξουσίᾳ ἐστίν·
εἴρηται δὲ ἡ παροιμία, παρόσον πέντε κριταὶ τοὺς κωμικοὺς ἔκρινον, ὥς φησιν Ἐπίχαρμος;
Hesych. s.v. πέντε κριταί· τοσοῦτοι τοὺς κωμικοὺς ἔκρινον, οὐ μόνον Ἀθήνησιν ἀλλὰ καὶ ἐν
Σικελίᾳ; schol. Aristoph. *Birds* 445 ἔκριναν ε' κριταὶ τοὺς κωμικούς, οἱ δὲ λαμβάνοντες τοὺς ε'
ψηφοὺς εὐδαιμόνουν. Lysias (quoted above) implies that the same system was in force for
dithyramb. A passage of an unknown literary critic of about the second century B.C. (*Ox.
Pap.* xiii, No. 1611), though very corrupt, seems to show that Lysippus in his Βάκχαι and
Cratinus in his Πλοῦτοι spoke of five judges, though the preceding words *may* refer to some
later period in which there were *four* judges of comedies; cf. G. Capovilla, *Menandro*, p. 34.

[6] Aristid. *Rhet.*, p. 2 (Dind.), and *Vit. Soph.*

[7] Aristid., loc. cit.; Plutarch, *An seni*, etc., p. 785 b; Alkiphron, *Epp.* IV. xviii, § 16
(Schepers); Athen. vi. 241 f., etc.

[8] *in Ctes.* § 232.

proceedings in the Assembly held after the festival and any subsequent legal proceedings.)

The very large number of victories won by Aeschylus and Sophocles is a testimony to the general fairness of the verdicts and the capacity of the judges in the fifth century B.C.; each of these poets was victorious with more than half his plays. Euripides won few victories, partly because his views and probably his technique were less popular in his lifetime than they afterwards became, partly because he had Sophocles to compete against. Now and then, of course, things went wrong. The *Oedipus Tyrannus* of Sophocles was defeated by the plays of Philokles, and Euripides was placed below Xenokles (in 415, the year of the *Troades*) and Nikomachos, who is otherwise unknown.[1] But we know nothing of the other plays produced by Sophocles and Euripides on these occasions, nor about the way in which the choregos or the chorus and actors discharged their functions. Although there may have occasionally been verdicts due to intimidation by the audience or by powerful persons,[2] Plato speaks in the *Laws*[3] as if the undue influence of the crowd had only recently become serious, and the instances of corruption mentioned by the orators also belong to the fourth century. Aristophanes[4] suggests that a poet's chances were affected by the order in which competitors had to appear. This was determined by lot, and the first place was regarded as the least and the last as the most advantageous.

37. Besides the plays or groups of plays entered for competition the festival was enlarged in the fourth century B.C., as inscriptions show,[5] by the performance of an old tragedy from 386 B.C. onwards, and of an old comedy from 339 B.C. (Whether these performances took place regularly before 341 B.C. in the case of tragedy and 311 B.C. in that of comedy the evidence does not suffice to show.) In the fifth century the only performances of old plays (with an exception to be noticed) were presentations of unsuccessful plays in a revised form—of comedies perhaps more frequently than of tragedies, though Euripides certainly

[1] Suid. s.v. Νικόμαχος . . . παραδόξως Εὐριπίδην καὶ Θέογνιν ἐνίκησε.
[2] See above, p. 97. On the taste and influence of the audience see below, ch. vi.
[3] Probably composed after 360 B.C. See 700 c–701 a (especially 700 c) and 659 a–c, and above, p. 98.
[4] *Ekkl.* 1158 ff.
[5] See above, p. 73.

revised and re-produced his *Hippolytus*, and possibly other plays.[1]
But the fact that two forms of a play were known does not
necessarily mean that both were performed at the City Dionysia,
as the programmes of the Rural Dionysia may often have included re-productions, in their original or in revised forms, of
plays which had appeared at the greater festival.[2] To the
memory of Aeschylus was accorded the singular honour of a
decree that a competitor who offered his plays was to be chosen
as one of the three competitors in the contest at the Dionysia,[3]
but this is quite a different thing from the practice introduced
in the fourth century, when it is evident that plays of Sophocles
and Euripides might be re-produced, and that the text of them
was liable to be tampered with by the actors who produced
them, so that Lycurgus passed a law to check this practice.[4] In
341 B.C. the old tragedy produced (by the famous actor Neoptolemus) was the *Iphigeneia* of Euripides; in the next year the
same actor produced Euripides' *Orestes*. We hear also,[5] apart
from inscriptions, of performances of a number of plays of
Sophocles, and of the *Kresphontes*, *Hecuba*, and *Oinomaos* of Euripides. In all these records some distinguished actor—Polos or
Theodoros or Aristodemos or Andronikos—is spoken of as
having 'acted the play', and in some of them, as Demosthenes
unkindly suggests, Aeschines failed badly. Polos seems to have
distinguished himself as protagonist in plays of Sophocles, Theodoros in the *Oinomaos* and *Hecuba* of Euripides. The only actor
who is recorded as having ventured upon Aeschylus at this
period was Likymnios, who according to Alkiphron defeated his

---

[1] Arg. Eur. *Hippolyt.* There were said to have been two editions of the *Autolycus* and the
Phrixus—but the evidence (see Nauck, *Fragm. Trag.*[2], pp. 441, 627) is not perfectly satisfactory—
and also of the Δημυνίαι of Sophocles (ibid., p. 215).

[2] It would not be safe to draw any inference as to competitions of actors with single plays
from the dream of Thrasyllus before the battle of Arginusae (Diod. Sic. xiii. 97) that he and
his colleagues as generals were acting the *Phoenissae* of Euripides in the theatre at Athens
in competition with the hostile generals who were performing the *Supplices*. But from Athen.
584 d it seems that Andronicus (fourth century) had been successful in a contest in acting
the *Epigonoi* (? of Aeschylus or Sophocles), and the story of Likymnios in Alkiphron (see
below), alluding to his defeat of two rivals in acting Aeschylus' Πρόπομποι, even if fictitious,
shows that such a contest in acting an old play was possible. Such contests might take place
at rural festivals.

[3] See above, p. 87.

[4] See below, p. 153; Page, *Actors' Interpolations in Greek Tragedy*, pp. 2, etc., and appendix
to Vürtheim's edition of Aeschylus' *Supplices*.

[5] See Plut. *Dem.*, p. 849 a, *Fort. Alex.*, p. 333 f; Dem. *de Cor.* §§ 180, 267, *F.L.* § 246;
Aelian, *V.H.* xiv. 40; Diod. Sic. xiii. 97; Stob. *Flor.* 97. 28; Athen. xiii. 584 d; schol. on
Soph. *Ajax* 865. The subject of actors will be resumed in the following chapter.

rivals in acting Aeschylus' Πρόπομποι,[1] but the evidence of the continued popularity of Sophocles and Euripides is very striking.

38. A revision of comedies for re-production is known to have been made in several instances in the fifth century. Aristophanes' *Clouds* was certainly produced in two versions, and ancient critics knew of two plays produced by him called Εἰρήνη, but were uncertain whether they were the same or not.[2] There was also a second Θεσμοφοριάζουσαι;[3] but the two plays called Πλοῦτος were probably independent and separated by a long interval of time. The *Frogs* was presented a second time in response to popular demand,[4] owing to the good advice contained in the parabasis, but there is no reason to suppose that it was revised. Eupolis is said to have revised his *Autolykos*,[5] and such revision seems to have been frequent in the time of the Middle and New Comedy, the second version being sometimes given a different name. Thus Diphilus revised his Συνωρίς[6] and Αἱρησιτείχης (perhaps renamed Εὐνοῦχος ἢ Στρατιώτης),[7] Antiphanes his Ἄγροικος (reproduced as Βουταλίων),[8] Alexis his *Demetrius*[9] and his Φρύξ or Φρύγιος,[10] and Menander his Ἐπίκληρος.[11] But such reproductions may have been at the Lenaia or Rural Dionysia or some other festival; they are in any case a different thing from the regular presentation of an old comedy outside the competition. In 311 B.C. the play so presented was the Θησαυρός of Anaxandrides; in the late third century an inscription records the presentation of the *Phocians* of Philemon, in 181 B.C. of the Ἀποκλειομένη of Poseidippus, in 167 of the Φάσμα of Menander, in 155 of the Φιλαθηναῖος of Philippides.

There is no evidence as to the way in which the actor and the play for re-production were selected. Some interpret the obscure references to ἀγῶνες χυτρινοί as having to do with a contest of

---

[1] He may have defeated them in competing for the privilege of producing the old play; but some scholars treat the story as fictitious (e.g. O'Connor, *Chapters on Actors*, etc., p. 105), and no actor named Likymnios is otherwise known.

[2] Argt. iii to Aristoph. *Peace*.

[3] Athen. i. 29 a; see Kock, *Com. Fragm.* i, pp. 472 ff.

[4] Argt. Aristoph. *Frogs*, quoting Dikaiarchos as authority.

[5] Galen v, p. 38 b; see Kock, op. cit., i, pp. 267–8.

[6] Athen. vi. 247 c.   [7] See Kock, op. cit., ii, p. 342.

[8] Athen. viii. 358 d.

[9] Id. xiv. 663 c. It is uncertain whether the title Δημήτριος ἢ Φιλέταιρος combines those of the two versions.   [10] Id. x. 429 e.

[11] Id. ix. 373 c; Harpokr. 139. 25. The remark of Athenaeus (374 c) that Anaxandrides destroyed his unsuccessful plays instead of revising them implies that revision was a common practice.

comic actors held at the time of the Anthesteria, to determine which should produce the old comedy at the next Dionysia, but we have already seen that there are serious difficulties in the way of this interpretation.[1]

APPENDIX TO CHAPTER II

THIS appendix contains a transcript of practically all the inscriptions bearing on the Dionysia and Lenaia, with introductions and notes where necessary, and concludes with a summary of the main chronological conclusions.

Introduction to I.G. *ii². 2318*

Since the inscription was printed in the *Corpus* some changes have been necessitated or suggested by the discovery of a new fragment, published by Capps in *Hesperia*, xii (1943), pp. 1 ff., and the transcription given below embodies these alterations.

The extant remains consist of parts of thirteen columns; these were preceded by two or three others now lost (col. vi and col. x are also missing); the first extant column begins with part of the record for 473–472 B.C., and the record goes down in a fragmentary form to 329–328 B.C. (in col. xiii). Under each year were included, in an unvarying order, the archon's name; the names of the victorious tribe in the boys' dithyrambic contest and of its choregos (but not the name of the poet); next, those of the victorious tribe and choregos in the men's contest; then the names of the victorious choregos and poet in comedy; and finally the same for tragedy—11 lines for each year until 450–449 B.C., when the name of the victorious tragic actor was added, making 12 lines. Cols. i and ii each consisted of 140 lines, cols. iii to ix of 141. (Capps's calculations in *Hesperia*, loc. cit., are virtually convincing.) In the year 406–405 some disturbance was caused by the introduction of synchoregia, necessitating 2 lines extra for that year; but if Capps's calculation (ibid., p. 8) is right, as it seems to be (see above, p. 88), this expedient was not carried beyond that year. Most of the catalogue appears to have been inscribed by the same hand, very soon after 346 B.C.; on the attribution of the later fragments to the same or different hands the experts are not agreed. Col. xi seems to have contained 153 lines, by means of crowding in the lower part of the column, while in the lower part of col. xii the lines were placed at longer intervals. The record probably ended at or before the time of the institution of the agonothetes (about 308 B.C.).

The question of the date of the beginning of the record is bound up with the problem of the heading. So far as this is preserved it runs over

[1] See above, p. 15.

the top of cols. i to iv, and reads (with undoubted restorations) [ΠΡΩ]ΤΟΝ ΚΩΜΟΙ ΗΣΑΝ Τ[ΩΙ ΔΙΟΝΥΣ]ΩΙ ΤΡΑΓΩΙΔΟΙ Δ[. . .

It seems possible that we have here part of a relative clause such as ἀφ' οὗ or ἐφ' οὗ πρῶτον κῶμοι ἦσαν τῷ Διονύσῳ, followed by the beginning of a main clause, which Capps conjectures to have run τραγῳδοὶ δημοτελεῖς . . . ἀγωνίσαντες ἐν ἄστει οἵδε νενικήκασιν (δημοτελεῖς being supported, as the appellation of a public festival, by Thucyd. ii. 15, and Plato, *Laws* xi. 935 b, etc.). The difficulty of this is that the inscription contains so much more than the names of victorious tragic poets, and Capps's solution does not seem at all certain. As regards the first part of the heading, up to about 18 letters are needed if there were two lost columns, or up to about 27 if there were three. It is possible, moreover, that the first part was not a relative clause at all, but something like ἐπὶ . . . ἄρχοντος πρῶτον κῶμοι ἦσαν τῷ Διονύσῳ, continuing τραγῳδοὶ δὲ ἐπὶ . . . κωμῳδοὶ δὲ ἐπὶ Τελεσίνου (487/6 B.C.), following a chronological order. This would be possible, whether κῶμοι referred to the festival as a whole (as instituted by the State), as is commonly assumed, or (as has been more recently urged) specifically to dithyrambs. Marx, Kirchner, and others believe that κῶμος was specially applied to the χοροὶ ἀνδρῶν, on the strength of (1) Pindar, *Pyth.* v. 22 δέδεξαι τόνδε κῶμον ἀνέρων (but ἀνέρων is here explicitly mentioned), and (2) the Law of Euegoros in Dem. *in Meid.* § 10 τοῖς ἐν ἄστει Διονυσίοις ἡ πομπὴ καὶ οἱ παῖδες καὶ ὁ κῶμος καὶ οἱ κωμῳδοὶ καὶ οἱ τραγῳδοί, where, if κῶμος = χοροὶ ἀνδρῶν, the order is that of this inscription. The contest of men's choruses may have been the only 'event' of the festival at first, and so have been called by the more general name of κῶμος, but when the boys' choruses were added, though they were distinctly spoken of as οἱ παῖδες, they may have been popularly included with the men's choruses under the name κῶμοι. (The lawgiver Euegoros is supposed to have reverted to the original use of κῶμος = χοροὶ ἀνδρῶν; but this is not very convincing, and many scholars suppose that after καὶ οἱ παῖδες in the law the words καὶ οἱ ἄνδρες may have dropped out.)

But if κῶμοι means dithyrambs generally, or men's choruses then, it might be argued, the record must have gone back to about 509 B.C., since the Parian Marble (Ep. 46) assigns to the archonship of Lysagoras (otherwise unknown) in a year which is either 510–509 or 509–508 B.C. the first contests of χοροὶ ἀνδρῶν, in which the victor was Hypodikos of Chalcis. (Some scholars suppose that the composer or stone-mason had mistakenly written Lysagoras for Isagoras who was archon in 508–507 B.C., the year of the reforms of Kleisthenes; there seems no justification for this. See Cadoux in *J.H.S.* lxviii (1948), p. 113.) But a record going back to that time would hardly fill three columns unless it began with some preliminary matter. The column next before the extant col. i would have included 6 lines of the year 473–472 at the foot, and 2 lines of 486–485 at the head. The column before that would have contained, at the foot, 9 lines of 486–485, and 11 lines of 487–486—the year in which contests in comedy were probably introduced. Capps[1] and Wilhelm reconstruct the whole column so as to make it begin in 502/1 or thereabouts, supposing that the festival was reorganized and the choregic system introduced at that time, and it is perhaps more probable that this was the beginning of the record than that there was another column to the left, going back to about 509 and only partly filled. If so, the contests before 502–501 B.C. would have been held under some less democratic system than that initiated in 502/1. But the dates of the introduction of the boys' contest and the competition in tragedy remain unknown, and without fresh information there can be no certainty as to the date when the record began.

There is a difference of opinion as to the relation of this inscription to the work of Aristotle entitled Νῖκαι Διονυσιακαὶ ἀστικαὶ καὶ Ληναϊκαί. (So the title is given by Hesychius. In Diog. Laert. v. 26 it appears as Νῖκαι Διονυσιακαὶ αʹ, i.e. a single book.) But as we have no knowledge of this work except the title, the problem is insoluble.[2] On the whole, the balance of probability is against connecting the two. The inscription in its original form (without the later additions) seems to have been compiled about 346 B.C. or within a few years of that date, and it must, of course, have been copied from official records in Athens; but it seems certain that Aristotle was not in Athens, at least not for any length of time, in the years 348–334 B.C. (Whether or not the inscription is in any way connected with the activities of Lycurgus in regard to the drama can only be conjectured.) The inscription itself reads like a transcript of an official record. It may have been continued down to the institution of an agonothetes (about 309) or may (as Reisch thinks) have ended at least by 319 B.C.

Reisch thinks that the wall or walls on which the record must have been inscribed may have been a temple-like structure in the eastern parodos of the Theatre of Dionysus, erected as part of the Lycurgean reconstruction. Against this is the fact to which Kirchner calls attention in *I.G.* ii. 2², p. 659, that all the fragments, except one of the latest, were

---

[1] See especially *Hesperia*, xii, p. 10.

[2] See especially on one side Reisch in Pauly–W. v, cols. 398 ff., and *Zeitschr. f. öster. Gymn.* 312 ff.; on the other Körte, *Class. Philol.* i (1906), pp. 391 ff. (with whom the view expressed in the text is most in agreement), and Oellacher, *Wiener Stud.* xxxviii (1916), pp. 81 ff. There is a good discussion in Flickinger, *Greek Theater*, ch. ix. There seems to be more probability that the Victors' Lists, *I.G.* ii². 2325, were based on Aristotle's Νῖκαι, but this also is no more than conjecture. Other important contributions to the discussion of the inscriptions are those of Wilamowitz in *Gött. gel. Anz.* 1906, pp. 617 ff.; Körte, *Rhein. Mus.* lx (1905), pp. 425–47; Jachmann, *de Aristotelis didascaliis* (1909); and Wilhelm's masterly survey of the whole field in his *Urkunden dramatischer Aufführungen* (1906) is as indispensable as ever.

found on the *northern* slope of the Acropolis; it is unlikely that the whole structure, or all its fragments, should have been transferred from south to north, and it seems more likely that the monument was originally placed in or near the Agora, perhaps among other records compiled by order of the archons and kept in their custody.

I.G. ii². 2318 ('*Fasti*')

The heading so far as extant ran (in a larger script) over the first four extant columns: viz. ΤΟΝ ΚΩΜΟΙ ΗΣΑΝ Τ[ΩΙ ΔΙΟΝΥΣ]ΩΙ ΤΡΑΓΩΙ-ΔΟΙ Δ[

Col. i	Col. ii	Col. iii
[473–472]	[460–459]	[448–447]
Ξε]νοκλείδης ἐχορήγε	Πανδιονί[ς ἀνδρῶν	ων] Λαμπτρ: ἐχορήγε
Μ]άγνης ἐδίδασκεν	Κλεαίνετ[ος ἐχορήγει	Σοφοκ]λῆς ἐδίδασκεν
τραγωιδῶν	κωμωιδῶ[ν	ὑποκριτὴς Ἡρ]ακλείδης
Περικλῆς Χολαρ: ἐχορή	Θαρ[ρίας ἐχορήγει	['Επὶ Τιμαρχίδου] [447–446]
Αἰσχύλος ἐ[δίδασκε		
['Επὶ Χάρητος] [472–471]	[τραγωιδῶν]	'Ε[ρεχθηὶς ἀνδρῶν
	]: ἐχορή	Βίω[ν ἐχορήγει
	] ἐδίδασκεν	κωμ[ωιδῶν
	['Επὶ Φιλ]οκλέους [459–458]	Ἀνδ[
	Οἰν]ηὶς παίδων	Καλ[λίας ἐδίδασκεν
	Δημόδοκος ἐχορήγει	τρα[γωιδῶν
ἐχ]ορήγει	Ἱπποθωντὶς ἀνδρῶν	Θαλ[
ἐδίδ]ασκεν	Εὐκτήμων Ἐλευ: ἐχορή	Κα[ρκίνος ἐδίδασκε
	κωμωιδῶν	ὑπ[οκριτὴς
ἐχ]ορήγει	Εὐρυκλείδης ἐχορήγει	'Επ]ὶ Καλλιμάχου [446–445]
Πολυφράσμω]ν ἐδίδασ	Εὐφρόνιος ἐδίδασκε	
['Επὶ Πραξιέργο]υ [471–470]	τραγωιδῶν	
πα]ίδων	Ξενοκλῆς Ἀφιδνα: ἐχορή	
ἐχο]ρήγει	Αἰσχύλος ἐδίδασκεν	
ἀνδρ]ῶν	'Επὶ Ἄβρωνος [458–457]	
ἐχ]ορήγ	'Ερεχθηὶς παίδων	
	Χαρίας Ἀγρυλῆ: ἐχορή	
	Λεοντὶς ἀνδρῶν	
	Δεινόστρατος ἐχο[ρήγ	
	κωμωιδῶν	
	ἐχο]ρήγ[ει	
['Επὶ Δημοτίωνος] [470–469]	[τραγωιδῶν]	
		['Επὶ Λυσιμαχίδου] [445–444]
	['Επὶ Μνησιθείδου] [457–456]	

Col. iv	Col. v	Col. vi (missing)
[436–435]	[424–423]	[412–411]
'Ισοκράτη[ς ἐχορήγει		['Επὶ Καλλίου]
Ἕρμιππος [ἐδίδασκεν		
τραγωιδ[ῶν		
Νίκων Ἀ[		
'Ιοφῶν ἐ[δίδασκεν		
ὑποκ]ρι[τὴς		
['Επὶ Ἀντιοχίδου] [435–434]		

Col. iv (cont.)	Col. v (cont.)	Col. vi (cont.) (missing)
	['Επὶ Ἀμεινίου] [423–422]	
		['Επὶ Θεοπόμπου] [411–410]
	Παια[νι ἐχορήγ Κάνθαρ]ος ἐδί[δασκεν τραγ]ωιδῶν	
['Επὶ Κράτητος] [434–433]	]ν Παιανιε[ὺς : ἐχορ Με]νεκράτης ἐδί[δασκε ὑπ]οκριτὴς Μυνν[ία]κος 'Επ]ὶ Ἀλκαίου [422–421] 'Ιπποθωντὶς παίδων Ἀρίσταρχος Δεκε : ἐχορή Αἰαντὶς ἀνδρῶν	
	Δημοσθένης ἐχορήγει κ]ωμωιδῶ[ν	['Επὶ Γλαυκίππου] [410–409]
	ἐχο]ρήγ [Εὔπολις ἐδίδασκεν]	
['Επὶ Ἀψεύδους] [433–432]		

Col. vii	Col. viii	Col. ix
[401–400]		
		['Επὶ Καλλίου] [377–376]
['Επὶ Λάχητος] [400–399]		
	['Επὶ Πυργίωνος] [388–387]	
	Ἀρα]ρὼς ἐδ[ίδασκ]εν τραγωιδ[ῶν	['Επὶ Χαρισάνδρου] [376–375]
ὑποκριτὴς Νικόστρ]ατος 'Επὶ Ἀριστοκράτου]s [399–398] παίδω]ν	Ἀριστοκράτ[ης] Φαληρ : [ἐχορ Σο]φοκλῆς ἐδίδασκεν ὑποκριτὴς Κλέανδρο[s	[ἰς παίδων] [ἐχορήγει] [ἰς ἀνδρῶν]
]ἐχορ	'Επὶ Θεοδότου [387–386]	χος Ἀ[. . . ἐχορήγει κω]μωιδῶν
]ε : ἐχορή	παλαιὸν δρᾶμα πρῶτο[ν παρεδίδαξαν οἱ τραγ[ωιδοί	. . . γνητος [ἐχορήγει Ἀνα]ξανδρί[δης ἐδίδασκεν
]ἐχορή ἐδίδα]σκεν	Ἀντιοχὶς παίδων Εὐηγέτης Παλλη : ἐχο[ρήγ Αἰγηὶς ἀνδρῶν Ἴασος Κολλυ : ἐχορήγ[ει	τρα]γωιδῶν . . . γένης [ἐχορήγει Σο]φοκλῆς [ἐδίδασκεν ὑπ]οκριτ[ὴς 'Επὶ 'Ι]ππο[δάμαντος [375–374]
['Επὶ Εὐθυκλέους] [398–397]		

I.G. ii². 2318 (*cont.*)

Column x is missing. The following fragments remain of cols. xi–xiii. (The lines in this transcript are not printed to correspond for these columns as they are for cols. i–ix.)

Col. xi

.... ιλ: [ἐχορήγει   [*348–347*]
Ἄ]λεξις ἐδ[ίδασκε
τραγωιδῶν
Κλ]εόμαχος Ἀχα[ρν : ἐχορή
Ἀ]στυδάμας ἐδίδασκε
ὑ]ποκριτὴς Θ[ετταλός
'Ε]πὶ Θεμιστο[κλέους   [*347–346*]
'Ερεχθηὶς π[αίδων
Διονυσ[ἐχορήγει
Ἀ]κ[αμαντὶς ἀνδρῶν
(53 lines missing)

ἐκ Κερ]αμ : ἐχορή   [*343–342*]
ἐ]δίδασκε
ὑποκριτὴς Ἀ]θηνόδωρος
'Επὶ Σωσιγένο]υς   [*342–341*]
Αἰγηὶς παίδ]ων
Εὐθύδημος Δι]ομε[εὺς ἐχορ]ήγει
'Ιπποθωντὶς] ἀνδρῶν
...... ἐκ Κοί]λης ἐχορή
[κωμωιδῶν]
.... Εὐω]νυ : [ἐχορή
[ἐ]δίδασκε]
[τραγωιδῶν]
.... ἐχ]ορ[ήγει
[Ἀστυδάμας ἐδίδασκε]
[ὑποκριτὴς Νεοπτόλεμος]

Col. xii

τρ]αγωιδῶν   [*341–340*]
Ἀρρενείδης Πα[ια]νι: ἐχο
Ἀστυδάμας ἐδίδ[ασκεν
ὑποκριτὴς Θετ[τα]λός
'Ε]πὶ Θεοφράστο[υ   [*340–339*]
πα]λαιὸν δρᾶμ[α πρ]ῶτο[ν
π]αρεδίδαξα[ν οἱ] κ[ω]μ[ωιδοί
Ἀ]ντιοχὶς παί[δων
(80 lines missing)

'Επὶ] Νι[κοκράτους   [*334–333*]
Κεκροπ[ὶς παίδων
Διόφαν[τος Ἀλαιεὺς ἐχο
Κεκροπὶς [ἀνδρῶν
'Ονήτωρ [ἐχο
κω[μ]ωιδ[ῶν
Διοπεί[θης .... ἐχο
τραγωιδ[ῶν]
Φρ[α? ..... ἐχο
(13 lines missing)

[ὑποκριτὴς] Νικ[όστρατος]   [*332–331*]
'Ε]πὶ Ἀριστοφάνους   [*331–330*]
Οἰνη[ὶς] παί[δων
Νικόστρατος Ἀ[χ]αρν[εὺς ἐχο
'Ιπποθωντὶς ἀνδρ[ῶν
Ἄρχιππος Πειραιε[ὺς ἐχο
[κωμωιδῶν]
.... ο[ς] Κηφισ[ιεὺς ἐχο
.... ἐδ]ί[δασκε

Col. xiii

[κωμωιδῶν]   [*330–329*]
..... ἐ]κ Κε[ραμέων
ἐ]χορήγ[ει
Θεόφιλος ἐδίδ[ασκεν
τραγωιδῶν
Θη]ραμένης Κηφισι
ἐχορήγ]ει
Τιμοκ]λῆς ἐδίδα[σκεν
ὑπο]κριτὴς
Ἀθηνόδωρος
'Επὶ Κηφισοφῶντος   [*329–328*]
'Ι]ππ[ο]θωντὶς παί[δων

Unplaced Fragments
Insignificant, except part of *k*.
[ἀνδρῶν]
Πολυά[ρατος? ... ἐχορήγει
κωμ[ωιδῶν

Notes on details of *I.G.* ii². 2318

Col. i. Αἰσχύλος ἐδίδασκε, 473–472 B.C. Cf. Argt. Aesch. *Pers.* ἐπὶ Μένωνος τραγῳδῶν Αἰσχύλος ἐνίκα Φινεῖ, Πέρσαις, Γλαύκῳ, Προμηθεῖ. Πολυφράσμω]ν, suggested by Lipsius.

Col. ii. Εὐφρόνιος ἐδίδασκε, 459–458 B.C. Cf. *I.G.* ii². 2325. Ξενοκλῆς Ἀφιδναῖος, 459–458 B.C. Cf. Argt. Aesch. *Agam.* ἐδιδάχθη τὸ δρᾶμα ἐπὶ ἄρχοντος Φιλοκλέους 'Ολυμπιάδι πῃ ἔτει β' πρῶτος Αἰσχύλος Ἀγαμέμνονι, Χοηφόροις, Εὐμενίσι, Πρωτεῖ σατυρικῷ, ἐχορήγει Ξενοκλῆς Ἀφιδναῖος.

Col. iii. Καλλίας ἐδίδασκεν. Cf. *I.G.* ii². 2325, and Capps, *Am. J. Phil.* 1899, p. 396.

Κα[ρκίνος. After Lipsius.

Col. iv. "Ερμιππος. Cf. *I.G.* ii². 2325, and Capps, *Hesperia*, xii, p. 3. This was his first victory (436–435 B.C.).

'Ιοφῶν, son of Sophocles. He was second in 429–428 B.C. (Argt. Eur. *Hippolytus*).

Col. v. Κάνθαρ]ος. Cf. Oellacher, op. cit., p. 116, and *I.G.* ii². 2325.

Μυνν[ίσ]κος. Cf. *I.G.* ii². 2325; O'Connor, *Hist. of Actors*, p. 118. He acted for Aeschylus.

Δημοσθένης. The general in the Peloponnesian War.

Col. vii. Νικόστρ]ατος. Cf. ii². 2325; O'Connor, p. 122.

Col. viii. Ἀρα]ρώς, son of Aristophanes, who after 388 B.C. brought out his father's Κώκαλος and Αἰολοσίκων; but the present entry must refer to a play of his own; cf. Oellacher, op. cit., pp. 101, 130. Capps (*Am. J. Phil.* 1907, pp. 89 ff., 181 ff.; cf. *Hesperia*, xii, p. 3) really disproves the view that any of these inscriptions entered the name of the nominal producer rather than of the victorious poet.

Σο]φοκλῆς ἐδίδασκεν, 388–387 B.C., son of Ariston the son of the great Sophocles; began to exhibit in 397–396 B.C. (Diod. XIV. liii. 6). Cf. also col. ix (376–375 B.C.).

Col. ix. Ἀναξανδρίδης ἐδίδασκεν, 376–375 B.C. His first victory at the Dionysia was in 376 B.C. (*Marm. Par.* Ep. 70).

Col. xi. Ἀστυδάμας ἐδίδασκε, 348–347 B.C., i.e. Astydamas the younger, whose *Parthenopaeus* and *Lycaon* were victorious in 341–340 B.C., *I.G.* ii². 2320. Cf. Capps, *Am. J. Phil.* (1900), 41; Wilamowitz, *Aischylos-interpretationen*, 1914. The name is supplied below (342–341 B.C.) by Capps, *Introd. of Comedy to City Dionysia*, p. 18, with the approval of Wilhelm.

Θετταλός. Cf. O'Connor, p. 103.

Col. xii. Νικόστρατος, 332–331 B.C. Cf. *I.G.* ii². 2320; O'Connor, p. 123.

Col. xiii. Τιμο]κλῆς ἐδίδασκεν, 330–329 B.C. Name completed on suggestion of Körte. On distinctness of Timokles tragic and T. comic poet, *vide* Th. Wagner, *Symbolarum . . . capita quattuor*; Körte, *B.Ph.W.* 1906, col. 903.

Unplaced. Πολυάρατος. Name suggested by Wilhelm, *Urkunden*, pp. 31, 33; he was a trierarch at about the end of the fifth or beginning of the fourth century B.C.

Introduction to I.G. ii². 2319–23

These inscriptions all form part of a record probably engraved on the inner walls of a square building, on the Ionic epistyle or architrave of which the lists of victors (*I.G.* ii². 2325) were inscribed in columns of 17 lines each. The record was arranged in the order: (1) tragedies at Dionysia, (2) comedies at Dionysia, (3) comedies at Lenaia, (4) tragedies at Lenaia. (The allocation of Nos. 2321 and 2322 to 'comedies at Lenaia' is practically certain.) The record of comedies at the Lenaia ended a very few years after 288 B.C., and it is not likely that the record of tragedies at the Lenaia continued longer; the whole quadripartite record in its original form was probably inscribed at about this date.

Reisch believes that the monument was the work of the agonothetes of 279–278 B.C., and that the dedicatory inscription survives in *I.G.* ii². 1193 as restored by Wilhelm (*Urkunden*, p. 90):

δ]ῶρον [*Φ*]ρεά[ρ]ριος [Διονύ]σωι ἀ[ν]έθηκεν
. . . καὶ ἀγω]νοθέτης [γενόμενος· Ἀναξ]ικράτης ἦρχεν.

But the list of victorious actors in comedy at the Lenaia continues until far down in the third century B.C., and that of victorious comic poets until 150 B.C., and as there is no ground for the suggestion, made by Reisch, that their victories were won with old plays, it must be inferred that contests in comedy at the Lenaia went on for more than a century after the main didaskalic inscription was erected. The contests in comedy at the Dionysia likewise continued, and the record of these (No. 2323) seems to have been made up at intervals by different hands and with some gaps. It is generally assumed that so far as the record refers to the time before the Διδασκαλίαι of Aristotle (Diog. Laert. v. 26), it was a copy of that work, or at least followed it closely, though omitting the part dealing with dithyramb, and that in continuing Aristotle's work it followed the same plan. It includes the names of the actors of each play and of the victorious actor, but does not mention the choregoi; the satyric play and the old plays which after certain dates the festival included are recorded.

I.G. ii². 2319–23 (Διδασκαλίαι)

No. 2320 (= ii. 973)

Tragedies at Dionysia

342/1 ['Επὶ Σωσιγένους σατυρι]
. . . .
παλαι]ᾶι Νε[οπτόλεμος
'Ιφιγε]νείαι Εὐρ[ιπ]ίδο[υ
πον]: Ἀστυδάμας
Ἀχι]λλεῖ ὑπε: Θετταλός
Ἀθάμαντι ὑπε: Νεοπτόλ[εμος

Ἀν]τιγόνηι ὑπε: Ἀθηνόδω[ρος
Εὐ]άρετος δ[εὐ:] Τεύκρωι
ὑπ]ε: Ἀθηνόδωρος
Ἀχι]λλεῖ ὑ[πε]: Θετταλός
. . . ε]ι ὑπ[ε: Ν]εοπτόλεμος
Ἀφαρεὺς] τρί: Πελιάσιν
ὑπε: Νεοππτ]όλεμος
'Ορέστηι [ὑπε: Ἀθηνόδωρος
Αὔγηι ὑπε: Θεττα[λός
ὑπο: Νεοπτόλεμος ἐνίκ[α

Appendix to Chapter II

111

No. 2320 (cont.)

341/0 Ἐπὶ Νικομάχου σατυρι
Τιμοκλῆς Λυκούργῳ
παλαιᾶι: Νεοπτόλεμ[ος
Ὀρέστηι Εὐριπίδο
ποη: Ἀστυδάμας
Παρθενοπαίωι ὑπε: Θετ[ταλός
Λυκά]ονι ὑπε: Νεοπτόλε[μος
Τιμο]κλῆς δεύ: Φρίξωι
ὑπε:] Θετταλός
Οἰδί]ποδι ὑπε: Νεοπτόλ[εμος
Εὐάρ]ετος τρί
Ἀλκ]μέ[ων]ι: ὑπε: Θεττα[λός
... λ]ηι ὑπε: Νεοπτό[λεμος
ὑπο Θ]ετταλὸς ἐνίκα

340/39 ἐπὶ Θεο]φράστου σα[τυρι
.... Φορκίσ[ι
παλαιᾶι ?Νικ]όστρ[ατος
.... Εὐ]ριπί[δου
ποη:........]ο

No. 2319 (= ii. 972), Col. ii

Tragedies at Lenaia

ειρ
ὑπε
ὑπο [.... ἐνίκα
420/19 Ἐπὶ Ἀ[στυφίλου ....
Ἀγα[μέμνονι
ὑπε
Ἡρα[κλείδης? δευ:
Θησῆ[ι
ὑπε
ὑπο
419/18 Ἐπὶ Ἀρχ[ίου
Τυροῖ Τι
ὑπε: Λυσικράτ[ης
Καλλίστρατος [δευ:
Ἀμφιλόχῳ Ἰξίο[νι

ὑπε: Καλλιππίδ[ης
ὑπ]ο: Καλλιππίδ[ης] ἐνίκα
418/17 Ἐπ' Ἀ]ντιφ[ῶ]ντος Σ ...

No. 2321 (= ii. 974)

Comedies at Lenaia (? 5th cent.)

......ηταις
['Επὶ ....]
... ς: Ἀριστοφ[άνης
... Ὀδομ]αντοπρέσ[βεσι?
ὑπο ... ἐ]νίκα
Ἐπὶ ... ο]υ

No. 2322 (= ii. 974 b)

Comedies at Lenaia? (4th cent.)

Ἄλεξις: [δεύ:
ὑπε: Καλλ
Ἡρακλεί[δης τρί
Θεόφιλο[ς Εὔβουλος? τέ:
Ναυ]σι[κάαι? ὑπε

No. 2319 (= ii. 972), Col. i

Comedies at Lenaia (3rd cent.)

.... τέ:] Λοτιδι (?)
ὑπε: Ἀριστόμα]χος
]ης πέμ: Ἀνασωιζομέν
ὑπε: Ἀντ]ιφάνης
ὑπο: Ἱερ]ώνυμος ἐνίκα
289/8 Ἐπὶ Δι]οτίμου Σίμυλος
Ἐφε]σίαι: ὑπε Ἀριστόμαχος
Διόδωρος: δεύ: Νεκρῶι
ὑπε Ἀριστόμαχος
Διόδωρος τρί Μαινομένωι
ὑπε Κηφίσιος
Φο]ινικ[ίδ]ης τέ: Ποητεῖ
ὑπε Ἀντιφάν]ης (?).

No. 2323 a (= ii. 974 c)

Comedies at Dionysia (4th cent.)

ὑπε: Ἀσκληπιόδ]ωρο[ς
Μένανδρος] πέμ: Ἡνιόχωι
ὑπε: Κάλ]λιππος πρεσβύτ
ὑπο: Κάλλι]ππος νεώ: ἐνικ
312/11 ἐπὶ Πολέμ]ωνος παλαιᾶι
...... Θ]ησαυρῶι Ἀνάξαν
ποη: Φιλιπ]πίδης Μύστιδι
ὑπε: Ἀσκ]ληπιόδωρος
Νικόστ]ρατος δεύ
..... οσκόπωι

ἐ[πὶ ..... παλαιᾶι
ι
γ
μ

¹ Adaeus, who was mentioned in a comedy of Herakleides, died 353 B.C. Theophilus was victor in 329 B.C.

No. 2323 a (*cont.*)

ὑπε : Κ]άλλιππος νεώτε	
Ἀμεινί]ας τρι : Ἀπολειπούσει	φ
οὗτος ἔ]φηβος ὢν ἐνεμήθη[1]	τ
ὑπε : Ἀσκ]ληπιόδωρος	Στ[τέ :
Θεόφιλο]s(?) τέ : Παγκρατιασ	ὑπ[ε
ὑπε : . . . . ιπ]πος	Νι[κόστρατος? πέμ
. . . . πέμ : Π]αιδίωι	ύ[πε
[ὑπε:]	ύ[πο : ἐνίκα
ὑπο : Ἀσκληπιόδωρο]s ἐνίκ[α	[ἐπὶ]

[*Note.* Some lines which are too fragmentary to be informative are omitted.]

No. 2323 (= ii. 975)

Comedies at Dionysia

Col. i (*c. 215–210 B.C.*)

'Ερχιεῦσιν
[ὑπε Νικόδη]μος
[ἐπὶ . . . .] οὐκ ἐγένετο
[ἐπὶ . . . . . . π]αλαιᾶι
. . . . Φωκεῦσι Φιλή
[ποη Ἀριστο]κράτης Ἀπε
. . . . ύ]πε Νικόδημος
. . . . Ἀ]νεψιοῖς
[ὑπε   ]os
[Πον]ήρᾳ
[ὑπε   ]της
[. . . 'Εμπ]όρωι
[ὑπε   ]ης
. . . . . ωι
[ὑπε   ]ης
[Ἀγν]οοῦντι

Col. ii (some omissions at beginning)

Τιμόθ[εος]
ὑπε Π
Κλέο
ὑπε
'Ολυ[μπ
            (3 lines omitted)
. . . . . Συν]εφήβοις
ὑπε
ὑπο . . .]ἐνίκα
c. 200 to 195 B.C.
['Επὶ . . . . οὐ]κ ἐγένετο
['Επὶ   ο]υ παλαιᾶι
[Μισογ]ύνει Μενάνδρου
[ποη   ]νης Ἀδελφαῖς
ὑπε   κ]ος
. . . . Δακτυλίωι
ὑπε   ]ων
. . . . Ἀθην[αίωι

Col. ii or Col. v

. . . . Προγαμοῦντι
ὑπε . . . . . .]ων
. . . . πρ]εσβύτερος τεθ
παρακαταθ]ήκει
ὑπε . . . .]μαχος

Col. iii

Τ]ι[μόστρα]τος Λυ[τρουμένωι
ὑπε [Δ]ιογείτων
ὑπο Κράτης ἐνίκα
c. 188–187
'Επὶ Συμμάχου οὐκ ἐγ[ένετο
c. 187–186
'Επὶ Θεοξένου οὐκ [ἐγένετο]
c. 186–185
'Επὶ Ζωπύρου [παλαιᾶι
'Εράτων Μεγ[
ποη Λαί[νης . . .
            (some lines omitted)
c. 184–183
ὑπε 'Ονή]σιμ[ο]s
    Κρίτων 'Εφεσίοις
ὑπε Σώφιλος
Παράμονος Ναυαγῶι
ὑπε 'Ονήσιμος
Τιμόστρατος Φιλοικείωι
ὑπε Καλλίστρατος
Σωγένης Φιλοδεσπότωι
ὑπε 'Εκαταῖος
Φιλήμων νεώ Μιλησίαι
ὑπε Κράτης
ὑπο 'Ονήσιμος ἐνίκα
183–182
'Επὶ 'Ερμογένου οὐκ ἐγένετο
182–181
'Επὶ Τιμησιάν[ακτος π]αλαιᾶι
Φιλόστρατο[s Ἀποκλε]ιομένει Ποσει
ποη[. . . .   ]κλήρωι
            (some lines omitted)
ποη

[1] Cf. Anon. *de Com.* (Kaibel, *Fragm.*, p. 9), of Menander, ἐδίδαξε δὲ πρῶτον ἔφηβος ὢν ἐπὶ Φιλοκλέους ἄρχοντος (322–321 B.C.).

Col. iii (cont.)

ὑπε Πο
’Ιόλαος
ὑπε Φ
Τιμο[Εὐ]εργετοῦντι
[ὑπε   ]
. . . Συνεξ]απατῶντι
[ὑπε   ]
[ω]ν Συντ[ρ
[ὑπε   ]ης
. . . . Συναγῶνι
ὑπε   ]ίδης
ὑπο   ξ]ένος ἐνί[κα
’Επὶ . . . . . παλαι]ᾶι Προ . .

Col. iv

[’Επὶ . . . παλαιᾶι]
. . . Μονο]τρόπωι
. . . .
ποη   Ἀν]ασωιζομ[έ
[ὑπε   ]
. . . . υμένωι
ὑπε . . . .]ος
. . . . Ἀγνοοῦντι
ὑπε Κριτόδημος
. . . . . . Ν]εμέσει
ὑπε Σίθ]νικος
Παρά]μονος Χορηγοῦντι
ὑπ]ε Μόνιμος
ὑπ]ο Κριτόδημος ἐνίκα
169–168
’Ε]πὶ Εὐνίκου οὐκ ἐγένετο
168–167
’Επὶ Ξενοκλέους παλαι[ᾶι
Μόνιμος Φάσματι Μενάνδρου
ποη Παράμονος τεθνηκὼς . . . . ις
ὑπε Δάμων
Κρίτων Αἰτωλῶι
ὑπε Μόνιμος
Βίοττος Ποητεῖ
ὑπε Δάμων
Λάμπυτος
ὑπε Κα . . . .
’Επικρ[άτης . . . .
[ὑπε   ]
[ὑπο   ἐνίκα]

167–166

[’Επὶ   ]
          (some lines lost)
[ὑπο] Εὐερ[γ . . . ἐνίκα
163/2
’Ε]πὶ ’Εράστ[ου οὐκ ἐγένετο
162/1
’Επὶ Ποσει[δωνίου οὐκ ἐγένετο
161/0
’Επὶ Ἀριστ[όλα παλαιᾶι
‘Ηρακλ . .

Col. v

ὑπε Καβεί]ριχος
’Επ]ιγέ[ν]ης Λυτρουμένῳ
ὑπε Καβείριχος
ὑπο Νικόλαος ἐνίκα
158–157
’Επὶ Ἀνθεστηρίου οὐκ ἐγένε[το
157–156
’Επὶ Καλλιστράτου οὐκ ἐγένε[το
156–155
’Επὶ Μνησιθέου παλαιᾶι
Δάμων Φιλαθηναίωι Φιλιππί[δου
πο Φιλοκλῆς Τραυματίαι
ὑπε Καλλικράτης
Χαιρίων Αὐτοῦ Καταψευδομέ[νωι
ὑπε Δάμων
Βίοττος Ἀγνοοῦντι
ὑπε Δάμων
Τιμόξενος Συγκρύπτον[τι
ὑπε Καλλικράτης
Ἀγαθοκλῆς ‘Ομονοία[ι
ὑπε Νι]κ[ό]λαος
[ὑπο   ἐνίκα]

Col. vi

ὑπ]ε Λυσίμαχος
    ακοντα
    Σαλαμινίαις
    Ἀτ]θίσιν
Φ]ίλων ἐνίκα
c. 143–142
’Επὶ   ο]ὐκ ἐγένετο
c. 142–141
[’Επὶ   οὐκ ἐγένε]το
(The record ended *c.* 120 B.C.)

I.G. *ii²*. 2325 = *ii*. 977 (*Lists of Victors*)

(Some portions which are practically uninformative are omitted in this transcript.)

Tragic Poets at Dionysia

Col. i	Col. iii
(about 10 lines missing)	(8 lines missing)
485–484 Αἰ]σχύ[λος	. . . . . ας
Εὐ]έτης Ι	Καρκί]νος ΔΙ
471–470 Πολ]υφράσμ[ων	*373–372* Ἀστ]υδάμας ΓΙΙ[-?
Νόθ]ιππος Ι	Θεο]δέκτας ΓΙΙ
469–468 Σοφ]οκλῆς ΔΓΙΙΙ	Ἀφα]ρεύς ΙΙ
. . . . τος ΙΙ[-?	. . . . ω]ν ΙΙ
c. 460 Ἀριστ]ίας	

Tragic Actors at Dionysia

Col. i	Col. ii (early 4th cent.)
ὑποκριτῶν τρ[αγικῶν	(4 lines missing)
450–449 Ἡρακλεί[δης	Νι
Νικόμαχο[ς	Θε
Μυ[ν]νίσκος	Ἀ]ς
Σαώνδας [Ι]	Ἀθη
Ἄνδρων ΙΙ	Ἀρι[στ
Χ]αι[ρ]έστρατος Ι	
Μενεκ]ράτης ΙΙΙ	Col. iii (late 4th cent.)
Λεπ]τίν[ης	Αἰσχ]ύλ[ος
	Πλ]εισθένης
	Γο]ργοσθένης ΙΙ
	Ἐπα]μείνων ΙΙ

Comic Poets at Dionysia

Col. i	Col. ii
[ἀστικαὶ ποιητῶν	Τηλεκλεί]δης ΙΙΙ
[κωμικῶν	. . . .]ς Ι
487–486 [Χιωνίδης]	. . .
. . . .	. . .
. . . .	*438–437* Φερ[εκράτης
. . . .]ς Ι	*436–435* Ἕρμ[ιππος
c. 480 Μάγνη]ς ΔΙ	*427–426* Ἀρι[στοφάνης
. . . .]ς Ι	*425–424* Εὔ[πολις
Ἀλκιμέν]η[ς?] Ι	*423–422* Κά[νθαρος
. . . . . .]ς Ι	Φρύ[νιχος
459–458 Εὐφρόν]ιος Ι	*455–454* Ἀμ[ειψίας
Ἐκφαν]τίδης ΙΙΙΙ	Πλά[των
Κρατί]νος ΓΙ	Φιλ[ωνίδης
Διοπ]είθης ΙΙ	Λύκ[ις
Κρά]της ΙΙΙ	Λεύ[κων
447–446 Καλλία]ς ΙΙ	

Comic Poets at Dionysia (cont.)

	Col. iii		Col. vi
	Νικοφῶ[ν		(6 lines missing)
	Θεόπομπ[ος		. . . . . . ος Ι
403–402	Κη]φισό[δωρος		θ]εος Ι
	Col. v		Ποσεί]διππος ΙΙ
c. 290	Πο]σείδιππος ΙΙΙΙ		. . . . . . ΙΙΙ
	Σατυρίων Ι		. . .
	Ἀ]πολλόδωρος ΙΙ		. . .
			Νίκαρχος Ι
c. 279–278	Φιλή]μων Γ·Ι		Νικόμαχος Ι
	Δαμό]ξενος Ι		Ἀριστοκράτης Ι–
	Φοινικ]ίδης ΙΙ	*186–185*	Λαίνης ΙΙΙ
		184–183	Φιλήμω[ν

Col. vii

156–155 Χα[ιρίων
Δη
    (5 lines missing)
Πο
Ο

Comic Actors at Dionysia

	Col. ii		Col. iii
289–288	Ἀριστόμα]χ[ος	*259/8*	Φιλοκ]ύδης ΙΙΙ
	Δημ]έας Ι		. . . . ης Ι
	Ἐχ]ένικος Ι		Εὐην?]ωρ ΙΙΙ
	Δ]έρκετος Ι		ν Ι
	Ἀριστίων ΙΙ		Κηφι]σόδωρος ΙΙ
	Φιλωνίδη[ς		Ἀρισ]τομένης ΙΙ
	Φιλοκλῆ[ς		Διον]ύσιος Ι
	Καλλίστ[ρατος		ν ΙΙ
	Ἐμμενί[δης		
	Πολυκ[λῆς		

Comic Poets at Lenaia

	Col. i		Col. ii
	Ληναϊκ]α[ὶ ποη]τῶν	*c. 412/11*	Πο[λίοχος] Ι
	[κωμικῶν]		Με[ταγένη]ς ΙΙ
c. 440	Ξ]ενόφιλος Ι		Θεό[πομπ]ος ΙΙ
	Τ]ηλεκλείδης Γ		Πολ[ύζηλο]ς ΙΙΙΙ
	Ἀριστομένης ΙΙ		Νικοφ[ῶν
	Κρατῖνος ΙΙΙ		Ἀπο[λλοφάνη]ς Ι
	Φερεκράτης ΙΙ		Ἀμ[ειψίας
	Ἕρμιππος ΙΙΙΙ		Ν[ικοχάρης?
429–428	Φρύνιχος ΙΙ		Ξενο[φ]ῶν Ι
	Μυρτίλος Ι		Φιλύλλιος Ι
427/6	Εὔ]πολις ΙΙΙ		Φιλόνικος Ι
			. . . .]ς Ι
			[Κηφισόδωρος .] (?)

The City Dionysia

Comic Poets at Lenaia (cont.)

Col. iii

c. 378–377 Φίλι[ππος .] ΙΙ
Χόρη[γος
Ἀναξα[νδρί]δης ΙΙΙ
Φιλέτα[ιρο]ς ΙΙ
Εὔβουλος ΓΙ
Ἔφιππος Ι
Ἀ]ντιφάν[ης] ΓΙΙΙ
Μ]νησίμ[αχος] Ι
Ναυ[σικράτ]ης ΙΙΙ
Εὐφάνη[ς -
Ἄλεξις ΙΙ-
Ἀρ]ιστ[οφῶν
. . . .
. . . .
. . . .
Ἀσκληπιόδω]ρος? Ι

Col. iv

-
Διο[νύσι]ος Ι
Κλέ[αρχ]ος [-
Ἀθηνοκλῆς
Πύρ[ρήν] Ι
Ἀλκήνωρ Ι
Τιμοκλῆς Ι
Προκλείδης Ι
after 321 Μ[έν]ανδρος Ι
Φ[ι]λήμων ΙΙΙ
Ἀπολλόδωρο[ς -
Δίφιλος ΙΙΙ
Φιλιππίδης ΙΙ-
Νικόστρατος -
Καλλιάδης Ι
after 311 Ἀμεινίας Ι
ΙΙΙ

Col vi

(12 lines missing)
. . Ι
]όδωρος Ι
Εὐμήδη[ς] ΙΙ
Πανδαί[τ]ης Ι
Μενεσ[θ]εύς Ι

Col. vii

(9 lines missing)
Πο]λυ
Θεμισ[τ
Θεω[ν
Θεοδ
Διοσκο[υρίδη]ς Ι
Εὐβου[λίδη]ς Ι
Θεόδω[ρος
Ὀ]νησι . . . . . . ΙΙΙ

Col. viii

(9 lines missing)
Ἐμμ]ενίδης Ι
Ἀρί]στων ΙΙΙ
Νούιος ΙΙΙ
Διονύσιος ΙΙ
156–155 Ἀγαθοκλῆς Ι
Ἀρχικλῆς ΙΙ
Βίοττος Ι
Νικόδημος ΙΙ

Tragic Poets at Lenaia

Col. iii

. . . .]ς ΙΙ
Ἀπολλόδω]ρος Γ
. . . . .]ας Ι
. . . . .]δης Ι
. . . . κ]ράτης Ι
c. 340 Ἀστυδ]άμας
. . . . .]δης

Col. iv

c. 330 Ἀχ[αιό]ς Ι
Φιλῖνος Ι
Ἀσκληπιάδης
Καίριος Ι
Τι]μόστρατ[ος

Tragic Actors at Lenaia

Col. i

ὑποκριτῶν τραγικῶν
c. 432 Χαιρέσ[τ]ρατος I
Με]ν[εκρά]της I
Λεπτίν]ης III

Μυννίσκ?]ος II
419–418 Καλλιππί]δης Γ
Νικόστρα]τος III

Col. ii

c. 400 Χαρίδημος -
Φίλιππος .
Φύτιος II
Εὐπόλεμο[ς
Θρασύβο[υλος
Ἀριστόδ[ημος
Μίρων II
Κλ]εο[δάμα]ς I
Θεόδωρος IIII
Ἵππαρχος ΓI
Ἀμεινίας I
Ἀν]δροσθένης I
Νεο]πτόλεμος I
348–347 Θεττ]αλός II
. . . . .]ς II
Ἀριστ]ίων I
. . . . . άδης I

Col iii

. . .
. . .
. . . .]ος II
. . . . . .]ς II
Εἰ[. . . . .]ς I
Ἀρ[ιστοφ]ῶν I
Πο
Ν
c. 330 Ἀρχίας
Πραξία[ς
Ἱερομν[ήμων] III
Φιλ
Νικ
Ἀρι

Col. iv

. . .
Ἐ[
Βακχ[
Στεμφ[ύλιος
Ξένων I
Χαρίας
Ἀντιμέ[νης
Τεισίλα[ς
Γο[ργοσθένης
Νίκων II .
Ἀριστόνι[κος
Πύρριχος
Ἀγήτωρ I
Θηραμέν[ης
Κλεῖτος

Col. v

Τ . . .
279 Κλεό[δωρος
Αἰσχύ[λος
Ἀρίμνη[στος
Ἐπαμε[ίνων
Ἐροτ[ίων
Ἀ]ρισ[τ

Col. vi

260–259 Ἡράκ[λειτος
257–256 Ἀλέξανδ[ρος
Καλλικλῆς III
Ε]ὐρήμων I
Ἰσο]κράτης I
. . . . ν]νος II
. . . . . κ]ος I
. . . .]ος I

Col. vii

Πάμφιλος
Σωσίθεος II
Πολύκριτος I
Ναύσων I
Ἀρίστων I

Col. viii

Ἔχετος IIII
Ἐ]πίνικος IIII

The City Dionysia

Comic Actors at Lenaia

Columns i and ii must have gone back to about 442 B.C.

Col. iii

c. 375 Σάτ]υρος ΓΙ
Φι]λήμων ΙΙ
Κα]λλίστρατ[ος
(8 lines missing)
. . .]κων ΙΙΙΙ
Παρμένων Ι
Λύκων ΙΙ
Ν[α]υσικ[ράτης
Ἀμ]φιχ[άρης
Φο]ρ[μίων

Col. v

before 312 Ἀρισταγόρας Ι
Κάλλιππος ΙΙΙΙ

Col. v (cont.)

290–289 Ἀσκληπιόδωρος Γ
Π]ολύευκτος Ι
Π]υρραλεύς Ι
Μ]οσχίων ΙΙ
Δη]μ[οφῶ]ν Ι
Ἱ]ερώνυμος ΙΙΙΙ
Ἀριστόμαχος ΙΙΙ
Δέρκετος Ι.
. . .
Φιλοκ[λῆς
Ἀριστοκράτης Ι
Ἐμμενίδης Ι
Αὐτόλυκος Ι
Φιλωνίδης Ι
Σωκράτης Ι

Col. vi

Πολ[υκλῆς?
Λυκίσ[κος
Σωσικλ[ῆς
Πολύζηλο[ς
Πυθάρατος Ι
Καλλίας ΙΙΙ
Μενεκ[λῆ]ς Ι
Δ[ημήτρ]ιος ΙΙ
Πιτθεύς Ι
Ἡρακλείδης ΙΙ
. . .

Col. vi (cont.)

. . . .]ρος ΙΙ
. . . . .] Ι
. . . .]ς Ι
Δ[ημο?]κράτης Ι
Φιλ[ο]στέφανος Ι
c. 240 Ἑρμόφαντος Ι

Col. vii

Φιλ[
Φερ[
Δημ[

Notes on *I.G.* ii². 2325

This record has been pieced together out of 41 marble fragments, nearly all found on the south slope of the Acropolis, most of them written by the same hand, but with some later portions added by others. The record was inscribed on the Ionic epistyles or architraves of the same building as carried the didaskalic *I.G.* ii². 2319–23, with 17 lines to each column. There is some reason for thinking (with Reisch) that the building was the votive offering of an agonothetes in the year 279–278 B.C., though it must have been continued later. The order of the names is that of the individual poet's or actor's first victory in his appropriate category. A number of dates are confirmed, or an approximate dating rendered possible, by entries in other inscriptions, particularly (for the later period) by those recording the Soteria of Delphi and performances at Delos. (References are given by Kirchner.)

Notes on details

Tragic Poets at Dionysia

Αἰσχύλος: first victory dated 485–484 B.C. by *Marm. Par.*, Ep. 50.
Νόθιππος: mentioned Athen. viii. 344 c, and identified by Wilhelm
(*Urkunden*, p. 102) with Gnesippus.
Ἀστυδάμας: i.e. the elder.
Ἀφαρεύς: his two victories were won with plays presented for him by
Dionysius (Plut. *Vit. X Orat.* 839 d).

A very fragmentary fourth column contains the beginning of names
which may have been those of Aiantides, Homeros, and Dionysius, who
were tragic poets of the Alexandrian Pleiad.

Comic Poets at Dionysia

Μάγνης: cf. Anon. *de Com.* α´ (Kaibel, *Com. Fr.*, p. 7) Ἀγωνισάμενος
Ἀθήνησι νίκας ἔσχεν ἔνδεκα.
Καλλίας: cf. No. 2318, col. iii (victory in 447/6 B.C.).
Ἕρμιππος: date proved by No. 2318, col. iv (and dating of Φερεκράτης
confirmed).
Ἀριστοφάνης: victory probably won with the *Babylonians*, 427/6 B.C.
The long controversy as between the rival readings Ἀριστοφάνης and
Ἀριστομένης seems to have been finally settled in favour of the
former. See Capps, *Hesperia*, xii, p. 3 and references there.
Εὔπολις: victory probably won with the Χρυσοῦν Γένος, 425/4 B.C.
Κάνθαρος: cf. No. 2318, col. v.
Φρύνιχος: first victory (which must have been at the Lenaia) in 430/29,
Anon. *de Com.* α´ (Kaibel, p. 8).
Ἀμειψίας: victorious with Κωμασταί in 415–414 B.C. (Argt. Aristoph.
Birds).
Νικοφῶν: his Ἀδωνίς competed against Aristoph. *Ploutos* in 389/8 B.C.
Κηφισόδωρος: cf. Lysias xxi. 4 ἐπὶ Εὐκλείδου ἄρχοντος (i.e. 403–402)
κωμῳδοῖς χορηγῶν Κηφισοδώρῳ ἐνίκων.
Ποσείδιππος: cf. Suidas s.v. τρίτῳ ἔτει μετὰ τὸ τελευτῆσαι τὸν Μένανδρον
διδάξας. (Menander died 293–292 B.C.)
Ἀπολλόδωρος in col. v is A. of Carystus; he also won three Lenaian
victories.
Φιλήμων in col. v is Philemon II, son of the elder Philemon.
Φοινικίδης: Lenaian victory in 289–288, No. 2318, col. i.
Φιλήμων in col. vi is Philemon III, who won at the Dionysia in 184–
183 B.C.

The contest in comedy at the Dionysia went on till about 120 B.C.;
cf. No. 2323, col. vi (Reisch, *Zeitschr. öst. Gym.* 1907, p. 299).

Comic Actors at Dionysia

Many of these names appear in the list of actors at the Lenaia and in the inscriptions from Delos and Delphi.

Comic Poets at Lenaia

The beginning of the contest in comedy, both for poets and actors, is to be placed in the period 445 to 440 B.C. See Reisch, *Zeitschr. öst Gym.* 1907, p. 308; Capps, *Am. J. Arch.* 1907, p. 187.

The six names lost at the end of col. i must include those of Aristophanes and Philonides.

Ἀναξανδρίδης (col. iii): first victory at Dionysia in 377–376 B.C. (*Marm. Par.*, Ep. 70).

Ἄλεξις: Kirchner dates his first victory before the death of Plato in 348–347 B.C., owing to the mention of Plato in fr. 1 (K.).

Μένανδρος: first appearance in 322–321 B.C. (Anon. *de Com.*); first victory at Dionysia, 316–315 B.C. (*Marm. Par.*, Ep. B. 14).

Φιλήμων: first victory at Dionysia in 328–327 B.C. (*Marm. Par.*, Ep. B. 7).

Ἀπολλόδωρος in col. iv is A. of Gela.

Φιλιππίδης: cf. No. 2323 a (victory at Dionysia in 312–311 B.C.); in the same year Νικόστρατος was second (ibid.).

Comic Actors at Lenaia

Φιλήμων (in col. iii), acted for Anaxandrides (Aristot. *Rhet.* iii. 1413ᵇ25).

Παρμένων: cf. Aeschines *in Tim.* i. 157 (345 B.C.).

Κάλλιππος (in col. v)—the younger: won at Dionysia in 313–312, 312–311 B.C. (No. 2323 a).

Μοσχίων (in col. v) = Μ. Εὐβούλου Γαργαρεὺς διδάσκαλος κωμικῶν in record of Soteria at Delphi, 258–257 B.C.

Tragic Poets at Lenaia

Ἀπολλόδωρος: of Tarsus, to whom Suidas ascribes six tragedies.

Ἀστυδάμας: i.e. the younger.

Ἀχαιός: of Syracuse (Suid. s.v.).

Tragic Actors at Lenaia

Some of these names appear in the list of actors at the Dionysia.

Καλλιππίδης, victorious at Lenaia in 419–418 B.C.; cf. No. 2319, col. ii.

Ἀριστόδημος: acted in the time of Philip of Macedon, as did Νεοπτόλεμος (victorious at Dionysia in 342–341 B.C. (Nos. 2318, col. xi; 2320).

Ἱερομνήμων: victorious in 307–306 B.C. (*I.G.* xi. 1289).

Ἡράκλειτος of Argos: mentioned in records of Soteria for 259 and 256 B.C.

Σωσίθεος: ? the same as the tragic poet of the late third century.

I.G. *ii². 3073* (*Monument of Xenokles*)

(Wilhelm, *Urkunden*, pp. 209 ff.; Capps, *Am. J. Arch.* iv, p. 76; Reisch, *de Mus. Gr. Cert.*, p. 83; *B.C.H.* iii, pl. 5.)

ὁ δῆμος ἐ[χορήγει ἐπ' Ἀναξι]κράτους ἄρχοντος·   *307–306* B.C.
ἀγωνοθέ[της Ξενοκλῆς Ξ]είνιδος Σφήττιος
ποιητὴς τραγωιδοῖς ἐνίκα [Φανόστρατο]ς ʿΗρακλείδου Ἀλικαρνασσεύς
ὑποκριτὴς τραγωιδοῖς ἐνίκ[α . . . .]ν Εὐανορίδου Κυδαθηναιεύς
ποιητὴς κωμωι[δ]οῖς ἐνί[κα Φιλήμω]ν Δάμωνος Διομειεύς
ὑποκριτὴς κ[ωμωιδοῖς ἐνίκα Κάλλιπ]πος Καλλίου Σουνιεύς.

The monument set up by Xenokles as agonothetes was about 14 feet high, and the tablet on which the inscription was carved was enclosed in a decorative architectural setting. That the monument refers to the Lenaia, not the Dionysia, is proved by the fact that tragedy is recorded before comedy.

I.G. *xiv. 1097 and 1098* (*Roman fragments*)

The texts here transcribed follow the restoration by W. A. Dittmer, *The Fragments of Athenian Comic Didaskaliai found in Rome* (1923), who assumes a line of 74 letters.

1098 a

(The poet first referred to is Telekleides, and the extant portion must have been preceded by an enumeration of his three Dionysiac and five Lenaian victories.)

δεύτερος] ἐν ἄ[στει
    ] Εὐμέ[νισι
   Ἐ]πὶ Εὐδ[
  κωμωιδί]αι Λήναια [
   Στ]έρρους ἀν[εδίδαξε
   ] τέταρτος [ἐν ἄστει
  ʿΗσ]ιόδοις σωίω[ι
  Στρατ]ιώταις [name of poet
ἐπὶ δὲ τὴν νίκ]ην καὶ ἐπὶ τὰ τ[ρίτα καὶ ἐπὶ τὰ τέταρτα οὐκ ἦλθε
  ] Ξενόφιλος [
ἐπὶ τὰ τ]ρίτα καὶ ἐπὶ τὰ [τέταρτα οὐκ ἦλθε.

Notes

l. 1. Telekleides' first Lenaian victory was won about 441–440 B.C. (*I.G.* ii². 2325). He is identified (for this inscription) by the titles Στερροί and ʿΗσίοδοι.

l. 3. There is no archon in this period beginning with Εὐδ[(l. 3):

Körte suggests that this is a mistake for Εὐθυδήμου (432–431 B.C.) : Capps proposes an alternative restoration 'Επὶ 'Α]ψεύδ[ους (archon 433–432 B.C.).

l. 4. κωμωιδίᾳ in this and the next fragment implies that when this record was compiled the name of the particular play (which failed to get the first prize) was lost.

l. 7. σωίωι probably implies that there was a copy in the Alexandrian Library.

1097

(The first poet referred to in this fragment is Kallias, whose first Dionysiac victory was in 446.)

'E]πὶ Ἀντιοχίδου Κύ[κλωψιν	434 B.C.
]ς κωμωιδίαι Δ ἐν ἄ[στει	
κω]μωιδίαι ἐπὶ Τιμοκλέ[ους	440 B.C.
ἐ]πὶ Θεοδώρου Σατύροις [	437 B.C.
5 Ὑπέ]ροις σιδεροῖς ἐπὶ Πυ[θοδώρου	431 B.C.
Βατράχ]οις Ε ἐπὶ Ἀντιοχίδου [	434 B.C.
Λ]ύσιππος ἐνίκα μὲν [ἐν ἄστει ἐπὶ	c. 440 B.C.
ἐπὶ Γλαυκίπ]που Καταχήναις [	409 B.C.
Βάκχ]αις αὗται μόναι σώι[ζονται	
10 ἐ]πὶ Διοφάντου Διονύ[σῳ	394 B.C.
Β ἐν ἄσ]τει ἐπὶ Νικοτέλου[ς	390 B.C.
ἀνεδίδαξ]ε ἐπὶ Λυσιμάχου [	435 B.C.
Γ ἐν ἄστε]ι ἐπὶ Μοριχίδου [	439 B.C.
ἐπὶ Στρατοκλέο]υς Κολεοφόροι.	424 B.C.

Notes

l. 9. Some fragments of Lysippos' Βάκχαι (the only play of which the Alexandrians had a copy) are preserved. The mention of Lampon in them (as in Kallias' Πεδηταί) dates it *c.* 432 B.C.

ll. 10–14. Are probably (as Capps and Dittmer propose) a record of Aristomenes, who must have had a long career; but the case is not perfectly made out.

1098

Begins with a record of the plays of Anaxandrides; the preceding portion must have recorded his seven Dionysiac victories (the first in 376 B.C. according to *Marm. Par.*) and three Lenaian. It begins with the plays placed second.

] ἐπὶ Χίωνος Μαι[νομένῳ	364 B.C.
]ς Διονύσου γοναῖ[ς	
] Ἀμπρακιωτίδι Γ ἐν [ἄστει	
ἐπὶ Λυσισ]τράτου 'Ερεχθεῖ ἐ[πὶ	368 B.C.

5 ‘Ηρακ]λεῖ ἐπὶ Χαρισάνδρο[υ   *375* B.C. (or Ἀχιλ]λεῖ)
 ἐπὶ ‘Ιπ]ποδάμαντος ’Ιοῖ ἐ[πὶ   *374* B.C.
 ] ’Οδυσσεῖ ἐπὶ Κηφισοδ[ότου *357* B.C. (or Κηφισοδ[ώρου.
                     365 B.C.)

 ] ἐπὶ Ἀπολλοδώρου Ἀγ[ροίκοις *349* B.C.
 διὰ Ἀνα]ξίππου Λήναια ἐπ[ὶ   (or διὰ Διω]ξίππου)
10]ποίῳ ἐπὶ Ναυσιγένου[ς   *367* B.C.
 Ε] ἐν ἄστει ἐπὶ Χίωνος [*364* B.C.
 Φαρμακομάν]τει ἐπὶ Ἀγαθοκλ[έους *356* B.C.
 ] ἐπὶ Θουδήμου Ἀ[*352* B.C.
 ]ου Ἀντέρωτι ἐ]πὶ
15 "Εφιππος ἐ]νίκα Λήναι[α
 ] Γ ἐν ἄστ[ει
 ]ι ἐπ[ὶ
 ἐπὶ] Ἀρ[ιστοδήμου

The whole inscription from which these three fragments come contained the lists of plays produced by each poet in order of the places awarded to each play, and under each rank (firsts, seconds, etc.), giving the Dionysian placings before the Lenaian. It is conjectured that 'the record probably extended back to the introduction of Comedy into each of the two festivals, about 486 B.C. for the City Dionysia and 442 B.C. for the Lenaia' (Dittmer, p. 7). It was probably derived from Alexandrian sources, e.g. from Callimachus' πίναξ κατὰ χρόνους τῶν ἀπ' ἀρχῆς γενομένων διδασκάλων, and beyond that from the official Διδασκαλίαι at Athens. Körte and others think that the great size of the inscription suggests that it occupied a wall in some great library in Rome, where the fragments were found.

Inscription in Hesperia, vii (1938), pp. 116–17

Two fragments discovered in the course of the excavations of the Agora are published by B. D. Meritt.

       c. 14
Fragm. A. [. . . . .]ς
        :. 8
    [. . . . .] δ[εύτ]ε
     c. 5
    [. . . . .]όδημος τρί
    [ἐπὶ Ἀλ]κιβιάδου ἄρχον
    [ἀγων]οθέτης Νικοκλῆς
    [παλ]αιᾶι κωμωιδίαι
    [Καλ]λίας ἐνίκα
    [Μισα]νθρώποις Διφι
    [Διοσκ]ουρίδης δεύ

[Φάσμ]ατι Μενάνδρ

[. . . . .]s τρί Πτωχε̃ Φιλ
[σατύροι]s παλαιοῖς

[. . . . . .]os ἐνίκ ῾Ερμεῖ

[. . . . . . .] δεύ Ἄτλαν[τ

[. . . . . . τρί] Μαθητ[αῖs (?)

[παλαιᾶι τρα]γ[ωιδιᾶι

Fragm. B.   [. . . . . τρί] Φυλ[

[. . . . . Μεν]εκρ

παλαιᾶι τρ]αγωιδιᾶι

[. . . . . . . ἐ]νίκα

[. . . . . Σ]οφο

[. . . . . δ]εύ ᾿Ιξί[ονι

[. . . . . . τρί Οἰ]δίπ[οδι

The inscription recorded the actors who were placed first, second, and third in each of the contests in old comedy, old satyr-play, and old tragedy, and Fragment A from line 4 to the end is for the year in which Alcibiades was archon, viz. 255–254 B.C. (Pritchett and Meritt, *Chronology of Hellenistic Athens* (1940), p. 97). The date to which Fragment B refers is undeterminable; it may be earlier or later.

Notes

A, *ll.* 1–3. Why should not these refer to the old tragedies of the year 256–255 B.C.?

Καλλίαs: cf. *I.G.* ii². 2325. His first victory was about 265 B.C.

Μισανθρώποιs: Capps (*Hesperia*, xi, pp. 1–3 ff.) stoutly defends this against Körte's proposal of Φιλάνθρωποι (*Hermes*, lxxiii (1938), pp. 123 ff.). There can be no certainty, but Capps makes out a strong case.

πτωχε̃: probably = πτωχεῖ = πτωχῇ.

῾Ερμεῖ: the only known play of the name was the *Hermes* of Astydamas.

The interest of the fragments is that they prove that instead of a single old play of each kind being acted, there was a contest between the old plays of each kind (or their actors), and that satyric plays were treated in the same way as tragedies and comedies. Körte connects this with the collection of old plays by the Alexandrians and the love of satyric plays at Alexandria, though perhaps he overstates the case.

Chronological Summary

City Dionysia

Contest of Tragic Poets. Thespis *c.* 534 B.C. Record of *I.G.* ii². 2318 (*Fasti*) began ? *c.* 501 B.C.

Contest of Comic Poets. Probably 486 B.C. (Suid. s.v. Chionides). Continued at least to *c.* 120 B.C. (*I.G.* ii². 2323).

Contest of Tragic Actors. c. 449 B.C. (*I.G.* ii². 2325; Wilhelm, p. 9. List begins with Herakleides). Latest names in No. 2325, *c.* 280 B.C.

Contest of Comic Actors. Began between 329 and 312 B.C. (*I.G.* ii². 2318 proves that there was no contest in 329, and *I.G.* ii². 2323a that there was a contest in 312 B.C.). Continued at least to about 120 B.C. (*I.G.* ii². 2323).

Performance of Old Tragedies. In 386 B.C. first performance (*I.G.* ii². 2318, παρεδίδαξαν may imply that it was an 'extra'); in 341–339 B.C. (*I.G.* ii². 2320) it is introduced by παλαιᾷ in each year, as if it was part of the regular programme.

Performance of Old Comedies. In 339 B.C. first performance (*I.G.* ii². 2318, παρεδίδαξαν); probably regular in 311 B.C. (παλαιᾷ, *I.G.* ii². 2323 a); last record 155 B.C. (*I.G.* ii². 2323).

Note. In the victors' list *I.G.* ii². 2325 there is no mention of prizes given to tragic or comic actors who brought out old plays, nor in the Fasti or Didaskaliai, but in the inscription published in *Hesperia*, vii, pp. 116–17, there *is* a record of contests of old comedies, old satyric plays, and old tragedies with a prize for the successful actor in each kind, in the year 254 B.C.

Satyric Plays. Not recorded in Fasti (*I.G.* ii². 2318), but in the Didaskaliai for 341–339 B.C. (*I.G.* ii². 2320) the list for each year begins with a single satyric play.

For competitions of old satyric plays in 254 B.C. see note above. They are evidently at this time placed on a level with tragedies and comedies.

Dithyrambs. Inscriptional record in Fasti begins in 473–472 B.C. Date of earliest contests uncertain. Record in Fasti goes down to 328 B.C. Performances probably continued to a late date (see p. 74).

Lenaia

Contest of Tragic Poets. c. 432 B.C. (Reisch, *Zeitschr. öst. Gym.* 1907, p. 308). Proved by tragic actors' list in *I.G.* ii². 2325. List of victorious poets goes down to about 320 B.C.; but as the tragic actors' list (so far as extant) goes down to end of third century B.C., the contest of poets doubtless also continued.

Contest of Comic Poets. c. 442–440 B.C. (*I.G.* ii². 2325. List of poets headed by Xenophilus and Telekleides whose first city victory was *c.* 455 B.C.). The extant didaskalic record (*I.G.* ii². 2319) terminated soon after 288 B.C., being immediately succeeded by a column recording tragedies at the Lenaia, but the list of victorious comic poets continues beyond 150 B.C. (*I.G.* ii². 2325).

Contest of Tragic Actors. Began *c.* 432 B.C. (*I.G.* ii². 2325). Extant victors' list goes down to end of third century B.C.

Contest of Comic Actors. Began *c.* 442 B.C. Extant victors' list in *I.G.* ii². 2325 begins about 375 B.C. but was preceded by two other columns, which would bring it up to about 442 B.C. Extant record goes down to end of the third century B.C., but contests probably continued until after 150 B.C.

Note. The early date 442 B.C. is confirmed if a statement in the Argument to Aristophanes' *Peace*, which runs ὑπεκρίνατο Ἀπολλόδωρος ἡνίκα Ἑρμῆν λοιοκρότης, is rightly emended ἐνίκα "Ἑρμων ὁ ὑποκριτής, and refers (as suggested by Körte, *Rhein. Mus.* lii (1897), p. 172) not to the extant *Peace*, which was produced at the City Dionysia in 421 B.C., but to the second play of the same name composed by Aristophanes. See O'Connor, *Chapters in Hist. of Actors*, etc., pp. 19, 95.

Satyric Plays. No record, and no room for satyric play in *I.G.* ii². 2319 (*c.* 432 B.C. onwards).

Old Tragedies. No record.

Old Comedies. No record. (In 288 B.C. the plays were all new.)

Dithyrambs. I.G. ii². 3779 records a dithyrambic victory at the Lenaia won by a citharode early in the third century B.C.

III

THE ACTORS

A. TERMINOLOGY, ETC.

1. The word regularly used to denote an actor in tragedy or comedy from the last quarter of the fifth century B.C. onwards was ὑποκριτής. It first occurs in literature in Aristophanes, *Wasps* 1279,[1] and if the inscriptional record commonly called *Fasti* (*I.G.* ii². 2318), though itself engraved in the middle of the fourth century, transcribes accurately the archons' records of the fifth, the word was used of the victorious protagonist in the actors' contest in tragedy, instituted about 449 B.C.[2]

The connected verb ὑποκρίνομαι is used in Epic poetry in two senses: (1) 'interpret' omens or dreams;[3] (2) 'answer' a question;[4] and both meanings are found later,[5] the second mainly in Herodotus. The meaning to 'act' a play or a particular part is first found in literature in the middle of the fourth century,[6] but no doubt went back as far as the use of ὑποκριτής for 'actor' —probably a century or more earlier. This and kindred words (ὑπόκρισις, ὑποκριτική) are also used by Aristotle of the orator's or actor's 'declamation' or 'delivery'.[7]

The question whether and when the word ὑποκριτής was used in a restricted sense, of actors other than the protagonist, will be considered shortly; but there seems to have been no other word at any time for 'actors' in general (including protagonists), and in Plato[8] and other writers it is used in this general sense. Once only it is used of the chorus—in the scholium on Aeschylus' *Agamemnon*, l. 1347 πεντεκαίδεκά εἰσιν οἱ τοῦ τραγικοῦ χοροῦ ὑποκριταί; but the reference here is to the passage in which the

---

[1] τὸν δ' ὑποκριτὴν ἕτερον ἀργαλέον ὡς σόφον.   [2] See pp. 114, 125.
[3] *Iliad* xii. 228; *Od.* xix. 535, 555, and probably *Od.* xv. 170, though either meaning would be possible here.   [4] *Iliad* vii. 407; *Od.* ii. 111; *Hymn to Apollo* 171.
[5] The first in Aristoph. *Wasps* 53; Hippocr. *Ep.* 15; Theocr. xxiv. 67; Philostr. *Vit. Ap.* ii. 37. The second in Herod. i .2, 164 and (of an oracle) 78, 91; also in v. 49 and viii. 101 and in Thucyd. vii. 44, but in these three passages the reading (ὑπο- or ἀπο-) is uncertain. ὑποκριτής is used of the 'interpreter' in Plato, *Tim.* 72 b (τῆς δ' αἰνιγμῶν οὗτοι φημῆς καὶ φαντάσεως ὑποκριταί), and in Lucian.
[6] Demosth. *F.L.* § 246; Aristot. *Eth. N.* vii. 1147ᵃ23, *Rhet.* iii. 1403ᵇ23.
[7] Ibid. 1413ᵇ23, etc.
[8] e.g. *Sympos.* 194 b (of Agathon ἀναβαίνοντος ἐπὶ τὸν ὀκρίβαντα μετὰ τῶν ὑποκριτῶν; cf. *Rep.* 373 b, 395 a; *Charm.* 162 d).

chorus break into dialogue with one another and so behave like ὑποκριταί. Aristotle's precept[1] καὶ τὸν χορὸν δὲ ἕνα δεῖ ὑπολαβεῖν τῶν ὑποκριτῶν, shows (in the context) that it was *not* generally so regarded. Mute persons also were not strictly ὑποκριταί: Hippocrates[2] lays down that such παρεισαγόμενα πρόσωπα στολὴν καὶ πρόσωπον ὑποκριτοῦ ἔχουσιν, οὐκ εἰσὶν δε ὑποκριταί.

2. There is more difference of opinion about the terms τραγῳδός, τραγῳδοί, κωμῳδός, κωμῳδοί. The plural is regularly used of the members of the tragic or comic chorus from Aristophanes onwards. It is also used quite commonly to denote the tragic or comic performance, contest, or festival, at least from the middle of the fourth century. Aeschines uses such expressions as γιγνομένων τῶν ἐν ἄστει τραγῳδῶν, τραγῳδῶν ἀγωνιζομένων καινῶν, τοῖς τραγῳδοῖς ('at the time of the tragic contest'), μελλόντων ὥσπερ νυνὶ τραγῳδῶν γίγνεσθαι.[3] The same use is found in an inscription[4] of the middle of the century—ἀνειπάτω δὲ αὐτὸν ὁ μετὰ Γνᾶθιν δήμαρχος Διονυσίων τῶν Ἐλευσῖνι τοῖς τραγῳδοῖς, in the law of Euegoros quoted by Demosthenes,[5] in the inscription of Xenokles in 306 B.C. ποιητὴς τραγῳδοῖς ἐνίκα κτλ.,[6] and possibly in the heading of the Fasti, but in default of any certain restoration of this heading this must remain in doubt.[7]

Closely connected with the above usages is that of the plural to represent the performers of a tragedy as a whole, without any conscious differentiation of actors and chorus. This is probably the sense throughout the *Fasti*, e.g. for the year 458 B.C.: κωμῳδῶν | Εὐρυκλείδης ἐχορήγει | Εὐφρόνιος ἐδίδασκε | τραγῳδῶν Ξενοκλῆς Ἀφιδνα: ἐχορη | Αἰσχύλος ἐδίδασκεν. (The genitives may depend on ἐχορήγει = χορηγὸς ἦν, or on one of the lost words of the heading.) Some scholars think that in the entries for 386 B.C.: ἐπὶ Θεοδότου | παλαιὸν δρᾶμα πρῶτο⟨ν⟩ παρεδίδαξαν οἱ τραγῳδοί, and for 339 B.C.: ἐπὶ Θεοφράστου | παλαιὸν δρᾶμα πρῶτον | παρεδίδαξαν οἱ κωμῳδοί, the words refer to the actors in particular, but there seems to be no reason why

---

[1] *Poet.* xviii.   [2] Νόμος (Littré, iv. 15), § 1.

[3] *In Ctes.* §§ 34, 41, 45, 154: cf. O'Connor, *Chapters in the History of Actors*, p. 23. In Demosth. *de Pace*, § 7 εἰ γὰρ ἐν Διονύσῳ τραγῳδοὺς ἐθεᾶσθε the meaning 'performance of tragedies' would be possible, but the rendering 'rival tragic actors' gives more point to the passage, the comparison being with Demosthenes and Aeschines as rival orators.

[4] *I.G.* ii². 1186; see above, p. 43. Cf. *I.G.* ii². 956, etc.

[5] *In Meid.* § 10; see above, p. 24.

[6] *I.G.* ii². 3073 (I differ from O'Connor about this). See above, p. 121.

[7] See above, p. 104.

they should do so, and the intrusion of a second meaning into an otherwise consistent inscription seems hardly natural, even though in *I.G.* ii². 2323 the old comedy performed is placed under the name of the protagonist.

The word τραγῳδός (with the plural τραγῳδοί) is rarely applied to the poet. It is possibly so used in Aristophanes' *Wasps* 1480, 1498, 1505, though the meaning 'actor' cannot be ruled out.¹ Other possible (though not quite certain) instances are Krates, fr. 24 (K.) τοῖς δὲ τραγῳδοῖς ἕτερος σεμνὸς πᾶσιν λόγος ἄλλος ὅδ᾽ ἔστιν; and (in the transition-period between Middle and New Comedy) Diphilus, fr. 30 (K.) ὡς οἱ τραγῳδοί φασιν, οἷς ἐξουσία | ἔστιν λέγειν ἅπαντα καὶ ποιεῖν μόνοις; and Timokles, fr. 6 (K.) τοὺς γὰρ τραγῳδοὺς πρῶτον εἰ βούλει σκόπει | ὡς ὠφελοῦσι πάντας.² The use of κωμῳδοί in Plato's *Laws* xi. 933 d is equally uncertain: τί δὲ δή; τὴν τῶν κωμῳδῶν προθυμίαν τοῦ γελοῖα εἰς τοὺς ἀνθρώπους λέγειν ἢ παραδεχώμεθα; The general meaning 'comedy' is not ruled out by the mention of poets (comic, iambic, lyric) in the next sentence, though it is at least likely that κωμῳδῶν should be rendered generally 'comic writers' (as by Rees). A more certain argument is derived from such passages as Aristoph. *Clouds* 1091, where τραγῳδοῦσ᾽ ἐκ τίνων; is used in a manner exactly parallel to συνηγοροῦσιν ἐκ τίνων; and δημηγοροῦσιν ἐκ τίνων; and seems to imply τραγῳδοί (meaning tragic poets) as a parallel to συνήγοροι and δημήγοροι. In a number of other passages³ the work of the individual comic poet is described by the verb κωμῳδεῖν, and probably implies that the poet himself could be called κωμῳδός. An almost certain instance in the Classical period is in Aristotle's *Poetics*, ch. xxii: Ἀριφράδης τοὺς τραγῳδοὺς ἐκωμῴδει ὅτι ἃ οὐδεὶς ἂν εἴποι ἐν τῇ διαλέκτῳ τούτοις χρῶνται.⁴ There is no doubt of this

---

¹ See O'Connor, op. cit., pp. 19, 20, for the meaning 'poet'. But the passage of Aristophanes may imply simply that Philocleon, dancing the dances employed by the oldest tragedians (Thespis and Phrynichus), challenges any contemporary actor to produce anything better. The uncertainty is caused by the fact that at least one of the sons of Karkinos, who accept the challenge, was a poet.

² This is followed by a number of references to tragic heroes and heroines, but there is no mention of poets, and τοὺς τραγῳδούς may be quite general (= 'tragedy').

³ e.g. Aristoph. *Acharn.* 631, *Peace* 751, and Aristot. *Poet.* xxii (see above): cf. Aristoph. *Thesm.* 85 ὅτιὴ τραγῳδῶ καὶ κακῶς αὐτὰς λέγω. The word, however, may in certain contexts refer to the style of the speaker's delivery, e.g. Dem. *de Cor.* § 13 ἡλίκα νῦν ἐτραγῴδει καὶ διεξῄει.

⁴ Another instance would be found in ch. v: καὶ γὰρ χορὸν κωμῳδῶν ὀψέ ποτε ὁ ἄρχων ἔδωκεν, if the emendation κωμῳδῷ, which Bywater once favoured, were adopted (see Gudeman's edition ad loc.).

usage in a few passages of late writers, such as Plutarch (τὸ τοῦ τραγῳδοῦ, followed by a quotation) and Lucian; Pollux[1] speaks of a poet (Eudoxus) τῶν νεῶν κωμῳδῶν, and a scholiast on Aristoph. *Frogs* 86 writes εἰσὶ δέ, ὥς φησι, δύο Ξενοκλεῖς τραγῳδοὶ γεγονότες.[2]

The use of τραγῳδός, κωμῳδός to denote the actor occurs in some fourth-century writers,[3] viz. Plato, *Phaedrus* 236 c ἵνα δὲ μὴ τὸ τῶν κωμῳδῶν φορτικὸν πρᾶγμα ἀναγκαζώμεθα ποιεῖν ἀνταποδιδόντες ἀλλήλοις (though even here the general sense 'comedy' is not impossible); Chares (a fourth-century historian), fr. 4 (Jacoby) ὑπεκρίθησαν τραγῳδοὶ μὲν Θέτταλος κτλ.; and Aristotle, *Oecon.* I. iv. 1344ᵃ20 ἡ δὲ διὰ τῆς κοσμήσεως οὐδὲν διαφέρουσά ἐστι τῆς τῶν τραγῳδῶν ἐν τῇ σκευῇ πρὸς ἀλλήλους ὁμιλία.[4] The words are regularly used of the actors in the inscriptional records of festivals at Delphi, Delos, and elsewhere from about 280 B.C. onwards,[5] as well as in late writers such as Plutarch, Athenaeus, and others. In these inscriptions τραγῳδός and κωμῳδός are normally used of the protagonists in old plays, the other actors being called either ὑποκριταί or συναγωνισταί,[6] though ὑποκριτής could be used of the protagonist as well, and if he produced an old play he was called πρωταγωνιστὴς παλαιᾶς κωμῳδίας or τραγῳδίας. There seems to be no instance of τραγῳδός or κωμῳδός being used of the protagonist of a new play; this is always ὑποκριτής.

The idiomatic use of τραγῳδός in later times to signify the protagonist, as distinct from the ὑποκριταί who took the lesser roles, seems to be confirmed by a scholium on Demosthenes' *de Pace*, § 6. Demosthenes uses the words κατιδὼν Νεοπτόλεμον τὸν ὑποκριτήν, and the scholiast states that in his own time (i.e. in that of the unknown scholar whom he is probably quoting) he would have called him τραγῳδός. Some words in the scholium are out of place, but (as restored by Capps[7]) it should run:

[1] vii. 201.

[2] The use of the word here may be a reminiscence of the scene in the *Wasps*, 1478 ff. (see above).

[3] On Dem. *de Pace*, § 7 εἰ γὰρ ἐν Διονύσου τραγῳδοὺς ἐθεᾶσθε, see above, p. 128, n. 3.

[4] Here the context requires that the τραγῳδοί shall be individuals, and excludes any more general meaning. (The *Oeconomicus*, however, is possibly a third-century work, and it is not Aristotelian as it stands, though much of its material may be.)

[5] See (for a brief account) *Theatre of D.*, pp. 240 ff., and below, Ch. vii.

[6] It is unnecessary to discuss here whether there are any exceptions to this general rule as laid down (for example) by O'Connor, op. cit., p. 15.

[7] *Am. J. Phil.* xxix (1908), pp. 206 ff.

ὑποκριτὰς ἐκάλουν οἱ ἀρχαῖοι τοὺς νῦν τραγῳδοὺς λεγομένους, [τοὺς ποιητάς, οἷον τὸν Εὐριπίδην καὶ Ἀριστοφάνην] τοὺς δὲ νῦν ὑποκριτὰς (οὗτοι δὲ ἦσαν δύο) τὸν μὲν δευτεραγωνιστὴν τὸν δὲ τριταγωνιστήν, αὐτοὺς δὲ τοὺς ποιητὰς τῶν δραμάτων τραγῳδοὺς καὶ τραγῳδοδιδασκάλους, followed by a further scholium, τραγῳδούς· τοὺς ποιητάς, οἷον τὸν Εὐριπίδην καὶ Ἀριστοφάνην. In the scholiast's time (or that of his authority, perhaps an Alexandrian of the third or second century B.C.) the tragic 'team' included a τραγῳδός and two ὑποκριταί.[1]

The attempt has been made (but wrongly) to carry this distinction between τραγῳδός and ὑποκριτής back to the earliest days of tragedy. Of these early days Aristotle in the *Poetics*[2] writes: καὶ τό τε τῶν ὑποκριτῶν πλῆθος ἐξ ἑνὸς εἰς δύο πρῶτος Αἰσχύλος ἤγαγε καὶ τὰ τοῦ χοροῦ ἠλάττωσε καὶ τὸν λόγον πρωταγωνιστὴν παρεσκεύασεν· τρεῖς δὲ καὶ σκηνογραφίαν Σοφοκλῆς. (The 'two actors' of Aeschylus are generally assumed to be the poet himself and one other. In his latest plays he required three actors who are similarly assumed to be himself and two others. The three actors of Sophocles did not include himself as he did not act.[3]) With this passage must be connected Themistius' account[4] of Aristotle's doctrine: καὶ οὐ προσέχομεν Ἀριστοτέλει ὅτι τὸ μὲν πρῶτον ὁ χορὸς εἰσιὼν ᾖδεν εἰς τοὺς θεούς, Θεσπὶς δὲ προλογόν τε καὶ ῥῆσιν ἐξεῦρεν, Αἰσχύλος δὲ τρίτον ὑποκριτὰς καὶ ὀκρίβαντας, τὰ δὲ πλείω τούτων Σοφοκλέους ἀπελαύσαμεν καὶ Εὐριπίδου; Assuming the text to be correct, Thespis, acting by himself, delivered a prologue and set speech—we do not know what he called himself or was called; this was the second stage in the history of tragedy—then Aeschylus (thirdly) introduced 'actors', i.e. two persons at least, not merely declaiming speeches but acting a plot and conversing with each other and probably with the chorus, and these would be called ὑποκριταί (he himself being one of them). The lost passage of Aristotle which Themistius cites was probably the basis of Diogenes Laertius:[5] τὸ

---

[1] See later (Ch. vii) on the Διονύσου τεχνῖται, of whom these teams were members.

[2] Ch. iv e.g.

[3] He played the harp in his *Thamyris*, and played ball in the *Nausicaa*, to the delight of the audience (*Vit. Sophocl.*; *Athen.* i. 20 f; Eustath. *ad Od.*, p. 1533. 63). See p. 94.

[4] *Orat.* 26, 310 d.

[5] iii. 56: cf. Suid. s.v. Σοφοκλῆς· οὗτος πρῶτος τρίσιν ἐχρήσατο ὑποκριταῖς καὶ τῷ καλουμένῳ τριταγωνιστῇ; and *Vit. Sophocl.* παρ' Αἰσχύλῳ δὲ τὴν τραγῳδίαν ἔμαθε, καὶ πολλὰ ἐκαινούργησεν ἐν τοῖς ἀγῶσι. πρῶτον μέν, καταλύσας τὴν ὑπόκρισιν τοῦ ποιητοῦ διὰ τὴν ἰδίαν μικροφωνίαν (πάλαι γὰρ καὶ ὁ ποιητὴς ὑπεκρίνετο αὐτός), τοὺς δὲ χορευτὰς ποιήσας ἀντὶ ιβ' ιε', καὶ τὸν τρίτον

παλαιὸν ἐν τῇ τραγῳδίᾳ πρότερον μὲν μόνος ὁ χορὸς διεδραμάτιζεν, ὕστερον δὲ Θέσπις ἕνα ὑποκριτὴν[1] ἐξεῦρεν ὑπὲρ τοῦ διαναπαύεσθαι τὸν χορόν, καὶ δεύτερον Αἰσχύλος, τὸν δὲ τρίτον Σοφοκλῆς καὶ συνεπλήρωσε τὴν τραγῳδίαν. Further, the *Life* of Aeschylus states : ἐχρήσατο δὲ ὑποκριτῇ πρώτῳ μὲν Κλεάνδρῳ, ἔπειτα καὶ τὸν δεύτερον αὐτῷ προσῆψε Μυννίσκον τὸν Χαλκιδέα· τὸν δὲ τρίτον ὑποκριτὴν αὐτὸς ἐξεῦρεν, ὡς δὲ Δικαίαρχος ὁ Μεσσήνιος, Σοφοκλῆς. (πρώτῳ does not of course mean that Kleander was the first ὑποκριτής ever so called, but that he was the first employed by Aeschylus in addition to himself. Mynniskos would only have acted in the poet's latest plays, as he was still active many years after Aeschylus' death.) Out of these notices a very probable account can be constructed. Tragedy began with a choral performance of τραγῳδοί: to this Thespis added a prologue and set speech delivered by himself.[2] The speech (which, at any rate, as Diogenes asserts, gave the chorus a breathing-space) may or may not have been an answer to questions by the chorus. If it was, the speaker may have been termed ὑποκριτής; or the term may have come into use at any time when he or his successors (before the time of Aeschylus), or Aeschylus himself, began not merely to declaim but to converse with the chorus, or, at latest, when Aeschylus called in Kleander as a second actor and conversed with him (and probably with the chorus as well). Aeschylus and Kleander would certainly be called ὑποκριταί, 'answerers' of each other or of the chorus;[3] so, of course, would Sophocles' three actors, and so in Aeschylus' last plays would Aeschylus, Kleander, and Mynniskos. But there seems to be no sufficient ground for supposing (with Else)[4] that when Themistius says that Aeschylus invented ὑποκριταί, the word excludes the part played by the poet himself as actor;

ὑποκριτὴν ἐξεῦρεν (I follow Else's punctuation.). If Aeschylus in his latest plays adopted the innovation of Sophocles, it is easy to see that the change might be attributed by some writers to himself.

[1] i.e. himself, but the writer is concerned only with the form of the drama, not with the names of the actors. We cannot tell whether Thespis called himself ὑποκριτής.

[2] Aristot. *Rhet.* III. i ὑπεκρίνοντο γὰρ αὐτοὶ τὰς τραγῳδίας οἱ ποιηταὶ τὸ πρῶτον, and Plut. *Solon* xxix ἐθεάσατο τὸν Θέσπιν αὐτὸν ὑποκρινόμενον, ὥσπερ ἔθος ἦν τοῖς παλαιοῖς. The note of Pollux, iv. 123, ἐλεὸς δ' ἦν τράπεζα ἀρχαία, ἐφ' ἣν πρὸ Θεσπίδος εἷς τις ἀναβὰς τοῖς χορευταῖς ἀπεκρίνατο may be true, and Thespis may have substituted his more dignified prologue and speech for this crude procedure; but the note is of very doubtful historical value (see *Dith. Trag. Com.*, pp. 118 ff.).

[3] Photius, s.v. ὑποκρίνεσθαι· τὸ ἀποκρίνεσθαι οἱ παλαιοί· καὶ ὁ ὑποκριτὴς ἐντεῦθεν, ὁ ἀποκρινόμενος τῷ χορῷ.

[4] *Trans. Am. Phil. Ass.* lxxvi (1945), pp. 1 ff.

or that in the *Life* of Aeschylus the writer implies that Kleander was a ὑποκριτής[1] and the poet was not. In the very sentence which precedes, ὑποκριταί is used in a sense which must cover the poet's own role as actor, and in many passages of Aristotle it is equally inclusive. Else supposes that Thespis and Aeschylus must have called themselves τραγῳδοί, as distinct from ὑποκριταί. They may or may not have called themselves or been called τραγῳδοί; about this there is no evidence, but it is most improbable that either Aristotle or the writer of the *Life* should have introduced in a particular sentence without warning a restricted sense of ὑποκριταί, inconsistent with their use of the word elsewhere. The partial specialization and differentiation of the words τραγῳδός and ὑποκριτής—it was never complete—belongs apparently to the organization of the Διονύσου τεχνῖται in the third century. (The victorious protagonist in the fifth and fourth centuries was always recorded under the title of ὑποκριτής in the *Fasti*, as also are the actors named in the Victors' Lists (*I.G.* ii². 2325).)

3. The words πρωταγωνιστής, δευτεραγωνιστής, and τριταγωνιστής, with the corresponding verbs, are occasionally, though rarely, used of actors in the theatre, and the first two of participants in other contests. πρωταγωνιστής and πρωταγωνιστεῖν could be used of the leader or most important agent in any activity involving effort, and they are several times found in this sense in the fourth century B.C., viz. Aristotle, *Pol.* v (VIII). iv. 1338ᵃ30 ὥστε τὸ καλὸν ἀλλ' οὐ τὸ θηριῶδες δεῖ πρωταγωνιστεῖν; *Poet.* iii τὸν λόγον πρωταγωνιστὴν παρεσκεύασεν; Clearchus (an historian of the fourth or third century), fr. 25 (Müller) πρωταγωνιστὴς τῆς ὑπηρεσίας. It is not known to what writers Suidas refers when he says of Chionides, ὃν καὶ λέγουσι πρωταγωνιστὴν γενέσθαι τῆς ἀρχαίας κωμῳδίας, but the word must mean 'originator', 'first *poet*', not 'first *actor*'. They are first used with reference to the theatre in extant literature by Plutarch, *Praec. ger. reip.* xxi. 816 f ἄτοπον γάρ ἐστι τὸν μὲν ἐν τραγῳδίᾳ πρωταγωνιστὴν Θεόδωρον ἢ Πῶλον ὄντα μισθωτὸν τῷ τὰ τρίτα λέγοντι πολλάκις ἕπεσθαι καὶ προσδιαλέγεσθαι ταπεινῶς, ἂν ἐκεῖνος ἔχῃ τὸ διάδημα καὶ τὸ σκῆπτρον, ἐν δὲ πράξεσιν ἀληθιναῖς κτλ.; and *Vit. Lysandr.* 23 οἷον ἐν τραγῳδίαις ἐπιεικῶς συμβαίνει περὶ τοὺς ὑποκριτάς, τὸν μὲν ἀγγέλου τινὸς ἢ θεράποντος ἐπικείμενον

---

[1] Else misunderstands πρωτῷ (see above).

πρόσωπον εὐδοκιμεῖν καὶ πρωταγωνιστεῖν, τὸν δὲ διάδημα καὶ σκῆπτρον φοροῦντα μηδὲ ἀκούεσθαι φθεγγόμενον. (Plutarch also uses πρωταγωνιστεῖν in its general sense, without reference to the drama.)[1] In Lucian, *Calumn.*, § 7, both the technical and the general senses are in mind: πρῶτον δὲ προσαγάγωμεν τὸν πρωταγωνιστὴν τοῦ δράματος, λέγω δὲ τὸν ποιητὴν τῆς διαβολῆς. The reference to the theatre is found in a note of Pollux with regard to the use of the stage-doors, which is certainly untrue of the Classical period:[2] τριῶν δὲ τῶν κατὰ τὴν σκηνὴν θυρῶν ἡ μέση μὲν βασίλειον ἢ σπήλαιον ἢ οἶκος ἔνδοξος ἢ πᾶν τοῦ πρωταγωνιστοῦ τοῦ δράματος, ἡ δὲ δεξιὰ τοῦ δευτεραγωνιστοῦντος καταγώγιον. It is not known of what period or play Pollux is speaking. It also appears in Plotinus III. ii ὥσπερ ἐν δράματι τὰ μὲν τάττει αὐτὸς ὁ ποιητής, τοῖς δὲ χρῆται οὖσιν ἤδη· οὐ γὰρ αὐτὸς πρωταγωνιστὴν οὐδὲ δεύτερον οὐδὲ τρίτον ποιεῖ, ἀλλὰ διδοὺς ἑκάστῳ τοὺς προσήκοντας λόγους ἤδη ἀπέδωκεν ἑκάστῳ, εἰς ὃ τετάχθαι δέον;[3] and in the scholiast on Euripides, *Phoenissae* 93 ταῦτα μηχανᾶσθαί φασι τὸν Εὐριπίδην ἵνα τὸν πρωταγωνιστὴν ἀπὸ τοῦ τῆς Ἰοκάστης προσώπου μετασκευάσῃ.

Apart from the passage of Pollux just quoted, we find δευτεραγωνιστής used in the general sense of 'seconder' or 'supporter' in Demosthenes, *F.L.*, § 10, ἔχων Ἴσχανδρον τὸν Νεοπτολέμου δευτεραγωνιστήν (where it would be pointless to suppose a reference to the actor's profession, even though Neoptolemus was an actor—he was now referred to solely as a politician), and in Lucian, *Peregr.* 36 ὁ ἐκ πατρῶν δᾷδα ἔχων, οὐ φαῦλος δευτεραγωνιστής. The only passages in which it is generally thought to be used with reference to the drama are in the lexicon of Hesychius where it is rendered by δεύτερος ἀγωνιζόμενος (and even this may be quite general), and the inaccurate scholium on Demosthenes, *On the Peace*, § 6, quoted above.[4]

On the contrary τριταγωνιστής and τριταγωνιστεῖν are always used (except in this same scholium) with reference to an actor,

[1] *de Alex. fortuna* 332 d, and *de Mus.* 1141 d (πρωταγωνιστούσης δηλόνοτι τῆς ποιησέως, sc. as compared with the flute).

[2] Pollux iv. 124. See *Theatre of D.*, p. 238.

[3] Apparently the poet has a protagonist etc. assigned to him, and so χρῆται οὖσιν ἤδη (accepts them as assigned), but he does give to each (αὐτὸς τάττει) the speeches adapted to his rank. Plotinus' date was in the third century A.D.

[4] p. 130. Some late instances of the general sense are found in the scholia to Demosthenes and in Suid. s.v. Ἀβρογάστης (quoted by Rees, *Rule of Three Actors*, pp. 33–34).

and this actor is nearly always Aeschines, taunted by Demosthenes. It cannot indeed be regarded as quite certain that this was its sole use or that the word was coined by Demosthenes. He uses it first in *F.L.* § 247. The whole passage (§§ 246–7) must be noted:

ταῦτα μὲν γὰρ τὰ ἰαμβεῖα ἐκ Φοίνικός ἐστιν Εὐριπίδου· τοῦτο δὲ τὸ δρᾶμα οὐδεπώποτ᾽ οὔτε Θεόδωρος οὔτ᾽ Ἀριστόδημος ὑπεκρίναντο, οἷς οὗτος τὰ τρίτα λέγων διετέλεσεν.... Ἀντιγόνην δὲ Σοφοκλέους πολλάκις μὲν Θεόδωρος, πολλάκις δ᾽ Ἀριστόδημος ὑποκέκριται, ἐν ᾗ πεποιημένα ἰαμβεῖα καλῶς καὶ συμφερόντως ὑμῖν πολλάκις αὐτὸς εἰρηκὼς καὶ ἀκριβῶς ἐξεπιστάμενος παρέλιπεν. ἴστε γὰρ δήπου τοῦθ᾽ ὅτι ἐν ἅπασι τοῖς δράμασι τοῖς τραγικοῖς ἐξαίρετόν ἐστιν ὥσπερ γέρας τοῖς τριταγωνισταῖς τὸ τοὺς τυράννους καὶ τοὺς τὰ σκῆπτρα ἔχοντας εἰσιέναι.[1]

This passage (delivered thirteen years before the speech *On the Crown*) does not suggest that τριταγωνιστής was anything but a current and understood equivalent for ὁ τὰ τρίτα λέγων, or that Demosthenes had invented it *ad hoc*. Besides this, the comic poet Antiphanes wrote a play called Τριταγωνιστής, which may or may not have had any reference to Aeschines, but may have been brought out at any date after the death in 380–379 B.C. of Philoxenus (the dithyrambic poet) who is the subject of the only extant passage. This passage seems likely to have been written while the memory of the poet was still fresh (and therefore before Aeschines was well known). The date of Antiphanes' death is uncertain, but may have been about 334–330 B.C. But in the speech *On the Crown* in 330, Demosthenes gives Aeschines the full benefit of both words (§ 129 τὸν καλὸν ἀνδριάντα καὶ τριταγωνιστὴν ἐξέθρεψέ σε; § 209 ὦ τριταγωνιστά; § 267 πονηρὸν ὄντα καὶ πολίτην καὶ τριταγωνιστήν; and § 262 μισθώσας σαυτὸν τοῖς βαρυστόνοις ἐπικαλουμένοις ὑποκριταῖς, Σιμύκᾳ καὶ Σωκράτει, ἐτριταγωνίστεις; § 265 ἐτριταγωνίστεις, ἐγὼ δ᾽ ἐθεώρουν); cf. Plutarch (?), *Vit. X Orat.* 840 a (on Aeschines) ὡς δὲ Δημοσθένης φησίν, ὑπογραμματεύων καὶ τριταγωνιστῶν Ἀριστοδήμῳ ἐν τοῖς Διονυσίοις διετέλει.

On the whole the probability is that πρωταγωνιστής and πρωταγωνιστεῖν were words of wide meaning, which were

---

[1] This obviously does not apply to plays in which (as in the *Oedipus Tyrannus*) the principal part was that of a king, but to plays in which the king or tyrant was a tyrant in the modern sense, and all that was required was violence and declamation, rather than subtlety or skilful display of emotion. The schol. on this passage says that, according to Iuba, the reason for assigning such parts to the tritagonist was that ἧττόν ἐστι παθητικὰ καὶ ὑπέρογκα.

applied (among other things) to the actor who took the principal
role in a play, though it was only late, if at all, that they became
officially recognized technical terms, and they never appear in
inscriptions; that δευτεραγωνιστής kept its general significance
of 'supporter', until very late, though it was evidently used
much more rarely; and that τριταγωνιστής, whenever it first
came into use, was specially attached in a derisory sense to
Aeschines. (So in the *Life* of Aeschines we read that τριτα-
γωνιστὴς ἐγένετο τραγῳδιῶν, and in Bekker's *Anecd. Gr.* 309.
32 τριταγωνιστής· ὁ Αἰσχίνης ἀδοκιμώτατος τῶν ὑποκριτῶν ἐν τῇ
τρίτῃ τάξει καταριθμούμενος; in Suidas, s.v. Σοφοκλῆς· οὗτος
πρῶτος τρίσιν ἐχρήσατο ὑποκριταῖς καὶ τῷ καλουμένῳ τριταγωνιστῇ,
the participle doubtless veils a reference to Demosthenes.) The
derisory sense does not attach to the word itself, which could
not mean '*third-rate* agonist', but to the implication that Aeschines
never rose above the lowest place in the troupes of three actors
(with their choruses) who toured the country-places in which
he acted.[1] It cannot be discovered when the three words acquired a semi-technical sense with reference to the stage. They
are, as has already been noticed, unknown to the inscriptions
of the third or second centuries, in which the actors other than
the principal one, the τραγῳδός or κωμῳδός, are sometimes
termed συναγωνισταί. But by the third century A.D. there seems
to have come about a division of the profession of actor into
three classes, and the three names had reference to these and
not to the position of the actor in a particular play as determined
by the poet.[2] Normally, at all periods, the best actor would have
taken the part of greatest importance in the play, but a story
told by Aristotle[3] may mean that Theodoros (in the fourth
century B.C.) always insisted on taking the part of the character
who appeared first, thinking that the first speaker always won
the sympathy of the audience.

---

[1] See esp. O. J. Todd, in *Class. Quart.*, 1938, pp. 30 ff. The implication may not have been
strictly true, but neither Demosthenes (nor his audience) are likely to have been over-
sensitive about this.

[2] Plotinus III. ii, p. 484. See above, p. 134.

[3] *Pol.* VII. xvii. 1336ᵇ28 ἴσως γὰρ οὐ κακῶς ἔλεγε τὸ τοιοῦτον Θεόδωρος ὁ τῆς τραγῳδίας
ὑποκριτής· οὐδενὶ γὰρ πώποτε παρῆκεν ἑαυτοῦ προεισάγειν, οὐδὲ τῶν εὐτελῶν ὑποκριτῶν, ὡς
οἰκειουμένων τῶν θεάτρων ταῖς πρώταις ἀκοαῖς. The interpretation given above is that of
Lüders, O'Connor, and others, and seems better than supposing that Theodoros rearranged
the play or the parts so as to bring the protagonist on first. (It will be seen below that the
prologue was often spoken by the second or third actor.)

B. NUMBER OF ACTORS AND DISTRIBUTION OF PARTS

1. The passage has already been quoted in which Aristotle traces the history of the form of tragedy, whereby it acquired first two and then (with Sophocles) three actors, and so attained its φύσις—its complete development. Plainly Aristotle (in the second half of the fourth century) knows nothing of any fourth actor, and it follows that (with some trifling exceptions to be considered shortly) every play had to be presented by three actors. It was a necessary consequence of this that not more than three speakers could take part in dialogue at any one time,[1] but ὑποκριταί in Aristotle and elsewhere—the plural of ὑποκριτής, actor—cannot possibly mean 'speaking persons present at one time', as Rees and others appear to assume.[2] The phrases often used, literally and metaphorically, for first, second, and third actors' parts, never hint at a fourth.[3] Nor is it likely that in a contest to which great importance was attached the State would have provided three actors for one competitor and four for another. Some tragedies in which the difficulties caused by this limitation have led certain scholars to treat them as exceptions to the rule will be considered later.

It may be assumed that in the fifth and fourth centuries satyric drama was subject to the same rule as tragedy. Three actors are required in the *Cyclops* of Euripides, the only complete satyric play extant; the *Ichneutai* of Sophocles, so far as the extant remains give any indication, could be performed with two.

As regards comedy there is less certainty. A late grammarian[4]

---

[1] This rule is referred to by Horace, *Ars P.* 190, and the commentators thereon (Diomedes 455 (Keil), and Porphyrio on Horace ad loc.), who note that a fourth person, if present, is always mute: cf. schol. on Aesch. *Choeph.* 899 μετεσκευάσται δ' ἐξάγγελος εἰς Πυλάδην, ἵνα μὴ δ' λέγωσιν.

[2] Rees, *The Rule of Three Actors in Classical Drama* (Chicago, 1908). Discussions on this point have been many; e.g. O'Connor, op. cit.; Kaffenberger, *Das Dreischauspielergesetz in der gr. Tragödie* (Darmstadt, 1911); O. J. Todd, loc. cit.; E. B. Ceadel, *Class. Quart.* 1941, pp. 139 ff.; A. C. Schlesinger, *Proc. Am. Phil. Assoc.* 1929, p. xxvi, and *Class. Philol.* xxv (1930), pp. 230 ff., xxviii (1933), pp. 176 ff., xlvi (1951), 32 ff.; Flickinger, *Greek Theater*[4], ch. iii. The treatment in the text is an attempt to adhere to the evidence and the possible meaning of words, without reciting the whole history of opinion on the subject.

[3] e.g. Strattis, fr. 1 (K.) μισθωσάμενος τὰ πρῶτα τῶν ἐπῶν λέγειν (of the actor Hegelochus); Demosth. *Fals. Leg.* § 246 τὰ τριτὰ λέγων (of Aeschines as third actor in a troupe: see above, p. 135); Menander, fr. 484 (K.) τὰ δεύτερ' ἀεὶ τὴν γυναῖκα δεῖ λέγειν | τὴν δ' ἡγεμονίαν τῶν ὅλων τὸν ἄνδρ' ἔχειν; Lucian, *Tyrannicid.* 22 τὰ μὲν πρῶτα ἐγὼ ὑπεκρινάμην, τὰ δεύτερα δὲ ὁ παῖς, τὰ δὲ τριτὰ ὁ τύραννος αὐτός.

[4] Tzetzes (Kaibel, p. 28) ἐπιγενόμενος δὲ ὁ Κρατῖνος κατέστησε μὲν πρῶτον τὰ ἐν τῇ κωμῳδίᾳ πρόσωπα μέχρι τριῶν, στήσας τὴν ἀταξίαν. (He has just said that οἱ περὶ Σουσαρίωνα τὰ πρόσωπα ἀτάκτως εἰσῆγον.)

states that it was not until the time of Cratinus (i.e. about
455 B.C.) that comedy, which had hitherto been a disorderly
performance, was reduced to order and the number of actors
reduced to three—a statement which must be received with
caution in view of Aristotle's admission of ignorance on the
subject[1]—and of the difficulty of distributing the parts of some
of Aristophanes' plays between three actors only. This will be
considered later, but in the meantime Tzetzes may be thought
to be perhaps handing down a tradition from some earlier
source. The 'disorderliness' even of Aristophanic comedy was
further reduced in the time of the New Comedy, and the evidence of the extant remains of Menander will have to be
considered.

2. In any case the performance of the three actors was supplemented by the employment when required of mute persons
(κῶφα πρόσωπα), or perhaps of persons who if not absolutely
mute could be left out of the reckoning. (Instances will be given
below.) Such additions to the cast are very often stated to be
covered by the term παραχορήγημα, but this name must be
used with caution.[2] The word appears only in four scholia, and
in a corrupt passage of Pollux :[3] ὁπότε μὴν ἀντὶ τετάρτου ὑποκριτοῦ δέοι τινὰ τῶν χορευτῶν εἰπεῖν ἐν ᾠδῇ, παρασκήνιον καλεῖται
τὸ πρᾶγμα, ὡς ἐν Ἀγαμέμνονι Αἰσχύλου· εἰ δὲ τέταρτος ὑποκριτής
τι παραφθέγξαιτο, τοῦτο παραχορήγημα ὀνομάζεται καὶ πεπρᾶχθαί
φασιν αὐτὸ ἐν Μέμνονι Αἰσχύλου. The first clause gives an otherwise unknown sense of παρασκήνιον, and the words ἐν Ἀγαμέμνονι
Αἰσχύλου are an obvious dittography from ἐν Μέμνονι Αἰσχύλου ;
the contingency described in it—the singing of words by a
member of the chorus instead of by a fourth actor—does not
appear to have occurred in any extant play. The second clause
describes the addition (παρα-) to the actors' parts of something
spoken by a fourth actor. The *Memnon* has perished, and the
scholia give only four instances of παραχορήγημα, viz. the parts
played by *Bία* in the prologue of the *Prometheus Vinctus* and by
the Areopagites in the *Eumenides* (both being silent, and so not
in accordance with the definition of Pollux), the children of
Trygaeus weeping for their father in Aristophanes' *Peace*, and

[1] Aristot. *Poet.*, ch. v.
[2] See especially Rees, 'The Meaning of Parachoregema', in *Class. Phil.* ii (1907), pp.
387 ff.; and above, p. 90.   [3] Poll. iv. 109.

the unseen chorus of Frogs in Aristophanes' play.[1] Evidently the word could be used loosely of any special extra provision of persons. It is in any case a late technical term,[2] though the thing denoted by it occurred occasionally in the fifth century.[3]

3. The chief disadvantages of the limitation of the number of actors to three, as exemplified in the extant remains, were the occasional necessity of dividing one role between two or more actors (a division rendered possible by the use of masks), the frequent necessity of assigning two or more parts in succession to the same actor, and the need in a few plays of 'lightning changes' of costume, in order to enable the actor to take up a different role after a very brief interval. There were also in some plays awkward situations which would have been got over if a fourth actor had been available, and at times some incongruity may have been felt by unusually severe spectators when the different roles taken by one and the same performer were very unlike one another.[4] A survey of the plays will illustrate these points.

4. The first play of Aeschylus, the *Suppliants*, though it requires two actors, hardly makes full use of them. Danaus is present from l. 234 to l. 523 while the King of Argos is conversing with the chorus, but for most of the time does not utter a word, and only a single word of the text shows that he is there at all (l. 319 Βῆλον δίπαιδα, πατέρα τοῦδ᾽ ἐμοῦ πατρός); he only speaks the short speech, ll. 490–9. At l. 775 he goes off to get help,[5] but does not himself come back with the rescuers. He returns as the Egyptian herald at l. 872, and departs just after 951, and reappears at 980 having resumed the person and costume of

---

[1] Schol. *Prom.* 12 ἐν παραχορηγήματι αὐτῷ εἰδωλοποιηθεῖσα Βία; schol. *Eumen.* 573 ἐν παραχορηγήματι αὐτῷ εἰσιν οἱ Ἀρεοπαγῖται μηδαμοῦ διαλεγόμενοι; schol. *Peace* 114 τὰ τοιαῦτα παραχορηγήματα καλοῦσιν, οἷα νῦν τὰ παιδία ποιεῖ καλοῦντα τὸν πατέρα· εἶτα πρὸς οὐδὲν ἔτι τούτοις χρήσεται; schol. *Frogs* 209 ταῦτα καλεῖται παραχορηγήματα, ἐπειδὴ οὐχ ὁρῶνται ἐν τῷ θεάτρῳ οἱ βάτραχοι, οὐδὲ ὁ χορός, ἀλλ᾽ ἔσωθεν μιμοῦνται τοὺς βατράχους. ὁ δὲ ἀληθῶς χορὸς ἐκ τῶν εὐσεβῶν νεκρῶν συνέστησεν.

[2] It has nothing to do with χορηγοί in the sense in which the word was used in the Classical period; these χορηγοί belonged to the remote past, and the significance of the word is connected with the secondary meaning of χορηγεῖν—'furnish'. The history of this and kindred words is well worked out by Rees, op. cit.   [3] See below (on *Oed. Col.*).

[4] Cf. Lucian, *Menipp.* 16 οἶμαι δέ σε καὶ τῶν ἐπὶ τῆς σκηνῆς πολλάκις ἑωρακέναι τοὺς τραγικοὺς ὑποκριτὰς τούτους πρὸς τὰς χρείας τῶν δραμάτων ἄρτι μὲν Κρέοντας, ἐνίοτε δὲ Πριάμους γιγνομένους ἢ Ἀγαμέμνονας, καὶ ὁ αὐτός, εἰ τύχοι, μικρὸν ἔμπροσθεν μάλα σεμνῶς τὸ τοῦ Κέκροπος ἢ Ἐρεχθέως σχῆμα μιμησάμενος μετ᾽ ὀλίγον οἰκέτης προῆλθεν ὑπὸ τοῦ ποιητοῦ κεκελευσμένος.

[5] ἐγὼ δ᾽ ἀρωγοὺς ξυνδίκους θ᾽ ἥξω λαβών. He hints, however, that he may be delayed and instructs the chorus how to behave in that case. See below on the failure of Xouthos to reappear in the last scene of Euripides' *Ion*.

Danaus. The brief but animated dispute between the King and the Herald (ll. 910–65) is the only dialogue between two actors in the play. The fact that the parts of Danaus and the Herald of the enemy are played by the same actor was of course concealed by the use of masks, and if the long actor's robe enveloped most of his body this may have assisted the concealment. At l. 234 the play illustrates a consequence of the simple structure of the drama when there was only one actor, in the fact that the King first addresses the chorus and not their father, whom he might have been expected to notice. In the same way Darius in the *Persians* addresses the chorus first, and not the widowed queen-mother, and Klytaimnestra in the *Agamemnon* makes an elaborate address to the Argive elders before saying a word to her husband after his ten years' absence, though her so doing is also a most effective stroke of characterization.

In the *Persians* there are again only two actors, of whom the first plays the part of Atossa until nearly the end of the play, the second those of the Messenger and Darius. The fact that when Atossa has gone off at l. 851 to get a change of raiment for Xerxes (expected to arrive immediately) she never returns, evidently means that she had to act the part of Xerxes from l. 907 to the end of the play, perhaps because she had a better singing voice than the actor who played the Messenger and Darius. There seems never to have been any difficulty in the same actor taking both male and female roles in the same play, though the idea is shocking to some modern scholars. Female roles were in any case taken by male actors. The *Seven against Thebes* down to l. 1004 requires only two actors, of whom one takes the parts of Eteokles and Antigone, the other those of the Scout and Ismene. The final scene in our texts (ll. 1005–78) requires three actors (Herald, Antigone, and Ismene), but there can really be no doubt, on many grounds, that the scene was added in some later revision of the play, probably not before the latter part of the century.

The *Prometheus Vinctus* apart from the opening scene could be acted by two actors, of whom one would play Prometheus throughout, the other Okeanos, Io, and Hermes. The first scene requires actors for Hephaistos and Kratos, as well as Prometheus and the mute *Bía*, and those who[1] wish to dispense

[1] Like Flickinger, *Greek Theater*, p. 174; Kaffenberger, op. cit., pp. 27 ff., and many others.

with a third actor here imagine that Prometheus was represented by a gigantic hollow puppet, and that when Hephaestos goes off at l. 81, the actor of that part goes behind the puppet and slips inside it, and thereafter speaks as Prometheus, having just time to perform the necessary manœuvre during the six lines uttered by Kratos (with a possible dramatic pause). This would not be impossible, but the improbability of Prometheus being so represented is so great that it is more likely that the opening scene of the play (which on other grounds is to be placed fairly late in Aeschylus' career) was one of his first ventures upon a three-actor cast.[1]

In the *Agamemnon* the protagonist is obviously Klytaimnestra; the second actor probably took the parts of the Herald and Cassandra, the third those of the Watchman and Agamemnon; either the second or the third may have played Aigisthos.

Apart from one short passage, the *Choephoroi* could easily be played by three actors—the first as Orestes, the second as Elektra, the Nurse, and Klytaimnestra, the third as the Servant, Pylades, and Aigisthos. This scheme involves a 'lightning change' from the costume of the Servant into that of Pylades between ll. 886[2] and 899—not at all impossible with practice, if it may be assumed that Pylades does not enter until a few moments after the entry of Orestes at l. 892—where again a dramatic pause would be most effective. But those who dislike lightning changes imagine the introduction of a fourth actor to speak the three tremendous lines assigned to Pylades (900–2). Aeschylus may well have been bold enough to transgress convention in this way, but it does not seem to be necessary to suppose it.[3] In the *Eumenides* each of the three principal characters—Orestes, Apollo, Athena—requires its actor; the third actor must have added the parts of the Pythia and the ghost of Klytaimnestra to that of Athena. The most striking feature of this play is the introduction of the jury of Areopagites, and of the members of the final great procession, who take part with the chorus in the united celebration.[4]

5. The plays of Sophocles, with the exception of the post-

---

[1] See *Theatre of D.*, p. 42, and the introduction to Thomson's edition of the play.

[2] Not 889, as there is no reason to suppose that the same attendant is addressed.

[3] Discussions of this scene are innumerable; for a different view from that given in the text see Rees, op. cit., p. 43.

[4] See especially W. Headlam, *J.H.S.* xxvi (1906), p. 268.

humously produced *Oedipus Coloneus*, could all be acted by three actors without serious objection, provided that no such objection were felt to the performance of male and female roles by the same actor,[1] and that reasonable care were taken in the choice of actors physically suited to the play. Thus in the *Ajax* the second actor plays Odysseus, Tekmessa, and Menelaus, and the third Athena, the Messenger, and Agamemnon, Tekmessa being represented in the latter part of the play (l. 1163 onwards) by a κωφὸν πρόσωπον dressed in her costume and mask. The protagonist played Ajax and then Teukros. The infant Eurysakes was mute throughout. In the *Antigone* the protagonist must have been Kreon, who appears throughout the play; the second actor took the parts of Antigone and the Messenger, the third those of Ismene, the Guard, Haimon, and Teiresias. (The suggestion that the same actor could not adopt such different tones as those of Ismene and the Guard would certainly be repudiated by any competent actor.) In the *Electra* the heroine is played by the first actor throughout, Orestes and Klytaimnestra by the second, and Paidagogos and Aigisthos by the third; Chrysothemis might be taken by either the second or third. Rees[2] is not justified in saying that 'it is beyond the power of an ordinary actor to play successfully characters so widely different as those of the girl Chrysothemis and the Old Pedagogue under any arrangement', especially in interlaced order. Chrysothemis was played in any case by a male actor, and if he could change from one tone to the other once in a play he could do so twice. In the *Trachiniae* the principal actor takes first the part of Deianeira and then that of Herakles. Rees considers this objectionable in every way, partly because of the difference in temperament between the two persons (a difference for which a good actor could certainly prepare himself in an interval extending over 150 lines), partly because the parts would need actors of very different physical proportions. But there is no reason to think that Herakles, though sturdy and strong, was particularly *tall*, and the rest would be a matter of make-up. The silence of Iole throughout is pathetic in itself, but if explanation is needed, the absence of a fourth actor will suffice. The *Oedipus Tyrannus* and the *Philoctetes* present no difficulties. In the former the first

---

[1] The fact that female roles were in any case played by a male actor really removes the objection which would arise on the modern stage. [2] Op. cit., p. 57.

actor plays Oedipus throughout, the second Kreon, Iokasta, and the Second Herdsman, the third the Priest, Teiresias, and the Messengers. In the latter, the principal actor will have played Neoptolemos, the second Philoktetes (or vice versa), the third Odysseus and Herakles. But in the *Oedipus Coloneus* the fact must be faced that the part of Theseus appears to be taken in turn by each of the three actors—by the third (who plays the Stranger in the prologue and afterwards Ismene, Kreon, and Polyneikes) in ll. 551–667, 1096–1210, and 1550–5; by the second (who otherwise plays Antigone throughout) in ll. 887–1043, when Antigone has been carried off by Kreon's ruffians; and by the first (the player of Oedipus until l. 1555, and afterwards of the Messenger) in the brief scene from l. 1751 to the end of the play. In view of this some scholars[1] postulate a fourth actor. This cannot be said to be really necessary provided that there were no marked difference of height between the three actors, that each were sufficiently skilled in the adaptation of his voice and manner, and that the mask and costume of Theseus could be properly fitted to each. Athenian theatrical attendants had probably acquired some experience in such matters in the course of a century, though anyone is at liberty to suppose that if Sophocles had lived he would have made some adjustments to meet any difficulty that may have been felt. But in fact the complete silence of Ismene from l. 1096 to l. 1555, when speech or lyric utterance seems to be demanded from her, is only to be explained by the absence of a fourth actor; it is clear that in these scenes she was represented by an extra mute figure dressed in her costume, because the poet had *not* a fourth actor at his disposal.

Many proposals have been made for the distribution of the parts between three actors,[2] but a more ingenious solution than any of the whole problem has been proposed by E. B. Ceadel,[3] which may commend itself to those who think the division of the role of Theseus impossible, on account of the importance of the character in the play and the possibility that a triple impersonation would not escape detection.[4] He suggests that Antigone,

---

[1] Rees, op. cit., p. 79, distributes the parts between six actors, but there is no evidence whatever that more than three were ever available.

[2] These are very well described and criticized by E. B. Ceadel, *Class. Quart.* 1941, pp. 136 ff.

[3] Loc. cit.

[4] Ceadel lays stress on Oedipus' words to Theseus on his entrance at l. 891 ὦ φίλτατ',

who from l. 509 to 847 speaks only a few disjointed words (the equivalent of three or four lines in all) just at the end of this long stretch, may be represented during that part of the play by a παραχορήγημα,[1] and that whereas in any case Ismene is represented by a mute from 1096 to 1555 this same mute may as a παραχορήγημα sing the very few lines assigned to her in the final scene. (Or they might be sung by a singer behind the scenes.) The contrast between her voice in dialogue in the scene ll. 310–509 and her lyric voice 1,200 lines later would hardly be noticed. If these changes were made, the following distribution of parts would be possible: first actor, Oedipus and Messenger; second actor, Antigone (except from 509 to 847) and Kreon; third actor, Stranger, Ismene (310–509), Theseus, Polyneikes. This seems to be a quite satisfactory compromise, since it neither splits the role of Theseus, nor requires so much of the παραχορήγημα (whether one or two) as to make him virtually a fourth actor.

6. There is no play of Euripides in which the parts cannot be distributed without serious difficulty between three actors, except in so far as, in four plays, brief speaking or singing parts are assigned to young children.[2] Obviously these cannot have been played by grown-up actors, and must either have been taken by a boy as a παραχορήγημα (with one or more as mutes if required), and spoken or sung either by the boy himself or by a singer behind the scene.[3] Such may have been the case in the *Alcestis* 393–415, and *Andromache* 494–545, where there is a lyric dialogue between the young Molossos and his mother, and the *Suppliants* 1113–64, where there is a κομμός between the children and the chorus. In the *Medea* the children's voices are only heard from behind the stage. The following is the distribution of parts which seems to be certain or most probable in the extant plays:

Alcestis. 1st actor, Admetus, Apollo; 2nd, Alkestis, Pheres, Herakles; 3rd, Thanatos, Servant. The silence of the restored Alkestis in the

ἔγνων γὰρ τὸ προσφώνημά σου, just when Theseus was being played for the first time by a *different* actor (with presumably a different voice) from the one who had previously taken the part. But Sophocles may be just saying (to the audience), 'You may think that Theseus has changed, but he hasn't!'

[1] On the term παραχορήγημα and its meanings see above, p. 138.

[2] There are also scenes in which children appear but do not speak, e.g. Eurysakes in Sophocles' *Ajax*, the children of Polymestor in the *Hecuba* 978, and the daughter of Teiresias (if she was a child) in the *Phoenissae* 834.

[3] Cf. Devrient, *Das Kind auf der antiken Bühne*. Many critics have felt the inappropriateness of the words put in the mouths of the supposed children, especially of Eumelos, the son of Alkestis, but whether this is due to the words being uttered by grown-up persons may be doubted.

last scene is often said to be due to the actor who had played the part earlier being required for Herakles; but it is dramatically and pathetically so effective as to require no such justification.

Medea. 1st, Medea; 2nd, Nurse, Iason; 3rd, Paidagogos, Aigeus, Messenger.

Heraclidae. 1st, Iophon, Eurystheus; 2nd, Demophon, Servant; 3rd, Herald, Makaria, Alkmene.

Hippolytus. 1st, Hippolytus; 2nd, Aphrodite, Phaedra, Theseus; 3rd, Servant, Nurse, Messenger, Artemis.

Andromache. 1st, Andromache, Orestes, Messenger; 2nd, Menelaus, Nurse, Thetis; 3rd, Hermione, Peleus.

Hecuba. 1st, Hecuba; 2nd, Polyxena, Talthybius, Agamemnon; 3rd,[1] Polydorus, Odysseus, Servant, Polymestor.

Suppliants. 1st, Adrastos; 2nd, Theseus, Euadne; 3rd, Aithra, Herald, Messenger, Iphis, Athena.

Hercules Furens. 1st, Amphitryon, Iris; 2nd, Megara, Lyssa, Messenger; 3rd, Herakles, Lykos.

(For lack of a fourth actor Herakles and Lykos never meet, but Kaffenberger[2] is perhaps going too far in suggesting that the death of Megara, which seems to have been an innovation in the story by Euripides, was necessitated by there being no actor for her in the latter part of the play. Euripides was much given to 'piling up the agony'.)

Ion. 1st, Ion; 2nd, Kreousa; 3rd, Xouthos, Paidagogos, Messenger, Prophetess, Athena.

(The lack of a fourth actor explains why Xouthos never reappears, as he might be expected to do, in the last scene. But in ll. 1130–1 he hints that he may be late in returning, and so far prepares the audience for his absence.)[3]

Troades. 1st, Hecuba; 2nd, Posidon, Talthybius, Menelaus; 3rd, Athena, Cassandra, Andromache, Helena.

Electra. 1st, Electra; 2nd, Orestes; 3rd, Peasant, Old Man, Messenger, Clytemnestra, Castor.

Pylades is a mute person throughout, and his silence in the first and last scenes, even when he is directly addressed, is unnatural and would certainly have been avoided if there had been a fourth actor at the poet's disposal.

Iphigenia in Tauris. 1st, Iphigeneia, Athena; 2nd, Orestes, Thoas; 3rd, Pylades, Messenger.

(Orestes and Pylades are represented by mute figures in ll. 1223–33.)

---

[1] Played by Aeschines, according to Dem. *de Cor.* §§ 180, 267.
[2] Op. cit., pp. 37–38.
[3] See above on the similar position of Danaus in Aeschylus' *Suppliants*.

L

Helena. 1st, Helena, Messenger II, Castor; 2nd, Teukros, Menelaus, Servant; 3rd, Portress, Messenger I, Theonoe, Theoklymenos.

Phoenissae. 1st, Iokasta, Antigone from 103 to 201 (?), Kreon; 2nd, Antigone (after 201), Polyneikes, Menoikeus; 3rd, Paidagogos, Eteokles, Messengers, Oedipus.

(Other arrangements have been suggested. If the scholiast on l. 93[1] is right, the appearance of the Paidagogos on the roof from ll. 88 to 102 is intended to give the actor of Iokasta time to change into the costume of Antigone, but they must afterwards have been represented by different actors, as they appear together in ll. 1270–82, and Antigone appears (1582–end) with Kreon, who is played by the same actor as Iokasta.)

Orestes. 1st, Orestes; 2nd, Electra, Menelaus; 3rd, Helena, Tyndareus, Pylades, Messenger, Hermione, Phrygian, Apollo.

(The complete silence of Hermione in the scene which ends at l. 135 is not altogether natural, but in this scene, though not from 1313 onwards, she must have been represented by a mute, there being no available actor. Much more unnatural is the silence of Pylades—for the same reason—from 1549 onwards, and the device by which at 1591 Orestes answers for him, while very unconvincing, is a clear proof of the want of a fourth actor. Between 1352 and 1369 the third actor makes a 'lightning change' from Hermione to the Phrygian.)

Bacchae. 1st, Dionysus, Teiresias; 2nd, Pentheus, Agaue; 3rd, Cadmus, Servant, Messenger.

Iphigenia in Aulis. 1st, Agamemnon, Achilles; 2nd, Menelaus, Clytemnestra; 3rd, Old Man, Iphigeneia, Messengers. (It would be possible to transpose the parts of the 1st and 3rd actors *in toto*.)

(A considerable distance separates the appearances of Iphigeneia between 607 and 1473 from those of the two Messengers at 414 and 1532, and the Old Man only appears between the two appearances of Iphigeneia during a very short scene (855–95), so that the alternation of different parts taken by the same actor, to which some critics object, need not have presented any serious difficulty to a competent and adaptable player.)

Hypsipyle. The remains are too fragmentary to allow of any certainty as regards the distribution of roles; but as Hypsipyle, Amphiaraus, and Eurydike appear in one scene, these parts must have been taken by the 1st, 2nd, and 3rd actors respectively. The difficulty in regard to the children of Hypsipyle—Euneos and Thoas—has not been

---

[1] ταῦτα μηχανᾶσθαί φασι τὸν Εὐριπίδην, ἵνα τὸν πρωταγωνιστὴν ἀπὸ τοῦ τῆς Ἰοκάστης προσώπου μετασκευάσῃ· διὸ οὐ συνεπιφαίνεται αὐτῷ Ἀντιγόνη, ἀλλ᾽ ὕστερον. The object may have been to give the singing of the elaborate lyrics of the two characters to the specially qualified protagonist (Iokasta, ll. 202 ff.; Antigone, ll. 1485 ff., 1710 ff.).

completely solved. Both appear to be speaking characters (ll. 304–6, Page), in a scene in which both Hypsipyle and Amphiaraus appeared. Possibly Thoas did not speak until Amphiaraus had left the scene; or the few words which he speaks may have been regarded as a παραχορήγημα or even spoken from behind the scene while the actor remained mute, though he was certainly a speaking character in the Prologue.

In the lost *Kresphontes* of Euripides Aeschines as third actor took the part of the tyrannical king—Kresphontes[1] (the leading part, that of Merope, being taken by Theodoros).

There are many reasons for thinking that the extant *Rhesus* is a fourth-century play, and not the work of Euripides. However this may be, many scholars are convinced that the scene ll. 645–73 requires four actors, representing Odysseus, Diomedes, Athena, and Alexandros, all present at once. But at l. 636 (before the entry of Alexandros) Athena clearly sends Diomedes away to kill Rhesus, while Odysseus must have gone off at 627, and must have captured the horses of Rhesus (as l. 671 shows) before she recalls them both at 668, while they are still off the scene. The actor of Odysseus, after a quick change, played Alexandros between 642 and 665, and made a lightning change back to the costume of Odysseus between ll. 668 and 674—a quite possible thing if prepared for, especially if the interval were prolonged by the excited entry and movements of the chorus at 675. If this be allowed, the distribution will be: 1st actor, Hector, Odysseus, Alexandros; 2nd, Aeneas, Rhesus, Athena, Muse; 3rd, Dolon, Messenger, Diomedes, Charioteer.

The general objection made by Rees and others to the assignment of incongruous parts to the same actor in many of the above schemes has already been briefly dealt with. Such incongruity would be serious if there were any elaborate acting attached to each part, and above all if there were scope for facial expression, which is one of the chief modern means of expressing individual character and feeling, but the use of masks (and probably the conventionality of costume), as well as the relatively statuesque acting,[2] left individual expression mainly to the tone of voice, which a competent actor would have been able to adapt as the part required, in so far as even this was possible when the voice was masculine throughout. To

---

[1] Dem. *de Cor.* § 180; Aelian, *Var. Hist.* xiv. 40. He similarly took the part of the cruel Oinomaos in Sophocles' play so named, again as third actor.

[2] But the statuesqueness of the acting in the fifth century must not be exaggerated; see below, p. 169.

The Actors

judge ancient acting by the standards of modern is a quite mistaken proceeding.

7. It is evident that the practice as regards the number of actors was not so strict in comedy as in tragedy, and that though there were three principal actors, there was much more freedom to introduce additional performers for very small parts. If comedy originated in a more or less disorderly revel, it can be understood that this did not include regularly constructed dramatic scenes, at least until elements from the Dorian mime were introduced into the revel,[1] and it is not difficult to accept the tradition recorded (probably after passing through many hands) by a late writer that it was Cratinus who reduced the disorderliness and fixed the number of regular actors at three.[2] Nor is it surprising that Aristophanes himself should have retained some of the old freedom. In his first extant play, the *Acharnians*, there is one scene (ll. 56–125) in which first four and then five speaking persons are present. Three of the parts— those of Dikaiopolis, Amphitheos, and the Ambassador—are obviously taken by the three principal actors, but the Herald throughout the scene (and down to l. 173) and Pseudartabas (who speaks only two lines) must have been presented by extra performers. In a later scene (ll. 1069–94) a Herald or Messenger probably performs a 'lightning change' between ll. 1077 and 1085: otherwise a fourth actor or supernumerary would be required for ll. 1069–77. The real difficulty in this play concerns the part of Nikarchos in the scene ll. 910–58, since he is described as a small person, and therefore could presumably not be played by any of the three regular actors who played full-grown persons. It has been suggested that he also is a supernumerary—or, since he speaks about a dozen lines in all—a fourth actor, who also took the small parts of the daughter of Dikaiopolis (2 lines only) and one of the Megarians' daughters. If this be granted, the *Acharnians* would be acted as follows: 1st actor, Dikaiopolis;

---

[1] Cf. *Dith. Trag. Com.*, ch. iii.
[2] Tzetzes, *Prol. de Com.* § 16 (Kaibel, *Com. Gr. Fragm.*, p. 18 = Dübner, *Anon. de Com.* v) καὶ αὐτὴ δὲ ἡ παλαιὰ ἑαυτῆς διαφέρει· καὶ γὰρ οἱ ἐν τῇ Ἀττικῇ πρῶτον συστησάμενοι τὸ ἐπιτήδευμα τῆς κωμῳδίας (ἦσαν δὲ οἱ περὶ Σουσαρίωνα) τὰ πρόσωπα ἀτάκτως εἰσῆγον καὶ γέλως ἦν μόνος τὸ κατασκευαζόμενον. ἐπιγενόμενος δὲ ὁ Κρατῖνος κατέστησε μὲν πρῶτον τὰ ἐν τῇ κωμῳδίᾳ πρόσωπα μέχρι τριῶν, στήσας τὴν ἀταξίαν, καὶ τῷ χαρίεντι τῆς κωμῳδίας τὸ ὠφέλιμον προσέθηκε τοὺς κακῶς πράσσοντας διαβάλλων καὶ ὥσπερ δημοσίᾳ μάστιγι τῇ κωμῳδίᾳ κολάζων. ἀλλ' ἔτι μὲν καὶ οὗτος τῆς ῥαχαιότητος μετεῖχε καὶ ἠρέμα πως τῆς ἀταξίας· ὁ μέντοι γε Ἀριστοφάνης μεθοδεύσας τεχνικώτερον τὴν κωμῳδίαν τῶν μεθ' ἑαυτοῦ ἀνέλαμψεν ἐν ἅπασιν ἐπίσημος φανείς.

2nd, Amphitheos (or Ambassador and Theoros), Euripides, Lamachos, Megarean, Boeotian, Farmer; 3rd, Ambassador and Theoros (or Amphitheos), Kephisophon, Sycophant, Lamachos' Servant, Paranymph, Messengers (if a second were required); 4th, Daughter of Dikaiopolis, Nikarchos (not more than 15 lines in all); two supernumeraries, Herald and Pseudartabas.

In the *Knights* three actors are sufficient, the first representing the Sausage Seller, the second Nikias and Kleon, the third Demosthenes and Demos.[1]

We have the *Clouds* only in a revised or partly revised form. Obviously Strepsiades is played by the first actor throughout, Socrates by the second, and Pheidippides by the third; the second also plays Pasias and the third Amynias. But in the text as it stands, four actors are required in ll. 889-1104, since it seems clear that both Strepsiades and Pheidippides must have been present during the dispute of the two $\Lambda\acute{o}\gamma o\iota$. Socrates was not,[2] but his actor cannot have taken the part of either of the $\Lambda\acute{o}\gamma o\iota$, as he returns at l. 1105, and would have no time at all to change his costume. But it is quite uncertain what happened in the play as originally constructed.[3]

The *Wasps* could not be performed without four actors. Two are required for the parts of Philokleon and Bdelykleon. The third may have played Sosias, the Reveller, and the Prosecutor (ll. 1415 ff.); the fourth, Xanthias and the $\mathcal{A}\rho\tau o\pi\omega\lambda\acute{\iota}s$,[4] but other arrangements would be possible. The Boy (ll. 230-315) and the three sons of Karkinos in the last scene must have been extra performers.

In the *Peace* the part of Trygaeus must have been taken by the first actor; the second took those of the First Servant (ll. 1-149), Hermes, Kydoimos, and the Priest; the third, those of the Second Servant (ll. 1-49 and 819-1126), Polemos, and the $\Delta\rho\epsilon\pi\alpha\nu o\nu\rho\gamma\acute{o}s$. The extra performers required include the children of Trygaeus, of Lamachos, and of Kleonymos, and the

---

[1] van Leeuwen puts ll. 1254-6 into the mouth of Nikias, against the evidence of the manuscripts and on what appear to be insufficient grounds. But if he is right, a fourth actor would be required for Nikias here, though not necessarily earlier in the play.

[2] l. 887 $\dot{\epsilon}\gamma\grave{\omega}$ δ' $\dot{\alpha}\pi\acute{\epsilon}\sigma o\mu\alpha\iota$.

[3] The witness who speaks three words at l. 1246 must have been a 'super'.

[4] The scene 1388-1449 requires four actors, as Philokleon and Bdelykleon are present throughout and the $\mathcal{A}\rho\tau o\pi\omega\lambda\acute{\iota}s$ who goes off at 1414 has no time to change into the $K\alpha\tau\acute{\eta}\gamma o\rho os$ who enters at 1415.

mute figures of Peace and Opora. The distribution of the parts from 1210 to 1264 depends upon whether the various Armourers, who in most texts appear in succession and under different names, are not (as some editors have suggested) in fact all one ὅπλων κάπηλος (l. 1209) offering different objects successively. In that case they would all be taken by the second actor and the different objects carried by various mutes. But this view is not easy to reconcile with the text. The Κρανοποιός and the Δορυξός are certainly two separate persons, and are present at the same time, and so are the Λοφοποιός and Δορυξός. The Δορυξός is present throughout the scene, and may have been represented by the second actor; the third actor may have played the Θωρακοπώλης, and the very brief parts of the Λοφοποιός (5½ lines), Σαλπιγγοπώλης (2 lines), and Κρανοποιός (3 lines) spoken by a fourth actor and one or two extra performers.

The *Birds* could nearly all be performed by three actors, if some rapid changes of costume were made. The first would act Pisthetairos throughout; the second, the Hoopoe, Priest, Oracle-monger, Inspector, First Messenger, Iris, Parricide, Sycophant, Poseidon, and Final Messenger; the third, Euelpides, the Poet, Meton, Ψηφισματοπώλης, Second Messenger, Second Herald (1263 ff.), Kinesias, Prometheus, Herakles. The First Herald (448-50) and Triballos would be extra performers speaking very few lines, and Basileia in the last scene would be a mute. Under this arrangement the Hoopoe would retire about l. 835, to return as the Priest at 851, and Poseidon would change into a Messenger during the lyrics, ll. 1693-1706. But obviously so large a number of characters could be more satisfactorily distributed if a fourth actor were employed.

The *Lysistrata* includes a conversation of four characters very early in the play (ll. 77-253), but could otherwise be acted by three, with a line or two spoken here and there by an extra performer. The part of Lysistrata would occupy the first actor throughout; the second would play Kalonike, the Proboulos, First Woman (ll. 729 ff.), Kinesias, Athenian (1072-188), and First Athenian (1216-46); the third, Myrrhine, First Woman (ll. 439-613), Third Woman (ll. 729-80), the Spartan Herald, and Spartan. This would leave to extra performers the speeches of a Woman at l. 136 (1 line), the Second Woman in the scene

439–613 (3 lines) and in 729 ff. (3 lines), and the Second Athenian (5 lines between ll. 1216 and 1246); most of these could have been taken by the fourth actor who played the part of Lampito in ll. 77–253. Kinesias' infant would be an 'extra' of the familiar kind.

In the *Thesmophoriazousai* the first actor must have played Mnesilochos; the second, Euripides and the First Woman; the third, the Servant, Agathon, the Κηρύκαινα, Second Woman and Third Woman, and Policeman (a lightning change between 924 and 930). A fourth actor is required at l. 929 for the Prytanis, who plays a very small part. The play is notable for the extra chorus which accompanies Agathon.

The *Frogs* could be played with Dionysus assigned to the first actor, Xanthias and Aeschylus to the second, and Herakles, Charon, Aiakos, the Maidservant, the Innkeeper, and Euripides to the third; a fourth would be required for the very small parts (so far as spoken lines are concerned) of the Corpse, Plathane, and Pluto. If the fourth actor were more fully employed it would be possible to give the parts of Xanthias and Aeschylus to separate performers. In ll. 548–89 there is a conversation between four characters, though one of them (Dionysus) only speaks two lines. There is an (unseen) chorus of Frogs in addition to the regular chorus of Initiated.

The *Ekklesiazousai* can also be arranged for three actors with a very little help from a fourth. The parts may be distributed thus: 1st actor, Praxagora, Chremes, Second Man (ll. 730 ff.), First and Third Old Women; 2nd actor, First Woman, Blepyros, Κηρύκαινα, Young Man; 3rd actor, Second Woman, First Man, Young Woman, Maidservant; 4th actor, Third Woman (who speaks 3 lines in a conversation of four persons, ll. 1–284), Second Old Woman (ll. 1049–65).

The *Ploutos* could well be acted by three actors only, if the part of Ploutos were divided between two actors with different masks—the one representing him before, the other after his restoration to health. If so, the first actor will take Karion, the Old Woman, and Ploutos from l. 771 onwards; the second, Chremylos, the Just Man, and Hermes; the third, Ploutos from ll. 1 to 286, Blepsidemos, Chremylos' Wife, the Sycophant, Young Man, and Priest.

It seems probable, therefore, that in the Old Comedy the

greater part of the work was done by three actors, but that for a particular scene, when required, or for very small parts, a fourth could be employed. When four persons converse, one of them takes a very small part (though the opening scene of the *Lysistrata* is somewhat exceptional) and the chorus does not join in the dialogue. It was obviously a less serious matter to provide an occasional or unimportant fourth actor for a single comedy, which is all that each competitor offered, than for three tragedies, and the structure of comedy was looser from the first than that of tragedy.

8. Whether there was any fixed custom in regard to the number of actors in the New Comedy it is not possible to say. The remains of Menander's plays[1] are too fragmentary, and the assignment of lines to particular characters sometimes too uncertain, and it is not safe to argue from the Roman comedy to the Greek; nor do we know whether or at what time a virtual division of the play into Acts came into vogue and with it the permission of intervals during which the scene was empty and changes of costume could be made. What is certain is that there are extant scenes of Menander's plays which could not be performed without four actors, e.g. the Arbitration scene in the *Epitrepontes*, and the one which follows it immediately, as there would be no time for Daos, the defeated litigant, to change his mask and dress and reappear as Onesimos.[2] In the *Perikeiromene* there is a scene in which Polemon, Sosias, Pataikos, and Habrotonon are all present at once and all take some part in the conversation, and a later scene in which Glykera, Pataikos, Doris, and Moschion (at first in hiding, but interjecting 'asides') all take part. (In both these plays the employment of three actors only would entail some very awkward divisions of the same role

[1] The number of actors in Menander's plays has been frequently discussed, e.g. in Legrand's *Daos*, pp. 365 ff.; K. Rees in *Class. Philol.* v (1910), pp. 291 ff.; Graf, *Szenisches zu Menander*, pp. 29–49, etc., but there are too many 'unknown quantities' to allow of any certain solution of the problems.

[2] In the *Epitrepontes* Onesimos and Smikrines would each require a single actor; a third could play Daos and Habrotonon; the fourth, Syriskos and Chairestratos; but the distribution of the parts of Simmias, Charisios, Pamphile, Sophrone, and the Cook is quite uncertain. In the *Samia* the first actor would play Demeas, the second Parmenon and possibly Chrysis also, the third, Nikeratos, Moschion, and the Cook. The division of the parts in the *Perikeiromene* is (with the text as it is) very difficult to ascertain; but Polemon obviously occupies the protagonist entirely, and Daos, Glykera, and Habrotonon could be played by one actor, and so could Sosias and Moschion; a fourth could take Doris and Pataikos (no part of Myrrhine's role is extant). But objections will easily suggest themselves to this arrangement.

between two or even three actors, but as the availability of four is certain from the scenes above referred to, there is no need to prove this in detail.)

The evidence as regards the number of actors employed in each play, after the organization of actors' guilds in all parts of the Greek world, is confined to the series of inscriptions recording the names of all the performers at the Soteria at Delphi from about 275 B.C. onwards.[1] At each festival three (or two) troupes of performers of tragedy and four or three troupes of performers of comedy are recorded, and in each troupe are three τραγῳδοί or κωμῳδοί (with a flute-player and in nearly every case a didaskalos).[2] This implies that for any one play only three actors were available—the protagonist and two others, who in some other inscriptions are referred to as συναγωνισταί. But there is reason to believe that the actors of the later period (like the Athenian actors whom Lycurgus compelled to keep to the authorized text of the great poets) took great liberties with the text of older plays, and may have got over difficulties by this means. They would naturally select for action only such of the newer plays as their companies could conveniently perform (that the same actor might take two very different parts in the same play is proved by references in Lucian and others; see above).

C. DELIVERY, SPEECH, RECITATIVE, SONG

1. The presentation[3] of a play, whether by actors or chorus, involves three elements—the utterance of the words, the use of gestures, and the movements (or absence of movement) from place to place on the scene of action, whether on the level ground or on the stage.

The practice of Greek actors included speech unaccompanied by music, speech accompanied by an instrument (or what is

---

[1] See *Theatre of D.*, p. 240 (and refs. there given), and Rees in *Am. J. Phil.* xxxi (1910), pp. 43 ff. The latter's difficulty, that no tragic chorus is mentioned (though there were seven comic choreutai until a late date) and that nevertheless each tragic troupe had its flute-player and didaskalos, may be solved if we consider that the flute-player would be needed to accompany any lyrics sung by a τραγῳδός, and that there may have been enough for the didaskalos to do in connexion with these musical portions.

[2] Where no didaskalos is mentioned, the protagonist or a leading member of the chorus may have fulfilled the task.

[3] The Greek word for 'present' is διατιθέναι; e.g. Plato, *Charmid.* 162 d ἀλλά μοι ἔδοξεν αὐτῷ ὥσπερ ποιητῆς ὑποκριτῆ κακῶς διατιθέναι τὰ ἑαυτοῦ ποιήματα; and *Laws* ii. 658 d ῥαψῳδὸν . . . καλῶς Ἰλιάδα καὶ Ὀδύσσειαν ἤ τι καὶ Ἡσιοδείων διατιθέντα.

conventionally termed recitative), and song. The first was normally employed for the portions of a play written in iambic trimeters (the metre considered most akin to prose speech), whether in dialogue or monologue, the second for the delivery of tetrameters and of iambics inserted in the midst of lyric systems, the third for lyrics. The texts which give direct evidence on this subject are few, and except as regards recitative raise no difficulties:

(1) Aristotle, *Poet.* iv. τό τε μέτρον (of the earliest tragedy) ἐκ τετραμέτρου ἰαμβεῖον ἐγένετο. τὸ μὲν γὰρ πρῶτον τετραμέτρῳ ἐχρῶντο διὰ τὸ σατυρικὴν καὶ ὀρχηστικωτέραν εἶναι τὴν ποίησιν. λέξεως δὲ γενομένης ('when a spoken part was introduced') αὐτὴ ἡ φύσις τὸ οἰκεῖον μέτρον εὗρε. μάλιστα γὰρ λεκτικὸν τῶν μέτρων τὸ ἰαμβεῖόν ἐστιν. σημεῖον δὲ τούτου· πλεῖστα γὰρ ἰαμβεῖα λέγομεν ἐν τῇ διαλέκτῳ τῇ πρὸς ἀλλήλους.

(2) Aristotle, *Rhet.* iii. viii. ἴαμβος αὐτή ἐστιν ἡ λέξις ἡ τῶν πολλῶν· διὸ μάλιστα πάντων τῶν μέτρων ἰαμβεῖα φθέγγονται λέγοντες.

(3) Aristotle, *Poet.* vi. λέγω δὲ ἡδυσμένον λόγον (as employed by tragedy) τὸν ἔχοντα ῥυθμὸν καὶ ἁρμονίαν καὶ μέλος, τὸ δὲ χωρὶς τοῖς εἴδεσι τὰ διὰ μέτρων ἔνια μόνον περαίνεσθαι καὶ πάλιν ἕτερα διὰ μέλους.

(4) Xenophon, *Symp.* vi. iii. ἢ οὖν βούλεσθε, ἔφη, ὥσπερ Νικόστρατος ὁ ὑποκριτὴς τετράμετρα πρὸς τὸν αὐλὸν ἔλεγεν, οὕτω καὶ ὑπὸ τὸν αὐλὸν ὑμῖν διαλέγωμαι; (Nikostratos was a famous tragic actor of the last part of the fifth century. See Rees, op. cit., pp. 122–3.)

(5) [Plutarch] *de Mus.*, p. 1140 f. ἀλλὰ μὴν καὶ Ἀρχίλοχος τὴν τῶν τριμέτρων ῥυθμοποιίαν προσεξεῦρε καὶ τὴν εἰς τοὺς ὁμογενεῖς ῥυθμοὺς ἔντασιν[1] καὶ τὴν παρακαταλογὴν καὶ τὴν περὶ ταῦτα κροῦσιν ('recitative and its accompaniment') . . . ἔτι δὲ τῶν ἰαμβείων τὸ τὰ μὲν λέγεσθαι παρὰ τὴν κροῦσιν ('uttered to an accompaniment') τὰ δ' ᾄδεσθαι, Ἀρχίλοχον φασὶ καταδεῖξαι, εἶθ' οὕτω χρήσασθαι τοὺς τραγικοὺς ποιητάς, Κρέξον δὲ λαβόντα εἰς διθυράμβων χρῆσιν ἀγαγεῖν.[2] οἴονται δὲ καὶ τὴν κροῦσιν τὴν ὑπὸ τὴν ᾠδὴν[3] τοῦτον πρῶτόν εὑρεῖν, τοὺς δ' ἀρχαίους πάντα πρόσχορδα ποιεῖν.

(6) Aristotle, *Problems* xix. 6. διὰ τί ἡ παρακαταλογὴ ἐν ταῖς ᾠδαῖς[4]

---

[1] τὴν . . . ἔντασιν: the combination of iambic with rhythms of another type, e.g. (as he explains later) an iambic+paeonic line.

[2] Krexos (4th cent. B.C.) was the first to introduce recitative (as distinct from singing) into dithyramb.

[3] ὑπὸ τὴν ᾠδήν, i.e. on a higher note or notes than the utterance of the reciter. The use of ὑπό for higher and ὑπέρ for lower was derived from the position of the higher and lower strings of the harp as held by the player. (Another terminology based on the position of the notes of the flute was also in vogue. See Weil and Reinach's edition of the *de Musica*, p. 111.)

[4] Probably refers to iambic lines inserted in or between lyric strophes. See Dale, *Lyric Metres of Gk. Drama*, p. 198, and below, pp. 160 f.

τραγικόν; ἢ διὰ τὴν ἀνωμαλίαν ('the contrast involved'); παθητικὸν γὰρ τὸ ἀνωμαλὲς καὶ ἐν μεγέθει τύχης ἢ λύπης· τὸ δὲ ὁμαλὲς ἔλαττον γοῶδες.

(7) Lucian, *de Saltat.* 27 (speaking with contempt of the actor who 'sings' the iambic parts of a play). εἶτ' ἔνδοθεν αὐτὸς κεκραγώς, ἑαυτὸν ἀνακλῶν καὶ κατακλῶν, ἐνίοτε καὶ περιᾴδων τὰ ἰαμβεῖα.

(8) Athenaeus xiv. 636 b. ἐν οἷς γάρ, φησί (sc. Phillis of Delos), τοὺς ἰαμβοὺς ᾖδον ἰαμβύκας ἐκάλουν· ἐν οἷς δὲ παρακατελογίζοντο τὸ ἐν τοῖς μέτροις κλεψιάμβους.

The term παρακαταλογή, applied to the recitation of lines to the accompaniment of the flute, the instrument best suited for tragic use,[1] is found only twice (in Aristotle's *Problems* and in 'Plutarch') and the corresponding verb once (in Athenaeus). The invention of παρακαταλογή was ascribed to Archilochus, from whom the tragic poets adopted it. The word is equivalent in meaning to καταλέγειν παρὰ τὴν κροῦσιν,[2] and it would appear that the accompaniment was on a higher note or notes than those employed by the actor. Whether the actor or the flautist kept to the same note or notes, wholly or mainly, is never stated; we have in fact very little notion what this 'recitative', later accompanied by the κλεψίαμβος, was like. (It can hardly have required a special instrument in Classical times if, as is generally believed, it was employed in the iambics inserted among lyrics. There would hardly have been time for the rapid change of instruments implied.) The use of the flute in the parabasis of comedy seems to be proved by Aristophanes' *Birds* 682–4 ἀλλ' ὦ καλλιβόαν κρέκουσ' | αὐλὸν φθέγμασιν ἠρινοῖς | ἄρχου τῶν ἀναπαίστων (schol. ad loc. πολλάκις πρὸς αὐλὸν λέγουσι τὰς παραβάσεις).[3] The transition in Aristophanes, *Peace* 1171, from sung lyrics to recited trochaic tetrameters in the same sentence would be much more difficult unless both were accompanied by the same instrument. The scholiast[4] on Aristophanes' *Clouds* 1352

[1] Plut. *de Ei ap. Delph.* xxi καὶ γὰρ ὁ αὐλὸς ὀψὲ καὶ πρῴην ἐτόλμησε φωνὴν ἐφ' ἱμερτοῖσιν ἀφιέναι· τὸν δὲ πρῶτον χρόνον εἷλκε τὸ πρὸς τὰ πένθη καὶ τὴν περὶ ταῦτα λειτουργίαν οὐ μάλα ἔντιμον οὐδὲ φαιδρὰν εἶχεν, εἶτ' ἐμίχθη πάντα πᾶσιν.

[2] καταλέγειν = recite (generally 'recite at length' or 'in full') with no suggestion of music, and in *I.G.* ix. 2. 531. 12 (Larissa, about 1 B.C.) καταλογή is distinguished from singing, Hesych. καταλογή· τὸ τὰ ᾄσματα μὴ ὑπὸ μέλει λέγειν is obscure, but καταλογή here is thought to = παρακαταλογή. (He also applies the term ᾄσματα to the anapaestic tetrameters of the parabasis, which were recited, not sung.)

[3] The distinction of *cantica* and *diverbia* in Plautus and Terence does not appear to admit any third variety of delivery.

[4] οὕτως ἔλεγον πρὸς χορὸν λέγειν, ὅτε τοῦ ὑποκριτοῦ διατιθεμένου τὴν ῥῆσιν ὁ χορὸς ὠρχεῖτο

(ἤδη λέγειν χρὴ πρὸς χορόν) speaks of the chorus's dancing during the delivery by an actor of the various tetrameter systems—trochaic, anapaestic, and iambic, and as the choral dance must in all probability have been accompanied by the flute, the same accompaniment must have served for the actor delivering his address. It is not surprising that this intermediate kind of delivery is sometimes called 'singing', sometimes 'speaking'. Hesychius speaks of ἀναπαιστά as τὰ ἐν ταῖς παραβάσεσι τῶν χορῶν ᾄσματα, though Aristophanes himself describes the chorus as 'speaking' the parabasis.[1] (There is the same inconsistency as regards the close (or exodos) of comedy, which generally took the form of recited or sung lines,[2] but is described by a late grammarian[3] as τὸ ἐπὶ τέλει λεγόμενον τοῦ χοροῦ—where, however, λεγόμενον may be used in the general sense of 'utterance', as λέξις often is.)

2. This account represents the general agreement of scholars based on the scanty evidence which has come down to us. But it raises or leaves unsolved a number of interesting questions. For instance, is it to be assumed that whenever trochaic tetrameters occurred they were accompanied (in the Classical period) by the flute, e.g. in the dialogues of Aeschylus' *Persae* 155–75 (between the Queen and the chorus), 702–58 (between Darius and the Queen—in which the narrative of the disaster is mainly drawn out in alternate question and answer); or in the altercation between Aigisthos and the chorus (with a speech of 8 lines by Klytaimnestra) in the *Agamemnon* 1639–73? The matter of these conversations does not suggest musical accompaniment, and we may have here simply a survival of the original use of this metre in tragedy before the iambic trimeter was introduced for the purpose of dialogue.[4] Similarly in Sophocles' *Philoctetes* 1402–8, although the brief dialogue between Neoptolemus and Philoctetes, as they are starting for the ship, shows an enhanced

διὸ καὶ ἐκλέγονται ὡς ἐπὶ τὸ πλεῖστον ἐν τοῖς τοιούτοις τὰ τετράμετρα ἢ τὰ ἀναπαιστικὰ ἢ τὰ ἰαμβικά, διὰ τὸ ῥᾳδίως ἐμπίπτειν ἐν τούτοις τὸν τοιοῦτον ῥυθμόν (schol. on Aristoph. *Clouds* 1352).

[1] *Knights* 507–9 εἰ μέν τις ἀνὴρ τῶν ἀρχαίων κωμῳδοδιδάσκαλος ἡμᾶς | ἠνάγκαζεν λέξοντας ἔπη πρὸς τὸ θέατρον παραβῆναι, | οὐκ ἂν φαύλως ἔτυχεν τούτων.

[2] Poll. iv. 108 ὁ ἐξιόντες ᾖδον, and schol. on Aristoph. *Wasps* 270 ἅπερ ἐπὶ τῇ ἐξόδῳ τοῦ δράματος ᾄδεται. At the end of the *Ploutos* the chorus (in two concluding anapaestic tetrameters) end with δεῖ γὰρ κατόπιν τούτων ᾄδοντας ἕπεσθαι.

[3] *Tract. Coisl.* (Kaibel, *Com. Gr. Fragm.* i, p. 53). Other late grammarians use the definition ἡ πρὸς τῷ τέλει τοῦ χοροῦ ῥῆσις.

[4] Aristot. *Poet.* iii.

degree of excitement, the words put in the mouth of each hardly suggest song or music. But it is in Euripides, and in his later period, that the use of this metre for dialogue is most frequent. (The *Philoctetes* is, of course, later than much of Euripides' work.) The first instance is in the *Ion* 510–65, in the excited dialogue between Ion and Xouthos, when the latter claims Ion as his son, and most of the conversation is in half-lines, the speakers interrupting one another constantly, but surely not to music? The exodos of the play ends with 16 lines of dialogue in this metre, indicating a certain intensifying of interest, but not obviously calling for musical accompaniment. Rapid dialogue, with each line divided between two speakers, is characteristic of many of these Euripidean scenes in tetrameters, e.g. *Iph. Taur.* 1203–33 (between Iphigeneia and Thoas), *Helena* 1621–41 (between Theoklymenos and the Attendant), *Phoenissae* 588–637 (between Eteokles and Polyneikes), *Orestes* 729–806 (between Orestes and Pylades—stichomythia followed by divided lines), *Iphig. Aul.* 1338–401 (between Iphigeneia and Klytaimnestra).[1] Stichomythia (alternate question and answer, each taking an entire line) is also common in these scenes, and there are a few connected speeches, as in *Troad.* 444–61 (the highly emotional ending of Cassandra's reply to Talthybius), *Iph. Taur.*, loc. cit. (when the dialogue is over), *Bacchae* 604–41 (mainly Dionysus' narrative of exciting events), *Iph. Aul.* 316–401 (where 18 lines of excited dialogue are followed by long speeches in the same metre, delivered by Menelaus and Agamemnon), 855–916 (where 45 lines of stichomythia, in which the Old Man, Achilles, and Klytaimnestra take part, are followed by a speech of Klytaimnestra), and 1338–1401 (where the excited dialogue ends with a long speech by Iphigeneia in the same metre).[2] It is difficult to imagine musical accompaniment associated, to whatever degree, with most of these dialogues and speeches, and it seems probable that in most of them the metre connotes excitement or eagerness, and that Euripides in particular developed its use in this sense.

3. It seems probable that the anapaestic dimeters used in every play of Aeschylus were generally given in recitative

---

[1] The brief dialogue in *Rhesus* 683–90 is also mainly in broken lines.

[2] Other tetrameter passages in Euripides are *Ion* 1250–60, where Kreousa is urged by the chorus to take refuge at the altar, *Phoen.* 1335–9, where the hurrying messenger announces bad news to Kreon, and *Orest.* 1549–53, where the chorus spies Menelaus approaching.

accompanied by the flute. This may be taken as certain where they are uttered by the chorus as they enter the orchestra, preceded by the flute-player, as at the beginning of the *Suppliants* and *Persae* and in the *Agamemnon* 40–103, or when they form an introduction to a sung choral ode, as in the *Persae* 532–47 and 623–32, and before the κομμός, 907–30, and also in the *Agamemnon* 40–103, already cited, and 355–66, and the *Eumenides* 307–20. It may also be assumed that these dimeters were recited in the long dialogue between Klytaimnestra and the chorus, 1462–1577, when the utterances of the Queen in this metre contrast with the lyric strophes and antistrophes of the chorus. A similar contrast with the lyrics appears in the great litany of the *Choephoroi*, where it is the chorus which from time to time speaks in a more subdued emotional tone than Electra and Orestes, and concludes (476–8) with the appropriate prayer. (A similar difference of tone seems to be marked in the two couplets in this metre in the *Septem* 879–80 and 887–8.) The metre is used sometimes to express the moral of what has gone before or to utter an appropriate prayer; e.g. in the *Agamemnon* 1331–42, and the *Choephoroi* 719–29, 855–68, 1007–9, 1018–20. In the *Prometheus* 93–191 we have an instance of the practice, common in Euripides, by which this metre is used for the whole first scene in which a principal character speaks, and the semi-musical mode of utterance may well have been employed. Aeschylus also occasionally uses the metre when the chorus first sees or greets one of the characters, as (for example) in the *Septem* 862–74, where Antigone and Ismene are discerned, and the *Agamemnon* 782–809, where their address of a not over-warm welcome to Agamemnon is couched in anapaestic dimeters. In the *Prometheus* 281–97 Okeanos announces himself in the same metre. (In these scenes the instrumental accompaniment and recitative utterance seem less appropriate.) In the spurious final scene of the *Septem* and in the *Choephoroi* the metre is employed in the exodos, and the flute may have been used, as it doubtless was when the chorus marched out.[1]

Sophocles employs anapaestic dimeters in the Aeschylean manner in the *Ajax* and *Antigone*. They are also used in the preludes to the *kommoi* of the *Trachiniae* and *Tyrannus*. (In

---

[1] Special cases are those of the *Prometheus* 276–83, where the chorus changes its position, and 877–87 where the cries of Io while rushing away are in this metre.

the *parodos* of the *Electra* they are sung.) In the *Philoctetes* 144–200 it is the metre in which Neoptolemus expresses himself in alternation with the lyrics of the chorus, when they are looking for Philoctetes, and in the *Oedipus Coloneus* 136–75 it is much used in the agitated scene when Oedipus first confronts the chorus, both in dialogue and in the last scenes of the strophe and antistrophe. In both these plays the matter seems neither to require nor to exclude recitative. In Euripides anapaestic dimeters are constantly in use. It may be in the parodos of the chorus (*Alcestis* 77–85, *Hecuba* 99–153) or in highly emotional scenes at or near the beginning of a play (*Medea* 96–203, *Hippol.* 170–266, *Hecuba* 59 ff., *Troad.* 98–121, *Iph. Taur.* 143–235) in all of which the emotional delivery of the recitative seems more natural than bare speech, and in the *Ion* 82–183 it suits the liveliness of the boy's utterance. Its appropriateness to the dialogue of Agamemnon and the Old Man at the beginning of the *Iphigeneia in Aulis* and to the opening dialogue of the *Rhesus* is perhaps more questionable. It may be doubted whether in the *Medea* 1081–116, where a passage in this metre virtually takes the place of a choral ode, and in the *Ion* 862–922, where dimeters form a considerable part of Ion's monody, the anapaests may not actually have been sung rather than recited. In the funeral procession in the *Alcestis* 862–95 Admetus laments in anapaestic dimeters, alternating with the lyric strophes and antistrophes of the chorus. It may be that this contrast is an element in the characterization of Admetus,[1] and if so, his part was probably recited. In the *Andromache* there is a similar contrast between the anapaests (515–22, 537–44) of the brutal Menelaus and the terrified lyrics of Andromache and her child, but it is difficult to be positive whether Menelaus required a flute accompaniment, or whether the metre merely expresses the urgency of his commands. Nor is it easy to be certain whether the brief moralizing lines, *Alcestis* 238–43, are to be thought of as spoken or as recited. (On the other hand, the prayer in 741–6 is virtually lyric in tone.) There is the same doubt about *Heraclidai* 288–96 and 702–8. The chorus's brief cry of sympathy in *Medea* 357–63 seems to call for more than mere speech. Almost all the plays of Euripides employ anapaestic dimeters to conclude the exodos, and in nearly all of these scenes recitative

---

[1] In ll. 273–9 also Admetus' distress does not go beyond anapaestic dimeters.

and the flute may be assumed; in most there are only a few formal or almost formal lines.[1] A few special cases do not fall clearly under any of the above heads; e.g. *Hippolytus* 1283-95, where Artemis begins her address to Theseus with 12 dimeters of fierce denunciation, whether accompanied or not; *Troades* 782-98, comprising the whole brief tragic episode in which Talthybius carries Astyanax away, and certainly calling for the more intensified tone; *Electra* 1292-1341, an emotional scene of parting between Orestes and Elektra in the presence of the Dioskouroi, who conclude with 14 lines in the same metre; and *Iphigeneia in Aulis* 1276-83, where 7 lines of dimeters, shared between Klytaimnestra and Iphigeneia, precede the latter's lyric monody.

There may be a difference of opinion as to the employment of recitative in many of the passages mentioned. But the most difficult class of passages consists of those, very numerous in Euripides,[2] in which a few lines in the metre are used to announce the approach of some human person or a god *ex machina* or of a procession or whatever it may be. In a few of these recitative to the flute seems not impossible, e.g. *Andromache* 494-500 at the end of a choral ode, in others it would be almost absurd. In the present state of our knowledge the test must be mainly subjective; but it is hard to believe that anapaestic dimeters were never simply spoken, the metre itself being in that case sufficient to emphasize the appropriate tone.

4. It should be noted that the word παρακαταλογή is not (in the few instances of its occurrence) applied to anapaestic dimeters, and poets were probably free to employ any of the three methods of delivery. The word does appear to apply to iambics delivered to an accompaniment, but it has already been noticed that there can be no certainty what exactly were these accompanied iambics adopted by the tragic poets from Archi-

---

[1] Four plays (*Alcestis, Medea, Andromache, Bacchae*) end with the lines πολλαὶ μορφαὶ τῶν δαιμονίων (or πολλῶν ταμίας Ζεὺς ἐν Ὀλύμπῳ) | πολλὰ δ᾽ ἀέλπτως κραίνουσι θεοί, | καὶ τὰ δοκηθέντ᾽ οὐκ ἐτελέσθη, | τῶν δ᾽ ἀδοκήτων πόρον ηὗρε θεός· | τοιόνδ᾽ ἀπέβη τόδε πρᾶγμα; and two (*Phoenissae* and *Orestes*) with a prayer for victory—ὦ μέγα σεμνὴ Νίκη, τὸν ἐμὸν | βίοτον κατέχοις | καὶ μὴ λήγοις στεφανοῦσα—which is really extra-dramatic. The schol. on Aristoph. *Wasps* 582 states definitely: ἔθος δὲ ἦν ἐν ταῖς ἐξόδοις τῆς τραγῳδίας χορικῶν προσώπων προηγεῖσθαι αὐλητὴν ὥστε αὐλοῦντα προπέμπειν. See above, p. 156.

[2] *Alc.* 28-37; *Hippol.* 1342-6; *Androm.* 496-500, 1166-72, 1226-30; *Suppl.* 794-7, 980-9, 1113-22; *Herc. F.* 442-50; *Troad.* 568-76, 1118-22, 1252-9; *Elec r.* 988-97, 1233-7; *Iph. Taur.* 455-66; *Orest.* 102-7; *Iph. Aul.* 590-606; *Phoeniss.* 1480-4.

lochus, or those described by Athenaeus (after the almost unknown Phillis of Delos) as ἐν οἷς παρακατελογίζοντο τὸ ἐν τοῖς
μέτροις. In fact a large proportion of the iambic trimeters associated with lyrics form part of symmetrical structures in which
the lyric strophe and antistrophe are each followed by the same
number of iambic lines—two, three, four, or five, or more rarely
by a single line; it seems at least possible that these iambics were
recited, and the contrast between these recited iambics and the
sung lyrics may be what is referred to as παθητικόν in the Aristotelian *Problems* xix. 6 (see above, p. 155). There are instances
in all three poets, affording impressive and symmetrical structures. Thus in Aeschylus' *Suppliants* 348–406 each choral strophe
and antistrophe is followed by five iambic lines in the mouth
of the King; and in ll. 736–63 the dochmiac strophes of three
lines alternate with four iambic lines divided between King and
chorus; in the *Persae* 256–89 choral strophes of four lines alternate with the iambic trimeter couplets of the Messenger; in the
Septem 203–44 and 686–711 Eteokles utters three-line groups of
trimeters in alternation with the choral lyrics, and it must be
admitted that Eteokles' sentiments seem to demand violent
speech rather than musical accompaniment. In the *Agamemnon*
1072–1113 also, the trimeter couplets of the chorus, in response
to Cassandra's wild lyrics, are extremely prosy, and may well
have been spoken. Cassandra's own lyrics end with trimeter
couplets (uttered by herself) at 1160–1 and 1171–2, and as there
is no break in the sense or change of tone, these may even have
been sung. In Sophocles' *Ajax*, ll. 348–93 are parallel in form
to the first of the instances from the *Agamemnon*, the lyrics of
Ajax being broken by one, two, or three trimeters of the chorus.
The same typical form is found in the *Electra* 1232–87, where
Orestes' trimeters occur between the lyric strophe, antistrophe,
and epode of Electra, and in the *Oedipus Coloneus* 1448–1504,
except that each group of five trimeters is a dialogue, and should
probably be thought of as spoken rather than recited. In other
passages of Sophocles the symmetry is more complicated (e.g.
Ajax 891–914 and 942–60, *Electra* 1232–87, *Oedipus Tyrannus*
649–88, and *Antigone* 1261–76 and 1284–1300) and in some of
these the use of recitative seems very doubtful, though there can
at present be no criterion but the reader's feeling. In Euripides
the typical symmetry of alternate strophes and iambics is found

in the *Alcestis* 244–65 and *Hippolytus* 571–97; but in the *Medea* 1273–81, *Heraclidai* 75–110, and *Andromache* 825–45 the iambic lines are included within the strophe and antistrophe, and in a number of plays we find iambic lines combined or mixed with the non-antistrophic lyrics to which Euripides was prone, e.g. *Hecuba* 684–720, *Supplices* 1123–63, *Hercules Furens* 875–905 and 1178–1213, *Iphigeneia in Tauris* 827–67, and *Phoenissae* 103–81. Whether or how in these passages the transitions between song and parakataloge were managed must be mainly a matter of conjecture. Our authorities, such as they are, do not require us to believe that *all* iambics found in combination with lyrics were delivered in parakataloge, and the poet was probably free to prescribe whatever delivery he required.

5. When we pass to the Old Comedy difficulties are not at an end. In the account given earlier in this chapter it has been made plain that the anapaests of the parabasis were accompanied by the flute, as also, in all probability, were any tetrameter speeches delivered by an actor while the chorus or a semi-chorus was dancing, and in particular the epirrhema and antepirrhema of the parabasis, which were commonly in trochaic or iambic tetrameters. This is all that is required to satisfy the statement of the scholiast on the *Clouds* 1352 (see above, pp. 155 f.), from which it is certainly impossible to infer that *all* tetrameters were accompanied by the flute. (They were certainly not all accompanied by choral dancing.) The word παρακαταλογή is never applied to comedy. But the Old Comedy included as a rule a number of epirrhematic systems besides the parabasis,[1] though not so perfectly symmetrical, such as the agon, almost entirely in tetrameters, the proagon, and the 'battle-scene'. (The parodos is also often in tetrameters, and here no doubt the chorus usually marched, or entered otherwise, to music.) In all of these scenes it is only possible to be guided by the character of the words in conjecturing the manner of delivery, and opinions will inevitably differ. It seems, however, at least improbable that very long passages of close argument between two or more persons were recited to the flute before a dancing chorus, while on the other hand instrumental accompaniment is practically

---

[1] The analysis of the plays in my *Dith. Trag. Com.*, pp. 312 ff., with the chapter preceding it, gives details. Some difficulties as to the rendering of certain metres in comedy are discussed by J. W. White, *The Verse of Greek Comedy* (1912), pp. 368–71, but there is room for wide differences of opinion about many details.

certain in the exodos of some plays; and it is unlikely that the freedom of the poet was restricted by rigid conventions.

Of the Middle and New Comedy too little has survived to allow of any profitable discussion of delivery. It is clear that scenes in trochaic tetrameters were not infrequent; there are fragments of some twenty such scenes in the Middle Comedy and three trochaic tetrameter scenes (with indications of another) survive in the remains of Menander's *Samia* and *Perikeiromene*, in which there is no reason to suppose that more is implied than the quickening of the pace which goes with the metre. A few other traces of such scenes in the New Comedy are found. In the fragments of the Middle Comedy, but not of the New (except in Menander, fr. 312 (K.)), we find over a dozen in anapaestic dimeters, some of considerable length,[1] and several resembling the πνῖγος of the Old Comedy. We do not know how they were spoken or sung, except that in some of them great rapidity may be assumed. There are a very few traces of iambic tetrameters[2] and Eupolideans.[3] Hexameters are sometimes introduced for special effects—parody, high-stilted language, riddles, prophecy; the delivery of these may have varied.

6. The instrument by which both singing and recitative were normally accompanied in tragedy and comedy was the flute.[4] In the *Problems* of Aristotle, xix. 43, it is argued that the flute gives a better accompaniment to the human voice than the lyre, because both flute and voice are wind-instruments and so blend better. There is no special reference to tragedy in the passage, but it appears probable that the lyre was used in the drama mainly for special effects, as when the young Sophocles played it in his *Thamyris*, and it may have been confined almost entirely to the occasional accompaniment of monodies. In his parody of the lyrics of both Aeschylus and Euripides in the *Frogs*,[5] Aristophanes has the lines which he collects from various plays of each author sung to the lyre; but, taking the context

---

[1] e.g. Anaxandrides, fr. 71 (K.) (71 lines); Mnesimachus, fr. 4 (65 lines); Epikrates, fr. 11 (38 lines).

[2] e.g. Antiphanes, fr. 25; Fr. Incert. 294. [3] Alexis, fr. 237.

[4] Schol. on Aristoph. *Clouds* 313 (μοῦσα βαρύβρομος αὐλῶν) προσηύλουν γὰρ καὶ ταῖς τραγῳδίαις καὶ τοῖς κυκλίοις χοροῖς. In Aristoph. *Wasps* 580–2 there is a reference to the flute-player in the *Niobe* (? of Aeschylus or Sophocles), and the schol. remarks (*inter alia*) ἔθος γὰρ ἦν ἐν ταῖς ἐξόδοις τῶν τῆς τραγῳδίας χορικῶν προσώπων προηγεῖσθαι αὐλητήν. For the flute in comedy cf. Aristoph. *Birds* 682–4 (quoted above) and *Eccles.* 890–2.

[5] See especially ll. 1286, 1304.

as a whole, this does not imply that all these passages were from odes or solos originally accompanied by the lyre. That Euripides punctuates some of the lines of the parodos of the *Agamemnon* with τοφλάττοθρατ τοφλάττοθρατ (having said that he is making up a passage, στάσιν μελῶν | ἐκ τῶν κιθαρῳδικῶν νόμων εἰργασμένην), and that Aeschylus in putting together a nonsensical selection of lines from Euripides calls for a lyre (ἐνεγκάτω τις τὸ λύριον—doubtless the lyre which his rival had just been using), is sufficiently explained if it is remembered that neither poet could sing the other's lines *and accompany them himself* (as the travesty demanded) on anything but the lyre—certainly not on the flute. The argument of Kranz[1] that the fact that the Furies in the *Eumenides*[2] describe their ὕμνος as ἀφόρμικτος implies that other *choral odes in tragedy* were accompanied by the φόρμιγξ is absurd; it is enough that the music of the lyre was the common accompaniment of cheerful songs in real life.[3] On the other hand, it is quite possible that in adopting the musical style of his friend Timotheos and the new school,[4] Euripides may also have employed the lyre, the instrument whose capacity was especially developed by Timotheos. A lyre—in fact two—are portrayed on the Pronomos vase,[5] in which the central figure is the flute-player Pronomos, surrounded by satyrs and actors in the presence of Dionysus, but it would not be safe to draw any inference from this as to the extent of the use of the lyre in tragedy or satyric drama. When theatrical companies were organized in the fourth century, each seems to have included a single flute-player.[6]

It is probable that the flute-player in tragedy and satyric drama wore no mask. There is indeed no direct evidence; but where satyrs are depicted as dancing to the flute, as on the

[1] *Stasimon*, p. 139.

[2] Cf. *Agam.* 990 τὸν δ᾽ ἄνευ λύρας ὅμως ὑμνῳδεῖ | θρῆνον Ἐρίννος αὐτοδίδακτος ἔσωθεν | θυμός.

[3] The application of the epithets ἄχορον ἀκίθαριν to Ares in the *Suppliants*, l. 681, and that the chorus (ibid. 691) in invoking blessings on Argos prays ἀγνῶν τ᾽ ἐκ στομάτων φερέσθω φάμα φιλοφόρμιγξ has no discernible bearing on the use of the lyre in tragedy; and Horace, *Ars Poet.* 216, which Kranz also quotes, has no reference to tragedy at all.

[4] See below, p. 265 f.

[5] Furtwängler–Reichhold, *Gr. Vasenmalerei* iii, pls. 143–5 and pp. 132 ff. (including Buschor's discussion). See below, pp. 179–80. The vase is certainly not the reproduction of a scene in a play.

[6] Cf. inscriptions recording performances at the Soteria, and others referred to in Ch. VII below. It is not known to what period Sextus Empiricus refers (p. 751. 17 Bekker) when he writes ὡσαύτως δὲ (sc. πρὸς λύραν ᾔδετο) καὶ τὰ παρὰ τοῖς τραγικοῖς μέλη καὶ στάσιμα φυσικόν τινα ἐπέχοντα λόγον (nor, it must be admitted, exactly what he means).

Pronomos Vase, and on the Pandora Krater of about 450 B.C.
in the British Museum[1] (though this may not be connected with
a theatrical performance at all), as well as on the Pompeian
Mosaic[2] representing the rehearsal of a satyric play, the flute-
player is not masked. As regards comedy, it seems uncertain
whether Procne in the *Birds* is to be regarded as wearing a bird-
mask or not when she comes forward to accompany the anapaests of the parabasis. On the vase-paintings representing birds
and horsemen, with a flute-player, the latter seems to be wearing
only the regular mouthpiece (φορβεία).[3]

We read little of instruments, other than the flute and lyre,
accompanying the actor's delivery; but in the *Hypsipyle* the
heroine accompanies her song to her infant with κρόταλα—
probably a rattle—which Aristophanes parodies by castanets
played (probably) by an ugly old woman (*Frogs* 1304 ff.):

καίτοι τί δεῖ
λύρας ἐπὶ τούτων; ποῦ 'στιν ἡ τοῖς ὀστράκοις
αὕτη κροτοῦσα; δεῦρο Μοῦσ' Εὐριπίδου,
πρὸς ἥνπερ ἐπιτήδεια ταῦτ' ᾄδειν μέλη.

D. VOICE AND ENUNCIATION

There is much evidence to show that Athenian audiences
attached great importance to the actor's voice, though the
Athenian sound-vocabulary is not always so clear as to indicate
exactly the qualities looked for, and most of the evidence is
comparatively late. Obviously the voice needed to be strong
enough to carry throughout the vast theatre without shouting
as bad actors were liable to do, but this must not be overstressed,
because (at least according to Lucian) the actors of the later
comedy found it unnecessary to strain their voices.[4] (He couples
the tragedian's exaggeration of sound with the grotesque costume which they wore at this period.) The large theatres demanded practised voice-production rather than violent effort,

---

[1] See *Dith. Trag. Com.*, pp. 156–7, fig. 14.

[2] Below, Fig. 69; cf. *Theatre of Dionysus*, fig. 98, etc. With this should be compared the
picture of a rehearsal of tragedy on an engraved stone in the British Museum, figured by
Wiesler, *Theatergeb.*, Taf. xii. 45, in which the flute-player is not masked, though the five
choreutai represented have masks thrown back on the top of their heads. (See also
Baumeister, *Denkm.* i. 392, Abb. 423.)

[3] *Dith. Trag. Com.*, pp. 245 ff.

[4] Lucian, *Anach.* 23 αὐτοὶ δὲ (οἱ τραγῳδοὶ) μέγαλα τε ἐκεκράγεσαν καὶ διέβαινον οὐκ οἶδ'
ὅπω ἀσφαλῶς ἐν τοῖς ὑποδήμασι . . . οἱ δὲ κωμῳδοὶ βραχύτεροι μὲν ἐκείνων καὶ πεζοὶ καὶ ἀνθρω-
πινότεροι καὶ ἧττον ἐβόων.

and in fact the acoustic properties of the theatre of Epidaurus are such that a clear but not forced delivery of the speaker's lines from the normal place is audible as far as the uppermost row of seats.[1] (The remains of the theatres at Athens and Syracuse give less good, though not bad, results; but their condition makes a satisfactory test impossible.) Thus, while μεγαλοφωνία, εὐφωνία, and λαμπρότης were commended, and it was by his voice that an actor was commonly judged, great stress is also laid on beauty of tone and adaptability to the personality or mood of the character represented. Plato indeed so far distrusted the influence of the actor's loud voice that he would not admit it to his ideal state (*Laws* vii. 817 c μὴ δὴ δόξητε ἡμᾶς ῥᾳδίως γε οὕτως ὑμᾶς ποτε παρ᾽ ἡμῖν ἐάσειν σκηνάς τε πήξαντας κατ᾽ ἀγορὰν καὶ καλλιφώνους ὑποκριτὰς εἰσαγαγομένους, μεῖζον φθεγγομένους ἡμῶν, ἐπιτρέψειν ὑμῖν δημηγορεῖν πρὸς παῖδάς τε καὶ γυναῖκας καὶ τὸν πάντα ὄχλον). Dionysius the tyrant of Syracuse (early in the 4th century), in choosing actors to perform his play at Olympia, chose τοὺς εὐφωνοτάτους τῶν ὑποκριτῶν . . . οὗτοι δὲ τὸ μὲν πρῶτον διὰ τὴν εὐφωνίαν ἐξέπληττον τοὺς ἀκούοντας;[2] and Demosthenes, when his voice failed to produce its effect on the Assembly, is said to have exclaimed τοὺς ὑποκριτὰς δεῖν κρίνειν ἐκ τῆς φωνῆς, τοὺς δὲ ῥήτορας ἐκ τῆς γνώμης.[3] Neoptolemus, the tragic actor in the fourth century, who was also employed as an ambassador between Philip II and Athens, is described as πρωτεύων τῇ μεγαλοφωνίᾳ καὶ τῇ δόξῃ.[4] But the need of adaptability is frequently emphasized—first of all by Aristotle, who is speaking primarily of the orator but illustrates the point, and particularly the necessity of naturalness, from the drama; e.g. (*Rhet.* iii. 1) ἔστι δὲ αὐτὴ μὲν ἐν τῇ φωνῇ, πῶς αὐτῇ δεῖ χρῆσθαι πρὸς ἕκαστον πάθος, οἷον πότε μεγάλῃ καὶ πότε μικρᾷ καὶ πότε μέσῃ, καὶ πῶς τοῖς τόνοις, οἷον ὀξείᾳ καὶ βαρείᾳ καὶ μέσῃ, καὶ ῥυθμοῖς τίσι πρὸς ἕκαστον, and (*Rhet.* iii. 2) δεῖ λανθάνειν ποιοῦντας καὶ μὴ δοκεῖν λέγειν πεπλασμένως ἀλλὰ πεφυκότως· τοῦτο γὰρ πιθανόν . . . οἷον ἡ τοῦ Θεοδώρου φωνὴ πέπονθε πρὸς

---

[1] This was demonstrated when the late Mr. H. A. L. Fisher recited a passage of Homer to myself and others there many years ago. (On the supposed effect of masks in increasing the volume of sound in the actor's voice see below, Ch. iv, § 14.)   [2] Diod. Sic. xv. 7.

[3] Plut. *Vit. X Orat.* p. 848 b. Cicero, on the other hand, (*de Orat.* iii, § 224) makes a good voice the first requisite for an orator also. The anecdote in Alciphron iii. xii (4th cent. A.D.) of an actor named Likymnios who defeated his rivals τορῷ τινι καὶ γεγωνοτέρῳ φωνήματι is probably fictitious, but illustrates the same standard of judgement some 600 years later.

[4] Diod. Sic. xvi. 42.

Voice and Enunciation

67

τὴν τῶν ἄλλων ὑποκριτῶν. ἡ μὲν γὰρ τοῦ λέγοντος ἔοικεν εἶναι, αἱ
δ' ἀλλότριαι. (Theodorus' skill in drawing tears from his audience
—even from so hardened a tyrant as Alexander of Pherai—may
have been as much the result of his voice as of his acting.)[1] At
a later date πλάσμα was used in a less unfavourable sense than
πεπλασμένως (the equivalent of 'artificial') in Aristotle, and
(with kindred words) signified adaptability, as in Plutarch,
Symp. Qu. VII. viii. 1 πρόσεστι δὲ ὑπόκρισις πρέπουσα τῷ ἤθει
τῶν ὑποκειμένων προσώπων, καὶ φωνῆς πλάσμα καὶ σχῆμα, καὶ
διαθέσεις ('delivery') ἐπόμεναι τοῖς λεγομένοις.[2] Lucian (*Piscat.* 31)
implies the same principle: καὶ τὸ πρᾶγμα ὅμοιον ἐδόκει μοι
καθάπερ εἴ τις ὑποκριτὴς τραγῳδίας, μαλθακὸς αὐτὸς ὢν καὶ
γυναικίας, Ἀχιλλέα ἢ Θησέα ἢ Ἡρακλέα ὑποκρίνοιτο αὐτόν, μήτε
βαδίζων μήτε φθεγγόμενος ἡρωικόν, ἀλλὰ θρυπτόμενος ὑπὸ τηλι-
κούτῳ προσωπείῳ; and (*Nigrin.* 11) μὴ καὶ κατ' ἄλλο τι γένωμαι
τοῖς ὑποκριταῖς ἐκείνοις ὅμοιος, οἳ πολλάκις ἢ Ἀγαμέμνονος ἢ
Κρέοντος ἢ καὶ Ἡρακλέους αὐτοῦ πρόσωπον ἀνειληφότες, χρυσίδας
ἠμφιεσμένοι καὶ δεινὸν βλέποντες καὶ μέγα κεχηνότες μικρὸν φθέγγονται καὶ ἰσχνὸν καὶ γυναικῶδες καὶ τῆς Ἑκάβης ἢ Πολυξένης
πολὺ ταπεινότερον.

The skill with which Polos, the famous actor of about 300 B.C.,
could perform the part of Oedipus, whether as king or as beggar,
is referred to by Plutarch (*de Amicit.* vii): ἢ οὐχ ὁρᾷς ὅτι οὐκ
εὐφωνότερον οὐδὲ ἥδιον ὁ Πῶλος τὸν τύραννον Οἰδιπόδα ὑπεκρίνετο
ἢ τὸν ἐπὶ Κολωνῷ ἀλητὴν καὶ πτωχόν;

The actor naturally had not only to adapt himself generally
to the character represented, but to control every inflexion of
his voice so as to express exactly the character's mind as reflected
in the text, and so Aristotle[3] treats a knowledge of the 'figures of
speech'—question, prayer, threat, command, narrative, and so
on—as an essential part of ὑποκριτική. He also[4] treats as essential to the actor's art the power to repeat the same thing in a
variety of tones: ἀνάγκη γὰρ τὸ μεταβάλλειν τὸ αὐτὸ λέγοντας,
ὅπερ ὥσπερ ὁδοποιεῖ τῷ ὑποκρίνεσθαι . . . οἷον καὶ Φιλήμων ὁ
ὑποκριτὴς ἐποίει ἔν τε τῇ Ἀναξανδρίδου Γεροντομανίᾳ, ὅτε λέγοι

---

[1] Aelian, *V.H.* xiv. 40; Plut. *de Alex. Fort.* 334 a. The same power was a boast of Kallippides
(Xen. *Symp.* iii. 11 Καλλιππίδης ὁ ὑποκριτής, ὃς ὑπερσεμνύνεται ὅτι δύναται πολλοὺς κλαίοντας
καθίζειν).
[2] Cf. Plut. *Cic.* 3 ἥ τε φωνὴ πολλὴ μὲν καὶ ἀγαθή, σκληρὰ δὲ καὶ ἄπλαστος, and ibid. 4 ἥ τε
φωνὴ λαμβάνουσα πλάσιν ἡδεῖα μὲν πρὸς ἀκοὴν ἐτέθραπτο.
[3] *Poet.* xix.
[4] *Rhet.* iii. 12.

''Ραδάμανθυς καὶ Παλαμήδης', καὶ ἐν τῷ προλόγῳ τῶν Εὐσεβῶν
τὸ 'ἐγώ' ... ἀναγκὴ γὰρ ὑποκρίνεσθαι καὶ μὴ ὡς ἐν λέγοντα τῷ
αὐτῷ ἤθει καὶ τόνῳ εἰπεῖν. (Unhappily the point of the examples
of Philemon's skill is lost to us. Anaxandrides was composing
from about 380 to 345 B.C.)

But there must have been plenty of actors even in the Classical
period who did not come up to the highest standard and performed at the Rural Dionysia rather than in the City. Such
were Simykas and Sokrates, the βαρύστονοι—the 'roarers'—to
whom, according to Demosthenes,[1] Aeschines joined himself
with poor success. Pollux[2] enumerates the terms which unkind
critics might apply to bad actors: εἴποις δ' ἂν βαρύστονος
ὑποκριτής, βομβῶν, περιβομβῶν, ληκυθίζων, λαρυγγίζων, φαρυγγί-
ζων καὶ βαρύφωνος δὲ καὶ λεπτόφωνος καὶ γυναικόφωνος καὶ στρηνό-
φωνος καὶ ὅσα σὺν τούτοις ἄλλα ἐν τοῖς περὶ φωνῆς εἴρηται. An
amusing story is told by Philostratus[3] of an actor in the time
of Nero who terrified the people of Ipola in Baetica, when pre-
tending to reproduce the melodies sung by Nero at Olympia
in a resounding voice (ἐπεὶ ἐξάρας τὴν φωνὴν γεγωνὸν ἐφθέγξατο),
so that they fled from the theatre ὥσπερ ὑπὸ δαίμονος ἐμβοηθέντες.
Another story[4] speaks of an actor who is called Ἠπειρώτης
(either because this was his name or because he came from
Epirus) who, ἄριστα φωνῆς ἔχων, εὐδοκιμῶν δ' ἐπ' αὐτῇ καὶ
θαυμαζόμενος λαμπροτέρα τοῦ εἰωθότος, dared to compete against
Nero himself and refused to lower his tone until Nero's own
actors used violence to force him to do so.

There are sundry allusions to the careful training to which
actors subjected themselves, fasting and dieting themselves and
using every opportunity before and in the intervals of the performances to test their voice and bring it into condition; e.g.
in Aristotle,[5] διά τί τοῖς μετὰ τὰ σιτία κεκραγόσιν ἡ φωνὴ δια-
φθείρεται; καὶ πάντας ἂν ἴδοιμι τοὺς φωνασκοῦντας, οἷον ὑποκριτὰς
καὶ χορευτὰς καὶ τοὺς ἄλλους τοιούτους ἕωθέν τε καὶ νήστεις ὄντας
τὰς μελέτας ποιουμένους.[6] Hermon, a comic actor of the late
fifth century, is said to have missed his turn to appear while he
was trying his voice outside the theatre.[2]

---

[1] *de Cor.* § 262.   [2] iv. 114.
[3] *Vit. Apoll.* v. ix.   [4] Lucian, *Nero* ix.
[5] *Probl.* xi. 22.   [6] Cf. Athen. viii. 343 e, 344 d.
[7] Pollux iv. 88 ὁ μὲν ἀπῆν τοῦ θεάτρου τῆς φωνῆς ἀποπειρώμενος. Cicero, *de Orat.* i, § 251,
speaks of tragic actors 'qui et annos complures sedentes declamitant, et cotidie, antequam

The keen sensitiveness of an Athenian audience to the quality
—especially, perhaps, the clearness—of an actor's voice is shown
by the pains taken by the actor to come up to the standard.
Their appreciation of the recitatives of Nikostratos in the fifth
century has already been noticed,[1] and the importance to the
protagonist (to whom, if successful, the prize for acting was
open) of winning their favour is quaintly illustrated at a later
date by Cicero's statement[2] that the Greek actors of his day,
who played the second or third part, modified their tone, even
if they had better voices than the protagonist, so as to give him
his chance. The sensitiveness of the audiences required not only
good voices but clearness and correctness of enunciation, and
the comic poets of the fifth century were never tired of mocking
the actor Hegelochus who had pronounced the line, Eur. *Orestes*
279, ἐκ κυμάτων γὰρ αὖθις αὖ γαλήν' ὁρῶ, as if it had ended with
γαλῆν ὁρῶ.[3] They were not above being amused by mere tricks
of voice—the imitation of animals and inanimate noises—if they
'came off', as when Parmenon imitated the squeaking of a pig
or Theodorus the sound of a windlass;[4] but few audiences do not
occasionally let cleverness get the better of good taste.

E. GESTURE

The actor's qualifications included a command not only of
voice but of gesture in the widest sense; and it is important not
to exaggerate the statuesqueness so often said to characterize
the actor's behaviour. The belief in this arises mainly from a
failure to distinguish between the earlier and the later periods
in the history of Greek costume. The thick-soled κοθορνοί—

---

pronuntient, vocem cubantes sensim excitant eandemque cum egerunt sedentes ab acutissimo
sono usque ad gravissimum sonum recipiunt et quasi quodammodo colligunt'; and Lucian,
(*de Saltat.* 27) with some contempt describes the tragic actor as ἔνδοθεν αὐτὸς κεκραγώς,
ἑαυτὸν ἀνακλῶν καὶ κατακλῶν, ἐνίοτε καὶ περιάδων τὰ ἰαμβεῖα, καὶ τὸ δὴ αἴσχιστον μελῳδῶν
τὰς συμφορὰς καὶ μόνης τῆς φωνῆς ὑπεύθυνον παρέχων ἑαυτόν.

[1] p. 154. Cf. *Prov. Coislin.* 124 ἐγὼ ποιήσω πάντα κατὰ Νικόστρατον· ἐπὶ τῶν ὀρθῶς πάντα
ποιούντων· ἦν γὰρ ὁ Νικόστρατος ὑποκριτὴς τραγικὸς ἄριστος καὶ μάλιστα ἐν ταῖς τῶν ἀγγέλων
ἐπαγγελίαις.

[2] *In Q. Caec. Divin.* § 48. Cicero also (*Orator*, §§ 25, 27) highly extols the impeccable taste
of Athenian audiences as judges of oratory.

[3] Aristoph. *Frogs* 303 and schol.; also schol. on Eur. *Orest.* 279; Sannyrion, fr. 8 (K.);
Suidas s.v. Ἡγέλοχος writes τοῦτον δὲ καὶ ὡς ἀτερπῆ τὴν φωνὴν Πλάτων σκώπτει.

[4] Plut. *de Aud. poet.* 3. Parmenon's rivals, resolved to defeat him, brought a real pig into
the theatre, and when it squealed the audience cried εὖ μέν, ἀλλ' οὐδὲν πρὸς τὴν Παρμένοντος
ὗν. The rivals then released the pig, confounding the audience, and so creating a new proverb.
(Plut. *Quaest. Symp.* v. 674 b.)

raising the actor's feet several inches above the ground—and the costume of the Rieti statuette would imply that the actor must as far as possible be stationary, and the narrow raised stage would make careless movements inadvisable. But (as will be shown below) these are not to be found in the Classical period, when, as the texts of the plays make clear, there was no difficulty in rapid movement, kneeling, prostration, and the free play of gesture. (This will be illustrated shortly.) It was only facial expression that was unalterable, owing to the use of masks. Two persons might embrace, and this happened often,[1] but kissing was impossible; nor could there be any display of tears, though they are often mentioned. Thus, according to the text, the eyes of the chorus in the *Prometheus* fill with tears of sympathy for the sufferer;[2] Electra bursts into violent weeping at the sight of the lock of Orestes' hair,[3] and later in the play[4] the Nurse enters in tears; the chorus weeps at the sight of Antigone being led away to death;[5] Antigone weeps at the loss of her father;[6] Admetus bursts into tears more than once;[7] so do Medea[8] and Kreousa.[9] In other scenes in Euripides, Andromache or Aithra or Klytaimnestra are seen weeping.[10] Or it may be Herakles or Menelaus or Ion or a faithful servant,[11] or the sympathetic chorus.[12] Sometimes the incongruity is concealed by the Greek habit of covering the head and face when in tears,[13] and the frequent tears of Agamemnon in the *Iphigeneia in Aulis*[14] recall the famous painting inspired by the play in which he is seen with head veiled[15] to conceal his grief. Changes of expression and signs of temper or mood which are mentioned in the text had to be imagined by the audience—as, for instance, when Klytaimnestra announces to the chorus the fall of Troy[16]:

> ΧΟ. χαρά μ' ὑφέρπει δάκρυον ἐκκαλουμένη.
> ΚΛ. εὖ γὰρ φρονοῦντος ὄμμα σοῦ κατηγορεῖ.

[1] Eur. *Hec.* 410, *Ion* 1438, *Phoen.* 306 ff., etc.   [2] ll. 145, 399.
[3] *Cho.* 185–6 ἐξ ὀμμάτων δὲ δίψιοι πίπτουσί μοι | σταγόνες ἄφρακτοι δυσχίμου πλημμυρρίδος.
[4] l. 731. Electra is also spoken of as weeping in Soph. *El.* 829 (ὦ παῖ, τί δακρύεις;).
[5] *Antig.* 803–4. (When Ismene enters in tears at l. 527, the tears may have been depicted on the mask and remained there during the short scene that follows.)
[6] *Oed. Col.* 1709–10 ἀνὰ γὰρ ὄμμα σε τόδ', ὦ πάτερ, ἐμὸν | στένει δακρῦον.
[7] *Alc.* 530, 1067.   [8] *Med.* 905, 922, 1012.
[9] *Ion* 241, 876, 940.   [10] *Androm.* 532, *Hiket.* 21, 770, *Iph. Aul.* 888, 1433
[11] *H.F.* 1394, *Helen.* 456, *Ion* 1369, *Electr.* 502.
[12] *Hippl.* 853, *H.F.* 449, 1045, *Hiket.* 49, 96.
[13] *Electr.* 1339, *Hiket.* 286, *Ion* 967, *Orest.* 280.   [14] *Iph. Aul.* 477, 496, 650, 684.
[15] Baumeister, *Denkm.* i. 755, fig. 807, etc.   [16] A. *Ag.* 270–1.

and now and then the impossibility of changing the expression is almost apologized for in the text. The Eumenides became friendly, but could not show it in their faces, and Athena has to reassure the Athenians[1] ἐκ τῶν φοβερῶν τῶνδε προσώπων | μέγα κέρδος ὁρῶ τοῖσδε πολίταις. Electra in Sophocles' play explains that she cannot show in her face the joy which she feels, owing to her long association with sorrow and hatred:[2]

> ΟΡ. οὕτως δ' ὅπως μήτηρ σε μὴ 'πιγνώσεται
> φαιδρῷ προσώπῳ νῶν ἐπελθόντοιν δόμους·
> ἀλλ' ὡς ἐπ' ἄτῃ τῇ μάτην λελεγμένῃ
> στέναζ'· ὅταν γὰρ εὐτυχήσωμεν, τότε
> χαίρειν παρέσται καὶ γελᾶν ἐλευθέρως. . . .
> ΗΛ. μήτηρ δ' ἐν οἴκοις· ἣν σὺ μὴ δείσῃς ποθ' ὡς
> γέλωτι τοὐμὸν φαιδρὸν ὄψεται κάρα.
> μῖσός τε γὰρ παλαιὸν ἐντέτηκέ μοι,
> κἀπεί σ' ἐσεῖδον, οὔποτ' ἐκλήξω χαρᾷ
> δακρυρροοῦσα.

and in Euripides' *Orestes*[3] she retains her gloomy expression to deceive Hermione:

> πάλιν κατάστηθ' ἡσύχῳ μὲν ὄμματι
> χροᾷ τ' ἀδήλῳ τῶν δεδραμένων πέρι·
> κἀγὼ σκυθρωποὺς ὄμματων ἔξω κόρας,
> ὡς δῆθεν οὐκ εἰδυῖα τἀξειργασμένα.

In the *Suppliants* of Aeschylus (ll. 70–6) and the *Choephoroi* (ll. 24–5) the gashes torn in their cheeks by the chorus had presumably to remain visible throughout the play—unless indeed they were left to the imagination from the first.

A sudden access of joy or grief could obviously be accompanied by embraces or other movements which would, for a few moments at least, hide the face, and so soften any sense of incongruity which the audience might feel. The look of astonishment or fear at the appearance by a god *ex machina* would not be missed, as the actors would have turned their backs to the audience. In comedy indeed the two sides of a mask might have different expressions (e.g. the angry and the kindly father), of which the actor turned the appropriate one to the spectators.[4] Opportunities for an actual change of mask are very few in

---

[1] *Eum.* 990–1. [2] Soph. *Electr.* 1296 ff., 1309 ff. [3] ll. 1317 ff.
[4] Quint. xi. iii, § 74; Bieber in Pauly–Wissowa, *Encycl.* gives other references (s.v. Masken). A. Rumpf, *A.J.A.*, lv. 8 traces this back to the fifth-century painter Parrhasios.

the extant plays. Such a change was certainly made in the
Oedipus Tyrannus and the *Helena*, and perhaps after the blinding
of Polymestor in the *Hecuba*, and in the *Cyclops*.[1]

The importance which the Athenians attached to gesture is
illustrated by Aristotle's precept[2] that the poet should not only
keep the scene before his eyes in composing his play, but should
also, if possible, include the gestures in his composition, and so
make the demonstration of passion or feeling by his characters
convincing (δεῖ δε τοὺς μύθους συνιστάναι καὶ τῇ λέξει συναπ-
εργάζεσθαι ὅτι μάλιστα πρὸ ὀμμάτων τιθέμενον, . . . ὅσα δὲ
δυνατὸν καὶ τοῖς σχήμασιν συναπεργαζόμενον· πιθανώτατοι γὰρ ἀπὸ
τῆς αὐτῆς φύσεως οἱ ἐν τοῖς πάθεσίν εἰσιν, καὶ χειμαίνει ὁ χειμα-
ζόμενος καὶ χαλεπαίνει ὁ ὀργιζόμενος ἀληθινώτατα). There is no
suggestion of statuesqueness here, though Aristotle does refer
later[3] to the possibility of overdoing the amount of gesture
(περιεργάζεσθαι τοῖς σημείοις) or using gestures inappropriate to
tragedy, and records that Mynniskos nicknamed Kallippides 'the
monkey' from his excess of gesture—a record which is sufficient
disproof of any inevitable statuesqueness in the last third of the
fifth century.[4] That Euripides' practice was in accordance with
Aristotle's precept is shown by the frequency with which the
movements and gestures of the actor are precisely indicated in
the text; e.g. twice in the *Hecuba*, first when Hecuba appears
(ll. 59 ff.) :

> ἄγετ' ὦ παῖδες τὴν γραῦν πρὸ δόμων,
> ἄγετ' ὀρθοῦσαι τὴν ὁμόδουλον,
> Τρῳάδες, ὑμῖν, πρόσθε δ' ἄνασσαν·
> λάβετε φέρετε πέμπετ' ἀείρατέ μου
> γεραιᾶς χειρὸς προσλαζύμεναι·
> κἀγὼ σκολιῷ σκίπωνι[5] χερὸς
> διερειδομένα σπεύσω βραδύπουν
> ἤλυσιν ἄρθρων προτιθεῖσα,

---

[1] See Hense, *Die Modifizierung der Maske in der gr. Trag.*, where there is a minute discussion
of all possible instances, including those in lost plays. It is perhaps doubtful whether the
avoidance of scenes of death and violence was really due to the obligation to employ masks,
which could not respond to such circumstances, but it was at least convenient.

[2] *Poet.* xvii. Cf. *Rhet.* ii. viii ἀνάγκη τοὺς συναπεργαζομένους σχήμασι καὶ φωναῖς καὶ
αἰσθήσει (what is present to the senses) καὶ ὅλως ἐν ὑποκρίσει ἐλεεινοτέρους εἶναι.

[3] *Poet.* xxvi.

[4] An otherwise unknown Pindaros was criticized on the same ground.

[5] The *Life of Sophocles* says that the crooked staff, according to Satyrus, was first introduced by Sophocles; cf. Plut. *de lib. educ.* iv τάς γε μὴν καμπύλας τῶν ὑποκριτῶν βακτηρίας
ἀπευθύνειν ἀμήχανον.

nd, secondly, when Polyxena describes the gestures of Odysseus
ll. 342–4):

> ὁρῶ σ᾽, Ὀδυσσεῦ, δεξίαν ὑφ᾽ εἵματος
> κρύπτοντα χεῖρα καὶ πρόσωπον ἔμπαλιν
> στρέφοντα, μή σου προσθίγω γενειάδος.

he second passage is very like Andromache's words to Peleus
Androm. 572–5):

> ἀλλ᾽ ἀντιάζω σ᾽, ὦ γέρον, τῶν σῶν πάρος
> πίτνουσα γονάτων—χειρὶ δ᾽ οὐκ ἔξεστί μοι
> τῆς σῆς λαβέσθαι φιλτάτης γενειάδος—
> ῥῦσαί με πρὸς θεῶν.

n these and very many other passages it is right to speak of
uripides as composing τοῖς σχήμασι συναπεργαζόμενον. It can,
f course, be assumed that passages of lamentation are accom-
anied by the usual gestures of mourning or distress such as
he rending of the garments, whether these are mentioned or
ot.[1] Hurried entries and exits are usually indicated in the words
f some speaker;[2] and so are many other instances of rapid or
iolent movement, such as the struggle of Philoctetes and Neo-
tolemus (*Philoct.* 816), the flight of Helen into sanctuary
Helen 543–4):

> οὐχ ὡς δρομαία πῶλος ἢ Βάκχη θεοῦ
> τάφῳ ξυνάψω κῶλον,

nd, most striking of all, Ajax rushing to fall on his sword (Soph.
j. 865).[3] There was nothing to prevent kneeling in supplication
s Andromache does (*Androm.* 529), or falling and lying pros-
ate on the ground, as do Iolaos (*Heraclid.* 75) and Hecuba
Troad. 36, 462), or crawling on all fours as the Pythia does in
he *Eumenides* and Polymestor in the *Hecuba* (l. 458). (Kneeling
r prostration as practised by Orientals is confined, in the extant
lays, to the *Persae* 152 ff. and the *Phoenissae* 293 and 610.) Scenes
f active violence, involving the actors—common in the Old
omedy, but rare in extant tragedy—are found near the end of

---

[1] Those who want a more minute classification of gestures and ways of expressing emotion,
cluding the most obvious, in the dramatists may find it in F. L. Shisler's article in *A.J.P.*
vi (1943) or in Spitzbarth, *Unters. zur Spieltechnik der gr. Tragödie* (1946).
[2] e.g. Sophocl. *Antig.* 766, *Electra* 871; Eur. *Androm.* 545.
[3] In the *Oinomaos*, Aeschines, as Oinomaos, tripped and fell when in hot pursuit of Pelops
d had to be picked up by Sannio, the chorus-trainer (Demosth. *de Cor.* § 180 and *Vit.
schin.*). But there is no justification for laying the blame on his κόθορνοι as some scholars
ve done.

Aeschylus' *Hiketides*, in the *Oedipus Coloneus* 820 ff., and the *Heraclidae* (687 ff.).

It need not be doubted that the pathetic acting of Theodoros and Polos and other great actors depended upon their use of gesture as well as upon their voice. It has already been mentioned how Theodoros could move even Alexander of Pherae to tears, and how Polos gave his impressive rendering of Oedipus as a wanderer; and before them Kallippides boasted of his power to draw tears from his audience.[1] (The same Kallippides, however, incurred censure for the introduction of vulgarity into his female roles.[2]) It is obvious that the Old Comedy allowed every kind of gesture and movement to the actor, and that no inconvenience of costume nor sense of delicacy restrained him. The lack of refinement became less in the later comedy, the masks and costume of which will be discussed later.

[1] Xen. *Symp.* iii. 11 Καλλιππίδης ὁ ὑποκριτής, ὃς ὑπερσεμνύνεται ὅτι δύναται πολλοὺς κλαίοντας καθίζειν.
[2] Aristot. *Poet.* xxvi.

IV
THE COSTUMES

IN considering the dress of the actors in tragedy, satyric drama, and comedy, it will be convenient to discuss the masks, the clothing of the body, and the footwear, for the most part separately. But it must first be observed that the general descriptions of the actor's appearance which have come down to us are all late, and their applicability to the actors of the Classical period often very doubtful. Lucian (in passages which will be referred to later) wrote at a time when it was the custom to exaggerate the height and size of the tragic actor to the point of grotesqueness, and the compiler of the *Life* of Aeschylus which appears in the scholia to his plays ascribes to that poet quite uncritically inventions which were introduced into tragedy at any period: his sources cannot be traced.[1] Iulius Pollux, whose catalogues are the chief written source of information, belongs to the second century A.D., and Iuba, on whose Θεατρικὴ ἱστορία he is often supposed to have drawn,[2] was himself only writing at the very end of the first century B.C. In fact, Pollux only mentions Iuba once,[3] in a sentence which has no reference to theatrical subjects and is bracketed by some editors. Others[4] think that the authority used by Pollux was Tryphon, of the latter half of the first century B.C., whom Pollux never mentions.[5] The great Alexandrian scholar, Aristophanes of Byzantium (*c.* 257–180 B.C.) is known to have written a work on masks (περὶ προσώπων), which is once referred to by Athenaeus,[6] but in the only passage

---

[1] Cf. Cramer, *Anecd. Par.* i. 19 εἰ μὲν δὴ πάντα τις Αἰσχύλῳ βούλεται τὰ περὶ τὴν σκηνὴν εὑρήματα προσνέμειν.

[2] e.g. by Rohde, *De Julii Pollucis in apparatu scenico enarrando fontibus* (1870). But his direct use of Iuba (though not their use of some common source) seems to be disproved by V. Gordziejew, *Quaestionum de Julii Pollucis fontibus caput* (Warsaw, 1936), who also argues acutely that Pollux and Athenaeus did not use a common source. [3] v, § 88.

[4] e.g. Bapp, 'De fontibus quibus Athenaeus in rebus mus. lyr., enarr. usus sit' (*Leipz. Stud.* viii (1885)).

[5] Latte, however (*De saltationibus Graecorum*), makes out a strong case for the use of Tryphon by Athenaeus in regard to dances.

[6] xiv. 659 a Χρύσιππος δ' ὁ φιλόσοφος τὸν μαίσωνα ἀπὸ τοῦ μασᾶσθαι οἴεται κεκλῆσθαι, οἷον τὸν ἀμαθῆ καὶ πρὸς γαστέρα νενευκότα, ἀγνοῶν ὅτι Μαίσων γέγονεν κωμῳδίας ὑποκριτὴς Μεγαρεὺς τὸ γένος, ὃς καὶ τὸ προσωπεῖον εὗρε τὸ ὑπ' αὐτοῦ καλούμενον μαίσωνα, ὡς Ἀριστοφάνης φησιν ὁ Βυζάντιος ἐν τῷ περὶ προσώπων, εὑρεῖν αὐτὸν φάσκων καὶ τὸ τοῦ θεράποντος πρόσωπον καὶ τὸ τοῦ μαγείρου. Aristophanes evidently treated the masks of μαίσων and θεράπων as distinct, whereas Pollux speaks of the μαίσων θεράπων, οὖλος θεράπων and θεράπων τεττίξ. See below, § 22.

of Pollux from which it is possible to argue the nomenclature is different from that of Aristophanes as quoted by Athenaeus. It is of course likely that Pollux used the work of so distinguished a scholar, and a strong case has been made[1] for thinking that he made direct use of Eratosthenes, the slightly senior contemporary of Aristophanes; but we have practically no knowledge of the literature which intervened in the course of the three or four centuries which separated them. The chief value of Pollux is probably in reference to the drama, and especially to the comedy, of the latest Hellenistic and of imperial Roman times, when the masks and costumes of the different types of character (and no doubt these types themselves) had become stereotyped and conventionalized to a degree probably quite unknown in the Classical period.

The archaeological evidence has also to be used with great caution. The masks of terra-cotta or marble which have been found (many of them, perhaps, votive copies) differ for the most part from original masks in linen, cork, or wood,[2] at least in not representing coverings for the whole or the greater part of the head, but only the face and part of the crown, and they may have differed in other ways.[3] The vase-paintings also, which depict scenes based on tragedy, can rarely, if ever, be taken to reproduce the scene as acted. As a general rule the persons shown on the vases wear no masks, and while the robes often correspond more or less to certain patterns, it is not certain how far these precise robes were worn when the corresponding scenes were performed in the theatre and how far they are a convention of vase-painting. (This applies particularly to the south Italian vases, whose dates are considerably later than those of the great period of Athenian tragedy.) This problem will be referred to later.

With these precautions—and others may prove to be necessary—we may proceed first to the consideration of the masks.

---

[1] By Gordziejew, op. cit. Other discussions of Pollux's sources will be found by Bethe in Pauly-W. *Real-Encycl.* s.v. 'Julius Pollux', and Robert, *Die Masken der neueren att. Komödie,* pp. 18 ff., etc., and in the *Oxford Classical Dictionary*, s.v. 'Pollux'.

[2] For wooden masks cf. Hesych. s.v. κυριττοί· οἱ ἔχοντες τὰ ξύλινα πρόσωπα κατὰ Ἰταλίαν καὶ ἑορτάζοντες τῇ Κορυθαλίᾳ γελοιασταί and also κυλίνθιον· προσωπεῖον ξύλινον, and κύριθρα προσωπεῖα ξύλινα. (Of course cork masks were ξύλινα.)

[3] The eyes, for instance, are sometimes painted in and not left blank. The treatment of the parts of the face round about the eyes in the theatrical masks themselves may well have varied greatly.

A. MASKS[1]

1. There is much uncertainty as regards the use of masks in the earliest period of Athenian tragedy. Aristotle probably did not regard them as having been worn from the first,[2] and the tradition followed in Suidas' lexicon held that Thespis, who gave the first performances of tragedy, first disguised his face, when acting, with white lead, then hung flowers over it, and only then took to plain linen masks, and that, after Choirilos had done something unspecified to the masks and robes and Phrynichus had introduced feminine masks,[3] it was Aeschylus who first used coloured and terrifying masks[4]—contrasting apparently with the masks ἐν μόνῃ ὀθόνῃ of Thespis. A similar tradition lies behind Horace's lines:[5]

> ignotum tragicae genus invenisse Camenae
> dicitur et plaustris vexisse poemata Thespis,
> quae canerent agerentque peruncti faecibus ora;
> post hunc personae pallaeque repertor honestae
> Aeschylus et modicis instravit pulpita tignis
> et docuit magnumque loqui nitique cothurno.

That Horace's history is in part confused or wrong does not affect the probability that he is recording a tradition prevalent in his day about Aeschylus.

2. It does not seem possible to go behind the tradition of the use of masks by Thespis and his successors, whatever may be the truth conveyed by it, to the use of masks with some special (or, as some scholars think, some magical) significance in the worship of Dionysus. The primitive use of masks in the worship of a number of deities in Greece is well attested—Artemis Orthia

---

[1] The study of these has been greatly facilitated by the work of Dr. Margarete Bieber, and especially by her article in Pauly–W. *Real-Encycl.* s.v. 'Masken'. Roberts's *Winckelmanns-programm* on the masks of the later comedy is also indispensable. Much relevant material is collected in Müller's *Lehrbuch*, pp. 270 ff., and in recent years Prof. T. B. L. Webster has contributed much new material and useful discussion (see later, p. 211, n. 1).

[2] He definitely regards them as having been 'introduced' into an already existing comedy (*Poet.* v), though he does not know who introduced them.

[3] γυναικεῖον πρόσωπον εἰσήγαγεν ἐν τῇ σκηνῇ may mean 'introduced a female character'. For the work of these early poets see *Dith. Trag. Com.*, where all passages are quoted.

[4] Suid. s.v. Αἰσχύλος· . . . οὗτος πρῶτος εὗρε προσωπεῖα δεινὰ καὶ χρώμασι κεχρισμένα ἔχειν τοὺς τραγικούς, καὶ ταῖς ἀρβύλαις τοῖς καλουμένοις ἐμβάταις κεχρῆσθαι.

[5] *Ars Poet.* 275–80; cf. *Dith. Trag. Com.*, pp. 105, 112–13, and on *cothurno* see below, pp. 228 ff. On the mistaken use of the words *magnumque loqui* to support the fancy that the mask was formed as a speaking-trumpet, to increase the loudness of the voice, see below, pp. 193 ff.

and Artemis Korythalia at Sparta and Demeter Kidaria in Arcadia will serve as illustrations[1]—and in some of these worships the identification of the worshipper with his god by the wearing of his likeness may have been felt to convey some special potency. But in tragedy and comedy and other forms of Dionysiac κῶμος the masks were for the most part not those of the god, and in some worships in which the god is represented by a pillar surmounted by a mask, the worshippers are not disguised.[2] It is known that masks were *de rigueur* for those who took part in Dionysiac κῶμοι,[3] in some cases perhaps because the revels were liable to become somewhat disreputable, and respectable citizens preferred to conceal their identity, but in most, probably, because they enjoyed the fun of 'dressing up'; and it is natural to suppose that when the particular forms of dance or revel which developed into drama crystallized into their formal shapes, the use of masks should have continued. Satyr-dances must always have been performed by masked dancers; and if the innovation of Thespis was the introduction of an actor (himself) to a chorus of masked dancers (though they were probably not satyrs),[4] he may well have thought it natural to disguise his own face also, and tried various experiments before settling down to linen masks—to be improved upon later by Aeschylus and others by the use of colour and the adaptation of the masks to the personality of the character represented by the actor.

3. The only archaeological evidence of the character of the tragic actor's mask in the time of Aeschylus is given by the fragments of an oinochoe of about 470 B.C. (Fig. 25) found by the American excavators of the Agora at Athens.[5] On one of these fragments a boy (perhaps attendant on an actor) is carrying a finely painted female mask, and Miss Lucy Talcott, who publishes the fragments, notes that it corresponds exactly with the description given by Pollux[6] of the mask of a maiden whose hair is cut short as a sign of mourning: ἡ δὲ κούριμος παρθένος ἀντὶ ὄγκου ἔχει τριχῶν κατεψηγμένων διάκρισιν, καὶ βραχέα ἐν

---

[1] See Dawkins, *Temple of Artemis Orthia*, p. 153, etc.; Hesych. s.v. Κυριττοί; Paus. VIII. xv, etc., and for a fuller list, Bieber, *Jahrb. Arch.* xxxii (1917), pp. 69–70.

[2] See below, p. 219.   [3] Cf. Dem. *de F.L.* § 287.

[4] See *Dith. Trag. Com.*, pp. 100 ff., 111–22, etc.

[5] *Hesperia*, viii, pp. 267 ff., fig. 1. The evidence of the vase as regards shoes and dress will be considered later, see p. 216.   [6] iv. 140.

FIG. 25. ATTIC OINOCHOE FROM AGORA, ATHENS

FIG. 26. RELIEF FROM PEIRAEUS

FIG. 27. MUSE FROM MANTUA

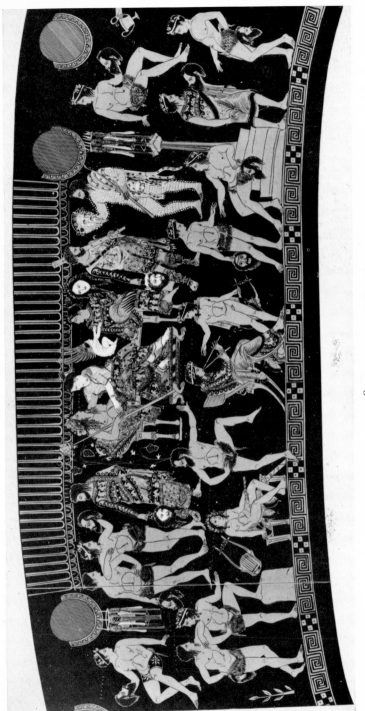

FIG. 28. PRONOMOS VASE

FIG. 29. SILENUS AND INFANT DIONYSUS

FIG. 30. ATTIC DINOS (SATYRS) IN ATHENS

κύκλῳ περικέκαρται, ὕπωχρος δὲ τὴν χροίαν. The absence of the ὄγκος, the peaked elevation above the forehead, regular in later tragic masks, is to be noted, and the fact that instead of the gaping mouth of the later masks, the lips are scarcely parted. In the original mask the eyes must have been at least partly blank, but here the artist has painted them in fully, and he must also be responsible for the closing of the lips. Miss Talcott conjectures that the heroine of the mask may have been the Antigone of the *Seven against Thebes*, but she may equally well have been a heroine from some lost play of the first third of the fifth century.[1]

4. The beautiful votive relief[2] of about 400 B.C. found in the Peiraeus (Fig. 26), in which the reclining Dionysus is visited by three actors, shows masks in the hands of two of them. One of these is a mask of a bearded man with a distinct, though not large, ὄγκος, raising but not distorting the outline of the head. The other has been too much damaged to allow of any certainty; it probably represents a female face, also with ὄγκος and open mouth. The mask of a bearded man in the hand of the statue of a Muse at Mantua (Fig. 27)[3] has also a marked ὄγκος, but the opening of the lips is not exaggerated. The statue is of about the same date as the relief from the Peiraeus, and so (or perhaps a few years earlier) is the well-known volute-krater from Ruvo at Naples[4] (Fig. 28), the painting on which seems to give the place of honour to the flute-player Pronomos. In addition to eleven members of a satyr-chorus, who wear masks with the familiar snub-nose, there is Silenus, their leader, holding up the mask of an aged and bearded man, with snub-nose and moderately wide-open lips, but not unduly grotesque—in this resembling the (roughly contemporary) statue of Silenus carrying the infant Dionysus (Fig. 29), found in the theatre at Athens.[5] In

---

[1] The picture suggests that the feminine mask was originally white, as distinct from the masculine, and this is confirmed by the Pronomos vase (below).

[2] There is much difference of opinion about the characters intended by the masks on this relief. See Studniczka in *Mélanges Perrot*, pp. 307 ff.; Bieber, *Denkm.* pp. 104–5 (and refs. given there), and Buschor in Furtw.–Reich. iii, pp. 134 f. (and Fig. 61), who thinks that the mask, which to Dr. Bieber seems feminine, is that of Teiresias. It seems to be that of an old man.

[3] Cf. Bieber in *Jahrb. Arch.* xxxii (1917), p. 79, Abb. 45.

[4] Furtw.–Reich. iii, pls. 143–5, pp. 132–50, where Buschor's discussion is most important. He dates the vase in the last years of the fifth century. See also Bulle, *Eine Skenographie*, pp. 27–29.

[5] Wieseler, *Theatergeb.* Taf. vi, No. 6; cf. Bieber, *Jahrb. Arch.* xxxii (1917), p. 80, Abb. 46.

the centre are three persons, one on the left, two on the right, of the couch on which Dionysus and Ariadne are seated, each of the three holding a mask and clad in the highly decorated garments which are generally regarded as theatrical. The figure on the left is Laomedon, that on the right Herakles, and between them, seated on the end of the couch, is a female personage, holding up a mask, which is generally agreed to be that of Hesione. None of the masks has an ὄγκος, but those of Hesione and Laomedon are surmounted by the cap conventionally associated with Asiatic characters. The lips are moderately wide open. None of the characters wears thick-soled κόθορνοι. It is disputed whether they are thought of as persons in a tragedy or in a satyric play.[1] In satyr-drama the ὄγκος and thick κόθορνοι appear not to have been employed until very late—satyrs were too nearly on the same plane as ordinary human beings to require the heroic grandeur which such devices were probably supposed to give—and they were probably not introduced into tragedy itself until after the date of the vase; the ὄγκος in its exaggerated form seems certainly not to have been early.[2]

5. Mention should be made in passing of two Attic vases (Figs. 30, 31) of the late fifth century B.C. by the 'painter of the Athens Dinos', in which satyrs are represented accompanied by a flute-player in the richly decorated costume worn by the actors and (in a less highly decorated form) by the flute-player on the Pronomos vase. (The first[3] is an Athenian dinos, the latter[4]—in fragments—a bell-krater in Bonn.) On these two

---

[1] The picture is probably not to be regarded as the reproduction of a scene in a play or of the preparations for a play behind the scenes or in a rehearsal, but as an imaginary picture of Dionysus in the midst of his thiasos, embracing both his satyrs and tragedy, if the three actors are regarded as the embodiment *ad hoc* of Tragedy, as Buschor believes. The three figures are not figures of actors dressing up (whether for a satyr-play or a tragedy), but figures, possibly of characters in a recently victorious play, but introduced here as members of a thiasos, and as imagined by the poet, though their theatrical function is indicated by their holding masks. The fact that one of the three is a woman, as imagined by the poet, not a male actor impersonating a woman, is really unmistakable; moreover, she has bare feet; and Laomedon, even without his mask, is Laomedon as imagined, with a beard, not the (probably beardless) actor who impersonated him. The same thing is true, *mutatis mutandis*, of the satyrs; they are a Dionysiac thiasos as imagined by the poet, though a thiasos connected by their masks with the theatre. The older view, which regards the three as characters in a satyric play recently performed, is maintained in spite of its difficulties by Dr. Bieber (Pauly–W. *Real-Encycl.* s.v. 'Masken', col. 2085). Some regard this 'Asiatic cap' as a mask-strap.   [2] See below, pp. 182, 194, and n. on p. 188.

[3] Brommer, *Satyrspiele*, Abb. 2; cf. *Ath. Mitt.* xxxvi (1911), Taf. 13.

[4] Brommer, op. cit., Abb. 3: the figure in the text is from a photograph lent by Sir John Beazley.

FIG. 31. FRAGMENTS OF ATTIC KRATER (SATYRS)

FIG. 32. ATTIC KRATER (PROMETHEUS AND SATYRS)

FIG. 33. ATTIC KRATER (ORPHEUS AND SATYR)

FIG. 34. GNATHIA KRATER IN WÜRZBURG

FIG. 35. DETAIL FROM KRATER IN WÜRZBURG (see Fig. 34)

FIG. 36. APULIAN KRATER IN VATICAN

vases, as in the case of one of the satyrs on the Pronomos vase, the loin-cloth is of linen, not of goatskin. But it is not justifiable to assume that the scenes come from a satyric play as performed. The subject of dancing satyrs—or men masked and dressed as satyrs—with a flute-player and in every kind of company was evidently a favourite one with painters, and it would not be right to draw inferences from their pictures, nor from the flute-player and the use of masks, to the performances in the theatre. This does not mean that the subjects of a number of vases on which satyrs appear may not have been suggested by plays. This was very probably so (for example) in two other vases figured by Brommer, one (Fig. 32)[1] depicting Prometheus in a decorated robe, but with short sleeves, bringing fire in a reed to the satyrs, the other (Fig. 33),[2] Orpheus, also in decorative dress but not of the 'tragic' pattern, with a satyr entranced by his song. (The former is an Athenian column-krater of the last third of the fifth century, the latter a column-krater in Naples.) But it cannot be inferred that the satyrs and others appeared in the theatre exactly as they do on these vases.[3]

6. We have next to consider a fragment from Tarentum (Figs. 34, 35) in the Wagner Museum at Würzburg, described by Bulle[4] and assigned by him to a date early in the fourth century B.C. On this is displayed a tragic actor, with a sword in his left hand, and in his right the noble mask of a bearded man, apparently golden-haired, the crown of the head being raised to support the abundant hair, but not distorted, since the hair follows in a natural manner the shape of the head. The eyes are fully painted in. The actor is still wearing his stage-costume— Bulle imagines him to be coming forward to receive the applause of the audience—and the poverty of the costume suggests to Bulle a king in exile, while the combination of it with a sword brings it into relation to a picture (Fig. 36)[5] of a royal figure on

[1] Brommer, op. cit., Abb. 42. Some, with much less probability, regard the central figure as Dionysus rather than Prometheus. See Beazley's art. on 'Prometheus the Firebringer', in *Am. J. Arch.* (1939), pp. 636, etc.; he figures other vases depicting Prometheus and satyrs. Aeschylus wrote a satyric play called Προμηθεύς, produced with the Πέρσαι, and also a Προμηθεὺς Πυρκαεύς. [2] Brommer, op. cit., Abb. 50.

[3] Pollux iv. 42, quoted below (p. 188), seems to indicate that the masks of the actors (as distinct from the chorus) in satyric drama did not differ from those employed in tragedy, and this may have been true also of their costumes (see below, p. 244).

[4] *Festschrift für James Loeb* (1930), pp. 5 ff., pl. ii, figs. 1, 2, 6. Cf. *Eine Skenographie*, p. 5.

[5] Ibid., p. 17, fig. 8. Bulle argues ingeniously for the suggestion that the amphora depicts the story of Thyestes and Pelopia. He reinforces his view of the vase (*Eine Skenographie*, p. 30,

an amphora of early Apulian make, bearing a sword, but taking refuge at an altar. (The date of the amphora is also placed by him early in the fourth century.)

A tragic mask in the small museum on the Acropolis (Fig. 37) is assigned to the fourth century owing to the lettering on the monument in which it is included.[1]

7. The most interesting conclusion from this scanty evidence is that in the early Classical period, whether in Athens or in Italy, there was an avoidance of exaggeration in the conformation and features of the mask,[2] and in this there is a strong contrast with the series of actors' masks which will shortly be considered. But first it will be well to notice some vases which give a little information about the masks worn by tragic choruses of the fifth and fourth centuries B.C.

On a peliké in Boston[3] (Fig. 39), of about the time of Pheidias, are two young men rehearsing or preparing to rehearse their parts as choreutai; they are to form part of a female chorus; the mask of the right-hand figure lies on the ground facing him; the left-hand figure is already in full costume, wearing a mask like that which lies on the ground, and with the same dressing of the hair. The mask is that of a beautiful female face, entirely free from exaggerations, though it is impossible to be certain how far the poet is giving a faithful and unbeautified picture of the theatrical masks of his day.

---

n. 5) by the conjecture that the object on the ground is a skin bag such as a wanderer might carry on his travels. But Rumpf (*Phil. Woch.* lii (1932), cols. 208–10) denies that the Würzburg actor represents a king in exile, and thinks that his costume may have been a normal actor's dress at this date, the lack of decoration being merely indicative of a difference in fashion (see below, p. 223). He dates the vase in the time of Alexander the Great.

[1] Walter, *Beschreibung der Reliefs im kleinen Akropolismuseum*, No. 413.

[2] I cannot follow Dr. Bieber (*Jahrb. Arch.* xxxii (1917), pp. 81 ff.) in deriving the ὄγκος from the archaistic style of hair-dressing found on such monuments as the Hermes of Alkamenes (Fig. 38) from Pergamon, which, with the hair over the brow following closely the shape of the head, seems quite remote from the 'lambda-shaped' ὄγκος (as Pollux described it) worn by actors after the fifth century, but not attributable on any evidence worth consideration to Aeschylus as part of the stage costume. Its absence on the oinochoe from the Agora described by Miss Talcott (see above, p. 178) suggests the contrary. Dr. Bieber also derives the pointed beard which appears on some of the earlier representations of actors' masks from the fashion in vogue before the Persian Wars. But the gap in time between that epoch and the Peiraeus relief—the earliest of her instances—makes the derivation very uncertain, and in fact most of the masks to which she refers (*History of Gk. and Rom. Theat.*, p. 37) are comic.

[3] Cf. Caskey and Beazley, *Att. Vases in Mus. of Fine Arts, Boston*, pl. 29. 2; Buschor in Furtw.–Reich. *Gr. Vasenmalerei*, iii, pp. 134–5, Abb. 62. That tragedy, and not comedy, as some have supposed, was in the painter's mind, is indicated by the absence of any feature suggestive of the Old Comedy.

FIG. 39. ATTIC PELIKE (BOSTON)

FIG. 37. TRAGIC MASK IN ATHENS

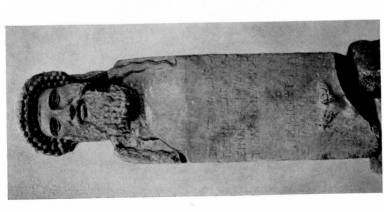

FIG. 38. HERMES OF ALKAMENES

a

b

FIG. 40*a*, *b*. ATTIC KRATER FROM TARANTO IN WÜRZBURG

FIG. 40c. ATTIC KRATER FROM TARANTO IN WÜRZBURG

FIG. 41. SOUTH ITALIAN KRATER FROM BARI

FIG. 42. APULIAN KRATER IN MUNICH

FIG. 43. PAINTING FROM HERCULANEUM

The fragments of an early-fourth-century krater from Tarentum in Würzburg are described by Bulle,[1] with some likely restorations by Wirsing (Fig. 40). The vase is probably by the Pronomos painter and, like the Pronomos vase in Naples, taken from the commemoration of a tragic victory, and the maidens who are depicted are no doubt the maidens in a tragic chorus, wearing their tragic robes, and carrying their masks. Four of these (or parts of them) can be discerned, and two others can be conjectured with fair certainty; the four are all alike, and are surrounded by bushy hair; the lips are open; the eyes are fully painted in. The expression is natural and unexaggerated, and the vase shows that there was no attempt at individual differentiation between the several members of the chorus.

A bell-krater from Bari[2] (Fig. 41), and apparently of about 400 B.C., shows Dionysus holding a female (?) mask with light curled hair, but no ὄγκος. The other figures are a satyr and two Maenads, and the vase may reproduce the votive tablet of a dramatic victor, though not a scene from the play. The mask may represent that worn by members of a Maenad chorus. A somewhat similar female mask is seen (Fig. 42) on a kalyx-krater in Munich,[3] painted in the later Apulian style of the fourth century. It is held out by Dionysus to a young man, who is probably thought of as about to take some part in a play. Two satyrs are depicted in the group, though without masks. In both these paintings the absence of an ὄγκος may indicate a member of a tragic chorus rather than an actor; but it may equally indicate an actor in a satyric play of a period before actors in satyric plays wore masks with an ὄγκος.

8. The texts of classical tragedies rarely give any indication of the character of the masks of the chorus; but in the *Suppliants*

---

[1] *Corolla Curtius*, pp. 151–60, pls. 54–56. The characters in the play, as in the Pronomos vase, are gathered to do honour to Dionysus, who is seated in company with a goddess. The figures are those of the characters as imagined by the poet, not strictly those of the performers, though the connexion of the characters with the theatre is denoted by their masks. The only figures from real life are those of the flute-player and the poet. The standing figure looking at the poet must be the Muse (or possibly Σκηνή, see below, p. 185), and behind her is a chest for the reception of literary rolls. Above (to the left of Dionysus) is a tripod holding a richly ornamented dinos. The person in the upper zone holding a mask is probably an actor, not, as Bulle thought, the chorus-leader (see below, p. 218). Bulle also finds a trace of a male figure (? a king) not wearing thick-soled κόθορνοι.

[2] Published by Dr. Bieber in *Jahrb. Arch.* xxxii (1917), p. 88, Abb. 59.

[3] Jahn in *Arch. Ztg.* for 1855, pp. 147 ff., Taf. 83. The figure in the text is from a photograph lent by Sir John Beazley.

of Aeschylus the masks must have presented a dark complexion
—the ἀπαλὰν Νειλοθερῆ παρειάν (ll. 70 ff.) of a μελανθὲς ἡλιο-
κτύπον γένος (l. 131), perhaps with traces of gashes in the
cheeks, self-inflicted in distress (ll. 24–25).

The texts also give very little information about the masks
worn by the actors. It may be that the masks in tragedy, as in
comedy, were far more individualized than they were when
(perhaps towards the end of the fourth century) the tendency
to standardization of typical masks had set in. A number of
instances suggest that a hero or heroine who was regarded as
beautiful or admirable wore fair hair; such were Phaedra,
Iphigeneia, and Helena;[1] Hippolytus and in some plays
Orestes;[2] in contrast with the wicked Polyneikes.[3] Orestes in
his distress in Euripides' play of the name may have had a
special mask displaying his squalor;[4] and it seems almost certain
that the feminine beauty of Dionysus in the *Bacchae* must have
been shown in his mask.[5] Personages in mourning were represented as shorn,[6] and the locks might be cut off during the play.[7]
Speaking generally, it seems likely that the poet and his mask-
maker enjoyed great freedom, and there is no hint of any un-
naturalness or exaggeration.[8]

9. We may now turn to the masks of actors later than those
which have so far been considered.

Among the wall-paintings found at Herculaneum is the copy
(Fig. 43) of a votive tablet[9] dedicated by a victorious tragic
actor, probably towards the end of the fourth or early in the
third century B.C. The principal figure is the actor, a man with
a fine face, who has just taken off his mask and ruffled his hair
in doing so. A kneeling female figure, probably identified rightly
as Skene,[10] is writing an inscription beneath the mask which

---

[1] Eur. *Hippol.* 220, *Iph. Taur.* 174, *Helena* 1224.

[2] Eur. *Hippol.* 1334, *Electr.* 515, *Iph. Taur.* 52.

[3] Eur. *Phoen.* 308 βοστρύχων τε κυανόχρωτα χαίτας πλόκαμον.

[4] Eur. *Or.* 223–6 ΟΡ. ὑπόβαλε πλευραῖς πλευρά, καὐχμώδη κόμην | ἄφελε προσώπου· λεπτὰ
γὰρ λεύσσω κόραις. | ΗΛ. ὦ βοστρύχων πινῶδες ἄθλιον κάρα, | ὡς ἠγριώσαι διὰ μακρᾶς ἀλουσίας.

[5] Eur. *Bacch.* 455 ff. πλόκαμός τε γὰρ σοῦ ταναός, οὐ πάλης ὕπο, | γένυν παρ᾽ αὐτὴν κεχυμένος,
πόθου πλέως· | λευκὴν δὲ χροίαν ἐκ παρασκευῆς ἔχεις, | οὐχ ἡλίου βολαῖσιν, ἀλλ᾽ ὑπὸ σκιᾶς, | τὴν
Ἀφροδίτην καλλονῇ θηρώμενος.

[6] Eur. *Or.* 458 Tyndareos is μελάμπεπλος | κουρᾷ τε θυγατρὸς πενθίμῳ κεκαρμένος.

[7] Soph. *Ajax* 1173, *El.* 448; Eur. *Helen.* 487.　　　　　　　　[8] See also above, p. 182.

[9] Pfuhl, *Mal. u. Zeichn.* iii, fig. 653; cf. Bieber, *Denkm.*, p. 110, Taf. lv; Bulle, *Festschr. für
James Loeb*, p. 12, fig. 4.

[10] Like the figure on the relief in Constantinople mentioned below. Others suppose her to
be a Muse.

stands in its receptacle above a low pillar. (There is a second actor in the background.) This mask is very different from those hitherto considered, with its high ὄγκος and long hair hanging on each side, its wide-open mouth and staring eyes. The naturalness of the earlier masks has gone, and the tragicalness is exaggerated; and this is true also of a somewhat similar mask (Fig. 44) probably derived from the same period.[1] A vase (Fig. 47)[2] is thought to represent a messenger in a tragedy of the fourth century. A mask in the hands of a tragic poet in the Vatican,[3] probably of the second half of the fourth century, has a moderate ὄγκος (Fig. 45), and so has a feminine mask[4] (Fig. 46) on a Gnathia vase of the third century.[5]

On a relief in Constantinople[6] (Fig. 48), Euripides is seen handing to Σκηνή a mask of Herakles, and two other masks, those of a woman and a bearded man, are imagined by Dr. Bieber to be those of Megara and Lykos in the *Hercules Furens.* This seems uncertain; but while there is only slight exaggeration in the mask of Herakles, the other two have a high ὄγκος. The lettering, and particularly the spelling ΕΥΡΕΙΠΙΔΗC, indicate a date hardly earlier than the second century B.C., though it remains possible that the masks, like the portrait of the poet, may be taken from some earlier source. The tragic mask with a large ὄγκος is well illustrated by three terra-cotta statuettes (Figs. 49–51) which Dr. Bieber places side by side[7]—one of a young actor, from Asia Minor, of Hellenistic date; the second from Rheneia (near Delos); the third also from Asia Minor, but not quite certainly tragic.[8] She figures also[9] a bearded actor (Fig. 52) carrying a mask with high ὄγκος and a club, wearing high-soled κόθορνοι; it was found at Amisos, and seems to be of Hellenistic date.

[1] Bulle, op. cit., p. 13, fig. 5. References to earlier discussions of these two masks are given by Bulle and Bieber.

[2] *Iapigia*, iii (1932), p. 259, fig. 41.

[3] Bieber, *Denkm.*, Taf. xlii. The head of Euripides does not belong to the original, and is here omitted. The eyebrows, nose, and beard of the mask are much 'restored'.

[4] Daremberg and Saglio, *Dict.* s.v. 'Persona', fig. 5587.

[5] Professor Webster finds the ὄγκος depicted on Gnathia vases of the early third century, *J.H.S.* lxxi. 222, nos. 3–5. No. 4 is Fig. 46.

[6] The figure is from a photograph kindly lent to me by Professor T. B. L. Webster; cf. Bieber, *Denkm.*, Taf. xlvi.

[7] Ibid., p. 121, Taf. lxi, and *Hist. Gk. and Rom. Th.*, pp. 161–2.

[8] Rayet thinks it may be an old man of the New Comedy. Cf. also Simon, *Comicae Tabellae*, 49 on Fig. 49.

[9] *Hist. of Gk. and Rom. Th.*, p. 150, fig. 203.

The frieze[1] of which fragments were found at Pergamon (Fig. 53) and which may belong to the second century B.C., when drama flourished under the Attalids, includes two feminine masks—those of a younger and an older woman—and a masculine one, with long hair falling from a semicircular erection above the forehead. The latter has been conjectured to represent Herakles.

There are also figured a terra-cotta mask from Thebes (Fig. 54)[2] of a bearded man wearing above the ὄγκος the cap which indicates an Oriental, and (Fig. 55)[3] one of a pair of terra-cotta masks in the Berlin Museum, from Selymbria, probably of Hellenistic date, and representing a young man and a young woman. A mosaic threshold (Fig. 56)[4] from the House of the Faun in Pompeii, attributed to the second century B.C., exhibits two masks of the ultra-tragical type, with the high ὄγκος which is exhibited in the paintings from Herculaneum already noticed. (The masks must be derived from Greek sources, as Roman actors had almost certainly not begun to wear masks so early.)

In the well-known relief (Fig. 57)[5] on the monument of P. Numitorius Hilarus on the Via Salaria, probably dating from quite late in the first century B.C., Andromache wears a large ὄγκος, and Odysseus (leading away the young Astyanax from his mother) a seafarer's cap, which partly obscures the ὄγκος. The theatrical setting is that of the Roman stage, and the scene probably comes from a Roman play, but the relief illustrates the persistence of the later Greek type of masks.

10. The date at which Roman tragic actors began to wear masks is not certain, but Diomedes[6] says that the practice began with Roscius, a great actor of both tragedy and comedy, who was defended by Cicero in an extant speech. The change was not at first popular. Donatus[7] seems to date it earlier and

[1] Altmann, *Ath. Mitt.* xxix (1914), pp. 179, 194, figs. 18, 27, 28. Cf. below, p. 207, n. 2.

[2] Bieber, *Denkm.*, Taf. lxv, fig. 1.

[3] Ibid., fig. 2. Others, however, interpret these as comic.

[4] Mau, *Pompeii in Leben und Kunst*, fig. 158 (p. 303).

[5] I have to thank Professor Webster for a photograph of the lower half of the monument. The two smaller figures on the monument have never been satisfactorily explained.

[6] *Gr. Lat.* i. 489 (Keil) 'personis vero uti primus coepit Roscius Gallus, praecipuus histrio, quod oculis perversis erat.' Cf. Cic. *de Orat.* iii, § 221 'sed in ore sunt omnia, in eo autem ipso dominatus est omnis oculorum; quo melius nostri illi senes, qui personatum ne Roscium quidem magnopere laudabant.' Before masks came into vogue, old, middle-aged, and young men were distinguished, according to Diomedes, by white, black, and red hair.

[7] *de Comoedia* (Kaibel, *Gr. Com. Fragm.* i, pp. 68, 69).

FIG. 44. PAINTING FROM HERCULANEUM

FIG. 45. STATUE IN VATICAN HOLDING MASK

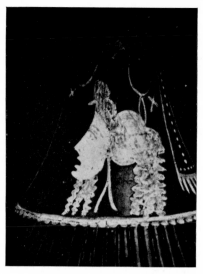

FIG. 46. TRAGIC MASK ON GNATHIA
OINOCHOE FROM RUVO IN LOUVRE

FIG. 47. APULIAN KANTHAROS FROM RUVO

FIG. 48. EURIPIDES—RELIEF IN CONSTANTINOPLE

FIG. 49. TERRACOTTA FIGURE
FROM MYRINA IN ATHENS

FIG. 50. TERRACOTTA FIGURE
FROM RHENEIA

FIG. 51. TERRACOTTA FIGURE FROM
PERGAMON

FIG. 52. TERRACOTTA FIGURE
FROM AMISOS IN LOUVRE

a

b

c

FIG. 53. FRAGMENTS OF FRIEZE IN PERGAMON

FIG. 54. TERRACOTTA MASK FROM THEBES

FIG. 55. TERRACOTTA MASKS FROM SELYMBRIA

FIG. 56. MOSAIC FROM THE HOUSE OF THE FAWN, POMPEII

FIG. 57. MONUMENT OF NUMITORIUS, ROME

FIG. 58. MARBLE MASK, NAPLES

FIG. 59. MARBLE MASK, NAPLES

FIG. 60. MARBLE RELIEF FROM POMPEII, NAPLES

FIG. 61. MARBLE RELIEF, MUNICH

FIG. 62. MARBLE RELIEF FROM POMPEII, NAPLES

FIG. 63. MARBLE MASK (TRAGIC), OXFORD, BEAZLEY

FIG. 63a. MARBLE MASK (TRAGIC), OXFORD, BEAZLEY

FIG. 64. MELPOMENE HOLDING
MASK, VATICAN

FIG. 66. IVORY STATUETTE
FROM RIETI, PARIS

FIG. 65. CAKE MOULD FROM OSTIA

FIG. 67. MARBLE MASK, ATHENS   FIG. 68. MARBLE MASK, BRITISH MUSEUM

FIG. 69. MOSAIC OF REHEARSAL FROM POMPEII, NAPLES

Masks 187

ascribes the use of tragic masks to Cincius Faliscus and of comic masks to Minucius Prothymus. (Nothing else is known of either.) However that may be—and the matter has been endlessly discussed[1]—there are many masks or representations of actors' masks from Italy, and particularly from Pompeii, though none of them can be exactly identified. The figures here given are as follows:

Fig. 58.[2] Marble mask (female) from Pompeii, in Naples Museum.

59.[3] Marble mask (female) in Naples Museum.

60.[4] Marble relief from Pompeii, in Naples Museum, showing masks of a man, a woman, and a girl. (Dr. Bieber suggests Herakles, Deianeira, and Iole.)

61.[5] Marble relief in Munich, showing heads (of an almost natural shape) of Perseus and Andromeda.

62.[6] Marble mask (male) from Pompeii in Naples, wearing a very high ὄγκος.

63. Marble mask (male) in Oxford (Beazley).

63 (a). Marble mask (female) in Oxford (Beazley).

64.[7] Marble mask, held by a statue of Melpomene in the Vatican. (Most of the nose and beard of the mask are 'restored'. The mask is conjectured to be that of Herakles.)

65.[8] The figures on a mould found at Ostia and dating probably from the first half of the third century A.D.

66.[9] The famous statuette from Rieti (formerly in the Castellani Collection and now in Paris)—a late Roman work, probably of the late second century A.D. The mask is probably that of a female figure, and Dr. Bieber and others think that it represents an elderly woman. It has a very high ὄγκος, long hair hanging down, and very wide-open mouth and eyes.

67.[10] A terrific female mask (not entirely unlike Fig. 58), found by the American excavators in the Agora at Athens among remains of the fourth and fifth centuries A.D.

[1] The materials for the discussion are assembled by C. Saunders, Am. J. Phil. xxxii (1911), pp. 58–73, who argues that the date was between 130 and 91 B.C. See now W. Beare, The Roman Stage, pp. 184 f.

[2] Museo Borbonico, xi, Tav. xlii. 4; cf. Bieber, Skenika, p. 13, fig. 8; Denkm., Taf. lxv. 4, p. 124.

[3] From photo lent by Sir John Beazley. Cf. Simon, Comicae Tabellae, 66, n. 126.

[4] Bieber, Denkm., Taf. lxiii, p. 122.   [5] Ibid., Taf. lxiv. 1.

[6] Cf. ibid., Taf. lxv. 3, p. 124. Figs. 62–64 and 66 are taken from photographs lent by Sir John Beazley.   [7] Cf. Bieber, Denkm., Taf. lxii, p. 122.

[8] The main subject of Dr. Bieber's Skenika (see also Denkm., Taf. lix, p. 118: she figures one or two similar objects). She interprets them as Klytaimnestra, Achilles, and an attendant, in a scene from Euripides' Iphigeneia in Aulis. I do not feel sure about this. Cf. Simon, Com. Tab. 49.

[9] Mon. dell' Inst. xi, Tav. 13; cf. Baumeister, Denkm. iii, Taf. 58 (a fine coloured picture); Bieber, Denkm., Taf. lxii, p. 122.   [10] Hesperia, ix (1940), p. 292.

Fig. 68.[1] A large marble mask of Roman date in the Rossie Collection in the British Museum.

11. At what date the exaggerated type of mask, with a high ὄγκος, found its way into satyric drama is uncertain.[2] But (with the exception of that of Silenus) those depicted in the Mosaic[3] from the House of the Tragic Poet in Pompeii (Fig. 69), representing the rehearsal or preparations for a satyric play, have a large ὄγκος—particularly the female mask. It is sometimes supposed that this mosaic really copies a votive tablet of a very much earlier date; but the scenery is more like that of a number of Pompeian wall-paintings than (as some scholars assert) like that of the work of Assteas in the fourth century, and it may not have been until relatively late (e.g. in the first century B.C.) that satyric drama followed tragedy in the use of the ὄγκος. The masks are those of a female character with wide-open lips, and of a bearded man with dark hair and beard, in addition to that of Silenus.

12. That there is little agreement among scholars about the relation of the dramatic scenes and costumes depicted in Italian wall-paintings to the drama of Greece is not surprising, as there is practically no evidence. The paintings—or some of them—may be copies of earlier works of art, or of votive tablets erected by successful choregoi, poets, or actors, but it is very doubtful whether any of them can be derived (as Robert thought they could) from Athenian originals of the fifth century B.C. Most of them can probably be used only as evidence of the dramatic costumes of the Augustan and the succeeding period, as worn on the Roman stage in performances either of Greek or of Roman plays. But they are worth reproducing as displaying the later developments of peculiarities which began to show themselves in the second and first centuries B.C. Those which are here

---

[1] Brit. Mus. 1950.7.71.

[2] A rather obscure phrase in Pollux iv. 142, at the end of his account of tragic masks, seems to indicate that apart from those of satyrs and Silenus, the masks in satyric drama did not differ from those of tragedy: σατυρικὰ δὲ πρόσωπα Σάτυρος πόλιος, Σάτυρος γενειῶν, Σάτυρος ἀγένειος, Σειληνὸς πάππος. τἆλλα ὅμοια τὰ πρόσωπα, πλὴν ὅσοις ἐκ τῶν ὀνομάτων αἱ παραλλαγαὶ δηλοῦνται, ὥσπερ καὶ ὁ πάππος Σειληνὸς τὴν ἰδέαν ἐστὶ θηριωδέστερος. But whether or not ὅμοια means 'like those of tragedy' is by no means certain; and in any case Pollux gives no indication of dates. In the earlier period, young satyrs are often represented as bald-headed, and they are so in Sophocles' *Ichneutai* 357–9 (Pearson), as is Silenus in Sophocles, fr. 171 (Pearson), and Eur. *Cyclops* 227. In the *Ichneutai*, l. 41, Silenus is a πρεσβευτής.

[3] See *Theatre of D.*, p. 231, fig. 98.

FIG. 70. PAINTING FROM HERCULANEUM, NAPLES

FIG. 71. PAINTING IN POMPEII (PERSEUS AND ANDROMEDA)

FIG. 72. PAINTING, CASA DEL CENTENARIO, POMPEII (HERAKLES)

FIG. 73. PAINTING, CASA DEL CENTENARIO, POMPEII (PRIAM AND HECUBA)

figured are the following. (The dresses and footwear will be noticed later.)

(1) A painting on marble (Fig. 70) from Herculaneum,[1] depicting three female figures—one wearing tall boots and in every way exaggerated; the mask has a high ὄγκος and is very large. It was long customary to think that the principal person was Phaedra (the others being the Nurse and the chorus-leader), but the characterization is entirely unlike that of the Phaedra of Euripides' *Hippolytus*, and Dr. Bieber suggests Electra, with an aged chorus-leader and Chrysothemis, as in Sophocles' play —a better conjecture, but not convincing. The costume generally cannot possibly go back, as Robert imagined, to the fifth century B.C., with its high kothornoi and the quite non-classical type of expression in the face of the principal character.

(2) A wall-painting (Fig. 71) in Pompeii,[2] probably of early Augustan date, shows masks of Perseus (wearing the cap of darkness on the top of his ὄγκος), Andromeda, and her parents— with a rather harmless-looking sea monster. It is impossible to accept Robert's reference of the picture back to the original performance of Euripides' *Andromeda* in 412 B.C. It takes its place naturally in the series of representations of the Roman period which include masks with a high ὄγκος and a characteristic expression.

(3) Four paintings from the Casa del Centenario in Pompeii, dating probably from the first century A.D., though they may be copied from earlier originals either Roman or possibly Greek. As to this there is no evidence.

   (a) A scene[3] (Fig. 72) in which Herakles is the principal figure. The identity of the other figures is quite uncertain. They are usually supposed to be Megara and Amphitryon, with Lykos taking refuge at the altar; but, at least in Euripides' play, Lykos does not do this, and the undignified little old man is more likely to be a servant than to be the noble Amphitryon. Whether the characters are taken from some other play on the subject, Greek or Roman, can only be conjectured.

---

[1] Robert, *Kentaurenkampf u. Tragödienszene* (1898), p. 14, Taf. ii; cf. Bieber, *Dresd. Schauspieler-relief*, pp. 64 ff.; *Denkm.*, p. 113, fig. 110.
[2] Robert, *Arch. Ztg.* 1878, Taf. 3; *Arch. Hermeneutik*, p. 196; cf. Bieber, *Denkm.*, p. 123, Taf. lxiv.
[3] Dieterich, *Pulcinella*, pl. i; cf. Bieber, *Skenika*, p. 17, fig. 10; *Denkm.*, p. 113, fig. 111.

(*b*) A picture of Priam and Hecuba[1] (Fig. 73), and
(*c*) A picture of Priam supplicating Achilles[2] (Fig. 74).
In both these the masks with their high ὄγκος are characteristic of the period. It is impossible to refer the scenes to any known Greek or Roman play.

(*d*) A picture of Medea[3] with a sword and her children being brought to her by the Paidagogos—obviously not taken from Euripides' play. Medea wears a lofty ὄγκος (Fig. 75).

(4) A painting from Pompeii[4] in the Museum at Palermo (Fig. 76) depicting a servant addressing his master, who wears a high ὄγκος and thick κόθορνοι. It reminds Dr. Bieber of the opening scene of Euripides' *Iphigeneia in Aulis*, but scenes between masters and servants must have been so common that no certain identification is possible. The servant's ὄγκος is lower; he has a hooked nose, and in this (as Dr. Bieber notices) resembles some other servants shown in these paintings.[5]

(5) A painting[6] from the Casa dei Dioscuri in Pompeii (Fig. 77) showing a lady of high rank, carrying a tiny infant, and vehemently haranguing a servant who seems to be protesting, and is carrying a jug. The ὄγκος of the mistress is much higher than that of the servant,[7] and her features are of the terrifying type which we have met with already.

It would be outside the scope of this book to discuss the late Roman mosaic[8] found at Porcareccia (Lorium) in Etruria, in some of the remains of which are figures wearing a high ὄγκος and standing almost on stilts. They show at best the continuity either of artistic tradition or of dramatic practice down to a late date (Fig. 78).

13. Pollux (iv. 132 ff.) enumerates 6 tragic masks of old men, 8 of young men, 8 of women of various ages, and 6 of servants, and Dr. Bieber[9] and others have tried with varying degrees of success to find specimens corresponding to each of them among

---

[1] *Mon. dell' Inst.* xi, Tav. 30, No. 3; cf. Bieber, *Denkm.*, p. 115, fig. 112.
[2] *Mon. dell' Inst.* xi, Tav. 30, No. 4; cf. Bieber, *Denkm.*, p. 115, fig. 113.
[3] *Mon. dell' Inst.* xi, Tav. 31, No. 11; cf. Bieber, *Denkm.*, p. 116, fig. 114.
[4] Wieseler, *Theatergeb.*, Taf. ix; cf. Bieber, *Skenika*, p. 20, fig. 12; *Denkm.*, p. 117, pl. lvii.
[5] e.g. in Fig. 65.
[6] Wieseler, op. cit., Taf. viii. 12; cf. Bieber, *Skenika*, p. 21, fig. 14; *Denkm.*, p. 117, pl. lviii.
[7] There is a similar distinction between master and servant in Fig. 76.
[8] They are discussed by Bieber, *Denkm.*, pp. 118 ff.; but the identification of all but a few of the characters is very doubtful. The examples in Fig. 78 are taken from Wieseler, op. cit., pls. vii and viii.
[9] Pauly–W. *Real-Encycl.* s.v. 'Masken', cols. 2077 ff. Cf. also T. B. L. Webster in *Festschrift A. Rumpf*, pp. 141 f.

FIG. 74. PAINTING, CASA DEL CENTENARIO, POMPEII (PRIAM AND ACHILLES)

FIG. 75. PAINTING, CASA DEL CENTENARIO, POMPEII (MEDEA)

FIG. 76. PAINTING FROM POMPEII (MASTER AND SERVANT), PALERMO

FIG. 77. PAINTING FROM CASA DEI DIOSCURI, POMPEII
(MISTRESS AND SERVANT), NAPLES

a

b

c

d

FIG. 78 (a–d). MOSAICS FROM PORCARECCIA, VATICAN

e

f

g

h

FIG. 78 (e–h). MOSAICS FROM PORCARECCIA, VATICAN

extant archaeological remains. (Some of the more probable of these identifications are mentioned below.) Of the old men, the oldest is the ξυρίας—white-haired, the hair attached to the ὄγκος, and the beard closely cut; he is 'long in the cheek' (ἐπιμήκης ὢν τὰς παρείας—the meaning of which is not quite clear without a certain specimen). It seems that Priam was so represented— at least at a late date. Suidas interprets πριαμωθῆναι as = ξυρη- θῆναι· τὸ γὰρ τοῦ Πριάμου πρόσωπον ξυρίας ἐστί, and Hesychius similarly explains the word πριαμωθήσομαι. But in the Pompeian paintings[1] Priam has a considerable beard. The λευκὸς ἀνήρ is grey-haired, with a low ὄγκος and curls round his head, a stiff beard (if this is the meaning of γένειον πεπηγός), projecting eye- brows, and a rather pale complexion (παράλευκον τὸ χρῶμα).[2] The σπαρτοπόλιος is a dark-haired man, turning grey, with a somewhat pale face (ὕπωχρος). The μέλας ἀνήρ has a dark com- plexion, curly hair and beard, a large ὄγκος, and a cruel face (τραχύς). Dr. Bieber thinks that some masks of Herakles fall under this head. The ξανθὸς ἀνήρ had light curls, a smaller ὄγκος, and a good complexion (εὔχρως),[3] while the ξανθότερος, though in other ways similar, was paler and was the mask of a sick man.[4]

The masks of the νεανίσκοι have no beards. The oldest of them is the πάγχρηστος νεανίας. He has thick dark hair and a good complexion inclining towards swarthiness (μελαινόμενος). Dr. Bieber is probably right in attributing this mask to the noble young hero, such as Achilles or Perseus. The οὖλος has hair closely attached to a large ὄγκος, his brows are raised, and he has a grim look (βλοσυρός). The πάρουλος is like him, but younger. The ἁπαλός has light-coloured curls, a pale complexion, and a bright expression (φαιδρός); the mask is πρέπων θεῷ ἢ καλῷ; Dr. Bieber suggests that it may have been worn by Dionysus in the *Bacchae*, but the description so carefully given in the text of the play probably implies a mask specially made to reproduce it. The πιναρός looks swollen (ὀγκώδης),[5] has

---

[1] See above, p. 190, Figs. 73–4.

[2] Dr. Bieber finds an example from Pompeii in *Arch. Ztg.* xxxvi (1878), Taf. iv. 2. The left-hand mask of the two, as there briefly described by Robert (ibid., p. 21), certainly corresponds fairly well with Pollux's description (Fig. 79).

[3] εὔχρως—generally of bright or healthy colour, as distinct from pale. Professor Webster brings the Würzburg actor under this head and some of the masks of Herakles.

[4] Such perhaps as Telephos or Philoctetes, though we cannot tell whether any of the masks described by Pollux were actually used several hundred years earlier.

[5] I do not feel certain what ὀγκώδης really means. Professor Webster thinks that it simply = ὄγκον ἔχει, though this does not quite explain the termination. The mask recalls the

downcast eyes and discoloured complexion, very dirty, with long light hair. This suggests to Dr. Bieber the young hero in distress —Philoktetes or Telephos (but were these classed as νεανισκοί?) —and (not very convincingly) the terra-cotta statuette from Rheneia. The δεύτερος πιναρός is thinner and younger. The ὠχρός is pale, with hair all round his head, and the complexion of a sick man—the mask is for a ghost or a wounded man; Dr. Bieber thinks it would suit the dying Hippolytus or the ghost of Polydorus in the *Hecuba*. The πάρωχρος is generally like the πάγχρηστος, but pale, to denote sickness or love; Dr. Bieber suggests that it would suit Haimon in the *Antigone* or the hero in Euripides' *Orestes*.

Of the three servants represented by masks the eldest is the διφθερίας, 'the leather-clad', who wears a cap (περίκρανον) instead of an ὄγκος, with white, straight-combed hair, a pale face, an unkind sneer,[1] his forehead drawn up, his eyes gloomy (σκυθρωπούς), and the cut of his beard long out of date (τὸ γένειον προπαλαίτερος).[2] This mask is very probably that associated with the παιδαγωγός. Next in age comes the σφηνοπώγων ('wedge-bearded'), who is in the prime of life, with a high ὄγκος, flat on the top and hollowed out at the sides, and light hair, a pointed beard, and a stern red face, suited to a messenger. The youngest of the three, the ἀνάσιμος,[3] has an upturned nose, a high ὄγκος, hair standing upright in the middle of his forehead, and a reddish face—he too is a messenger.

Of the women represented the oldest and most dignified is the πολιὰ κατάκομος, with long white hair and a moderate ὄγκος, and rather pale—such as, Dr. Bieber thinks, Hecuba in the Pompeian fresco.[4] The ἐλεύθερον γρᾴδιον has her grey hair tinged with yellow, a small ὄγκος, and her hair falling to her shoulders the mask is significative of calamity. The οἰκετικὸν γρᾴδιον—the old slave-woman—wears a lamb's-wool cap instead of an ὄγκος and has a wrinkled face. (Pompeian paintings illustrate both these.[5]) The οἰκετικὸν μεσόκουρον (half-shorn) has moderately long hair, only partly grey, a low ὄγκος, and a pale complexion while the διφθερῖτις (leather-clad) is younger and has no ὄγκος

description of Orestes at the beginning of Euripides' play, but this too may have been special one. See above, p. 184.

[1] μυκτῆρα τραχύν—meaning perhaps not quite certain.
[2] The emendation προπαλέστερος (Hemsterhuis) would mean 'prominent', 'pointing forward'.   [3] C has variant ἀνάσιλλος.
[4] Above, p. 190. But in the play Hecuba in deep mourning would not be wearing long hair
[5] Above, p. 189, Fig. 70 (Nurse); p. 190, Fig. 73 (Hecuba).

FIG. 79. PAINTED MASKS FROM POMPEII

FIG. 80. ATTIC CHOUS IN LENINGRAD

The κατάκομος ὠχρά has long black hair, a pale face, and a look of pain. The μεσόκουρος ὠχρά differs from the last only in having shorter hair; so has the μεσόκουρος πρόσφατος (recently half-shorn), but she is not so pale. The κούριμος παρθένος[1] has no ὄγκος but her hair parted, combed back, and cut short, and a somewhat pale complexion, and the second κούριμος παρθένος is similar, but without the parting and close-cut hair, ὡς ἐκ πολλοῦ δυστυχοῦσα. The κόρη has a youthful face, such as that of Danae or some other young girl.

Besides all these, tragedy employed special masks—ἔκσκευα πρόσωπα—such as those of Actaeon wearing horns, the blind Phineus, Thamyris with one blue eye and one dark, Argos with his many eyes, Euhippe changing into a horse, Tyro with her face bruised by her mother Sidero, Achilles shaven in mourning for Patroklos, Amymone, Priam, or the masks of a Titan, a Giant, a River, a Triton, a Fury, Death, or personifications such as Λύσσα, Οἶστρος, Ὕβρις, Ἀπάτη, Μέθη, Ὄκνος, Φθόνος, Muses, Nymphs, Horai, Pleiades, etc.

Unfortunately Pollux gives no indication of dates, and this list—based probably in the main on the fixed types of a post-Classical period—cannot give much information about the earlier periods, in which there may have been less exaggeration and more freedom.[2]

14. It is only necessary to refer briefly to two suggestions which have been made with regard to the peculiarities of the tragic masks: (1) that they served to make the actor's voice more resonant, so that it could carry throughout the vast theatres; (2) that the grotesqueness of the later masks, and particularly the high ὄγκος, was in some way connected with the introduction of the raised stage.

The first suggestion is supported by a passage of Aulus Gellius (v. vii) who is quoting the work of an earlier writer, Gavius Bassus, *de Origine Vocabulorum*: 'Caput' inquit 'et os coperimento personae tectum undique unaque tantum vocis emittendae via pervium, quoniam non vaga neque diffusa est, in unum tantummodo exitum collectam coactamque vocem ciet ⟨et⟩ magis claros canorosque sonitus facit. Quoniam igitur indumentum illud oris

[1] See above, p. 178.
[2] It may be assumed that if masks adapted to special characters were employed in the revived tragedies in his own day, they would equally have been allowed in the great period of tragedy. See above, p. 184.

clarescere et resonare vocem facit, ob eam causam "persona" dicta est, litera propter vocabuli formam productiore.' The suggested derivation, of course, does not bear looking into, and some modern experiments with masks manufactured so far as possible on ancient lines make it extremely doubtful whether in fact masks ever did anything to increase sound. Certainly no 'megaphone effect' could be produced by linen masks such as Thespis is said to have used, so that it cannot have been their original object; and it is doubtful whether such effects could be satisfactorily achieved without the use of metal.[1] When Roscius introduced masks into tragedy in Rome (if he did so),[2] it was not to enhance the resonance of his voice, but to conceal his squint.

15. The theory that the introduction of the less natural type of mask coincided with the introduction of the raised stage is supported by Bulle,[3] but he dates the latter change in the second half of the fourth century B.C., and this is probably more than a century too early,[4] at least as far as Athens is concerned. It may be that when action began to be confined to the relatively narrow stage instead of the wide orchestra, it was necessarily more restrained and statuesque, and masks of the newer type, which were suited to actors facing the audience (and that from a greater distance) and seldom seen in the round, would commend themselves as suitable; but the earliest of the masks with a high ὄγκος seem to belong to the years about 300 B.C., and cannot have been suggested by the alteration in the place of action, unless indeed these masks came first into vogue in theatres away from Athens. So much is obscure with regard to the relevant dates that it would be rash to lay down any positive statement. The most repulsive forms of tragic mask, at which Lucian scoffs, were the result of the depraved taste of the imperial period.[5]

16. The double derivation of Attic comedy, from animal-masqueraders in Attica and from such impersonations of coarsely padded and phallic beings as are depicted on early Corinthian vases, is reflected in the appearance of the Athenian performers

[1] Cf. Dingeldein, *Haben die Theatermasken der Alten die Stimme verstärkt?* (1890), which I have not been able to see.   [2] See above, p. 186.
[3] *Festschrift für James Loeb*, p. 19.   [4] See *Theatre of D.*, pp. 182, etc.
[5] Lucian, *de Salt.* § 27 πρόσωπον ὑπὲρ κεφαλῆς ἀνατεινόμενον ἐπικείμενος καὶ στόμα κεχηνὸ πάμμεγα ὡς καταπιόμενος τοὺς θεατάς, κτλ.

in the fifth century. There were many animal choruses in the comedies, and these doubtless wore appropriate masks;[1] and when the choruses were not strictly animal, but at the same time not human, as in Aristophanes' *Clouds*, grotesque masks were invented to suit the poet's fancy. Thus the 'Clouds' were like women, only half-disguised (ll. 340 ff.) :

ΣΤ.   λέξον δή μοι, τί παθοῦσαι,
εἴπερ νεφέλαι γ' εἰσὶν ἀληθῶς, θνηταῖς εἴξασι γυναιξίν;
οὐ γὰρ ἐκεῖναί γ' εἰσὶ τοιαῦται.   ΣΩ. φέρε ποῖαι γάρ τινές εἰσιν;
ΣΤ. οὐκ οἶδα σαφῶς· εἴξασιν γοῦν ἐρίοισιν πεπταμένοισιν,
οὐχὶ γυναιξὶν μὰ Δί' οὐδ' ὁτιοῦν· αὗται δὲ ῥῖνας ἔχουσιν.

—which Socrates justifies by recalling the fanciful shapes which clouds in the sky frequently assume. But whereas it is probable that the members of a tragic chorus were all masked alike, this was not always so in comedy, for, for example, in the *Birds* (268–304) all kinds of birds are represented in the chorus. How the choruses which represented ordinary human beings were masked there is no precise evidence to show, but old men and women were doubtless rendered grotesque in some way.

Nor is it possible to tell how the comic poets disguised such collective personifications as the Πλοῦτοι of Cratinus, or the Πόλεις and Δῆμοι of Eupolis. It can only be assumed that the poet's wit was not fettered by any stereotyped conventions, and that (as in the *Birds*) the members of a chorus need not have been all alike. But the tight-fitting and grossly padded dress of the Athenian comic actors, cut short so as to display the phallos, seems to have been Doric and to have originated in mime-like performances in Sparta and Corinth and probably elsewhere.[2] Its first certain appearance in art as an actor's costume (though passages in Aristophanes virtually prove its use in his plays) is on an Attic vase (Fig. 80) in Leningrad,[3] on which these gross figures carry masks and evidently form part of a dressing-room

[1] For early dances of Birds, Riders on Horseback, etc., see *Dith. Trag. Com.*, pp. 244 ff., and for an enumeration of animal dances in comedy, ibid., p. 247. To this list should be added the *Bees* of Diokles and the *Swine* of Cephisodoros. For choruses of Riders on Dolphins and Ostriches see Brommer in *Jahrb. Arch.* lvii (1942), Anz., pp. 65 ff.; Bieber, *Hist. Gk. Rom. Theat.*, pp. 66–67; and Bielefeld, *Jahrb. Arch.* lxi–lxii (1946–7), Anz., cols. 48–54. For Ἰχθύες Χορευταί see L. B. Lawler in *Class. Phil.* xxxvi (1941), pp. 142 ff.; and for a possible Thracian pig-dance (κολαβρισμός) see Lawler and Kober, ibid. xl (1945), pp. 98 ff.
[2] See *Dith. Trag. Com.*, pp. 254 ff.
[3] Ibid., pp. 262–3; cf. Körte, *Jahrb. Arch.* viii (1893), p. 69. The two central figures are grossly phallic in the original.

scene. The vase is probably contemporary with the Middle Comedy,[1] but the costume is likely to have been traditional rather than a new invention of the fourth century,[2] when the grossness of comedy, to judge from the fragments, was at least tending to abate, though the change was very gradual. If so, the vase may be used tentatively as evidence for the Old Comedy.

Masks like those on the Leningrad vase appear also on a number of terra-cotta statuettes of padded and phallic actors, which are also attributed to the fourth century and may exemplify a tradition carried on from an earlier period.[3]

In addition Attic comedy probably derived ultimately from Dorian sources the masks of certain typical or recurrent characters—the wrinkled and gap-toothed old woman, the old man with his stick, and possibly others. These types are found among the votive masks excavated at Sparta and corresponding closely to some descriptions of characters in Aristophanes.[4] Other stock characters—the food-stealer and the quack-doctor, for instance —may have brought their masks with them to Athens, but we do not know what they were like. So may such favourite characters of mythological burlesque as Herakles and possibly Odysseus, but, again, precise evidence is lacking.[5] The attribution of the masks of the μαίσων (Fig. 81) and the θεράπων ἡγέμων to Maison of Megara has difficulties of its own, but may point to Dorian origin at an early date, and again the discussion involves some terra-cotta figures.[6]

17. It is clear that the Old Comedy enjoyed complete freedom

---

[1] Or at least very little earlier. Sir John Beazley tells me that it probably dates from early in the fourth century. But the figure of a child dressed as a comic actor in a scene on a 'Children's Χοῦς' (see above, p. 10), published by S. P. Karouzou (*Am. J. Arch.* l (1946), pp. 132 ff., fig. 10), has all the characteristics described, and is probably somewhat earlier than the Leningrad vase.

[2] The Dorian origin of the costume is more or less confirmed by its partial resemblance to that which appears on a sixth-century Corinthian amphora (Bieber, *Denkm.*, p. 129, Abb. 123; after Körte, *Jahrb. Arch.* viii (1893), p. 91). On this some of the figures wear no masks, but this was regularly so in some forms of mime-like performance in the Peloponnese.

[3] Körte, op. cit. pp. 77 ff., enumerates over a hundred of these. See Bieber, *Denkm.*, Taf. lxix–lxxi, and below, pp. 199, 200, Figs. 81–88, 90–91. For the need of caution in using these indiscriminately as evidence for comedy see below, p. 198.

[4] See *Dith. Trag. Com.*, pp. 254 ff., where figures are given and passages quoted.

[5] Ibid, p. 269.

[6] Ibid., pp. 278 ff., and see below on Pollux' description, pp. 202 f. For the terra-cotta statuette generally identified with the μαίσων see R. Zahn in *Die Antike*, ii (1926), Taf. 23. The figure has a blue mantle and white tunic, and carries a basket from which the head of a goose protrudes. It obviously represents a cook who has just come from market. Its date probably falls early in the fourth century B.C.

in the production of masks to suit its characters. The masks of living persons burlesqued by the poet might be recognizable portraits, though possibly with some degree of caricature.[1] In the *Knights*,[2] indeed, the poet says that none of the mask-makers dared to produce a portrait of Kleon:

καὶ μὴ δέδιθ'· οὐ γάρ ἐστιν ἐξηκασμένος,
ὑπὸ τοῦ δέους γὰρ αὐτὸν οὐδεὶς ἤθελεν
τῶν σκευοποιῶν εἰκάσαι. πάντως γε μὴν
γνωσθήσεται· τὸ γὰρ θέατρον δεξιόν.

But it may be assumed that the two slaves would be at once recognizable by their masks as Nikias and Demosthenes. In Cratinus, fr. 71, Pericles was similarly represented with his abnormal head, ὁ σχινοκέφαλος Ζεὺς ὁδὶ προσέρχεται. That the mask of Socrates in the *Clouds* was likewise a portrait is confirmed rather than disproved by the story,[3] true or false, that Socrates himself stood up in the theatre so that everyone (and particularly the many strangers present) might see who was meant. The mask of Agathon in the *Thesmophoriazousai*[4] was probably an effeminate-looking caricature. Other living characters introduced by Aristophanes were Lamachos,[5] Meton, Kinesias, and the three great tragedians; and his contemporary Eupolis introduced Pericles, Nikias, Alcibiades, and Kallias. All of these may have been made immediately recognizable by their masks. The use of portrait-masks probably went out of fashion by the end of the fifth century, and Platonios[6] makes it characteristic of the Middle and New Comedy that they deliberately avoided such resemblances and made use of masks with features so exaggerated that they could not possibly be like any real human being. (He ascribes the change to the fear lest any mask should even by accident resemble some Macedonian ruler.)

---

[1] Pollux iv. 143 τὰ δὲ κωμικὰ πρόσωπα τὰ μὲν τῆς παλαιᾶς κωμῳδίας ὡς τὸ πολὺ τοῖς προσώποις ὧν ἐκωμῴδουν ἀπεικάζετο ἢ ἐπὶ τὸ γελοιότερον ἐσχημάτιστο, τὸ δὲ τῆς νέας κτλ.

[2] ll. 230 ff. (See Neil's note ad loc.) What truth there may be in the scholiast's statement that Aristophanes played the part himself it is impossible to say.

[3] Aelian, *Var. Hist.* ii. xiii (end).　　　　　　　　　　　　　　　　　　[4] See ll. 191–2.

[5] Whether Lamachos' mask included some traditional features of the Boastful Soldier, who seems to belong to all periods of comedy, there is no evidence to show. His bombastic crests are certainly mentioned.

[6] περὶ διαφορᾶς κωμῳδιῶν, § 13 (Kaibel, *Com. Gr. Fragm.*, p. 5). He states expressly that the characters of Menander, very human though we feel them to be, wore these hideously exaggerated masks; see below, p. 201. (There is, of course, no necessary inconsistency between the statement of Platonios and the derivation of certain grotesque types from Dorian sources.) Alexis, fr. 116, speaks of the first-class parasite wearing ὀφρῦς χιλιοταλάντους.

Aristophanes, and no doubt the other poets of the Old Comedy, gave full rein to their instinct for the comic, when they invented such masks as those of Βασιλέως ’Οφθαλμός in the *Acharnians*, consisting, according to the usual interpretation, of a huge eye and a Persian beard,[1] and of the Servant of the Epops in the *Birds*.[2]

There is practically no more evidence than has been given as to the masks used in the theatre in the time of the Old Comedy; these included a few traditional types, and we may perhaps assume that the slave and the female characters who appear in the last scenes of a number of plays could be recognized at once by their masks and dress. But probably great freedom prevailed. There are very few, if any, certain representations of scenes or characters taken from comedy on Attic vases of the fifth or fourth centuries.[3] Robert[4] is satisfied that he can trace back to the fifth century not only the μαίσων and θεράπων ἡγέμων, as described by Pollux, and some conventional types of old woman, but also the masks of bearded men differentiated as Ἑρμώνιος and Λυκομήδειος and some others, but his reasoning is very doubtful. (Some references to his identifications will be found below.)[5]

18. The statuettes and other figures enumerated and repro- duced by Körte, Winter, Dr. Bieber, and others, though infer- ences have been drawn from them to the practice of comedy in an earlier generation,[6] are in general more safely treated as parallel to the dramatic figures of the Middle and New Comedy[7] rather than to those of the Old; and if this is so, caution is even more necessary when evidence is sought from masks, statuettes, and wall-paintings of the Roman period or of Italian origin. In these the artists very probably had in view the comic per- formances of the Roman stage (after the introduction of masks in the first century B.C.), or those of the Greek towns of south Italy, rather than those of Athens or the Greek cities of the East and the mainland. Robert is doubtless right in attaching im-

---

[1] *Ach.* 91 ff. (For details see Starkie's note ad loc., and for a different interpretation of the passage see Damste in *Mnemos.* xliii (1915), pp. 433–41.) [2] ll. 60 ff.

[3] The few suggested instances appear to me to be so uncertain that I do not discuss them here.

[4] *Die Masken der neueren Att. Komödie* (Winckelmannspr. 1911), especially pp. 63 ff., 85 ff., 108 ff. See also Webster, *The Masks of Comedy*, p. 18 (= *Rylands Bulletin*, xxxii. 114).

[5] pp. 200–10. [6] See above, p. 196.

[7] Some may also have been suggested by contemporary mimes; see p. 237.

FIG. 81. MAISON

FIG. 82. HERAKLES

FIG. 83. SLAVE

FIG. 84. HERAKLES

FIG. 85. NURSE AND CHILD

FIG. 86. SLAVE MARKETING

FIG. 87. HYDROPHOROS

FIG. 88. SEATED SLAVE

portance to the reliefs (including representations of masks) and the terra-cottas of Myrina, Pergamon, and Priene, which lay within the district of Teos,[1] the greatest centre of dramatic artists, for a time, in the Near East; but their evidence does not affect the fourth and scarcely the third century. For the same reason the paintings and other works of art from Pompeii, Herculaneum, and Rome, while they doubtless reproduce masks in vogue at the time, with others conjecturally thought to be copied from earlier works, can (as has already been indicated) throw little light on the masks and costumes of earlier periods. Still less, except for passing comparison or illustration of particular points, can the figures in the manuscripts of Terence, which have been the subject of endless discussion. On the other hand, any descriptions of the facial appearance of characters in the texts of Plautus and Terence, although they used no masks, may be taken with some confidence to be translated from New Comedy plays in which masks were worn, and so to indicate what the masks were like, and Robert[2] notices a few correspondences between some of these descriptions and those given by Pollux, though the correspondences are seldom complete.

19. Of the archaeological evidence which may itself date from the early part of the fourth century, the vase at Leningrad, bearing a picture of a dressing-room scene in which the grotesquely padded actors are carrying masks, and the statuette generally agreed to represent the Maison, have already been noticed.[3] A terra-cotta figure of Herakles in the British Museum (Fig. 82)[4] probably dates from about 400 B.C., and a figure of a slave (Fig. 83), perhaps taking refuge at an altar, is dated by H. Luschey, who publishes it,[5] about the turn of the fifth and fourth centuries; the slave wears the padded and indecent costume. This figure closely resembles some of a series of fourteen terra-cotta statuettes in the Metropolitan Museum of Fine Art in New York,[6] some of which are figured here (Figs. 84–88).

[1] See below, p. 298. The ubiquity of the 'Artists of Dionysus' makes it probable that from the third century onwards much the same masks were employed wherever in the Greek world the same companies played, but there must also have been variations; and the evidence from other places does not necessarily hold good for Athens.

[2] Op. cit., pp. 54–58.   [3] Above, pp. 195–6.

[4] *Bulletin of Rylands Library*, xxxii. 97 f., fig. 7. I am indebted to Professor Webster for a photograph.   [5] *Ganymed* (1949), p. 71.

[6] Published by G. M. A. Richter, *Bull.Metr.Mus.* ix (1914), pp. 235 ff.; the whole series is figured by Bieber, *Hist. of Gk. and Rom. Th.*, pp. 85 ff. I have to thank Professor Webster for the photographs reproduced here, and the authorities of the Museum for permission to print them.

These are important as having all been found at Athens, in the same grave, and as being almost certainly contemporary with the Middle Comedy, since replicas of some of them have been found in the ruins of Olynthus and must therefore date from before the destruction of the town in 348 B.C. They include figures of Herakles, of fat men and women, standing or seated, and some carrying objects; the mask of an old man is several times repeated; nearly all the figures are grotesquely padded and wear the indecently short tunic. A remarkable relief from Athens at Lyme Park (Fig. 89)[1] shows a seated figure, probably a poet, holding in one hand a scroll, in the other the mask of a slave, and is probably of the early fourth century.

To these may be added a group of terra-cotta figures of actors from the necropolis of Halai in Boeotia,[2] of which one is reproduced here (Fig. 90). From the same site, but of a date much later in the century, is a mask of a slave (Fig. 91).[3] Two figures on Italian vases, treated by Bulle[4] as comic actors and belonging probably to the middle or end of the century, are perhaps connected with the phlyakes. A Campanian vase at Cambridge, of about the third quarter of the century, shows the mask of a slave hanging on the wall (Fig. 91 a).[5]

Some objects from Pergamon probably date from the latter part of the second century—especially a portion of the frieze which has already been mentioned[6] in connexion with the tragic masks, and which bears also a grinning comic mask, commonly supposed to be that of a cook (though this is perhaps not certain); and a mask which is certainly that of the loquacious cook called τέττιξ (Fig. 92), and corresponds exactly to the description of Pollux.[7]

[1] Again I am indebted to Professor Webster for the photograph (cf. *Studies for D. M. Robinson*, p. 590). His belief that the seated figure is a poet is reinforced by a comparison with the Menander relief (see below, p. 201). The second mask is probably that of an old man. The relief was found in a tomb in Athens in 1812, and its date seems to be about 380 B.C.

[2] See *Hesperia*, xi (1942), p. 405, pl. xxiii; reproduced by permission of Miss Hetty Goldman, the owner of the negative.　　　　　　　　　　　　　　　[3] Ibid., p. 409, pl. xx.

[4] *Festschrift für James Loeb*, pp. 29 and 31, figs. 17 and 20. Walters (*Brit. Mus. Cat. of Gk. Vases*, iv, F. 543, p. 225) calls the former a comic actor, and Bulle argues that it is so from the absence of the phallos. But the phlyakes may have shed some of their indecency in the course of time or in the hands of some painters (see below, p. 235). In other respects these two figures conform to the phlyakes-type.

[5] Professor Webster has kindly furnished me with a photograph of this, which is here reproduced by permission of the Board of Archaeology and Anthropology at Cambridge.

[6] Above, p. 186; cf. Bieber, *Denkm.*, Taf. civ.

[7] Robert, op. cit., fig.29; *Dith. Trag. Com.*, p. 279, fig. 46. Cp. Simon, *Tabellae*, p. 189, n. 15.

20. To the first century belongs the famous Menander relief[1]
(Fig. 93) in the Lateran Museum, in which the poet, seated, is
gazing at a mask which he holds in his left hand, while on the
table in front of him are two other masks, and beyond it the
figure of a Muse (though some prefer to identify it as Glykera)
holding some object now lost. In the background (behind and
above the table) is what appears to be a reading-desk, on which
is a manuscript roll, partly opened. Robert identifies the three
masks with those classified by Pollux as the νεανίσκος μέλας,
λαμπάδιον (or certainly a ἑταίρα of some description) and
ἡγέμων πρεσβύτης. (Dr. Bieber, perhaps less probably, would
identify them with the νεανίσκος πάγχρηστος, ψευδοκόρη, and
πρεσβύτης μακροπώγων καὶ ἐπισείων.) Both the masculine masks
wear a conspicuous στεφάνη or roll of hair above the forehead.

A second relief[2] in Naples—far inferior in artistic value—may
be mentioned here, since, though its date is uncertain and the
theatrical architecture represented does not help to fix it, the
scene and the masks certainly belong to the later comedy
(Fig. 94). A young man, supported by a slave and accompanied
by a flute-player, is returning intoxicated from a feast, and is
encountered by his father and an elderly friend, who is trying
to calm the paternal indignation. The masks seem to be those
of the πρεσβύτης μακροπώγων, the πρεσβύτης ἡγέμων (the father),
the νεανίσκος δεύτερος ἐπίσειστος, and the θεράπων ἡγέμων ἐπίσειστος of Pollux's catalogue. The masks worn by the three
women—one old and two young—depicted in the mosaic of
Dioskorides (Fig. 95) may well be derived from comedy, but
there is much uncertainty about both the date and the interpretation of the picture (or of its original).[3]

21. Two striking wall-paintings also illustrate masks of the
New Comedy type, whether the plays which the painter has
in view were Greek originals or (as is more likely) Roman
imitations. The first (Fig. 96) (from Pompeii and now in the
Museum at Palermo)[4] depicts an angry mistress and a θεράπων

[1] Studniczka in *N. Jahrb.* xli (1916), p. 25; Robert, op. cit., pp. 77 ff., fig. 96; Bieber, *Denkm.*, pp. 136–7, Taf. lxxxviii, etc. The figure of Menander reproduces earlier likenesses, which probably go back to the third century. This is not the place to discuss the many questions raised about details in the relief, but see Webster, *Bull. Rylands Libr.* xxxii. 1, pp. 102 ff.
[2] Robert, op. cit., pp. 61 ff., fig. 85; Bieber, *Denkm.*, p. 137, fig. lxxxix; cf. *Theatre of D.*, p. 219, fig. 77.
[3] Ibid., p. 223 and fig. 86, and refs. given there.
[4] Bieber, *Skenika*, fig. 13; cf. also *Denkm.*, Taf. xc. 1.

ἡγέμων in attitudes of mutual protest. The second (Fig. 97) (from Herculaneum)[1] shows a slave and two women. The slave seems to be a θεράπων πάππος; the younger woman a ἑταίρα of the λαμπάδιον type, though Robert would call her a ψευδοκόρη; the elder is variously named by different scholars. From Pompeii come also a wall-picture[2] (Fig. 98) of a Boastful Soldier and the Parasite who flatters him; these are no doubt based on Roman comedy, but the typical masks may have descended from a Greek origin; the two characters are found in all the epochs of Greek comedy; they appear in the painting in the company of a number of unmasked persons, never quite satisfactorily explained.

To these may be added two paintings from the Casa del Centenario in Pompeii, the one (Fig. 99)[3] representing a θεράπων πάππος and his aged master, the other (Fig. 100)[4] a slave on the watch, though the dates of the originals are indeterminable; and a painting from the House of the Dioscuri (Fig. 101),[5] now in Bonn, depicting a young woman, an old man with a staff, and a (half-obliterated) slave.

22. The preceding descriptions have sometimes made use of the nomenclature of Pollux's catalogue of the masks of comedy and applied it tentatively to some of the archaeological remains. It will be convenient now to give Pollux's classification in order, and to mention, so far as probability allows, the masks and figures illustrated in the following pages, under the various headings. It cannot of course be assumed that every terra-cotta (or marble) mask or figure of an actor is good evidence for the practice of the theatre; the makers may well have made fancy figures of actors without adhering precisely to theatrical costumes; they may have taken figures from mimes; some figures, such as the bronze caricature (Fig. 102) from Dodona,[6] in which the ὄγκος of the tragic hero is combined with the grotesque

---

[1] Robert, op. cit., p. 42, fig. 72; Bieber, *Denkm.*, p. 158, Taf. xc. 2. Dr. Bieber follows this with a description and figure of a much less distinct painting from Herculaneum, showing an old man, a slave, and a flute-player (Taf. xci. 1).

[2] Ibid., p. 159, fig. 136; Robert, op. cit., pp. 5, 22–23.

[3] *Mon. dell' Inst.* xi, pl. 32; Robert, op. cit., p. 24.

[4] Dieterich, *Pulcinella*, Taf. 2; cf. Robert, op. cit., p. 25, fig. 54.

[5] A. K. H. Simon, op. cit., Taf. ii. 1. She describes all the paintings just mentioned (with others, mostly less well preserved) with careful accounts of colours. She takes the 'elder woman' (Fig. 97) as a πάγχρηστος and the 'parasite' (Fig. 98) as a slave.

[6] Caraponos, *Dodona et ses ruines*, pl. xiii, no. 5.

FIG. 89. RELIEF OF COMIC POET

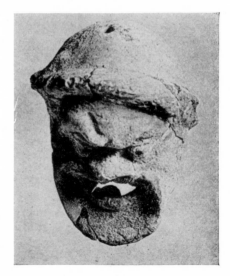

FIGS. 90–1. TERRACOTTAS FROM HALAI

FIG. 92. TETTIX (?)

FIG. 91*a*. CAMPANIAN VASE

FIG. 93. MENANDER RELIEF

features and costume of comedy, must have been the work of imagination. But the majority of terra-cotta and other masks and figures here cited doubtless give, as a whole, a true general idea of the range and character of comic actors' masks, and illustrate roughly the catalogue given by Pollux.

Older men

(1) The πρῶτος πάππος, the oldest; his head is close-shaved, but with a full beard; his eyebrows indicate gentleness (ἡμερώτατος τὰς ὀφρῦς); he has thin cheeks, a downcast expression, a pale complexion, and a cheerful forehead (τὸ μέτωπον ὑποφαιδρός—i.e. he does not frown).

(2) The δεύτερος πάππος is thinner, with a more intense and gloomy look, a rather pale complexion, a full beard, red hair, and bruised ears.

(3) The ἡγέμων πρεσβύτης has his hair raised in a στεφάνη—a kind of roll or 'wreath' of hair, running round his head, a hooked nose, a flat face, and the right eyebrow raised. The angry father on the Naples relief (Fig. 94) is thought to exemplify this type, though obviously at a relatively late date.

(4) The πρεσβύτης μακροπώγων καὶ ἐπισείων has a στεφάνη, but his hair hangs loose beneath it; his eyebrows are not raised, and he looks lethargic (νωθρός).

(5) The Ἑρμώνιος is growing bald (ἀναφαλαντίας), has a good beard, raised eyebrows, and a piercing look (τὸ βλέμμα δριμύς). According to the *Etymologicum Magnum*,[1] the name is derived from Hermon, a comic actor mentioned by Pollux,[2] and almost certainly in the Argument to Aristophanes' *Peace*.[3] If so, the type goes back to the fifth century.

(6) The σφηνοπώγων is going bald, has a wedge-shaped beard, raised eyebrows, and a rather obstinate expression (ὑποδύστροπος).

(7) The Λυκομήδειος has curly hair, a long beard, one eyebrow raised,[4] and the look of a busy-body (πολυπράγμων). (Several plays of the Middle period are entitled Πολυπράγμων.)

(8) The πορνοβόσκος is like the Λυκομήδειος, but his lips have a slight grin, his brows are contracted, and he is wholly or

---

[1] p. 376. 48.   [2] iv. 88; see above, p. 168.
[3] τὸ δὲ δρᾶμα ὑπεκρίνατο Ἀπολλόδωρος· ἐνίκα Ἕρμων ὁ ὑποκριτής—Rose's emendation for ἡνίκα ἑρμῆν λοιοκρότης.
[4] Cf. Rumpf, *A.J.A.*, lv. 8 for raised eyebrows of nos. 3 and 7.

partly bald. Robert compares the description of the *leno* in Plautus' *Rudens*, ll. 317–18.

(9) The Ἑρμώνιος δεύτερος has a shaven head and a pointed beard.

The following figures illustrate this group. (Unless it is otherwise stated, they are full-length terra-cotta figures.)

Fig. 103. Old man in a rage. (In Berlin, from Athens.)[1]
104. Old man sitting. (In Louvre, from Myrina.)[2] A σφηνοπώγων.
105. Old man. (In Dresden, from Boeotia.)[3] A σφηνοπώγων.
106. Old man. (In Louvre, from Myrina.)[4] Perhaps a πορνοβόσκος; some identify with the Ἑρμώνιος.
107. Mask of old man. (In Athens, probably from Myrina.)[5]
108. Conversation piece; old man and old woman. (In Würzburg.)[6]
109. Two drunken men. (In Berlin, perhaps from Tanagra.)[7]
110. Heavily laden soldier. (In Berlin, from Asia Minor.)[8] Robert regards the mask as of the Λυκομήδειος type. Possibly a traveller carrying his luggage.
111. Pedlar. (In Munich, from Athens.)[9]
112. Water-carrier. (In Palermo, from Centuripe.)[10] Other copies are known from Athens[11] and (probably) Boeotia. Robert thinks the mask is a specimen of the Ἑρμώνιος.

Younger men

(1) The πάγχρηστος νεανίσκος, 'the Perfect Young Man', has the appearance of good training (γυμναστικός), a rather sunburnt complexion, light hair with a στεφάνη, a few wrinkles on the forehead, eyebrows raised. He seems to be represented by one of the masks on the Menander relief (Fig. 93), and Robert and Simon find the type also in Plesidippus in Plautus, *Rudens* 314.

(2) The μέλας νεανίσκος is younger, more like a cultured youth than an athlete, with his eyebrows lowered (Robert takes

---

[1] Bieber, *Denkm.*, p. 132, Taf. lxix. 1.   [2] Robert, *Masken*, p. 19, fig. 40.
[3] Ibid., fig. 44.
[4] Pottier and Reinach, *Nécropole de Myrine*, pl. xlvi. 4; cf. also Robert, ibid., fig. 33; Bieber, *Denkm.*, p. 164, Taf. xcvii. 4.
[5] Robert, ibid., p. 18, fig. 37; Bieber, *Denkm.*, p. 168, Taf. ciii. 1. Cf. Simon, op. cit. 88, n. 39.
[6] Photograph lent by Professor Webster. See also Bulle, *Zeitschr. des Münch. Altertumsvereins*, N.F. xi (1900), p. 22, Abb. 4.
[7] Bieber, *Denkm.*, p. 132, Taf. lxix. 2.
[8] From a photograph lent by Sir John Beazley; cf. Robert, op. cit., p. 21, fig. 17; Bieber, *Denkm.*, Taf. lxxiii. 3.
[9] From photographs lent by Sir John Beazley; cf. Bieber, *Denkm.*, p. 133, Taf. lxxi.
[10] Ibid., p. 132, Taf. lxx. 2.   [11] Cf. Fig. 87 (above).

FIG. 94. COMEDY RELIEF NAPLES

FIG. 95. MOSAIC OF DIOSKOURIDES

FIG. 96. PAINTING OF COMEDY (MISTRESS AND SERVANT), PALERMO

FIG. 97. PAINTING OF COMEDY, NAPLES

FIG. 98. LOST PAINTING OF COMEDY FROM POMPEII

FIG. 99. PAINTING, CASA DEL CENTENARIO, POMPEII

FIG. 100. PAINTING, CASA DEL CENTENARIO, POMPEII

FIG. 101. PAINTING FROM CASA DEGLI DIOSCURI, BONN

FIG. 102.* BRONZE FROM DODONA   FIG. 103.* EXCITED MAN, BERLIN

FIG. 104. SEATED SLAVE   FIG. 105. OLD MAN   FIG. 106. PORNOBOSKOS

FIG. 107. MASK

FIG. 108.* OLD WOMAN AND MAN

FIG. 109.* DRUNKEN MEN

FIG. 110. SOLDIER (?)

Charisios in the *Epitrepontes* and one of the masks on the Menander relief as examples).

(3) The οὖλος νεανίσκος is still younger,[1] and ruddy, with curly hair, raised eyebrows, and one wrinkle across his forehead. Robert takes the Tyndarus of Plautus' *Captivi*[2] as an example.

(4) The ἁπαλὸς νεανίσκος is the youngest of all, with hair like the πάγχρηστος, as if reared in the shade (σκιατροφίας) and delicate.

The following figures are thought to illustrate this group:

Fig. 113. Young man. (In Athens, from Myrina.)[3] Probably a πάγχρηστος νεανίας.

114. Young man returning from revel. (In Berlin, from Myrina.)[4] Wears a wreath, and probably played a tympanum. (He may be a νεανίας δεύτερος ἐπίσειστος—see below.)

115. Mask of young man. (In Munich, from Amisos (Samsun).)[5]

116. Marble mask. (In British Museum.)[6] ? A ἁπαλὸς νεανίσκος.

Some special types

(1) The ἀγροῖκος (the Rustic) has a dark complexion, broad lips, a snub nose, and a στεφάνη round his hair.

(2) The ἐπίσειστος—a Soldier and a Braggart—has a dark skin and dark hair hanging down.

(3) The δεύτερος ἐπίσειστος is similar, but less coarse, and light-haired. (See above.)

(4) The κόλαξ and (5) the παράσιτος—the Flatterer and the Parasite—are of dark complexion with hooked noses; they have frequented the palaestra and are of good physique. The flatterer has his eyebrows raised more mischievously. The parasite has his ears more battered and is more cheerful; he carries his patron's toilet-necessities, the στλεγγίς and λήκυθος.[7] Dr. A. K. H. Simon takes Gnatho in Menander's *Κόλαξ* and Gelasimus in Plautus' *Stichus* as examples of the two types. A fragment of

[1] The readings vary between καλὸς καὶ νέος and μᾶλλον νέος.
[2] ll. 647 f.
[3] Robert, op. cit., p. 80, fig. 98; Bieber, *Denkm.*, p. 163, Taf. xcv. 2. Contrast Simon, op. cit. 64.
[4] Froehner, *Terres cuites de la Colln. Gréau*, i. 26, pl. 27; cf. Robert, op. cit., p. 66, fig. 87; Bieber, *Denkm.*, p. 163, Taf. xcvi. 1.
[5] Ibid., p. 169, Taf. ciii. 3.
[6] Webster, in *Bull. Rylands Libr.* xxxii (1949), fig. 1.
[7] These characters are found in Epicharmus and in the Old Comedy, but whether they wore the same masks as mentioned by Pollux there is no evidence to show. See Giere, *De parasito capita selecta* (Diss. Kiel, 1908), and A. K. H. Simon, *Die Szenenbilder zur gr. Neuen Komödie*, pp. 47–48, 53.

Alexis (116 (K.)) distinguishes between the μέλανες παράσιτοι and the 'swell' parasites of whom the speaker says:

θάτερον ζητῶ γένος
σεμνοπαράσιτον †ἐκ μέσου† καλούμενον,
σάτραπας παρασίτους καὶ στρατηγοὺς ἐπιφανεῖς,
ὑποκρινόμενον εὖ τοῖς βίοις, ὀφρῦς ἔχον
χιλιοταλάντους ἀνακυλιόν τ᾽ οὐσίας.

For the parasite attendant on a boastful soldier see above, Fig. 98.

(6) The εἰκονικός, a second type of parasite (?), has scattered grey hairs and his beard shaved off; he is richly clad and foreign.

(7) The Σικελικός is a third type of parasite—probably derived from Sicilian farces or even from Epicharmus who has a striking portrait of a parasite.[1]

The above types may be illustrated by the following figures:

Fig. 117. Mask of young rustic. (In Paris, from Kyme.)[2]
118. Mask of parasite. (In Berlin, from Myrina.)[3]
119. Parasite. (In Berlin, from Capua.)[4]
120. Flatterer (κόλαξ). (In Athens, probably from Myrina.)[5]

Slaves

Seven masks of slaves are catalogued by Pollux.

(1) The θεράπων πάππος is a freedman and is the only grey-haired servant.[6] (See above Figs. 97, 99.)

(2) The ἡγέμων θεράπων has a roll of red hair (σπεῖραν τριχῶν πυρρῶν) on his forehead, his eyebrows raised, and his brow contracted, being among slaves what the πρεσβύτης ἡγέμων is among free men. He probably appears in Fig. 96. Robert compares Leonidas in Plautus *Asinaria*, ll. 400–1.

(3) The κάτω τριχίας is red-haired but going bald, with eyebrows raised.

---

[1] Some scholars find a reference to the type in Diphilus, fr. 119 (K.), παχὺς ὠνθυλευμένος στέατι Σικελικῷ, but Sicilian luxury was proverbial quite apart from parasites; cf. Suidas, s.v. Σικελικὴ τράπεζα; Athen. xii. 518 c, 527 c, d, etc.

[2] Robert, op. cit., p. 27, fig. 55; Bieber, *Denkm.*, p. 169, Taf. ciii. 2.

[3] Ibid., Taf. civ. 1. Cf. Simon, op. cit. 181, n. 10. [4] Ibid., p. 165, Taf. xcvii. 3.

[5] Robert, op. cit., p. 23, figs. 51–52; Bieber, *Denkm.*, p. 164, Taf. xcvii. 2. But cf. Simon, loc. cit.

[6] The fact that almost all the slave-masks in Pollux's list are red-haired must not be taken to mean that no free man's mask was ever red-haired; and W. Beare (*Class. Quart.* xliii (1949), pp. 30 ff.) makes it clear that in Roman comedy, and therefore probably in the Greek originals, a slave might sometimes appear in the costume of a free man.

FIG. 111. PEDLAR

FIG. 111*a*. PEDLAR

FIG. 112. HYDROPHOROS

FIG. 113. YOUNGISH MAN

FIG. 114. YOUTH

FIG. 115. TERRACOTTA MASK

FIG. 116. MARBLE MASK

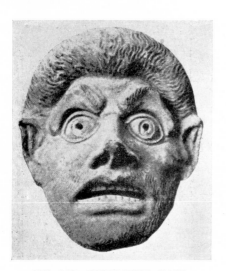

FIG. 117. TERRACOTTA MASK

FIG. 118. TERRACOTTA MASK

FIG. 119. PARASITE

FIG. 120. PARASITE

FIG. 123.* TRAVELLER

121. SLAVE WITH CHILD

FIG. 122. SLAVE WITH CHILD

FIG. 124. COOK

FIG. 125. SLAVE

FIG. 126. SLAVE

FIG. 127. SLAVE

(4) The οὖλος θεράπων has red curly hair, a red complexion, and a squint, and is going bald.

(5) The μαίσων θεράπων is red-haired and bald.[1]

(6) The θεράπων τεττίξ is dark-haired, with a bald head, but two or three black curls on head and chin, and a squint.[2]

(7) The θεράπων ἐπίσειστος ἡγέμων is like the θεράπων ἡγέμων, but has his hair hanging down loose.

A few of the innumerable statuettes and masks of slaves are here figured.

Fig. 121. Slave carrying infant. (In Bonn, from Boeotia.)[3] Cf. the scene in Menander's *Epitrepontes*, where the slave carries an exposed infant. The subject is one which recurs in the New Comedy.

122. Slave carrying infant. (In British Museum.)[4]

123. Slave carrying luggage. (In British Museum, from Athens.)[5]

124. Cook. (In Berlin, from Myrina.)[6] The identification of the figure as a μαίσων seems to be generally agreed, but is perhaps not quite certain.

125. Seated slave. (In Berlin, probably from Myrina.)[7] A θεράπων οὖλος.

126. Slave. (In Berlin, from Etruria.)[8] A θεράπων οὖλος.

127. Mask of slave. (In Berlin, from the Komnos Collection.)[9] A θεράπων οὖλος.

128. Slave advancing. (In Athens, from Myrina.)[10]

129. Slave advancing. (In Athens, probably from Myrina.)[11]

130. Slave seated on altar. (In British Museum.)[12] Probably Italian.

131. Ditto. (At Stoke-on-Trent.)[13]

132. Ditto. (In British Museum; said to be from Tanagra.)[14]

133. Ditto. (In Copenhagen.)[15]

[1] See above, p. 196, Fig. 81.
[2] See above, p. 186. fig. 53c, p. 200, Fig. 92, and *Dith. Trag. Com.*, pp. 278–9.
[3] Bieber, *Denkm.*, p. 135, Taf. lxxiii. 2.
[4] Brit. Mus. C. 237; photograph by Mr. R. A. Higgins.
[5] Ibid. 238; photograph by Mr. R. A. Higgins.
[6] *Dith. Trag. Com.*, fig. 44; cf. Robert, op. cit., p. 14, fig. 26; Bieber, *Denkm.* p. 163, Taf. xcvi. 2.
[7] Berlin Mus., no. 5030; Robert, op. cit., fig. 21.
[8] Ibid., fig. 20 (from *Arch. Ztg.* 1854, Taf. 69, figs. 21, 22).
[9] Robert, op. cit., fig. 57.
[10] Phot. Nat. Mus. Athens, no. 191; cf. Robert, op. cit., fig. 90; Bieber, *Denkm.*, Taf. c. 1.
[11] Phot. Nat. Mus. Athens, no. 1124; cf. Robert, op. cit., fig. 27; Bieber, *Denkm.*, Taf. c. 2.
[12] Brit. Mus. D. 322. (British Museum photograph.)
[13] Webster, *Bull. Rylands Libr.* xxxii. 1, fig. 6. (Photograph lent by Professor Webster.)
[14] Brit. Mus. C. 90. (Photograph by Mr. R. A. Higgins.)
[15] Copenhagen, Nat. Mus. 1067. (Photograph from Sir John Beazley.)

Fig. 134. Slave seated on altar.[1] (In British Museum.) Early Hellenistic, probably Attic.

135. Mask of slave. (From Athens.)[2]

136. Mask of slave. (In British Museum, from Melos.)[3]

137. Marble mask of slave. (From Athens, near Dipylon Gate.)[4]
Probably a θεράπων ἡγέμων. Roman date.

138. Soldier slave (?). (In British Museum.)[5]

139. Slave carrying a kid. (In Louvre.)[6]

Women

The female masks in Pollux' list include three old women:

(1) The λυκαίνιον ('wolfish')—withered and long-faced, with
many wrinkles, a pale-yellowish complexion, and a squint.

(2) The γραῦς παχεῖα who has fat cheeks, wrinkles, and a
narrow band round her hair.

(3) The οἰκουρὸν γράδιον ἢ οἰκετικὸν ἢ ὀξύσιμον, the house-
keeper, who has about two teeth in each jaw, and a snub nose;
followed by five young women:

(1) The λεκτική ('chatterbox') has hair all round her head
(περίκομος), smoothed back on the top (παρεψησμέναι αἱ τρίχες),
straight eyebrows, and a white skin.

(2) The οὔλη is like the λεκτική, but has curly hair.

(3) The κόρη has hair brushed back, with a parting, straight
dark eyebrows, and a sallow complexion.

(4) The ψευδοκόρη (the wronged girl) is paler and has her
hair bound round her head, and 'is like a newly wedded bride'.
The context makes plain that the hair was parted. See perhaps
Fig. 97 (the younger woman). Glykera in the Περικειρομένη of
Menander may be an instance.

(5) The second ψευδοκόρη is distinguished from the first by
the absence of the parting.

There are seven masks of ἑταῖραι:

(1) The σπαρτοπόλιος λεκτική, the chatterbox with scattered
grey hair, is a retired member of the profession. See Fig. 149

[1] Brit. Mus. 1910.1.6.16. (British Museum photograph.)

[2] *Hesperia*, iv, pp. 337–8, fig. 25. (By permission of the American School in Athens.)

[3] Brit. Mus. C. 81. (British Museum photograph.)

[4] Brueckner, *Skenika*, Taf. iv.

[5] Webster, *Bull. Rylands Libr.* xxxii. 1, fig. 8. (Photograph lent by Professor Webster.) It
seems very uncertain what this statuette represents.

[6] Photograph lent by Sir John Beazley.

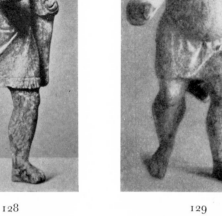

128   129

130   131

FIGS. 128–31. SLAVES

132

133

134

FIGS. 132-4. SLAVES

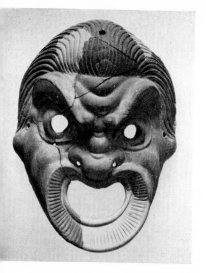

FIG. 135. SLAVE

FIG. 136. ? SLAVE

FIG. 137. SLAVE

FIG. 138. SOLDIER SLAVE

FIG. 139.* SLAVE WITH KID

FIG. 140. WOMAN

FIG. 141. NURSE WITH CHILD

FIG. 142. WOMAN WEEPING (?)

FIG. 143. WOMAN WEEPING

FIG. 144. WOMAN WEEPING

FIG. 145. WOMAN

FIG. 146. OLD WOMAN   FIG. 147. OLD WOMAN

FIG. 148. OLD WOMAN

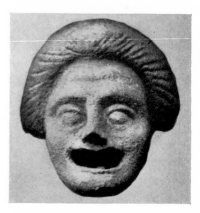

FIG. 149. YOUNG WOMAN   FIG. 150. WOMAN (?)

Masks

(assigned by Robert to this type, and almost certainly λεκτική, if not σπαρτοπόλιος).

(2) The παλλακή (concubine) is like the last, but has hair all round her head.

(3) The τέλειον ἑταιρικόν is redder than the ψευδοκόρη and has curls about her ears.

(4) The ἑταιρίδιον ὡραῖον is unadorned and has her hair bound with a ribbon. See Fig. 151.

(5) The διάχρυσος ἑταίρα has much gold ornamentation about her hair.

(6) The διάμιτρος has her hair bound with a multicoloured band (μίτρα).

(7) The λαμπάδιον is distinguished by a coiffure rising upwards to a point. See Fig. 157.

Finally, there are two maidservants (θεράπαιναι):

(1) The ἅβρα περίκουρος has her hair cut short, and wears only a white χιτών with a girdle. (The ἅβρα was the ordinary young domestic slave-girl.)

(2) The παράψηστον θεραπαινίδιον has her hair brushed back, with a parting, and a somewhat upturned nose; she wears a saffron χιτών and is the servant of ἑταῖραι.

The following illustrations are here given of some of these feminine types:

Fig. 140. Young woman. (In British Museum, probably Attic, fourth century B.C.)[1]

141. Old woman carrying infant. (In British Museum, from Athens.)[2]

142. Woman weeping (?). (In British Museum, from Olbia, probably middle of fourth century B.C.)[3]

143. Woman weeping (?). (In Athens.)[4]

144. Woman weeping. (In British (?) Museum, from Tarentum; probably early Hellenistic.)[5]

145. Mask of old woman. (In Paris, said to be from Tanagra.)[6]

146. Mask of old woman. (In Berlin.)[7]

[1] Brit. Mus. 1907.5.18.7. This illustration and the next two are from photographs by Mr. R. A. Higgins.
[2] Ibid. C. 4. Cf. above, Fig. 85.   [3] Ibid. 1907.5.20.79.
[4] Nat. Mus. Athens, 13015; from a photograph lent by Sir John Beazley.
[5] Brit. Mus. E. 31. (British Museum photograph.)
[6] Dith. Trag. Com., fig. 29. (See Robert, op. cit., pp. 45–46, fig. 81.)
[7] Berlin, Antiquarium, no. 436; Robert, op. cit., p. 46, fig. 82; Bieber, Denkm., p. 169, Taf. cvii. 3.

P

Fig. 147. Mask of old woman. (In Berlin.)[1]
  148. Mask of old woman. (In Berlin, from Corneto.)[2]
  149. Statuette of woman. (In Athens, probably from Myrina.)[3] Probably a λεκτική.
  150. Mask of woman (?). (In Berlin, from Greece.)[4]
  151. Masks of young woman and slave in a painting from Pompeii.[5] (The woman is classed by Robert as ἑταιρίδιον ὡραῖον.)
  152. Marble mask of woman. (In Naples, from Pompeii.)[6]
  153. Marble mask of young woman. (In Naples.)[7]
  154. Ditto. (In Naples, from Pompeii.)[8]
  155. Bronze. Ditto. (In Paris).[9]
  156. Marble. Ditto. (In Vatican, from Tivoli.)[10] Probably a διάχρυσος ἑταίρα.
  157. Terracotta. Ditto. (In Oxford, from Smyrna.)[11] Probably the ἑταίρα known as λαμπάδιον.

A few miscellaneous illustrations are also included:

Fig. 158. Mosaic showing masks of flute-player and slave (in Rome, from the Aventine);[12] possibly the ἑταιρικὸν τέλειον and the οὖλος θεράπων of Pollux.
  159. Marble relief of masks (in Naples, from Pompeii);[13] a young man, an old man, a θεράπων ἡγέμων, and a satyr-mask (?) in the background.
  160. Marble relief showing masks (in Vatican, from Ostia);[14] an old man and a young man (? νεανίσκος ἁπαλός) above; a young man (? νεανίσκος οὖλος) and a θεράπων ἡγέμων below.
  161. Bronze statuette of actor (from the Agora, Athens),[15] probably first to third century A.D. Doubtfully comic.

23. The attempt to assign the right mask out of Pollux's list to each character in the scanty remains of the New Comedy or

---

[1] *Dith. Trag. Com.*, fig. 30. (See Robert, op. cit., p. 46, fig. 83.)
[2] Berlin Mus. 7138; Robert, op. cit., fig. 99.
[3] Ibid., fig. 64.   [4] Ibid., fig. 68.
[5] *Arch. Ztg.* xxxiv (1878), Taf. 4; Robert, op. cit., fig. 69.
[6] Naples Mus., no. 6612; Robert, op. cit., fig. 63.
[7] Naples Mus., no. 6625; Museo Borbonico xi, Taf. xlii. 2; cf. Bieber, *Denkm.*, Taf. cvi. 2.
[8] Naples Mus., no. 6616; Bieber, *Denkm.*, Taf. cvi. 4.
[9] Paris, Bib. Nat. 994. From photo lent by Sir John Beazley.
[10] Robert, op. cit., Taf. i.
[11] From photo lent by Sir John Beazley.
[12] Stuart Jones, *Cat. of Capit. Mus. Mon.*, pl. 35 (part); cf. Bieber, *Denkm.*, p. 162 Taf. xci. 2.
[13] Naples Mus., no. 6619; Bieber, *Denkm.*, p. 162, Taf. xciv. 1.
[14] Ibid. 2 = Robert, op. cit., fig. 14.
[15] *Hesperia*, vi, p. 351, fig. 15.

FIG. 151. YOUNG WOMAN AND SLAVE

FIG. 152. YOUNG WOMAN

FIG. 153. YOUNG WOMAN

FIG. 154. YOUNG WOMAN

FIG. 155. BRONZE MASK

FIG. 157. TERRACOTTA MASK

FIG. 156. MARBLE MASK

FIG. 158. MOSAIC IN ROME

FIG. 159. MARBLE RELIEF IN NAPLES

FIG. 160. MARBLE RELIEF IN NAPLES

FIG. 161. BRONZE STATUETTE OF ACTOR

in Plautus and Terence is a pleasant game and may now and
then yield results which command some confidence; but it requires much guess-work, as well as, not infrequently, the assumption that the several types admit of considerable deviations from
the descriptions of them in Pollux. It may be doubted also how
far it is legitimate to eke out the meagre descriptions of Pollux
with the observations contained in the pseudo-Aristotelian
Physiognomonika—a conflation of two treatises, perhaps of the
third century B.C., based on the study of the men and women
of real life, without any special reference to the stock characters
of the stage, such as may sometimes be detected in Theophrastus.
But the reader may derive plenty of interest and enjoyment from
the attempt, as it is made, for example, most recently, by Professor Webster.[1] It is a pity that it is impossible to follow up
(for lack of sufficient evidence) his ingenious suggestion that the
members of different households in a play were distinguished by
their different styles of hairdressing—all those of one household,
for example, whether father, son, or slave, having curly hair,
while all those of the other household agreed in some other style
of hair-control. But the suggestion can hardly be taken to be
proved. The same doubts suggest themselves about the classification of terra-cotta figures and of characters represented in other
artistic remains under the headings offered by Pollux,[2] whose
descriptions are often quite insufficient to distinguish related
types of masks with precision, and in any case refer to a comedy
which may have changed much before his day. If it is urged
that his own authorities were Alexandrian,[3] this is at best a
generalization which does not help to determine whether a
particular description has Alexandrian authority, or to what
period or century it applies; though of course the lists in Pollux
and the artistic remains undoubtedly help at times to interpret
each other. Professor Webster has worked out very interestingly
the chronology of the masks depicted on the (south Italian)
Gnathia vases, mostly of the fourth century, and has distinguished those contemporary with the Middle and with the
New Comedy respectively; but even if he establishes a certain

---

[1] 'South Italian Vases and Attic Drama' in *Class. Quart.* xliv (1948), pp. 15 ff.; *The
Masks of Greek Comedy* (1949) and 'Masks on Gnathia Vases' (*J.H.S.* lxxi. 222).
[2] Dr. A. K. H. Simon pursues the subject at length in *Die Szenenbilder zur gr. Neuen Komödie*;
the identifications are often very inconclusive, but the book contains a valuable collection
and classification of material.   [3] See above, p. 175.

parallelism between the subjects and characters of the vases and those of Attic comedy, more proof seems to be required before the one can be said to be 'derived' from the other. Greek legend and Greek life in both countries provided a common range of stories, subjects, and characters, on which it was possible to draw in any Greek country without imitating anyone and, as has been suggested earlier in this chapter, many of the terra-cotta and other figures may be works of imagination, without any direct dependence on the stage. But there will probably always be room for differences of opinion on this subject, and the studies of Professor Webster and others are providing and will, it is to be hoped, continue to provide a very valuable contribution to our knowledge of the less heroic aspects of Greek and Roman civilization.

B. DRESS AND FOOTWEAR

1. The costume of the tragic actor—or at least of the principal actors, as distinct from servants, messengers, and other minor characters—is very commonly identified by scholars with that which is worn by deities, heroes, and heroines on a large number of south Italian vases ranging from the last quarter of the fifth century B.C. to a late period in the fourth. This consists essentially of a long robe (σύρμα) reaching to the ground, with a shorter garment over it falling to just below the knee. Very frequently the upper garment is furnished with sleeves—it is a χειριδωτὸς χιτών—though sometimes it is the wider and longer garment which has the sleeves; the whole costume is very richly decorated with embroidered patterns in which certain elements frequently recur—stripes, pointed rays, palmettes, spirals, heads of sphinxes and horses, Νικαί, and the wave-like ornament which is sometimes called the 'running hound'. Personages in rapid motion or preparing for action often wear a decorated tunic falling only to the knee—such persons as warriors, hunters (including Artemis), and other active characters.

To what extent these paintings are in fact a safe guide to the theatrical costume of the Classical period is a question to which, as has already been hinted, only a cautious reply can be given; the evidence is for the most part too late for the purpose, and there has been endless controversy in regard to the decorative robe, which Pollux[1] terms the ποικίλον, and the sleeved tunic, the χειριδωτὸς χιτών in particular.

Some have declared it to be of foreign origin. A short χιτών with sleeves, the κανδύς, was certainly worn by Persians and appears in representations and descriptions of Persians and Phrygians from the middle of the fifth century, and it was also in use in Athenian private life in the fourth century.[2] A number of instances have been collected of its use as a woman's garment.[3] But these facts belong to too late a date to reveal the source from which the sleeved tunic came into tragedy. It is found on vases in the representations of a few Thracian figures—such as Orpheus, Thamyras, and Bendis—and the fact that a similar garment to that of the tragic actor was worn in the fifth century by the hierophant and δᾳδοῦχος at Eleusis[4] suggests that it may have come into Athens from Thrace with the worship of Dionysus, and to Eleusis, also from Thrace, with Eumolpos. (It occurs occasionally as the costume of Scythians, Dacians, and other barbarians, but always in the form of a short tunic, not of the long robe commonly regarded as most characteristic of tragedy.) Scholars have often supposed[5] that the tragic costume was taken from the regular festal robe of the Peisistratean epoch; but it appears that in fact this festal robe was not decorated or fitted with sleeves, but was a sleeveless garment of white linen;[6] the vases give plenty of evidence of its character.

There is much more likelihood in the derivation of the use of the decorated χιτών, with narrow, close-fitting sleeves, in tragedy from the worship of Dionysus at an early date. A vase figured by Dr. Bieber—an Attic black-figured amphora of about 500 B.C.[7] (Fig. 162)—shows Dionysus in such a robe, differing

---

[1] Pollux iv. 115 ff. καὶ ἐσθῆτες μὲν τραγικαὶ ποικίλον (οὕτω γὰρ ἐκαλεῖτο ὁ χιτών), ἐπιβλήματα δὲ κτλ. (see below). He gives no indication of the date of which he is speaking.

[2] Cf. the inventories of garments dedicated to Artemis Brauronia about the middle of the fourth century (*I.G.* ii². 1514, 1523, 1524), in which the κανδύς occurs several times; e.g. in No. 1514 Teisikrateia dedicates κανδὺν ποικίλον, and in No. 1524 Olympias dedicates κανδὺν ἀμόργινον. There are here many instances of sleeved garments entirely independent of the theatre. [3] Amelung in Pauly-W., *Real-Encycl.* s.v. χειριδωτὸς χιτών.

[4] Athen. i, p. 21 d (see below). [5] e.g. Pringsheim, *Arch. Beitr. zur Gesch. des Eleus.-Kultes*, p. 14; Körte, *Festschr. Deutscher Philologen in Basel*, 1907, p. 202.

[6] See Rumpf, *Philol. Woch.* (1932), cols. 208–10; Bieber, *Jahrb. Arch.* xxxii (1917), pp. 18, 102.

[7] Ibid., pp. 19 ff., Taf. i. Dr. Bieber cites many later representations of Dionysus in a not dissimilar costume—continuing the tradition into the Roman epoch, though these are mostly not dramatic in subject. (It should be noted that in the vases depicting Dionysus in the processions of the *currus navalis* the god does not wear the sleeved χιτών; but this was

in some points from the 'tragic robe' of the fourth-century vases, but to a great extent similar, and although the scene (Dionysus amidst his thiasos) may be imaginary, Dr. Bieber may be right in thinking that it recalls a cult-performance, and the alleged resemblance (alluded to above) of the tragic actor's dress to that of the officials of Eleusis at a later date[1] at least suggests that such a dress was regarded as appropriate to a solemn ritual, and that if it was characteristic of Dionysus, it may have been transferred to actors who were in a sense his ministers.

2. That the characteristic tragic costume, whatever it was, was the invention of Aeschylus was a strong tradition in the later Hellenistic age, the statements to this effect being associated with the attribution to him (undoubtedly false, as will be seen below) of the thick-soled kothornoi. The earliest of these statements is that of Horace,[2] according to whom Aeschylus was *personae pallaeque repertor honestae*. The same tradition is found in Athenaeus and Philostratus (both about A.D. 200).

Athen. i, p. 21 d καὶ Αἰσχύλος δὲ οὐ μόνον ἐξεῦρε τὴν τῆς στολῆς εὐπρέπειαν καὶ σεμνότητα, ἣν ζηλώσαντες[3] οἱ ἱεροφάνται καὶ δᾳδοῦχοι ἀμφιέννυνται, ἀλλὰ καὶ πολλὰ σχήματα ὀρχηστικὰ αὐτὸς ἐξευρίσκων ἀνεδίδου τοῖς χορευταῖς. Χαμαιλέων γοῦν πρῶτον αὐτόν φησι σχηματίσαι τοὺς χορους ὀρχηστοδιδασκάλοις οὐ χρησάμενον, ἀλλὰ καὶ αὐτὸν τοῖς χοροῖς τὰ σχήματα ποιοῦντα τῶν ὀρχήσεων, καὶ ὅλως πᾶσαν τὴν τῆς τραγῳδίας οἰκονομίαν εἰς ἑαυτὸν περιϊστᾶν. ὑπεκρίνετο γοῦν μετὰ τοῦ εἰκότος τὰ δράματα. Ἀριστοφάνης γοῦν—παρὰ δὲ τοῖς κωμικοῖς ἡ περὶ τῶν κωμικῶν ἀπόκειται πίστις—ποιεῖ αὐτὸν Αἰσχύλον λέγοντα 'τοῖσι χοροῖς αὐτὸς τὰ σχήματ' ἐποίουν'.

quite a different type of ritual from any that has been connected with tragedy.) The decorated dresses of figures on the François vase (sixth century; Furtw.–Reich., pls. 1–3, 11, and 12) are quite different in shape and decoration from the 'tragic robe'.

[1] Dr. Bieber and others cite a late-fourth-century hydria from Cumae (Fig. 163—Froehner, *Coll. Tyszkiewicz*, pl. x) showing the sleeved robe worn in an Eleusinian ceremony (Bieber, *Hist. Gk. and Rom. Theat.*, p. 37, fig. 42). It is, however, so different from the 'tragic' robe that it can hardly be used for argument. She also cites a pelike (figured by Pfuhl, fig. 596), but here again, apart from the mere fact of sleeves being worn, the differences are more striking than the resemblances. Cf. also Attic lekane in Tübingen, hydria in Istanbul, Nilsson, *Gesch.*, pl. 45/1, 44/1.

[2] *Ars Poet.* 278 (see above, p. 177). On this Porphyrion comments *Aeschylus primus tragoediis coturnos et syrma et personam dedit; horum enim trium auctor est.*

[3] Most writers known to me think it improbable that the Eleusinian officials should have waited for Aeschylus to provide them with robes suitable to their office. Some conjecture (without evidence) that Aeschylus really borrowed from Eleusis. Pringsheim (*Arch. Beitr. zur Gesch. des Eleus.-Kultes*, p. 1) conjectures that στολή was a technical name for both costumes, on the strength of Athenaeus and Lysias vi. 81; Plut. *Alcib.* 22; Pollux iv. 116. But στολή (like 'robe') is used in many non-religious applications, and neither the tragic nor the Eleusinian costume is always called by this name.

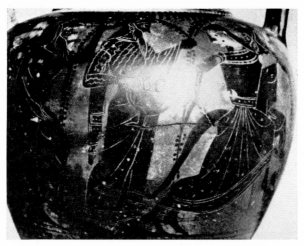

FIG. 162. DIONYSUS (BLACK FIGURE VASE)

FIG. 163. ELEUSINIAN CEREMONY (RED FIGURE VASE)

FIG. 164. ANDROMEDA (ATTIC RED FIGURE VASE)

Philostr. *Vit. Apoll.* vi. xi, p. 219 K. (after enumerating many improvements of tragedy by Aeschylus) ὁ δ' ἐνθυμηθεὶς μὲν ἑαυτὸν ὡς ἐπάξιον τοῦ τραγῳδίαν ποιεῖν φθέγγοιτο, ἐνθυμηθεὶς δὲ καὶ τὴν τέχνην ὡς προσφυᾶ τῷ μεγαλείῳ μᾶλλον ἢ τῷ καταβεβλημένῳ τε καὶ ὑπὸ πόδα, σκευοποιίας μὲν ἥψατο εἰκασμένης τοῖς τῶν ἡρώων εἴδεσιν, ὀκρίβαντος δὲ τοὺς ὑποκριτὰς ἐνεβίβασεν, ὡς ἴσα ἐκείνοις βαίνοιεν, ἐσθήμασί τε πρῶτος ἐκόσμησεν, ἃ πρόσφορον ἥρωσί τε καὶ ἡρωίσιν ἠσθῆσθαι, ὅθεν Ἀθηναῖοι πατέρα μὲν αὐτὸν τῆς τραγῳδίας ἡγοῦντο.

Philostr. *Vit. Soph.* i. ix, p. 11 K. Σικελία Γοργίαν ἐν Λεοντίνοις ἤνεγκεν, ἐς ὃν ἀναφέρειν ἡγώμεθα τὴν τῶν σοφιστῶν τέχνην, ὥσπερ ἐς πατέρα· εἰ γὰρ τὸν Αἰσχύλον ἐνθυμηθεῖμεν, ὡς πολλὰ τῇ τραγῳδίᾳ ξυνέβαλετο ἐσθῆτί τε αὐτὴν κατασκευάσας καὶ ὀκρίβαντι ὑψηλῷ καὶ ἡρώων εἴδεσιν ἀγγέλοις τε καὶ ἐξαγγέλοις καὶ οἷς ἐπὶ σκηνῆς χρὴ πράσσειν, τοῦτο ἂν εἴη καὶ Γοργιάς τοῖς ὁμοτέχνοις.

A certain caution is necessary here. Athenaeus ascribes to Chamaeleon (about 300 B.C.) certain statements about Aeschylus' treatment of the chorus, but he does not refer to him as his authority in regard to costume, and in his phrasing (ἀλλὰ καὶ . . .) he seems to distinguish the two statements and to refer to Chamaeleon only for what follows. Moreover, the last sentence of the passage seems to imply that, whether for himself or for Chamaeleon, the recognized authority on Aeschylus was the *Frogs* of Aristophanes,[1] and this is plainly the case with Philostratus. But all that Aristophanes[2] (half a century after the death of Aeschylus) says is that Aeschylus' heroes wore more dignified robes than ordinary men:

AI. κάλλως εἰκὸς τοὺς ἡμιθέους τοῖς ῥήμασι μείζοσι χρῆσθαι·
καὶ γὰρ τοῖς ἱματίοις ἡμῶν χρῶνται πολὺ σεμνοτέροισιν,
ἁμοῦ χρηστῶς καταδείξαντος διελυμήνω σύ.   *EY.* τί δράσας;
AI. πρῶτον μὲν τοὺς βασιλεύοντας ῥάκι' ἀμπισχών . . .

These more dignified robes may or may not have been like the decorative robes of the south Italian vases. (It should be added in passing that there was also a tradition that Choirilos exercised some influence on the costumes of tragedy.[3]) Moreover, it may be of some significance that Aristotle in enumerating the innovations made by Aeschylus in tragedy never refers to costume,

---

[1] All these writers must have used also some authority, now lost, for Aeschylus' supposed use of the high-soled kothornos. See below, p. 230.

[2] *Frogs* 1060 ff.

[3] Suid. s.v. Χοιρίλος says that κατά τινας τοῖς προσωπείοις καὶ τῇ σκευῇ τῶν στόλων ἐπέχειρησε. But the exact meaning of the last word is uncertain.

except that, if Themistius is right,[1] he did ascribe ὀκρίβαντας (some kind of footwear) to him.

No mention has been made of the statement in the very unreliable *Life of Aeschylus*,[2] compiled from many sources and of unknown date. It evidently repeats the same tradition as the passages already quoted, but in a rather strange phrase it does allude to the sleeves: πρῶτος Αἰσχύλος πάθεσι γεννικωτέροις τὴν τραγῳδίαν ηὔξησεν . . . τούς τε ὑποκριτὰς χειρῖσι σκεπάσας καὶ τῷ σύρματι ἐξογκώσας μείζοσί τε τοῖς κοθόρνοις μετεωρίσας.

The result of this discussion can only be that it was believed, fifty years after the death of Aeschylus, that he had given the kings and heroes of tragedy, in the form of a full-length robe (σύρμα), a more distinguished costume than they previously wore, and that writers of a much later date interpreted this to mean that he had invented the costume to which they, and probably at least a generation or two before them, had become accustomed in tragedy. Whether the costume devised by him was essentially that of the vases of the end of the fifth and the fourth centuries (many of them Italian) can only be conjectured; an affirmative conjecture would not seem to be wholly improbable, but it would be no more than a conjecture.

3. There is unfortunately no artistic evidence as regards the tragic costume of the first half of the fifth century except the fragments of the oinochoe of about 470 B.C., published by Miss Talcott, to which reference has already been made.[3] One of them shows the lower part of a finely pleated, but not decorated, skirt, reaching to the feet and with traces of an upper garment above it, worn by a female figure in rapid motion. The scene cannot have been taken directly from the theatre, as the boy who is carrying a mask is completely nude, but the woman's costume may have been theatrical.[4]

Accordingly, apart from the Boston pelike with its two choreutai, which has already been described,[5] and which indicates an undecorated robe as the dress of the chorus, we are

---

[1] See below, p. 230. Aristotle's low rating of the art of the σκευοποιός is hardly sufficient explanation. [2] § 14.

[3] *Hesperia*, viii, pp. 267 ff., fig. 1. See above, pp. 179, 182.

[4] Dr. Bieber's interpretation of a red-figured Athenian vase of the same date (480–470 B.C.), in which there are two groups each consisting of four singers and a flute-player, appears to involve too much conjecture to be used as evidence (*Am. J. Arch.* xlv (1941), pp. 529–36 and pl. xiv).

[5] See above, p. 182; the date is probably about 430 B.C.

left without information until about the last decade of the century. Then three Attic vases in particular deserve special attention—the Andromeda krater[1] from Capua (Fig. 164), generally dated before the end of the century, the Pronomos vase from Ruvo,[2] which has already been partly discussed, and which must be of very nearly the same date, and the Taranto fragments,[3] which have also been reproduced above, and which are considered to be not much later.

In the centre of the Andromeda krater the heroine stands with her arms fastened to the rock, clothed in a robe reaching the ground; the lower and upper parts of this robe show bands of decorative figures or patterns. It is a single garment—not an upper and an under—such as are so often worn by heroes in south Italian vases. The sleeves reaching the wrist bear a conspicuous band of decoration. Cepheus the father of Andromeda, and Perseus her deliverer are on either side of her; Hermes and Aphrodite (in a robe without sleeves but bearing some of the same patterns as that of Andromeda) stand on a somewhat higher level; and to the left is the sitting figure of an Ethiopian in a sleeved costume richly decorated in every part, and reaching to the knee; below it the legs are encased in tight and highly ornamented trousers. The scene depicted is plainly not one which can have been presented in the theatre, though it has been commonly assumed that since the *Andromeda* of Euripides was presented at Athens in 412 B.C. and attained great popularity, and since the vase must date from not many years after this, the costumes presented on the vase must be those used in the play. If the Andromeda vase stood alone it could not be claimed with much confidence as evidence for the practice of the theatre.[4]

The Pronomos vase, however, does seem to be more definitely

---

[1] Engelmann, *Arch. Stud.*, fig. 20; Bieber, *Denkm.*, Taf. lii.

[2] See pp. 164, 179, 183, Fig. 28.

[3] *Corolla Curtius*, pp. 151–60, Taf. 54–56 (see above, p. 183, Fig. 40).

[4] In some of the many vase-paintings of the Andromeda story (obviously a popular subject) the costumes are of a quite different type. Some of these are collected by Engelmann, *Arch. Stud.*, pp. 60 ff. and Séchan, *Études*, pp. 256 ff.; cf. also C. M. Dawson, *Romano-Campanian Landscape Painting*, p. 143. The only reason why the costumes on the krater described in the text, and not these others, should be supposed to be theatrical is that the former, and not the latter, bear a close resemblance to the costumes on the Pronomos vase, which seem certainly to stand in some relation to those of the theatre. It has been suggested that the Ethiopian on the krater described may have represented a member of the chorus, which would have been Oriental like that of the *Persae* and other plays, though female (fr. 117 N.).

connected with the theatre, since the masks which the characters hold cannot be anything but theatrical masks, and they
would hardly be wearing costumes which did not go naturally
with the masks—in other words, which were not also theatrical.
The decorations on some of these costumes, including the sleeves,
are very like (and some almost identical with) those on the
Andromeda krater; such costumes are worn by Laomedon,
Hesione, Herakles, and the flute-player, though that of Laomedon falls to his ankles only, not to the ground, and that of
Herakles reaches only to the knee.[1]

The Taranto fragments published by Bulle are in general ana-
logous to the Pronomos vase as presenting not a scene from
a play but the commemoration of a dramatic victory, in which
a number of figures are identified by their masks as theatrical,
and their costumes, therefore, as probably theatrical also. The
flute-player in a highly decorative and sleeved chiton is especially noticeable,[2] as is the fact that the members of the chorus
also wear decorative robes—though not so ornate as that of the
flute-player. One figure, whom Bulle regards as the chorus-
leader, is more richly apparelled than the others, but Sir John
Beazley is doubtless right in regarding this figure as an actor.
(So far as is known the chorus did not wear sleeves, at least unless
they were orientals.) Sir John Beazley tells me that the poet is
wrongly given sleeves in Bulle's reconstruction (Fig. 40).

4. Many painted vases of the same period (shortly before and
for many years after the end of the fifth century) show personages wearing costumes closely akin to those shown on the three
vases described. A large number of these paintings have no
traceable dependence on the theatre in subject or treatment;
others, while presenting subjects which were also mentioned or
described in drama, are evidently not intended to reproduce
scenes as they were presented in the theatre—the absence of

---

[1] Some fragments of an Attic krater of the late fifth century in Bonn, published by Bieber,
Dresd. Schauspieler-relief, p. 17, show figures of Poseidon and Amymone in decorative robes
with sleeves, and parts of two satyrs and a flute-player. But the connexion of this picture with
a satyr-play is apparently disproved (Bieber in *Ath. Mitt.* xxxvi (1911), p. 273; cf. Buschor
in Furtw.–Reich. iii, p. 139). The scene is an imaginary one and shows that the use of ornamental sleeves does not of itself afford any evidence about theatrical costumes.

[2] Dr. Bieber (loc. cit.) notes the frequent occurrence of the χιτών χειριδωτός, decorated,
but without a girdle, as the dress of flute-players on vases; e.g. of the flute-player at a
symposium on an Athenian red-figured bell-krater (Fig. 166) of the early fourth century;
cf. p. 180 above.

FIG. 166. FLUTE PLAYER (ATTIC RED FIGURE VASE)

FIG. 165. ANDROMEDA (ENLARGED)

FIG. 167. PELOPS AND HIPPODAMEIA (ATTIC RED FIGURE VASE)

FIG. 168. PELOPS AND HIPPODAMEIA (ATTIC RED FIGURE VASE)

masks and the nudity of the male characters are enough to prove
this. An examination of all the material suggests that towards
the end of the fifth century, and through a considerable part of
the fourth, the vase-painters of south Italy adopted these highly
decorated costumes as the dress of gods, kings, queens, princes,
and princesses, as well as of priests, prophets, and others attached
to cults—among whom flute-players may have been included.
The vase-painters of Athens did so at the end of the fifth century; it has already been mentioned that one form of decorative dress—the kandys—was fashionable in Athens during part
of the fourth century, and it is quite probable that these decorative robes (which on the vases appear in long or short forms,
and with or without sleeves) may have been employed by the
tragic poets among others; though the later vases on which
they occur are almost entirely south Italian, and these costumes
appear in representations of both dramatic and non-dramatic
subjects.

Some illustrations may be given. The Attic stamnos of the
late fifth century, on which Dionysus himself appears as a pillar
wearing a mask and draped in a decorated robe, over a longer,
undecorated, finely folded skirt, has already been referred to[1]
and figured in connexion with the Lenaian festival at which he
was worshipped (as on the vase) by women. (With it may be
compared a richly draped cult-image of Artemis standing on a
pillar in a vase-painting[2] representing a scene in which Oeno-
maus and Pelops are the chief figures.)

An Attic amphora from Arezzo[3] (Fig. 167), about 410 B.C.,
shows Pelops and Hippodameia driving rapidly in a chariot,
both in decorated robes (that of Pelops falling only to the knee);
Pelops has no sleeves, Hippodameia has them only to the elbow.
On an Attic bell-krater from Naples (Fig. 168)[4] of the early
fourth century, the dress of Pelops is even more ornate and
includes long sleeves with decorative bands, while other figures
—Artemis on her pillar, Athena, and Myrtilos—show different
degrees of decoration. A number of Italian vases depict parts of
the same story; on one of these (Fig. 169),[5] an amphora of the
fourth century from Ruvo, Hippodameia wears a long, richly

[1] See above, p. 31, Fig. 16.   [2] See below, Fig. 168; Robert, *Archäol. Hermen.*, fig. 222.
[3] Furtw.–Reich., pl. 67. For other Attic examples of this period period see e.g. Metzger,
Représentations, pls. xxiv, xxxvi, xli.
[4] Ibid., pl. 146.   [5] *Annali dell' Instituto*, xii (1840). Tav. d'aggregazione N.

ornamented robe; on another (Fig. 170),[1] a kalyx-krater of the fourth century from Ruvo, Sterope is similarly costumed. (Both are in the British Museum.) A vase of the fourth century in Bari (Fig. 171)[2] shows Merope slaying Melanippos—a scene which cannot have been represented in the theatre. He wears a sleeved χιτών with rich ornamentation.

Another well-known non-theatrical scene, the punishment of Talos, is seen on an Attic volute-krater from Ruvo (Fig. 172a). On this Kastor and Pollux wear richly decorated costumes down to the knee, without sleeves, the decoration including a band bearing human figures. On the other side of the vase (Fig. 172b)[4] Jason's dress is very richly embroidered, without sleeves.

On a volute-krater from Ruvo (Fig. 173)[5] which is Apulian of the fourth century, in a picture of the Ransoming of Hector, Priam wears a decorated robe with sleeves; the two goddesses depicted, Athena and Thetis (in the lower register), wear long robes but no sleeves, and Athena her gorgon breastplate. In an Attic picture of the death of Actaeon (Fig. 174)[6] on a bell-krater of about 440–430 B.C. from Vico Ecquense, Lyssa wears a very short decorative tunic with sleeves, as well as tall 'kothornoi'.

Some special interest is attached to the vases showing scenes from the story of Orestes, which, while obviously inspired by the drama, are yet very free from its influence in details. Two pictures of the purification of Orestes give quite different costumes to the Furies. The first is on a bell-krater in the Louvre from Armento (Fig. 175),[7] manufactured probably in the earlier part of the fourth century, the second on a bell-krater in London from Paestum (Fig. 176),[8] the work of Python in the middle of the century. The resemblances and differences between the different figures as depicted on each are obvious, and both contrast strongly with the kalyx-krater from Ruvo in Leningrad (Fig. 177),[9] where Orestes is surrounded by sleeping Furies wearing quite undecorated costumes. Where there are such differences, any inference as to the costumes actually worn in the theatre is obviously impossible. The consideration of the

---

[1] *Mon. ined. dell' Instit.* v, pl. 23 (lower half).

[2] Bieber, *Skenika*, Abb. 1.   [3] Furtw.–Reich., pl. 38.

[4] Ibid., vol. i, p. 197.   [5] *Mon. ined. dell' Instit.* v. 11.

[6] From a photograph lent by Sir John Beazley; cf. Pfuhl, *Mal. u. Zeich.*, fig. 515.

[7] Furtw.–Reich., pl. 120. 3.

[8] Trendall, *Paestan Pottery*, pl. 17, pp. 60–62; Tillyard, *Hope Vases*, pl. xxxvi. I am indebted to Sir John Beazley for a photograph.   [9] *Theatre of D.*, fig. 11.

FIG. 169. PELOPS AND HIPPODAMEIA (APULIAN AMPHORA)

FIG. 170. PELOPS AND HIPPODAMEIA (APULIAN KRATER)

FIG. 171. MELANIPPOS (APULIAN KRATER)

FIG. 172*a*. TALOS (ATTIC KRATER)

FIG. 172*b*. JASON, ETC. (REVERSE OF ATTIC KRATER)

FIG. 173. RANSOMING OF HECTOR (APULIAN KRATER)

FIG. 174. LYSSA (ATTIC KRATER)

FIG. 175. ORESTES (SOUTH ITALIAN KRATER)

FIG. 176. ORESTES (PAESTAN KRATER)

FIG. 177. ORESTES (GNATHIA KRATER)

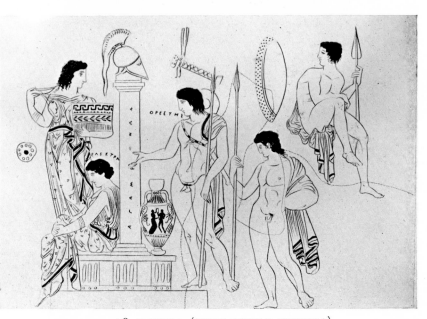

FIG. 178. ELECTRA (SOUTH ITALIAN AMPHORA)

FIG. 179. ELECTRA (LUCANIAN HYDRIA)

FIG. 180. IPHIGENEIA (PAESTAN KRATER)

several representations of Iphigeneia as priestess *in Tauris* leads
to the same conclusion.[1] In all she wears a decorative robe,
probably in virtue of her sacred office (cf. *Iph. Taur.* 798–9,

ξέν', οὐ δικαίως τῆς θεοῦ τὴν πρόσπολον
χραίνεις, ἀθίκτοις προσβαλὼν πέπλοις χέρα) ;

but the decoration differs considerably on the several vases,
though in three of them the robe bears a broad central band
from neck to foot. In one the robe is much nearer to the 'Andromeda' type than in the others. On a number of fourth-century
vases[2] Electra seated at her father's tomb wears a decorated
robe (without sleeves), probably simply indicative of rank,
though in the *Choephoroi* it is practically certain that she was
clad in black, and in other plays in mourning or rags.[3] The
scene as painted diverges in a number of ways from the scene
as it must have been presented in the theatre.

The highly decorative costume appears in a fragment of a
Paestan fourth-century amphora (Fig. 181)[4] from Paestum,
now generally regarded as representing Tereus in his fury—the
subject of Sophocles' *Tereus* (probably many years earlier)—and
in representations of the madness of Lycurgus, in which a
decorative robe is worn by the flying figure of Lyssa, as well as
by some human characters (Fig. 182).[5] These scenes of violence
would not have been presented in the theatre at all, though
they may have been described; but the painter doubtless gives
his own imaginative treatment. Another fourth-century vase
(Fig. 183) showing a non-theatrical scene is a Paestan bell-krater
of Python,[6] on which Alkmene on the pyre, and Amphitryon and

---

[1] Ibid., figs. 14, 15, 16, 19, pp. 86 ff.

[2] e.g. an amphora at Naples (Fig. 178) (from Millingen, *Peintures de Vases*, pl. xiv), a
Lucanian hydria (Fig. 179) also at Naples (Raoul-Rochette, *Mon. Inédits*, pl. xxxiv), and
many others. The Paestan kalyx-krater (Fig. 180) at Syracuse (Pace, *Monumenti Antichi*,
xxviii (1922), Tav. 1) has generally been regarded as also a representation of Electra at the
tomb, but has been almost conclusively shown by Anti (in *Dioniso*, x, pp. 124 ff.) to present
a situation based on the *Iphigeneia in Tauris*, including Iphigeneia, Orestes, Pylades, and a
kanephoros, the central object being an altar, not a tomb. It has often been pointed out that
painters may have had Stesichorus, as well as Aeschylus, in mind, and that the subject was
treated in art even before the date of the *Choephoroi*—e.g. in a relief from Melos in the Louvre;
cf. *Mon. dell' Inst.* vi, pl. lvii; Robert, *Bild und Lied*, pp. 177–8.

[3] *Choeph.* 11–18; cf. Soph. *Electra* 191 (ἀεικεῖ σὺν στολᾷ) ; Eur. *Electra* 108, 185, 1107.

[4] *Arch. Anz.* vi, 1891, fig. 9; cf. Bieber, *Ath. Mitt.* l (1925), pl. ii, and *Hist. Gk. Rom. Th.*,
fig. 58; Trendall, op. cit., no. 290.

[5] A volute-krater from Anzio in Naples, Millingen, *Peintures de Vases*, p. 93, pl. i; cf. kalyx-
krater from Ruvo (*Mon. dell' Inst.* v. 22; Séchan, fig. 21). See above, fig. 170 for other side.

[6] *J.H.S.* xi (1890), pl. vi; Trendall, op. cit., no. 107.

Antenor engaged in lighting it, wear very ornate dress of the general type under discussion, but differing as regards sleeves, and with the costume of the two men only reaching the knees. Alkmene's dress has bands of the same chess-board pattern as is worn by Zeus in the upper register. A south Italian volute-krater (Fig. 184),[1] now lost, shows Teiresias in a long robe with sleeves and decorated above the waist—perhaps in virtue of his office as a minister of the gods. On other vases[2] recalling the story of Antigone Kreon wears an ornamental dress, probably as a royal robe. In other vase painting reminiscent of the drama in subject, but not reproducing exactly scenes from the theatre, Polymestor on a fourth-century amphora in the British Museum (Fig. 185),[3] staggering forward in his blindness, wears a short ornamental chiton; on a Lucanian lekythos[4] of the fourth century the heroine appears in an extremely rich costume; Medea, a favourite subject of the painters,[5] sometimes wears sleeves as part of her decorative dress, sometimes not. On one (Fig. 188)[6] she wears a plain white dress, but very ornamental sleeves. A Paestan hydria (Fig. 189) in the British Museum,[7] on which (according to one interpretation) Agrios is shown taking refuge on the altar from Oineus and Diomedes, displays some striking variations of the ornamental dress. On the krater from Bari[8] which represents the death of Thersites Agamemnon wears a rich (doubtless royal) costume with sleeves. Costumes of this type are very conspicuous on a number of vases which can have nothing to do with the theatre—e.g. the Attic amphora from Melos in the Louvre (Fig. 190),[9] where all the goddesses are dressed in this style; the 'Persian vase', a fourth-century Apulian

---

[1] Raoul-Rochette, *Mon. Inéd.*, pl. 78. This is different from the network of woollen threads assigned to Teiresias by Pollux iv. 116.

[2] e.g. an Apulian amphora from Ruvo (*Mon. dell' Inst.* x, pl. 26; *Theatre of D.*, fig. 13).

[3] Brit. Mus. 1900.5–19.1. (British Museum photograph.)

[4] Fig. 186. Millingen, *Peintures de Vases*, pl. xli. The identification of the heroine as Phaedra is certainly wrong.

[5] e.g. (besides the famous Canosa Vase, Furtw.–Reich., pl. xcix; *Theatre of D.*, fig. 21), a fourth-century amphora (Fig. 187) from Nola (Raoul-Rochette, *Choix de Peintures*, p. 277).

[6] A fourth-century amphora from Cumae in the Louvre (*Arch. Ztg.* xix (1867), Taf. ccxxiii; *Encyclop. photogr. de l'Art*, iii, no. 36 A).

[7] Brit. Mus. F. 155. (Photograph lent by Sir John Beazley.) The identification of Agrios is very uncertain, and therewith the subject of the painting; cf. Trendall, *Paestan Pottery*, pp. 58–60, pl. 16 b).

[8] *Theatre of D.*, fig. 17; Séchan, *Études*, fig. 156. The vase is assigned to the second half of the fourth century.

[9] Furtw.–Reich., pl. 96.

FIG. 181. TEREUS (PAESTAN AMPHORA)

FIG. 182. LYCURGUS AND LYSSA (APULIAN AMPHORA)

FIG. 183. ALKMENE (PAESTAN KRATER)

FIG. 184. TEIRESIAS (APULIAN KRATER)

FIG. 185. POLYMESTER (APULIAN AMPHORA)

FIG. 186. LUCANIAN LEKYTHOS

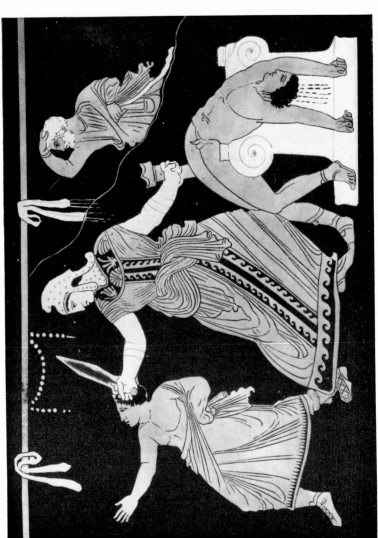

FIG. 188. CAMPANIAN AMPHORA
(MEDEA)

FIG. 187. CAMPANIAN AMPHORA (MEDEA)

FIG. 189. PAESTAN HYDRIA (AGRIOS?)

FIG. 190. ATTIC AMPHORA FROM MELOS

FIG. 191. APULIAN KRATER (PERSIANS)

krater in Naples (Fig. 191),[1] and several vases on which Orpheus,
doubtless as inspired by the gods, wears a dress of this type,
whether on earth[2] or in Hades.[3] This selection of illustrations
may conclude with an Attic vase (Fig. 192)[4] on which a very
similar costume is worn by the flute-player in the very secular
surroundings of a symposium.

The great variety of contexts in which the ornamental costume, with or without sleeves, and very variable in details is
found, confirms the suggestion made earlier that for half a century or perhaps somewhat longer, it became a favourite or
fashionable costume with artists for personages whose station or
function demanded some distinction or mark of sanctity; and
that (as the three vases described at the beginning of this discussion show) it was sometimes adopted in the theatre. Whether
it had any special significance before this period of a religious
or other character there is little to show, and the greater part
of the fourth-century evidence comes from south Italy, except in
so far as the kandys, a shortened form of decorative dress, seems
to have been familiar in Athenian 'real life' in the fourth century. That in all the contexts in which it appears it was derived
from the theatre seems a much less likely hypothesis than that
for a time the theatre may have followed a fashion prevailing
in Athens in the late fifth century and continuing in Italy, and
we have to be content to be without any satisfactory evidence
of the appearance of the characters in the plays of Aeschylus,
Sophocles, and Euripides in the fifth century, except in so far
as the texts themselves give us information.[5]

5. From the texts we learn that the chorus was dressed according to its supposed nationality or occupation, and in some plays
its un-Greek costume is specially noticed; e.g. in the *Suppliants*
of Aeschylus the King on first meeting them cries:[6]

ποδαπὸν ὅμιλον τόνδ' ἀνελληνόστολον
πέπλοισι βαρβάροισι κἀμπυκώμασι
χλίοντα προσφωνοῦμεν; οὐ γὰρ Ἀργολὶς
ἐσθὴς γυναικῶν οὐδ' ἀφ' Ἑλλάδος τόπων.

[1] Ibid., pl. 88.
[2] *Mon. dell' Inst.* viii. 431; Baumeister, *Denkm*, ii, fig. 1318.
[3] *Theatre of D.*, figs. 24 and 27. Cf. the Attic Apollo, Furt.–Reich., pl. 87, about 335 B.C.
[4] Tischbein, *Vases Hamilton*, ii. 55; see also above, p. 218, Fig. 166.
[5] See Dierks, *de tragicorum histrionum habitu scenico apud Graecos* (Göttingen, 1883).
[6] ll. 234–7, cf. 121 (Σιδονίᾳ καλύπτρᾳ).

Probably their dress was of some rich fabric,[1] and it was held by a girdle. (In l. 719 of the same play Danaos describes the Egyptian invaders, who afterwards break into the orchestra, as wearing white garments over their dark skins.) The chorus of the *Persians* must have worn the dress of elderly Persian nobles. (It may have been richly decorated and may have included trousers,[2] such as were regularly associated in Greek art with Persians; but there is no direct evidence.) The *Phoenissae* of Euripides may also have worn an Oriental costume, but it is not definitely indicated. In the *Agamemnon* the text is a little puzzling; the aged men have to support themselves on sticks,[3] and yet carry swords.[4] In the *Choephoroi* the chorus wear the black robes of mourners; in Euripides' *Alcestis* they change into such robes at the appropriate moment;[5] and in his *Suppliants* they wear, if not actual mourning, at least πεπλώματ' οὐ θεωρικά.[6] In the *Eumenides* the chorus are themselves black-skinned, but we are not told how they were dressed until at the end of the play they are adorned with scarlet cloaks.[7] In Sophocles' *Ajax* and *Philoctetes* the chorus consists of seamen, who were doubtless appropriately habited, and Philoktetes notices with pleasure[8] that they were dressed as Greeks (σχῆμα μὲν γὰρ Ἑλλάδος | στολῆς ὑπάρχει προσφιλεστάτης ἐμοί). In the *Rhesus* the chorus must have been in military uniform. That in the *Bacchae* the followers of Dionysus wore fawn-skins, such as characterize Maenads in art, may be taken for granted.[9]

6. Individual characters frequently appear in mourning. Electra is doubtless in black in the *Choephoroi*,[10] in Sophocles' *Electra*[11] she is shown ἀεικεῖ σὺν στολᾷ, in Euripides' *Electra* she is at first mistaken for a slave[12] and wears rags.[13] Mourning is worn by Admetus in the *Alcestis*, by Helen in the *Helena*,[14] by Iokasta in the *Phoenissae*,[15] and by Tyndareus in the *Orestes*.[16] The

---

[1] πολυμίτων πέπλων in l. 432 is generally rendered 'damask'.

[2] Trousers are worn by the Ethiopian on the Andromeda krater above described, who is conjectured by some scholars to represent the chorus. See p. 217.

[3] l. 75.　　　　　　　　　　　　　　　　　　　　　　　　　[4] ll. 1351, 1651.

[5] They are not in mourning at ll. 215 ff. They go out with Admetus for the funeral at 740–6, and possibly return in mourning at 861.　　　　[6] l. 97.

[7] l. 1028.　　　　　　　　　　　　　　　　　　　　　　　[8] ll. 223, 224.

[9] It seems almost to be implied by ll. 110 ff.　　　[10] ll. 16–18 imply this.

[11] l. 191.　　　　　　　　　　　　　　　　　　　　　　[12] ll. 109–10.

[13] l. 185, τρύχη τάδ' ἐμῶν πέπλων.　　　　　　　　[14] l. 1186—here it is a pretence.

[15] ll. 325–6 ἄπεπλος φαρέων λευκῶν, ὦ τέκνον, | δυσόρφναια δ' ἀμφὶ τρύχη τάδε | σκότι ἀμείβομαι.　　　　　　　　　　　　　　　　[16] l. 457.

FIG. 192. ATTIC KRATER, SYMPOSIUM

FIG. 193. RELIEF OF TRAGIC ACTOR

FIG. 194. RELIEF OF ARCHELAOS OF PRIENE

FIG. 195. ATTIC KYLIX

plight of Philoctetes and of Oedipus at Kolonos in Sophocles
and of the shipwrecked Menelaus[1] and the sick Orestes[2] in
Euripides is indicated by their garments, and his introduction
of Telephos and many other heroes in rags is one of the innovations with which Euripides is taunted by Aristophanes.[3] There
is no description in any extant play of the dress in which kings
and queens and their children would naturally appear in the
theatre, and it is therefore impossible to compare their costume
with the decorative robes shown in vase-paintings. But a passing
mention may be made of the special 'effects' of which Euripides
sometimes made use—such as the black and horrible Thanatos
of the *Alcestis*; the fine clothes in which Hermione decks herself
in the *Andromache*;[4] and the robes, perhaps bridal garments, in
which Euadne arrays herself before leaping into her husband's
funeral pyre in the *Suppliants*.[5] Ion also appears to have been
richly clad as the minister of Apollo.[6] In the *Rhesus*, Rhesus'
golden armour must have made a sensation. But what we learn
from the texts of dramatic costume in the period of the great
poets is meagre in the extreme, and for the later period we have
only the evidence supplied by vases and sculpture.

7. The vases painted by Assteas in the fourth century do not
seem to be sufficiently closely related to theatrical performances
to afford reliable evidence,[7] though the long robe worn by
Megara in the picture of the Mad Herakles, with its central
stripe and bands of chess-board pattern, so far resembles the
costumes seen on some of the vases already discussed, whether
or not similar dresses were worn by actors in Italy or Athens.
But two monuments of the fourth century, both already figured,
seem to indicate either that the highly decorative robe was not
an essential feature in the tragic actor's make-up or that it had
gone out of fashion before the end of the century. On the relief
from the Peiraeus[8] Dionysus is receiving three actors, dressed

---

[1] Eur. *Helena* 416, 421, 554, 1079, 1204.   [2] *Orestes* 391.
[3] *Acharn.* 412 ff.; *Frogs* 1063 ff. (The *Philoctetes* and *Oed. Col.* of Sophocles are later than
most plays of Euripides.)
[4] ll. 1477 ff. κόσμον μὲν ἀμφὶ κρατὶ χρυσέας χλιδῆς | στολμόν τε χρωτὸς τόνδε ποικίλων πέπλων |
οὐ τῶν Ἀχιλλέως οὐδὲ Πηλέως ἄπο | δόμων ἀπαρχὰς δεῦρ' ἔχουσ' ἀφικόμην, | ἀλλ' ἐκ Λακαίνης
Σπαρτιάτιδος χθονὸς | Μενέλαος ἡμῖν ταῦτα δωρεῖται πατήρ.
[5] ll. 1054–5 *ΙΦ.* σκευῇ δὲ τῇδε τοῦ χάριν κοσμεῖς δέμας; | *ΕΥ.* θέλει τι κλεινὸν οὗτος ὁ στολμός,
πάτερ.
[6] ll. 326–7 *ΚΡ.* ἔχεις δὲ βίοτον· εὖ γὰρ ἤσκησαι πέπλοις. | *ΙΩΝ.* τοῖς τοῦ θεοῦ κοσμούμεθ' ᾧ
δουλεύομαι.   [7] On the 'Mad Herakles' vase see *Theatre of D.*, p. 222, etc.
[8] Above, pp. 179, 182 and refs. there, and Fig. 26.

in long robes reaching the ground, sleeved, girdled, and pleated, but no decoration appears. One wears a shorter robe above the long one. It cannot, however, be assumed that they are in full stage costume, even though they carry masks; the scene is obviously a work of free imagination. The relief is generally dated early in the fourth century, and to the same period is ascribed by Bulle the remarkable figure of a tragic actor on a Tarentine krater at Würzburg.[1] Here the costume is unmistakably that of the play in which the actor is supposed to have just ended his part, and it is quite different from the decorative robe seen on so many vases. It consists of a brown, sleeved tunic, with a fringe of tassels round the lower edge, and falling only to the knee; a dark violet mantle hangs on the actor's left arm. It has already been noticed that while Bulle regards the figure as that of a king in exile or distress, Rumpf thinks that it is probably a normal tragic actor's costume of the Alexandrian period. That it is at least not something unique is indicated by the occurrence of a very similar costume in the figure of an altar-suppliant on an amphora in the Vatican, which Bulle regards as contemporary with the Würzburg vase. The actor depicted on the wall-painting at Herculaneum[2] which is regarded as a copy of a Greek original (probably a votive tablet) of the late fourth or early third century, wears a white robe, falling to the ground, with a gold-coloured girdle (not unlike the costumes of the Peiraeus relief); a purple mantle, indicative (like his sceptre) of royalty, lies across his knees as he sits. It can hardly be doubted that we have here good evidence for a costume actually worn by an actor in the theatre, but in what theatre it is impossible to say. The statuette from Amisos in the Louvre figured by Dr. Bieber,[3] of Hellenistic date, also shows a long pleated robe, with the girdle worn high up; and the terra-cotta statuettes from eastern Greece[4] probably show the costume there conventional for young men.

There is hardly any further evidence before the late Roman Republic and the early Empire. To the former probably belongs the actor shown on a striking relief in Dresden (Fig. 193);[5] but

---

[1] See above, p. 181 and Fig. 34, and refs. there given.
[2] See above, p. 184, Fig. 43.
[3] *Hist. Gk. and Rom. Th.*, fig. 203; see above, p. 185, Fig. 52.
[4] See above, p. 185, Figs. 49–50.
[5] Bieber, *Das Dresdener Schauspieler-relief* (frontispiece), and *Denkm.*, Taf. lv; Bulle, *Festschr.*

the dress is that of the Roman not of the Greek theatre, as are also those shown on the monument of Numitorius.[1]

Some of the Pompeian wall-paintings reproduced on earlier pages[2] as illustrating tragic masks also display costumes, but whether they are those of Roman plays (as seems very likely) or copies of lost Greek originals, it is impossible to say with any certainty.

One late statuette demands notice, if only because generations of scholars have, without justification, treated it as representative of the costumes of the Classical Greek theatre. This is the ivory statuette from Rieti[3]—an actor in a long blue robe, sleeved, with vertical yellow stripes from the girdle downwards and decorated with geometrical figures arranged vertically. The sleeves are crossed by yellow bands. But the date is probably not earlier than the latter part of the second century A.D., and the decoration is not unlike that of the figures in the late Roman mosaics from Porcareccia; the statuette cannot be used as evidence for any costume belonging to the Greek theatre.

8. The above account of the tragic actors' costume has been mainly confined to the χιτών, with some mention of the χλαμύς or mantle which was often carried on the arm. But Pollux enumerates a number of accessory garments, though he gives no indication of the dates at which they may have been in vogue. He says:[4]

καὶ ἐσθῆτες μὲν τραγικαὶ ποικίλον (οὕτω γὰρ ἐκαλεῖτο ὁ χιτών),[5] τὰ δ' ἐπιβλήματα ξυστίς, βατραχίς, χλανίς, χλαμὺς διάχρυσος, χρυσόπαστος, στατός, φοινικίς, τιάρα, κάλυπτρον, μίτρα, ἀγρηνόν· τὸ δ' ἦν πλέγμα ἐξ ἐρίων δικτυῶδες περὶ πᾶν τὸ σῶμα, ὃ Τειρεσίας ἐπεβάλλετο ἤ τις ἄλλος μάντις, κόλπωμα, ὃ ὑπὲρ τὰ ποικίλα ἐνεδέδυντο οἱ Ἀτρεῖς καὶ οἱ Ἀγαμέμνονες καὶ ὅσοι τοιοῦτοι. ἐφαπτὶς συστρεμμάτιόν τι πορφυροῦν ἢ φοινικοῦν, ὃ περὶ τὴν χεῖρα εἶχον οἱ πολεμοῦντες ἢ θηρῶντες. ὁ δὲ κροκωτὸς ἱμάτιον· Διόνυσος δὲ αὐτῷ ἐχρῆτο καὶ μασχαλιστῆρι ἀνθινῷ καὶ θύρσῳ.

The ξυστίς is described by the scholiast on Aristoph. *Clouds* 70 as τὸ κροκωτὸν ἱμάτιον ὃ οἱ ἡνίοχοι μεχρὶ τοῦ νῦν φοροῦσι

---

für James Loeb, pp. 13–14. The latter somewhat boldly contends that the figure is a representation of Q. Roscius himself. (See above, p. 186.)

[1] See above, p. 186, Fig. 57. [2] See above, pp. 187 f., Figs. 70–77.

[3] See above, p. 187, Fig. 66. A coloured figure of this is to be found in Baumeister, *Denkm.* iii, Taf. 58 (see p. 1576). The dress is discussed by Bieber, *Dresd. Schausp.*, pp. 37, 38, 67.

[4] iv. 116–17.

[5] This garment is also called a χιτὼν ζωτός or ζῳδιωτός (Poll. vii. 55), from the character of the ornament.

πομπεύοντες· χρῶνται δὲ αὐτὸ καὶ οἱ τραγικοὶ βασιλεῖς; the βατραχίς (green) and φοινικίς may have been distinguished from this principally by their colour, as may also the 'golden' or 'gold-sprinkled' χλαμύς. The κροκωτός (saffron-coloured) was already worn by Dionysus in Aristophanes' *Frogs*.[1] Of the κόλπωμα, worn to give the importance of increased size to royalty, there is no certain illustration, nor of the network of woollen threads worn by seers (the ἀγρηνόν). The στατός or στατὸς χιτών seems to have been a stiff garment falling from head to foot without a girdle.[2] The 'flowery girdle' of Dionysus is not mentioned elsewhere.

At a late date tragic actors used padding above and below the waist (προστερνίδια and προγαστρίδια) to increase their size and so incurred the ridicule of Lucian.[3] The word σωμάτιον is sometimes said to be used of the actor's robe generally,[4] and sometimes to mean such padding as has just been mentioned.

9. With regard to the footwear of the principal tragic actors, the statements of the older textbooks to the effect that the actors wore shoes in which the thickness of the soles was increased to four or even to eight or ten inches, as in the Rieti statuette, are no longer supported by any scholar of reputation. They are due mainly to an indiscriminate use of evidence without any regard for chronology. The facts are really simple.[5]

(1) There is no evidence at all of the use of such thick soles until late in the Hellenistic age, and many scenes in the extant plays would have been impossible if such shoes had been worn. Reference has already been made[6] to the frequent scenes of rapid and even violent movement included in the tragedies,

---

[1] l. 46 and schol.; cf. W. Headlam's note on Herodas viii. 28.

[2] See Liddell and Scott, s.vv. στατός and στάδιος; and Suid. s.v. ὀρθοστάδια· οἱ στατοὶ χιτῶνες ὀρθοστάδιοι, οἱ δὲ συρόμενοι συρτοί.

[3] Lucian, *Iup. Trag.* 41 ἀνάγκη δυοῖν θάτερον ἤτοι Πῶλον καὶ Ἀριστόδημον καὶ Σάτυρον ἡγεῖσθαί σε θεοὺς εἶναι τότε ἢ τὰ πρόσωπα τῶν θεῶν αὐτὰ καὶ τοὺς ἐμβάτας καὶ τοὺς ποδήρεις χιτῶνας καὶ χλαμύδας καὶ χειρῖδας καὶ προγαστρίδια καὶ τἆλλα, οἷς ἐκεῖνοι σεμνύνουσι τὴν τραγῳδίαν, ὅπερ γελοιότατον οἶμαι; *de Salt.* 27 ἐῶ λέγειν προστερνίδια καὶ προγαστρίδια, προσθετὴν καὶ ἐπιτεχνητὴν παχύτητα προσποιούμενος. It can hardly be inferred from the former passage that the great actors of an earlier age used these devices, though Lucian uses their names to represent the profession.

[4] Poll. ii. 235; iv. 115; Phot. s.v. σωμάτια· τὰ ἀναπλάσματα οἷς οἱ ὑποκριταὶ διασάττουσιν αὑτούς. (But the reference may be to comedy.)

[5] The whole matter was independently (and almost simultaneously) cleared up by K. K. Smith, 'Use of the High-heeled Shoe or Buskin in Greek Tragedy' (*Harvard Studies*, xvi, 1905), and A. Körte, 'Der Kothurn im fünften Jahrhundert' (*Festschr. Deutscher Philologen u. Schulmänner in Basel*, 1907).

[6] Above, pp. 169 f. A number of instances are collected by K. K. Smith, op. cit., pp. 135 ff.

and a sufficient disproof of the use of soles several inches thick
is afforded by the scene[1] where Agamemnon orders an attendant
to remove his shoes as he dismounts from his chariot. Can we
suppose that he suddenly became several inches shorter, or that
(as some have suggested) what the attendant really did was to
fasten the thick-soled shoes on, and that the king trampled on
the purple carpet (and probably up some steps) with these?
Such shoes are not seen in the Peiraeus relief, and in fact the
earliest certain occurrences of them in connexion with tragedy
are on a marble base[2] of about 100 B.C., or a little earlier, found
at Halicarnassus, in which the Tragic Muse is distinguished from
others by ornamental shoes with soles probably somewhat less
than 3 inches high; and (probably a little later) on the relief
of Archelaos of Priene (the so-called Apotheosis of Homer) in
the British Museum (Fig. 194),[3] in which again the Tragic Muse
wears a thick-soled shoe. After this date there are many (though
not many extreme) instances. The actors of the monument of
Numitorius have been figured earlier in this chapter,[4] and in
some of the paintings from Herculaneum and Pompeii some of
the principal characters are shod in this manner,[5] but not in
all—not, for example, in the paintings of Priam and Hecuba
and of Priam and Achilles, so that if these are, as is often supposed, copies of early Hellenistic works, they would suggest that,
at the date of the originals, no such shoes were worn. The Rieti
statuette, which is a late Roman work,[6] has them, but concealed
by the robe, the visible supports being in effect pegs to hold the
statuette in place on its base. The date of the statuette from
Amisos (on the Black Sea), which was figured above,[7] is not
known; it is probably late Hellenistic. Nor is the date of the
original of the fine painting at Herculaneum,[8] of an actor in the
part of a king. He appears to be wearing shoes soled with two
layers of leather, but this painting is probably late and it would

---

[1] Aesch. *Agam.* 934 ff. ἀλλ' εἰ δοκεῖ σοι ταῦθ' ὑπαί τις ἀρβύλας | λύοι τάχος, πρόδουλον ἔμβασιν ποδός, | καὶ τοῖσδ' ἐμβαίνοντ' ἀλουργέσιν θεῶν | μή τις πρόσωθεν ὄμματων βάλοι φθόνος.
[2] Trendelenberg, *Der Musenchor* (36th Winckelmannsprogr. Berlin, 1876).
[3] This picture of the lower portion of the relief was furnished by the British Museum.
[4] See pp. 186, 227 and Fig. 57.
[5] See above, pp. 187 ff. In some the long robe reaching the ground hides the thick soles, which are either discernible through it or can be inferred from the proportions of the figure. In some the principal actor has a taller sole than the less important.
[6] See p. 187, Fig. 66.   [7] See p. 185, Fig. 52.
[8] See above, p. 184, Fig. 43. It was not improbably of the late fourth or early third century B.C.

not be safe, though it is perhaps not too venturesome, to ascribe such soles to the figure in the original. The Dresden actor[1] seems to represent a further stage in the transition from the fifth-century custom to the period of high-soled κόθορνοι, his shoes being fitted with soles consisting of several thin layers; and he is conjectured to belong to the late Republican period. It has also been suggested[2] that we have in the Peiraeus relief of about 400 B.C. an earlier stage in the transition, in which the actors wore a sole consisting of a single layer only; and it is very credible that in the great period of drama, the fifth century, a soleless shoe—not so very unlike a sock—should have been found inadequate for the comfortable execution of the vigorous movements which the texts of the plays demand, though at what point the single sole was introduced there is no evidence to show. That Aeschylus did something to improve the footwear of his actors is quite probable, but the only statement about this is in the very unreliable *Life*, which speaks of him as τούς τε ὑποκριτὰς χειρῖσι σκεπάσας καὶ τῷ σύρματι ἐξογκώσας μείζοσί τε τοῖς κοθόρνοις μετεωρίσας, a passage which is evidently based on the corrupt tradition ascribing the thick-soled κόθορνοι to him—a tradition which has already been shown to be impossible;[3] and μετεωρίσας would be a very exaggerated expression if it referred to a sole of an ordinary single layer.

10. But if the grotesque thick soles[4] were not worn by actors of the Classical period, what did they in fact wear? The fragments of the vase[5] published by Miss Talcott (the date is about

---

[1] See above, p. 226, Fig. 193, and Bieber, *Das Dresd. Schausp.-relief*, pp. 69, 70.

[2] Ibid., p. 52.

[3] See above, p. 216. The same tradition is probably found in Horace, *Ars Poet.* 280 'et docuit magnumque loqui *nitique* cothurno'; as it is in Philostratus, *Vit. Apoll.* VI. xi ὀκρίβαντος δὲ τοὺς ὑποκριτὰς ἀνεβίβασεν. Themist. *Or.* 316 d also ascribes ὀκρίβαντας to Aeschylus, and ὀκρίβας is a synonym for κόθορνος in Lucian, *Nero* 9, and in the *Life of Sophocles*, i. 9. (In classical Greek, e.g. Plato, *Sympos.* 194 b, it denotes a platform.) ἐμβάτης is also used of the thick-soled shoe in a number of passages of Lucian; cf. Suidas, s.v. Αἰσχύλος ... οὗτος πρῶτος εὗρε ταῖς ἀρβύλαις τοῖς καλουμένοις ἐμβάταις κεχρῆσθαι. Pollux iv. 115 is mistaken in identifying ἐμβάτης with the *comic* shoe: καὶ τὰ ὑποδήματα κόθορνοι μὲν τὰ τραγικὰ καὶ ἐμβάδες, ἐμβάται δὲ τὰ κωμικά. Possibly ἐμβάδες and ἐμβάται have been accidentally transposed, but ἐμβάς seems to have been used in the Classical period for any ordinary shoes—such as would also be worn in comedy; it was probably never confined strictly to one type. Cf. Pollux vii. 85 ἐμβάδες· εὐτελὲς μὲν τὸ ὑπόδημα, Θρᾴκιον δὲ τὸ εὕρημα, τὴν δὲ ἰδέαν κοθόρνοις ταπεινοῖς ἔοικεν. ἐμβάτης is found in classical literature only in Xenophon, *de Equit.* xii. 10, where it means a riding-boot. In Aristoph. *Eccles.* 345, 507, the same pair of shoes are called λακωνικαί and ἐμβάδες.

[4] Their absurdity did not escape Lucian, e.g. *de Salt.* 27 εἰς μῆκος ἄρρυθμον ᾐσκημένος ἄνθρωπος ἐμβάταις ὑψηλοῖς ἐποχούμενος; *Somn.* 26 τῶν ἐμβάδων τὴν ὑπόδεσιν ἀμορφοτάτην καὶ οὐ κατὰ λόγον τοῦ ποδός—an absurdity exposed to view when an actor tumbled down.

[5] *Hesperia*, viii, pp. 267 ff.; see above, pp. 178, 182, 216, Fig. 25.

470 B.C.) and those of the pelike in the Boston Museum[1] (of about 440 B.C.) may perhaps be taken as attesting the wearing of a simple soft shoe, reaching some way up the leg, by members of a female chorus. They probably wore it not as a dramatic 'property' but as a normal woman's shoe, such as is sometimes seen on vases. (A kylix in the Torlonia Museum in Rome is here figured as an example; Fig. 195.)[2] A statement is said (in the *Life of Sophocles*) to have been made by Istros, an Alexandrian scholar of the late third century B.C., which seems to imply that in Sophoclean drama the footwear of chorus and actors was alike: φησὶ δὲ ῎Ιστρος καὶ τὰς λευκὰς κρηπῖδας αὐτὸν (Sophocles) ἐξευρηκέναι, ἃς ὑποδοῦνται οἵ τε ὑποκριταὶ καὶ οἱ χορευταί. There must surely have been some differentiation according to the characters represented; it seems improbable that all should have worn white shoes; but the word κρηπῖδες does seem to imply some kind of sole,[3] though there is no further evidence for their use by Sophocles. In fact the earliest direct evidence for the footwear of actors seems to be that of the Pronomos Vase,[4] on which the figures holding masks may be taken with great probability to be wearing their dramatic costume, and if so, a soft decorated shoe, reaching some way up the leg, may be claimed for the contemporary theatre. This type of shoe is also worn by the actor on the Tarentine krater at Würzburg[5] (probably of the early fourth century B.C.) and is here richly ornamented; there can be no doubt about its connexion with the theatre, though it is with the theatre of south Italy, and not necessarily that of Athens. The same type appears continually on south Italian vases of the fourth century, presenting subjects both connected and unconnected with the theatre; the figures given earlier will furnish illustrations. It seems, however, safe to say that though the use of this type was extended far beyond theatrical subjects, it was probably in vogue in the late fifth and fourth century for actors.

If we look for a possible ancestry of this type, we find that shoes of soft material, reaching some way up the leg and often

---

[1] See above, p. 182, Fig. 39.
[2] Furtw.–Reich. ii, p. 238, Abb. 83. See also Bieber, *Dresd. Schausp.-relief*, p. 51, for other instances. There is no direct evidence to show that such shoes were called κόθορνοι, but see below, p. 233.
[3] Bekker, *Anecd.*, p. 237. 19 κρηπίς· εἶδος ὑποδήματος ἀνδρικοῦ ὑψηλὰ ἔχοντος τὰ καττύματα.
[4] See above, p. 179, Fig. 28.
[5] See above, p. 181, Fig. 34.

turned up at the tip, are known from Athenian vases going back
to an early period. From the illustrations here given[1] it will be
seen that they differ considerably among themselves; e.g. some
are close-fitting, others loose and open widely at the top, some
are more ornamental than others, and some differ strongly in
shape and ornamentation from those of the Pronomos Vase.
The following are the figures given.[2]

Fig. 196.[3] Dionysus on psykter by Dikaios-painter in London; *circa*
520–510 B.C.

197.[4] Dionysus on amphora in London (E. 265); late sixth
century B.C.

198.[5] Dionysus on stamnos in London (E. 443); *circa* 490–480 B.C.

199.[6] Satyr as Hermes on psykter of Douris in London (E. 768);
circa 490–480 B.C.

200.[7] Hermes on hydria in Leningrad; *circa* 470 B.C.

201.[8] Hermes on stamnos in Trieste; *circa* 470–460 B.C.

202.[9] Athenian lekythos of about 460–450 B.C.

203.[10] Amphora by Achilles-painter in Paris, *circa* 450 B.C.

204.[11] Thamyras on Athenian hydria, soon after 450 B.C.

On several of these vases Dionysus wears a shoe reaching
high up the calf and decorated in varying degrees with frills and
otherwise at its upper edge, and these shoes in their more ornamental varieties suggest that the type of shoe which appears on
the Pronomos Vase may have been taken over by the tragic
drama, as a form of Dionysiac worship, from Dionysus and his
circle as conceived in ancient art, though the same kind of shoe
is found worn, on the vases, by Hermes, Hephaistos, Thamyras,[12]
and Artemis.

[1] I have to thank the Trustees of the British Museum for leave to print Figs. 196 to 199,
and for providing me with photographs, and Sir John Beazley for figs. 200–1.

[2] Dr. Bieber, *Dresd. Schausp.-relief*, pp. 46–8, gives a much longer list of pre-Aeschylean
shoes worn by revellers, musicians, etc.—nearly all of the same general type as those here
figured.

[3] Brit. Mus. E. 767.   [4] Brit. Mus. E. 265.
[5] Brit. Mus. E. 443.   [6] Brit. Mus. E. 768.
[7] Hermitage 627 (St. 1538).
[8] S 424.

[9] Published by S. P. Karouzou in *J.H.S.* lxv (1945), pp. 38 ff., fig. 1, and pl. iv a. The
latter is reproduced here by her kind permission. She argues that the figure wearing the shoes
is that of an actor, or of the caricature of an actor in a satyric play, but I am not convinced
by this, though there are some attractive arguments which deserve careful study. If it were
so, this would be the earliest known painting of an actor, as distinct from a member of a chorus.

[10] *Monuments Piot*, vii, pl. 2; but the face of Dionysus and the top of his head are 'restored'.
[11] *J.H.S.* xxv (1905), pl. i.
[12] Instances are collected by Séchan, *Études*, figs. 60–63. These suggest to Körte (op. cit., p.
205), along with the stories told by Herodotus, that the original home of the κόθορνος was in

11. The instances given, and others, suggest that this type of footwear, reaching up the calf and more or less decorative, may be identified with the κόθορνος which was certainly regarded as a characteristic part of Dionysus' dress in the fifth century, and which was generally familiar as a feminine and hence as an effeminate kind of footwear; and so Herakles in Aristophanes' *Frogs*[1] laughs at Dionysus' attempt to combine it with a club: τίς ὁ νοῦς; τί κόθορνος καὶ ῥόπαλον ξυνηλθέτην;[2] Elsewhere in Aristophanes[3] the κόθορνος is a woman's shoe, as also it is in Herodotus i. 155 κέλευε δέ σφεας κιθῶνάς τε ὑποδύνειν τοῖς εἵμασι καὶ κοθόρνους ὑποδέεσθαι ... ταχέως σφεάς γυναῖκας ἀντ᾿ ἀνδρῶν ὄψεαι γεγονότας. Its shape—or at least its looseness in some of its forms—is indicated by the story in Herodotus vi. 125 of Alkmaion wearing κόθορνοι (which must have been tall loose boots) when he went to collect the gold of Croesus, and filling them so full of gold that he could scarcely stagger along. (The shoes on the Athenian lekythos in Fig. 202 seem to approximate to this type.) So also Theramenes[4] from his adaptability to the politics of either party was nicknamed κόθορνος—evidently a shoe that was loose and easy and fitted either foot (and obviously cannot have had a hard, thick sole). There is no definite evidence that in the Classical period the tragic boot was specifically named κόθορνος. This was evidently the name of a boot in common use, especially by women, but also associated in art with Dionysus; and this association it continued to have. Pausanias[5] compares the image of Zeus Philios at Megara with Dionysus: κόθορνοί τε γὰρ τὰ ὑποδήματά ἐστιν αὐτῷ καὶ ἔχει τῇ χειρὶ ἔκπωμα, τῇ δ᾿ ἑτέρᾳ θύρσον, and Virgil[6] bids the god come to the winepress in the words:

Thrace or Lydia. S. P. Karouzou distinguishes such shoes as appear on the Athenian lekythos (Fig. 202) from 'the Thracian *endromides*, which fit close to the foot, worn for example by Orpheus, Thamyras, or Hermes on the psykter by Duris'. There is indeed a distinction between the looser and closer-fitting types, but the term ἐνδρομίδες seems to be entirely confined in Greek to the hunting-shoes worn by Artemis; it is only found in Callim. *Hymn to Artemis* 16 and *to Delos* 238, and *Anthol. Planud.* iv. 253, and once, of a soldier's tall boot, in the *Belopoeica* of Philo Mechanicus (3rd–2nd cent. B.C.).

[1] l. 47.
[2] In the *Birds* 996 the question addressed to Meton—τίς ἡ 'πίνοια, τίς ὁ κόθορνος τῆς ὁδοῦ; —is probably a hint at Meton's effeminacy. (He had shirked military service.)
[3] *Lysistr.* 657–8; *Ekkles.* 311 ff. (with 344–6). The specimens shown in Fig. 231, and others figured by Dr. Bieber in *Dresd. Schausp.-relief*, p. 51, may have been like those mentioned by Aristophanes.
[4] Xen. *Hellen.* III. iii. 30, 31; Pollux vii. 90, 91.   [5] VIII. xxxi. 4.
[6] *Georg.* ii. 7. In *Ecl.* vii. 32 and *Aen.* i. 336 it belongs also to Diana.

Huc, pater o Lenaee, veni nudataque musto
tingue novo mecum dereptis crura cothurnis.[1]

The name may naturally have been applied from the first to the actor's boot among others, and though there is still no answer to the question at what date some kind of sole was introduced, the name could still be applied to a soled shoe or boot of the appropriate shape, no less than to a hunting-boot, which certainly would not fit either foot. In time the usage of the word seems to have become specialized and much more closely confined to the thick-soled tragic shoe of the late Hellenistic and imperial periods, though Pausanias could still use it of the footwear of Dionysus in art.

12. The costumes worn by the choruses and actors of the Old Comedy have been almost sufficiently described in the course of the account given of their masks. It is evident that the poets enjoyed complete freedom to clothe their choruses and their actors in accordance with the characters which they represented, but that the actor's dress often differed from that of real life by its gross indecency, the tight χιτών being cut short so as to show the phallos, and by the grotesque padding of the body.[2] That these characteristics continued into the period of the Middle Comedy seems to be indicated by a number of fourth-century statuettes.[3] But the coarseness of the show gradually abated, and with Menander and his successors it may gradually

[1] On this Probus writes: 'cothurni sunt calceamentorum genera venatorum, genibus crura etiam muniuntur, cujus calceamenti effigies est in simulacris Liberi et Dianae.' That this type of shoe could be regarded in classical times *inter alia* as a hunting-boot is indicated not only by its association with Artemis (see especially the Iphigeneia vase figured in *Theatre of D.*, p. 89, fig. 16), but by its being worn by Lyssa (see above, p. 220), and by a Fury on one of the Orestes vases (see above, p. 220). There is some difficulty in the calling of the feminine (and Dionysiac) shoe by the same name as the hunting-boot, which must have been of stouter material, and presumably had a stronger sole (though not of the unnatural kind used in later tragedy). Perhaps the essence of the κόθορνος was simply that it came some way up the leg, and any shoe or boot which did this may have borne the name, until, late in its history, the name became specialized.

[2] The literary evidence is also unmistakable: e.g. Aristoph. *Ach.* 158, 592, 1216; *Wasps* 1342 ff.; *Peace* 1349; *Lysistr.* 928 ff., 982 ff., 1073 ff.; *Thesm.* 62, 643 ff.; Eupolis, fr. 244 (K.). Aristophanes' resolution (*Clouds* 537 ff.) to avoid such indecencies does not seem to have lasted long; cf. *Dith. Trag. Com.*, p. 237. For padding see *Clouds* 1215; *Frogs* 200 (Dionysus is γάστρων); and perhaps Antiphanes, fr. 19 (K.), and Anaxandrides, fr. 69 (K.).

[3] See above, pp. 194–200, and Figs. 82 ff., 108 ff. The attempt to prove the wearing of the phallus in Diphilus' *Epitrope* from Plautus' *Rudens* (which is taken from that play), ll. 428–9, can hardly succeed. See W. Beare, *Class. Quart.* xliii (1949), p. 30, who refers to Cicero, *de Off.* i. 129 'scaenicorum quidem mos tantam habet vetere disciplina verecundiam ut in scaena sine subligaculo prodeat nemo'. In Antiphanes, fr. 33 (K.), the Academic philosopher's dress shows the elegancies which such persons affected, and also in Ephippus, fr. 14 (K.).

FIG. 196. ATTIC PSYKTER, DIONYSUS

FIG. 197. ATTIC AMPHORA, DIONYSUS

FIG. 198. ATTIC STAMNOS, DIONYSUS

FIG. 199*. ATTIC PSYKTER, SATYR AS HERMES

FIG. 200. ATTIC HYDRIA, HERMES

FIG. 201. ATTIC STAMNOS, TRIESTE

FIG. 202. ATTIC LEKYTHOS

FIG. 203. ATTIC AMPHORA, DIONYSUS

FIG. 204. ATHENIAN HYDRIA, THAMYRAS

have disappeared; the costumes became those of ordinary life, though some degree of caricature appears to have been allowed at times in the masks and the figures of slaves and to a lesser extent of angry fathers and others who invited it.

Pollux[1] gives a brief account of the costumes worn in comedy; he does not say of what epoch he is speaking, but it was evidently a time when conventionality was more stereotyped than in the Classical period. The regular comic garment, he says, was the ἐξωμίς, a plain white garment with no seam on the left side. Old men wore a white ἱμάτιον, younger men a red or purple one, parasites black or grey; slaves wore over the ἐξωμίς a short white cloak called ἐγκόμβωμα or ἐπίρρημα;[2] old women wore green or light blue, except priestesses, who were dressed in white; some women also wore a χιτών reaching the feet and edged with purple. Young women wore white, which for heiresses was fringed or tasselled. The πορνοβόσκος had a coloured tunic with a flowered mantle over it; and so on.

On their feet the comic actors normally wore ἐμβάδες—the shoes of everyday life.[3]

13. The attempt has sometimes been made[4] to discover more exactly the costume worn by actors of the Middle Comedy by a study of that of the φλύακες, whose performances are depicted on a large number of south Italian vases of the fourth century B.C.—a period covering practically the same years as those of the Middle Comedy itself. The subjects of these—the parody of heroic legends, and particularly of those of Zeus, Herakles, and Odysseus, and scenes depicting revelry or the trickeries and punishment of slaves and the ways of old men and women (and young)—are often found in the Middle Comedy, but most of them, and possibly all, go far back behind both comedy and the vases to the early Dorian mimes or mime-like performances of the Peloponnese, from which Attic comedy and the Italian

---

[1] iv. 119–20. In Aristoph. *Lysistr.* there are mentioned the ἐξωμίς (661), the χλαμύς (987), and the ἔγκυκλον (113)—a ἱμάτιον with a decorative border—all probably garments of ordinary life.

[2] For the costumes of slaves, etc., in Roman comedy and in the New Comedy, see W. Beare, loc. cit., and *The Roman Stage*, 176 ff. There were obvious differences between town and country slaves, corresponding to their occupations.

[3] See above, p. 230, n. 3. For the confusion of ἐμβάδες and ἐμβάται in Pollux iv. 115, etc., see K. K. Smith in *Harvard Studies*, xvi, pp. 149–51.

[4] Most recently by T. B. L. Webster, *Class. Quart.* xlii (1948), pp. 17 ff., who makes a valuable collection of relevant material, though I cannot always agree with his interpretation of it. See above, p. 211.

phlyakes alike derived much.[1] Athenaeus[2] classes the Italian
φλύακες with the primitive Spartan δεικηλίσται and with the
φαλλοφόροι who under various names were found in many parts
of the Greek world; and in their common origin we have a
sufficient explanation of the resemblances between the subjects
and costumes of comedy and those of the φλύακες,[3] without
having to suppose that either the φλύακες or the Middle Comedy
imitated the other directly. They probably represented parallel
but independent and somewhat different lines of development.
The particular form of gross indecency in which each indulged
—the body-garment cut short so as to display a phallos of
exaggerated size—probably goes back to the common origin of
both, as also the grotesque padding of the body which mime and
comedy alike found amusing, as human nature does generally
in its less exalted moods. But the masks of the phlyakes in general
display a different type of hideousness (quite easily recognizable)
from those of the terra-cottas contemporary with the Middle
Comedy, and it has been well observed (by Wüst)[4] that the
expression on them is that required by the momentary situation
depicted on the vase, not that of a character-mask which could
be worn throughout a whole dramatic performance. Further,
the phlyakes regularly wear tights, such as very rarely appear
on Attic vases but are often shown on terra-cottas.[5] Besides
this the phlyakes are almost always represented as performing
on a low temporary stage, raised on short posts or columns,
with or without curtains as part of the setting, and usually with
a few steps leading up to it—something totally different from
the theatres of the period—so far as our evidence goes.

[1] See *Dith. Trag. Com.*, pp. 228 ff. [2] xiv. 621 f., 622.
[3] The noun φλύακες (φλύαξ) sometimes signifies the performers, sometimes the performance (cf. τραγῳδοί = τραγῳδία). The derivation and exact meaning of the word still
remain uncertain. Hesychius explains φλύαξ as μέθυσος ἢ γελοιάστης, and it is variously
connected with φλυαρεῖν, φλύω, φλύζω. Körte (*Jahrb. Arch.* viii. 86 ff.) thinks that φλύαξ
was originally a vegetation-deity, and Radermacher, while approving this, connects the
word with φλέω, φλόος (in what sense he does not make quite plain), thinking that
φλύαξ : φλέω, φλόος : : ῥύαξ : ῥέω, ῥόος (*Sitzb. Akad. Wien*, 1924).
[4] Pauly–W. *Real-Encycl.* xx. 1, col. 302, s.v. φλύακες.
[5] e.g. Attic terra-cottas figs. 86 ff. On a late-fifth-century oinochoe (Pfuhl, *Mal. u. Zeichn.*,
fig. 572; Beazley, *A.R.V.* 848/22; Bieber, *Denkm.*, fig. 125; Rumpf, *A.J.A.* lv. 8, figs. 5–7) is a
caricature of Herakles in a chariot driven by Nike and drawn by centaurs, with a grotesque
phallic figure, apparently wearing tights, dancing in front; but this cannot be based on any performance and must be purely imaginary, though the costume of the dancer and the particular
style of caricature of Herakles may be borrowed from some mime-like show. A vase of Brygos
(Pfuhl, op. cit., fig. 424) depicts a half-caricatured Herakles as a Scythian *toxotes* wearing
long striped trousers and sleeves, drawing his bow against a crowd of Sileni attacking Hera.

14. It seems more likely that if a parallel in Athens to the phlyakes of south Italy is sought, it is to be found in the mimes, still surviving in the fourth century, of which Attic vases, and probably terra-cottas also, have preserved traces—performances on a much smaller scale than comedy and in a different setting. These performances appear to have been given on a low stage, bearing a general resemblance to that of the Italians, and to have employed one or more grotesque dancing figures. Such is the figure shown on an oinochoe, an Attic vase of about 425 B.C.[1]—almost nude, apparently a dwarf, and carrying the attributes, the pouch and sickle (κίβισις and ἅρπη), of Perseus. An older and a younger man are sitting together in front of the platform and gravely looking on. Such also is another dancing dwarf on a low platform, on an Attic stemless cup of about 430 B.C. from Al Mina, published by Sir John Beazley,[2] who cites parallel instances. Another vase of about 410 B.C., from the same place, and published by the same scholar,[3] shows the figure of a Persian, wearing the decorative sleeves and trousers characteristic of Persians in Attic art, dancing on a low platform; Dionysus and a Maenad are looking on, and a satyr plays the flute. (The scene is, of course, imaginary, but the type of performance represented may be one in vogue in Athens at the time.) None of these vases has anything to do with comedy, though they do suggest the continuance in Athens, at least on a small scale, of a lower type of entertainment corresponding to that of the phlyakes, and it may be that some of the many extant statuettes (including some of the more indecent) are to be related to these mime-like performances rather than to the Middle Comedy itself,[4] though there is probably sufficient evidence for the persistence of some degree of grossness in comedy until the latter

[1] First published by G. Caputo in *Dioniso*, iv (1935); well figured in *J.H.S.* lxv (1945), pl. v (see p. 42), and by Bulle, *Das Theater zu Sparta*, pl. v. In *Theatre of D.*, p. 74, I wrongly doubted its Attic origin.

[2] *J.H.S.* lix (1939), pp. 10, 11, fig. 30.

[3] Ibid., pp. 23–24, fig. 60.

[4] The development of mimes as the most popular form of entertainment—non-Dionysiac and often non-theatrical and not confined to festivals—is traced in detail in Reich's *Mimus*. The performers were perhaps normally travelling professionals. (They were not admitted to the companies of 'Artists of Dionysus' as, of course, comedians were.) A certain number of the terra-cottas and other artistic remains recall characters from the literary mimes (Sophron, Theocritus, Herodas) at least as much as characters from New Comedy, and the vulgar non-literary mime probably furnished the artists with plenty of suggestions; for some varieties of these see Aristokles (2nd cent. B.C.) *ap.* Athen. xiv. 621 c, and Hippolochus (*c.* 300 B.C.) *ap.* Athen. iv. 130 c, and for other references to mimes see Oeri, *Der Typ der komischen Alten*, pp. 81 ff.

part of the fourth century.[1] (By this date it may also have begun to disappear from the Italian performances.)[2] If the view here taken of the substantial independence of the phlyakes from Attic comedy is correct, it is unnecessary to discuss the former more fully here. A large number of the vases are figured in their full hideousness and disgustingness in several easily accessible publications.[3]

[1] See above, p. 234.

[2] Cf. a kalyx-krater figured by Bulle, *Festschr. für Loeb*, p. 31, fig. 20 (which is probably a phlyax-vase), and a bell-krater, ibid., p. 34, fig. 24 = Bieber, *Hist. Gk. Th.*, fig. 394.

[3] Besides the primary sources (Heydemann in *Jahrb. Arch.* i (1886) and Zahn in Fürtw.–Reich. iii. 180 ff.) reference may be made to Bieber, *Denkm.*, pp. 138 ff., figs. 126–32, and Taf. 76–86; and *Hist. Gk. and Rom. Theat.*, pp. 258–300; Trendall, *Paestan Pottery* (1936); Radermacher, 'Zur Gesch. der gr. Komödie' (*Sitzb. Akad.-Wiss. Wien*, 1924); Bulle, *Festschr. für Loeb* (1930), pp. 29 ff.; Wüst, art. Φλύακες in Pauly–W. xix (1941), cols. 392–406. Some new specimens are recorded in *Dioniso*, vol. vi. The φλύακες became literary about 300 B.C. in the hands of Rhinthon; the meagre fragments are to be found in Olivieri, *Frammenti della Commedia Greca e del Mimo nella Sicilia e nella Magna Grecia* (1930).

V

THE CHORUS

A. CHARACTER, FUNCTION, AND MOVEMENTS OF THE CHORUS

1. A COMPLETE account of the chorus as it presented itself in the Greek theatre could hardly be given without a full history of dithyramb, tragedy, satyric drama, and comedy—a more ambitious undertaking than can be contemplated here. For the present purpose dithyramb will be left out of consideration; there is little to add to its history since the author wrote of it in 1927,[1] and a brief account of its production is given in Chapter II of this book.

The tragic chorus, from having occupied the whole performance before Thespis introduced an actor, came gradually to take up less and less time and interest. At the outset it might be actually the fortune of the chorus, more than that of any character in the play, that was at stake; so it was in the *Suppliants* of Aeschylus, where the chorus occupies considerably more than half the play. In the *Persai* and the *Seven against Thebes* the chorus is still vitally affected by the issue. In the *Agamemnon* and *Choephoroi* also it is very closely bound up with the royal house to which the personages of the drama belong, and in the *Eumenides* it may almost be said to have the principal role. Of the extant plays of Aeschylus there is only the *Prometheus Vinctus* (probably one of his latest plays)[2] in which the chorus is little more than a very sympathetic spectator. In Sophocles and Euripides the choral element in the play scarcely ever exceeds a quarter of the whole, and is often very much less, and though in Sophocles the chorus is generally closely attached to or interested in a principal character, in Euripides it may often be relatively independent as regards both the intimacy of its interest and the immediate connexion of its songs with the events of the plot. Intelligent

---

[1] In *Dithyramb, Tragedy and Comedy*. A few new fragments have been found, mainly from papyri. (See especially *Mitt. aus der Papyrus-sammlung Rainer*, Neue Folge, i. 19,996 ab., ed. Oellacher.)

[2] See Introduction to G. Thomson's edition. Kranz (*Stasimon*, pp. 226–8) thinks that the second and third stasima were substitutes, written about 440–430 B.C. for Aeschylus' original work, but this conclusion is not adequately proved.

reading will indeed show that actual irrelevance is very rare
and, where it exists, has a real dramatic justification, and in two
of the latest plays of the fifth century, the *Bacchai* and the
Oedipus Coloneus, the choral odes present some very striking
examples of dramatic effectiveness as well as of poetic beauty.
But the practice, said to have been begun by Agathon, of writing
choral interludes (ἐμβόλιμα) which could be transferred from
one play to another, like the music of a modern theatre band,
seems to have become common by the time of Aristotle, who
deprecates it and demands that the chorus shall be treated as
one of the actors and be interwoven with the plot,[1] though there
is reason to think that at least from time to time in the fourth
century choral odes, with words and not merely dances, were
still composed and indeed Aristotle's prescription implies that
it must have been so. It was natural that when full use came to
be made of three actors the dialogue should be more between
them and less between actor and chorus; and conversely the
actors themselves came to sing lyric monodies.

The want of all texts, except a relatively small number of
fragments, makes it impossible to trace the later history of the
tragic chorus, but it is significant that in the records of the
'Artists of Dionysus' from the latter part of the third century
onwards, there is very little mention of tragic choreutai, and it
is probable that the few who appeared did in fact contribute
nothing but *entr'actes*.[2] A satyric play without a satyr-chorus is
not easy to imagine, but very little is known of the satyric drama
after the fifth century, and the name may have been given to
plays very different from those of the fifth century and more
like comedy;[3] but, in whatever form, satyric plays were still
composed under the early Roman Empire and presumably as
a rule with a chorus, of whatever kind.

In comedy the chorus was a very important element down to
the end of the fifth century, after which the parabasis, and the
epirrhematic structure generally,[4] disappear, and in many plays
the chorus simply sing interludes to break up the dialogue into
scenes. This is so, for example, in Aristophanes' *Ploutos*, and no

---

[1] Aristot. *Poet*. ch. xviii. Cf. *Probl*. xix. 48 where the chorus is spoken of as κηδευτὴς ἄπρακτος· εὔνοιαν γὰρ μόνον παρέχεται οἷς πάρεστιν; cf. *Theatre of D*., pp. 160–3.
[2] See below, pp. 312 ff.
[3] See *Theatre of D*., pp. 161–2, 196, 242–4; and above, pp. 80 ff..
[4] On these see *Dith. Trag. Com*., pp. 292 ff.

words are provided by the poet for such interludes. But that
some plays of the Middle and early New Comedy still included
a chorus is proved by Aristotle's statement[1] that a tragic and
a comic chorus might be composed of the same persons, and a
few comic choreutai are mentioned[2] as members of dramatic
companies down to the time of the early Roman Empire.

2. The number of the tragic chorus appears to have been
twelve in the plays of Aeschylus, and fifteen in those of Sophocles[2]
and Euripides. Some scholars indeed suppose that the Danaid
trilogy (including the *Suppliants*) of Aeschylus had choruses of
fifty; this view partly depends upon the (probably mistaken)
derivation of tragedy from the dithyramb with its fifty singers,[3]
partly on the fact that legend gave Danaus fifty daughters,
partly on a very improbable story narrated by Pollux,[4] that
there were fifty choreutai until the irruption of the fifty *Eumenides*
so scared the Athenian audience that the chorus was henceforth
reduced. Some also suppose that in the *Oresteia* Aeschylus
adopted the change introduced by Sophocles, and employed
fifteen choreutai. (That the number was twelve in the *Persai* and
Septem is not disputed.)[5] That this was so is stated in two scholia,[6]
but these, being doubtless inferences from *Agam.* 1343 ff., carry
no more weight than modern inferences from the same passage.
In this passage the cry of the king is heard at l. 1343.

AΓ. ὤμοι πέπληγμαι καιρίαν πληγὴν ἔσω.

ΧΟ. σῖγα· τίς πληγὴν αὐτεῖ καιρίως οὐτασμένος;

AΓ. ὤμοι μάλ' αὖθις, δευτέραν πεπληγμένος.

ΧΟ. τοὔργον εἰργάσθαι δοκεῖ μοι βασιλέως οἰμώγματι.
ἀλλὰ κοινωσώμεθ' ἤν πως ἀσφαλῆ βουλεύματ' ⟨ῇ⟩.

---

[1] *Politics* III. iii ὥσπερ γε καὶ χορὸν ὅτε μὲν κωμικὸν ὅτε δὲ τραγικὸν ἕτερον εἶναί φαμεν,
τῶν αὐτῶν πολλάκις ἀνθρώπων ὄντων, and *Eth. Nic.* IV. vi κωμῳδοῖς χορηγῶν ἐν τῇ παρόδῳ πορφύραν εἰσφέρων; cf. Aeschines, *in Tim.* § 157 πρῴην ἐν τοῖς κατ' ἀγροὺς Διονυσίοις κωμῳδῶν
ὄντων ἐν Κολλυτῷ καὶ Παρμένοντος τοῦ ὑποκριτοῦ εἰπόντος τι πρὸς τὸν χορὸν ἀνάπαιστον. Cf.
Theatre of D., pp. 163–5. The χοροὶ μεθυόντων who break into some plays of Menander cannot
be regarded as part of the play.

[2] Ibid., pp. 240 ff., and below, pp. 312 ff.

[3] *Vit. Soph.*, and Suid. s.v. Σοφοκλῆς; cf. Pollux iv. 109, and a number of scholia, etc.
(In some of these the number is given as 14, the coryphaeus being excluded.)

[4] For the arguments against this derivation see *Dith. Trag. Com.*, pp. 87–89, *Theatre of D.*,
p. 32. The distinction between the κύκλιος χορός of the dithyramb and the τετράγωνος χορός
of tragedy is strongly against it. The arguments for a chorus of fifty in Aeschylus' earliest
plays are well presented by Lammers, *Die Doppel- und Halb-chöre in der ant. Tragödie*, but seem
to be less strong than the objections. [5] iv. 110.

[5] Vide Muff, *De choro Persarum fabulae Aeschyleae* (1878), pp. 16 ff., and *Der Chor in den
Sieben des Aischylos* (1882), pp. 1, 2.

[6] On Aristophanes' *Knights*, l. 586, and Aesch. *Eumen.*, l. 585.

Then follow twelve iambic couplets each of which is plainly the utterance of a single choreutes. The last of these twelve runs (1370–1):

ταύτην ἐπαινεῖν παντόθεν πληθύνομαι
τρανῶς Ἀτρείδην εἰδέναι κυροῦνθ᾽ ὅπως.

Some scholars suppose that the three trochaic lines 1344, 1346–7, are uttered by three choreutai other than the twelve who deliver the iambic couplets. It seems much more likely that they are spoken by the coryphaeus. In lines 1346–7 he asks for advice from the rest; in the eleven following iambic couplets he gets it, and in the twelfth he sums up. There is certainly no argument here for fifteen choreutai.

That the satyric chorus consisted at the end of the fifth century of twelve persons has been argued with great probability from the Pronomos vase,[1] on which there are eleven choreutai in addition to Silenus, their leader. Whether the reduction by more than half in the number of tragic choreutai in the time of the 'Artists of Dionysus' was accompanied by a similar reduction in the satyric drama there is no evidence to show.

That the chorus of the Old Comedy consisted of twenty-four members is agreed by all authorities,[2] and that towards the end of the third century B.C. performances were given at Delphi by seven choreutai and later still by even fewer is attested by inscriptions. Of numbers in the intervening period nothing is known.

3. In some few plays of Aeschylus and Euripides the employment of a second chorus in at least one scene of the play is beyond doubt. In the final scene of Aeschylus' *Suppliants* the handmaids, of whom each member of the Danaid chorus had one, join in the choral ode. (They had doubtless been present all the time, distinguished from the Danaids by their costume and conveniently grouped in or round the orchestra.) At the end of the *Eumenides* a chorus of Πρόπομποι escorts the Eumenides themselves to their sanctuary.[3] The *Phoinissai* of Phrynichus, performed in 476 B.C.

---

[1] Above, p. 179. The only evidence to the contrary consists of statements in two passages of Tzetzes, whose authority is worthless anyhow, giving the number as 11 (said to be 'the same as in tragedy'), or as 16—both wrong.

[2] e.g. Pollux iv. 109 and a number of scholia, e.g. on Aristoph. *Ach.* 211, *Birds* 297. On the possible earlier history and affinities of the comic chorus see *Dith. Trag. Com.*, ch. iii.

[3] Lammers, op. cit., pp. 40–53, argues also for a second chorus in the second and third plays of the Danaid trilogy, and in Aeschylus' Καβειροί and Ὅπλων Κρίσις and Ἡλιάδες, and the satyric Θεωροὶ ἢ Ἰσθμιασταί and Τρόφοι; but I am not convinced as regards all of these.

—certainly later than the Danaid trilogy of Aeschylus—had a chorus of councillors as well as the main chorus of Phoenician women, though whether the councillors did more than deliver a prologue through the mouth of their leader or take part in an introductory scene there is no evidence to show.[1] There is no certain instance of a second chorus in Sophocles,[2] but in the *Suppliants* of Euripides, the handmaids may have formed a separate group; the situation, however, is full of difficulties which have not been wholly solved. In the lost *Phaethon* there is no doubt that there were two choruses—one of maidservants attendant upon Klymene, the other the wedding choir which enters with Merops at a later point in the play;[3] and in the *Alexandros*[4] there was a chorus of shepherds accompanying Paris, as well as the main chorus of Trojans—whether male or female is uncertain. The shepherds when they appear (in the middle of the play) seem to have been on the scene at the same time as the Trojan chorus, and so contrast with the supplementary chorus of huntsmen which accompanies the hero in the *Hippolytus* but disappears before the parodos. In the *Antiope*, besides the chorus of Attic shepherds,[5] there was an additional chorus of Maenads who entered (and departed) with Dirke. In this play also both choruses were on the scene at once. ·

4. Of the costumes worn by the chorus in tragedy, comedy, and satyric play some account has already been given. For the early period of tragedy the texts are almost the only evidence,[6] and they afford no reason to distrust, and sometimes confirm, the natural assumption that the chorus was dressed according to the character which it assumed in the play. We have considered also the slight information furnished by the Boston pelike[7] and by a krater in Taranto[8]—the former suggesting that the

[1] Argt. to Aeschylus, *Persai* . . . πλὴν ἐκεῖ (i.e. in the *Phoinissai*) εὐνοῦχός ἐστιν ἀγγέλλων ἐν ἀρχῇ τὴν Ξέρξου ἧτταν στορνύς τε θρόνους τινας τοῖς τῆς ἀρχῆς παρέδροις, ἐνταῦθα δὲ προλογίζει χορὸς πρεσβυτῶν. (The πάρεδροι and the πρεσβυταί were presumably the same.) See Lammers, op. cit., pp. 55–63, for a full discussion.

[2] Lammers, op. cit., p. 82, thinks there may have been one in the *Thamyras*, an early work of the poet, but the argument is not convincing.

[3] See *New Chapt. in Gk. Lit.* iii, pp. 143 ff., and Lammers, op. cit., pp. 122–5.

[4] On this play see B. Snell's edition of the fragments (*Hermes*, Einzelschriften v (1937), as well as Lammers, op. cit., pp. 107–9.

[5] This is not the place to discuss whether they were Attic or Theban. See *New Chapters*, iii, p. 107; Lammers, op. cit., pp. 109 ff.

[6] See above, p. 223.

[7] See pp. 182, 216, Fig. 39.

[8] See pp. 183, 217, 218, Fig. 40.

choreutai wore undecorated robes, the latter that they might, if desired, be decorative—that of the leader of the chorus more so than the rest. But of the costume of the chorus after the beginning of the fourth century we know really nothing. From the time when (as in Aristotle's day) they sang mainly ἐμβόλιμα —interludes which had nothing to do with the play—they may not have been dressed 'in character' at all.

It is not doubted that the choruses of satyr-plays were distinguished by the loin-cloth of goatskin (more rarely linen drawers) with the phallos and the horse's tail appended. As the satyrs appear on vases they are otherwise naked;[1] in the theatre they may have worn close-fitting flesh-coloured skins.[2] When, however, as was frequently the case, they appeared as hunters, reapers, shepherds, or what-not, they doubtless wore some appropriate additions to the purely satyric dress.[3] In the mosaic representing the rehearsal of a satyr play in the Hellenistic period,[4] the costume is no longer indecent. (Nor was it so at this period in comedy.) Silenus, who was leader of the chorus, always wore, with slight modifications, a tunic resembling a fleece (μαλλωτὸς or χορταῖος χιτών). As regards comedy, reference has already been made to the choruses partially disguised as animals, birds, or fishes, which figured frequently in the Old Comedy,[5] and to the freedom of the poets to clothe their dancers in any guise which suited the play, and this freedom doubtless persisted to later periods, though in the Middle and New Comedy the old grotesqueness was soon abandoned, and in so far as choruses appeared they appeared as ordinary human beings. In more than one play the purpose was served by a band of intoxicated young men or revellers.[6] Neither in tragedy nor in comedy was the chorus ever a mixed crowd, such as Shakespeare was apt to introduce; but in comedy there might be, as in the *Lysistrata*, a division into male and female semichoruses, and in the *Birds* the birds composing the chorus were not only

---

[1] See pp. 179 f. None of the vases known to me reproduces an actual scene from a satyric play.

[2] Cf. Horace, *Ars P.* 221 'mox etiam agrestes satyros *nudavit*'; but this does not necessarily exclude the close-fitting garment of skin. On the whole subject see *Dith. Trag. Com.*, pp. 151–9.

[3] The shepherd-slaves of Polyphemus in Eur. *Cyclops* probably wore a goatskin cloak; cf. l. 80 σὺν τῇδε τράγου χλαίνᾳ μελέᾳ.

[4] See pp. 165, 188, Fig. 69.

[5] See p. 234 and *Dith. Trag. Com.*, pp. 244 ff.

[6] See pp. 88, 241.

of many species, but consisted of roughly equal numbers[1] of cock- and hen-birds, though the division has not the same significance in this play as in the *Lysistrata*.

5. The characteristic which distinguished the dramatic choruses, of all three kinds, from the κύκλιος χορός of the dithyramb was that their formation was rectangular. The positive statements to this effect[2] are indeed late, but they are unanimous, and the rectangular formation is presupposed in many references to the position of particular choreutai. It is not, of course, implied that in particular circumstances, at least in comedy, the chorus might not break into a round dance, as it does in Aristophanes' *Thesmophoriazousai*, where they join hands in such a fling—ll. 953 ff.:

> ὅρμα χώρει·
> κοῦφα ποσὶν ἄγ᾽ ἐς κύκλον,
> χειρὶ σύναπτε χεῖρα,
> ῥυθμὸν χορείας ὕπαγε πᾶσα·
> βαῖνε καρπαλίμοιν ποδοῖν.
> ἐπίσκοπεῖν δὲ πανταχῇ
> κυκλοῦσαν ὄμμα χρὴ χοροῦ κατάστασιν.

and again in ll. 966 ff.:

> ἀλλὰ χρῆν
> ὥσπερ ἔργον αὖ τι καινὸν
> πρῶτον εὐκύκλου χορείας εὐφυᾶ στῆσαι βάσιν.

Whether this ever occurred in tragedy seems less certain,[3] but it may have happened at times, and the invention of new dances was doubtless not confined to Phrynichus and Aeschylus. The

---

[1] Schol. Aristoph. *Knights* 589 συνειστήκει δὲ ὁ χορὸς ὁ μὲν κωμικὸς ἐξ ἀνδρῶν ἤδη καὶ γυναικῶν ὁμοῦ δὲ καὶ παίδων κδ΄, ὡς καὶ οὗτος ἀπηρίθμησεν ἐν Ὄρνισιν ἄρρενας μὲν ὄρνεις ιβ΄, θηλείας δὲ τοσαύτας. The same scholiast, however, goes on to say that when there was a division into men and women, or adults and children, the men, or the adults, were in a majority of 13 to 11.

[2] Tzetzes, *Prol. ad Lycophr.*, p. 254 (M.) τραγικῶν δὲ καὶ σατυρικῶν καὶ κωμικῶν ποιητῶν κοινὸν μὲν τὸ τετραγώνως ἔχειν ἱστάμενον τὸν χορόν; Bekker, *Anecd.*, p. 746. 27 οἱ γὰρ χορευταὶ αὐτῶν ἐν τετραγώνῳ σχήματι ἱστάμενοι τὰ τῶν τραγικῶν ἐπεδείκνυντο; *Etym. Magn.* τραγῳδία· τετράγωνον εἶχον οἱ χορευταὶ σχῆμα. Pollux iv. 108 implies the same thing (see below).

[3] S. Ferri in *Dioniso*, iii, pp. 336 ff., attempts to prove that a number of choral odes in extant plays were danced in circular formation, but in none of these does the text give any evidence of this, and his argument is really based on the assumption that any magical or invocational dance must have been circular. In the few passages quoted by him in which a cyclic dance is referred to, it is *not* the dance in which the chorus itself is engaged (e.g. Eur. *Herc. F.* 687–93, *Iph. T.* 1089 ff., *Iph. Aul.* 1475 ff. In the last the reading at the crucial point is uncertain). He also seems to assume that *any* invocation of Apollo in particular must have been associated with a cyclic dance, but this cannot be substantiated.

rectangular formation consisted in tragedy of three files (ζυγά) and five ranks (στοῖχοι),[1] in comedy of four files and six ranks, and its movements, in tragedy, when marching and not dancing, might be κατὰ ζυγά (with a front of three members) or κατὰ στοίχους (with a front of five). The military character of its movements has already been referred to.[2] Although in particular the entry (πάροδος) of the chorus might be in single file or in some less orderly manner (particularly in comedy, but also in the *Eumenides*), and in some might be κατὰ στοίχους (though there is no certain extant instance of this), it is probable that the normal entry, when it was made in regular formation was κατὰ ζυγά. In the rare instances in which the chorus left the scene for a time (μετάστασις),[3] the manner of its re-entry (ἐπιπάροδος) evidently varied. In the *Eumenides* 243 ff. the text does not suggest a formal march—the chorus plainly enter σποράδην; in Sophocles' *Ajax* 866 ff. the two semi-choruses, as the scholiast states, come in from opposite directions; in Euripides' *Alkestis* 872 ff. they are following Admetus in a mourning procession— possibly κατὰ ζυγά, but the utterances are perhaps (as in the *Eumenides*) those of individual choreutai; at l. 515 of the *Helena* they re-enter with a short lyric ode, which was sung as they came out of the house, but they can hardly have marched out of the door in formation. (In the *Ekklesiazousai* of Aristophanes, after a μετάστασις at l. 310, the chorus returns at l. 478, and after a very brief march breaks into strophe and antistrophe.)

---

[1] Pollux iv. 108–9 μέρη δὲ χοροῦ στοῖχος καὶ ζυγόν. καὶ τραγικοῦ μὲν χοροῦ ζυγὰ πέντε ἐκ τριῶν καὶ στοῖχοι τρεῖς ἐκ πέντε· πεντεκαίδεκα γὰρ ἦσαν ὁ χορός. καὶ κατὰ τρεῖς μὲν εἰσῄεσαν, εἰ κατὰ ζυγὰ γίγνοιτο ἡ πάροδος, εἰ δὲ κατὰ στοίχους, ἀνὰ πέντε εἰσῄεσαν. ἔσθ' ὅτε δὲ καὶ καθ' ἕνα (in single file) ἐποιοῦντο τὴν πάροδον. ὁ δὲ κωμικὸς χορὸς τέτταρες καὶ εἴκοσιν ἦσαν οἱ χορευταί, ζυγὰ ἕξ, ἕκαστον δὲ ζυγὸν ἐκ τεττάρων, στοῖχοι δὲ τέτταρες, ἐξ ἄνδρας ἔχων ἕκαστος στοῖχος.

[2] pp. 156 ff.

[3] Pollux iv. 108 καὶ ἡ μὲν εἴσοδος τοῦ χοροῦ πάροδος καλεῖται, ἡ δὲ κατὰ χρείαν ἔξοδος ὡς πάλιν εἰσιόντων μετάστασις, ἡ δὲ μετὰ ταύτην εἴσοδος ἐπιπάροδος, ἡ δὲ τελευταῖα ἔξοδος ἄφοδος. The term πάροδος is also used of the opening chant of the chorus (e.g. Aristot. *Poet.* xii where it is ἡ πρώτη λέξις ὅλη χοροῦ, if the almost necessary emendation of ὅλου to ὅλη is accepted), and of the passages which gave entry to the theatre. ἐπιπάροδος is also used in Cramer, *Anecd. Paris.* i. 20, and by Tzetzes, who cites Eukleides as his authority, of the entry of a second chorus when the original one has left the scene (ἐπιπάροδος δὲ ἔστιν, ὅταν ἕτερος χορὸς ἀφ- ικνεῖται τοῦ προτέρου παρελθόντος). The word seems not to occur elsewhere, and there is no extant example of an ἐπιπάροδος in the second sense, unless the entry of the main chorus of the *Hippolytus* at l. 121 is treated as such, the brief appearance of the χορὸς κυναγῶν (ll. 61 ff.) being regarded as the πάροδος; cf. de Falco, *L'Epiparodo nella Tragedia Greca*, p. 11. (Eukleides seems to have been a grammarian known to Tzetzes, but nothing more is known of him.) Reference should be made to the careful analysis of the forms of parodos by Kranz in Pauly- W. *Real-Encycl.* s.v. 'Parodos'.

The following diagram will illustrate the normal arrangement of the tragic chorus:

στ. 5	στ. 4	στ. 3	στ. 2	στ. 1	
(5)	(4)	(3)	(2)	(1)	ζυγὸν πρῶτον
(10)	(9)	(8)	(7)	(6)	ζυγὸν δεύτερον
(15)	(14)	(13)	(12)	(11)	ζυγὸν τριτόν

When, as appears to have been usual in Athens, the chorus entered by the western passage, with the auditorium on its left,[1] the left-hand file (the ἀριστεροστάται), which was nearest to the spectators, was composed of the best choreutai, the middle file (the λαυροστάται 'men in the alley' or δευτεροστάται) of the least efficient, and the third file (τριτοστάται or ἔσχατοι or δεξιοστάται) might be of intermediate quality. (They would confront the audience directly in those manœuvres in which the first file faced the skene instead of the audience.) The men numbered 1, 6, 11, 5, 10, 15 were sometimes spoken of as κρασπεδῖται, 'men on the fringe', or ψιλεῖς 'unprotected' (though this may only refer to Nos. 5, 10, 15).[2] The leader of the chorus (the κορυφαῖος) was No. 3, τριτὸς ἀριστεροῦ or πρωτοστάτης; Nos. 2 and 4, on each side of him, were his παραστάται and next to him in importance.[3] A passage of Menander's Ἐπίκληρος[4] suggests that the complement of choreutai may have been made up of mutes placed in the rank farthest from the audience:

ὥσπερ τῶν χορῶν
οὐ πάντες ᾄδουσ', ἀλλ' ἄφωνοι δύο τινες

[1] Schol. Aristid. iii, p. 535 (Dind.) ὅτε εἰσῇεσαν οἱ χοροὶ πλαγίως βαδίζοντες ἐποιοῦντο τοὺς ὕμνους καὶ εἶχον τοὺς θεατὰς ἐν ἀριστερᾷ αὐτῶν καὶ οἱ πρῶτοι τοῦ χοροῦ ἀριστερὸν στοῖχον, and p. 536 τοὺς οὖν καλοὺς τῶν χορευτῶν ἔταττον εἰσιόντες ἐν τοῖς ἑαυτῶν ἀριστέροις, ἵνα εὑρεθῶσι πρὸς τὸν δῆμον ὁρῶντες. Pollux ii. 161 τάχα δὲ καὶ ὁ ἀριστεροστάτης ἐν χορῷ προσήκοι ἂν τῇ ἀριστερᾷ, ὡς ὁ δεξιοστάτης τῇ δεξιᾷ, and iv. 106 δεξιοστάτης, ἀριστεροστάτης, δευτεροστάτης, τριτοστάτης. Hesych. s.v. ἀριστεροστάτης· ὁ πρωτοστάτης τοῦ χοροῦ; and s.v. λαυροστάται· οἱ ἐν τοῖς μέσοις ξυγοῖς ὄντες ἔν τισι στενωποῖς μὴ θεωρούμενοι· οἱ δὲ χείρους μέσοι ἵστανται· οἱ δὲ ἐπιτεταγμένοι (i.e. those who have to fulfil the allotted task of the chorus) πρῶτοι καὶ ἔσχατοι (i.e. third); and s.v. ὑποκόλπιον τοῦ χοροῦ· τῆς στάσεως χῶραι αἱ ἄτιμοι.

[2] Plut. *Symp. Q.*, p. 678 d ὥσπερ χοροῦ τοῦ συμποσίου τὸν κρασπεδίτην τῷ κορυφαίῳ συνήκοον ἔχοντες; Hesych. s.v. ψιλεῖς· οἱ ὕστατοι χορεύοντες; Suid. s.v. ψιλεύς· ἐπ' ἀκροῦ χοροῦ ἱστάμενος.

[3] Photius, s.v. τριτὸς ἀριστεροῦ· ἐν τοῖς τραγικοῖς χοροῖς τριῶν ὄντων στοίχων καὶ πέντε ζυγῶν, ὁ μὲν ἀρίστερος πρὸς τῷ θεάτρῳ ἦν, ὁ δὲ δέξιος πρὸς τῷ προσκηνίῳ. συνέβαινεν οὖν τὸν μέσον τοῦ ἀριστεροῦ τὴν ἐντιμοτάτην καὶ οἵαν τοῦ πρωτοστάτου χώραν ἐπέχειν καὶ στάσιν; cf. Aristot. *Met.* IV. xi ταῦτα δ' ἐστιν ὅσα πρὸς τὸ ὡρισμένον διέστηκε κατὰ τὸν λόγον, οἷον παραστάτης τριτοστάτου πρότερον καὶ παρανήτη νήτης· ἔνθα μὲν γὰρ ὁ κορυφαῖος, ἔνθα δὲ μέση ἀρχή, and Pol. III. iv ἀναγκὴ μὴ μίαν εἶναι τὴν τῶν πολιτῶν ἀρετήν, ὥσπερ οὐδὲ τῶν χορευτῶν κορυφαίου καὶ παραστάτου. The terms χορηγός, ἡγέμων, χοροστάτης, χορολέκτης, and others are found applied to the κορυφαῖος in a few passages. (See Müller, *Bühnenalt.*, p. 207.)

[4] Fr. 165 (K.).

ἢ τρεῖς παρεστήκασι πάντων ἔσχατοι
εἰς τὸν ἀριθμόν, καὶ τοῦθ᾽ ὅμοιόν πως ἔχει
χώραν κατέχουσι, ζῶσι δ᾽ οἷς ἔστιν βίος.

Hesychius seems to say that the mutes were in the central rank; but it cannot be taken as certain that Menander is speaking of dramatic and not of dithyrambic choruses. (Fifty good voices would be less easy to find than fifteen.)

In its entry and its departure from the scene the chorus, at least in tragedy, was normally preceded by the flute-player,[1] who, if the Pronomos vase is good evidence, might be richly dressed, but only exceptionally wore a mask.[2]

But the modes of entry displayed by the choruses even of extant plays are too varied to be comprised within the simple formula of a march κατὰ ζυγά. This phrase primarily describes the marching entry found in several early plays in which the first lyric strophe and antistrophe are preceded by about 40 to 65 anapaestic dimeters, probably delivered in recitative by the whole chorus[3]—the *Suppliants*, *Persai*, and *Agamemnon*, and the *Ajax* of Sophocles. In the *Alcestis* of Euripides also, and in the *Rhesus*, there is a brief anapaestic opening, and there is a variant of this form in Sophocles' *Electra*, where Elektra utters 35 anapaestic dimeters while the chorus are coming in. In the *Hecuba*, ll. 98–153, the chorus delivers 56 anapaestic dimeters, and there is no lyric entrance-song, properly speaking. (There is no ode in strophe and antistrophe until l. 444.) The long anapaestic openings of the early plays suggest a march of the chorus round the orchestra before taking up its position (στάσις).[4] In a number of plays in which there is no anapaestic opening, such as the *Antigone*, *Oedipus Tyrannus*,[5] *Trachiniai*, *Philoctetes*, and the *Hippolytus*,[6] *Andromache*, *Hercules Furens*, *Ion*, *Electra* (of Euripides), and *Iphigeneia in Aulis*, the chorus may have begun to sing the anti-

[1] Schol. on Aristoph. *Wasps* 582 ἔθος δὲ ἦν ἐν τοῖς ἐξόδοις τῆς τραγῳδίας χορικῶν προσώπων προηγεῖσθαι αὐλητήν, ὥστε αὐλοῦντα προπέμπειν. When two semi-choruses entered separately, as in the *Lysistrata*, we do not know what the flute-player did, if there was one; nor is it known what happened as regards the flute-player when a second chorus entered (see above, p. 242).

[2] See above, pp. 89, 218.

[3] See above, pp. 157 ff. Some scholars suppose that they were recited by the coryphaeus alone. This, to judge from some modern performances, would have been much less impressive.

[4] Hesychius says that lines were marked in the orchestra to help them to form a straight front: s.v. γραμμαί· ἐν τῇ ὀρχήστρᾳ ἦσαν, ὡς τὸν χορὸν ἐν στοίχῳ ἵστασθαι.

[5] In the *O.T.* they may have been present from the first as part of the group of the citizens addressed by Oedipus in l. 1; but ll. 151 ff. have the look of an entrance-song.

[6] Disregarding the χορὸς κυνηγῶν which occupies part of the prologue.

strophic parodos while entering, or (perhaps more probably)
may have marched in quietly κατὰ ζυγά, preceded by the flute-
player, and faced the audience to sing. In one or two plays the
chorus were either present from the first, as in the *Suppliants* of
Euripides,[1] or entered with the principal character, as in the
Bacchae. In the *Choephoroi* they enter silently, while Orestes is
speaking the prologue. In the *Helena* the strophe and antistrophe
in the normal place of the parodos are sung in turn by Helen
and the chorus. In the *Orestes* the chorus creep in, almost
whispering, for fear of disturbing the sick hero, and join in a
lyric dialogue with Elektra. In two extant plays, the *Eumenides*[2]
and the *Oedipus Coloneus*, the chorus hurried in σποράδην, one by
one: they are in pursuit. The *Herakleidai*, *Troades*, and *Iphigeneia
in Tauris* have each peculiarities of form, and (much earlier) the
entry of the Ocean-nymphs in the *Prometheus Vinctus* was evidently unique.[3]

Of the movements or attitude of the chorus during the main
part of the play there is little or no direct information. When
the leader engaged in dialogue with the actors, he must have
faced them, as did probably the whole chorus, and in the absence
of the actors, when not dancing, they must have faced the
audience; but by what manœuvres they changed their direction
is unknown. At moments of crisis they doubtless reacted as the
crisis demanded.[4]

6. There is also little direct information as to the movements
of the chorus in comedy, except in so far as the texts testify to
a great variety and freedom in the mode of entry, to great liveliness during the play, and to a marching departure, headed by
the flute-player and varied at times (as in the *Wasps* and *Ekklesiazousai*) by a vigorous dancing exit. It has been supposed
that in the parabasis of the Old Comedy the two semi-choruses
stood facing one another, but the evidence for this is only a confused note of Hephaestion.[5] It seems more likely that during the

---

[1] They must have entered unobtrusively before the play began.
[2] There is a different mode of entry in each of the three plays of the *Oresteia*. It is not worth
while to pursue the purely academic question, which is the 'real parodos' of the *Eumenides*.
[3] See *Theatre of D.*, pp. 39 ff.
[4] For their behaviour during choral odes see below, pp. 256 f.
[5] Hephaest. 14, p. 131 C. ἔστι δέ τις ἐν ταῖς κωμῳδίαις καὶ ἡ καλουμένη παράβασις, ἐπειδὰν
εἰσελθόντες εἰς τὸ θέατρον καὶ ἀντιπρόσωπον ἀλλήλοις στάντες οἱ χορευταὶ παρέβαινον. But the
words εἰσελθόντες εἰς τὸ θέατρον do not really apply to the παράβασις. In Aristoph. *Ach.* 629,
Knights 508, *Peace* 735 παραβαίνειν πρὸς τὸ θέατρον is plainly used of the chorus coming forward

delivery of the epirrhematic parts of the parabasis each semi-chorus at least should have faced the audience in turn, whether the whole chorus did so at once or not. That some part of the parabasis was accompanied by lively dancing—perhaps by the semi-chorus whose leader was not addressing the audience—is suggested by their partially discarding their dramatic costume and performing ἀποδύντες, unencumbered by dress.[1]

7. Something has already been said in regard to the manner of delivery of the choral parts of the drama.[2] Where the chorus takes part in the dialogue, speaking normally in iambic trimeters or more rarely in trochaic tetrameters, the leader doubtless spoke for the whole, as he (or the leaders of the two semi-choruses in turn) almost certainly did (in recitative) in the parabasis of the Old Comedy, and at particular moments (especially in comedy) the leader might address his fellow choreutai.[3] In tragedy the parodos and stasima (the choral odes in the body of the play, after the chorus had reached its στάσις or normal position)[4] were as a rule sung by the whole chorus in unison, and there is no evidence for the regular delivery of strophe and antistrophe by separate semi-choruses; but there were exceptional scenes in which a division into semi-choruses was made,[5] as for a brief space in the *Ajax*, when they are searching for the hero, in the parodos of the *Alcestis*, and, in comedy, throughout the *Lysistrata* and probably the ode and antode of the parabasis generally;[6] and also scenes in which the lyric utterances of individual choreutai take the place of united song —as, for instance, the opening scene of the *Eumenides* and the parodos of the *Ion*.[7] It is fashionable with scholars at the present

to face the spectators for the delivery of the 'anapaests'—the long formal address. See *Dith. Trag. Com.*, p. 242.

[1] See ibid., p. 235. On the delivery of the parabasis in song and recitative see above, p. 162.   [2] pp. 156 ff.

[3] e.g. Aristoph. *Wasps* 1516, *Thesm.* 655, *Frogs* 382, etc.   [4] See below, p. 256.

[5] Cf. Pollux iv. 107 καὶ ἡμιχόριον δὲ καὶ διχορία καὶ ἀντιχόρια· ἔοικε δὲ ταὐτὸν εἶναι ταῦτα τὰ τρία ὀνόματα· ὁπόταν γὰρ ὁ χορὸς εἰς δύο μέρη τμηθῇ, τὸ μὲν πρᾶγμα καλεῖται διχορία, ἑκατέρα δὲ ἡ μοῖρα ἡμιχόριον, ἃ δ' ἀντᾴδουσιν, ἀντιχόρια. The division in the final extant scene of the *Seven against Thebes*, of which the date and authorship are unknown, is a striking instance, the two halves of the chorus siding with Antigone and Ismene respectively.

[6] The evidence is that of the Ravenna and Venetian MSS. as regards several of the plays; see Arnoldt, *Die Chorpartieen bei Aristophanes*, pp. 180 ff.

[7] Cf. schol. on Aesch. *Sept.* 97 ταῦτα δέ τινες τῶν τοῦ χοροῦ γυναικῶν πρὸς τὰς ἑτέρας φασίν. But the schol. on Aristoph. *Frogs* 375 shows that there was no unanimity among the old commentators on such suggestions: ἐντεῦθεν Ἀρίσταρχος ὑπενόησε μὴ ὅλου τοῦ χοροῦ εἶναι τὰ πρῶτα· τοῦτο δὲ οὐκ ἀξιόπιστον· πολλάκις γὰρ ἀλλήλοις οὕτω παρακελεύονται οἱ περὶ τὸν χορόν.

time to multiply instances of this by splitting up choral systems into individual ejaculations, but this may easily be overdone, and the process is anyhow guided mainly by the scholar's personal fancy. In the κομμός, in which chorus and actors join in a lamentation or other lyric dialogue, the poet was doubtless free to employ individual or combined utterance as he chose, and the form varied greatly.[1] There is some reason for thinking that a division into semi-choruses may have been more frequent in satyric drama than in tragedy, but the *Cyclops* and the *Ichneutai* hardly afford a sufficient basis for a general statement. In both plays there are also passages of non-antistrophic choral lyrics, satyric drama being in this as in other respects less formal than tragedy. It may be added that the modern literature on the subject of the methods of delivery in Greek drama is as immense as the evidence is slight and inconclusive.

B. DANCING IN DRAMA

1. The place of dancing in Greek culture and its various manifestations was much more important than it is in modern life.[2] Plato regards dancing as a form, regulated and rendered orderly, of the instinctive delight in active motion[3] which characterizes all human beings, and lays great stress on the importance of developing it in conformity with the moral and artistic sense of educated men (*Laws* ii. 654 b):

ΑΘ. ὁ καλῶς ἄρα πεπαιδευμένος ᾄδειν τε καὶ ὀρχεῖσθαι δυνατὸς ἂν εἴη καλῶς. ΚΛ. ἔοικεν. ΑΘ. ἴδωμεν δὴ τί ποτ' ἐστὶ τὸ νῦν αὖ λεγόμενον. ΚΛ. τὸ ποῖον δή; ΑΘ. 'καλῶς ᾄδει', φαμέν, 'καὶ καλῶς ὀρχεῖται' πότερον 'εἰ καὶ καλὰ ᾄδει καὶ καλὰ ὀρχεῖται' προσθῶμεν ἢ μή; ΚΛ. προσθῶμεν.

and later (vii. 798 d):

ΑΘ. τί οὖν; τοῖς ἔμπροσθεν λόγοις πιστεύομεν, οἷς ἐλέγομεν ὡς τὰ περὶ τοὺς ῥυθμοὺς καὶ πᾶσαν μουσικήν ἐστιν τρόπων μιμήματα βελτιόνων καὶ χειρόνων ἀνθρώπων; ἢ πῶς; ΚΛ. οὐδαμῶς ἄλλως κτλ.

The Greeks tended to regard all dancing as 'mimetic', or expressive, especially in its employment of rhythmical gestures

---

[1] See Haigh, *Tragic Drama of the Greeks*, pp. 359–61.

[2] A brief summary of the ways in which dancing entered into every phase of Greek life is conveniently given by A. Brinkmann, 'Altgr. Mädchenreigen' (in *Bonner Jahrb.* cxxx (1925), pp. 118–21).

[3] He connects χορός with χαρά (*Laws* ii. 654 a). Lucian, *de Salt.* 25, records a tradition that Socrates οὐ μόνον ἐπήνει τὴν ὀρχηστικήν, ἀλλὰ καὶ ἐκμαθεῖν αὐτὴν ἠξίου μέγιστον ἀπονέμων εὐρυθμίᾳ καὶ εὐμουσίᾳ καὶ κινήσει ἐμμελεῖ καὶ εὐσχημοσύνῃ τοῦ κινουμένου. In spite of which Libanius in the fourth century A.D. still found it necessary (ὑπὲρ τῶν ὀρχηστῶν) to defend the practice of dancing against the censure of the Fathers of the Church.

and motions. So Aristotle[1] can say of dancers that διὰ τῶν σχηματιζομένων ῥυθμῶν (the rhythms embodied in gesture) μιμοῦνται καὶ ἤθη καὶ πάθη καὶ πράξεις. Athenaeus[2] quotes Damon, the friend and musical adviser of Plato, as stressing the moral implications of dancing:

οὐ κακῶς δ᾽ ἔλεγον οἱ περὶ Δάμωνα τὸν Ἀθηναῖον ὅτι καὶ τὰς ᾠδὰς καὶ τὰς ὀρχήσεις ἀνάγκη γίγνεσθαι κινουμένης πως τῆς ψυχῆς· καὶ αἱ μὲν ἐλεύθεριοι καὶ καλαὶ ποιοῦσι τοιαύτας, αἱ δ᾽ ἐναντίαι τὰς ἐναντίας.

He illustrates this by the story of Hippokleides, who 'danced away his wedding' with the daughter of Kleisthenes of Sikyon by a clever but vulgar performance,[3] and continues:[4]

καὶ γὰρ ἐν ὀρχήσει καὶ πορείᾳ καλὸν μὲν εὐσχημοσύνη καὶ κόσμος, αἰσχρὸν δὲ ἀταξία καὶ τὸ φορτικόν. διὰ τοῦτο γὰρ καὶ ἐξ ἀρχῆς συνέταττον οἱ ποιηταὶ τοῖς ἐλευθέροις τὰς ὀρχήσεις καὶ ἐχρῶντο τοῖς σχήμασι σημείοις μόνον τῶν ᾀδομένων, τηροῦντες ἀεὶ τὸ εὐγενὲς καὶ ἀνδρῶδες ἐπ᾽ αὐτῶν, ὅθεν καὶ ὑπορχήματα τὰ τοιαῦτα προσηγόρευον.[5] εἰ δέ τις ἀμέτρως διαθείη τὴν σχηματοποιίαν καὶ ταῖς ᾠδαῖς ἐπιτυγχάνων μηδὲν λέγοι κατὰ τὴν ὄρχησιν (i.e. allowed his dancing to become independent of the words), οὗτος δ᾽ ἦν ἀδόκιμος.

Nor, he continues, ought the words to be left without the assistance of appropriate dancing.

διὸ καὶ Ἀριστοφάνης ἢ Πλάτων[6] ἐν ταῖς Σκευαῖς, ὡς Χαμαιλέων φησίν, εἴρηκεν οὕτως

> ὥστ᾽ εἴ τις ὀρχοῖτ᾽ εὖ, θέαμ᾽ ἦν· νῦν δὲ δρῶσιν οὐδέν,
> ἀλλ᾽ ὥσπερ ἀπόπληκτοι στάδην ἑστῶτες ὠρύονται.

He goes on to compare choral dancing with military drill, in a passage which has already been quoted,[7] and speaks, very interestingly, of the connexion between dancing (in the wide sense, including manual gestures) and the work of the ancient sculptors:

ἐστὶ δὲ καὶ τὰ τῶν ἀρχαίων δημιουργῶν ἀγάλματα τῆς παλαιᾶς ὀρχήσεως λείψανα· διὸ καὶ ξυνέστη τὰ κατὰ τὴν χειρονομίαν ἐπιμελεστέρως διὰ ταύτην τὴν αἰτίαν. ἐζήτουν γὰρ κἂν ταύτῃ κινήσεις καλὰς καὶ ἐλευθερίους. . . . καὶ τὰ σχήματα μετέφερον ἐντεῦθεν εἰς τοὺς χορούς, ἐκ δὲ τῶν χορῶν εἰς τὰς παλαίστρας.

---

[1] *Poet.* i.
[3] Herod. vi. 129.
[5] ὑπ-όρχημα being essentially a dance which accompanied or was secondary to something else—here, to the temperament expressed. See below, p. 260.
[6] It was Plato (the comic poet), fr. 636 (K.).

[2] xiv. 628 c.
[4] xiv. 628 d, e.
[7] Above, p. 246.

In pursuance of his general doctrine, as quoted above, Plato,[1] having distinguished warlike and peaceful dancing, describes the latter as τὴν ἐν εὐπραγίαις τε οὔσης ψυχῆς σώφρονος ἐν ἡδοναῖς τε ἐμμέτροις· εἰρηνικὴν ἄν τις λέγων κατὰ φύσιν τὴν τοιαύτην ὄρχησιν λέγοι, and he banishes[2] from his Ideal State all orgiastic, drunken, and indecent dancing: ὅση μὲν βακχεία τ᾽ ἐστὶν καὶ τῶν ταύταις ἑπομένων, ἃς Νύμφας τε καὶ Πᾶνας καὶ Σειληνοὺς καὶ Σατύρους ἐπονομάζοντες, ὥς φασιν, μιμοῦνται κατῳνωμένους, περὶ καθαρμούς τε καὶ τελετάς τινας ἀποτελούντων, σύμπαν τοῦτο τῆς ὀρχήσεως τὸ γένος οὔθ᾽ ὡς εἰρηνικὸν οὔθ᾽ ὡς πολεμικὸν οὔθ᾽ ὅτι ποτὲ βούλεται ῥᾴδιον ἀφορίσασθαι; such dancing was certainly not πολιτικόν, fit for citizens. Nor were the music and dances that are characteristic of comedy; at most they must be allowed to remain so as to illustrate the higher type by contrast, and must be left to slaves and hireling foreigners.[3]

2. Two characteristics of ancient Greek dancing have already been mentioned in passing—the use made of the hands (χειρονομία), and the predominantly expressive or mimetic character of the performance. The former, possibly with other gestures but without necessarily any motion of the body from place to place, was enough to constitute ὄρχησις in the Greek sense, the word covering any series of rhythmical movements. Such manual gesticulation seems certainly to have been more elaborately developed when pantomimic dancing, apart from drama, became the most popular form of entertainment, so that Demetrius the Cynic after watching Nero 'dance' the story of Ares and Aphrodite, without words or music, cried: ἀκούω, ἄνθρωπε, ἃ ποιεῖς, οὐχ ὁρῶ μόνον, ἀλλά μοι δοκεῖς ταῖς χερσὶν αὐταῖς λαλεῖν,[4] and Lesbonax of Mytilene (in the Augustan age) called dancers by the name χειρίσοφοι.[5]

---

[1] *Laws* vii. 814 e.   [2] Ibid. 815 c.

[3] Ibid. 816 d, e. Cf. *Rep.* iii. 396 a γνωστέον μὲν γὰρ καὶ μαινομένους καὶ πονηροὺς ἄνδρας τε καὶ γυναῖκας, ποιητέον δὲ οὐδὲν τούτων οὐδὲ μιμητέον.   [4] Lucian, *de Salt.* 63.

[5] Ibid. 69. It must be remembered that when Lucian writes about dancing he has in mind primarily the pantomimic dancing of his own day, not the drama. At this time every kind of *tour de force* was open to a dancer who chose to employ it. He might imitate (ibid. 19) ὕδατος ὑγρότητα καὶ πυρὸς ὀξύτητα καὶ δένδρου δόνημα. Athenaeus xiv, p. 629 f records a dance entitled κόσμου ἐκπύρωσις as mentioned by the Cynic Menippus of Gadara, who perhaps invented it to travesty Stoic doctrines of the fiery consummation of all things, just as (according to the conjecture of Latte, *de Saltationibus Graecorum*) another 'comic dance' mentioned by Athenaeus and called χρεῶν ἀποκοπή may have travestied the agitators who demanded *novae tabulae*. (For the proposed emendation κρεῶν ἀποκλοπή cf. Pollux iv. 104 and *Dith. Trag. Com.*, p. 230.) Athenaeus' list includes also ἀλφίτων σύγχυσις, θερμαυστρίς (a μανιώδης ὄρχησις), and ἀπόκινος or μακτρισμός (cf. Aristoph. *Knights* 20 ἀλλ᾽ εὑρέ τιν᾽ ἀπόκινον

Plutarch[1] speaks of a well-known dancer as χειρονομῶν ἐν ταῖς παλαίστραις. But it is not to be doubted that in the drama itself from the first the use of the hands was one of the most effective methods of expression. Athenaeus[2] says that Τέλεσις ἢ Τελέστης ὁ ὀρχηστοδιδάσκαλος πολλὰ ἐξεύρηκε σχήματα, ἄκρως ταῖς χερσὶ τὰ λεγόμενα δεικνύς,[3] and the texts of the great dramatists make it plain that grief and joy, welcome and horror must have found expression by such gestures of the chorus, no less than of the actors.

3. Plutarch,[4] analysing the elements of ὄρχησις, distinguishes motions (φοραί), postures or attitudes (σχήματα), and indications (δείξεις). The latter, the mere pointing to objects or persons, need no further elucidation. 'Postures', σχήματα, he describes as the attitudes in which each motion resulted—suggesting, it might be, Apollo or Pan or a Bacchant. Like Plato and Aristotle he lays stress on the mimetic character of dancing (οὕτως ἐν ὀρχήσει τὸ μὲν σχῆμα μιμητικόν ἐστι μορφῆς καὶ ἰδέας, καὶ πάλιν ἡ φορὰ πάθους τινος ἐμφαντικὸν ἢ πράξεως ἢ δυνάμεως), and of the gestures being intimately associated with the words from moment to moment (ὀρχηστικῇ δὲ καὶ ποιητικῇ κοινωνία πᾶσα καὶ μέθεξις ἀλλήλων ἐστι—especially in the ὑπορχηματικόν γένος, of which something will be said below—as if the words and the parts of the body were connected by strings which the former pulled).[5] The lists given by Pollux[6] and others show that in time the σχήματα of the dance—the postures or attitudes—had come to be standardized and named, but how far those which Pollux enumerates were employed by choruses as well as by individual actors is a matter of conjecture. As regards tragedy he writes: καὶ μὴν τραγικῆς ὀρχήσεως σχήματα σιμὴ χείρ,[7] καλαθίσκος, χείρ

ἀπὸ τοῦ δεσπότου, where the schol. describes it as εἶδος ὀρχήσεως φορτικῆς. Athen. xiv. 629 c refers to its mention in Cratinus' *Nemesis*, Cephisodorus' *Amazones*, and Aristophanes' *Centaur*).

[1] *Symp. Quaest.* ix. 747 b.　　　　　　　　　　　　　　　　[2] i, p. 21 f.

[3] There is some uncertainty about the identity of 'Telesis or Telestes'. Both names appear in inscriptions as those of κωμῳδοί at the Soteria in the third century B.C., but Telestes is described by Athenaeus a few lines later as ὁ Αἰσχύλου ὀρχήστης; see below, p. 256.

[4] *Symp. Quaest.* ix. 747 b ff.

[5] Ibid. 748 a–c.

[6] iv. 103–5. Latte (*de Salt. Graec.*, pp. 7 ff.) argues that the chief authority on which both Athenaeus and Pollux drew was Tryphon (see above, p. 175), though they also used Didymus.

[7] σιμή and καταπρηνής = 'upturned' and 'downturned'. τραγικῆς probably covers satyric drama, and σιμὴ χείρ is abundantly illustrated in the posture of satyrs on vases. (See Latte, op. cit., pp. 19, 20.) καλαθίσκος may indicate holding the hands above the head, basket-wise, like a caryatid; cf. Séchan, *La Danse grecque antique* (1930), pp. 135–6. θερμαυστρίς means

καταπρανής, ξύλου παράληψις, θερμαυστρίς, κυβίστησις, παραβῆναι τέτταρα.¹ A somewhat similar list is given by Athenaeus,² who seems to enumerate tragic and comic postures together.³ The interest of the passage lies in the quotations, which show that some of the names go back to the fifth century B.C. :

σχήματα δέ ἐστιν ὀρχήσεως ξιφισμός, καλαθίσκος, καλλαβίδες,⁴ σκώψ, σκώπευμα. ἦν δὲ ὁ σκὼψ τῶν ἀποσκοπούντων τι σχῆμα ἄκραν τὴν χεῖρα ὑπὲρ τοῦ μετώπου κεκυρτωκότων. μνημονεύει Αἰσχύλος ἐν Θεωροῖς

καὶ μὴν παλαιῶν τῶνδέ σοι σκωπευμάτων,

καλλαβίδων δ' Εὔπολις ἐν Κόλαξιν

καλλαβίδας δὲ βαίνει
σησαμίδας δὲ χέζει,

θερμαυστρίς, ἑκατερίδες, σκοπός, χεὶρ καταπρηνής, χεὶρ σιμή, διποδισμός, ξύλου παράληψις, ἐπαγκωνισμός, καλαθίσκος, στρόβιλος.

4. Little is known of the history of dancing in the drama after the earliest period, when Phrynichus and Aeschylus invented many dances and σχήματα ὀρχήσεως. Phrynichus boasted :⁵

σχήματα δ' ὄρχησις τόσα μοι πόρεν, ὅσσ' ἐνὶ πόντῳ
κύματα ποιεῖται χείματι νὺξ ὀλοή.

and it is natural to connect this with Aristophanes' praise⁶ of the beauty of Phrynichus' lyrics. Another passage of Aristophanes, quoted by Athenaeus,⁷ records the claim of Aeschylus :

καὶ Αἰσχύλος δὲ οὐ μόνον ἐξεῦρε τὴν τῆς στολῆς εὐπρέπειαν καὶ σεμνότητα, ἣν ζηλώσαντες οἱ ἱεροφάνται καὶ δᾳδοῦχοι ἀμφιέννυνται (see above, p. 213) ἀλλὰ καὶ πολλὰ σχήματα ὀρχηστικὰ αὐτὸς ἐξευρίσκων ἀνεδίδου τοῖς χορευταῖς. Χαμαιλέων γοῦν πρῶτον αὐτόν φησι σχηματίσαι τοὺς χοροὺς ὀρχηστοδιδασκάλοις οὐ χρησάμενον, ἀλλὰ καὶ αὐτὸν τοῖς χοροῖς τὰ σχήματα ποιοῦντα

'a pair of tongs', and may indicate the position of the legs; it is given as the name of a dance, as well as of a σχῆμα. But some of the names are unintelligible. We can only guess how the chorus in Eur. *Electra* 859 ff. may have behaved when it danced ὡς νεβρὸς οὐράνιον πήδημα κουφίζουσα σὺν ἀγλαΐᾳ. E. Roos, *Tragische Orchestik*, Lund, 1951, was published too late for me to use.

¹ Possibly some trick by which a dancer or a στοῖχος took up a position by passing the other four στοῖχοι in a chorus of five.
² xiv. 629 f ξιφισμός, the attitude of a sword-thrust. This was employed in tragedy (Hesych. s.v. σχῆμα ὀρχηστικὸν τῆς λεγομένης ἐμμελείας ὀρχήσεως. So also Phot. and Suid.).
³ It is not certain how far Athenaeus' list of 'comic' σχήματα and dances included those practised in mimes which were for centuries the most popular forms of entertainment, and were not primarily theatrical or Dionysiac, nor confined to festivals, but were the favourite amusement of the common people and provided by travelling actors (see Reich, *Mimus*, p. 320 and *passim*).
⁴ Phot. s.v. καλλαβίδες· τὸ διαβαίνειν ἀσχημόνως καὶ διελκεῖν τὰ ἰσχία ταῖς χερσίν.
⁵ Plut. *Symp. Quaest.* viii, p. 732 f.   ⁶ *Birds* 748 ff.
⁷ i, p. 21 e, f. The quotations are frs. 677–8 (K.).

τῶν ὀρχήσεων, καὶ ὅλως πᾶσαν τῆς τραγῳδίας οἰκονομίαν εἰς ἑαυτὸν περιϊστᾶν. ὑπεκρίνετο γοῦν μετὰ τοῦ εἰκότος τὰ δράματα. Ἀριστοφάνης γοῦν (παρὰ δὲ τοῖς κωμικοῖς ἡ περὶ τῶν τραγικῶν ἀπόκειται πίστις) ποιεῖ αὐτὸν Αἰσχύλον λέγοντα

τοῖσι χοροῖς αὐτὸς τὰ σχήματ' ἐποίουν,

καὶ πάλιν

τοὺς Φρύγας οἶδα θεωρῶν
ὅτε τῷ Πριάμῳ συλλυσόμενοι τὸν παῖδ' ἦλθον τεθνεῶτα
πολλὰ τοιαυτὶ καὶ τοιαυτὶ καὶ δεῦρο σχηματίσαντας.

Athenaeus[1] continues (after a few lines):

Ἀριστοκλῆς[2] οὖν φησιν ὅτι Τελέστης ὁ Αἰσχύλου ὀρχηστὴς οὕτως ἦν τεχνίτης ὥστε ἐν τῷ ὀρχεῖσθαι τοὺς Ἑπτὰ ἐπὶ Θήβας φανερὰ ποιῆσαι τὰ πράγματα δι' ὀρχήσεως.[3] φασὶ δὲ καὶ ὅτι οἱ ἀρχαῖοι ποιηταί Θέσπις Πρατίνας [Κρατῖνος] Φρύνιχος ὀρχησταὶ ἐκαλοῦντο διὰ τὸ μὴ μόνον τὰ ἑαυτῶν δράματα ἀναφέρειν εἰς ὄρχησιν τοῦ χοροῦ, ἀλλὰ καὶ ἔξω τῶν ἰδίων ποιημάτων διδάσκειν τοὺς βουλομένους ὀρχεῖσθαι.

Sophocles was himself an accomplished dancer, who 'danced with the lyre' round the trophy erected after the battle of Salamis and joined in the game of ball in his own tragedy of *Nausicaa*,[4] but nothing is known of the dancing of his choruses, nor of those of Euripides. The falling off in dancing lamented by Plato the comic poet (probably about the turn of the century) has already been mentioned,[5] as has the evidence of Diogenes of Babylon in regard to the performance of tragic choruses with little or no dancing.[6]

5. To the most interesting problem—the action of the chorus while delivering the strophe and antistrophe of the stasimon[7] (and of the lyric portion of the parodos)—there is unfortunately

---

[1] i, p. 22 a.

[2] Aristocles of Rhodes perhaps lived about the beginning of the Christian era.

[3] I cannot feel absolutely certain that this Telestes was not in fact a dancer employed by Aeschylus but identical with the dancer of the late third century B.C. (mentioned by Athenaeus a few lines earlier) who specialized in presenting subjects taken from Aeschylus. It is difficult to know exactly how (in the *Seven against Thebes* as we know it) a single actor could 'dance the play'. See above, pp. 92, 254. Haigh (*Att. Th.*[3], p. 317) interprets the phrase of 'dumb show' accompanying the long descriptive speeches. But dumb show by whom? Not Eteocles or the Messenger surely, and there was no one else.

[4] Athenaeus i, p. 20 e, f Σοφοκλῆς δὲ πρὸς τῷ καλὸς γεγενῆσθαι τὴν ὥραν ἦν καὶ ὀρχηστικὴν δεδιδαγμένος καὶ μουσικὴν ἔτι παῖς ὢν παρὰ Λάμπρῳ. μετὰ γοῦν τὴν ἐν Σαλαμῖνι ναυμαχίαν περὶ τρόπαιον γυμνὸς ἀληλιμμένος ἐχόρευσε μετὰ λύρας· οἱ δὲ ἐν ἱματίῳ φασί. καὶ τὸν Θάμυριν διδάσκων αὐτὸς ἐκιθάρισεν· ἄκρως δὲ ἐσφαίρισεν, ὅτε τὴν Ναυσικάαν καθῆκε.

[5] Above, p. 252.

[6] Philodemus, *de Mus.* iv. 7, p. 70 (K.). See *Theatre of Dionysus*, p. 195.

[7] See above, pp. 249 f.

no answer. That they remained absolutely immobile, as some scholiasts[1] assert, is very improbable, and the idea is generally recognized as due to a misinterpretation of the word στάσιμον, which means not that they were standing but that they had reached their station (στάσις) in the orchestra (they had not yet done this in the parodos; in the exodos they were leaving it). In a few plays the texts[2] prove that they danced, and it can scarcely be doubted that as a rule they went through suitable— probably not as a rule violent—motions and gestures, not only while themselves singing the choral odes, but also as they followed the action of the play and reacted to the speech and behaviour of the actors. It may be with such movements in view that a scholiast[3] speaks of ἡ πρὸς τὰς ῥήσεις ὑπόρχησις. There is no reason why the movements executed by the chorus should have been precisely the same in the antistrophe as in the strophe of the chorus. The music was probably repeated,[4] but the gestures made while they were singing may have been accommodated to the words, which may have been quite different in tone in the two positions—violent, for instance, in one and reflective in the other. It has been pointed out[5] that in the *Bacchae*, ll. 977 ff., the lines ἴτε θοαὶ Λύσσας κύνες, ἴτ᾽ εἰς ὄρος and ὃς ἀδίκῳ γνώμᾳ παρανόμῳ τ᾽ ὀργᾷ suggest very different movements or gestures; as do the strophe and antistrophe, 923 ff., of the *Hecuba*, the one calling for mimetic action, the other for a sorrowful gaze upon the city the women are leaving. In comedy the dances both in singing choral odes and during the action must often have been much livelier, as the texts suggest,[6] though it can hardly be doubted that (for example) the incomparable lyrics of the Mystai in the *Frogs* were wedded to equally lovely movement.[7]

[1] e.g. schol. on Eur. *Phoin.* 202; Suid. s.v. στάσιμον; *Etym. Magn.* 20, etc. Aristotle (*Poet.* xii) evidently regards the characteristic of the στάσιμον as the absence of *marching* (not *dancing*) rhythms: στάσιμον δὲ μέλος χοροῦ τὸ ἄνευ ἀναπαίστου καὶ τροχαίου, though the phrase is not quite correct as regards fifth-century tragedy.

[2] e.g. Aesch. *Eum.* 307 ἄγε δὴ χορὸν ἅψωμεν; Eur. *Herc. Fur.* 761 πρὸς χοροὺς τραπώμεθα.

[3] On Aristoph. *Frogs* 894. The words are given as one of the current interpretations of ἐμμέλεια, but this must be a mere confusion.

[4] A. M. Dale, *Lyric Metres of Greek Drama*, p. 196.

[5] Ibid., pp. 203–4.

[6] See above, p. 249.

[7] See L. B. Lawler, 'The Maenads' (*Mem. of American Acad. in Rome*, vi, pp. 69–112), especially p. 109 'The variety of metres seems to bear out the evidence of the monuments that the Maenad dance could be calm, restrained, spirited or ecstatic; medium, fast or slow; further that it could be measured or dignified, or a wild, almost rhythmless rout, each dancer keeping his own rhythm.'

6. Certain difficulties attach to some of the technical terms traditionally applied to the Greek dramatic dances. These are enumerated by Aristoxenus :[1] Ἀριστόξενος δὲ ἐν τῷ περὶ τραγικῆς ὀρχήσεως ἡ καλουμένη ἐμμέλεια, καθάπερ τῆς σατυρικῆς ἡ καλουμένη σίκιννις, τῆς δὲ κωμικῆς ὁ καλούμενος κόρδαξ, and almost in the same words by Pollux.[2] The same list is assumed by Athenaeus.[3] Besides these the term ὑπόρχημα is frequently used, in meanings which will be discussed presently.

The word ἐμμέλεια seems to be originally an abstract term, indicative of the quality of harmonious or graceful modulation of words; as such it is sometimes used of an orator's style or delivery,[4] and it may well mean this in Aristophanes' *Frogs* 895–8

καὶ μὴν ἡμεῖς ἐπιθυμοῦμεν
παρὰ σοφοῖν ἀνδροῖν ἀκοῦσαι
τίνα λόγων ἐμμέλειαν
ἔπιτε δαΐαν ὁδόν.

(The reference here must be to style rather than to music and dancing.[5]) The transition from the abstract meaning to the concrete name for a type of dance is explained in Plato's *Laws* :[6]

διὸ μίμησις τῶν λεγομένων σχήμασι γενομένη τὴν ὀρχηστικὴν ἐξηργάσατο τέχνην σύμπασαν. ὁ μὲν οὖν ἐμμελῶς ἡμῶν, ὁ δὲ πλημμελῶς ἐν τούτοις πᾶσι κινεῖται. πολλὰ μὲν δὴ τοίνυν ἄλλα ἡμῖν τῶν παλαιῶν ὀνομάτων ὡς εὖ καὶ κατὰ φύσιν κείμενα δεῖ διανοούμενον ἐπαινεῖν, τούτων δὲ ἓν καὶ τὸ περὶ τὰς ὀρχήσεις τῶν εὖ πραττόντων, ὄντων δὲ μετρίων αὐτῶν πρὸς τὰς ἡδονάς, ὡς ὀρθῶς ἅμα καὶ μουσικῶς ὠνόμασεν ὅστις ποτ' ἦν, καὶ κατὰ λόγον αὐταῖς θέμενος ὄνομα συμπάσαις ἐμμελείας ἐπωνόμασε, καὶ δύο δὴ τῶν ὀρχήσεων τῶν καλῶν εἴδη κατεστήσατο, τὸ μὲν πολεμικὸν πυρρίχην, τὸ δὲ εἰρηνικὸν ἐμμέλειαν, ἑκατέρῳ τὸ πρέπον τε καὶ ἅρμοττον ἐπιθεὶς ὄνομα.

That the concrete use was early in vogue is indicated by the story of Hippokleides (already referred to)[7] who ἐκέλευσέ οἱ τὸν αὐλητὴν αὐλῆσαι ἐμμέλειαν, πειθομένου δὲ τοῦ αὐλητέω ὠρχήσατο, as well as by the threat (referring to a tragic poet) in Aristophanes' *Wasps*,[8] ἀπολῶ γὰρ αὐτὸν ἐμμελείᾳ κονδύλου.

---

[1] Bekker, *Anecd.*, p. 101. 16.   [2] iv. 99.

[3] Athen. xiv. 630 b–e, etc.; Lucian, *de Salt.* 22, who describes these three as the γενικώταται ὀρχήσεις, and 26.

[4] e.g. in Dion. Hal. *Dem.* 50, where ἐμμέλεια is a characteristic of Demosthenes, and Plutarch, *De rect. rat. aud.* 7 τὴν φωνὴν ἐμμελείας τισὶ μαλακότησι καὶ παρισώσεσιν ἐφηδύνοντες ἐκβακχεύουσι καὶ παραφέρουσι τοὺς ἀκροωμένους.

[5] A scholiast on this passage evidently regarded Aristophanes' use as a solecism, ὅτι καταχρηστικῶς νῦν εὐρυθμίαν, κυρίως γὰρ ἡ μετὰ μέλους τραγικὴ ὄρχησις, οἱ δέ, ἡ πρὸς τὰς ῥήσεις ὑπόρχησις.   [6] 816 a, b (cf. Lucian, *de Salt.* 25, quoted above, p. 251).

[7] Herod. vi. 129.   [8] l. 1503.

It is consistent with Plato's account that Athenaeus characterizes the ἐμμέλεια as marked by τὸ βαρὺ καὶ σεμνόν, 'gravity
and dignity', and calls it σπουδαία as compared with the vulgar
κόρδαξ,[1] but the nature of its movements is not further explained.
The scholiast on Euripides' *Hecuba*, 1. 647 says: ἰστέον δὲ ὅτι
τὴν μὲν στροφὴν κινούμενοι πρὸς τὰ δεξιὰ οἱ χορευταὶ ᾖδον, τὴν δὲ
ἀντιστροφὴν πρὸς τὰ ἀριστερά, τὴν δὲ ἐπῳδὸν ἱστάμενοι ᾖδον. But
what was the nature of this κίνησις to right and left does not
appear. (Epodes are relatively rare in tragedy, and some suppose
that the scholiast is thinking of dithyramb, with a circular chorus
revolving as required.) However this may be, the name ἐμμέλεια
seems to cover a considerable variety of dances (in some of
which the σχήματα enumerated were introduced), ranging from
the fine serenity of the Colonus ode to the raging of the Furies
and the ecstatic devotions of the Bakchai, adapting itself to every
kind and degree of emotion, and presenting every form of lyric
beauty.[2]

7. The name σίκιννις, denoting the satyric dance, is variously
derived[3] from an eponymous Sikinnos—a barbarian or a
Cretan—or from σείεσθαι, or from σείεσθαι καὶ κινεῖσθαι, or (as
Athenaeus puts it) ἀπὸ τῆς κινήσεως, ἣν καὶ οἱ σάτυροι ὀρχοῦνται
ταχυτάτην οὖσαν· οὐ γὰρ ἔχει πάθος αὕτη ἡ ὄρχησις, διὸ οὐδὲ
βραδύνει. (The meaning of this sentence is not very clear, and
some editors emend πάθος to ἦθος.) Some said that the dance
originated in Crete, others that it came from the Phrygian worship of Dionysus Sabazios,[4] and modern scholars offer a number
of unprovable suggestions.[5] It is natural to conjecture that it is
the dance which is being executed by a satyr on the Pronomos
vase, though this gives no idea of the *pace* of the σίκιννις. It may
have included a good deal of leaping; at least the Cyclops in
Euripides' play[6] says to the satyrs:

[1] Athen. xiv. 630 e, 631 d.
[2] Plutarch, *Symp. Quaest.* ix. 747 b has never been satisfactorily explained: ὀρχουμένων δὲ
πολλῶν προθυμότερον ἢ μουσικώτερον, δύο τοὺς εὐδοκίμους καὶ βουλομένους ἀνασώζειν τὴν
ἐμμέλειαν ἠξίουν τινὲς ὀρχεῖσθαι φορὰν παρὰ φοράν. On the whole subject see Chr. Kirchhoff,
Dramatische Orchestik der Hellenen (Leipzig, 1898), and on the ἐμμέλεια in particular, pp. 242 ff.
(I have not been able to get this.)   [3] Athen. xiv, p. 630 b, c; *Etym. M.* s.v., etc.
[4] Eustath. 1078. 20 ἦν δὲ καὶ σίκιννις κωμικωτέρα, ἣν πρῶτοί φασιν ὠρχήσαντο Φρύγες ἐπὶ
Σαβαζίῳ Διονυσίῳ, ὀνομασθεῖσα κατὰ τὸν Ἀρριανὸν ἐπὶ μιᾷ τῶν ὀπαδῶν τῆς Κυβέλης νυμφῶν, ᾗ
ὄνομα ἦν Σίκιννις.
[5] Some of these are collected by Latte, op. cit., p. 89, and Séchan, *La Danse grecque
antique*, p. 213. Herbig (*Sitz. Akad. München*, 1914, 2 Abh., p. 10) compares the Etruscan
termination *-enna*. Cf. also E. Roos, *Tragische Orchestik*, pp. 166 f.   [6] ll. 220-1.

ἐπεὶ μ᾽ ἂν ἐν μέσῃ τῇ γαστέρι
πηδῶντες ἀπολέσαιτ᾽ ἂν ὑπὸ τῶν σχημάτων

—which may have been the σχήματα of the σίκιννις. The mention[1] of a tune called σικιννοτύρβη and the figure on a vase of a satyr called Τυρβάς are hardly enough to relate the σίκιννις to the τυρβασία, which was the characteristic dance of the dithyramb.[2] The name Σίκινος or Σίκιννος, attached to a satyr, occurs on several vases, Athenian and Italian, from about 510 B.C. onwards, with or without καλός.[3]

8. The term ὑπόρχημα is not used with absolute consistency throughout the long course of Greek literary history. In its strict sense it seems to denote a performance in which the dancers (not themselves singing) accompany one or more singers, the dance being closely related to and illustrating the words. It was said to have originated in Crete, where Thaletas was the first to compose the πυρρίχη or armed dance in this form,[4] but Athenaeus (rightly) traces the type back to Homer.[5] In Sparta Xenodamos of Cythera was an early composer of hyporchemes, and we are told of a ὑπορχηματικὴ ὄρχησις in which men and women joined. Such dances, in which the dancers accompanied singers who did not dance, continued outside the drama down to a late date and are often mentioned. Pindar composed two books of hyporchemes (Clement of Alexandria[6] even makes him the inventor of the hyporcheme), and one or two fragments of Bacchylides are ascribed to this species. Aeschylus makes a fine use of a metaphor from the hyporcheme which implies the division of the performers into two groups—*Choeph.* 1024–5 πρὸς δὲ καρδίᾳ φόβος | ᾄδειν ἕτοιμος, ἡ δ᾽ ὑπορχεῖσθαι κότῳ—and nearly six

---

[1] Athen. xiv, p. 618 c.   [2] See *Dith. Trag. Com.*, pp. 49, 50.

[3] A list is given in Pauly-W., *Real-Encycl.* s.v. Σίκινος.

[4] Sosibius *ap.* schol. Pind. *Pyth.* ii. 127.

[5] *Il.* xviii. 590; *Od.* viii. 262 ff.; *Hymn to Apollo Pyth.* 10 ff. See Athenaeus i. 15 d οἶδε δὲ ὁ ποιητὴς καὶ τὴν πρὸς ᾠδὴν ὄρχησιν· Δημοδόκου γοῦν ᾄδοντος κοῦροι πρωθῆβοι ὠρχοῦντο· καὶ ἐν τῇ Ὁπλοποιΐᾳ δὲ παιδὸς κιθαρίζοντος ἄλλοι ἐναντίοι μολπῇ τε ὀρχηθμῷ τε ἔσκαιρον. ὑποσημαίνεται δὲ ἐν τούτοις ὁ ὑπορχηματικὸς τρόπος, ὃς ἤνθησεν ἐπὶ Ξενοδήμου καὶ Πινδάρου. καὶ ἔστιν ἡ τοιαύτη ὄρχησις μίμησις τῶν ὑπὸ τῆς λέξεως ἑρμηνευομένων πραγμάτων; and xiv. 628 d διὰ τοῦτο γὰρ καὶ ἐξ ἀρχῆς συνέταττον οἱ ποιηταὶ τοῖς ἐλευθέροις καὶ ἐχρῶντο τοῖς σχήμασι σημείοις μόνον τῶν ᾀδομένων, τηροῦντες ἀεὶ τὸ εὐγενὲς καὶ ἀνδρῶδες ἐπ᾽ αὐτῶν, ὅθεν καὶ ὑπορχήματα τὰ τοιαῦτα προσηγόρευον. (Cf. also Plut. *Symp. Quaest.* ix. 748 a, b, and for Xenodamos Plut.(?) *de Mus.* ix.) Athenaeus quotes (from Polycrates, an historian of uncertain date) a description of the dances at the Spartan Hyacinthia: iv, p. 139 e χοροί τε νεανίσκων παμπληθεῖς εἰσέρχονται καὶ τῶν ἐπιχωρίων τινα ποιημάτων ᾄδουσιν, ὀρχησταί τε [ἐν] τούτοις ἀναμεμιγμένοι τὴν κίνησιν ἀρχαϊκὴν ὑπὸ τὸν αὐλὸν καὶ τὴν ᾠδὴν ποιοῦνται.

[6] *Stromat.* i, p. 365.

hundred years later Lucian[1] describes the dances at sacrifices in Delos (without mentioning any date): παιδῶν χοροὶ συνελθόντες ὑπ' αὐλῷ καὶ κιθαρᾷ οἱ μὲν ἐχόρευον, ὑπωρχοῦντο δὲ οἱ ἄριστοι προκριθέντες ἀπ' αὐτῶν. τὰ γοῦν τοῖς χοροῖς γραφόμενα τούτοις ᾄσματα ὑπορχήματα ἐκαλεῖτο, and he contrasts[2] the elegance of the dancer's facial appearance (since he could keep his mouth shut) with the gaping lips of the dramatic actor's mask, and adds that πάλαι μὲν γὰρ οἱ αὐτοὶ καὶ ἦδον καὶ ὠρχοῦντο· εἶτ' ἐπειδὴ κινουμένων τὸ ᾆσθμα τὴν ᾠδὴν ἐτάραττεν ἄμεινον ἔδοξεν αὐτοῖς ὑπᾴδειν. (He is probably thinking of the development of pantomime, which was very popular in his day—often with only a single dancer.)[3]

But because the song and dance of this type were of a very lively kind,[4] the word came to be used more loosely of a joyful choral song generally.[5] It can only be in this sense that modern scholars, following the example of one or two scholiasts, incorrectly apply the name to a number of choral odes occurring at moments of sudden joy or expectation in plays of Sophocles,[6] and distinct in character from normal tragic stasima. The distinction is expressed by the scholiast on Sophocles, *Trachiniai* 205 ff., who writes τὸ γὰρ μελιδάριον οὔκ ἐστι στάσιμον ἀλλ' ὑπὸ τῆς ἡδονῆς ὀρχοῦνται. Similar odes are found in the *Ajax* 693 ff., the *Antigone* 1115 ff., the *Oedipus Tyrannus* 1086 ff.; and in all these cases the excited joy of relief or anticipation darkens by contrast the calamity which falls or becomes known immediately afterwards. The language of the ode in the *Trachiniai* strongly suggests that it would have been termed a paean, but there is plenty of evidence of hyporchemata addressed to Apollo, and the ode in the *Ajax* was called a ὑπόρχησις by Eukleides (the authority of Tzetzes).[7] The essential difference between the two

[1] *de Salt.* 16.
[2] Ibid. 29, 30.
[3] Ibid. 63.
[4] So lively that Athenaeus, xiv. 630 e, compares it with the kordax.
[5] Ibid. 631 c ἡ δ' ὑπορχηματική ἐστιν ἐν ᾗ ᾄδων ὁ χορὸς ὀρχεῖται. (This is really inconsistent with what he says earlier, unless ὁ χορός includes both singers and dancers as in the Delian hyporchemes described by Lucian.) Cf. Cramer, *Anecd. Par.* i. 20 ὑπόρχημα δ' ἂν εἴη μᾶλλον τῶν σατύρων, ἐκεῖνοι γὰρ ᾄδοντες ὀρχοῦνται, and Proclus, *Chrestom.* 246. 7 W. ὑπόρχημα τὸ μετ' ὀρχήσεως ᾀδόμενον μέλος.
[6] The absence of all mention of hyporchemata by Aristotle in the *Poetics* (especially ch. xii) probably means that he regarded ὑπόρχημα in the strict sense as a species of poetry no less distinct from drama than (for example) the paean. The application of the word and its derivatives to choral odes in tragedy and satyric drama is much later than Aristotle.
[7] Tzetzes, *de Trag.* 114 ff. (see above, p. 246).

species was that the dance in the paean was not mimetic and (probably) that the singers were also dancers.

The long fragment of Pratinas, in which he protests against the threatened predominance of the flute over the words in the dithyramb, is called a hyporchema by Athenaeus,[1] and while it is probable that this came in a satyric play, this is not universally accepted,[2] and it may have been an independent poem.[3]

In the ancient lists of dances characteristic of the several kinds of dramatic performance, the κόρδαξ is always mentioned as the special dance of comedy; but as it was evidently a solo dance, it falls outside the scope of this chapter.[4] (The movements of the comic chorus have already been briefly considered.[5])

C. MUSIC IN DRAMA

1. The use of speech, recitative, and song by actors and chorus has been briefly discussed earlier in this volume, with special reference to παρακαταλογή or recitative and its uses by actors and chorus; but the greater part of the choral odes in Greek drama was sung, and there is no subject on which it is more difficult—if it is not virtually impossible—to reach a clear understanding, not to speak of appreciation, than that of the music to which the words were set and the character of the instrumental accompaniment. In the first place the structure of ancient Greek music was itself extremely complicated; and in the second, our knowledge of it begins (except for one slight fragment) at a period which was perhaps two hundred years later than that at which choral odes were a regular part of the structure of a Greek play, and it cannot be assumed that it had not changed considerably in that long interval, so that as regards the Classical period—from Aeschylus to Menander—we are virtually without any direct evidence, and are dependent upon a few passages in writers who refer to the subject.

2. Greek music, no less than modern, consisted of a succession of notes separated from one another by intervals, but the inter-

---

[1] xiv. 617 d.

[2] See *Dith. Trag. Com.*, pp. 28 ff. and references there; also Pohlenz, *Gött. Nachr.*, 1926, pp. 298 ff., and Kranz, *Stasimon*, p. 15. On the Hyporchema generally see Diehl, s.v. in Pauly–W. ix, cols. 338 ff., and Th. Reinach, s.v. in Daremberg–Saglio, *Dict. des Antiq.*

[3] See A. M. Dale, 'Stasimon and Hyporcheme', in *Eranos*, xlviii (1950), p. 19.

[4] For this and some other comic dances see *Dith. Trag. Com.*, pp. 256, 259 ff., and references there given, and art. 'Kordax' (by Warnecke) in Pauly–W. xxii, cols. 1382 ff.

[5] pp. 249–50; cf. also *Theatre of D.*, pp. 163 ff.

vals might be not only tones and semitones as in modern music, but fractions of a semitone, and the succession was not divided into lengths of approximately similar structure, as modern music is by bars. Further, 'A Greek musician,[1] as we learn from theoretical treatises, had at his disposal a number of modes (ἁρμονίαι or εἴδη τοῦ διὰ πασῶν) which differed from one another in the order of the larger and smaller intervals of which they were composed. Each mode might, within limits, be modified by decreasing the size of the smaller intervals and increasing the size of the larger, and so have a diatonic or a chromatic or an enharmonic form; furthermore, these modes could be sung or played in a number of keys (τόνοι)—that is to say, their absolute pitch might be varied.'

Aristoxenus (who as a pupil of Aristotle may be assumed to be trustworthy in regard to tragedy) recorded that the modes proper to tragedy were the pathetic Mixolydian and the stately and majestic Dorian; but that these were not exclusively used is shown by Aristoxenus' own statement recorded in the *Life of Sophocles* that Sophocles had introduced the Phrygian mode (which was the special mode of dithyramb),[2] and by a passage in the Aristotelian *Problems* which justifies the use of the Hypodorian and Hypophrygian modes for the lyrics sung by actors, when realistic action was called for, but not for those of the chorus. It will be convenient to set out these passages at length:

(1) Plutarch (?) *de Mus.* xvi. καὶ ἡ Μιξολύδιος δὲ παθητική τίς ἐστι, τραγῳδίαις ἁρμόζουσα. Ἀριστόξενος δέ φησι Σαπφὼ πρώτην εὑρᾶσθαι τὴν Μιξολυδιστί, παρ' ἧς τοὺς τραγῳδοποιοὺς μαθεῖν· λαβόντας γοῦν αὐτοὺς συζεῦξαι τῇ Δωριστί, ἐπεὶ ἡ μὲν τὸ μεγαλοπρεπὲς καὶ ἀξιωματικὸν ἀποδίδωσιν, ἡ δὲ τὸ παθητικόν, μέμικται δὲ διὰ τούτων τραγῳδία.

(2) *Vit. Soph.* (ad fin.). φησὶ δὲ Ἀριστόξενος ὡς πρῶτος τῶν Ἀθήνηθεν ποιητῶν τὴν Φρυγίαν μελοποιίαν εἰς τὰ ἴδια ᾄσματα παρέλαβε καὶ τοῦ διθυραμβικοῦ τρόπου κατέμιξεν.

(3) Aristot. *Probl.* xix. 48. διὰ τί οἱ ἐν τραγῳδίᾳ χοροὶ οὔθ' ὑποδωριστὶ οὔθ' ὑποφρυγιστὶ ᾄδουσιν; ἢ ὅτι μέλος ἥκιστα ἔχουσιν αὗται αἱ ἁρμονίαι, οὗ δεῖ μάλιστα τῷ χορῷ; ἦθος δὲ ἔχει ἡ μὲν ὑποφρυγιστὶ πρακτικόν, διὸ καὶ ἔν τε τῷ Γηρυόνῃ ἡ ἔξοδος καὶ ἡ ἐξόπλισις ἐν ταύτῃ πεποίηται, ἡ δὲ ὑποδωριστὶ μεγαλοπρεπὲς καὶ στάσιμον, διὸ καὶ

---

[1] I here quote J. F. Mountford, 'Greek Music in the Papyri and Inscriptions', in *New Chapters in Greek Literature*, ii (1929), pp. 146–83—a brief and most valuable summary of the subject. In the article on music in the *Oxford Classical Dictionary* Dr. Mountford and Mr. R. P. Winnington-Ingram give a very clear (and concise) account of Greek music, with a useful bibliography.   [2] Cf. *Dith. Trag. Com.*, pp. 62, 63, etc.

κιθαρῳδικωτάτη ἐστὶ τῶν ἁρμονιῶν. ταῦτα δ᾽ ἄμφω χορῷ μὲν
ἀνάρμοστα, τοῖς δὲ ἀπὸ σκηνῆς (lyrics sung by actors) οἰκειότερα.
ἐκεῖνοι μὲν γὰρ ἡρώων μιμηταί· οἱ δὲ ἡγέμονες τῶν ἀρχαίων μόνοι
ἦσαν ἥρωες, οἱ δὲ λαοὶ ἄνθρωποι, ὧν ἐστὶν ὁ χορός. διὸ καὶ ἁρμόζει
αὐτῷ τὸ γοερὸν καὶ ἡσύχιον ἦθος καὶ μέλος· ἀνθρωπικὰ γάρ. ταῦτα δ᾽
ἔχουσιν αἱ ἄλλαι ἁρμονίαι, ἥκιστα δ᾽ αὐτῶν ἡ ὑποφρυγιστί· ἐνθουσι-
αστικὴ γὰρ καὶ βακχική. κατὰ μὲν οὖν ταύτην πάσχομέν τι· παθητικοὶ
δὲ οἱ ἀσθενεῖς μᾶλλον τῶν δυνατῶν εἰσι, διὸ καὶ αὕτη ἁρμόττει τοῖς
χοροῖς· κατὰ δὲ τὴν ὑποδωριστὶ καὶ ὑποφρυγιστὶ πράττομεν, ὃ οὐκ
οἰκεῖόν ἐστι χορῷ· ἔστι γὰρ ὁ χορὸς κηδευτὴς ἄπρακτος· εὔνοιαν γὰρ
μόνον παρέχεται οἷς πάρεστιν.

3. It will be seen that the appropriateness of certain modes to
tragedy and to the several lyric elements in tragedy depends
upon a natural association (which we cannot, with our limited
information, appreciate) of the several modes with a special
range of feeling or action. It was because they were θρηνώδεις
that Plato[1] had excluded the Mixolydian, Syntonolydian, and
similar harmonies from his Ideal State, as well as the Ionian and
Lydian which were μαλακαὶ καὶ συμποτικαί, and had retained
only the Dorian and Phrygian, believing, as he did, that the
ἁρμονίαι had in themselves the power to influence men's characters and emotions.[2] Aristotle is even more emphatic than
Plato as to this influence, and writes:

Politics v (VIII). v. 1340 b. ἐν δὲ τοῖς μέλεσιν αὐτοῖς ἐστὶ μιμήματα τῶν
ἠθῶν. καὶ τοῦτ᾽ ἐστὶ φανερόν· εὐθὺς γὰρ καὶ ἡ τῶν ἁρμονιῶν διέστηκε
φύσις ὥστε ἀκούοντας ἄλλως διατίθεσθαι καὶ μὴ τὸν αὐτὸν ἔχειν τρόπον
πρὸς ἑκάστην αὐτῶν, ἀλλὰ πρὸς μὲν ἐνίας ὀδυρτικωτέρως καὶ συνεστη-
κότως μᾶλλον, οἷον πρὸς τὴν μιξολυδιστὶ καλουμένην, πρὸς δὲ τὰς
μαλακωτέρως τὴν διάνοιαν, οἷον πρὸς τὰς ἀνειμένας· μέσως δὲ καὶ
καθεστηκότως μάλιστα πρὸς ἑτέραν, οἷον δοκεῖ ποιεῖν ἡ δωριστὶ μόνη
τῶν ἁρμονιῶν, ἐνθουσιαστικῶς δ᾽ ἡ φρυγιστί.[3]

With regard to the Phrygian mode he differs from Plato, whom
he regards as inconsistent in accepting it, while rejecting the
flute as over-emotional:[4]

Politics v (VIII). v. 1342 b. ἔχει γὰρ τὴν αὐτὴν δύναμιν ἡ φρυγιστὶ τῶν
ἁρμονιῶν ἥνπερ αὐλὸς ἐν τοῖς ὀργάνοις· ἄμφω γὰρ ὀργιαστικὰ καὶ

---

[1] *Rep.* iii. 398 e, 399 a.

[2] In the *Laws* ii. 699 d, e he somewhat modifies this view, and is not sure that they have
always a quality independently of the words which are set to them.

[3] The whole passage which intervenes between this quotation and the next should be
carefully studied.

[4] Plato's special objection to the flute is based on the great multiplicity of notes possible
in it, as compared with the kithara (cf. Aristot. *Probl.* xix. 48, quoted above).

παθητικά. δηλοῖ δ' ἡ ποίησις· πᾶσα γὰρ βακχεία καὶ πᾶσα ἡ τοιαύτη
κίνησις μάλιστα τῶν ὀργάνων ἐστὶν ἐν τοῖς αὐλοῖς, τῶν δ' ἁρμονιῶν ἐν
τοῖς φρυγιστὶ μέλεσι λαμβάνει τὸ πρέπον, οἷον ὁ διθύραμβος ὁμολογου-
μένως εἶναι δοκεῖ φρύγιον . . . περὶ δὲ τῆς δωριστὶ πάντες ὁμολογοῦσιν
ὡς στασιμωτάτης οὔσης καὶ μάλιστα ἦθος ἐχούσης ἀνδρεῖον.

In confirmation of Aristotle's opinion of the Phrygian mode
it is remarkable that the one scrap of music set to fifth-century
drama which survives—a passage of Euripides, *Orestes* 338–44—
appears to be in this mode,[1] though it is too fragmentary to be
enlightening, both text and notation being uncertain.

A writer of perhaps a century later than Aristotle[2] rejects
somewhat violently the view that different types of music influenced character—that, for instance, the enharmonic genus
(which was normal in tragedy) made men brave—and it is
possible that such influence had grown less in the course of
time; but it cannot be seriously doubted that Plato and Aristotle
and Aristoxenus knew what they were talking about, and that
the music employed helped to give a certain emotional colour
to the performances with which it was associated,[3] though it is
impossible to trace the effects in detail.

4. At first there can be no doubt that the music, or at least
the musical accompaniment, was strictly subordinate to the
words. Pratinas' protest against the attempt to give predominance to the flute implies this.[4] Indeed it was essential that the
words should be heard clearly throughout the vast theatre, as
words seldom are even indoors when set to modern music and
sung in parts, and it must have been necessary even for singers
in unison (as ancient Greek singers always sang) to spend in-
finite pains on the enunciation of the words.[5] But what seemed
to the orthodox to be corruption[6] set in when a new school of

---

[1] Mountford, op. cit., p. 168. (The passage comes from the *Rainer Papyri*, 1892.) Euripides'
use of the Mixolydian mode is referred to by Plutarch, *de recta ratione audiendi*, p. 46 b (see
above, p. 163).

[2] *Hibeh Papyri*, vol. i. 13 (quoted by Mountford, op. cit., p. 181).

[3] Even today there are types of music which would be felt to be inappropriate in church,
and the inspiriting effect of a great march-tune is quite different from the emotions commonly
associated with a waltz, though different sorts of people experience such effects in very
different degrees, as Aristotle himself pointed out (*Pol.* v (VIII). v. 1340 a).

[4] Athen. xiv. 617 b. See *Dith. Trag. Com.*, pp. 28 ff.

[5] When Plutarch, *Symp. Quaest.* vii. 713 c says τὸ δὲ μέλος καὶ τὸν ῥυθμὸν ὥσπερ ὄψον ἐπὶ
τῷ λόγῳ καὶ μὴ καθ' αὐτὰ προσφέρεσθαι the context shows that he is thinking mainly of singing
at a symposium.

[6] *Dith. Trag. Com.*, pp. 55 ff. The guilty poets are enumerated in Pherekrates, fr. 145 (K.),
and include Melanippides, Phrynis, Kinesias, and Philoxenus as well as Timotheus.

poets, and above all Timotheos, introduced, first into dithyrambs and νόμοι, music of a much more elaborate and florid
type, and this was adopted in tragedy by Agathon and Euripides, who are mocked by Aristophanes for their innovations,[1]
—their notes, running hither and thither, which are compared
with the runs leading to an ants' nest, and probably also the
setting of a single syllable to several notes. (This actually occurs
once in the fragment of Euripides' *Orestes* already referred to.)
Such things could hardly fail to rob the words of the required
precision in utterance. Timotheos was kindly encouraged by
Euripides when the theatre hissed him, and was assured that
before long he would have the applause of every audience;[2] but
it may be that the obscurity imparted to the words of the tragic
chorus was one, among others, of the causes of its rapid decline
in the fourth century. Poets might not care to compose what
their hearers could not follow.

The problem of the relation between the music and the ac-
centuation, and between the music and the quantities and
scansion of the words sung, at present admits of no certain
solution, and the evidence is conflicting. The statements of
Dionysius of Halicarnassus[3] on both points appear to contradict
such evidence as the musical fragments afford; but the reader
who desires to pursue the matter farther may be referred to
more specialist treatises, with only this caution, that we do not
know how or to what music lyric excerpts (or lyric passages in
reproductions of classical plays) may have been sung in the
time of Dionysius some three hundred years later.

5. Little use seems to have been made in the classical drama
of instrumental music apart from words; but a few notes are
sometimes interjected in comedy for special purposes—the song

---

[1] Aristoph. *Thesm.* 100 μύρμηκος ἀτραπούς, ἢ τί διαμινύρεται (sc. Ἀγαθών); cf. *Frogs* 1301 ff.
See especially l. 1314, εἰειειειλίσσετε. Kranz (*Stasimon*, pp. 228 ff.) dates Euripides' adoption
of the new style from the *Troades* in 415 B.C. (cf. *Troad.* 511 ἀμφί μοι Ἴλιον, ὦ Μοῦσα | καινῶν
ὕμνων ἄεισον ᾠδάν), and notices that from this time Euripides' choruses were all feminine,
and therefore, he supposes, especially suited to the new style.

[2] Plutarch, *An Seni*, etc., p. 795 c.

[3] *de Comp. Vb.* xi τάς τε λέξεις τοῖς μέλεσιν ὑποτάττειν ἀξιοῖ (sc. ἡ ὀργανικὴ καὶ ᾠδικὴ μοῦσα)
καὶ οὐ τὰ μέλη ταῖς λέξεσιν, ὡς ἐξ ἄλλων τε πολλῶν δῆλον καὶ μάλιστα ἐκ τῶν Εὐριπίδου μελῶν,
ἃ πεποίηκεν τὴν Ἠλέκτραν λέγουσαν ἐν Ὀρέστῃ πρὸς τὸν χορόν (*Or.* 140-2) . . . τὸ δ' αὐτὸ
γίγνεται καὶ περὶ τοὺς ῥυθμούς. ἡ μὲν γὰρ πεζὴ λέξις οὐδενὸς οὔτε ὀνόματος οὔτε ῥήματος βιάζεται
τοὺς χρόνους, ἀλλ' οἵας παρείληφε τῇ φύσει τὰς συλλαβὰς τάς τε μακρὰς καὶ τὰς βραχείας,
τοιαύτας φυλάττει· ἡ δὲ μουσική τε καὶ ῥυθμικὴ μεταβάλλουσιν αὐτὰς μειοῦσαι καὶ παραύξουσαι,
ὥστε πολλάκις εἰς τἀναντία μεταχωρεῖν· οὐ γὰρ ταῖς συλλαβαῖς ἀπευθύνουσι τοὺς χρόνους, ἀλλὰ
τοῖς χρόνοις τὰς συλλαβάς. Cf. Mountford, op. cit., pp. 156 ff.; Dale, op. cit., pp. 194-6.

of the nightingale imitated on the flute in the *Birds*,[1] or the twanging of the lyre between the lines of Aeschylus travestied by Euripides in the *Frogs* (τοφλαττόθρατ τοφλαττόθρατ). Such effects were termed διαύλιον[2] or μεσαύλιον.[3]

To lead the singing the first note (ἐνδόσιμον) was given not by an instrument but by the coryphaeus, though it is to be feared that the start was sometimes assisted by the flute-player, not with his instrument only but with a wooden shoe (κρούπεζα) which he wore for the purpose. (Hesychius also speaks of a rattle.)[4]

---

[1] l. 222 where the text contains the παρεπιγραφή 'αὐλεῖ' and the schol. explains ὅτι μιμεῖται τις τὴν ἀήδονα ὡς ἔτι ἔνδον οὖσαν ἐν τῇ λοχμῇ.

[2] Schol. Aristoph. *Frogs* 1264, and Hesych. s.v. διαύλιον· ὁπόταν ἐν τοῖς μέλεσι μεταξὺ παραβάλλῃ ὁ ποιητὴς παρασιωπήσαντος τοῦ χοροῦ.

[3] Eustath. *ad Il.* xi. 547, p. 862. 19 μεσαύλιον, κροῦμά τι μεταξὺ τῆς ᾠδῆς αὐλούμενον.

[4] [Aristot.] *de Mundo* vi καθάπερ δὲ ἐν χορῷ κορυφαίου κατάρξαντος συνεπηχεῖ πᾶς ὁ χορός . . . οὕτως ἔχει καὶ ἐπὶ τοῦ τὸ σύμπαν διέποντος θεοῦ· κατὰ γὰρ τὸ ἄνωθεν ἐνδόσιμον ὑπὸ τοῦ φερωνύμως ἂν κορυφαίου προσαγορευθέντος κινεῖται μὲν τὰ ἄστρα ἀεὶ καὶ ὁ σύμπας οὐρανός; Aelian, *V.H.* xv. v δίδωσιν ὡσπεροῦν . . . χορολέκτης τὸ ἐνδόσιμον; cf. Dion. Hal. vii. 72 ἡγεῖτο δὲ καθ᾽ ἕκαστον χορὸν εἰς ἀνήρ, ὃς ἐνεδίδου τοῖς ἄλλοις τὰ τῆς ὀρχήσεως σχήματα πρῶτος; and Poll. vii. 87 ἡ δὲ κρούπεζα ξύλινον ὑπόδημα, πεποιημένον εἰς ἐνδόσιμον χοροῦ; Hesych. κρουπέζαι· . . . οἱ δὲ κρόταλον ὃ ἐπιψοφοῦσιν οἱ αὐληταί.

VI

THE AUDIENCE

1. In the description of the general character of the festival of the City Dionysia which has already been given[1] mention has been made of the presence in the theatre of an immense audience of citizens, increased by the attendance of a great number of visitors from abroad, some of them being persons of distinction specially invited to seats of honour. (At the Lenaia only citizens and μέτοικοι were present.)[2] The size of the audience at different periods cannot be exactly determined. Plato, writing in the *Symposium*[3] of Agathon's brilliant victory in 416 B.C., speaks of it as gained ἐν μάρτυσι τῶν Ἑλλήνων πλέον ἢ τρισμυρίοις. The dialogue itself is probably to be dated in or soon after 385 B.C.;[4] the reference, in any case, is to the theatre as it was before Lycurgus. But a figure of 30,000 greatly overestimates the seating capacity of the theatre at any period,[5] and it is possible that πλέον ἢ τρισμύριοι was a colloquial expression for 'a vast number'. It is so used at about the same date in Aristophanes' *Ekklesiazousai* 1132–3 ὅστις πολιτῶν πλεῖον ἢ τρισμυρίων | ὄντων τὸ πλῆθος οὐ δεδείπνηκας μόνος. There may, of course, have been many spectators standing—for instance, in the roadway which ran above and afterwards across the auditorium—but not enough to bring the total up to 30,000.

2. That the audience included women and boys as spectators of both tragedy and comedy can only be doubted by those whose sense of what would have been fitting, in view of the vulgarity and indecency of comedy for at least a century and a half, outruns their appreciation of the evidence. For the fifth century there is the story of the terrifying effect of the *Eumenides* on the women and children present—a story which though resting on very poor authority[6] would (as Haigh remarks) hardly have been invented unless women and children had in fact been

---

[1] See p. 98. [2] Aristoph. *Ach.* 504–8.
[3] 175 e.
[4] See Robin's edition (Budé), Introd., pp. viii ff.
[5] See *Theatre of D.*, pp. 140–1, where the number of seats in the Lycurgean theatre is estimated at about 14,000 (as compared with 17,000 at Epidaurus and 19,000 at Megalopolis). Also Fiechter, *Das Dionysos-Theater in Athen*, i, p. 73.
[6] *Vit. Aeschyli.* (See Haigh, *Att. Theatre*[3], p. 327. Haigh's discussion of the matter is so complete and conclusive that I follow it closely.)

admitted. There are also direct references to their presence in several passages of Aristophanes[1] and Eupolis.[2] Athenaeus[3] records that Alcibiades, entering the theatre in a procession dressed in a purple robe, was admired not only by the men but by the women. (Here, however, the reference may not be to a dramatic festival.) In a somewhat confused note a scholiast on Aristophanes[4] speaks of a psephisma of Phyromachus or Sphyromachus ordaining that there should be separate seats for men and women, and for free women and courtesans; the context shows that the reference must be to the theatre, and the date may be late in the fifth century or early in the fourth.

For the early fourth century there are passages of Plato which are conclusive. In the *Gorgias*[5] the drama is condemned as a form of rhetoric aiming solely at pleasure and addressed to children, women, and men alike, both slaves and free. In the *Laws*[6] the Athenian speaker declares that if all forms of public entertainment were passed in review, to be judged by the pleasure they gave, little boys would put the conjuror first, older boys the comic poet, while educated women and young men and the public generally would prefer tragedy.[7] Later in the century Aristotle[8] would forbid young men by law to be spectators of comedy, until they were of an age to take part in wine-parties and had been protected against harm by good education. It is one of the characteristics of Theophrastus' Ἀναίσχυντος[9] that he smuggles his boys and their attendant into the theatre

---

[1] *Clouds* 537–9; *Peace* 765–6, 962–7; *Frogs* 1050–1. The lines in the *Peace* 962–7 are most easily explained if we suppose that the women were seated at the back of the theatre, so that barleycorns scattered from in front of the σκηνή would not reach them. Rogers (Introd. to the *Ekklesiazousai*) argues from the omission of women from the list of persons addressed in the *Peace* 50–53 that they were not present; but the list is clearly an enumeration of boys and men in an ascending scale of manliness, and none of the other passages which he quotes can be used to prove the absence of women from the audience. The *Birds* 793 ff. and *Thesm.* 395 ff. only show that some women stayed at home, as is natural.

[2] Προσπάλτιοι, fr. 244 (K.).

[3] xii, p. 534 c—probably quoting Satyrus (3rd cent. B.C.).

[4] On *Ekkles.* 22 ὁ δὲ Φυρόμαχος ψήφισμα εἰσηγήσατο, ὥστε τὰς γυναῖκας καὶ τοὺς ἄνδρας χωρὶς καθέζεσθαι καὶ τὰς ἑταίρας χωρὶς τῶν ἐλευθέρων. The previous sentence brings the tragic actor Kleomachos into the story.

[5] 502 b–c; see especially 502 d ΣΩ. ἢ οὐ ῥητορεύειν δοκοῦσί σοι οἱ ποιηταὶ ἐν τοῖς θεάτροις; ΚΑΛ. ἔμοιγε. ΣΩ. νῦν ἄρα ἡμεῖς ηὑρήκαμεν ῥητορικήν τινα πρὸς δῆμον τοιοῦτον οἷον παίδων τε ὁμοῦ καὶ γυναικῶν καὶ ἀνδρῶν, καὶ δούλων καὶ ἐλευθέρων, ἣν οὐ πάνυ ἀγάμεθα. Cf. *Laws* vii. 817 c.

[6] ii. 658 a–d.

[7] At about the same date the speaker in Isaeus' eighth oration tells how his grandfather used to take him as a boy to see the plays at the Rural Dionysia.

[8] *Polit.* IV (VII). xvii. 1336 b.

[9] *Char.* ix.

with tickets which he has bought for someone else, and of his
Αἰσχροκερδής that he will only take his sons to the theatre if he
can get admission free.[1] The fictitious correspondence between
Menander and Glykera[2] speaks of Glykera ὁρώσης καὶ καθημένης
ἐν τῷ θεάτρῳ. On a throne in the third row from the front in
the theatre is an inscription[3] (probably of the second century
A.D.) ΙΕΡΙΑΣ ΑΘΗΝΑΣ ΑΘΗΝΙΟΥ, showing that at this time
priestesses might be admitted, and many other seats in other
parts of the theatre are assigned both to a great variety of
priestesses and to other ladies of distinction by inscriptions[4] cut
during the imperial epoch, some of the Augustan period or soon
after, but for the most part not to be more nearly dated. Among
the places so reserved are seats for the priestess of Antonia (the
wife of Drusus, deified after her death), the 'priestess of Vesta,
Livia, and Julia', of 'the Roman Vesta', of Γῆ Θέμις, and of
Helios; for two ἐρσηφόροι of Χλόη Θέμις, two ἐρσηφόροι of
Εἰλειθυῖα ἐν Ἄγραις, three κανηφόροι ἀπὸ Παλλαδίου, the ὑμνητρίαι
Νύσας (?) νύμφης, and others. Some inscriptions merely name
the deity (Δήμητρος Ἀχαίας, Μοιρῶν, etc.) whose priestess doubtless took the seat. Ladies who were not apparently priestesses,
but who were given seats, were Laodamia, Philippa wife of
Medeus, Theoxene, and others, and three seats in different
places are inscribed Μεγίστης κατὰ ψήφισμα.[5]

3. One thing which is certain with regard to the conditions
for admission to the theatre (apart from the seats specially reserved) is that the cost of a seat was two obols a day in the time
of Demosthenes, who protests[6] that if he had not provided that
Philip's ambassadors should be given seats of honour, they would

---

[1] *Char.* xxx καὶ ἐπὶ θέαν τηνικαῦτα πορεύεσθαι ἄγων τοὺς υἱούς, ἡνίκα προῖκα ἀφίασιν οἱ θεατρῶναι. (Holland proposes ἐπιθέατρον, but Dilke, in *B.S.A.* xliii, p. 130, disproves this.)

[2] Alkiphr. *Epp.* IV. xviii, § 10 (Schepers). The meaning of καθημένης ἐν τῷ θεάτρῳ in this passage can hardly be disputed even if in another passage (quoted by Rogers, loc. cit.) Glykera was only standing in the wings.

[3] *I.G.* iii¹. 5063 A.

[4] Ibid. 5093–164.

[5] There may have been more than one person of the name at different times; and she may have been a priestess. (See Kirchner's commentary in *I.G.* ad loc.) What a wealth of forgotten social and religious history must lie behind all these inscriptions.

[6] *de Cor.* § 28 ἀλλ' ἐν τοῖν δυοῖν ὀβόλοιν ἐθεώρουν ἄν. Cf. [Dem.] Περὶ συντάξεως (*circa* 352 B.C.), § 9 πολλῶν καὶ μεγάλων καὶ καλῶν ὄντων τούτων ἁπάντων, τῶν μὲν ἄλλων οὐδεὶς μέμνηται, τοῖν δυοῖν δ' ὀβολοῖν ἅπαντες. The comment of the confused scholium on *de Cor.* § 28—δύο γὰρ ὄντων τῶν πρεσβέων δύο ἦσαν οἱ ὀβολοί—is impossible as an interpretation of the 'two-obol' seats mentioned in the text, but there was in later times a belief that of the two obols only one was paid to the lessee of the theatre, and the other was for refreshments. (See quotation from his scholiast Ulpian, below.)

have watched the play from the two-obol seats. These were the seats which citizens were enabled to buy by means of the distributions from the theoric fund, which was then securely established; the payment was termed διωβολία or διωβελία. Apart from this the history of the charge for admission is uncertain. Plutarch,[1] apparently on the authority of Aristotle, attributes the introduction of θεωρικά, 'money for watching the play', to Pericles, as one of his devices for bribing the people, and Ulpian (in his commentary on Demosthenes' first Olynthiac)[2] agrees with this, but gives the further reason (which is repeated by the lexicographers) that the struggle of both citizens and foreigners for seats in the theatre had become so violent and the buying up of seats (presumably from the lessee of the theatre) such an abuse that to give the poor their chance Pericles instituted a theoric fund from which they were given money to buy seats. According to Philochorus and others the sum paid was originally a drachma, but this may have covered the three days of tragedies. It is very uncertain whether the statement of Aristotle in the *Constitution of Athens*[3] of the institution of διωβελία by Kleophon (and the promise of Kallikrates to increase it to three), refers to the θεωρικά at all, and not rather to special measures of poor relief, and it is impossible to say what, if any, historical event is

---

[1] Plut. *Per.* ix τούτοις (sc. Kimon's lavishness) ὁ Περικλῆς καταδημαγωγούμενος τρέπεται πρὸς τὴν δημοσίων διανομήν, συμβουλεύσαντος αὐτῷ Δαμωνίδου τοῦ ῞Οαθεν, ὡς Ἀριστοτέλης ἱστόρηκε· καὶ ταχὺ θεωρικοῖς καὶ δικαστικοῖς λήμμασιν ἄλλαις τε μισθοφορίαις καὶ χορηγίαις συνδεκάσας τὸ πλῆθος ἐχρῆτο κατὰ τῆς ἐξ Ἀρείου πάγου βουλῆς.

[2] On Dem. *Ol.* i. i (p. 33 Dindorf) ἰστέον δὲ ὅτι τὰ χρήματα ταῦτα δημόσια θεωρικὰ ἐποίησεν ἐξ ἀρχῆς ὁ Περικλῆς δι' αἰτίαν τοιαύτην· ἐπειδὴ πολλῶν θεωμένων καὶ στασιαζόντων διὰ τὸν τόπον, καὶ ξένων καὶ πολιτῶν, καὶ λοιπὸν τῶν πλουσίων ἀγοραζόντων τοὺς τόπους, βουλόμενος ἀρέσαι τῷ δήμῳ καὶ τοῖς πένησιν, ἵνα ἔχωσι καὶ αὐτοὶ πόθεν ὠνεῖσθαι τόπους, ἔγραψε τὰ προσοδευόμενα χρήματα τῇ πόλει γενέσθαι θεωρικὰ τοῖς πολίταις. Cf. Harpocr. s.v. θεωρικά . . . θεωρικὰ ἦν τινα ἐν κοινῷ χρήματα ἀπὸ τῶν τῆς πόλεως προσόδων συναγόμενα, ταῦτα δὲ πρότερον μὲν εἰς τὰς τοῦ πολέμου χρείας ἐφυλάττετο, καὶ ἐκαλεῖτο στρατιωτικά, ὕστερον δὲ κατετίθετο εἰς τε τὰς δημοσίας κατασκευὰς καὶ διανομάς, ὧν πρῶτος ἤρξατο Ἀγύρριος ὁ δημαγωγός. Φιλόχορος δὲ ἐν τῇ πρώτῃ τῆς Ἀτθίδος φησί 'τὸ δὲ θεωρικὸν ἦν τὸ πρῶτον νομισθὲν δραχμὴ τῆς θέας, ὅθεν καὶ τοὔνομα ἔλαβε'; and Suidas, s.v. θεωρικά (and also Photius): πλεονεκτουμένων δὲ τῶν πενήτων διὰ τὸ ῥᾳδίως τοῖς πλουσίοις πλείονος τιμῆς τοῦτο γενέσθαι, ἐψηφίσαντο ἐπὶ δραχμῇ μόνον εἶναι τὸ τίμημα; cf. schol. on Lucian, *Tim.* 49 δραχμὴ δὲ ἦν τὸ διδόμενον καὶ οὔτε πλέον ἐξῆν δοῦναι δραχμῆς οὔτε ἔλαττον.

[3] Ἀθ. Πολ. xxviii τοῦ δὲ δήμου (προειστήκει) Κλεοφῶν ὁ λυροποιός, ὃς καὶ τὴν διωβελίαν ἐπόρισε πρῶτος καὶ χρόνον μέν τινα διεδίδου, μετὰ δὲ ταῦτα κατέλυσε Καλλικράτης Παιανιεὺς πρῶτος ὑποσχόμενος ἐπιθήσειν πρὸς τοῖν δυοῖν ὀβολοῖν ἄλλον ὀβόλον. Sandys (ad loc.) thinks that this refers to the θεωρικά, but see M. N. Tod, *Greek Historical Inscriptions*, i, p. 206. The accounts of the ταμίαι ἱερῶν χρημάτων τῆς Ἀθηναίας for 410–409 and 407–406 B.C. (*I.G.* i². 304) mention a number of payments by them to the Hellenotamiai εἰς τὴν διοβελίαν, and Xenophon (*Hellen.* i. vii. 2) speaks of Ἀρχέδημος ὁ τοῦ δήμου τοτὲ (406 B.C.) προεστηκὼς ἐν Ἀθήναις καὶ τῆς διωβελίας ἐπιμελόμενος.

concealed in Suidas' statement[1] that ἐπὶ Διοφάντου (395–4 B.C.) τὸ θεωρικὸν ἐγένετο δραχμή. But it was certainly a payment of two obols a day for θεωρικά to which Demosthenes wished to refuse that priority among objects of public expenditure which had been given it by Eubulus,[2] though his contemporary Aristotle[3] speaks of attempts to get the διωβελία increased, and towards the end of Demosthenes' lifetime we seem to have a mention of payments of five drachmae under the head of θεωρικά, though the circumstances are not sufficiently clear to justify any certain inference. A certain Konon[4] drew his son's theoric money to the amount of five drachmae, and was fined a talent for so doing; but of course Konon may have had a family who might have gone to the theatre if they had been at home, or he may have claimed for more than one festival.

The distribution was possibly made not in cash but in the form of free tickets distributed through the authorities of each deme, and only full citizens were entitled to share in it.[5] The payment for them was made by the State to the lessee to whom the State granted the contract for the care of the theatre, and who went by the name of ἀρχιτέκτων (superintendent of buildings), θεατρώνης (lessee of the theatre),[6] or θεατροπώλης (seller of seats).[7] This official, in the case of the theatre at the Peiraeus, undertook to keep the theatre in repair,[8] and the same arrangement was doubtless in force at Athens. He was also responsible for the seating of those to whom the State assigned places of honour;[9] it is not known whether he was paid for these seats.

---

[1] s.v. δραχμὴ χαλαζῶσα. See also Harpocr., quoted above.

[2] Ulpian on Dem. *Olynth.* 1. i (p. 32 Dindorf) ἐπειδὴ χρήματα ἔχοντες στρατιωτικὰ ἔναγχος αὐτὰ πεποιήκασι θεωρικά, ὥστε λαμβάνειν ἐν τῷ θεωρεῖν ἕκαστον τῶν ἐν τῇ πόλει δύο ὀβόλους, ἵνα τὸν μὲν ἕνα κατασχῇ εἰς ἰδίαν τροφήν, τὴν δὲ ἄλλην παρέχειν ἔχωσι τῷ ἀρχιτέκτονι τοῦ θεάτρου, οὐδὲ γὰρ εἶχον τότε θέατρον διὰ λίθων κατεσκευασμένον· εἶτα βουλόμενος Δημοσθένης ταῦτα μεταβαλεῖν κτλ.

[3] *Pol.* II. vii. 1267 b ἔτι δ' ἡ πονηρία τῶν ἀνθρώπων ἄπληστον, καὶ τὸ πρῶτον μὲν ἱκανὸν διωβολία μόνον, ὅταν δ' ἤδη τοῦτ' ᾖ πάτριον, ἀεὶ δέονται τοῦ πλείονος. But again the reference may not be to the θεωρικά (see above, p. 271, n. 3).

[4] Hypereid. *in Dem.* col. 26 καὶ Κόνων μὲν ὁ Παιανεύς, ὃς ὑπὲρ τοῦ υἱοῦ ἔλαβεν τὸ θεωρικὸν ἀποδημοῦντος, πέντε δραχμῶν ἕνεκεν ἱκετεύων ὑμᾶς τάλαντον ὦφλεν ἐν τῷ δικαστηρίῳ, τούτων κατηγορευόντων. Cf. Deinarch. *in Dem.* § 56 πάλιν τὸν τὴν πεντεδραχμίαν ἐπὶ τῷ τοῦ μὴ παρόντος ὀνόματι λαβεῖν ἀξιώσαντα καὶ τοῦτον ἀπέφηνε (sc. ἡ βουλή).

[5] For distribution of θεωρικά by the authorities of the deme to citizens only see Dem. *in Leocharem*, § 37, but if Ulpian (see above, n. 2) is right, at least one of the two obols must have been paid in cash.

[6] Theophr. *Char.* xxx, if the reading θεατρῶναι is right (see above, p. 270, n. 1). The plural was possibly right as regards some theatres.

[7] Pollux vii. 199 θεατροπώλης ὁ θέαν ἀπομισθῶν.   [8] *I.G.* ii². 1176.

[9] Dem. *de Cor.* § 28, and Ulpian on *Olynth.* 1. i.

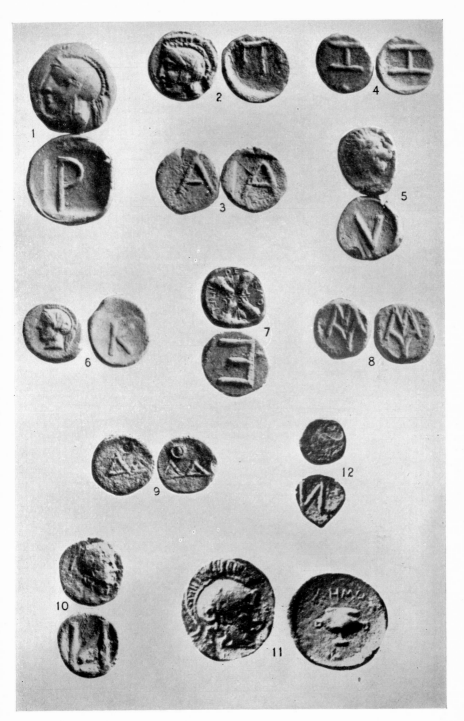

FIG. 205. BRONZE TOKENS

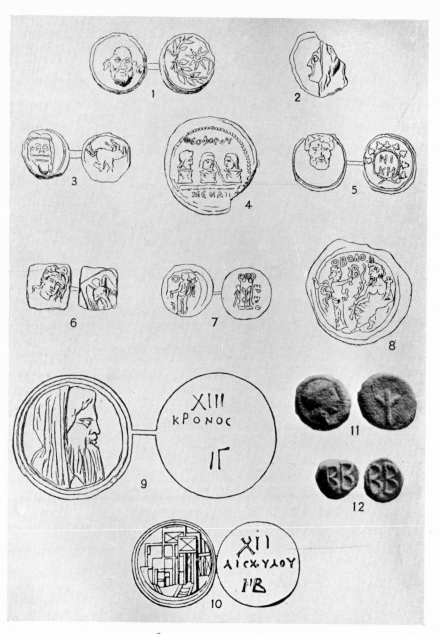

FIG. 206. LEADEN OR OTHER TOKENS

For all other seats he could only charge the authorized price. A passage of Theophrastus, already cited, suggests that there might be circumstances in which some seats were free at his discretion, but it is possible that the reference is not to the Athenian theatre.

4. The actual admission was by ticket, and many of these tickets or tokens (σύμβολα) survive, as part of an immense number of coin-like objects made of bronze, lead, ivory, bone, or terra-cotta, of which most appear to have given access to seats in the law-courts, the council chamber, the assembly, or the theatre, or the right of entrance to the market, while some indicate values of various kinds. They have been collected from all parts of the Greek world, but a large number are certainly of Athenian origin and of these many certainly, and many others with great probability, gave entrance to the theatre of Dionysus, and some of them undoubtedly to dramatic performances.[1] Three main series can be distinguished. The first consists of a number of bronze objects, like coins in their general appearance, practically all Athenian or Attic, and shown with virtual certainty by Svoronos to be tickets of admission to the theatre, whether for the assembly or for the drama, and to date from about 343 B.C. till late in the third century. They are stamped on one side with the head of Athena or a lion's head or some other emblem, and on the other with a letter of the alphabet, indicative, as Svoronos argues, of blocks of seats in the theatre. Some are stamped with letters on both sides. On some (probably late in the third century) the symbol is a κέρνος (a vessel particularly connected with the cult of Eleusis).[2] Specimens of various types are figured on my Plate (Fig. 205).[3] It would have been impossible to assign individual seats and to control the occupation

[1] They have been the subject of exhaustive study by Benndorf, *Beiträge zur Kenntniss des attischen Theaters* (1875), and Svoronos, *Journ. internat. d'archéologie numismatique*, i (1898), pp. 37 ff.; iii (1900), pp. 197 ff., 322 ff.; viii, pp. 323 ff.

[2] For the κέρνος (or κέρχνος) as a symbol see *Hesperia*, iii, p. 449; cf. also Head, *Hist. Nummorum*, p. 377. It was an earthenware dish with smaller vessels for offerings attached to it.

[3] Those figured are taken from Svoronos, *J. Arch. Num.* i and *Trésor des monnaies d'Athènes*, pl. 102. Nos. 1 and 2 show the head of Athena with a letter, Nos. 3 and 4 a letter on both sides; these are dated *c.* 342–338 B.C. The next group, Nos. 5–9, are placed between 338 and 307 B.C.; No. 5 has a lion's head and letter, No. 6 the head of Athena and letter; No. 7 the indication Θεσμοθετῶν with four owls and a letter; Nos. 8 and 9, two letters on each side. No. 10 (dated *c.* 307–296 B.C.) has the head of Athena with a letter and an owl. Nos. 11 and 12 bear the κέρνος, and are dated by Svoronos between 255 and 220 B.C. There is not absolute unanimity among numismatists as to the dating, nor can it always be certain that it was for dramatic performances that the tickets were used and not (for example) political assemblies.

of them in so vast a theatre, and each ticket would give only the right to a place in a particular block, within which there would still be room for plenty of struggling for desirable places.

A second series of tickets or tokens, representing by far the largest number of specimens, was made of lead—also in the shape of coins, and ranging from the end of the fifth century B.C.[1] until a late period in the early Christian era. Of these the large majority have been found in Italy and Sicily, but very many (over 1,000 of them known to Benndorf in 1875) come from Athens and Attica,[2] and they have been found in large quantities in Asia Minor and in all parts of the Greek world. There is no doubt that many of these gave entrance to the theatre, but the relation between these and the bronze series, which coincides with them in time for over a century, has not been made quite clear. That lead was a convenient material for the purpose is obvious, as leaden tokens could easily be melted down after they had been surrendered, and then re-stamped and used again. Many of them are stamped with a tragic or comic mask, or with the head of Silenus, and some with the name of a tribe—doubtless the tribe to which a particular κερκίς or block of seats in the theatre had been allotted. One of these is figured here (No. 7). Perhaps the most interesting is one which bears the name of the play, Menander's Θεοφορουμένη,[3] to which admission was given. (It can only have been one of the plays performed on the particular day on which the ticket gave the right of entry.) No. 7 is stamped with a figure of Bacchus and the name of the Erechtheid tribe, with a tripod indicative of the expected victory; others bear the word Νίκη.

A third type belongs to the imperial period,[4] and implies an audience of mixed Greek and Roman composition, since the number of the block of seats is given in both Greek and Roman notation.[5] Tickets of this type (which are relatively few) are made of ivory or bone, and it is conjectured that they were intended for a class of persons superior to the mass who had to be

---

[1] This is argued by Benndorf from the partial use on one or two of them of the Euclidean forms of letters of the alphabet.

[2] The figures here reproduced on Fig. 206 are taken from Benndorf, op. cit., nos. 19, 20, 22, 23, 27, 28, 42, 45; No. 8 was found at the Serapeum in Memphis, and shows Isis and the Nile, as well as the price (2 obols). The square shape of No. 6 is to be noted.

[3] See *Theatre of D.*, pp. 165–6. [4] Fig. 206, Nos. 9, 10. Cf. Dilke, *B.S.A.*, xliii, 181, n. 2.

[5] The numbers never go beyond fifteen, which was probably the highest number of κερκίδες at any period.

content with lead—possibly for the occupants of the front rows.
They are usually stamped on one side with a head or emblem,
to which a name is attached, and as it is known that in some
theatres,[1] and especially at Syracuse in the third century B.C.,
the names of personages, human, heroic, or divine, were attached
to particular blocks, it is thought that the heads or emblems on
these tickets refer to such blocks. A ticket of this type found in
the Odeion at Athens bears the name of Aeschylus.

In some theatres the admission tickets were made of clay or
terra-cotta, and Svoronos enumerates a few such from Athens.[2]
A large number, which cannot be further considered here, were
discovered in the theatre at Mantinea,[3] marked not only with
an indication of the place allotted, but with the holder's name.
They range from the fifth to the third century B.C.

5. The right to a seat of honour (προεδρία) was given by the
State and was probably enjoyed *ex officio* by certain officials such
as the archons and (at least in the course of time) by the generals;
but at the time of Aristophanes' *Knights*[4] the generals seem not
to have received it as a matter of course, since they are said to
have threatened to go on strike if they did not get it:

> καὶ στρατηγὸς οὐδ' ἂν εἷς
> τῶν πρὸ τοῦ σίτησιν ἤτησ' ἐρόμενος Κλεαίνετον·
> νῦν δ' ἐὰν μὴ προεδρίαν φέρωσι καὶ τὰ σιτία,
> οὐ μαχεῖσθαί φασιν.

Many priests also received the privilege, and (of unofficial persons) the orphan sons of those who had fallen in battle,[5] great
public benefactors, such as Demosthenes,[6] and (on a vote of the
Council) ambassadors from foreign states.[7] Persons so privileged
were honourably escorted to their seats[8]—in the Peiraeus by the

[1] See *I.G.* xiv. 3 for such names in Syracuse. They include those of Zeus, Herakles, Hieron, Philistis, Nereis. (See Rizzo, *Il teatro greco di Siracusa*, pp. 46 ff.) Tacitus (*Ann.* ii. 83) alludes to a similar practice in Rome ('equester ordo cuneum Germanici appellavit, qui Iuniorum dicebatur'). [2] Fig. 206, Nos. 11, 12.
[3] Fougères, *Mantinée et l'Arcadie orientale* (1898), pp. 530 ff.; Svoronos, *J. Arch. Num.* iii, pp. 197 ff.; in the latter volume, pp. 55 ff., is a description by Kastriotis of such tokens from Megalopolis.
[4] ll. 573 ff. Kleainetos was the father of Kleon. [5] Aeschin. *in Ctes.* § 154.
[6] The psephism quoted in [Plut.] *Vit. X Orat.*, p. 851, extends the privileges to Demosthenes' descendants.
[7] Dem. *de Cor.* § 28; Aeschin. *in Ctes.* § 76; cf. *C.I.A.* ii. 164 (ambassadors from Kolophon assigned prohedria in the Peiraeus).
[8] Schol. Aristoph. *Knights* 575 ἐξῆν δὲ τοῖς τῆς τιμῆς ταύτης τυχοῦσι καὶ ἐν βουλευτηρίῳ καὶ ἐν ἐκκλησίᾳ καὶ ἐν θεάτροις καὶ ἐν ἄλλῳ παντὶ συλλόγῳ τοὺς προκαταλαμβάνοντας, οἵτινες ἦσαν, ἐξεγείραντας αὐτοὺς εἰς τὸν ἐκείνων τόπον καθίσαι.

demarch;[1] and Aeschines taunts Demosthenes with his undue
servility towards the ambassadors of Philip in performing this
duty and providing them with cushions and purple rugs or
carpets (φοινικίδες) with his own hand.[2]

In the front row of the theatre of Dionysus as it is are sixty
seats inscribed[3] with the names of persons or officials (mainly
priests) for whom places were thus reserved; in the row behind
and in other suitable places other reservations are similarly
marked. A few of these seats are no longer in their original
positions, and a few which were in the front row are now missing.
Most of the extant inscriptions date from the time of Hadrian,
and all but about a dozen are carved over earlier inscriptions
wholly or partially erased. The central position in the front row
was occupied by the priest of Dionysus Eleuthereus, and in the
front seats of the same block or κερκίς were the priests of Ζεὺς
Πολιεύς ('Protector of the City') and of the Olympian Zeus; the
inscription Ἱερέως Διὸς Πολιέως probably goes back to the
second century B.C.[4] There were many other seats reserved for
priests and others connected with the worship of Zeus—for the
Ἱερεὺς Βουζύγης of Ζεὺς Τέλειος and of Zeus ἐν Παλλαδίῳ (the
latter post-Hadrianic), for the priests of Ζεὺς Φίλιος, of Ζεὺς
Σωτήρ and Athena, of Ζεὺς Βουλαῖος and Athena Βουλαία,[5]
whose altars were in the Council Chamber, and for the Φαιδρυνταί[6] who had the care of the statues of the Olympian Zeus in
the City and of Zeus in Pisa. Besides the priest of Dionysus
Eleuthereus there is a seat for the priest of Dionysus Αὐλωνεύς
(otherwise only known from a private dedication of the Roman
period, and interpreted by Farnell as the 'god of the flute', by
others as 'of Aulon'—there were several places of the name);

[1] *C.I.A.* ii. 589 καὶ εἰσαγέτω αὐτὸν ὁ δήμαρχος εἰς τὸ θέατρον καθάπερ ἱερεῖς καὶ τοὺς ἄλλους οἷς δέδοται ἡ προεδρία παρὰ Πειραιέων.
[2] Aeschin. *in Ctes.* § 76. The colour makes it improbable that the φοινικίδες were awnings.
[3] *I.G*². iii¹. 5021–164. (A few minor corrections have been made in *Hesperia*, xvi (1947), pp. 76–77, and by O. A. W. Dilke in *B.S.A.* xliii (1948), p. 178.)
[4] Other inscriptions dating from before the Christian era are those of the priests of the Pythian Apollo (5029) in the second row of the middle κερκίς and of 'Poseidon Γαιήοχος and Erechtheus', and two in the fourth row of the same κερκίς which read Διογένους Εὐεργέτου and Ἱερέως Ἀττάλου Ἐπωνύμου which Kirchner (*I.A.*, loc. cit.) dates 200–197 B.C. For the throne of the priest of Dionysus Eleuthereus see *Theatre of D.*, pp. 141 ff. The inscription on this is regarded as relatively early (probably pre-Christian).
[5] It is strange that there are no reservations (at least none extant) for other priests, etc., of Athena.
[6] In the inscriptions (5072 and 5064) the form is ΦΑΙΔΥΝΤΟΥ as in some other inscriptions; but Pausanias v. xiv. 5 reads φαιδρυνταί, and describes them as descendants of Pheidias.

and two for the priests of Dionysus Μελπόμενος described respectively as ἐκ τεχνειτῶν and ἐξ Εὐνειδῶν (a clan especially associated with music at Athens). These two are of interest because
Dionysus Μελπόμενος was especially an object of worship of the
'Artists of Dionysus'.[1] The close association of the cults of Athens
and of Dionysus with those of Eleusis is illustrated by seats
reserved for the priest of Demeter and Persephone, for the
Hierophant and the Δᾳδοῦχος (in the second row), and for
priests bearing the titles of 'Ιακχαγωγός (who carried the statue
of Iakchos in processions) and Λιθοφόρος (carrier of the sacred
stone in an Eleusinian ceremony). The priests of Apollo under
some of his many titles—Δαφνηφόρος, Λύκηος,[2] Πατρῷος, Δήλιος,
Ζωστήριος, and (in the second row) Πύθιος—also had seats, as
well as the Hieromnemon, the representative of Athens at the
Amphictyonic Council at Delphi. Two seats were assigned to
priests of Artemis and two to priests of Poseidon, and one each
to priests of Theseus, of Hephaestus, of the Twelve Gods,[3] of
the Muses, of Asklepios, of Eukleia and Eunomia, and some
others whose appellations are not all easy to interpret with certainty.[4] There were also seats for two of the ἐξηγηταί—the
official interpreters of religious law, one appointed for life by
popular vote out of the Eupatridai,[5] another by the oracle of
Delphi[6]—and for the 'Ιεροκῆρυξ 'the Sacred Herald'. The State
was recognized by the reservation of seats for the three archons
(two of those assigned to the thesmothetai have now disappeared), and of at least one General and a Herald (conjectured
to be the Herald who served the Council of Areopagus). Finally,
there were seats for the priests of human beings recently deified
—Diogenes the Benefactor, who (for a consideration) restored independence to Athens in 229 B.C. after the death of Demetrius,[7]
Attalus I at the beginning of the second century B.C. (both
already mentioned), Augustus (the inscription on the seat being

---

[1] See below, p. 308. His cult in the theatre of Priene is attested by an inscription of the
second century B.C. (Hiller von G., no. 174) and Pausanias (I. ii. 5) found a τέμενος dedicated
to him near the Dipylon Gate in Athens.
[2] Probably an inscription of the Augustan age, when this cult was in vogue.
[3] See above, p. 61.
[4] e.g. 5026 ἱερέως θυηχόου; 5046 ἱερέως πυρφόρου ἐξ ἀκροπολέως; 5047 ἱερέως δήμου καὶ
Χαρίτων καὶ 'Ρώμης; 5071 ἱερέως Ἀνάκων καὶ 'Ηρῷος ἐπιτελείου.
[5] No. 5049 ἐξηγητοῦ ἐξ Εὐπατριδῶν χειροτονητοῦ ὑπὸ τοῦ δήμου διὰ βίου.
[6] No. 5023 πυθοχρήστου ἐξηγητοῦ.
[7] See *Cambr. Anc. Hist.* vii, pp. 748–9.

probably contemporary),[1] Hadrian, and Hadrian's favourite, Antinous—the last under the title Ἀντινόου Χορείου ἐκ τεχνειτῶν.

Besides the seats assigned for prohedria, there were special parts of the theatre reserved for the Council[2] and for the Epheboi, and a psephisma has already been quoted[3] which assigned women separate places from men and courtesans from other women; there is some reason to suppose that women were seated at a distance from the skene.[4] Whether it can be inferred from a fragment of Alexis' Γυναικοκρατία that foreigners (or foreign women) were placed in one of the extreme left or right blocks is not quite certain without the context :[5]

> ἐνταῦθα περὶ τὴν ἐσχάτην δεῖ κερκίδα
> ὑμᾶς καθιζούσας θεωρεῖν ὡς ξένας.

It is very probable that each of the tribes (φυλαί) had its own block of seats out of the thirteen wedge-shaped blocks (κερκίδες) into which the auditorium was divided. In the time of Hadrian a statue of the emperor, of which the base is preserved, stood at the foot of the central block, erected by the Areopagus, the Council, and the People of Athens in A.D. 112; the bases of three statues of Hadrian are also preserved, erected respectively by the tribes Erechtheis, Akamantis, and Oineis, at the foot of the first and sixth blocks from the east and the sixth block from the west, and as the places of these correspond with the order of the tribes in the official list,[6] it is probable that the series of statues was once complete, and that each stood at the foot of a block appropriated wholly or in part to a tribe which had dedicated it, and the fact that the names of tribes appear on some of the 'theatre tickets' which have been found confirms this. In Hadrian's time, when there were twelve tribes, the central block may perhaps have been the βουλευτικόν, or official quarter. What was the distribution in the fifth century, when there were ten tribes, can only be conjectured.

6. With performances going on continuously from dawn till evening, the audience naturally provided itself with refresh-

---

[1] See Graindor, *Athènes sous Auguste*, p. 137.

[2] Aristoph. *Birds* 794 ἐν βουλευτικῷ: schol. ad loc. οὗτος τόπος τοῦ θεάτρου ὁ ἀνειμένος τοῖς βουλευταῖς, ὡς καὶ τοῖς ἐφήβοις ἐφηβικός; Poll. iv. 122 ἐκαλεῖτο δέ τι καὶ βουλευτικὸν μέρος τοῦ θεάτρου καὶ ἐφηβικόν. An inscription, *C.I.G.* ii. 2436, appears to refer to special places in the theatre at Melos for νεανίσκοι and ὑμνῳδοί.

[3] Schol. on Aristoph. *Ekkles.* 22, see above, p. 269.

[4] See above, p. 269.   [5] Fr. 41 (K.).

[6] For this point see Benndorf, op. cit., pp. 16, 17, and refs. given there.

ments. Some may have left the theatre for a time and gone home for a meal—as, Aristophanes[1] suggests in the *Birds*, it would be easy to do if they had wings; but there was also some circulation of provisions in the theatre itself, which were consumed, as Aristotle tells us, when the acting was bad,[2] and perhaps not only then. Philochorus[3] (half a century after Aristotle) gives a picture of the habits of the Athenian spectators in the past, who had a good meal before they came to the theatre, wearing garlands on their heads, and kept themselves refreshed throughout the performances with wine and with dried fruits and confectionery, which might also be used to pelt actors whom they did not like.[4] There is more than one allusion also to the scattering of such things among the audience by comic actors.[5] The discomfort of the hard seats was mitigated by the use of cushions, but the ostentatious placing of cushions for guests or patrons was a form of compliment which might suggest interested motives.[6] In the time of Hadrian there seem to have been awnings to shelter the two front rows in the Athenian theatre from sun and rain.[7]

There is plenty of evidence of the noisiness of Athenian audiences, both in their approval and their disapproval of a performance. Plato speaks[8] of the ἄμουσοι βοαὶ πλήθους and the κρότοι ἐπαίνους ἀποδιδόντες which had been carried so far as to establish a kind of θεατροκρατία over the poets; Demosthenes[9] records how the spectators hissed Meidias when he entered the theatre, and if an actor or a poet were forced to retire, the

---

[1] *Birds* 786-9 αὐτίχ' ὑμῶν τῶν θεατῶν εἴ τις ἦν ὑπόπτερος | εἶτα πεινῶν τοῖς χοροῖσι τῶν τραγῳδῶν ἤχθετο, | ἐκπτόμενος ἂν οὗτος ἠρίστησεν ἐλθὼν οἴκαδε, | κᾆτ' ἂν ἐμπλησθεὶς ἐφ' ἡμᾶς αὖθις αὖ κατέπτατο.

[2] *Eth. Nic.* x. v καὶ ἐν τοῖς θεάτροις οἱ τραγηματίζοντες, ὅταν φαῦλοι οἱ ἀγωνιζόμενοι ὦσι, τότε μάλιστα αὐτὸ δρῶσιν.

[3] *ap.* Athen. xi. 464 f λέγει δὲ περὶ τούτων ὁ Φιλόχορος οὑτωσί· 'Ἀθηναῖοι τοῖς Διονυσιακοῖς ἀγῶσι τὸ μὲν πρῶτον ἠριστηκότες καὶ πεπωκότες ἐβάδιζον ἐπὶ τὴν θέαν καὶ ἐστεφανωμένοι ἐθεώρουν, παρὰ δὲ τὸν ἀγῶνα πάντα οἶνος αὐτοῖς ᾠνοχοεῖτο καὶ τραγήματα παρεφέρετο, καὶ τοῖς χοροῖς εἰσιοῦσιν ἐνέχεον πίνειν καὶ διηγωνισμένοις ἐνέχεον πάλιν· μαρτυρεῖν δὲ τούτοις καὶ Φερεκράτη τὸν κωμικόν, ὅτι μέχρι τῆς καθ' ἑαυτὸν ἡλικίας οὐκ ἀσίτους εἶναι τοὺς θεωροῦντας.' The early start is referred to in Xen. *Oecon.* iii. vii, but perhaps with reference to the Rural Dionysia.

[4] Dem. *de Cor.* § 262—who, however, is speaking of the Rural Dionysia at which Aeschines acted. Whether he is to be taken seriously when he speaks (*F.L.* § 337) of Aeschines having been almost stoned to death may be doubted.

[5] Aristoph. *Wasps* 58, and schol.; *Ploutos* 797.

[6] Aesch. *in Ctes.* § 76, *Fals. Leg.*, § 111; Theophr. *Char.* ii (the κόλαξ takes the cushion from the slave and lays it for his patron himself).

[7] See *Theatre of D.*, p. 263. [8] *Laws* 700 c ff.; cf. *Rep.* vi. 492 b.

[9] *in Meid.* § 226.

hissing might be accompanied by the noise of heels kicking against the seats.[1] Pollux[2] speaks of a day on which the audience (evidently in a bad mood) hissed off one comic actor (and his play) after another, and Athenaeus[3] has a story of the comic poet Diphilus being violently ejected from the theatre. But physical violence in the theatre was legally a capital offence, even if it were prompted by a real grievance (as when a man turned out the usurper of his seat),[4] and there were beadles (ῥαβδοῦχοι or ῥαβδοφόροι)[5] to keep order, as well as the special officials who had to curb disorder among the singers.[6] The fight in the theatre between Alcibiades and Taureas, when they were rivals as choregi in a dithyrambic contest and Alcibiades drove Taureas away with blows, was doubtless exceptional,[7] but the story, which narrates that, despite his conduct, the judges were intimidated into awarding the victory to Alcibiades, although the spectators were in favour of Taureas, at least illustrates the uncertainty of decisions in the theatre. At a much later date Plutarch[8] speaks of tragic actors needing the support of a claque in the theatre, and Philemon is said to have won many victories over Menander through the help of such supporters, despite Menander's superior merits.[9] The theatre-beadles are not re-

---

[1] Pollux iv. 120 τὸ μέντοι τὰ ἐδώλια ταῖς πτέρναις κατακρούειν πτερνοκοπεῖν ἔλεγον· ἐποίουν δὲ τοῦτο ὁπότε τινα ἐκβάλοιεν. It is not known, however, if Pollux is speaking of Athens, and the practice is thought by some to imply wooden seats (as well as wooden shoes); see *Theatre of D.*, p. 19, and Dilke in *B.S.A.* xliii, p. 148. For hissing cf. Dem. *de Cor.* § 265 ἐξέπιπτες, ἐγὼ δ᾿ ἐσύριττον, and many passages of Lucian, e.g. *Nigrin.* 8, *Pro mercede cond.* 5, etc. The hissing might be reinforced by the peculiar sound denoted by κλώζειν; cf. Harpocr., etc., κλωσμὸν ἔλεγον τὸν γενόμενον ἐν τοῖς στόμασι ψόφον, ᾧ πρὸς τὰς ἐκβολὰς ἐχρῶντο τῶν ἀκροαμάτων, ὧν οὐχ ἡδέως ἤκουον.

[2] iv. 88; cf. p. 168, above.   [3] xiii. 583 f.

[4] Dem. *in Meid.* §§ 178–9; see above, pp. 66 f.

[5] Cf. Aristoph. *Peace* 734 and schol.

[6] See above, pp. 68, 93.   [7] Andocid. *in Alcib.* §§ 20, 21.

[8] *De adul. et amico* 22 ἀλλ᾿ ὥσπερ οἱ τραγῳδοὶ χοροῦ δέονται φίλων συνᾳδόντων ἢ θεάτρου συνεπικροτοῦντος, and there are references to the organization of supporters in Alkiphron's fictitious correspondence of Menander (2nd cent. A.D.), though this is no evidence for the Classical period, e.g. *Epp.* III. xxxv. 3 (Schepers) σὺ δὲ ἡμῖν μετὰ τῶν συνηθῶν ἐπίσειε τοὺς κρότους, ἵνα κἄν τι λάθωμεν ἀποσφαλέντες, μὴ λάβῃ χώραν τὰ ἀστικὰ μειράκια κλώζειν ἢ συρίττειν, ἀλλ᾿ ὁ τῶν ἐπαίνων κρότος τὸν θροῦν τῶν σκωμμάτων παραλύσῃ, and IV. xix. 5 τί γὰρ Ἀθῆναι χωρὶς Μενάνδρου; τί δὲ Μένανδρος χωρὶς Γλυκέρας, ἥτις αὐτῷ καὶ τὰ προσωπεῖα διασκευάζω καὶ τὰς ἐσθῆτας ἐκδύω, κἂν τοῖς προσκηνίοις (παρασκηνίοις edd.) ἕστηκα τοὺς δακτύλους ἐμαυτῆς πιέζουσα καὶ τρέμουσα, ἕως ἂν κροταλίσῃ τὸ θέατρον.

[9] Gellius, *Noct. Att.* xvii. 4. Menander is said to have asked Philemon if he was not ashamed of defeating him: 'Menander a Philemone, nequaquam pari scriptore, in certaminibus comoediarum ambitu gratiaque et factionibus saepenumero vincebatur. Eum cum forte habuisset obviam, "Quaeso," inquit, "Philemo, bona venia dic mihi, cum me vincis, non erubescis?" '

corded to have dealt with such bad manners as those of Theophrastus' βδελυρός and ἀναίσθητος—of whom the former[1] deliberately hissed when others applauded, and applauded when the
rest of the audience were silent, not to speak of other breaches of
good taste, while the latter[2] slept soundly throughout the performances and was left sleeping when the theatre had emptied.

7. That the audience as a whole followed a play intently is
shown by the stories which tell of their bursting into tears when
moved by a skilled actor such as Kallippides,[3] or of their dread
lest the old man who was to arrest Merope's blow, when she
was about to murder her son, should not arrive in time.[4] But
though Aristophanes may for his own purposes flatter their
judgement[5] with an allusion, it might be not without a touch
of irony, to their literary sense,[6] it may be doubted whether their
critical capacity was great. Their possession of books[7] (and probably not more than a small fraction of the audience possessed
them) does not prove very much, though at the beginning of the
Frogs[8] Dionysus—the embodiment of the average Athenian—
tells of his enjoyment in reading Euripides' *Andromeda*, and it
must not be forgotten that the Athenians imprisoned in the
quarries at Syracuse solaced themselves and their companions
in misfortune by repeating passages of Euripides which they
knew by heart.[9] The sentiment which Aristophanes puts in the
mouth of Aeschylus in the *Frogs*[10]—that there were no judges of
poets in the world like the Athenians—has to be counter-
balanced by the appeal of Euripides in Hades to the baser elements in the crowd,[11] and when Aristophanes flatters he is hardly

[1] *Char.* xi.

[2] *Char.* xiv.

[3] Xen. *Symp.* III. xi; cf. Isocr. *Paneg.* § 168 ἐπὶ μὲν ταῖς συμφοραῖς ταῖς ὑπὸ τῶν ποιητῶν
συγκειμέναις δακρύειν ἀξιοῦσιν.

[4] Plut. *De esu carnis* II. v σκόπει δὲ καὶ τὴν ἐν τραγῳδίᾳ Μερόπην, ἐπὶ τὸν υἱὸν αὐτὸν ὡς φονέα
τοῦ υἱοῦ πέλεκυν ἀραμένην καὶ λέγουσαν ' ὁσιαιτέραν δὲ τήνδ' ἐγὼ δίδωμί σοι | πληγήν ', ὅσον ἐν
τῷ θεάτρῳ κίνημα ποιεῖ, συνεξορθιάζουσα φόβῳ καὶ δέος μὴ φθάνῃ τὸν ἐπιλαμβανόμενον γέροντα
καὶ τρώσῃ τὸ μειράκιον.

[5] e.g. *Knights* 233 τὸ γὰρ θέατρον δέξιον.

[6] *Frogs* 1109 f. εἰ δὲ τοῦτο καταφοβεῖσθον, μή τις ἀμαθία προσῇ | τοῖς θεωμένοισιν ὡς τὰ | λεπτὰ
μὴ γνῶναι λεγόντοιν | μηδὲν ὀρρωδεῖτε τοῦθ' · ὡς οὐκέθ' οὕτω ταῦτ' ἔχει. | ἐστρατευμένοι γάρ
εἰσι, | βιβλίον τ' ἔχων ἕκαστος μανθάνει τὰ δεξιά.

[7] There are references to book shops in the *Birds* 1288 and Eupolis, fr. 304 (K.), and later
in Plato's *Apology* 26 d.

[8] l. 52.

[9] Plut. *Nikias*, ch. xxix. No doubt some of them had been members of dramatic choruses.
That Pheidippides in the *Clouds* 1371 declaimed an unedifying passage of Euripides of course
proves nothing.

[10] ll. 809–10 λῆρόν τε τἄλλ' ἡγεῖτο τῆς φύσεως πέρι | γνῶναι ποιητῶν.

[11] Ibid., ll. 771 ff.

to be taken more seriously than Demosthenes, who half a century later told the Assembly that no one was more acute than they.[1]

There was, at least in the fourth century, intense interest in the performance of rival actors,[2] and there might at any time be tumultuous applause for some sentiment of Euripides with which the crowd agreed[3]—or equally tumultuous hissing, if they disapproved, as they did when in the *Danae* they heard an eloquent passage in praise of money, and were only quieted when the poet sprang forward and advised them to wait and see what happened to the character who uttered the sentiment.[4] There are also the well-known stories of the attack on Aeschylus when he was supposed to be 'revealing the mysteries'[5] and on Euripides, when his *Melanippe Σοφή* opened with the line, Ζεύς, ὅστις ὁ Ζεύς, οὐ γὰρ οἶδα πλὴν λόγῳ.[6] (Socrates himself is said to have called for a repetition of the first three lines of the *Orestes*, which contain a not very profound observation, but Cicero, who tells the story, does not say what happened.)[7] At a much later date Philo records the excitement of an audience at the performance of a Euripidean play (it can hardly, however, have been at Athens) when they heard a couplet in praise of freedom.[8] But such stories do not prove the possession of any real critical sense, and when Cicero speaks of the fine taste of the Athenians, he is obviously thinking not of popular audiences but of the approval of the 'Attic style' in the schools of oratory in contemporary Athens.[9] In favour of the Athenian public it must never be forgotten that they approved of Sophocles from the beginning to

---

[1] *Olynth.* iii, § 32 καὶ γνῶναι ὑμεῖς ὀξύτατοι τὰ δέοντα.

[2] Dem. *de Pace*, § 6. The interest in the fourth century had largely shifted from the poets to the actors (see above, pp. 94 ff.).

[3] Such as τί δ' αἰσχρὸν ἦν μὴ τοῖσι χρωμένοις δοκῇ; (Stob. *Serm.* v. 82).

[4] Nauck², fr. 324 ὦ χρυσέ, δεξίωμα κάλλιστον βροτοῖς | ὡς οὔτε μήτηρ ἡδονὰς τοιὰς ἔχει, | οὐ παῖδες ἀνθρώποισιν, οὐ φίλος πατήρ, | οἵας σὺ χοἴ σε δώμασιν κεκτημένοι. | εἰ δ' ἡ Κύπρις τοιοῦτον ὀφθαλμοῖς ὁρᾷ, | οὐ θαῦμ' ἔρωτας μυρίους αὐτὴν τρέφειν. The story is told by Seneca, *Ep.* 115, who ascribes the fragment to the *Bellerophon*, while Stobaeus quotes it as from the *Danae*.

[5] Aristot. *Eth. Nic.* iii. i. 2.

[6] Plut. *Amator.* xiii, p. 756 c. See *New Chapters in Gk. Lit.* iii, p. 115, for this line and the substitute which he is said to have provided later, Ζεὺς ὡς λέλεκται τῆς ἀληθείας ὕπο.

[7] Cic. *Tusc. Disp.* iv, § 63. The lines run: οὐκ ἔστιν οὐδὲν δεινὸν ὧδ' εἰπεῖν ἔπος | οὐδὲ πάθος οὐδὲ ξυμφορὰ θεήλατος | ἧς οὐκ ἂν ἄραιτ' ἄχθος ἀνθρώπου φύσις.

[8] Philo Iud. (*circa* 30 B.C.–A.D. 45), *Quod omnis prob. lib.*, p. 886 πρώην ὑποκριτῶν τραγῳδίαν ἐπιδεικνύντων καὶ τὰ παρ' Εὐριπίδῃ τρίμετρα διεξιόντων ἐκεῖνα ' τοὐλεύθερον γὰρ ὄνομα παντὸς ἄξιον, | κἂν σμίκρ' ἔχῃ τις, μεγάλ' ἔχειν νομίζεται' τοὺς οὖν θεατὰς ἅπαντας εἶδον ἐπ' ἄκρων ποδῶν ὑπ' ἐκπλήξεως ἀναστάντας καὶ φωναῖς μείζοσι καὶ ἐκβοήσεσιν ἐπαλλήλοις ἔπαινον μὲν τῆς γνώμης, ἔπαινον δὲ καὶ τοῦ ποιητοῦ συνείροντας.

[9] *Orat.* §§ 25, 27.

the end of his career—there may have been some special reason
for the failure of the *Oedipus Tyrannus*, the greatest of all his
extant plays, to win the first prize—though it is impossible to
say whether it was his glorious poetry or his safe orthodoxy and
unassailable morality that most appealed to them. On the other
hand, nearly a century later they seem to have preferred Philemon to Menander,[1] and perhaps not solely because Philemon
whipped up his supporters. It may be that Menander's style was
too fine to be appreciated by the crowd, or, as some have suggested, that his friendship with Demetrius of Phalerum dimin-
ished his popularity. But Aristotle, in the generation before
Menander, does not really give a much better impression of
Athenian audiences than Plato had done,[2] and both alike speak
of poets and actors as lowering themselves to suit the depraved
taste of a public dominated by the less cultivated elements in it.
Lucian[3] in the second century A.D. is not much more complimentary, though he takes a rather more favourable view of the
influence exercised by the small handful of really competent
judges on the vulgar herd.

Aristotle's judgement of the theatrical audience and its influence on the poets is not necessarily inconsistent, as it is sometimes
stated to be, with the view which he states elsewhere in the
Politics that the opinion of the multitude on literary works (not
necessarily on particular performances) is worth more than that
of the single critic, which may be one-sided.[4]

There is not really much conflict of evidence as to the amount
of knowledge of the legends, the traditional subjects of tragedy,

---

[1] Quintil. x. i, § 72 'Philemon, qui ut pravis sui temporis iudiciis Menandro saepe praelatus est, ita consensu omnium meruit credi secundus'. See above, p. 280.

[2] *Laws* ii. 659 b, c. Cf. Aristot. *Pol.* v (VIII). vi. 1341 b ὁ γὰρ θεατὴς φορτικὸς ὢν μεταβάλλειν εἴωθε τὴν μουσικήν, ὥστε καὶ τοὺς τεχνίτας τοὺς πρὸς αὐτὸν μελετῶντας αὐτούς τε ποιούς τινας ποιεῖ καὶ τὰ σώματα διὰ τὰς κινήσεις, and vii. 1342 a ἐπεὶ δ' ὁ θεατὴς διττός, ὁ μὲν ἐλεύθερος καὶ πεπαιδευμένος, ὁ δὲ φορτικὸς ἐκ βαναύσων καὶ θητῶν καὶ ἄλλων τοιούτων συγκείμενος, ἀποδοτέον ἀγῶνας καὶ θεωρίας καὶ τοῖς τοιούτοις πρὸς ἀνάπαυσιν . . . ποιεῖ δὲ τὴν ἡδονὴν ἑκάστοις τὸ κατὰ φύσιν οἰκεῖον. διόπερ ἀποδοτέον ἐξουσίαν τοῖς ἀγωνιζομένοις πρὸς τὸν θεατὴν τὸν τοιοῦτον τοιούτῳ τινι χρῆσθαι τῷ γένει τῆς μουσικῆς. In *Poet.* xiii he speaks of the love of 'poetic justice'—of the play which ends well for the good and badly for the bad—as due to the ἀσθένεια of the spectators, ἀκολουθοῦσι γὰρ οἱ ποιηταὶ κατ' εὐχὴν ποιοῦντες τοῖς θεαταῖς.

[3] *Harmon.* § 2 ὁ γάρ τοι πολὺς οὗτος λέως αὐτοὶ μὲν ἀγνοοῦσι τὰ βελτίω, βάναυσοι ὄντες οἱ πολλοὶ αὐτῶν, ὄντινα δ' ἂν οἱ προύχοντες ἐπαινέσωσι, πιστεύουσι μὴ ἂν ἀλόγως ἐπαινεσθῆναι τοῦτον, ὥστε ἐπαινέσονται καὶ αὐτοί· καὶ γὰρ οὖν καὶ ἐν τοῖς ἀγῶσιν οἱ μὲν πολλοὶ θεαταὶ ἴσασι κροτῆσαί ποτε καὶ συρίσαι, κρίνουσι δὲ ἑπτὰ ἢ πέντε ἢ ὅσα δή.

[4] *Pol.* III. xi, p. 1281ᵃ42 διὸ καὶ κρίνουσιν ἄμεινον οἱ πολλοὶ καὶ τὰ τῆς μουσικῆς ἔργα καὶ τὰ τῶν ποιητῶν· ἄλλοι γὰρ ἄλλο τι μόριον, πάντα δὲ πάντες; cf. xvi, p. 1286ᵃ30 (without special reference to poetry) διὰ τοῦτο καὶ κρίνει ἄμεινον ὄχλος πολλὰ ἢ εἰς ὁστισοῦν.

which might be expected of an Athenian audience. The better educated could be assumed to be familiar with much of Homer and with many other legendary stories, but that Euripides did not think such knowledge to be general is implied in a significant passage of the *Hippolytus* :[1]

> ὅσοι μὲν οὖν γραφάς τε τῶν παλαιτέρων
> ἔχουσιν, αὐτοί τ᾽ εἰσὶν ἐν μούσαις ἀεί,
> ἴσασι μὲν Ζεὺς ὥς ποτ᾽ ἠράσθη γάμων
> Σεμέλης, ἴσασι δ᾽ ὡς ἀνήρπασέν ποτε
> ἡ καλλιφεγγὴς Κέφαλον εἰς θεοὺς Ἔως
> ἔρωτος οὕνεκ᾽.

This is quite consistent with Aristotle's statement in the *Poetics*[2] that even the well-known stories are well known only to a few, and when Antiphanes,[3] probably a little earlier, lays stress on the advantage possessed by tragedy, as against comedy, in being able to count on a general knowledge of its themes, he only chooses as his illustrations two of the most famous legends— those of Oedipus and Alkmaeon. In any case a previous knowledge of the plot is only one of the minor qualifications for a critical judgement or even for enjoyment of a play. That Aristophanes' own audience, or at least a considerable proportion of them, must have had some knowledge of literature is proved by the abundance of parodies and allusions in his plays, though many of these are allusions to plays very recently produced or consist of parodies of the tragic style rather than of particular passages.

We get very few hints of any special tastes of the Athenian audiences. They liked stock jokes,[4] and they disliked monotony.[5] What audience does not? Agathon is said to have failed through crowding too many events into a single plot,[6] and the word used (ἐξέπεσεν) implies that the audience as well as the judges showed their disapproval. But the anecdotes which have already been

---

[1] ll. 451 ff.

[2] Ch. ix ἐπεὶ καὶ τὰ γνώριμα ὀλίγοις γνώριμά ἐστιν, ἀλλ᾽ οὐχ ἧττον εὐφραίνει.

[3] Fr. 191 (K.) μακάριόν ἐστιν ἡ τραγῳδία | ποίημα κατὰ πάντ᾽, εἴ γε πρῶτον οἱ λόγοι | ὑπὸ τῶν θεατῶν εἰσιν ἐγνωρισμένοι, | πρὶν καί τιν᾽ εἰπεῖν· ὥστ᾽ ὑπομνῆσαι μόνον | δεῖ τὸν ποιητήν· Οἰδίπουν γὰρ ἂν μόνον | φῶ, τἄλλα πάντ᾽ ἴσασιν· ὁ πατὴρ Λάϊος | μητὴρ Ἰοκάστη, θυγατέρες, παῖδες τίνες, | τί πείσεθ᾽ οὗτος, τί πεποίηκεν. ἂν πάλιν, | εἴπῃ τις Ἀλκμέωνα, καὶ τὰ παιδία | πάντ᾽ εὐθὺς εἴρηχ᾽, ὅτι μανεὶς ἀπέκτονεν | τὴν μητέρ᾽, ἀγανακτῶν δ᾽ Ἄδραστος εὐθέως | ἥξει πάλιν τ᾽ ἄπεισι.

[4] Aristoph. *Frogs* 1 εἴπω τι τῶν εἰωθότων, ὦ δέσποτα, | ἐφ᾽ οἷς ἀεὶ γελῶσιν οἱ θεώμενοι;

[5] Aristot. *Poet.* xxiv τὸ γὰρ ὅμοιον ταχὺ πληροῦν ἐκπίπτειν ποιεῖ τὰς τραγῳδίας.

[6] Ibid. xviii, where Aristotle says that poets who do this ἢ ἐκπίπτουσιν ἢ κακῶς ἀγωνίζονται, ἐπεὶ καὶ Ἀγάθων ἐξέπεσεν ἐν τούτῳ μόνῳ.

mentioned, and the popular demand for the repetition of the *Frogs* on account of the political wisdom contained in the parabasis, suggest that the Athenian people were mainly sensitive in regard to anything which appealed to or conflicted with their moral and political sentiments, and in the *Frogs* itself most of the tests by which the rival poets are tried, so far as they are serious, have a moral or utilitarian background.

Our general conclusion must be that an audience which could follow devotedly the three great tragedians day after day, and could enjoy the wit of Aristophanes, must have possessed on the whole a high degree both of seriousness and intelligence, and though there was always a possibility of lower elements gaining the upper hand for a moment, the great poets, at least of the fifth century, never played down to them. Euripides, who has sometimes been accused of so doing, did no more than show his sympathy with new movements in thought and the new style in music, and though at first he might be regarded as dangerous and might suffer for it he too received in time a full measure of appreciation. The problem which is baffling to modern and Christian readers—how it was possible for the same audience, possibly even on the same day, to be absorbed in the noblest tragedy and pass immediately to the grossness which, along with the higher qualities of wit and humour, comedy displayed for at least a century and a half—would not have been appreciated by the Athenians of the fifth century, and is perhaps one which will never be completely solved.

VII

THE ARTISTS OF DIONYSUS[1]

1. THE organization of dramatic and musical performers into guilds or colleges at Athens and elsewhere is first definitely recorded about the end of the first quarter of the third century B.C., but it had been rendered almost inevitable by the growing importance of such performers during the fourth century, in the second half of which not only did small groups of actors go from deme to deme of Attica, but more famous actors toured the Greek world, visited the courts of Macedonian kings, and became persons of such significance that they were employed as accredited diplomatists both by Athens and by Philip. Demosthenes might ridicule Aeschines for his association with groups of inferior actors in performances in the demes,[2] but Demosthenes himself more than once refers (with an obvious sense of their importance) to the diplomatic activities of such famous actors as Neoptolemus and Aristodemus in the negotiations between Athens and Philip.[3] The fact that the profession of these actors conferred upon them[4] freedom of travel and immunity from hostile action indicates that they had a recognized status. Immunity from military and naval service may also have been commonly conceded, but that it cannot have been claimed as a right is shown by the cases of Sannio, a chorus-trainer of repute, and Aristeides, a choral singer, whom Demosthenes mentions as having been punished for evading service; and the attempts of Meidias to prevent the chorus to which Demosthenes was choregus from obtaining exemption imply that it was not

---

[1] See Welcker, *Die Griech. Tragödien*, i ii, pp. 1303 ff. (1839); Foucart, *De collegiis scaenicorum artificum apud Graecos* (1873); Lüders, *Die dionysischen Künstler* (1873); Sauppe, *Comm. de collegiis artificum scaenicorum Atticorum* (1876); Reisch, *De musicis Graecorum certaminibus*, pp. 71 ff. (1885); Brinck, *Diss. philol. Halenses* (1886), pp. 187 ff.; Poland, *De collegiis artificum Dionysiacorum* (1895), and *Gesch. des gr. Vereinswesens* (1909), pp. 129–47, and art. 'Technitai' in Pauly–W. *Real-Encycl.*; Ziebarth, *Das gr. Vereinswesen* (1896), pp. 79 ff.; Öhler, *Epigraph. Beitr. zur Gesch. der Dion. Künstler* (1908); Klaffenbach, *Symbolae ad historiam collegiorum artificum Bacchiorum* (1914); Daux, *Delphes au IIe et Ie Siècle* (1936), pp. 350 ff., 520 ff., 722 ff.; Flacélière, *Les Aitoliens à Delphes* (1937), pp. 121–3, 143, 162, 261–3. The small attention given to this subject by English scholars is the excuse for the present chapter.

[2] See above, pp. 46 f.

[3] See p. 287, n. 2, below.

[4] Under what kind of international law actors and musicians at this date obtained and enjoyed these immunities remains very obscure. About 277 B.C. they are guaranteed by a decree of the Amphiktyonic Council; see below, p. 289.

given as a matter of course.[1] Passages in Demosthenes imply that there must have been a large number of such professionals available, when called upon, to meet at Philip's court or camp, as, for instance, after the fall of Olynthus in 348, when he held an 'Olympian festival' there, with competitions, prizes, and presents for the performers.[2] But there is no indication that the actors of this time formed an organized body, nor can this be inferred from the references to them in Aristotle,[3] who says that while they called themselves τεχνῖται, others termed them Διονυσοκόλακες and in the *Problems* (if it is his work)[4] asks the reason for their general depravity and attributes it to their having to spend most of their time in making a living and to their habitual intemperance. (There were doubtless persons of all kinds in the profession then as now.)

2. Alexander showed an even greater passion for musicians and actors than his father.[5] After the capture of Thebes in 335 B.C. he held a nine-days festival at Dion, devoted mainly to dramatic contests,[6] and another such festival in 332 at Tyre,[7] where he is said to have been distressed at the defeat of Thettalos by Athenodoros in the competition for the actors' prize.[8] An account given by Chares in his *History of Alexander* of the great 'Wedding-Feast' celebrated at Susa is preserved by Athenaeus.[9]

---

[1] Dem. *in Meid.* §§ 15, 58–60.

[2] Dem. *de F.L.* § 192 ἐπειδὴ γὰρ εἷλεν "Ολυνθον Φίλιππος, 'Ολύμπι' ἐποίει, εἰς δὲ τὴν θυσίαν ταύτην καὶ τὴν πανήγυριν πάντας τοὺς τεχνίτας συνήγαγεν, ἑστιῶν δ' αὐτοὺς καὶ στεφανῶν τοὺς νενικηκότας ἤρετο Σάτυρον τουτονὶ τὸν κωμικὸν ὑποκριτήν, τί δὴ μόνος οὐδὲν ἐπαγγέλλεται. For the public activities of Neoptolemus, Aristodemus, Ktesiphon, and others, see Dem. *de Pace*, § 6 πάλιν τοίνυν ὦ ἄνδρες Ἀθηναῖοι, κατιδὼν Νεοπτόλεμον τὸν ὑποκριτήν, τῷ μὲν τῆς τέχνης προσχήματα τυγχάνοντ' ἀδείας, κακὰ δ' ἐργαζόμενον τὰ μέγιστα τὴν πόλιν, καὶ τὰ παρ' ὑμῶν διοικοῦντα Φιλίππῳ καὶ πρυτανεύοντα . . .; also *de F.L.* §§ 12, 18, 94, 315; *de Cor.* § 21; Aeschin. *de F.L.* §§ 15, 16, and passages in the 'Arguments' to the speeches of both orators *de F.L.*

[3] *Rhet.* III. ii.

[4] *Probl.* xxx. 10 διὰ τί οἱ Διονυσιακοὶ τεχνῖται ὡς ἐπὶ τὸ πολὺ πονηροί εἰσιν; ἢ ὅτι ἥκιστα λόγου σοφίας κοινωνοῦσι διὰ τὸ περὶ τὰς ἀναγκαίας τέχνας τὸ πολὺ μέρος τοῦ βίου εἶναι, καὶ ὅτι ἐν ἀκρασίαις τὸ πολὺ τοῦ βίου εἰσίν, τὰ δὲ καὶ ἐν ἀπορίαις; ἀμφότερα δὲ φαυλότητος παρασκευαστικά.

[5] Plut. *Alex.* 4.

[6] Diod. xvii. 16. (Arrian I. xi. 1 says it was at Aigai.) Similar festivals had been held earlier by Archelaus. [7] Plut. *Alex.* 29, and *De fortuna Alex.* ii. 2.

[8] Thettalos was fined by the Athenians for his failure to appear at the Dionysia, and the fine was paid by Alexander. The liability of artists to fines of this kind is laid down in the Euboean law (*I.G.* xii. 9. 207), c. 290 B.C., and elaborate provisions are made. See below, p. 289.

[9] xii. 538 c–539 a. See especially 538 f καὶ ἔκτοτε οἱ πρότερον καλούμενοι Διονυσοκόλακες Ἀλεξανδροκόλακες ἐκλήθησαν διὰ τὰς τῶν δωρεῶν ὑπερβολάς, ἐφ' οἷς καὶ ἥσθη ὁ Ἀλέξανδρος. ὑπεκρίθησαν δὲ τραγῳδοὶ μὲν Θέτταλος καὶ Ἀθηνόδωρος καὶ Ἀριστόκριτος, κωμῳδοὶ δὲ Λύκων καὶ Φορμίων καὶ Ἀρίστων. παρῆν δὲ καὶ Φασίμηλος ὁ ψάλτης. οἱ δὲ πεμφθέντες, φησί, στέφανοι ὑπὸ τῶν πρεσβευτῶν καὶ τῶν λοιπῶν ταλάντων ἦσαν μυρίων πεντακισχιλίων.

The performers included, besides conjurors, a rhapsode, solo performers on the harp and flute, singers accompanied by each instrument, tragedies, and comedies, and the rewards given were enormous. There are also accounts[1] of an even more extravagant festival at Ecbatana, where three thousand Greek 'Artists' had assembled. The example of Alexander was followed by his successors. Antipater made the actor Archias his agent in the pursuit of Demosthenes and other Athenian orators; and Antigonus held a festival in 302 B.C. on a great scale, gathering the most famous performers from the whole of Greece, at Antigoneia.[2] But there is still no suggestion of organized guilds,[3] such as are spoken of a quarter of a century later (and from then onwards) in connexion with festivals regularly celebrated at Delphi or organized by great patrons, and we can only conjecture the reasons which led to the almost sudden springing into existence of guilds, κοινά or σύνοδοι,[4] of Dionysiac artists, including musicians (both soloists and accompanists) and actors. Those who joined in them may have been impelled by their own interest and convenience; theatres were being built everywhere, to which they travelled to earn their livelihood, and some degree of organization would be almost necessary; while, on the other hand, local associations may have been encouraged by the authorities of the more important towns, so as to secure performers for their own festivals. The records show that dramatic and musical contests were far from being confined to festivals of Dionysus, and it is evident that the drama and music thus circulating throughout the Greek world was the most popular and influential form of culture for several hundred years. New festivals[5] were instituted from time to time in honour of kings and princes and of Rome also, when Rome acquired the empire of Greece and Asia Minor. Local 'Olympian' and 'Pythian' festivals sprang up in many places. At all of these the services of the Artists of Dionysus might be

[1] Plut. *Alex.* 72; Arrian VII. xiv.   [2] Diod. xx. 108.

[3] It is probable that Chamaileon (quoted by Athen. ix. 407 c) was guilty of an anachronism when he said of Hegemon, the parodist of the fifth century, ὁ δὲ παραγενόμενος καὶ συναγαγὼν τοὺς περὶ τὸν Διόνυσον τεχνίτας προσῆλθε μετ' αὐτῶν, Ἀλκιβιάδην βοηθεῖν ἀξιῶν, but in any case his language does not necessarily imply a κοινόν or σύνοδος.

[4] On the slight distinction sometimes implied between κοινόν and σύνοδος, and the history of the two terms in application to the artists' guilds, see Poland in Pauly–W. *Real-Encycl.* art. 'Technitai'. The distinction is generally almost imperceptible, but σύνοδος seems gradually to have prevailed over κοινόν as the name of a guild.

[5] For lists and accounts of these see Ferguson, *Hellenistic Athens*, pp. 296 ff.; Tarn, *Hellenistic Civilization*, pp. 97–98.

demanded and required that there should be a recognized organization of the artists, and some regular connexion between their guilds and the cities or courts at which they appeared.

3. The birth of the guilds can be approximately dated. The remarkable law or agreement[1] between the cities of Euboea, which was passed in a year falling between 294 and 288 B.C., shows no knowledge of them, and assumes that arrangements were made by the cities for their several festivals with individual artists. The law makes elaborate regulations for the Dionysia at Karystos, Eretria, Chalkis, and Oreos,[2] the Demetrieia at Oreos, and the Aristonikeia[3] at Karystos. It appoints agents or contractors (ἐργολάβοι) who are put on oath and required to engage performers and take guarantees from them, and to provide for them during the festivals; each of the four cities of Euboea is required to send θεωροί to each festival at its own expense, and is to give 600 drachmae of Demetrian currency (the coinage of Demetrius I of Macedonia, c. 294–288 B.C.) to each flute-player, 400 to a κωμῳδός, 300 to a costumier (ἱματιομίσθης)—the figure for a τραγῳδός is lost—and daily rations to all, including trainers (διδάσκαλοι) and members of cyclic choruses. Ἐργολάβοι, τεχνῖται, and their guarantors are subjected to fines and other penalties for default, though excuses on oath (ἐξωμοσίαι) are allowed under very elaborate provisions.

But shortly afterwards a decree[4] was passed by the Amphiktyonic Council at Delphi, which implies that artists' guilds had been regularly organized. This is now generally dated about 277 B.C. The same inference is clearly to be drawn from the resolution of the guild of Artists in Egypt,[5] found at Ptolemais and belonging to the reign of Ptolemy Philadelphus (283–247 B.C.) and probably to the earlier part of the reign.

4. It will be convenient to consider the Ptolemaic inscription

---

[1] *I.G.* xii, pt. 9, no. 207. See Klaffenbach, op. cit., p. 11.

[2] The Dionysia at Eretria and Oreos were in the month Lenaion.

[3] Aristonikos was a companion of Alexander.

[4] *I.G.* ii². 1132 (= Dittenb.³ no. 399). The Amphiktyonic decree (*I.G.* ii². 1134) asserts the priority of the Athenian guild: ἐπειδὴ γεγονέναι καὶ συνειλέχθαι τεχνιτῶν σύνοδον παρ᾽ Ἀθηναίοις συμβέβηκε πρῶτον, and (ὁ δῆμος ὁ Ἀθηναίων) πρῶτός τε πάντων συναγαγὼν τεχνιτῶν σύνοδον [καὶ ἀγωνιστῶν] θυμελικοὺς καὶ σκηνικοὺς ἀγῶνας ἐποίησεν.

[5] *B.C.H.* ix (1885), pp. 133 ff.; Dittenb. *Orient. Gr. Inscr. Sel.* (1903), nos. 50, 51; and see generally San Nicolò, *Ägyptische Vereinswesen* (1915), and Plaumann, *Ptolemais in Oberägypten* (1920).

first. It is a decree in honour of Lysimachus and runs as follows:

ἔδοξεν τεχνίταις τοῖς περὶ τὸν Διόνυσον καὶ Θεοὺς Ἀδελφούς· ἐπειδὴ Λυσίμαχος Πτολεμαίου Σωστρατεὺς ὁ ὕπαρχος καὶ πρύτανις διὰ βίου τήν τε εἰς τὸν βασιλέα καὶ τοὺς τούτου γονεῖς εὔνοιαν καὶ πρότερον μὲν ἔτι καὶ νῦν δὲ διὰ πλειόνων ἀποδέδεικται, καὶ πρὸς τὸν Διόνυσον καὶ τοὺς ἄλλους θεοὺς εὐσεβῶς καὶ ὁσίως διακείμενος τυγχάνει, τοῖς τε τεχνίταις φιλανθρώπως ἅπαντα χρῆται, καὶ κατ' ἰδίαν ἑκάστου καὶ κατὰ κοινὸν πάντων ἀντιλαμβάνεται, προθύμως καὶ ἐκτενῶς ἑαυτὸν συνεπιδιδοὺς εἰς τὸ συναύξεσθαι τὸ τεχνί-τευμα,[1] καλῶς δὲ ἔχει τοὺς τοιούτους τῶν ἀνδρῶν ἐπισημαινομένους τιμᾶν ταῖς πρεπούσαις τιμαῖς, δεδόχθαι τῷ κοινῷ τῶν περὶ τὸν Διόνυσον τεχνιτῶν, ὧν καὶ τὰ ὀνόματα ὑπογέγραπται, στεφανῶσαι Λυσίμαχον κίττου στεφάνῳ κατὰ τὰ πάτρια τῇ ια΄ τοῦ Περιτίου μηνὸς τοῖς Διονυσίοις ἀρετῆς ἕνεκα καὶ εὐσεβείας τῆς εἴς τε βασιλέα Πτολεμαῖον καὶ τὸν Διόνυσον καὶ τοὺς ἄλλους θεοὺς καὶ εὐνοίας τῆς εἰς τὸν βασιλέα καὶ τοὺς τούτου γονεῖς καὶ τῆς εἰς τοὺς τεχνίτας τύχῃ τῇ ἀγαθῇ, ἀναθεῖναι δ' αὐτοῦ καὶ εἰκόνα γραπτὴν ἐν τῇ παραστάδι τοῦ πρυτανείου, ἀναγράψαι δὲ καὶ τὸν γραμματέα τοῦ κοινοῦ Δήμαρχον τὸ ψήφισμα τόδε εἰς στήλην καὶ ἀναθεῖναι πρὸ τοῦ νεὼ τοῦ Διονύσου, τὸ δ' εἰς ταῦτ' ἀνάλωμα δοῦναι τὸν οἰκόνομον Σωσίβιον.

Then follow the names first of Ζώπυρος ὁ πρὸς τοῖς ἱεροῖς τῆς τριετηρίδος καὶ ἀμφιετηρίδος καὶ τούτου ἀδελφοὶ Διονύσιος Ταυρῖνος, and then those of 2 τραγῳδιῶν ποιηταί, 2 κωμῳδιῶν ποιηταί, 3 ἐπῶν ποιηταί (one of them being Δήμαρχος the γραμματεύς), 1 κιθαρῳδός, 1 κιθαριστής, 1 ὀρχηστής, 1 τραγῳδός, 6 κωμῳδοί, 4 συναγωνισταὶ τραγικοί, 1 αὐλητὴς τραγικός, 1 σαλπικτής, 1 σκευοποιός, 5 πρόξενοι, and 6 (or more) φιλοτεχνῖται.

The inscription presents much that later becomes familiar— the close association of the cult of Dionysus with a royal house, the proclamation in honour of a benefactor at the Dionysia, the statue and inscription, the mention of priest, secretary, and ac-countant, and the long and varied list of members, including poets, instrumental soloists and accompanists, principal actors and συναγωνισταί, with trumpeter, costumier, πρόξενοι (of whom something may be said later), and patrons of art.

Another inscription[2] of the same epoch and district illustrates some of the same points:

ἔδοξεν τοῖς τεχνίταις τοῖς περὶ τὸν Διόνυσον καὶ Θεοὺς Ἀδελφοὺς καὶ τοῖς τὴν σύνοδον νέμουσιν στεφανῶσαι Διονύσιον Μουσαίου πρύτανιν διὰ βίου κίσσου στεφάνῳ κατὰ τὰ πάτρια εὐνοίας ἕνεκα τῆς εἰς τὴν πόλιν τῶν Πτολε-

---

[1] τεχνίτευμα, 'the profession'.   [2] *B.C.H.* ix (1885), p. 140.

μαιέων καὶ τοὺς τεχνίτας τοὺς [περὶ] τὸν μέγαν Διόνυσον καὶ Θεοὺς Ἀδελφούς, ἀναγορεῦσαι δὲ τὸν στέφανον τοῖς Διονυσίοις καὶ ἀναγραφήν, καὶ ἀναθεῖναι πρὸ τοῦ νεὼ τοῦ Διονύσου, τὸ δὲ ἀνάλωμα τὸ εἰς στήλην δοῦναι τὸν οἰκόνομον Σωσίβιον.

An account by the historian Kallixenos, preserved by Athenaeus,[1] of a great procession organized at Alexandria in the reign of Ptolemy Philadelphus mentions the part taken by the τεχνῖται there, led by the poet Philiskos, who was 'priest of Dionysus'—an expression which probably implies that he was president of the local guild.

It is convenient to notice, along with these Egyptian records, some references of a rather later date to the activities of a Dionysiac guild in Cyprus, where, as in Egypt, the guild was dedicated to the reigning princes as well as to Dionysus. Two of these may be quoted, both recording the erection of statues to public officials at Paphos who also held the highest offices in the guild:

(1)[2] Ἀφροδίτῃ Παφίᾳ ἡ πόλις Παφίων Κάλλιππον Καλλίπου δὶς γραμμα-τεύσαντα τῆς βουλῆς καὶ τοῦ δήμου καὶ ἀρχιερεύοντα τῆς πόλεως καὶ τῶν περὶ τὸν Διόνυσον καὶ Θεοὺς Εὐεργέτας τεχνιτῶν, τὸν γραμματέα τῆς πόλεως κτλ.; and (2)[3] Ἀφροδίτῃ Παφίᾳ τὸ κοινὸν τὸ Κυπρίων Ποταμῶνα Αἰγύπτου τῶν ἐν Πάφῳ γεγυμνασιαρχηκότων καὶ ἡγητορευκότων καὶ τῶν περὶ τὸν Διόνυσον καὶ Θεοὺς Εὐεργέτας τεχνιτῶν εὐνοίας χάριν.

5. The Amphiktyonic decree, passed in or about the year 277 B.C. and conferring special privileges on the Athenian guild of Artists of Dionysus, almost coincides in time with the first of the series of inscriptions relating to the Soteria at Delphi, to which artists gathered from all over the Greek world. It may be assumed, though there is no proof of this as regards the earliest festivals of the series, that these artists were sent by or with the encouragement of their guilds. This is certain for the year 234 B.C., when the Isthmian and Nemean guild made its contribution to the Soteria,[4] and it may probably be inferred also for a year about 247 B.C.[5] It is certain again much later about 130 B.C.[6]

---

[1] v, p. 198 c.
[2] *C.I.G.* 2620; cf. 2619, but the restoration of this is very uncertain.
[3] *J.H.S.* ix (1888), p. 250, no. 105. ἡγήτωρ was the title of the chief priest of Aphrodite (Hesych. s.v.). [4] Dittenb.[3] 489.
[5] Ibid. 460 Δελφοὶ ἔδωκαν τῷ κοινῷ τῶν τεχνιτῶν τοῖς ἐς ᾿Ισθμὸν καὶ Νεμέαν συμπορευομένοις προμάντειαν, προεδρίαν, προδικίαν ἄρχοντος Αἰνησίλα.
[6] Ibid. 690. The exact date is uncertain (see Daux, op. cit., p. 357); it must fall between 145 and 125 B.C. In this year they sent only one κωμῳδός with two συναγωνισταί and four χορευταὶ κωμῳδοῦ. This inscription refers to the 'Winter Soteria'—probably a less important

The classes of performers at the Soteria are for the most part
the same as appear regularly in the notices which directly concern the guilds—tragic and comic actors (with διδάσκαλοι and
αὐληταί), rhapsodes, κιθαρισταί, and κιθαρῳδοί, as well as choruses
of boys and men, seven χορευταὶ κωμικοί at each festival, and
one or more ἱματιομίσθαι or costumiers, corresponding to the
σκευοποιός at Ptolemais.

Little is recorded of the τεχνῖται in the third century, but it
may be assumed that they continued to participate in all the
major festivals of the Greek world, profiting by the organization
and the privileges which various inscriptions attest. The Amphiktyonic decree of about 277 B.C. gave the Athenian τεχνῖται
freedom from arrest in war and peace, exemption from military
and naval service and, generally, safety of person and property,
any offender against them, and even the city in which the
offence was committed, being made responsible to the Amphiktyons.[1] While the Athenian guild was the first to be regularly
organized,[2] the guild of the artists especially connected with the
Isthmian and Nemean festivals must have come into existence
soon afterwards.[3] An inscription,[4] apparently from a sanctuary
of the τεχνῖται near the Dipylon at Athens, and dating probably
from the middle of the third century, records honours paid by
the Athenian guild to two of their officials, a tragic actor and a
singer; and another inscription[5] of the same century comes from
the basis of the statue of the tragic poet Xenokrates erected by
the guild.

About the year 250 B.C. the Isthmian and Nemean guild
received an invitation to the revived and ennobled festival of

festival than that to which the third-century inscriptions refer (ranging from about 277 to
225 B.C.; Dittenb.³ 424, 489, 509).

[1] Diodorus iv. 5 records a tradition that Dionysus himself invented both musical festivals
and the privileges of the artists: ἀλειτουργήτους ποιῆσαι καὶ τοὺς ἐν ταῖς στρατείαις μετα-
χειριζομένους τι τῆς μουσικῆς ἐπιστήμης, ἀφ' ὧν τοὺς μεταγενεστέρους μουσικὰς συνόδους
συστήσασθαι τῶν περὶ τὸν Διόνυσον τεχνιτῶν καὶ ἀτελεῖς ποιῆσαι τοὺς τὰ τοιαῦτα ἐπιτηδεύοντας.

[2] *I.G.* ii². 1134, etc. (see above, p. 289).

[3] See above, p. 291, and below.

[4] See Wilhelm, *Urkunden*, pp. 22–25. The text (with suggested supplements) runs: [ἐπεμελή-
θησαν δὲ καὶ] τῆς συν[όδου τῶν] τεχνιτῶν μετὰ τῶν προσαιρεθέντων ἐπιμελητῶν ὡς ἠδυνήθησαν
φιλοτιμότατα προσαναλώσαντες ἐκ τῶν ἰδίων· ἀγαθῇ τύχῃ· δεδόχθαι τοῖς τεχνίταις ἐπαινέσαι τοὺς
ἱεροποιοὺς Σωσίθεον τραγῳδόν, Σώφιλον ᾠδόν, καὶ στεφανῶσαι ἑκάτερον αὐτῶν κίττου στεφάνῳ
εὐσεβείας ἕνεκα τῆς πρὸς τοὺς θεοὺς καὶ φιλοτιμίας τῆς εἰς τὸ κοινὸν τῶν τεχνιτῶν· ἀναγράψαι
δὲ τόδε τὸ ψήφισμα καὶ τὰ ὀνόματα αὐτῶν ἐν στήλῃ λιθίνῃ καὶ στῆσαι ἐν τῷ Ποσειδίππου ἀνα-
θήματι.

[5] *I.G.* ii². 3211 τὸ κοινὸν τῶν τεχνιτῶν Ξενοκράτην Κυδαυτίδην ποιητὴν τραγῳδιῶν.

the Muses at Thespiai. The inscription which records this[1] is not uninteresting:

ὁ θυμελικὸς ἀγὼν στεφανίτης πρῶτον ἐγένετο ἀγωνοθετοῦντος Ἱεροκλέος, ἱερέως δὲ τῶν Μουσῶν Μνασίωνος, ἀπὸ δὲ τῶν τεχνιτῶν Αἰσχύλου, καὶ δόγματα περὶ τοῦ ἀγῶνος τῶν Μουσείων τεχνιτῶν· ἔδοξε τοῖς τεχνίταις τοῖς ἐξ Ἰσθμοῦ καὶ Νεμέας· ἐπειδὴ παραγενόμενος πρεσβευτὴς Ἱεροκλῆς παρὰ τῆς πόλεως Θεσπιέων καὶ τοῦ κοινοῦ τῶν Βοιωτῶν ψηφίσματά τε ἀπέδωκεν καὶ ἐπιστολήν, ἐν ᾗ παρεκάλει τοὺς τεχνίτας, τῆς πόλεως τῶν Θεσπιέων προκεχειρισμένης τὸν ἀγῶνα τὸν ἐν τῷ Ἑλικῶνι γινομένην στεφανίτην εἶναι τὸν θυμελικὸν κτλ.

The inscription goes on to record the acceptance of the invitation by the τεχνῖται to send a deputation to the festival.

That the Isthmian and Nemean guild was honoured late in the third century by the Amphiktyons (or the Aetolians who were virtually in control of Delphi) as the Athenian artists had been in 277 B.C. is proved by a decree[2] of about 227 B.C.:

ἐπὶ Λυκώπου στραταγέοντος τὸ τέταρτον ἔδοξε [τοῖς Αἰτωλοῖς ἀπο]δόμεν τοῖς τεχνίταις τάν τε ἀσφάλειαν καὶ τὰν ἀσυλίαν τοῖς ἐπ᾽ Ἰωνίας καὶ Ἑλλησπόντου τοῖς ἐγγεγραμμένοις καθὼς καὶ τοῖς εἰς Ἰσθμὸν καὶ Νεμέαν συμ[πορευομένοις].

This inscription contains also the first mention of the third great guild of actors, those of Ionia and the Hellespont, of which more will be heard in the next century.

Late in the third century—in 226 or 225 B.C.—we hear of Artists of Dionysus in the Peloponnese being caused to perform for the pleasure of Cleomenes III after his conquest of Megalopolis,[3] and (probably about the same time) of artists travelling to Kythera.[4] (Both inscriptions contain some points of human interest.) Plutarch[5] also speaks of the participation of the Dionysiac artists in the festival founded in commemoration of Aratos after his death at Sikyon in 213 B.C. A monument erected by a

[1] Dittenb.³ 457. Hierokles appears as a special envoy to Athens in *I.G.* vii. 1735. The δόγμα of the τεχνῖται follows, but that of the Thespieans is lost.

[2] Dittenb.³ 507.

[3] Plut. *Cleom.* 12 ἐμβαλὼν οὖν εἰς τὴν Μεγαλοπολιτικὴν ὠφελείας μεγάλας ἤθροισε ... τέλος δὲ τοὺς περὶ τὸν Διόνυσον τεχνίτας ἐκ Μεσσήνης διαπορευομένους λαβὼν καὶ πήξας θέατρον ἐν τῇ πολεμίᾳ καὶ προθεὶς ἀπὸ τεσσαράκοντα μνῶν ἀγῶνα μίαν ἡμέραν ἐθεᾶτο καθήμενος, οὐ δεόμενος θέας ἀλλ᾽ οἷον ἐντρυφῶν.

[4] Aelian, *N.H.* xi. 19 Παντα*κλῆς ὁ Λακεδαιμόνιος ἀναστείλας διὰ τῆς Σπάρτης ἐλθεῖν τοὺς ἐς Κύθηρα ἀπιόντας τῶν περὶ τὸν Διόνυσον τεχνιτῶν, εἶτα καθήμενος ἐν τῷ ἐφορείῳ ὑπὸ κυνῶν διεσπάσθη.

[5] *Arat.* 53 μέλη δὲ ᾔδετο πρὸς κιθάραν ὑπὸ τῶν περὶ τὸν Διόνυσον τεχνιτῶν.

travelling actor at Tegea,[1] of which he was a native, in commemoration of his victories away from home, probably belongs
to the same period; the festival of the Naia at Dodona, where
one of his successes was won, is not likely to have lasted after
the destruction of Dodona by the Aetolians in 219 B.C. He was
victorious at the Great Dionysia at Athens in Euripides' *Orestes*,
at the Soteria in Euripides' *Herakles* and Archestratos' *Antaios*, at
the Heraia at Argos in Euripides' *Archelaos* and *Herakles*, and
at the Naia in Euripides' *Archelaos* and Chaeremon's *Achilles*.
The list is interesting as illustrating the continued popularity
of Euripides.

6. There is more information about the guilds in the second
century B.C., and particularly about the increasing rivalry of the
Athenian and the Isthmian guilds, and the activities of the
Ionian and Hellespontine guild, whose centre was at Teos.

The exact causes of the dispute between the two mainland
guilds, which came to a head in the latter part of the century,
are nowhere quite clearly stated, but it may have turned in part
on an attempt of the Isthmian artists to prevent the Athenians
from performing at festivals at which they themselves claimed
prescriptive rights, or to interfere in other ways with their free
pursuit of their profession; and, perhaps because the Athenian
people seems to have been solidly behind its guild, the matter
was not without its political importance. An inscription[2] is
thought to record a letter from the proconsul Mummius in 146
B.C. after the destruction of Corinth, giving or confirming to the
artists of the Isthmian guild freedom from taxation and from
other public services.[3] However this may be—and the matter
is not certain—about the year 134 B.C. the Athenian guild sent
a deputation to request the Amphiktyons to renew the privileges
which had been conferred on them by the decree of 277 B.C.,
and these were now revived by a formal decree[4] which concludes
significantly: εἶναι δὲ ταῦτα τοῖς ἐν Ἀθηναῖς τεχνίταις, ἐὰν μή τι
Ῥωμαίοις ὑπεναντίον ᾖ. A decree of a few years later (perhaps
about 125 B.C.)[5] shows that the Athenian guild was in high

[1] *I.G.* v, pt. 2, no. 118. The entries are adorned with appropriate garlands.
[2] *I.G.* vii. 2413-14. See Klaffenbach, op. cit., pp. 24 ff.
[3] Among other privileges the technitai are to be ἀνεπιστάθμευτοι—free from liability to have soldiers quartered on them (cf. Polybius xv. 24. 2 for the word).
[4] *I.G.* ii². 1132 (latter part), dated 130-129 in the *Corpus*, 134 by Daux.
[5] Dittenb.³ 698 (cf. 697). A decree of the same year honours the σύνοδος τῶν ἐν Ἀθηναῖς ἐποποιῶν for their part in the same festival. Whether these were distinct from the τεχνῖται

favour with the Amphiktyons for its participation in 128–127
B.C. in the Pythais, a festival which seems to have been essentially
a sacred mission from Athens to Apollo,[1] and confirms and aug-
ments the privileges of the Athenian artists, though at the same
time they must have been on good terms with the Isthmian
guild, which they had invited to the Winter Soteria about 130
B.C.[2] In 128 B.C., in the praetorship of P. Cornelius Lentulus,
a *senatusconsultum* seems to have imposed terms on the two guilds,
perhaps requiring the Athenian to become part of the Isthmian,
and the Isthmian guild erected a statue to Lentulus at Delphi.
But the quarrel was only quiescent for a time, and (after various
moves of which only the most fragmentary information exists)
in 117 B.C. the Athenian guild carried its grievances to Sisenna,
proconsul of Macedonia, who summoned both parties to a hear-
ing at Pella; he imposed an agreement upon them and required
the Isthmian guild to pay ten talents to the Athenian; the agreement as a whole was plainly favourable to Athens. The Isthmian
guild repudiated the action of its delegates in signing it, and a
schism followed, the authorities of the guild calling an assembly
of their members at Sikyon, while the dissentients, supported by
the Athenian artists, established themselves at Thebes. The
Athenians then appealed to the Roman Senate, alleging that
the Isthmians had contravened the agreement made before
Sisenna, and had appropriated funds belonging in part to
themselves. The Isthmians in reply disowned the agreement
made πρὸς τοὺς ἐν Ἀθηναῖς φάσκοντας εἶναι τεχνίτας, and accused
the Athenians of conspiring with 'some of the τεχνῖται in Thebes
and Boeotia' to cause a schism and appropriate funds (probably
lodged in the treasury of the Isthmian guild at Thebes) and
offerings dedicated there. A remarkable *senatusconsultum* in 112
B.C., in determining the dispute in response to an appeal from
the people of Athens, was generally favourable to the Athenian
guild confirming the order of Sisenna, and sending the allegations
about theft of funds to an arbitrator.[3]

or a subdivision of them is uncertain. There is a record of a Pythais in 138–137 B.C., but no
express mention of the guild.

[1] See Daux, op. cit., p. 525. The festival had probably lapsed, and was revived by Athens
in the latter half of the second century (see ibid., p. 532). The two paeans with musical
notation are attributed by Daux to the festival of 128–127 B.C., but see below, p. 302.

[2] See above, p. 291, n. 6.

[3] The details of the whole story are uncertain at various points, but as given above seem
to emerge from the inscriptions in Dittenb.[3] 704, 705; cf. Klaffenbach, op. cit., pp. 29 ff.

In the meantime the Amphiktyons had continued to show favour to Athens, and in 117 B.C. a decree passed by them, after fulsome laudations of the services of Athens to culture and religion, and compliments to its τεχνῖται, gave the priests chosen by the τεχνῖται the right to wear crowns of gold and purple robes[1] in all cities, an honour about which difficulties might have been made in places where their Isthmian rivals were at home; and (probably in the spring of 116 B.C.), after further protests by the Isthmian guild, they confirmed the privileges of the Athenian guild in strong terms:

ἐκρίναμεν τὰ κεχρηματισμένα ἐν τῇ μεθοπωρινῇ πυλαίᾳ ἐπὶ ἄρχοντος ἐν Δελφοῖς Εὐκλείδου κύρια εἶναι καὶ βέβαια εἰς τὸν ἅπαντα χρόνον καὶ μηδὲν ὑπεναντίον αὐτοῖς ἐπιχρηματίζειν δίκαιον ἡγεῖσθαι, καὶ διαφυλάσσειν τὰς δεδομένας ὑφ' ἡμῶν τῷ δήμῳ τιμάς, ὁμοίως δὲ καὶ τοῖς παρ' ὑμῖν τεχνίταις τὰ ὑπάρχοντα φιλάνθρωπα περί τε τῆς ἀσυλίας καὶ ἀσφαλείας καὶ χρυσοφορίας ἔτι δὲ καὶ τῆς συνεργασίας, θεωροῦντες καὶ τοὺς κοινοὺς εὐεργέτας Ῥωμαίους ἐπὶ τῆς αὐτῆς γεγονότας γνώμης.[2]

The last words may refer to the terms imposed upon the two guilds by Sisenna at Pella late in 117 B.C. After this there are further decrees of the Amphiktyons paying honour in extravagant terms to the Athenian guild for its help in the Pythais in 105 B.C. (probably)[3] and again in 96 B.C.[4] In 105 the Athenians had sent ἐπιμελητὰν μὲν καὶ ἀρχιθέωρον—the comic poet Alexander—7 θεωροί (including a tragic ὑποδιδάσκαλος, 2 κωμῳδοί, 2 tragic poets, and 2 tragic συναγωνισταί), a διδάσκαλος τοῦ μεγαλοῦ χοροῦ, singers of paeans and instrumentalists; ἐξαπέστειλαν δὲ καὶ τοὺς συναγωνιξαμένους τὸν θυμελικὸν ἀγῶνα καὶ τὸν σκανικόν—3 epic poets, 3 rhapsodes, 4 κωμῳδοὶ καὶ τοὺς συναγωνιξαμένους τούτοις (6 names), 2 τραγῳδοὶ καὶ τοὺς τούτοις συναγωνιξαμένους (7 names), 2 tragic poets, and 5 satyric poets.[5] The enumeration of honours and statues conferred ends with the words καὶ εἶμεν πάντοις τοῖς ἐν Ἀθήναις τεχνίταις ἀσυλίαν καὶ προμάντειαν καὶ προπομπείαν καὶ προξενίαν, αὐτοῖς τε καὶ ἐκγόνοις αὐτῶν. In the later inscription the same ἀρχιθεωρός, the comic poet Alexander, receives honour.

---

[1] *I.G.* ii². 1134. For the reading χρυσοφορεῖν . . . καὶ [πορφυρο]φορεῖν (rather than [στεφανη]φορεῖν) see Daux, op. cit., p. 367.

[2] Dittenb.³ 704; *I.G.* ii². 1134. [3] Dittenb.³ 711.

[4] Ibid. 728 (see Daux, op. cit., pp. 564 ff.).

[5] There is a similar enumeration in Dittenb.³ 698 for 128–127 B.C., but with no mention of satyric poets. On these lists see Daux, op. cit., pp. 725 ff.

Another side of the activities of the guilds is illustrated by a vote of the Athenian guild itself, paying honour to Ariarathes, king of Cappadocia, soon after the middle of the second century.[1] Similar actions are recorded on the part of other guilds, which seem to have been to some extent dependent upon the patronage and benefactions of princes, and received from them, as also from friendly towns,[2] grants of ἀσυλία and other privileges.

Apart from the dispute with the Athenian guild, the chief interest of the Isthmian and Nemean guild in the second century B.C. lies in its wide extension over the Greek mainland, where a number of separate branches were established. The relation between the Isthmian guild and the τεχνῖται of Thebes has been much discussed, and the problem is probably not capable of solution; but it appears that the treasury of the guild was at one time placed at Thebes.[3] There is no evidence to show what happened after the schism in 117 B.C., the setting up (apparently) of rival σύνοδοι at Thebes and Sikyon, and the *senatus-consultum* of 112 B.C. Various inscriptions[4] mention τεχνῖται in Thebes without always making it clear whether they were independent of the Isthmian guild or were a branch of it, and the dates are not certain. Another record,[5] probably of the second century, may indicate the extension of the guilds' activities into Macedonia.

That there was a branch at Chalkis in Euboea is attested by an inscription of the early second century.[6] Another inscription of the second century is in honour of Soteles and his wife Xenola,

---

[1] Dittenb. *Or. Gr. Inscr. Sel.* 352 = *I.G.* ii². 1330.

[2] See below, p. 311.

[3] *C.I.G.* 1689 a. The inscription cannot be certainly restored. [ἔδοξε τοῖς Ἀμφικτύ]οσιν· ὅπως ἂν ἡ θυσία τῷ Διονύσῳ ... οἶνον τῶν τεχνιτῶν τῶν εἰς Ἰσμόν ... τοὺς ἱερομνήμονας, οἳ ἂν ὦσιν ἐν τῷ ... ταμείῳ ἐν Θήβαις ὑπὲρ τοῦ ... οἶνον τόν τε σῖτον. Restorers read τῶν εἰς Ἰσμήνιον or τῶν εἰς Ἰσθμὸν [καὶ Νεμεάν].

[4] e.g. *I.G.* vii. 2484 τὸ κοινὸν τῶν περὶ τὸν Διόνυσον τεχνιτῶν τῶν ἐν Θήβαις Διοκλῆν Τιμόστρατον Διονύσῳ. ἔστησεν Βρομίῳ Διοκλῆν Τιμοστράτου υἱὸν | ἐσθλὴ τεχνιτῶν μουσοπόλων σύνοδος (perhaps 2nd cent.), but cf. ibid. 2485 τὸ κοινὸν τῶν περὶ τὸν Διόνυσον τεχνιτῶν τῶν ἐξ Ἰσθμοῦ καὶ Νεμέας σ[υντελούντων] δὲ ἐν Θήβαις Καλλίστρατον Α ... (no date). Ibid. 2447, found at Thebes, refers to τεχνῖται (probably early 1st cent. B.C.), but with no reference to the guild.

[5] Ibid. 2486 [τὸ κοινὸν τῶν περὶ τὸν Διόνυσον τεχνιτῶ]ν τῶν εἰς Ἰσθ[μὸν καὶ Νεμέαν καὶ] Πιερίαν συντελούντων ... Ζευξίππου τὸν πρόξενον τὸν ἑαυτῶν Διονύσῳ ἀρετῆς ἕνεκεν καὶ εὐνοίας ἣν ἔχων διατελεῖ εἴς τε τοὺς τεχνίτας καὶ τῆς εἰς τὸν θεόν εὐσεβείας. But there is no agreement as to the restoration of the lost words in the second bracket.

[6] *B.C.H.* xvi (1892), p. 91 τὸ κοινὸν τῶν περὶ τὸν Διόνυσον τῶν ἐξ Ἰσθμοῦ καὶ Νεμέας, συντελούντων δὲ ἐν Χαλκίδι; cf. p. 107 Σάτ]υρος Σω ... ος Διο ... [Αὐ]τοκράτους ... ης ἀπὸ κοινοῦ Ταραντῖνος ἀπὸ τῆς αὐτῆς συ[νόδου Χαλκιδεύς (no express reference to τεχνῖται).

munificent subscribers to the funds of the branch at Opus.[1] But the most striking evidence of a certain independence enjoyed by the branches of the guild is to be found in a long decree[2] in honour of Zenon who was treasurer, and also a conspicuous benefactor, of the branch at Argos; among other things he had superintended extensive repairs to the buildings belonging to the branch and the erection of a statue to Nikomedes, king of Bithynia, who had given assistance to the branch. A statue is voted to Zenon, with a crown and a proclamation he made at the next Nemean games.[3] The date is uncertain; it is commonly considered to be about 114–113 B.C., but may well be earlier, though not before 146 B.C.[4]

7. The third of the guilds which divided the Greek world between them makes its appearance first in an Aetolian decree of about 227 B.C.,[5] which has already been noticed, conferring ἀσφαλεία and ἀσυλία on the registered members of the guild, and next in the records which date from just before the beginning of the second century. It was known as the κοινὸν τῶν περὶ τὸν Διόνυσον τεχνιτῶν ἐπ' Ἰωνίας καὶ Ἑλλησπόντου. Its centre was at Teos, and when the people of Teos, on the strength of their legendary connexion with Dionysus, sought and obtained special privileges for themselves and their territory from Delphi and the Aetolians in power there, as well as from many other Greek states and finally from Rome, these privileges were modelled upon those already given to the Artists of Dionysus. The decree of the Amphiktyons[6] may be quoted as typical:

ἔδοξε τοῖς Ἀμφικτίονοις τὰμ πόλιν καὶ τὰν χώραν τῶν Τηΐων ἱερὰν εἶμεν καὶ ἄσυλον Διονύσου ἀπὸ πάντων, καὶ ὑπάρχειν τοῖς Τηΐοις καὶ τοῖς ἐν Τέῳ κατοικεόντοις παρ' Ἀμφικτιόνων τὰ φιλάνθρωπα καὶ τίμια πάντα ὅσα καὶ τοῖς Διονυσιακοῖς τεχνίταις δέδοται παρὰ τῶν Ἀμφικτιόνων.

---

[1] *I.G.* ix. 278 Ἄρχοντος Ὀρθομενίδα ἔδοξε τοῖς περὶ τὸν Διόνυσον τεχνίταις τοῖς ἐξ Ἰσθμοῦ καὶ Νεμέας, συντελοῦσι δὲ ἐν Ὀποῦντι.

[2] *I.G.* iv. 558 ἐπειδὴ Ζήνων Ἑκατοδώρου Ἀργεῖος ἐν παντὶ καιρῷ διατελεῖ εὐσεβῶς μὲν διακείμενος τὰ πρὸς τοὺς θεούς, εὐνοϊκῶς δὲ πρὸς τὸ κοινὸν τῶν περὶ τὸν Διόνυσον τεχνιτῶν τῶν ἐξ Ἰσθμοῦ καὶ Νεμέας τῆς ἐν Ἄργει συνόδου κτλ.

[3] ἐν τοῖς πρώτοις Νεμείοις ἐν τῷ ἀγῶνι τῷ γυμνικῷ.   [4] See Comm. in *I.G.* ad loc.

[5] Dittenb.[3] 507; see above, p. 293. See further Hahland in *W. Jahreshefte*, xxxviii (1950), 67 ff.; Ruge in Pauly–W., s.v. Teos.

[6] Dittenb.[3] 564. The decrees of the Aetolians (ibid. 563) and the Delphians (ibid. 565) use very similar language. In another decree the Delphians give to the special ambassadors sent from Teos, and to their posterity, προξενίαν, προμαντείαν, προεδρίαν, προδικίαν, ἀσυλίαν, ἀτελείαν πάντων καὶ τἆλλα ὅσα τοῖς ἄλλοις προξένοις καὶ εὐεργεταῖς. The decrees of a number of Cretan townships, passed after the visit of the ambassadors of Teos, are to be found in Cauer, *Delectus Inscriptionum*, nos. 122–9.

FIG. 207. THE THEATRE OF PERGAMON

The dates of these decrees seem to fall between 205 and 201 B.C., and in 193 B.C. the Roman Senate sent a dispatch acknowledging the sanctity of Teos and ordering that it should be ἄσυλον καὶ ἀφορολόγητον ἀπὸ τοῦ δήμου τῶν Ῥωμαίων.[1]

About the same time the guild—on this occasion termed simply τὸ κοινὸν τὸν περὶ τῶν Διόνυσον τεχνιτῶν—accepted[2] an invitation to a musical and gymnastic festival at Magnesia on the Maeander in honour of Artemis Leukophryene, the great goddess of Magnesia, and conferred on the people of Magnesia a crown, the award of which was to be proclaimed both ἐν τῇ πανηγύρει τῶν τεχνιτῶν and in Magnesia. An inscription[3] very shortly afterwards recorded a complimentary vote by the guild of crowns for the people of Magnesia and the representatives sent by it to Teos, as well as a stele to be erected in the Temple of Artemis Leukophryene, and the same inscription records the acceptance of these compliments by the Magnesian people.

8. In the reign of Eumenes II of Pergamon (205–159 B.C.) Teos, and with it the guild, fell under the domination of the Pergamene king, and this is reflected in an interesting series of inscriptions, dating probably from shortly before the middle of the century, in which the guild appears under the title τὸ κοινὸν τῶν περὶ τὸν Διόνυσον τεχνιτῶν τῶν ἐπ' Ἰωνίας καὶ Ἑλλησπόντου καὶ τῶν περὶ τὸν καθηγεμόνα Διόνυσον. The original guild had become fused or allied with the society of worshippers of Διόνυσος καθηγεμών, who was a special object of worship to the Attalid house,[4] and was also the god to whom the theatre at Pergamon,[5]

---

[1] An inscription variously dated from the middle of the third to the middle of the second century also records an offer to the Artists by the city of Teos of land free of the taxes imposed by the city (no doubt as distinct from those levied by the Attalid monarchy). See *B.C.H.* xlvi (1922), pp. 312–19, and *Suppl. Epigr. Gr.* ii. 580; cf. A. H. M. Jones, *Cities of the Eastern Roman Provinces*, pp. 55–56; Robert, *Ét. Anatoliennes*, 39 ff.   [2] Kern, *Inschrift. von Magn.* 54.

[3] Ibid. 89. Some scholars ascribe to the same date (which must be anterior to the close connexion of Teos with Pergamon) a list of names in an inscription from Samothrake (Conze, *Reise auf den Inseln des Thrakischen Meeres*, p. 65; Benndorf, *Neue arch. Untersuch. auf Samothrake*, ii, p. 97, no. iv, l. 85) giving a list of names in the last part of which are the words: Τήϊοι (3 names follow) τοῦ κοινοῦ τῶν ἐ...... τεχνιτῶν τῶν [ἀπὸ Ἰωνίας] καὶ Ἑλλησπόντου. But the lettering is thought by some to be later, perhaps after the extinction of the Attalids.

[4] Eumenes II (205–159 B.C.) was preceded by Attalos I (241–205 B.C.) and succeeded by Attalos II (159–133 B.C.). On the whole subject see von Prott, *Ath. Mitt.* xxvii (1902), pp. 161 ff., and Hansen, *The Attalids of Pergamon* (1947). On the cult of Διόνυσος καθηγεμών see especially ibid., pp. 409, 418, and works quoted above, p. 298, n. 5. Whether he was claimed as their ancestor by the Attalids is doubtful.

[5] This fine theatre (whether or not it had a more modest predecessor) was built in the reign of Eumenes II. See Dörpfeld u. Reisch, p. 151; von Gerkan, *Das Theater von Priene*, p. 101; Bulle, *Untersuchungen*, p. 256.

which must have been the chief scene of the guild's performances, was consecrated. (There is no proof that he was worshipped in Teos itself, and after the extinction of the Attalid dynasty the additional words disappear from the title of the guild.)

Most of these inscriptions, the chief of which are printed in the appendix to this chapter, have to do with honours paid to the flute-player Kraton of Chalkedon, who had held high office in the guild and had been a munificent benefactor to it. He had brought distinction to it by his performance at many Greek festivals—at Delphi (at the Soteria and Pythia), at Thespiai (at the Μουσεῖα), at Thebes (at the Herakleia), and others[1]—and had won for it the commendation of the Amphiktyons, described as οἱ ἐκ πάντων τῶν Ἑλλήνων εὐσεβέστατοι. His personal character also is warmly praised, and he was in high favour at Pergamon, where he had founded the thiasos of Ἀτταλισταί, attached to the cult of the Attalid house, and had built the Ἀτταλεῖον close to the theatre. He had been given the citizenship of Pergamon. The longest of the decrees of the guild[2] orders that he shall be crowned annually 'on the day of the procession' and that a statue of him shall be erected in the theatre at Teos,[3] where it is to be crowned at the Dionysia and on other occasions, and a second at Delos, to be crowned by the τεχνῖται there, and a third elsewhere.[4] The guild is to send special representatives to the municipality of Teos and the people of Delos to secure the appropriate sites. In the second of the longer decrees of the guild it is not only ordered that the proclamation of the crown awarded to Kraton shall be made annually by the agonothetes and priest of Eumenes[5] ἐν τῇ βασιλέως Εὐμένου ἡμέρᾳ ὅταν ᾖ τε πομπὴ διέλθῃ καὶ αἱ στεφανώσεις συντελῶνται, but also (somewhat amusingly) ὁμοίως δὲ καὶ παρὰ τὸν πότον γενέσθω τῇ αὐτῇ ἡμέρᾳ μετὰ τὰς σπονδὰς ὑπὸ τῶν ἀρχόντων ἡ ἀναγγελία τοῦ στεφάνου. A tripod and altar of incense (which is to be offered annually) is to be placed by his statue in the theatre.

A special decree[6] in his honour was passed at the same time

---

[1] e.g. at Iasos, where the guarantors of a festival had engaged him to play. See Brinck, *Inscr. Gr. ad choregiam pertinentes*, p. 225, no. 110.

[2] *I.G.* xi. 1061 (= *C.I.G.* 3067, with emendations).

[3] On this theatre and the Dionysion connected with it (the masterpiece of Hermogenes) see Vitruv. III. iii, § 8; VII, praef., § 12.

[4] οὗ ἂν [ἀναθ]ῇ Κράτων, 'wherever a statue of Kraton is set up'.

[5] This double function of the presiding official corresponds to the double title of the guild.

[6] *C.I.G.* 3068 B.

by the κοινὸν τῶν συναγωνιστῶν, which is now generally agreed to have been a subordinate guild or club within the general guild, and to have included, in all probability, members other than the leading tragic and comic actors.[1] Kraton had been a member of this. The honours voted to him are somewhat less resplendent than those in the decrees of the general guild, but include a stele to be set up by the Dionysion in the most conspicuous situation, and a statue.

Another inscription[2] records the gratitude of the Ἀτταλισταί to Kraton as their founder and benefactor. This tribute was paid after his death and in the reign of Attalos III, and mentions his bequests to the Ἀτταλισταί. (The date must be later than 152 B.C., when a letter from Kraton to the Ἀτταλισταί, of which the heading survives,[3] was written.) Apart from this striking personality, the chief interest of the inscriptions of this group relates to the courtesy and generosity of the guild in sending a group of performers to Iasos to enable the people of Iasos to maintain their festivals at a time (about the middle of the second century B.C.) when they had fallen on evil days.[4] Two flute-players are sent, two tragic and two comic actors, a κιθαρῳδός and a κιθαριστής, with the necessary attendants; and it was expressly provided that the performances should be in accordance with the customs of the people of Iasos, and that the artists selected by the assembly of the guild should be bound to serve, on pain of a heavy fine. A friendly delegation is to carry this decree to Iasos.[5]

Unhappily the prosperity of the guild did not continue. Even in the reign of Eumenes II there had been disputes between the guild and the people of Teos, which had been settled by the king;[6] and at some time in the reign of Attalos II (later than 152 B.C.) the quarrel was renewed. The guild first migrated to

---

[1] The fact that a συναγωνιστὴς τραγικός was sent as the envoy of the guild to Iasos seems to prove that they were recognized members of the guild. It cannot be assumed that the title συναγωνιστής was always used in precisely the same sense.

[2] *C.I.G.* 3069. Some details of Kraton's bequests are recorded in no. 3071.

[3] *C.I.G.* 3070.

[4] Lüders, op. cit., no. 91 (p. 181). See appendix.

[5] A series of 47 inscriptions from Iasos, printed by Brinck, op. cit., pp. 216–44, gives lists of those who undertook to be responsible for engaging and paying for each festival (see above, p. 300, on the engagement of Kraton). This payment of individual performers was evidently preferred, though with the alternative of a lump sum paid down, as a method of financing the festivals.

[6] Fränkel, *Inschr. von Pergamon*, no. 163; cf. Hansen, op. cit., p. 158.

Ephesus, but Attalos ordered its removal to Myonnesos, and when the people of Teos protested to the Roman authorities that this was dangerously near Teos, the Romans moved the guild to Lebedos, where it was welcomed as increasing the population of that desolate town.[1] (Horace[2] speaks of it a century and a half later as a particularly unattractive place.) They were still at Lebedos in the time of Strabo (*circa* 64 B.C.–A.D. 19), by whom these facts are narrated. It is possible that at some time in their wanderings they had been settled at Priene, but this is only a conjecture based on a passage of Plutarch.[3] The τεχνῖται seem, nevertheless, to have had a centre in Teos itself in imperial times.[4]

9. Some few further fragments of the history of the guilds in the second century B.C. are not without interest. Two of the three hymns discovered at Delphi[5]—both of them accompanied by musical notation—were sung by the Athenian guild of Artists of Dionysus. Both are paeans addressed to Apollo, and were probably the offering of the guild, and both are dated on epigraphical grounds by Pomtow between 185 and 135 B.C. In the first the dedication runs ὁ δὲ τεχνι|τῶν πρόπας ἑσμὸς Ἀτθίδα λαχὼν | τὸν κιθαρίσει κλυτὸν παῖδα μεγάλου Διὸς ὑ|μνοῦσί σε παρ' ἀκρονιφῆ τόνδε πάγον κτλ.; in the second ἀνθ' ὧν | ἐκείνας ἀπ' ἀρχᾶς Παιήονα κικλήσκομεν ἅπας λαὸς αὐ|τοχθόνων ἠδὲ Βάκχου μέγας θυρσόπληξ [ἑσμὸς ἱ]ερὸς τεχνι|τῶν ἔνοικος πόλει Κεκροπίᾳ. They were doubtless composed for one of the great Delphic festivals—probably not the Soteria, but there are no certain indications.

There survive also some fragments of a decree[6] of the Athenian guild in honour of Aribazus son of Seleucus of the Peiraeus for his benefactions and goodwill towards them. The inscription is dated by Wilhelm about 130 B.C., but parts of it are too fragmentary to admit of certain interpretation.

---

[1] Strabo iv. i. 29 ἔπειτα Λέβεδος . . . ἐνταῦθα τῶν περὶ τὸν Διόνυσον τεχνιτῶν ἡ σύνοδος καὶ κατοικία τῶν ἐν Ἰωνίᾳ μεχρὶ Ἑλλησπόντου, ἐν ᾗ πανηγύρεις τε καὶ ἀγῶνες κατ' ἔτος συντελοῦνται τῷ Διονύσῳ· ἐν Τέῳ δὲ πρότερον τῇ ἐφεξῆς πόλει τῶν Ἰώνων· ἐμπεσούσης δὲ στάσεως εἰς Ἔφεσον κατέφυγον κτλ.

[2] *Epp.* i. xi. 7 scis Lebedus quid sit, Gabiis desertior atque | Fidenis vicus.

[3] *Anton.*, c. 57. It is not at all certain that those whom Antony settled at Priene belonged to the group associated with Teos a century earlier; and some think that they were the world-wide guild in its early stages; see Klaffenbach, op. cit., p. 8.

[4] *C.I.G.* 3082 (see below, p. 309).

[5] *B.C.H.* xviii (1894), pp. 345 ff.; Fairbanks, *Study of the Greek Paean* (1900), pp. 119 ff.

[6] *I.G.* ii². 1331, 1332; Wilhelm, *Urkunden*, pp. 225–8, who discusses difficulties and dates.

Polybius[1] records the lavish expenditure (about 201 B.C.) of Tlepolemos, governor of Pelusium and regent of Egypt, upon the Artists of Dionysus and others.

There is very little evidence in regard to activities of the guilds in the West at this period unless the long Corcyrean inscription[2] relating to a benefaction of Aristomenes and Psylla can be treated as such. The benefaction was an endowment for the hiring of τεχνῖται annually to perform at the Dionysia at Corcyra, and the deed contained elaborate provisions for its administration, but there is no actual mention of the guilds. There are also inscriptions dedicating rewards voted by the κοινὸν τῶν περὶ τὸν Διόνυσον τεχνιτῶν to benefactors at Syracuse[3] and at Rhegium,[4] but the dates are unknown.

An undated inscription from Kos[5] records the award of a crown by resolution τῶν περὶ τὸν Διόνυσον τεχνιτῶν (presumably the Ionian and Hellespontine guild) to a citizen of Kos, and the dispatch of two special messengers from the τεχνῖται to Kos to deliver the resolution.

10. From the first century B.C., as from the second, there are records which may imply the use of the services of the guilds, but do not actually mention them. Such are the well-known inscriptions of 92–91 B.C. regulating the mysteries of Andania in Messene,[6] and the lists of victors in Charitesia and Homoloia at Orchomenos,[7] and in the Μουσεῖα at Thespiai.[8] But there is a remarkable inscription from Eleusis,[9] which is now generally dated soon after 86 B.C., recording how the σύνοδος τῶν περὶ τὸν Διόνυσον τεχνιτῶν had always done its best to promote the worship of the gods, and particularly of Demeter and Koré, and had

---

[1] xvi. 21 διερρίπτει τὰ βασιλικὰ χρήματα τοῖς ἀπὸ τῆς Ἑλλάδος παραγεγονόσι πρεσβευταῖς καὶ τοῖς περὶ τὸν Διόνυσον τεχνίταις, μάλιστα δὲ τοῖς περὶ τὴν αὐλὴν ἡγεμόσι καὶ στρατιώταις.

[2] *I.G.* ix. 694: the inscription is of the second century B.C.; cf. Lüders, op. cit., pp. 121–4.

[3] *I.G.* xiv. 12 and 13. The names of the destined recipients of a crown and a statue are lost.

[4] Ibid. 615 ἀρχόντων δὲ (four names) τὸ κοινὸν τῶν περὶ τὸν Διόνυσον τεχνιτῶν καὶ προξένων Αἰσηνοῦν Νίκωνος τῆς εὐνοίας ἕνεκεν τῆς εἰς ἑαυτούς.

[5] Paton and Hicks, *Inscr. of Cos*, no. 24.

[6] Dittenb.[3] 736. The relevant passage runs: τεχνιτᾶν εἰς τὰς χοριτείας. οἱ ἱεροὶ προγραφόντω κατ' ἐνιαυτὸν τοὺς λειτουργήσοντας ἔν τε ταῖς θυσίαις καὶ μυστηρίοις αὐλητὰς καὶ κιθαριστάς, ὅσους ἂν εὑρίσκωντι εὐθέτους ὑπάρχοντας, καὶ οἱ προγράφοντες λειτουργούντω τοῖς θεοῖς.

[7] *I.G.* vii. 3195–7. The victors come from many parts (including a few from Athens), but many are naturally Boeotian.

[8] Ibid. 1760–2; but one of the indications of date given was the name (lost) of the priest of the τεχνῖται, who was an Argive and therefore a member of the Isthmian and Nemean guild. He was mentioned next to the priest of the Muses. A number of the victors are Athenians.

[9] *I.G.* ii[2]. 628.

provided an altar and a τέμενος where they offered libations and sang paeans at the time of the mysteries; and how the altar and τέμενος had been destroyed during the disturbances of the time, but the traditional sacrifices and the expenses of the σύνοδος had been provided by Philemon, their ἐπιμελητής, at his own cost, and the sanctuary and altar had been rebuilt and all the costs connected with the services had been given freely by him, when he had accepted office for the fourth time on the urgent request of the guild—all of which is set out in language of enthusiastic approval.

The Athenian guild appears perhaps in a less honourable light, but at least its importance in the life of the time is indicated, in the part which they played in the extravagant welcome given by Athens to Athenion, the envoy of Mithradates in 88 B.C.[1] The envoy was greeted as the 'messenger of the new Dionysus'[2] and made an honoured guest at the ceremonies of the guild, which offered sacrifices in his honour in its τέμενος.[3] The action of the guild obviously indicated hostility towards Rome and it is not surprising that after the ruin inflicted on Athens by Sulla little is heard of the Athenian guild for some time.[4]

The continued life of the Isthmian and Nemean guild in the first century, with a centre at Elis (among other places), is attested by the dedication of a statue to a benefactor[5] at Olympia, and the Asiatic artists are mentioned by Plutarch[6] as having been collected by Tigranes in great numbers at Tigranocerta and used by Lucullus to entertain his victorious army when he captured the city in 69 B.C.

In the last half of the century Naples seems to have been a

---

[1] Athen. v. 212 d, ε ὑπήντησαν δ' αὐτῷ καὶ οἱ περὶ τὸν Διόνυσον τεχνῖται, τὸν ἄγγελον τοῦ νέου Διονύσου καλοῦντες ἐπὶ τὴν κοινὴν ἑστίαν καὶ τὰς περὶ ταύτην εὐχάς τε καὶ σπονδάς . . . ἐν δὲ τῷ τεμένει τῶν τεχνιτῶν θυσίαι τ' ἐπετελοῦντο ἐπὶ τῇ Ἀθηνίωνος παρουσίᾳ καὶ μετὰ κήρυκος προαναφωνήσεως σπονδαί.

[2] The title of νέος Διόνυσος here given to Mithradates Eupator was frequently accorded to his contemporary Ptolemy Philopator (Dittenb. *Or. Gr. Inscr.*, nos. 186–93 and 741) and much later to Hadrian and Antoninus Pius (see below, pp. 307, 308, 310).

[3] Where this was is unknown. The βουλευτήριον τῶν τεχνιτῶν at a very much later date was παρὰ τὰς τοῦ Κεραμεικοῦ πύλας, near the theatre called Ἀγριππεῖον (Philostr. *Vit. Soph.* II. viii. 2); but there is no ground for identifying this with the τέμενος.

[4] The inscription *I.G.* ii². 2955 in which τὸ κοινὸν τῶν περὶ Διόνυσον τεχνιτῶν at Athens dedicates a statue to a person whose name is lost may belong to the first or the second century.

[5] Dittenb. and Purgold, *Inschr. von Olympia*, no. 405 τεχνῖται περὶ τὸν Διόνυσον [ἐξ Ἰσθμοῦ καὶ] Νεμέας οἱ εἰς Ἦλιν συμπορευόμενοι . . . . α Μεσσήνιον τὸν αὐτῶν πρόξενον καὶ εὐεργέτην Διὶ Ὀλυμπίῳ.

[6] *Lucull.* 29.

resort of the Artists. According to Plutarch,[1] Brutus found many there in 44 B.C., and arranged for the collection of famous performers for his purposes. (He was collecting wild beasts for shows at the same time.) In 32 B.C. the Διονύσου τεχνῖται from the whole of the Eastern Greek world were obliged to assemble at Samos for the delectation of Antony and Cleopatra, and, as Plutarch remarks somewhat bitterly, τῆς ἐν κύκλῳ σχεδὸν ἁπάσης οἰκουμένης περιθρηνουμένης καὶ περιστεναζομένης μία νῆσος ἐφ᾽ ἡμέρας πολλὰς κατηυλεῖτο καὶ κατεψάλλετο, πληρουμένων θεάτρων καὶ χορῶν ἀγωνιζομένων.[2]

A letter[3] is extant written by the triumvir M. Antonius in 33/2 B.C. to the assembly of Asiatic Greeks which had sent him a petition on behalf of a σύνοδος of τεχνῖται, and its language has suggested that the organization of a world-wide σύνοδος, which was in full activity in the reign of Trajan, had already begun when Antony wrote, though the full title of σύνοδος τῶν ἀπὸ τῆς οἰκουμένης περὶ τὸν Διόνυσον τεχνιτῶν is not given, and the organization may not have been complete. Part of the letter must be quoted in full:

Μᾶρκος Ἀντώνιος αὐτοκράτωρ τριῶν ἀνδρῶν δημοσίων πραγμάτων ἀπὸ καταστάσεως τῷ κοινῷ τῶν ἀπὸ τῆς Ἀσίας Ἑλλήνων χαίρειν. καὶ πρότερον ἐντυχόντος μοι ἐν Ἐφέσῳ Μάρκου Ἀντωνίου Ἀρτεμιδώρου, τοῦ ἐμοῦ φίλου καὶ ἀλείπτου, μετὰ τοῦ ἐπωνύμου τῆς συνόδου τῶν ἀπὸ τῆς οἰκουμένης ἱερονικῶν καὶ στεφανειτῶν ἱερέως Χαροπείνου Ἐφεσίου, περὶ τοῦ ⟨τὰ⟩ προϋπάρχοντα τῇ συνόδῳ μένειν ἀναφαίρετα, καὶ περὶ τῶν λοιπῶν ὧν ᾐτεῖτο ἀπ᾽ ἐμοῦ τιμίων καὶ φιλανθρώπων τῆς ἀστρατευσίας καὶ ἀλειτουργησίας πάσης καὶ ἀνεπισταθμείας καὶ τῆς περὶ τὴν πανήγυριν ἐκεχειρίας καὶ ἀσυλίας καὶ πορφύρας, ἵνα συγχωρήσω γράψαι παραχρῆμα πρὸς ὑμᾶς, συγχωρῶ βουλόμενος καὶ διὰ τὸν ἐμὸν φίλον Ἀρτεμίδωρον καὶ τῷ ἐπωνύμῳ αὐτῶν ἱερεῖ εἴς τε τὸν κόσμον τῆς συνόδου καὶ τὴν αὔξησιν αὐτῆς χαρίσασθαι.

But it may be doubted whether the reference is to the Artists of Dionysus at all; Antony had summoned them to perform before him, as has been noted above; but in the letter there is no mention of Dionysus, and the mention of Artemidorus as ἀλείπτης suggests that it is concerned with the parallel σύνοδος of athletes.

[1] *Brut.* xxi καὶ τῶν περὶ τὸν Διόνυσον τεχνιτῶν αὐτὸς εἰς Νέαν Πόλιν καταβὰς ἐνέτυχε πλείστοις· περὶ δὲ Κανουτίου τινος εὐημεροῦντος ἐν τοῖς θεάτροις ἔγραφε πρὸς τοὺς φίλους ὅπως πείσαντες αὐτὸν εἰσαγάγωσιν· Ἑλλήνων γὰρ οὐδένα βιασθῆναι προσήκειν. [2] *Anton.* 56.

[3] In a papyrus, published by Kenyon, *Class. Rev.* vii (1893), pp. 476 ff., and fully discussed by Brandis in *Hermes*, xxxii (1897), pp. 509 ff., to whom reference may be made for some difficulties of interpretation.

11. In that case the earliest reference to a world-wide organization of Dionysiac artists is in the letter addressed to them by the emperor Claudius in A.D. 43.[1] He writes τοῖς ἀπὸ τῆς οἰκουμένης περὶ τὸν Διόνυσον ἱερονείκαις στεφανείταις καὶ τοῖς τούτων συναγωνισταῖς, and (after a good many words which are missing) τὰ δὲ ὑπὸ τοῦ θεοῦ Σεβαστοῦ δεδομένα ὑμῖν νόμιμα καὶ φιλάνθρωπα συντηρῶ. Very similar language is found in an inscription[2] from Miletus containing a letter of the same emperor τοῖς περὶ τὸν Διόνυσον ἱερονείκαις καὶ τεχνείταις, again confirming τὰ ὑπὸ τῶν πρὸ ἐμοῦ Σεβαστῶν καὶ τῆς συγκλήτου δεδομένα δίκαια. From these two sources it would appear that the grant of privileges to a world-wide organization by emperors and senate goes back as far as Augustus.

Otherwise there are no references to the world-wide σύνοδος until the reign of Trajan. Then it appears in an inscription discovered at Gerasa (Jerash)[3] and dating probably between A.D. 105 and 114. This records a decree in honour of Titus Flavius Gerrenus, who had served as agonothetes on a great occasion: ψήφισμα τῆς ἱερᾶς συνόδου τῶν ἀπὸ τῆς οἰκουμένης περὶ τὸν Διόνυσον καὶ τὸν κύριον ἡμῶν Αὐτοκράτορα Νέρουαν Τραϊανὸν Καίσαρα Σέβαστον Γερμανικὸν Δακικ[ὸν τεχνιτῶν στεφανιτῶν] καὶ τῶν τούτων συναγωνιστῶν. The relation of these συναγωνισταί to the world-wide society is not definitely ascertainable; but from this and other inscriptions,[4] as has already been suggested, the subordinate performers appear to have formed a special society within the larger. In the same way the local guilds may have retained a separate though subordinate existence, or may only gradually have become merged in the world-wide guild. Thus a stele erected at Ephesus[5] in the second century by Ulpia to her two sons describes one of them as (inter alia) ἀγωνοθετήσαντα τῶν μεγάλων Πυθίων καὶ ἀρχιερατεύσαντα τῶν ἐπ' Ἰωνίας καὶ Ἑλλησπόντου καὶ ἀγωνοθετήσαντα τῶν χρυσοφόρων, and Smyrna appears to have kept its own guild in some special connexion with the mystic cult of Dionysus Briseus.[6] The loyalty of the guild was acknowledged in a letter from M. Aurelius,[7] and in another

---

[1] In a papyrus in Berlin, printed and fully discussed by Viereck, *Klio*, viii (1908), p. 413.
[2] Rehm, *Milet.* i. 3. 383.
[3] Kraeling, *Gerasa*, pp. 442 ff.; cf. *J. Rom. Stud.* xviii (1928), p. 173.
[4] See above, p. 301.
[5] *Ancient Gk. Inscr. in Brit. Mus.* iii, no. 618.
[6] *C.I.G.* 3176 συνόδῳ τῶν περὶ τὸν Βρισέα Διόνυσον χαίρειν. Brisa, the centre of the cult, was a promontory of Lesbos. [7] *C.I.G.* 3190.

inscription¹ the ἱερὰ σύνοδος τῶν περὶ τὸν Βρισέα Διόνυσον τεχνιτῶν καὶ μυστῶν commemorates the services of another M. Aurelius, son of Charidemus.

A decree from the σύνοδος at Aphrodisias,² which includes a request to the city of Aphrodisias, is evidently that of a local unit, and in a decree at Nysa³ in honour of M. Apollonius the σύνοδος is separately named (ἡ βουλὴ καὶ ὁ δῆμος καὶ ἡ γερουσία καὶ οἱ νέοι καὶ ἡ σύνοδος) and must also be a local guild. Later in the same century we find what is perhaps the last evidence of a more or less local unit within the whole in an inscription from Rhodes, which speaks of a ἱερὰ σύνοδος εἰς Νέμεα καὶ Πύθια, a guild performing especially at these two great festivals.

At Athens the τεχνῖται had a council-chamber in the Kerameikos,⁴ and it was probably they who in the latter half of the second century set up a monument⁵ to a famous comic actor and περιοδονείκης named Strato, who had been honoured with an ivy crown:

τῆδε Μενανδρείων ἐπέων δεδαηκότα πάσας
τύξιας εὐιέροις ἄγλαον ἐν θυμέλαις
ἐκτέρισαν θεράποντες ἀερσίφρονος Διονύσου
αὐτῷ κισσοφόρῳ τοῦτο χαριζόμενοι.

An inscription from Rhodiapolis,⁶ dated (somewhat doubtfully) late in the first or early in the second century, records that, along with others, Ἀθηναῖοι καὶ ἱερωτάτη Ἀρεοπαγείτων βουλὴ καὶ οἱ Ἀθήνησιν Ἐπικούρειοι φιλόσοφοι καὶ ἡ ἱερὰ θυμελικὴ σύνοδος paid honour to the physician Herakleitos. An inscription⁷ of the time of Antoninus Pius is probably Athenian in origin—it was brought to London with the Elgin Marbles—and describes itself as ψήφισμα τῆς ἱερᾶς Ἀδριάνης Ἀντωνείνης θυμελικῆς περιπολιστικῆς μεγάλης συνόδου τῶν ἀπὸ τῆς οἰκουμένης περὶ τὸν Διόνυσον καὶ Αὐτοκράτορα Καίσαρα Τίτον Αἴλιον Ἀδρίανον Ἀντώνεινον Σέβαστον Εὐσεβῆ νέον Διόνυσον τεχνιτῶν.

¹ Le Bas, *As. Min.* 1620; see below, p. 308.
² *B.C.H.* vii (1883). 273.
³ *C.I.G.* 2529 ὁ δᾶμος ὁ Ῥοδίων καὶ ἁ βουλὰ Τίτον Αὐρηλίανον Νικόστρατον Νικοστράτου ἀμώμητον σοφιστάν, τετιμαμένον καὶ ὑπὸ τοῦ μεγίστου Αὐτοκράτορος καθέδρᾳ καὶ λογιστείᾳ τᾶς ἱερᾶς συνόδου εἰς Νέμεα καὶ Πύθια.
⁴ Philostratus, *Vit. Soph.* ii. 8, p. 251.
⁵ *Ath. Mitt.* xvii (1892), p. 272, no. 1. For τύξιας cf. Hesych. τύξιν· τεῦξιν, παρασκευήν ('device'). For περιοδονείκης see below, p. 314.
⁶ *C.I.G.* iii. 4315 n, Add. See Ziebarth, op. cit., p. 88, n. 1.
⁷ *I.G.* ii². 1350. Another inscription (ibid. 1348) contains fragments of a letter of the τεχνῖται to Hadrian or Antoninus Pius and his reply.

The importance of the guild at Athens at this period is illustrated by the appropriation of two front seats in the theatre of Dionysus to members of it holding certain priesthoods. The seats are inscribed ἱερέως Διονύσου Μελπομένου ἐκ τεχνιτῶν and ἱερέως Ἀντινόου Χαρείου ἐκ τεχνιτῶν (of the time of Hadrian, whose visit is also commemorated otherwise in the theatre). The priest of Διόνυσος Μελπόμενος ἐξ Ἐννειδῶν had also a seat.[1]

The guild and its operations are referred to in inscriptions from all over the world. A census return in Egypt,[2] A.D. 145–6, mentions οἰκίαν ἐν τόπῳ καλουμένῳ Διονύσου τεχνιτῶν. From Ankyra[3] comes a ψήφισμα τῶν ἀπὸ τῆς οἰκουμένης περὶ τὸν Διόνυσον καὶ Τραϊανὸν Ἀδρίανον Σεβαστὸν Καίσαρα νέον Διόνυσον τεχνιτῶν ἱερονικῶν στεφανιτῶν καὶ τῶν τούτων συναγωνιστῶν καὶ τῶν νεμόντων τὴν ἱερὰν θυμελικὴν σύνοδον, in which the last words seem to distinguish the local association from the world-wide. (The inscription, dated A.D. 128, decrees a statue and other honours for Aelius Pompeianus.)

A decree from Aphrodisias,[4] of Hadrian's reign, illustrates the close association or even fusion in a number of these records of the Dionysiac artists with parallel associations of athletes. Other decrees of Eastern origin include a fragment from Thyatira of the time of Antoninus Pius;[5] a decree,[6] of the reign of M. Aurelius, from Pessinus, in which a crown is awarded to someone by the ἱερὰ μουσικὴ περιπολιστικὴ σύνοδος τῶν περὶ τὸν Διόνυσον τεχνιτῶν; and the dedication of a statue of Iulius Philippus at Tralles,[7] which seems to retain, even in the third

---

[1] *I.G.* iii. 274. The importance of Διόνυσος Μελπόμενος in connexion with theatrical performances is illustrated by an important inscription of the second century B.C. from Priene (*Inschr. von Priene*, no. 174), where public sacrifices and prayers to him in the theatre are prescribed.

[2] *Oxyrh. Pap.* ii, p. 208.

[3] Buckler in *J. Rom. Stud.* xvi (1926), pp. 245 ff., who prints also a second (very fragmentary) inscription of similar purport and wording.

[4] Le Bas, *As. Min.*, no. 1620. The decree is that of ἡ ἱερὰ περιπολιστικὴ εὐσεβὴς σεβαστὴ σύνοδος καὶ ὁ σύμπας ξυστὸς τῶν περὶ Τραϊανὸν Ἀδριανὸν Σεβαστόν; cf. an inscription in *Ath. Mitt.* xxiv (1899), p. 433, of the early third century A.D. from Prusias: τῶν ἱερῶν συνόδων οἰκουμενικῶν περιπολιστικῶν τῆς τε ξυστικῆς καὶ τῆς θυμελικῆς; and other parallels (e.g. a ἱερὰ θυμελικὴ καὶ ξυστικὴ σύνοδος at Alexandria (3rd cent. A.D.). To modern readers this may suggest a fusion of the Old Vic with the Association Football League. An inscription of the same date (Le Bas, 1619; Lüders, *Dion. Künstler*, p. 183) begins: ψήφισμα τῆς ἱερᾶς συνόδου· ἔδοξε τῇ ἱερᾷ συνόδῳ τῶν ἀπὸ τῆς οἰκουμένης περὶ τὸν Διόνυσον καὶ Αὐτοκράτορα Τραϊανὸν Καίσαρος θεοῦ Τραϊανοῦ Παρθικοῦ υἱὸν, θεοῦ Νερούα υἱωνόν, Ἀδριανὸν Καίσαρα Σέβαστον νέον Διόνυσον τεχνιτῶν . . . καὶ συναγωνιστῶν.

[5] *C.I.G.* 3476 b. 　　　　　　　　　　　　　　　[6] *C.I.G.* 4081.

[7] *C.I.G.* 2933.

century, the old title ἡ σύνοδος ⟨τῶν περὶ τὸν Διόνυσον τεχνιτῶν⟩ τῶν ἀπ᾽ Ἰωνίας καὶ Ἑλλησπόντου, implying that this great guild had maintained its identity with the larger organization; as does an inscription found in the theatre at Teos:[1] οἱ περὶ τὸν Διόνυσον τεχνῖται οἱ ἀπὸ Ἰωνίας καὶ Ἑλλησπόντου καὶ οἱ τούτων συναγωνισταὶ ἐτίμησαν Τιβέριον Κλαύδιον ἀγνωοθέτην τὸ τρίτον τῶν πενταετηρικῶν ἀγώνων Διονυσιακῶν Καισαρήνων κτλ. The continuance of some traditional association with Teos and Pergamon is further confirmed by two inscriptions probably of the early years of the third century, viz. (1)[2] ἐπὶ Ἀντιόχου φυλῆς Εὐμενίδος ἄρχων Παγκλῆς Παγκλέους ἱερονείκης ἀπὸ συνόδου τῆς ἱερᾶς, ὁ καὶ περιοδονείκης, ἄρχων τὸ δεύτερον ἐπὶ κτλ., where the tribe Eumenis probably derived its name from the royal house of Pergamon, and (2)[3] which mentions Septimius Tryphon as ἱερεὺς κατὰ τὸ ἑξῆς δίς of the ἱερὰ σύνοδος and ἀρχιερεὺς τοῦ καθηγέμονος Διονύσου (the special god of the Attalids), as well as ἀρχιερεὺς Μάρκου Αὐρηλίου Ἀντωνείνου Σεβαστοῦ τοῦ νέου Διονύσου διὰ βίου.

An inscription from Hierapolis[4] distinguishes two associations in a manner not quite satisfactorily explained, speaking of ἡ εἱροτάτη σύνοδος καὶ οἱ ἀπὸ τῆς οἰκουμένης ἱερονίκαι. There may have been many different groupings within the larger whole, which was probably associated with most of the festivals mentioned in many inscriptions in honour of one emperor after another.[5]

In Greece proper, apart from Athens, there are very few records. An inscription from Epidaurus,[6] probably of the first or second century, tabulating fines inflicted upon τεχνῖται who had failed to keep their engagements, may or may not imply the action of a guild: ἐπὶ ἀγωνοθέτα τῶν Ἀσκληπιείων καὶ Ἀπολλωνίων Σωστράτου τοῦ Πατροκλείδα κατάδικοι οἱ γενόμενοι τῶν τεχνιτῶν διὰ τὸ μὴ ἀγωνίσασθαι κεκομισμένοι τὸν μισθόν (2 lines missing) κωμῳδὸς Διονύσιος Διονυσίου Ῥόδιος μνᾶν τεττάρων.

In the West the headquarters of the world-organization was naturally in Rome, and there are several references to this in

---

[1] *C.I.G.* 3082 (probably early 3rd cent. A.D.); see above, p. 302.
[2] *C.I.G.* 6820.
[3] *C.I.G.* 6829. The date must be between A.D. 198 and 210. See above, pp. 299 ff. Various performers are styled περιοδονείκης and παράδοξος.
[4] Judeich, *Alterthümer von Hierapolis*, p. 84, no. 36.
[5] See Müller, op. cit., p. 410.   [6] *I.G.* iv². 99.

inscriptions, especially in the time of Antoninus Pius,[1] under the title of ἡ ἱερὰ ἡμῶν Ἀδριανὴ Ἀντωνεινὴ περιπολιστικὴ θυμελικὴ μεγάλη νεωκόρος ἐπὶ Ῥώμῃ σύνοδος. The epithet περιπολιστική which occurs frequently from the time of Antoninus or a little earlier indicates that the members of the guild travelled from place to place. There was a great multiplication of festivals, many of them connected with the cult of the Emperor, during this century, and the services of the Artists were constantly in demand in places far apart. The title νεωκόρος connotes the guardianship of a sanctuary of the cult, usually that of the Divine Emperor, and here especially of the central sanctuary in Rome. Philostratus[2] describes the control exercised over the Dionysiac artists in Rome by Euodianus of Smyrna, whose task appears to have been none too easy. In a Neapolitan inscription of the time of Antoninus[3] the ἱερὰ σύνοδος commemorates the series of victories won by Aelius Antigenidas, a flute-player, including a victory at the Eusebeia instituted by Antoninus in honour of his appellation Εὐσεβής (Pius); and earlier in the century there seems to have been a centre of the Artists at Nemausus (Nîmes).[4]

12. The inscriptions and passages of various authors selected for quotation in this account of the Artists of Dionysus will have given some idea of the character and importance of the guilds. The Artists stood on a higher plane in public regard than the actors of mimes and similar performers; these were never admitted to the guilds. The fact that each artist is named in inscriptions—there are at least very few exceptions—with the addition to his own name of that of his country virtually proves that they were citizens with full rights, however widely they may have been scattered and mingled in the guilds with the citizens of strange towns and countries.[5] The guilds were evidently or-

---

[1] e.g. *Ath. Mitt.* xiv. (1889), p. 316, and others quoted by Poland, op. cit., p. 594.

[2] *Vit. Soph.*, p. 260 (Kays.) ἐπιταχθεὶς δὲ καὶ τοῖς ἀμφὶ τὸν Διόνυσον τεχνίταις, τὸ δὲ ἔθνος τοῦτο ἀγέρωχοι καὶ χαλεποὶ ἀρχθῆναι, ἐπιτηδειότατος τὴν ἀρχὴν ἔδοξεν, καὶ κρείττων ἢ λαβεῖν αἰτίαν.

[3] Lüders, p. 185, no. 102.

[4] *C.I.G.* 6785 ψήφισμα συνόδου θυμελικῆς ἐν Νεμαύσῳ τῶν [περὶ τὸν Αὐτοκράτορα Νέρ]ουαν Τραϊανὸν Καίσαρα Σεβαστὸν [τεχνιτῶν or συναγωνιστῶν] and 6786, an inscription in honour of T. Iulius Dolabella by the σύνοδος in Nemausus: ψήφισμα τῆς ἱερᾶς Τραϊανῆς συνόδου τῶν περὶ τὸν Αὐτοκράτορα Καίσαρα Τραϊανὸν Ἀδριανόν, νέον Διόνυσον, συναγωνιστῶν.

[5] It would be rash to infer that there was a general distinction between ἐγγεγραμμένοι—registered members—and μετέχοντες from the use of the words in the decree sent from Teos to Iasos (see above, p. 301).

ganized with some thoroughness,[1] and their corporate existence and independence recognized not only in the grants of special privileges which have been noticed, but in the reception of envoys from them by cities almost as if they were independent states, in the appointment and recognition of their πρόξενοι both by states and by other guilds, and in the sending of θεωροί by the guilds, in addition to those of the cities, to great festivals. Their officers were annually appointed; all appointments, whether of officers, envoys, or πρόξενοι, were normally made by the κοινόν—the whole body of each guild—and it was the whole κοινόν that voted statues and crowns to famous actors and to kings and benefactors. The whole body was probably the authority which inflicted and adjudicated upon the fines which actors might have to pay, particularly for failing to appear at festivals to which they were sent—as the performers were sent from Teos to Iasos,[2] and were liable to such fines. Whether such performers were always selected by the assembly or authorities of their guild is uncertain; but in some inscriptions—e.g. those concerning Kraton— they are evidently regarded as the representatives of the guild and as reflecting upon it some of the credit of their own honours. It was doubtless the guild as a corporate body which (as at Eleusis and Magnesia) determined the part which it should play in the worship and festivals of gods other than Dionysus[3]— Demeter and Kore, Artemis, the Muses, Herakles, Sarapis, and others—and the close association of the Artists with Apollo of Delphi needs no further illustration, though the many lists of victors at Delphi and elsewhere leave it uncertain whether in these particular festivals they performed as individuals or as representatives sent by the guilds.

The chief official of a guild was probably, as a rule, the ἱερεύς, the priest of Dionysus, of whom most is to be learned from the inscriptions of Teos. He was elected annually and was re-eligible,

---

[1] Each had its own νόμοι and some at least their common seal.

[2] The Euboean Law (*I.G.* xii. 9. 207), which is earlier than the institution of guilds, also provided for various fines, and the fining of actors for non-appearance was evidently a legal proceeding in the time of Demosthenes and Alexander (see above, p. 303). The Corcyrean decree (see p. 287) regulating the newly endowed Dionysia also inflicts fines. In all these cases the authority must have been that of the State. But the guilds may have assumed the right of fine as they became constituted.

[3] It is incorrect to speak of the guilds as θίασοι of Dionysus. They formed a professional body, who worked under the patronage of Dionysus, but not a body consisting primarily of voluntary devotees of a particular cult, like the Διονυσιασταί, Ἀτταλισταί, and others. (The θίασοι often included women and slaves. The σύνοδοι did not.)

and a performing artist might be chosen, as Kraton was, at Teos.[1] (It happens that the title does not occur in Athenian records before Hadrian.) In Cyprus in the third century[2] and also in imperial times in Asia Minor the title ἀρχιερεύς is found; the same man, in Cyprus, was ἀρχιερεύς both of the city and of the τεχνῖται. One of the sons of Ulpia at Ephesus[3] was ἀρχιερεύς τῶν ἐπ' Ἰωνίας καὶ Ἑλλησπόντου, and (at least in the East) a 'chief priest' might be appointed for life.[4] In other cities Dionysus and the emperor might share the same high-priest. The ἀγωνοθέτης mentioned in the inscriptions from Teos was probably an official of the city, charged with the superintendence of public festivals, but the σύνοδος gave him orders as regards proclamations in the theatre. The office was sometimes combined with another. The decree from Eleusis in honour of Philemon[5] names the chief administrative officer ἐπιμελητής; he also offered sacrifices to the two goddesses. He was annually re-eligible, and his functions seem to have been comprehensive. In other decrees —particularly in that of the σύνοδος of Argos[6]—we find mentions of a ταμίας or financial officer, a γραμματεύς or secretary, and an ἐπιστάτης, appointed for special duties *ad hoc*. The νομοδείκτης[7] seems to have settled disputes between the members. In imperial times we hear also of a λογιστής[8]—not an officer of a guild, but an external commissioner, appointed apparently by the emperor, to keep an eye on its affairs.[9]

The members of the guild included poets of various kinds (dramatic, epic, and lyric), actors of tragedy, comedy, and satyric plays, singers in the choruses, instrumentalists, rhapsodes, and before long reciters of encomia and similar compositions, and διδάσκαλοι—trainers of choruses—who might themselves be actors or singers; the names of some occur from time to time both as διδάσκαλοι and as choreutae. ὑποδιδάσκαλοι are also mentioned. These were probably at first professional trainers em-

[1] See pp. 300 ff.
[2] Above, p. 290.
[3] See above, p. 306.
[4] e.g. *C.I.G.* 6829.
[5] *I.G.* ii². 628; see p. 303.
[6] *I.G.* iv. 558; see p. 298.
[7] *C.I.G.* 6829. The title is also found in an inscription at Ankyra (*J.R.S.* xvi, p. 246); see above, p. 308, and it occurs among those of the officials of certain mysteries.
[8] *C.I.G.* 2529; see p. 307.
[9] There were evidently differences as regards the precise functions and conditions of tenure of some of the chief offices in the different guilds and at different times, as would be expected.

ployed by the poets who were the διδάσκαλοι proper,[1] but later the title may have been applied at Athens of the producers of old plays, the original poets being still regarded as the true διδάσκαλοι. The costumiers (ἱματιομίσθαι) were doubtless also members of the guild. Their importance is attested, even before the existence of guilds, in the Euboean inscription to which reference has already been made,[2] as well as later. In the inscription from Ptolemais[3] the term used is σκευοποιός, as in Aristotle's *Poetics*. Whether the σαλπιγκτής, the trumpeter who announced the beginning of each 'event' in the contests,[4] and the κῆρυξ were members or servants of the guild is not quite certain. It has already been noted that within the guild the actors of secondary rank, the συναγωνισταί, might form a special society of their own.[5] In the time of Plato tragic and comic actors appear to have been rigidly separate;[6] in Cicero's day exceptional performers might excel in both kinds,[7] but the inscriptional records show that this must have been very rare.

There is little satisfactory evidence as to the payments made to artists.[8] The sums prescribed in the Euboean decree are not likely to have been exceptional for the early part of the third century B.C.; the Corcyrean inscription[9] of the second century B.C. gave each tragic or comic troupe and its flute-player $8\frac{1}{3}$ Corinthian minae in addition to rations, and in imperial times inscriptions from Aphrodisias[10] enumerate payments of very varying amounts to performers and composers of different kinds—whether as fees or as prizes does not appear certain; the poets, such as composers of new plays and of epic poems, come off worse than the performers. Probably the sums offered differed widely at different festivals, and the festivals themselves were correspondingly distinguished as θεματικοί ('paid in money-down'—apparently the least remunerative), ἀργυρῖται, ἡμι-ταλανταῖοι, and ταλανταῖοι.

---

[1] Phot. s.v. ὑποδιδάσκαλος· ὁ τῷ χορῷ καταλέγων. διδάσκαλος γὰρ αὐτὸς ὁ ποιητής, ὡς Ἀριστοφάνης. This is implied also in the enumeration in Plato, *Ion*, p. 536 a ὁρμαθὸς πάμπολυς ἐξήρτηται χορευτῶν τε καὶ διδασκάλων καὶ ὑποδιδασκάλων.

[2] See above, p. 289.　　　　　　　　　　　　　　[3] See above, p. 290.

[4] Cf. Poll. iv. 87, 91.　　　　　　　　　　　　[5] See above, pp. 301, 306.

[6] *Rep.* iii. 395 a οὐδὲ μὴν ῥαψῳδοί γε καὶ ὑποκριταὶ ἅμα· οὐδέ τοι ὑποκριταὶ κωμῳδοῖς τε καὶ τραγῳδοῖς οἱ αὐτοί.　　　　　　　　　　　　　　　　　　[7] Cic. *Orat.* 109.

[8] A story is told in various forms that Polos or Aristodemos (second half of the fourth century) boasted that he had made a talent in two days (Plut. *Vit. X Orat.* 848 b; Gell., *Noct. Att.* xi. 9).　　　　　　　　　　　　　　　　[9] See above, p. 303.

[10] *C.I.G.* 2758, 2759; Le Bas, *Asie Min.* 1620 c, d; *vide* Foucart, op. cit., p. 99.

Inscriptions show that each guild might have its annual παν-ήγυρις, as well as monthly feasts, celebrations of the birthdays of princes and benefactors, common dinners, and wine-parties, and that the guilds took a conspicuous part in the public sacrifices of sanctuaries or towns, and might march in processions clad in purple and gold.

13. The flattery of successful actors and instrumentalists in the imperial age seems to have reached the same height of absurdity as that of film-stars in the present day. In addition to the title ἱερονείκης, which could be used of any victor in sacred games or belonging to a ἱερὰ σύνοδος, we find περιοδονείκης used to indicate a victor in all the four great festivals of Greece, and πλειστονείκης of one who broke the record in the number of his victories; παράδοξος is constantly used of the victor, and παρα-δοξονείκης is attested by Plutarch. An inscription from Pessinus,[1] already referred to, is typical:

εἰσηγησαμένου Τ. Ἀντωνιανοῦ Εὐτυχιανοῦ . . . καὶ Ἀθηναίου, κιθαρῳδοῦ
περιοδονείκου παραδόξου, ἐπιψηφισαμένου Μ. Αὔρ. Γλυκωνιανοῦ Ἐφεσίου
κυκλίου αὐλητοῦ Πυθιονείκου, Ἀκτιονείκου, πλειστονείκου παραδόξου καὶ
πάσης τῆς συνόδου· εὐχάριστος ὑπάρχουσα ἡμῶν εἰς τοὺς Γαλάτας ἡ ἱερὰ
μουσικὴ περιπολιστικὴ σύνοδος τῶν περὶ τὸν Διόνυσον τεχνιτῶν . . . στεφανοῖ
τιμῶσα καὶ . . .

Two inscriptions at Delphi[2] were set up by their respective cities in honour of the record numbers of victories of the flute-players Zosimus of Gortyn and T. Aelius Aurelianus Theodotos of Nikomedeia; the latter had been accorded the citizenship of Thebes, Athens, Smyrna, Ephesos, Pergamon, and Antioch. (This was in the time of Commodus as emperor.) A third-century inscription[3] found at Athens contains an immense list of the victories of a κῆρυξ. A performer who was the outstanding success of a whole festival might be described as victorious διὰ πάντων.[4]

But in spite of all this flattery it is not easy to get a clear general idea of the social position and reputation of the actor at different periods. The depreciatory estimate of Aristotle has already been quoted,[5] but the language used of Kraton by his σύνοδος at Teos is that of warm personal regard, and there are

---

[1] *C.I.G.* 4081; see p. 308. Full references for these epithets are given by Müller, op. cit., p. 413. [2] *C.I.G.* 1719, 1720.
[3] Published in Φιλίστως (1861), vol. i, p. 329.
[4] e.g. *C.I.G.* 1585, 1586 (both at the Μουσεῖα of Thespiai), 1720 (see above), etc.
[5] Above, p. 287.

similar expressions in inscriptions of later periods. Yet Philostratus[1] speaks of actors as haughty and undisciplined, and
Lucian has little good to say of them. But the actors of whom
Lucian[2] speaks as being whipped, at the pleasure of the audience,
if they acted badly, or at best as being hissed off the stage, and
as wandering about in beggary and starvation when they had
put off the fine stage robes which they wore as gods and kings
and heroes, seem to belong to a different world from Kraton
and from others mentioned in inscriptions of Lucian's own time.
Probably most of the actors whose names appear in the inscriptions are those who were specially selected to perform at
great or special festivals, while Lucian is thinking of theatrical
performances which were commonly held in all towns, large or
small, and at many seasons.

APPENDIX

INSCRIPTIONS RELATING TO TEOS

1. *I.G.* xi. 1061 (= *C.I.G.* 3067, with emendations).

ἔδοξεν τῷ κοινῷ τῶν περὶ τὸν Διόνυσον τεχνιτῶν τῶν ἐπ᾽ Ἰωνίας καὶ Ἑλλησ-
[πόντου καὶ τῶν περὶ τὸν καθηγε]μόνα Διόνυσον· ἐπειδὴ Κράτων Ζωτίχου
αὐλητὴς πρότερόν τε γενόμενος [ἱερεὺς τοῦ Διονύσου καὶ ἀγω]νοθέτης καλῶς
καὶ ἐνδόξως προέστη τῆς τε ἱερωσύνης καὶ τῆς ἀγων[οθεσίας καὶ δοκιμασθ]εὶς
ἄξιος εἶναι ταύτης τῆς τιμῆς ὑπὸ τοῦ πλήθους τῶν τεχνιτῶν καὶ αἱρεθε[ὶς
πάλιν ἱερεὺς] τοῦ Διονύσου καὶ ἀγωνοθέτης ἐν τῷ αὐτῷ ἔτει, ὑπερθέμενος
τοὺς [πρὸ αὐτοῦ γενομένους πάντ]ας ἀγωνοθέτας τῇ τε χορηγίᾳ καὶ τῇ δαπάνῃ
καὶ τῇ αὐτοῦ μεγαλο[πρεπείᾳ καλῶς καὶ πρεπόν]τως καὶ ἀξίως τῆς συνόδου
πάντα τὰ πρὸς τιμὴν καὶ δόξαν ἀνήκοντα ἐπ[οίησε τῷ τε Διονύ]σῳ καὶ ταῖς
Μούσαις καὶ τῷ Ἀπόλλωνι τῷ Πυθίῳ καὶ τοῖς ἄλλοις θεοῖ[ς πᾶσι καὶ τοῖς
τε βασι]λεῦσι καὶ ταῖς βασιλίσσαις καὶ τοῖς ἀδελφοῖς βασιλέως Εὐμένου καὶ

---

[1] See above, p. 310.

[2] e.g. *Piscator* 33 ἐπεὶ καὶ οἱ ἀθλοθέται μαστιγοῦν εἰώθασιν, ἤν τις ὑποκριτὴς Ἀθηνᾶν ἢ Ποσει-
δεῶνα ἢ τὸν Δία ὑποδεδυκὼς μὴ καλῶς ὑποκρίνοιτο μηδὲ κατ᾽ ἀξίαν τῶν θεῶν, καὶ οὐ δή που ὀργί-
ζονται αὐτοῖς ἐκεῖνοι (sc. οἱ θεοί), ὅτι τὸν περικείμενον αὐτῶν τὰ προσωπεῖα καὶ τὸ σχῆμα
ἐνδεδυκότα ἐπέτρεψαν παίειν τοῖς μαστιγοφόροις, ἀλλὰ καὶ ἥδοιντ᾽ ἄν, οἶμαι, μαστιγουμένων·
οἰκέτην μὲν γὰρ ἢ ἄγγελόν τινα μὴ δεξίως ὑποκρίνασθαι μικρὸν τὸ πταῖσμα, τὸν Δία δὲ ἢ τὸν
Ἡρακλέα μὴ κατ᾽ ἀξίαν ἐπιδείξασθαι τοῖς θεαταῖς ἀποτρόπαιον ὡς καὶ αἰσχρόν; *Apol. de mercede
cond.* 5 (ὑποκριταὶ) ὑπόμισθοι τραγῳδοῦντες, ἐκπίπτοντες καὶ συριττόμενοι, ἐνίοτε δὲ καὶ μαστι-
γούμενοί τινες αὐτῶν, ὡς ἂν τῷ θεάτρῳ δοκῇ; *Nigrin.* 8 ἤδη τραγικοὺς ἢ νὴ Δία κωμικοὺς φαύλους
ἑώρακας ὑποκριτάς, τῶν συριττομένων λέγω τούτων καὶ διαφθειρόντων τὰ ποιήματα, καίτοι τῶν
δραμάτων πολλάκις εὖ ἐχόντων τε καὶ νενικηκότων; *ET.* πολλοὺς οἶδα τοιούτους; *Menipp.* (Νεκυο-
μαντεία) 16 the actor, who has been playing the King in lordly robes, when the play is
over πένης καὶ ταπεινὸς περίεισιν; *Navig.* 46 ὥσπερ οἱ τοὺς βασιλεῖς ὑποκρινόμενοι τραγῳδοὶ
ἐξελθόντες ἀπὸ τοῦ θεάτρου λιμώττοντες οἱ πολλοὶ καὶ ταῦτα πρὸ ὀλίγου Ἀγαμέμνονες ὄντες ἢ
Κρέοντες.

τῷ [κοινῷ τῶν περὶ τὸν Διόνυ]σον τεχνιτῶν ἀποδεικνύμενος τὴν αὑτοῦ καλο-
κἀγαθίαν καὶ εὐσέβε[ιαν καὶ . . . ἐν παντὶ και]ρῷ καὶ ἰδίᾳ καὶ κοινῇ ἀεί τινος
ἀγαθοῦ παραίτιος γενόμενος ὅπως [διαμένῃ εἰς τὸν ἀεὶ] χρόνον ἡ παρὰ τῶν
τεχνιτῶν ἀθάνατος δόξα, οὓς καὶ θεοὶ καὶ βασιλ[εῖς καὶ πάντες Ἕλ]ληνες
τιμῶσιν, δεδωκότες τήν τε ἀσυλίαν καὶ ἀσφάλειαν πᾶσι τεχ[νίταις πολέμου
καὶ εἰ]ρήνης, κατακολουθοῦντες τοῖς τοῦ Ἀπόλλωνος χρησμοῖς δι' οὓς [καὶ
τοῖς ἀγῶσι τοῖς τοῦ] Ἀπόλλωνος τοῦ Πυθίου καὶ τῶν Μουσῶν τῶν Ἑλικωνιά-
δων καὶ τοῦ [Ἡρακλέους, ἐν Δελφοῖς μὲν τοῖς] Πυθίοις καὶ Σωτηρίοις, ἐν
Θεσπιαῖς δὲ τοῖς Μουσείοις, ἐν Θήβαις δὲ τοῖ[ς Ἡρακλείοις ἐνέκριναν
αὐτοὺς (?) οἳ] ἐκ πάντων τῶν Ἑλλήνων εὐσεβέστατοι· ἀγαθῇ τύχῃ· δεδόχθαι
[τῇ συνόδῳ· ἵνα φαίνηται τιμῶ]σα τοὺς αὑτῆς εὐεργέτας καταξίως τῶν
εὐεργετημάτων· στεφανῶ[σαι Κράτωνα Ζωτίχου αὐλητ]ὴν εὐεργέτην καθ'
ἕκαστον ἔτος εἰς ἀεὶ ἐν τῷ θεάτρῳ ἐν ᾗ ἡμέρᾳ ἡ π[ανήγυρις τελ]εῖται μετὰ
τὴν στεφάνωσιν τῶν δήμων στεφάνῳ τῷ ἐκ τοῦ νόμο[υ ἀρετῆς ἕνεκα καὶ
εὐν]οίας ἣν ἔχων διατελεῖ εἰς τὸ κοινὸν τῶν περὶ τὸν Διόνυσον τεχνιτῶ[ν· τῆς
δὲ ἀναγορευσέως τοῦ στεφ]άνου ἐπιμέλειαν ποιεῖσθαι τὸν ἑκάστοτε γινόμενον
ἀγωνοθέτην· [ἀναθεῖναι δὲ αὐτοῦ εἰκόνας τ]ρεῖς· τὴν μὲν μίαν ἐν Τέῳ ἐν τῷ
θεάτρῳ ὅπως οἱ καθ' ἕκαστον ἔτος ἀ[γωνοθέται ἐν τῇ π]ανηγύρει καὶ ὅταν
ἡ Τηΐων πόλις συντελῇ Διονύσια ἢ ἄλλον τινὰ ἀγ[ῶνα στεφανῶσαι (τὴν
εἰκόνα)] τὴν Κράτωνος στεφάνῳ τῷ ἐκ τοῦ νόμου ᾧ πάτριόν ἐστι τοῖ[ς
τεχνίταις στεφανοῦν τοὺς αὑ]τῶν εὐεργέτας· τὴν δὲ ἄλλην ἐν Δήλῳ ὅπως καὶ
ἐκεῖ στεφανω[θήσεται ὑπὸ τοῦ κοινοῦ τῶν τε]χνιτῶν· τὴν δὲ τρίτην οὗ ἂν
ἀναθῇ Κράτων, ἵνα εἰς ἅπαντα τὸν [χρόνον ὑπόμνημα ᾖ τῆς τε πρὸς] τὸ θεῖον
εὐσεβείας καὶ τῆς εἰς τοὺς βασιλέας καὶ βασιλίσσας [καὶ τοὺς ἀδελφοὺς τοῦ]
βασιλέως Εὐμένου καὶ τὸ κοινὸν τῶν περὶ τὸν Διόνυσον τεχ[νιτῶν εὐνοίας,
ἅμα δὲ] καὶ τῇ συνόδῳ τῆς εὐχαριστίας διότι τὸν αὑτῆς εὐεργέτ]ην Κράτωνα
ἐτίμησαν ἀπο]διδοῦσα χάριτας τὰς δικαίας τῶν εὐεργετημάτων· ἀναγρ[άψαι
δὲ τόδε τὸ ψήφισμα] εἰς στήλην λιθίνην καὶ στῆσαι παρὰ ταῖς εἰκόσι ταῖς
Κράτ[ωνος· πέμψαι δὲ πρέσβεις] δύο πρὸς τὸν δῆμον τὸν Τηΐων οἵτινες
αἰτήσονται τόπον [ἐν τῷ θεάτρῳ ἐν ᾧ σταθήσεται] ἡ εἰκὼν Κράτωνος καὶ
ἄλλους πρὸς τὸν δῆμον τῶν Δηλίων [- - - - - - οἵτινες] ἐπελθόντες ἐπὶ τὸν
δῆμον καὶ τὴν βουλὴν ἀξιώσουσιν α[ὐτοὺς καὶ τοὺς πρυτά]νεις δοῦναι τῇ συνόδῳ
τῶν τεχνιτῶν τὸν τόπον ἐν ᾧ [σταθήσεται ἡ εἰκών].

2. *C.I.G.* 3068 A.

ἐπὶ ἱερέως Σατύρου, καὶ ἀγωνοθέτου κ[αὶ] ἱερέως βασιλέως Εὐμένου
Νικοτέλου[ς]. ἔδοξεν τῷ κοινῷ τῶν περὶ τὸν Διόνυσον τεχνιτῶν τῶν ἐπ'
Ἰωνίας καὶ Ἑλλησπόντου καὶ τῶν πε[ρὶ] τὸν καθηγεμόνα Διόνυσον· ἐπειδὴ
Κράτων Ζωτίχου αὐλητὴς εὐεργέτης ἔν τε τῷ πρότερον χρόνῳ τὴ[ν] πᾶσαν
σπουδὴν καὶ πρόνοιαν εἶχεν τῶν κοινῇ συμφερόντων τῇ συνόδῳ καὶ τιμηθεὶς
ἀξίως ὧν εὐεργέτηκεν ὑπερτίθεται τῇ εὐνοίᾳ καὶ φιλοτιμίᾳ τῇ εἰς τοὺς τεχνίτας,
πάντα πράττων τὰ συμφέροντα· — δεδόχθαι τῷ κοινῷ τῶν περὶ τὸν Διόνυσον
τεχνιτῶν· ἐπαινέσαι μὲν Κράτωνα Ζωτίχου αὐλητὴν εὐεργέτην ἐπὶ τῷ τὴν
αὐτὴν ἔχειν αἰεὶ προαίρεσιν τῆς εὐεργεσίας τῆς εἰς ἅπαντας τοὺς τεχνίτας·

προσδοῦναι δὲ αὐτῷ πρὸς ταῖς προϋπαρχούσαις τιμαῖς ἀνακήρυξίν τε στεφάνου
τοῦ ἐκ τοῦ νόμου ἣμ ποιήσεται αἰεὶ ἐν τῷ θεάτρῳ ὁ ἑκάστοτε γινόμενος
ἀγωνοθέτης καὶ ἱερεὺς βασιλέως Εὐμένου ἐν τῇ βασιλέως Εὐμένου ἡμέρᾳ
ὅταν ἥ τε πομπὴ διέλθῃ καὶ αἱ στεφανώσεις συντέλωνται· ὁμοίως δὲ καὶ παρὰ
τὸν πότον γινέσθω τῇ αὐτῇ ἡμέρᾳ μετὰ τὰς σπονδὰς ὑπὸ τῶν ἀρχόντων ἡ
ἀναγγελία τοῦ στεφάνου. παρατίθεσθαι δὲ καὶ ἐν ταῖς θέαις καὶ ἐν ταῖς
πομπαῖς παρὰ τὸν ἀνδριάντα τὸν Κράτωνος τὸν ἐν τῷ θεάτρῳ τρίποδά τε
καὶ θυμιατήριον, καὶ τῆς ἐπιθυμιάσεως τὴν ἐπιμέλειαν καθ' ἕκαστον ἔτος
αἰεὶ ποιεῖσθαι τὸν ἀγωνοθέτην καὶ ἱερέα βασιλέως Εὐμένου γινόμενον. —

3. *C.I.G.* 3068 B.

ἔδοξεν τῷ κοινῷ τῶν συναγωνιστῶν· ἐπειδὴ Κράτων Ζωτίχου Καλχη-
δόνιος αὐλητὴς εὔνους ὣν διατελεῖ τῷ κοινῷ τῶν συναγωνιστῶν καὶ λέγων
καὶ πράττων αἰεὶ τὰ συμφέροντα τοῖς συναγωνισταῖς, ἱερεύς τε αἱρεθεὶς
πρότερον τὴν πᾶσαν ἐπιμέλειαν ἐποιήσατο, τάς τε θυσίας συνετέλεσεν πάσας,
ὁσίως μὲν τὰ πρὸς τοὺς θεοὺς καὶ τοὺς βασιλεῖς, καλῶς δὲ καὶ ἐνδόξως τὰ
πρὸς πάντας τοὺς συναγωνιστάς, οὔτε δαπάνης οὔτε φιλοτιμίας οὐθὲν ἐλλείπων, καὶ νῦν δὲ ἀγωνοθέτης γενόμενος καλῶς τῶν ἀγώνων προστὰς καὶ τοῖς
νόμοις ἀκολουθήσας αἰείμνηστον τοῖς ἐπιγινομένοις κατέλιπεν τὴν ἀρχήν· —
ἵνα οὖν καὶ οἱ συναγωνισταὶ ἐμ παντὶ καιρῷ φαίνωνται τιμῶντες τοὺς ἐξ
ἑαυτῶν· δεδόχθαι τῷ κοινῷ τῶν συναγωνιστῶν· στεφανοῦν Κράτωνα Ζωτίχου
Καλχηδόνιον διὰ βίου ἔν τε τῷ κοινῷ δείπνῳ τῶν συναγωνιστῶν καὶ ἐν τῷ θεάτρῳ, ποιουμένους τὴν ἀναγόρευσιν τήνδε· — {το} τὸ κοινὸν τῶν συναγωνιστῶν
στεφανοῖ Κράτωνα Ζωτίχου Καλχηδόνιον στεφάνῳ τῷ ἐκ τοῦ νόμου ἀρετῆς
ἕνεκεν καὶ εὐνοίας ἧς ἔχων διατελεῖ εἰς τοὺς συναγωνιστάς. τῆς δὲ ἀναγγελίας
τῆς τοῦ στεφάνου ἐπιμελεῖσθαι τοὺς ἄρχοντας τοὺς κατ' ἐνιαυτὸν αἱρουμένους.
ἵνα δὲ καὶ τοῖς ἄλλοις πᾶσιν φανερὰ ᾖ εἰς τὸν ἅπαντα χρόνον ἡ τῶν συναγωνιστῶν εὐχαριστία, ἀναγράψαι τὸ ψήφισμα τόδε εἰς στήλην λιθίνην καὶ στῆσαι
πρὸς τῷ Διονυσίῳ ἐν τῷ ἐπιφανεστάτῳ τόπῳ. ἀναθεῖναι δὲ αὐτοῦ καὶ εἰκόνα
ἐν τῷ Διονυσίῳ γραπτὴν τελείαν ἐπιγράψαντας· τὸ κοινὸν τῶν συναγωνιστῶν
στεφανοῖ Κράτωνα Ζωτίχου Καλχηδόνιον ἀρετῆς ἕνεκεν καὶ εὐνοίας τῆς εἰς
αὐτούς.

4. *C.I.G.* 3068 C.

τῶν ἐν Ἰσθμῷ καὶ Νεμέᾳ τεχνιτῶν. ἐπειδὴ Κράτων Ζωτίχου Περγα-
μηνὸς αὐλητὴς κύκλιος πρότερόν τε πολλὰς καὶ μεγάλας παρέσχηται χρείας
κατ' ἰδίαν τε τοῖς ἐντυγχάνουσιν - - - - - -

5. *C.I.G.* 3069.

ψήφισμα Ἀτταλιστῶν· γνώμη τοῦ κοινοῦ τῶν Ἀτταλιστῶν· ἐπειδὴ ὁ ἱερεὺς
τῆς συνόδου Κράτων Ζωτίχου ἔν τε τῷ ζῆν πολλὰς καὶ μεγάλας ἀποδείξεις
ἐποιεῖτο τῆς πρὸς τοὺς Ἀτταλιστὰς εὐνοίας καὶ κατ' ἰδίαν ὑπὲρ ἑκάστου καὶ
κατὰ κοινὸν τῶν ὑφ' ἑαυτοῦ συνηγμένων καὶ κειμένων, τὴν πλείστην ποιούμενος πρόνοιαν, σπουδῆς καὶ φιλοτιμίας οὐδὲν ἐλλείπων, καὶ πολλὰ μὲν καλὰ

καὶ φιλάνθρωπα τῇ συνόδῳ παρὰ τῶν βασιλέων ἐποίησεν, ἀποδεχομένων
αὐτῶν τήν τε ἐκείνου ἅπαντα τρόπον πρὸς ἑαυτοὺς εὔνοιαν καὶ τὴν ἡμετέραν
αἵρεσιν καὶ συναγωγὴν ἀξίαν οὖσαν τῆς ἑαυτῶν ἐπωνυμίας, οὐκ ὀλίγα δὲ τῶν
ἰδίων ἐπιδιδοὺς καὶ χορηγῶν διετέλει, βουλόμενος δὲ τοῖς προϋπηργμένοις
ἀκόλουθα πράσσειν καὶ μεταλλάσσων τὸν βίον ἐν Περγάμῳ, προενοήθη τῆς
συνόδου, καὶ γράψας ἐπιστολὴν πρὸς τοὺς Ἀτταλιστὰς καὶ νόμον ἱερὸν ἀπολι-
πών, ὃν ἀπέστειλεν ἡμῖν βασιλεὺς Ἄτταλος, ἐπισημοτέραν ἐποίησεν τὴν
ὑπάρχουσαν εἰς τὴν σύνοδον εὔνοιαν, δι᾽ ὃν τό τε Ἀττάλειον τὸ πρὸς τῷ
θεάτρῳ, ὃ καὶ ζῶν καθιερώκει τοῖς Ἀτταλισταῖς, ἀνατίθησιν καὶ τὴν συνοικίαν
τὴν πρὸς τῷ βασιλείῳ τὴν πρότερον οὖσαν Μικρίου, ἀνατίθησιν δὲ καὶ καθιεροῖ
τῇ συνόδῳ καὶ ἀργυρίου Ἀλεξανδρείου δραχμὰς μυρίας καὶ πεντακοσίας, ἀφ᾽
ὧν ἐκ τῆς προσόδου θυσίας τε καὶ συνόδους πεποιήμεθα καθὼς ἐν τῇ νομο-
θεσίᾳ περὶ ἑκάστων διατέταχεν, ἀνάθησιν δὲ καὶ σώματα τοῖς Ἀτταλισταῖς
τὰ περιόντα· ἃ κατὰ μέρος ὑπὲρ ἁπάντων ἐν τῷ καθιερωμένῳ ὑφ᾽ ἑαυτοῦ
νόμῳ δεδήλωκεν· ἀπέλιπεν δὲ καὶ τὰ πρὸς συσκήνωσιν ἐν τῷ τεμένει χρηστήρια
ἱκανά, παραλῦσαι βουλόμενος καὶ τῆς εἰς ταῦτα δαπάνης καὶ χορηγίας τοὺς
Ἀτταλιστάς· ἵνα οὖν καὶ ἡ σύνοδος τῶν Ἀτταλιστῶν ἀξίας φαίνηται τοῖς
εὐεργέταις ἀπονέμουσα χάριτας, δεδόχθαι τοῖς Ἀτταλισταῖς κυρῶσαι μὲν τὸν
ἱερὸν νόμον τὸν ἀπολελειμμένον ὑπὸ Κράτωνος, συν[τελεῖσθαι δ]ὲ ἐπωνύμους
ἡμέρας Κράτωνός τε καὶ - - - -

[The inscriptions *C.I.G.* 3070, 3071 contain respectively the initial
greeting of Kraton's letter above-mentioned, and part of the list of
articles—mostly furniture—bequeathed by him to the Attalistai.]

6. Le Bas, *Asie Min.*, no. 281.

γνώμη τοῦ κοινοῦ τῶν περὶ τὸν Διόνυ[σον τεχ]νιτῶν [τῶ]ν ἐν Ἰωνίᾳ [κ]α[ὶ]
Ἑλλησπόντῳ καὶ τῶν περὶ τὸν καθηγεμόνα Δι[όνυ]σον. ἐπειδὴ Ἰασεῖς φίλοι
καὶ οἰκεῖο[ι κ]α[ὶ] εὐ[εργε]ταὶ ὑπάρχοντες καὶ [τὴν μεγίστην σπουδὴν καὶ]
φιλίαν ἔργ[ῳ καὶ λόγῳ δηλ]οῦντες τὴν πρὸς τού[ς πρεσβευτὰς - - -]ον κα[ὶ
Με]νέδημον, [διατηρ]οῦντες δὲ καὶ τὰ δεδο[γμένα τῷ κ]οινῷ τῶν περὶ τὸν
Διόνυσον τεχνιτῶν ὑπο[κρινομέ]νων κατὰ τὰς [διαγραφὰς τῶν Ῥωμ]αίων
τῶν κοινῶν [τῶν] τ[εχνι]τῶν Ἀσ[ίας] σωτήρων ἔν τε τοῖς πρότερον χρόνοις
[πᾶσ]αν σπουδὴν καὶ φιλοτιμίαν δείξαν[τες] περὶ τῆς τῶν ἀγώνων ερ - - - - - -
τὴν αἵρεσιν ἔχοντες - - τ[- - - - - - - - - - κ]αὶ ἐκτένειαν ἐν δὲ τῷ ν[ῦν καιρῷ]
σκ[- - - - - χ]ρήματα καλ - - - - - αιρ - - - ἀγ[αθῇ τ]ύχῃ, δεδόχθαι [τῷ] κοινῷ
[τῶν περὶ τ]ὸν Διόνυσον τεχνιτῶν· ἵνα - - - - - - σωτηρίας τ[- - - τῷ] Διονύσῳ
καὶ Ἰασεῦσιν εἰς τοὺς - - - - παρὰ τοῖς τῷ Διονύσῳ ἀγ - - τῶν ἐνγεγραμ-
μένων τεχνιτῶν καὶ μετεχόντων τῆς [ἐ]ν [Ἰ]α[σῷ] ἐ[κτενείας] καὶ φιλίας
ὑπαρχούσης ἡμῖν ἐκ παλαιῶν χρόνων αὐλητὰς δύο, τραγῳδοὺς δύο, κωμῳδοὺς
δύο, κιθαρῳδόν, κιθαριστήν, ὅπως [συν]άγωσιν τῷ θεῷ τοὺς [χ]ορούς κατὰ
τὰς πατρίας αὐτῶν διαγραφάς, προσμεῖναι δὲ τούτων καὶ τὰς ὑπηρεσίας
- - - - - · τοὺς δὲ νεμηθέντας πάντας ἐπιτελεῖσαι τοὺς τῶν Διονυσίων ἀγῶνας
ἐν τοῖς ὡρισμένοις καιροῖς πάντα παρασχόντας ἀκολούθως τοῖς Ἰασέων

νόμοις· ὃς δὲ τῶν νεμ[η]θέντων ὑπὸ τοῦ πλήθους μὴ παραγένηται εἰς Ἰασόν,
ἢ μὴ [τε]λ[εί]σῃ τοὺς ἀγῶνας ἀποτεισάτω τῷ κοινῷ τῶν περὶ τὸν Διόνυσον
τεχνιτῶν Ἀντιοχ[ι]κὰς δραχμὰς χιλίας ἱερὰς ἀπαραιτητοὺς τοῦ θεοῦ, ἐὰν μή
τις δι᾽ ἀσθένειαν ἢ διὰ χειμῶνα ἀδύνατος γένηται· τούτῳ δὲ ἔστω παραίτησις
τῆς ζημίας ἀπολογισαμένῳ ἐπὶ τοῦ πλήθους καὶ ἐμφανεῖς τὰς δείξεις εἰσ-
ενεγκαμένῳ καὶ ἀπολυθέντι ψήφῳ κατὰ τὸν νόμον· ἵνα δὲ καὶ Ἰασεῖς ἐπι-
γειν[ώ]σκωσιν τὴν τοῦ πλήθους ἡμῶν σπουδὴν καὶ ἣν ἔχομεν πρὸς τοὺς
φίλους ἐκτένειαν ἐν τοῖς ἀναγκαιοτάτοις καιροῖς, ἑλέσθαι πρεσβευτάς, οἵτινες
ἀφικόμενοι εἰς Ἰασὸν καὶ ἀναδόντες τόδε τὸ ψήφισμα τοῖς προστάταις καὶ
ἐπελθόντες ἐπὶ τὴν βουλὴν καὶ τὸν δῆμον καὶ ἐμφανίσαντες περὶ τῶν ἐψηφι-
σμένων τιμῶν αὐτοῖς καὶ ἀνανεωσάμενοι τὰ διὰ προγόνων ὑπάρχοντα πρὸς
ἀλλήλους φιλάνθρωπα παρακαλέσουσιν Ἰασεῖς διαφυλάσσειν τὴν πρὸς τὸ
κοινὸν τῶν περὶ τὸν Διόνυσον τεχνιτῶν οἰκειότητα συναύξοντας τὴν φιλίαν
ἀκολούθως τῇ διὰ προγόν[ω]ν ὑπαρχούσῃ εὐνοίᾳ. πρεσβευταὶ [ᾑ]ρέθησαν
Πλουτιάδης κιθαρῳδός, Λυσίμαχος ποιητὴς τραγῳδιῶν, — Νικόστρατος
συναγωνιστὴς τραγικός. — οἵδε ἐνεμέθησαν σὺν ταῖς ὑπηρεσίαις· — αὐληταί,
Τιμοκλῆς, — Φαίτας· — τραγῳδοί, Ποσειδώνιος, Σωσίπατρος· κωμῳδοί, —
Ἀγάθαρχος, Μοιρίας· κιθαρῳδός, Ζηνόθεος· κιθαριστής, Ἀπολλώνιος Σά—μιος.
— ἐπὶ στεφανηφόρου Ἀπόλλωνος τοῦ τρίτου μετὰ Μένητα Τυρταίου, Ἀπα-
τουριῶνος ἕκτῃ, ἐκυρώθη.

7. R. Demangel et A. Laumonier, *B.C.H.*, xliv (1922), 312, no. 2 (See
above, p. 299, n. 1).

εὔξασθαι δὲ τοὺς δ]ύο κήρυκα[ς ἐν τ]αῖς ἐκλησίαις γίνεσθαι τἀγαθὰ καὶ τῶι
κοινῶι τῶ[ν περὶ τ]ὸν Διόνυσον τεχνιτῶν· ἀγοράσαι δὲ αὐτοῖς καὶ κ[τῆμα]
ἔγγεον ἐν τῆι πόλει ἢ τῆι χώραι ἀπὸ δρα(χμῶν) Ⴔ Χ [καὶ] προσαγορεύεσθαι τὸ
ἀγορασθὲν κτῆμα ἱερὸν ὃ ἀν[ατίθησι] ὁ δῆμος τῶι κοινῶι τῶν περὶ τὸν Διόνυσον
τ[εχ]νιτῶν, ὃν ἀτελὲς ὢν ἡ πόλις ἐπιβάλλει τελῶν· ἀ[πο]δεῖξαι δὲ καὶ ἄνδρας δύο
οἵτινες κτηματωνήσου[σιν ἐ]π᾽ ἀναφορᾶι τῆι πρὸς τὸν δῆμον· ἵνα δὲ τὸ ἀργύριο[ν
ὑπ]άρχηι εἰς τὴν κτηματωνίαν, τοὺς ταμίας τοὺς [ἐν]εστηκότας δοῦναι τοῖς
ἀποδειχθησομένοις δρα(χμάς) [Χ]ΧΧ ἐκ τοῦ μετενηνεγμένου ἐκ τοῦ λόγου τῆς
ὀ[χυρ]ώσεως ὃ δέδοται εἰς τὴν τιμὴν τοῦ σίτου· τὸ δὲ ὑπ[ολι]πὲς δρα(χμὰς)
ΧΧΧ δότωσαν οἱ εἰσιόντες ταμίαι ἐκ τ[ῶν πρ]ώτων δοθησομένων αὐτοῖς ἐγ
βασιλικοῦ εἰς τὴν τ[ῆ]ς πόλεως διοίκησιν· δεδόσθαι δὲ αὐτοῖς καὶ ἐπο[χὴ]ν ἔτη
πέντε ἀπὸ μηνὸς Λευκαθεῶν καὶ πρυτ[άνεως] Μητροδώρου· ὅπως δὲ καὶ τὰ
δόξαντα τῶι δήμ[ωι πά]ντες εἰδῶσιν, ἀναγράψαι τόδε τὸ ψήφισμα εἰς [στήλη]ν
λιθίνην καὶ τὸν στέφανον καὶ ἀναθεῖναι παρὰ [τὸ]ν νεὼ τοῦ Διονύσου· ἀναγράψαι
δὲ καὶ εἰς τὴν παρ[αστά]δα τοῦ θεάτρου τὸ ψήφισμα τόδε καὶ τὸν στέφαν[ον· τῆ]ς
δὲ ἀναγραφῆς τῶν στεφάνων ⟨ι⟩ καὶ ψηφίσματ[ος καὶ τ]ῆς στήλης τὴν κατασκευὴν τὴν ἔγδοσιν π[οιείσθ]ωσαν οἱ ἐνεστηκότες ταμίας καὶ τὸ ἀνάλωμ[α
δότ]ωσαν οἱ ἐνεστηκότες ταμίαι· τοὺς δὲ π(ρ)εσβ[ευτὰς] τοὺς ἀποδεδειγμένους
ἀποδοῦναι τὸ ψήφι[σμα τόδ]ε τοῖς περὶ τὸν Διόνυσον τεχνίταις καὶ ἐπ[αινέσαι
α]ὐτοὺς ἐπὶ τῆι εὐνοίαι ἣν ἔχοντες διατε[λοῦσι] περὶ τὸν δῆμον τὸν Τηΐων.

BIBLIOGRAPHY

THIS Bibliography makes no claim whatever to completeness. Nearly every one of the histories of Greek literature, Greek tragedy, and Greek comedy contains some treatment of the subjects of this volume, and so also do many of the more considerable editions of Aeschylus, Sophocles, Euripides, Aristophanes, and Menander, and the numerous books about them. In view of their number I have not attempted (except in a few special cases) to include references to these.

A. MÜLLER. *Lehrbuch der griechischen Bühnenaltertümer.* 1886.

W. SCHMID. *Geschichte der griechischen Litteratur* (Otto's *Handbuch der Altertumswissenschaft*), vol. ii. 1934.

F. WIESELER. *Theatergebaüde und Denkmäler des Bühnenwesens.* 1851.

W. DÖRPFELD u. E. REISCH. *Das griechische Theater.* 1896.

A. E. HAIGH. *The Attic Theatre* (ed. iii, revised and partly rewritten by A. W. Pickard-Cambridge). 1907.

O. NAVARRE. *Le Théâtre grec.* 1925.

H. BULLE. *Untersuchungen an griechischen Theatern.* 1928.

J. T. ALLEN. *Stage Antiquities of the Greeks and Romans.* 1927.

R. C. FLICKINGER. *The Greek Theater and its Drama* (ed. iv). 1936.

M. BIEBER. *History of the Greek and Roman Theater.* 1939.

A. W. PICKARD-CAMBRIDGE. *The Theatre of Dionysus in Athens.* 1946.

O. A. W. DILKE. 'Details and chronology of Greek theatre caveas.' In *B.S.A.* xliii (1948) 125 ff.; xlv (1950), pp. 21 ff.

E. BETHE. *Prolegomena zur Geschichte des griechischen Theaters im Altertum.* 1896.

H. WEIL. *Études sur le drame antique.* 1897.

U. VON WILAMOWITZ-MÖLLENDORFF. *Einleitung in die griechische Tragödie.* 1907.

A. W. PICKARD-CAMBRIDGE. *Dithyramb, Tragedy, and Comedy.* 1927.

W. KRANZ. *Stasimon.* 1933.

O. NAVARRE. *Dionysus.* 1895.

L. R. FARNELL. *Cults of the Greek States,* vol. v. 1909.

W. WREDE. 'Der Masken-Gott.' In *Athen. Mitt.* liii (1928), pp. 66–95.

M. P. NILSSON. *Studia de Dionysiis Atticis.* 1900.

—— *Griechische Feste von religiöser Bedeutung.* 1906.

E. PFUHL. *De Atheniensium pompis sacris.* 1900.

J. FREI. *De certaminibus thymelicis.* 1900.

M. P. NILSSON. 'Die Prozessionstypen im griechischen Kult.' In *Jahrb. Arch.* xxxi (1916), pp. 309–39.

P. STENGEL. 'Die εἰσαγωγὴ τοῦ Διονύσου ἀπὸ τῆς ἐσχάρας.' In ibid., pp. 340–4.

E. BETHE. 'Programm und Festzug der grossen Dionysien.' In *Hermes,* lxi (1926), pp. 459–64.

A. B. Cook. *Zeus*, vol. i, pp. 645 ff. 1915. (Discussed in A. W. Pickard-Cambridge, *Dith. Trag. Com.*, pp. 208–18.)

J. T. Allen. *On the Program of the City Dionysia during the Peloponnesian War.* 1938.

L. Deubner. *Attische Feste.* 1932.

H. Schneider. Art. 'Σκηνικοὶ Ἀγῶνες' in Pauly–W., *Real-Encycl.* 1927.

A. Frickenhaus. *Lenäen-Vasen* (Winckelmannsprogramm). 1912.

E. Capps. 'The Dramatic Synchoregia at Athens.' In *Am. J. Phil.* xxiii (1902), pp. 319–28.

W. S. Ferguson. 'Demetrius Poliorcetes and the Hellenic League.' In *Hesperia*, xvii (1948), pp. 112–36.

P. Wiesmann. *Das Problem der tragischen Tetralogie.* 1929.

F. Brommer. *Satyroi.* 1937.

P. Guggisberg. *Das Satyrspiel.* 1947.

P. E. Legrand. *Daos.* 1910.

E. Capps. 'The Chorus in the Later Greek Drama.' In *Am. J. Arch.* xi (1895), pp. 287 ff. and 325 ff.

K. J. Maidment. 'The Later Comic Chorus.' In *Class. Quart.* xxix (1935), pp. 1–24.

L. Radermacher. *Zur Geschichte der griechischen Komödie.* 1924.

A. Olivieri. *Frammenti della Commedia Greca e del Mimo nella Sicilia e nella Magna Grecia.* 1934.

E. Wüst. Art. 'Φλύακες' in Pauly–W., *Real-Encycl.* 1941.
[Other references for Phlyakes at end of Chap. IV above.]

H. Reich. *Der Mimus.* 1923.

A. Baumeister. *Denkmäler des klassischen Altertums* (3 vols.). 1889.

C. Robert. *Bild und Lied.* 1881.

—— *Archäologische Hermeneutik.* 1919.

T. B. L. Webster. *Greek Art and Literature.* 1939.

M. Bieber. *Die Denkmäler zum Theaterwesen im Altertum.* 1920.

—— *Das Dresdener Schauspieler-relief.* 1907.

—— und A. Brueckner. *Skenika* (Winckelmannsprogramm). 1915.

D. Raoul-Rochette. *Monuments inédits.* 1833.

—— *Choix de peintures.* 1867.

Monumenti inediti pubblicati dall' Instituto di correspondenza archeologica (especially vol. xi). 1879–85.

A. Furtwängler u. K. Reichhold. *Griechische Vasenmalerei.* 1900–32.

P. Hermann. *Denkmäler der Malerei des Altertums.* 1901–31.

E. Pfuhl. *Malerei und Zeichnung der Griechen.* 1923.

A. D. Trendall. *Paestan Pottery.* 1936.

A. Mau. *Geschichte der dekorativen Wandmalerei in Pompeii.* 1882.

L. Curtius. *Die Wandmalerei Pompeiis.* 1929.

J. H. Huddilston. *Greek Tragedy in the Light of the Vase-paintings.* 1898.

R. Engelmann. *Archäologische Studien zu den Tragikern.* 1900.

M. Bieber. 'Die Herkunft des tragischen Kostums.' In *Jahrb. Arch.* xxxii (1917), pp. 15–104.

L. Séchan. *Études sur la Tragédie grecque dans ses rapports avec la Céramique.* 1926.

A. Rumpf. (Review of Séchan, op. cit.) In *Philolog. Woch.* 1932, pp. 210 ff.

F. Messerschmidt. *Bühnenbild und Vasenmalerei.* In *Röm. Mitt.* xlvii (1932), pp. 122–51.

H. Bulle. *Eine Skenographie* (Winckelmannsprogramm). 1934.

—— 'Von griechischen Schauspielern und Vasenmalern.' In *Festschrift für James Loeb,* 1930, pp. 5 ff.

—— 'Weihebild eines tragischen Dichters.' In *Corolla Curtius.* 1937.

C. Robert. *Kentaurenkampf und Tragödienszene* (Winckelmannsprogramm). 1898.

L. Talcott. Κούριμος Πάρθενος. In *Hesperia,* viii (1939), pp. 267 ff.

H. Dierks. *De tragicorum histrionum habitu scenico apud Graecos.* 1883.

F. Brommer. *Das Satyrspiel, Bilder griechischer Vasen.* 1944.

A. Dieterich. *Pulcinella.* 1897.
[For dances in animal costumes, etc., see note on p. 194.]

A. Körte. 'Archäologische Studien zur alten Komödie.' In *Jahrb. Arch.* viii (1893), pp. 61 ff.

H. Schnabel. *Kordax.* 1910.

A. Greifenhagen. *Eine attische schwarzfigurige Vasengattung.* 1929.

T. B. L. Webster. 'South Italian Vases and Attic Drama.' In *Class. Quart.* xlii (1948), pp. 15 ff. (cf. A. W. Pickard-Cambridge, ibid. xliii (1949), p. 57).

A. K. H. Simon. *Comicae Tabellae; die Szenenbilder zur griechischen neuen Komödie.* 1938.

H. Goldman and F. Jones. 'Terracottas from the Acropolis of Halai.' In *Hesperia,* xi (1942), pp. 365–421.

M. Bieber. Art. 'Masken' in Pauly–W., *Real-Encycl.* 1930.

C. Robert. *Die Masken der neueren attischen Komödie.* 1911.

W. Beare, *The Roman Stage,* 1950.

T. B. L. Webster. 'The Masks of Greek Comedy.' In *Bulletin of Rylands Library,* xxxii (1949), pp. 97–135.

—— 'Masks on Gnathia Vases.' In *J. Hell. Stud.* lxxi. 222.

—— 'Notes on Pollux' list of tragic masks.' In *Festschrift für A. Rumpf,* 141 ff.

O. Hense. *Die Modificierung der Masken in der griechischen Tragödie.* 1905.

P. R. Löhren. *Mienenspiel und Maske in der griechischen Tragödie.* 1927.

O. Dingeldein. 'Haben die Theatermasken der Alten die Stimme verstärkt?' In *Berliner Stud. für klass. Philologie u. Archäologie,* xl. 9. 1890.

K. K. Smith. 'The Use of the High-heeled Shoe or Buskin in Greek Tragedy.' In *Harvard Studies,* xvi. 1905.

A. Körte. 'Der Kothurn im fünften Jahrhundert.' In *Festschrift Basel.* 1907.

E. Rohde. *De Julii Pollucis in apparatu scenico enarrando fontibus.* 1870.

C. A. Bapp. *De fontibus quibus Athenaeus in rebus musicis enarrandis usus sit.* 1885.

V. Gordziejew. *Quaestionum de Julii Pollucis fontibus caput.* 1936.

W. Christ. *Metrik der Griechen und Römer.* 1879.

P. Masqueray. *Théorie des formes lyriques de la tragédie grecque.* 1895.

W. R. Hardie. *Res Metrica.* 1920.

U. von Wilamowitz-Möllendorff. *Griechische Verskunst.* 1921.

G. Thomson. *Greek Lyric Metre.* 1929.

W. J. W. Koster. *Traité de métrique grecque.* 1936.

J. D. Denniston. Art. 'Metre' in *Oxford Class. Dict.* 1949.

O. Schroeder. *Grundriss der griechischen Versgeschichte.* 1930.

A. M. Dale. *Lyric Metres of Greek Drama.* 1948.

—— 'Stasimon and Hyporchema.' In *Eranos,* xlviii (1950), pp. 14–20.

J. W. White. *The Verse of Greek Comedy.* 1912. [With an extensive bibliography.]

A. Gross. *Die Stichomythie in der griechischen Tragödie u. Komödie.* 1905.

J. Kanz. *De tetrametro trochaico.* 1913.

W. Christ. 'Die Parakatalogé im griechischen u. röm. Drama.' In *Abhandl. der bayrischen Akad.* xiii. 3, pp. 155 ff.

—— *Die Theilung des Chors im attischen Drama.* 1877.

J. Lammers. *Die Doppel- und Halbchöre in der antiken Tragödie.* 1931.

F. Heimsoeth. *Vom Vortrag des Chors in den griechischen Dramen.* 1841.

F. Bamberger. *De carminibus Aeschyleis a partibus chori cantatis.* 1832.

N. Wecklein. 'Technik und Vortrag der Chorgesänge des Aischylos.' In *Neue Jahrb.,* Suppl. xiii, pp. 215 ff.

K. Münscher. 'Der Bau der Lieder des Aischylos.' In *Hermes,* lix (1924), pp. 204–31.

Chr. Muff. *De choro Persarum fabulae Aeschyleae.* 1878.

—— *Der Chor in den Sieben des Aischylos.* 1882.

R. Arnoldt. *Der Chor im Agamemnon des Aischylos scenisch erläutert.* 1881.

O. Schroeder. *Aischyli cantica.* 1916.

O. Hense. *Der Chor des Sophokles.* 1877.

—— 'Ueber die Vortragsweise sophokleischen Stasima.' In *Rhein. Mus.* xxxii (1877), pp. 489 ff.

Chr. Muff. *Die chorische Technik des Sophokles.* 1877. (Reviewed by O. Hense, *Neue Jahrb.,* 1878, pp. 1 ff., 81 ff., 145 ff.)

O. Schroeder. *Sophoclis cantica.* 1923.

V. de Falco. *La Technica corale di Sofocle.* 1928.

O. Hense. *De Ionis fabulae Euripideae partibus choricis.* 1876.

R. Arnoldt. *Die chorische Technik des Euripides.* 1878.

Fecht. *Quaestiones choricae Euripideae.* 1878.

O. Schroeder. *Euripidis cantica.* 1928.

Chr. Muff. *Ueber den Vortrag der chorischen Partieen bei Aristophanes.* 1872.

R. Arnoldt. *Die Chorpartieen des Aristophanes scenisch erläutert.* 1873.

O. Schroeder. *Aristophanis cantica.* 1930.

Th. Zielinski. *Die Gliederung der altattischen Komödie.* 1885.

W. Kranz. Art. 'Parodos' in Pauly–W., *Real-Encycl.* 1949.

V. de Falco. *L'Epiparodo nella tragedia greca.* 1925.

K. Haym. *De puerorum in re scenica Graecorum partibus.* 1897.

H. Devrient. *Das Kind auf der antiken Bühne.* 1904.

G. Richter. *De mutis personis quae in tragoedia atque comoedia Attica in scenam prodeunt.* 1934.

H. Fischl. *De nuntiis tragicis.* 1909.

O. Ribbeck. *Alazon.* 1882.

—— *Kolax* (Abh. der sächs. Ges. der Wissenschaften, xxi).

—— *Agroikos* (ibid. xxiii).

E. M. Rankin. *The Rôle of the* Μαγειροί *in the Life of the Ancient Greeks.* 1907.

E. Giese. *De parasiti persona capita selecta.* 1908.

P. E. Legrand. *Daos.* 1910.

H. G. Oeri. *Der Typ des komischen Alten in der griechischen Komödie.* 1948.

J. B. O'Connor. *Chapters in the History of Actors and Acting in Ancient Greece.* 1908.

K. Rees. *The Rule of Three Actors in the Classical Drama.* 1908.

—— 'The Three-Actor Rule in Menander.' In *Class. Philol.* v (1910), pp. 291–302.

—— 'The Meaning of Parachoregema.' In ibid. ii (1907), pp. 387–400.

H. Kaffenberger. *Das Dreischauspielergesetz in der griechischen Tragödie.* 1911.

O. J. Todd. '*ΤΡΙΤΑΓΩΝΙΣΤΗΣ*, a Reconsideration.' In *Class. Quart.* xxxii (1938), pp. 30–38.

E. B. Ceadel. 'The Division of Parts among the Actors in Sophocles' *Oedipus Coloneus.*' In ibid. xxxv (1941), pp. 139 ff.

F. W. Dingnau. *The Idle Actor in Aeschylus.* 1905.

J. T. Allen. *Greek Acting in the Fifth Century.* 1916.

G. Capone. *L'Arte scenica degli Attori tragici greci.* 1930.

A. Spitzbarth. *Untersuchungen zur Spieltechnik der griechischen Tragödie.* 1946.

K. Sittl. *Die Gebärden der Griechen u. Römer.* 1890.

F. Völker. *Berühmte Schauspieler im griechischen Altertum.* 1899.

V. Flach. *Der Tanz bei den Griechen.* 1881.

M. Emmanuel. *La Danse grecque antique.* 1895. (Engl. tr. *The Antique Greek Dance,* 1916.)

Chr. Kirchhoff. *Die dramatische Orchestik der Hellenen.* 1898.

K. Latte. *De saltationibus Graecorum capita quinque.* 1913.

F. Weege. *Der Tanz in der Antike.* 1926. [Very fully illustrated.]

—— *Dionysische Reigen.* 1926.

L. Séchan. *La Danse grecque antique.* 1930.

V. Festa. 'Sikinnis.' In *Mem. del R. Accad. di Archeologia, Lettere e belle Arti di Napoli,* iii. 2 (1918), pp. 35–74.

M. Wegner. *Das Musikleben der Griechen,* 1949.

E. Roos. *Die tragische Orchestik im Zerrbild der altattischen Komödie.* 1951.

L. B. Lawler. 'The Maenads.' In *Memoirs of Amer. Academy in Rome,* vi, pp. 69–112.

H. Huchzermayer. *Aulos und Kithara in der griechischen Musik.* 1931.

J. B. Mountford. 'Greek Music in the Papyri and Inscriptions.' In *New Chapters in Greek Lit.* ii (1929), pp. 146–83.

—— and R. P. Winnington-Ingram. Art. 'Music' in *Oxford Class. Dict.* 1949. [With a good bibliography.]

O. NAVARRE. *Utrum mulieres Athenienses ludos scenicos spectaverint.* 1900.

A. ROEMER. *Ueber den litterarisch-aesthetischen Bildungsstand des attischen Theater-publikums.* 1905.

W. ELSPERGER. 'Reste und Spüren antiker Kritik gegen Euripides.' In *Philologus*, Suppl. 11. 1907.

J. GEFFCKEN. *Die Wirkung der Tragödie und ihre Beurteilung.* 1927.

O. BENNDORF. *Beiträge zur Kenntniss des attischen Theaters.* 1875.

J. N. SVORONOS. Arts. on theatre-tickets in *Journal International d'Archéologie numismatique*, i (1898), pp. 37 ff.; iii (1900), pp. 197 ff., 322 ff.; viii (1905), pp. 323 ff.

—— *Trésor des monnaies d'Athènes.*

O. LÜDERS. *Die dionysischen Künstler.* 1873.

P. FOUCART. *De collegiis scaenicorum artificum apud Graecos.* 1873.

E. REISCH. *De musicis Graecorum certaminibus.* 1885.

F. POLAND. *De collegiis artificum Dionysiacorum.* 1895.

—— *Geschichte des griechischen Vereinswesens*, pp. 129–47. 1909.

—— Art. 'Technitai' in Pauly–W., *Real-Encycl.* 1934.

E. ZIEBARTH. *Das griechische Vereinswesen*, pp. 79 ff. 1896.

J. OEHLER. *Epigraphische Beiträge zur Geschichte der dionysischen Künstler.* 1908.

G. KLAFFENBACH. *Symbola ad historiam collegiorum artificum Bacchiorum.* 1919.

A. SCHNEIDER. Art. 'Σκηνικοὶ Ἀγῶνες' in Pauly–W., *Real-Encycl.* 1927.

G. DAUX. *Delphes au IIᵉ et Iᵉ siècle.* 1936.

R. FLACÉLIÈRE. *Les Aitoliens à Delphes.* 1937.

E. V. HANSEN. *The Attalids of Pergamon.* 1947.

W. S. FERGUSON. *Hellenistic Athens.* 1911.

W. W. TARN. *Hellenistic Civilization.* 1927.

—— In *Cambridge Anc. Hist.* vi, pp. 495 ff.

Corpus Inscriptionum Graecarum (Boeckh). 1828–77.

Inscriptiones Graecae (vols. i–xiv). 1877–90.

Inscriptiones Graecae, Editio Minor (in progress). 1924– (especially ii², nos. 2318–25, ed. by Kirchner, 1931).

W. DITTENBERGER. *Sylloge Inscriptionum Graecorum* (ed. iii). 1915–24.

—— *Orientis Graecae Inscriptiones Selectae.* 1903–5.

P. LE BAS and W. H. WADDINGTON. *Inscriptions grecques et latines recueillies en Grèce et en Asie Mineure*, tome iii. 1870.

W. HAHLAND. 'Der Fries des Dionysostempels in Teos.' In *Wiener Jahresh.* xxxviii (1950), pp. 67 ff.

A. WILHELM. *Urkunden dramatischer Aufführungen in Athen.* 1906.

A. BRINCK. 'Inscriptiones Graecae ad choregiam pertinentes.' In *Diss. philol. Halenses* (1886), pp. 71–274.

E. CAPPS. 'The Catalogue of Victors at the Dionysia and Lenaea.' In *Am. J. Phil.* xx (1899), pp. 388 ff.

—— 'Chronological Studies in the Greek and Latin Poets.' In ibid. xxi (1900), pp. 38 ff.

—— 'The Dating of some Didascalic Inscriptions.' In *Am. J. Arch.* iv (1900), pp. 74 ff.

—— 'Studies in Greek agonistic Inscriptions.' In *Trans. Am. Phil. Ass.* xxxi (1900), pp. 114–37.

—— *The Introduction of Comedy into the City Dionysia.* 1903.

—— 'The Roman fragments of Athenian Comic Didascaliae.' In *Class. Philol.* i (1906), pp. 201 ff.

E. CAPPS. Review of Wilhelm's *Urkunden.* In *Am. J. Phil.* xxviii (1907), pp. 82 ff.

—— 'Epigraphical problems in the History of Attic Comedy.' In ibid., pp. 179 ff.

—— 'A new fragment of the List of Victors at the City Dionysia.' In *Hesperia*, xii (1943), pp. 1 ff.

E. REISCH. Art. 'Didaskalien' in Pauly–W., *Real-Encycl.* 1905.

—— 'Urkunden dramatischer Aufführungen in Athen.' In *Zeitschr. öst. Gymn.* 1907, pp. 289 ff.

—— 'Eine monumentale Chronik der athenischen Theateraufführungen.' In *Verhandl. der 55 Versammlung deutscher Philologen in Erlangen*, 1925, pp. 26 ff.

A. KÖRTE. 'Inschriftliches zur Geschichte der att. Komödie.' In *Rhein. Mus.* lx (1905), pp. 425 ff.

—— 'Aristotle's Νῖκαι Διονυσιακαί.' In *Class. Philol.* i (1906), pp. 391 ff. (Other articles by Körte on dramatic inscriptions will be found in *Woch. klass. Philol.* 1904, col. 393; *Berl. Phil. Woch.*, 1906, col. 1313 ff.; *Gött. gel. Anz.*, 1906, pp. 614 ff.; Bursian, *Jahresbericht*, 1911, pp. 218 ff.; *Philol. Woch.*, 1925, cols. 1 ff.; *Deutsch. Littztg.*, 1925, col. 2285; *Gnomon*, 1932, pp. 302 f.)

G. JACHMANN. *De Aristotelis Didascaliis.* 1909.

W. A. DITTMER. *The Fragments of Athenian Comic Didaskaliai found in Rome.* 1923.

B. D. MERITT. 'Greek Inscriptions.' In *Hesperia*, vii (1938), pp. 116–17. (See A. Körte in *Hermes*, lxxiii (1938), pp. 123 ff.; E. Capps in *Hesperia*, xii (1943), pp. 1 ff.)

H. OELLACHER. 'Zur Chronologie der altattischen Komödie.' In *Wiener Stud.* xxxviii (1916), pp. 81–155.

P. GEISSLER. *Chronologie der altattischen Komödie.* 1925.

T. B. L. WEBSTER. 'Chronological Notes on Middle Comedy.' In *Class. Quart.* N.S. ii (1952), pp. 13 ff.

INDEX